A Millennium of Family Change

A Millennium of Family Change

Feudalism to Capitalism in Northwestern Europe

WALLY SECCOMBE

VERSO

London · New York ·

First published by Verso 1992
© Verso 1992
All rights reserved

Verso
UK: 6 Meard Street, London W1V 3HR
USA: 29 West 35th Street, New York, NY 10001-2291

Verso is the imprint of New Left Books

ISBN 0-86091-332-5

British Library Cataloguing in Publication Data
A catalogue record for this book is available from the British Library

Library of Congress Cataloging-in-Publication Data
A catalogue record for this book is available from the Library of Congress

Typeset in Monotype Bembo by NorthStar, San Francisco, Calif.
Printed in Great Britain by Bookcraft (Bath) Ltd

Contents

Acknowledgements   vii

Introduction   1

1 Labour-Power, Family Forms and the Mode-of-Production Concept   **9**

    Towards an Expanded Mode-of-Production Concept   10
    Human Labour-Power and Its Production   14
    Conceiving of Family Forms in Modes of Production   22
    Patriarchal Power and Family Relations   30

2 Peasant Family Forms in the Feudal Mode of Production   **37**

    Origins of Feudal Land Inheritance and Peasant Family Forms   43
    Feudal Synthesis in the Early Middle Ages   56
    The Manor, the Village and the Peasant Holding   78
    The Division of Labour between Spouses   83
    Peasant Stratification   87
    The Mode of Seigneurial Exploitation and the Reproduction
       Cycle of Labour-Power   91
    Peasant Inheritance Customs and Strategies   96
    Marriage as a Facet of Property Devolution   103
    Mate Selection, Betrothal and Wedding Rituals   108
    Widows and the Family Cycle   117
    Household Composition and Divergent Family Cycles   121
    From Overextension to Crisis   126

3 Population and Changing Family Forms in the Transition from Feudalism to Capitalism   **133**

    PART I Late Medieval Crisis and the Origins of the Western
    European Marriage Pattern   133
       The Shifting Balance of Power in the Wake of the Black Death   136

Continuity and Change in Peasant Stratification 141
Tenure Shifts and Inheritance Forms 143
Land Availability and Inheritance Norms 148
Origins of the Western European Late Marriage System 150
Demographic Recovery: 1450–1600 157
Economic Recovery and Deteriorating Wages: 1450–1600 159
Peasant Polarization 162

PART II Proletarianization and Changing Family Forms 166

Proletarianization and Capital Accumulation 172
The Land-Poor and the Landless, the Settled and the Vagrant 174
Early Proto-industrialization: The Kaufsystem 181
Foundations of the Western European Marriage Pattern 184
Seventeenth-Century Stagnation and the Last Feudal–Agrarian
    Cycle 190
Proletarian Self-Expansion before 1750? 194
Domestic Service in Husbandry 197

PART III The Population Boom: Springboard to Industrial Capitalism 200

The Agricultural Revolution and the Decline of Service 202
The Verlagssystem's Expansion and Shifts in the Conjugal
    Division of Labour 205
The Mortality Decline after 1750 208
Explaining the Population Boom 212
Migration and Regional Demographic Trends 216
Proletarianization and the Vital Revolution 219
Proletarianization and the Rise of Extramarital Childbirth 225
The Demographic and Industrial Revolutions 229

4 Conclusion 233

Family Change from Feudalism to Capitalism 233
Western European Marriage and the Rise of Industrial Capitalism 239
Women and Patriarchy in the Transition to Capitalism 242

Appendix: A Note on the Brenner Debate 247

Notes 255

Bibliography 307

Index 333

Acknowledgements

In the course of researching my doctoral dissertation, which forms the sequel to this study, curiosity got the better of me and I made a brief detour (a minor digression, I assured the sceptics) into the medieval mists. You have the product of that imprudence before you – appearing a decade, and several incarnations, later. Time has not dimmed the gratitude I feel for the members of my thesis committee – Richard Lee, David Levine, David Livingstone, Meg Luxton, Mary O'Brien and Rayna Rapp – who managed to digest and criticize inchoate early versions of the work, stimulating its development. David Levine – in person, and through his own scholarship on the same general terrain – has probed my perspective, suggested countless references, and provoked numerous clarifications, as have June Corman, David Livingstone and Meg Luxton as we worked together on another study. Along the way, others generously read the manuscript in whole or in part: Perry Anderson, Michèle Barrett, Ernst Benz, Robin Blackburn, Susan Caldwell, Philip Corrigan, Anna Davin, Diane Elson, Nancy Folbre, John Gillis, Alan Greer, Roberta Hamilton, Harold Lavender, Richard Smith, Richard Wall and Ellen Woods. Their incisive criticisms have often sent me 'back to the drawing board', thus delaying, but immeasurably improving, the end-product. I alone remain responsible for its deficiencies. A special thanks is due Richard Wall, who has treated me with unfailing kindness and my work with an open mind, despite my vociferous opposition to the Cambridge paradigm.

For their love, support and inspiration, my deepest appreciation to Varda Burstyn and Jackie Larkin, who have remained comrades long after the term became unfashionable. And finally, to Helena Wehrstein, who has, upon occasion, implored the author to turn his attention to domestic matters rather closer to home; she has been the light of my life for even longer than this manuscript, and her love glows brighter than all the midnight oil I burnt finishing it.

I dedicate this work to Ruth, who fights her own battles with dignity and courage.

Introduction

Western family forms are changing in far-reaching ways. A quarter-century is a brief moment in family history, yet in the past twenty-five years we have witnessed: the demise of the male breadwinner family economy, with the mass employment of married women outside the home; skyrocketing rates of divorce and remarriage; birth rates dipping to unprecedented levels, well below replacement rates; the proliferation of single-parent households, mostly female-headed; and a sharp rise in the proportion of adults living alone.

These changes leave no room for detached observation or cool indifference. The current public mood is one of deep foreboding about the future of the family and a pervasive nostalgia for a simpler and more stable past. Public distress has been fuelled by popular sociologists who have written alarmingly of a 'crisis of the family'.[1] Such scholarly consternation has been cultural grist to the New Right's political mill; the more dire the prediction, the more dramatic the effect. Since, in conservative thought, 'the family' is the most natural and enduring of all human institutions, the rapidity of recent change is interpreted as an aberrant process that courts disaster unless 'traditional family values' are reinstated. There is a limited recognition that family forms *do* differ cross-culturally. But within our own culture it is commonplace to speak of 'the family' in universal terms, as if it were an eternal and unchanging essence. This prevailing image of domestic perdurance in the past – of a rock of private stability in a sea of public storms – imbues contemporary perceptions of rapid change with the fear of family dissolution. How accurate is this viewpoint historically? *Is* familial change, of the pace and scope witnessed in the past quarter-century, unprecedented? Or is there a collective act of myth-making involved in the prevailing account of 'the history of the Western family'?

Following Peter Laslett's lead, most historians and sociologists argue that the nuclear family prevailed in pre-industrial times and underwent no far-reaching structural changes in the transition to industrial capitalism. The survival of 'the

1

family' is thus equated with the preservation, come what may, of this irreducible matrix of human relations – the small life-support group formed by the bonds between a heterosexual couple, partnered for life, and their dependent children. While correctly stressing the resilience of Western families in the past, the thesis of nuclear continuity implies that the changes we have witnessed recently are historically unprecedented. In reference to the scale of marital breakdowns in the West since the 1960s, for example, Lawrence Stone has recently written that 'there has been nothing like it in the last two thousand years, and probably much longer.'[2]

I shall argue that there has been a great deal more change in family forms over the past millennium than the current consensus allows for. What we now term, in retrospect, 'the traditional family' is a recent invention, the product of a period of exceptional stability and uniformity in family relations, culminating in the 1950s. Against the backdrop of this quiescence, lived out by our parents' generation, the present phase of flux seems remarkable indeed. In a longer-term perspective, it does not seem so unusual. At the risk of repeating the historian's cliché, it is impossible to assess what is genuinely new in the present situation unless one has a reasonably accurate appreciation of what has gone before. In analysing family forms in particular – where lasting change must be distinguished from cyclical flux – it is advisable to take the long view of history. My hope is that this book, together with its sequel, will contribute modestly to that end.

The text presents a broad sketch of a millennium of economic and family change in Northwestern Europe, from the early Middle Ages to the brink of the Industrial Revolution. Throughout, I have sought to locate the family forms of labouring classes within prevailing modes of production. The theoretical approach is outlined in the first chapter. The second chapter situates peasant family forms within the feudal mode of production, while digressing to explore their formative roots in the transition from Antiquity. The third chapter begins with the generalized crisis of the feudal order in the fourteenth and fifteenth centuries, and finds evidence for the emergence of the distinctive Western European pattern of late and non-universal marriage in the aftermath of the Black Death; thenceforth, the chapter traces the rural evolution of family forms through the protracted process of proletarian formation in the early modern era. The concluding chapter offers a summary of the changes involved in the transition from peasant to proletarian family cycles, and then assesses the contribution of the Western European marriage pattern to the advent of industrial capitalism in the northwestern corner of the continent. The synoptic account of this book is linked with a sequel, *Weathering the Storm: Working-Class Families from the Industrial Revolution to the Fertility Decline*, the latter presenting an overview of changing urban working-class family forms in the nineteenth and early twentieth centuries.

Across this vast historical canvas, I try to show that there is an active inter-dependence between the development of modes of production and the evolution of family forms. Interdependence does not imply lock-step congruence, of course. As well as functional complementarity and structural alignment, there are moments of stress and contradiction between family forms and modes of production. But if reciprocal interaction is sustained and deep, then it is necessary to comprehend their development in relation with one another. On the one hand, 'no family system can be understood apart from the political and economic context in which it is found.'[3] On the other hand, no economic system can be adequately understood apart from the family forms with which it is associated, since families people societies and supply their labour forces.

Readers may be inclined to accept or reject this proposition a priori, depending on their theoretical dispositions. But are there empirical grounds on which it might be judged? While hypothesis testing, in a rigorous sense, is beyond the scope of historical argument, hypothesis-checking is often possible. One such check of the interaction thesis advanced above is to examine what happened to family forms in the passage from feudalism to capitalism, as the prevailing mode of production was revolutionized. Were families transformed in the process? Laslett and his associates have answered in the negative; if they are right, then my conception of 'deep reciprocal interaction' is vitiated, and instead one ought to emphasize the high degree of autonomy of family forms from socioeconomic developments. In the face of a formidable consensus, I shall argue that the difference between peasant and proletarian families was profound, and that domestic relations underwent a cultural revolution in the making of the modern working class.

While intensely critical of marxism, I seek to enrich historical materialism, not to abandon or surpass it. Yet this contribution can never simply be a matter of 'fitting' family forms into an otherwise sound structure – as if one were inserting the final piece of a jigsaw puzzle into the formed space left waiting for it – but more a case of opening marxism in an area in which it has been blocked.[4] For the inescapable fact of the matter is that marxism, as a historically constituted body of thought, has had precious little to say about family forms. The problem is not that most marxists are completely disinterested in families, or fail to appreciate their importance in shaping people's daily lives. To the contrary: there has been a growing willingness to concede the deficiency, as Western marxists have become increasingly critical of their own heritage and as cultural studies have come to the fore. However welcome this belated recognition is, it does not rectify the basic problem, which is conceptual in nature. The standard categories of marxist political economy, centred on relations of production, make no reference to family forms. The more deeply one is immersed in this discourse, the more seriously its analytical categories are taken, the thicker is the curtain brought down on family life and domestic relations. Even where an author intends to include the subject within. a broader purview, the results are too often gestural and insubstantive.[5]

The inspiration for this book lies in the challenge that modern feminism has issued to all bodies of 'malestream' knowledge: to rethink their paradigms from the ground up, building in a full account of gender relations at every level of analysis. Within a materialist framework, there are several ways to effect this integration. One might begin from the concept of the gendered division of labour, pivoting around the allocation of tasks between co-resident spouses; or alternatively, one might theorize a distinct mode of reproduction and then bring the modes of production and reproduction into historically specified relationship with one another. Others have found these to be fruitful lines of inquiry. I have opted for a rather different strategy: expanding the mode-of-production concept by including the reproduction of the species *as a form of production* with the same ontological status as goods production. There are trade-offs – strengths and limitations – in different theoretical approaches to the multifaceted task of revising historical materialism to take adequate account of gender relations. We ought to eschew a quest for the Holy Grail, the one and only key to situating class and gender relations within a unified framework. At particular points in the text, where alternative perspectives speak directly to my argument, I shall enjoin the debate. But I feel under no compulsion, by way of introduction, to negate roads not taken before setting out on my own.

If the main inspiration of the text is to take up the challenge which feminists have laid at marxism's door, the principal bodies of historical knowledge it draws upon – economic and social history, demographic and family history – are not deeply imbued with feminist insight; herein lies one of the tensions and difficulties of the text. For the most part, women's history has developed alongside family history, while scholars of the latter discipline have taken far too little notice. Despite this (and other) weaknesses, great strides have been taken in family history in the past two decades. Formerly, the domestic lives of common people were presumed to be lost forever in the black hole of folk-myth and unrecorded experience, but recently, these darkened interiors of the past have been illuminated in astonishing ways. Computer-assisted record linking techniques and population-simulation procedures have breathed new life into traditional sources of historical knowledge such as court rolls and parish registers. If we are still peering through a glass darkly, it is none the less exhilarating to be able to see anything at all. These breakthroughs have engendered a burst of intellectual creativity and attracted a swarm of graduate students, with the result that a burgeoning library of primary research has now been published. Its prevailing form has been the family reconstitution study of a single parish. A great number of these have been reported in scholarly journals, published as research monographs, and compiled in edited collections; hundreds more exist in the form of doctoral theses. My survey would not have been possible without this great leap forward in social history. The problem with a plethora of local studies, however, is that the big picture tends to dissolve into a mass of disparate keyholes, allowing tantalizing glimpses into the interior of a great many rooms while a coherent sense of the building's architecture as a whole is lost. This is a situation ripe for synthetic overview. The density of local studies in the main countries of Northwestern Europe is sufficient to warrant the attempt to discern enduring structures, identify recurrent sequences of development, and draw out regional contrasts.

The text proceeds at an intermediate level of analysis, poised between the epochal abstraction of modes of production and the histories of specific social formations. There is a paucity of work on the medial plane in historical materialism (and in other paradigms as well), with the result that the connections between modes of production (determinant cores) and social formations (mixed wholes) are too often conceived in an unduly schematic and mechanical fashion. While the merits of mid-range studies are readily appreciated, they are not easy to control. Registering the conceptual tension between a dissection of social structure and a rolling account of historical process, chapters 2 and 3 address thematic points as they first arise within a chronological progression of roughly demarcated periods, resuming the discussion of the same topic at a later stage, if necessary. The interlacing of theme and period often makes for an awkward presentation; the crucial Western European marriage system, for example, is taken up at four different points in the text. But I felt that to resolve the tension arbitrarily for the sake of expository ease would defeat the attempt to sustain an intermediate level of analysis.

What the historical survey surrenders in depth of detail is potentially compensated for in breadth of scope across time and space. Temporally, I have taken the long view of history, peering back at the murky contours of the transition from Antiquity to feudalism and scanning briskly forward across the centuries. This perspective seems especially apposite in a study of family forms, where the rapid pace of political change, demographic vicissitudes and short-term economic fluctuations must be distinguished from enduring changes in underlying socioeconomic relations, which proceed at a relatively glacial pace.[6] Changes in family structure tend to sneak up on contemporaries and may not become apparent at all until they are already firmly established.

Spatially, I have drawn from a very broad set of regions, though concentrating on the core zones of Northwestern Europe (and within that, too heavily on England). By selecting the entire zone as the unit of analysis, regional contrasts within Northwestern Europe are minimized. In addition, there are fluctuating inclusions and omissions around the adjacent zones of the Mediterranean and Central Europe, depending on the availability of evidence and the subject under discussion. This flux would ideally be eliminated by more complete and uniform coverage, or controlled through sustained comparisons between regions. I have attempted the latter, to some degree, particularly with the Mediterranean materials, but the limits of my own knowledge, time and foreign-language competence have necessitated a less rigorous form of overview.

Just as the focus on general trends across regions flattens spatial diversity, so the demarcation of stages of development straightens out temporal unevenness, downplaying the leads and lags between regions. In reality, the operation of uneven and combined development stretches out sequential progressions in vanguard regions and compresses them in the laggards. A broad survey cannot possibly do justice to this concatenation. It attempts a kind of mental averaging (for the most part non-numerical) to arrive at 'representative' portraits, discounting the exceptional, thus rendering a deceptively neat and uniform depiction of historical reality. The basic limitation is in the level of generalization (although it may be compounded by the author's errors), which is bound to downplay the rich diversity of history in favour of the typical case, even when relatively few instances actually reside in close proximity to the mean. This does not negate the attempt to draw up a broad historical survey; it does, however, caution against the uncritical digestion of its generalizations.

Historical sociology of this sort is a dependent discipline; the derivative aspect of the enterprise must be recognized. The raw materials of this survey were extracted and first interpreted by others; any originality in the finished composition is due solely to the way its elements have been combined. Standing on the shoulders of historians whose archival credentials and mastery of documentary detail can never be matched from on high, I have tried to make sense of their studies, assembling a myriad of meticulously stitched patches and working them up into a huge, patterned quilt. There are gaping holes in the finished product, where the fabric is held together by a few speculative threads, but in one sense that is the least of our problems. Even where the work of social historians has been taken into account and their results have been cited, one is bound to lose its rich detail, colour and texture as the larger design is imposed. To some extent, distortion is inevitable when research that is tightly delimited in time and space is surveyed from the commanding heights of generalization, through the prism of a different theoretical framework, by an author whose abiding interests and working hypotheses are far removed from those of the original scholar. I am aware of the potential pitfalls and inherent limits of this type of overview, where one's reach is bound all too frequently to exceed one's grasp. Sweeping and incautious assertions in these pages will undoubtedly vex historians who have spent their entire academic lives researching a particular region and period as they watch a neophyte tread clumsily across their beloved and well-tended fields. I must apologize to them in advance.

These caveats are not meant to depreciate the potential benefits of well-crafted work on the upper tiers of the pyramid of knowledge; it is simply to recognize an immense scholarly debt. For while the methodological protocols of historical sociology and social history are markedly different, the synthetic overview of the former is a complementary endeavour to the ground-level monograph of the latter. Whether they realize it or not, social historians need the sweeping generalizations and high theory furnished by historical sociology. Those who keep their noses pressed to the empirical grindstone, eschewing 'grand schemas' so as not to distort their view of reality, labour in the thrall of common sense – commonplace theories unconsciously held. Percept without concept is nonsense. It is far better to render one's theoretical framework explicit, checking and modifying it continuously in the light of empirical investigation, than to proceed 'by intuition and common sense'. The acid test of any theory, of course, is the analytical results achieved through its use. With this in mind, I have kept the first chapter as brief as possible, so as to get on with the historical account.

1

Labour-Power, Family Forms and the Mode-of-Production Concept

It is historical materialism's great merit to take as its starting point a close examination of the daily activities of working people, the vast majority of the population and the direct producers of society's wealth. Yet this strength is vitiated in so far as families are largely absent from marxism's established accounts of people's lives. Humans eat and sleep, work and procreate in family groups. Our deepest bonds are with family members. Families place us in society and shape our lives from cradle to grave. Yet families are nowhere to be found in most studies of modes of production. The result is that marxism has nothing to say about how the key microcosm of personal life is shaped by, and aligned within, the most basic macro-structure of society. Feminists have justly criticized marxists for elaborating the mode-of-production concept in a 'sex-blind' fashion.[1] For women's first labour (whatever else they may produce in the way of material goods) has been consistently excluded from the conceptual field of historical materialism's central theoretical construct. The result of this displacement has been to assign the social organization of childbirth, infant-care and early socialization to the realm of nature by default.[2] In this text and its sequel I shall endeavour to rectify this deficiency, making room for families at the heart of modes of production.

Modes of production facilitate and foster the reproduction of certain family forms and preclude or hamper the development of others. The crucial factors in this regard are the ways labour-power is harnessed and consumed, and producer families obtain the means of their members' subsistence. If modes of production shape family forms, the obverse is also true. Family forms are active elements in the constitution and development of modes of production, above all because they are central in the production of people and their capacities for work, compliance and resistance. These causal dynamics operate in an intricate and dialectical fashion. Structural-functionalist models – of the whole determining the action and alignment of its parts – are rejected at the outset. This,

9

in a nutshell, is the theoretical orientation of the book. My purpose in this chapter is to explain its key elements.

The potential benefits of such an approach are dependent upon unifying two kinds of analysis which have heretofore been disjoined: a marxist political economy, centred on the development and transformation of modes of production; and a historical sociology of population dynamics and family structures, tracing change in the long run. On each side of the family/economy divide, the terms of established discourse must be revised, laying the groundwork for integration. First, the standard version of the mode-of-production concept must be expanded to make room for the family-based production of human beings and their labour-power. Second, a superstructural and formalist discourse on kinship needs to be grounded in the organization of domestic subsistence in order to furnish an adequate conception of the family economy. In each case, the argument is informed by a feminist critique of the conventional paradigm.

Towards an Expanded Mode-of-Production Concept

'Mode of production' is undoubtedly the most important, and vexed, concept in historical materialism. Most marxist analyses – of entire social formations or of their major regions – are elaborated within the terms of this complex category. Controversies in historical materialism frequently centre on differences as to the proper elaboration of a given mode in analysing social formations where it is held to prevail. For better or for worse, used and abused, this concept has been historical materialism's theoretical keystone.

A mode of production is defined conventionally as a set of productive forces mobilized within, and in latent or manifest contradiction to, a given ensemble of social relations of production.[3] The major theoretical problem is that this forces/relations combination has been conceived in an arbitrarily constricted fashion. This is what has come to be known as the problem of economism, widely acknowledged by marxists of diverse persuasions in the past two decades. There is a broad consensus that the original sin of economism stems from an overemphasis on the economic dimension in conceptualizing modes of production, and a reduction of their political and ideological 'levels' to derivations of the economic base. While agreeing that the consequences of economism have indeed been pernicious for marxism, I find the standard diagnosis of this ill to be misconstrued. In my view, the economist error has stemmed not from an exaggeration of the weight of the socioeconomic dimension but instead from a false narrowing of its field, and a failure to conceptualize adequately the integration of the socioeconomic with politico-legal relations of the state and the cultural formation of groups and classes. In short, while others have faulted the reduction of superstructures to infrastructure, I focus here on the arbitrary constriction of the infrastructure itself. The 'relative autonomy of superstructures' cannot possibly compensate for a truncated conception of the infrastructure which has been left intact and unchallenged.

All human societies are necessarily involved in three interrelated productions: the production of the means of production; the production of the means of subsistence; and the production of labour-power. The reproduction cycle of each is constituted by means of the regular repair and periodic replacement of the productive force in question. Standard marxist accounts of the mode-of-production concept are confined to the first two 'departments'. The ongoing production of labour-power – its daily rejuvenation and generational replacement – is missing.[4] Yet this is primarily what families do: they people societies, restoring their members' energies and replacing worn-out labourers with the 'fresh blood' of youth. The exclusion of labour-power's daily and generational reproduction from the conception of modes of production has made it almost impossible to see families, as labour teams, pumping the life-blood through socioeconomic systems. From a feminist perspective, this tunnel vision is deadly, since the social control of women is based upon the control of their reproductive capacity in a broad range of societies.

In standard marxist discourse, the field of production is reduced to the production of material goods, the productive forces to the instruments of labour, and the social relations of production to those relations found at the site of goods production. Labour is treated as a vital input to production, but nowhere is labour-power taken seriously as an output of production. From this vantage point, subsistence is seen one-sidedly as a process of consumption. For the purpose of illuminating family forms and domestic relations, we need to invert our perspective, analysing goods production as a process of labour-power's consumption, while seeing the domestic consumption of food and shelter as a process of labour-power's production. This will be my perspective in this text.

The families of producers mediate the relationship between labour supply and demand; this equilibration must be conceived as a two-way street. Yet in doing so, we confront one of the enduring shibboleths of historical materialism. Ever since Marx denounced Malthus's population theories, orthodox marxists have remained deeply suspicious of any model of socioeconomic development that accords an active role to demographic forces.[5] Typically, the 'laws of economic development' have been counterposed to 'the laws of population', as if these were distinct mechanisms, separately housed, with a single drive-shaft running from the former to the latter. While marxist hostility was certainly justified in countering reactionary Malthusian *policies*, the *analytical* impact of discounting the ramified effects of population dynamics in studying societies has been disastrous for historical materialism. We have abandoned the terrain to our adversaries.

'Every particular historical mode of production has its own special laws of population, which are historically valid within that particular sphere', Marx declared in *Capital*.[6] More than a century later, this statement remains an unsubstantiated assertion which very few marxists have shown the slightest interest in investigating. Since I wish to evaluate its relevance in the following chapters, several of its implications ought to be spelled out here. We should understand by 'laws of population' what Marx means by laws in other contexts in political economy: a set of long-run forces and tendencies which never operate purely or unimpeded in the real world, but none the less persist as long as the mode of production is in place. We are not then speaking of a law in the sense of a set of forces which guarantee a uniform outcome in diverse settings. We are speaking of a characteristic interplay of forces and relations of fertility and mortality which allows for developments within a given mode of production as well as entailing discontinuities in the transition from one mode to another. The aggregate population outcome – the balance of births, deaths and migration – might be similar in societies where different modes of production prevail, but the *way* this result was generated would be distinctive in each case. Consistent with his entire orientation to political economy, Marx upholds the principle of historical specificity, rejecting any natural or eternal law of population growth or overpopulation. As he writes in *Grundrisse*: 'population is an abstraction if I leave out, for example, the classes of which it is composed ... [population in abstraction] is a chaotic conception of the whole.'[7] This point retains its validity, rendering a telling indictment of a great deal of contemporary demography which treats population dynamics divorced from the socioeconomic structures of the societies in question. However, historical materialism can hardly be exonerated from Marx's critique. The processes of mate selection and marriage structure childbearing in all known societies, but marxist studies typically ignore this crucial matrix of demographic reproduction.

In the statement quoted above, Marx insists that the principal determinants of population dynamics are endogenous to prevailing modes of production, and we should seek to locate them there. Yet this cannot simply be a matter of passive alignment within an overarching structure. Most modes of production generate their own internal 'contradictions' (in Marx's terms), and these conflicts propel their development through space and time. If this is generally true, then we would expect to find that demographic forces periodically get out of alignment with other elements of the socioeconomic system (such as its subsistence capacity and labour demand). The resulting disruptions alter the contours of the mode of production or push it towards a full-blown crisis. I state this as an initial hypothesis consistent with the theoretical tenets of historical materialism, but it also appears to receive compelling empirical confirmation. The most momentous transformations of the productive forces in human history are arguably the Agricultural Revolution (when semi-nomadic foragers began to turn the soil, sow and reap) and the Industrial Revolution (when fuel-powered machinery replaced hand tools and animal traction as the dominant means of production). In both cases, it seems that sharp disruptions in earlier population checks occurred immediately prior to sweeping changes in the technology at hand. The resulting population explosion furnished its own accelerators in the build-up of momentum, effecting a transition from one mode of production to another.[8]

By confining the productive forces to a narrow conception of tools and technology, orthodox marxists have fostered a bilateral reduction: on the one side, the effective omission of labour-power as humanity's first productive force; on the other, the marginalization of raw materials supplied by nature.[9] I shall be mainly concerned to criticize the first facet of this reduction, but the second must at least be recognized, for the two are deeply connected. The effect of leaving raw materials out of a conception of the means of production is to cut the productive forces off from nature, reintroducing the latter from the outside as a peripheral consideration. This is a fatal error, since it places the mode of production 'on top' of a natural template, as opposed to being embedded *in* nature, as in reality all modes of production are. The techno-structure of a mode of production directly reflects the insertion of the human community into its natural environment, and can never be a 'pure' expression of the mode of production as such, since it bears the profound impress of a particular community's natural habitat. Because a mode of production is normally disposed over a range of terrains, the social formations it dominates are differentiated by the adaptations their inhabitants have made to nature's diversity (soil, flora, fauna, climate and seasons). This is particularly true of pre-industrial formations. In every society and in every habitat, food, clothing and shelter are the stuff of daily life, the perennial objects of the labouring class's toil and concern. Subordinate classes live closer to nature than their superiors. They work with their hands transforming nature and lack the means to insulate themselves from nature's calamities, as classes wielding a social surplus are partially able to do. Especially in studies undertaken from the standpoint of labouring classes – marxism's proclaimed perspective – human interaction with nature ought to be fully recognized.

Classical marxism's predilection for seeing modes of production unfolding on top of a natural template was wholly consistent with the tendency to leave the regulation of fertility and women's reproductive labour out of the account. The implicit assumption of both omissions was the same: these were natural processes. As such, whatever their effects on human development, they were not really socially shaped and hence amenable to historical explanation. A more subtle version of this dismissal is still common today. It is conceded that family relations are socially determined, but in a deeply naturalized way. Other social relations – of production and of politics – must first be transformed before domestic relations can be worked on and changed. For critically minded marxists, the feminist movement has effectively discredited this 'secondary contradiction' position. The question we now confront is this: what happens to the major categories of historical materialism when gender hierarchy is no longer treated as a subsumed and derivative phenomenon?

Reacting against the narrow fixation of orthodox marxists on 'the point of production', marxist–feminists have generally thought of 'reproduction' as a separate process. While it is certainly preferable to the complete omission of labour-power's production, this approach has injected a conceptual duality into the heart of historical materialism. Symptomatic of such bifurcation has been the tendency of many marxist–feminists to conceive of a separate domestic mode of production under capitalism, or indeed wherever households stand apart from the main sites of goods production.[10] The paradoxical effect of this response, in 'adding on' a new sphere, is that it has left the conventional conception of production unaltered instead of tackling the problem head on. Doubled vision, however, is no alternative to tunnel vision. An expanded conception of modes of production is required, one that integrates the production of labour-power with goods production in a unitary matrix where neither is highlighted at the cost of obscuring the impact of the other.[11]

Human Labour-Power and Its Production

Before embarking on a historical analysis of labour-power's production through specific family forms, it will be useful to clarify the common foundations of its production in all family formations. The terrain of the universal is adequately approached not through idealist rumination on the essence of human nature but by means of an anthropologically informed comparison of the human species with others, particularly our closest primate relations. Recent advances in primatology have dramatically altered the traditional perception of a vast gap between the behavioural capacities of the individual members of our species and other primates.[12] On closer examination, the higher primates look more like us, and we like them. Chimpanzees, for instance, not only use but also fashion tools (peeling sticks and straightening plant stems) and carry them from one place to another to employ them in locations remote from where they were made. These were formerly thought to be exclusively human attributes. The symbol learning capacities of chimps and gorillas are also far in advance of what had formerly been assumed.

It is undeniable, however, that the evolutionary trajectory of humankind is sharply divergent from that of all other species on earth, including our closest primate relations. What ability accounts for this departure? The marxist reply is 'labour-power' – the capacity for complex co-operative production through an extensive division of labour. Able to adapt to, and acquire the means of subsistence in, a wide range of climates and habitats, we are not confined to a particular ecological niche, as are other species. Not only have we developed this capacity, but we are compelled to exercise it; we have become incapable of living *in* nature, in a fully immersed sense, as other species do.

All primates live and move about in groups (loose-knit or tightly organized in different circumstances), gathering food as they go; they certainly socialize with one another. What then distinguishes human communities from other primate groups? We produce the means of our own subsistence collectively, while other primates lead a hand-to-mouth existence, gathering and eating their own food and functioning as nutritionally self-sufficient units. They may share food, but their survival does not depend on doing so.[13] Even though human foragers do not plant seeds or store foodstuffs, they do obtain the means of subsistence in one location and then distribute goods for consumption elsewhere. The members of a foraging band thus depend on one another's production for survival and are compelled to organize the overall distribution of their labour-power to different tasks accordingly. In short, they organize a mode of production. 'Men can be distinguished from animals by consciousness, by religion or anything else you like. They themselves begin to distinguish themselves from animals as soon as they begin to produce their means of subsistence.'[14] The special quality of human labour-power is not confined to the production of goods; the way in which we produce *ourselves* is also unique. Through the social regulation of fertility (by means of marriage and within it) we shape our procreative capacity as no other species does. This process will be discussed more fully below.

Food-sharing entails the formation of a domestic group that pools its resources at a stable home-base site. Foodstuffs and other products are deposited, stored, prepared and then consumed jointly. Commensality is universal in the human species. Usually (but not invariably) the same group which eats together will build or obtain a dwelling of some form in which its members can rest and sleep 'under one roof'. The separation of food production from consumption gives rise to a specific labour of food preparation in the domestic setting, which, from the discovery of fire onwards, has involved cooking (once again, unique to the human species). Food preparation becomes a basic ingredient of domestic labour in all societies. Similarly, the erection of dwellings, with interior structure and furnishings, involves a minimal labour of maintenance, housework, which becomes a second universal component of domestic labour. While nothing other than spatial proximity or pragmatic convenience suggests that food preparation and housework would be 'naturally' combined

15

with one another, and with childcare, the three task-sets nevertheless appear to be amalgamated and assigned to women in virtually all societies. These domestic labours are far from being all that women do in most societies; but they are primarily theirs to do almost everywhere.[15] This consistency is based on a socially determined division of labour and is not the inevitable by-product of women's natural responsibility for childbearing and breastfeeding. Since food preparation, housework and childcare are, by their very nature, integral to the renewal of our capacity for labour, their joint assignment to women places them, much more than men, at the centre of labour-power's ongoing production. By omitting the production of labour-power from the conception of modes of production, mainstream marxism has ignored women's core contribution to the production of life; the masculine bias of the traditional framework is manifest.

The replacement of labour-power consumed in production involves a daily and a generational cycle in all societies. The members of a household eat together, socialize, rest and sleep; in the process, adult producers restore their energies to be able to work again tomorrow. Since consumption of the means of subsistence never stops, the domestic labour directly associated with it (food preparation and cleaning) is the most ceaseless year-round labour of all in human societies. Domestic labour knows no holidays; holidays taken from other labours tend to increase the time and effort required in domestic labour. Domestic labour is skilled labour, universally. A series of technological breakthroughs in human history originated in domestic activities and were probably the result of women's ingenuity and diligence: fire, cooking, earthenware pottery, tanning and cloth-making.[16] Furthermore, women, as food-gatherers, almost certainly discovered seed cultivation and initiated hoe agriculture.[17]

All societies must establish an overall relationship between the schedule of labour-power's exhaustion in production and its demographic replacement through the medium of its domestic groups. The way in which this relation is regulated and upset furnishes an important insight into the dynamics of the society as a whole. For whole periods, producer families may inadvertently align their demographic regime with the labour demands of the socio-economic system by flexibly adjusting the ratio of hands to mouths in their own households. At other times, the family-formation strategies of the producers come into conflict with the labour requisites of the system as a whole. Inefficiencies accumulate; if unresolved, they lead eventually to stagnation and crisis. In modern societies, where the great majority of people die in old age, we tend to ignore the centrality of the procreative imperative in the course of human history. But in pre-industrial societies, where life expectancy is twenty-five years and almost half of all infants die before their fifth birthdays, women must produce, on average, five children just to sustain the population at its present size.

A key aspect of demographic regulation is to be found in the way societies organize the relationship of sexuality to procreation, since this linkage is not naturally established in *Homo sapiens*. Even in societies with high mortality, most people have a surfeit of libidinal energy above and beyond the societal need, and parental desire, to bear more children. Unlike other primates, human females possess a continuous erotic capacity outside ovulation. More importantly, they experience no powerful drive at the time of ovulation to copulate with any available male, which other female primates do in oestrus. The suppression of oestrus in hominid development cleared the way for the cultural regulation of sexual expression. It was now possible to foster a community interest in monogamy and paternity, link the mother–child dyad with the adult pair, and build a role fusing biological paternity with social father-hood. Discriminating mate selection became the potential prerogative of women, with significant implications for evolution.[18]

The dissociability of sexuality from procreation leaves both capacities open to a great variety of developments. There is therefore 'no determined and species-specific mode of relationship [between the sexes], but rather gener-alized features which make it necessary to define specific modes. Therein lies not only man's adaptiveness, but also his problem.'[19] Conception itself be-comes, for the first time with the human species, a matter of practical knowl-edge and conscious determination. Birth control is not a recent invention in history. Various forms of fertility restriction (abstention, withdrawal, abortion and infanticide) have been detected in virtually all societies.[20] An estimated 90 to 99 per cent of human history has been spent in small nomadic bands prior to settled agriculture; these communities could not have survived unregulated fertility. Birth spacing in gathering and hunting bands averages three or four years, as prolonged and vigorous nursing suppresses ovulation, thus permitting mothers to remain mobile as food-gatherers throughout their childbearing years, carrying a single child as they travel.[21] Only under sedentary conditions do birth intervals shorten, curtailing the mobility of women caring for child-ren.[22] While this form of regulation is obviously very different from modern contraceptive practice, there is no reason to discount it as a form of birth control.[23] Today in Third World countries experiencing a 'population explo-sion', fertility rates reach only 40 to 60 per cent of natural capacity.[24] Nowhere do we find evidence for sustained birthrates which would naturally result from heterosexually active populations breeding freely.

The means of birth control are many and varied: some promote celibacy and fear of sex (e.g., abstinence); others facilitate sex play free of fear (e.g., effective contraceptives); some are the result of societal pressures and deter personal choice (e.g., the prohibition of premarital sex); others are employed as the personal choice of women or couples. The objectives of different modes of fertility control are also antithetic: while some policies may be designed to repress the birth rate and control population size, others seek to boost population growth, repress sexuality and control women. Whenever the disposition of property depends on paternity, older men seek to control women's sexuality since, as the Roman jurist Gaius remarked, 'while maternity is a fact, paternity is a matter of opinion' which depends on community perception of the mother's sexual fidelity for the socially legitimate father to be accepted as the actual sire. In short, fertility regulation is a combat zone of conflicting forces struggling over incompatible objectives. This is evident today in Western states where bitter social antagonisms have erupted in a protracted political struggle over women's right to make their own decisions on abortion. Women have rarely been autonomous agents in matters of sexuality and procreation, able to exercise self-control over their own biological capacities. As the contemporary women's movement has understood, the fight for reproductive autonomy is central to the struggle for women's emancipation.

Physiological changes accompanying the evolution of early hominids made childbirth more difficult. The shift to an upright walking posture altered the structure of the pelvic girdle, narrowing the birth canal; at the same time, infant skull size grew to make room for an enlarged brain. These changes increased the hazards of childbirth for both infants and mothers. Human parturition is extraordinarily arduous and draining at the best of times, but when complications arise, maternal injury and death occur more frequently than in other primates. Childbearing is not normally accomplished in solitude but is assisted by one or more attendants (midwives in most societies); this intervention is also distinct to the human species. Before the modern decline in fertility, women bore children more or less continuously from marriage until menopause, with an average of eight to ten pregnancies, three or four miscarriages, five or six live births, and two or three deaths before the age of five. The toll of such a burden on women's health and vitality must have been considerable.[25] Roughly 8 per cent would have died in childbed.

Yet child*bearing*, by nature a female burden, was only part of the reproductive load. The rest of the onus – child*care* – fell to women through a social division of labour and the concomitant delineation of a domestic sphere of diminished male obligation. The care of young children has always been a lengthy, time-consuming responsibility. The evolutionary bind of a shrinking birth canal and an expanding head size was resolved through neoteny, the immaturity of the human infant at birth, resulting in a prolonged period of child dependency. Since human behaviour is less tightly tied to instinctual drives and physiological maturation than that of other primates, the scope for reflexive reasoning, language and learning is correspondingly enlarged. Primary socialization has been intensified to bridge the gap between instincts and behaviour. Hand–eye co-ordination and prehensile skill mature much more slowly in humans than in other primates; children do not become self-sufficient eaters or defecators until they are three or four. Competent mobility develops more slowly as well, as a function of our upright stance. Constant adult surveillance is required to keep toddlers from stumbling into danger, and it is five or six years before children can keep up with adults travelling at any distance over rough terrain. In all these areas, non-human primates achieve competent self-sufficiency much more quickly than we do; consequently, the children of these species absorb much less of their parents' attention and energy.[26] The investment human adults must sink into the care of their progeny before the new generation is independently productive and recovering the costs of its extended upbringing is unique to our species.

While fathers have a highly variable involvement with their children's upbringing, it is rare that the actual work of childcare (cleaning and feeding) is taken to be men's regular responsibility or shared at all equally between parents. Practically universally, life begins with mother, not only for the first few months of life but for years thereafter. The mother–child bond is the first social relation through which we are inducted into the community. Feminist scholars have underlined the profound cultural significance of the asymmetry of parental involvement in childcare for the reproduction of polarized sex roles and gender identities.[27] They have postulated a powerful compensatory drive to assert male power in community life, in response to alienation from the labour of infant nurture and early socialization.[28]

Since the practices and customs of mothering vary widely cross-culturally, we cannot infer that the mother–child relationship has a uniform quality globally; we *can*, however, recognize its ubiquitous importance. It seems reasonable to postulate that the strength of the maternal bond will be proportional to the investment of time, energy and concern a mother spends in caring for a child. Since this outlay is unique to human reproduction, our mother–child ties tend accordingly to be intense and enduring.

Those who play a central role in the upbringing of children must themselves be highly skilled if the latter are to be brought up to be productive members of the community. Because of the pervasive assumption that mothering is instinctive, the knowledge and skills requisite to this role have been seriously underestimated. The devaluation of women's normal domestic skill repertoire is both an effect, and reciprocally a cause, of women's subordination in a broad range of societies. Feminists have subverted this naturalist assumption, forcing a belated appreciation of the maternal contribution to human development. In anthropology, the standard 'Man the Hunter' version of early human evolution has been vigorously criticized. Sally Slocum writes:

A major point in the Man the Hunter argument is that co-operative hunting among males demanded more skills in social organization and communication, and thus provided selection pressure for increased brain size. I suggest that longer periods of infant dependency, more difficult births, and longer gestation periods also demand more skill in social organization and communication. ... Caring for a curious, energetic, but still dependent human infant is difficult and demanding. Not only must the infant be watched, it must be taught the customs, dangers, and knowledge of its group. For the early hominids, as their cultural equipment and symbolic communication increased, the job of training the young would demand more skill.[29]

Because infant survival is precarious and child dependency prolonged, these burdens cannot be treated casually. Regular arrangements must be made (responsibilities assigned, labour-power set aside, space and time provided) to nurture and socialize the dependent young. As primary care-givers, women have a compelling interest in securing the putative father's devotion to the well-being of his children and his reliable assistance in the maintenance of mother and child. Where enduring paternal commitment was first achieved, Stone Age bands would have experienced a better chance of survival than groups where adult males roamed freely and women with children had to rely on their own resources. We know from the study of contemporary societies teetering on the brink of a subsistence crisis that their durable existence is jeopardized whenever investment in childcare is severely curtailed. Colin Turnbull has described the impoverished Ik people in these terms: under severe ecological strain, they scrimp on investment in the next generation – abandoning newborn babies and neglecting infants, causing an excess of deaths over births.[30] The Ik's failure must be kept in perspective. Western Europe in the early modern era was a demographic success story, yet at least 40 per cent of infants died before reaching their tenth birthdays. Even in 'healthy' pre-industrial circumstances, vast quantities of maternal labour-power were squandered. The efficiency of a society's labour force will be raised to the extent that this waste is reduced.

If human reproduction poses undeniable difficulties for our species, and particularly for women, biology is not destiny. We ought to avoid extending a benign version of patriarchy to the whole of human history, as Peter Laslett has in the following passage: 'The rules which forbid the begetting of children outside marriage have to a large extent succeeded in ensuring to every person born a male protector and provider. This appears to be true for all societies at all times.'[31] As Michèle Barrett and Mary McIntosh have pointed out, arguments which extrapolate from biological function to family structure 'for all societies at all times' are extremely dubious: 'Without denying the physical and mental demands of pregnancy, childbirth, lactation and childcare, we can properly question the assumption that these inevitably lead to women's dependence.'[32] We have only to recognize the great variety of labour assignments that societies have developed to deal with these problems to acknowledge that fully historical explanations for persistent patterns are required.

What, then, are the key variables that determine how women's reproductive responsibilities will affect their general social standing in the community? A critical factor is how readily women are able to combine their reproductive labours with other tasks: are various productive responsibilities congruent with infant nurture? Compatibility is essential if women are to participate with men on an equal footing in a society's overall division of labour. George Murdock assessed the division of labour by sex in 224 societies, finding a tremendous variety in what women (and men) did. Females were absent from only two areas: big game hunting and metalworking.[33] Evidently, it is not so much the nature of the work itself but the way it is socially organized which determines how easy or difficult it is for women to combine it with infant-care. Wherever childbearing and breastfeeding force women to withdraw from extra-domestic labour for extended periods, they tend to lose public presence and power in their communities. The deterioration of childcare compatibility was one of the causes of women's generally declining position in the transition from hoe to plough agriculture.[34] Whenever the prevailing mode of production in a society strongly prioritizes the production of wealth over and above the production of people, it tends to jeopardize the smooth integration of the two labour processes. This has occurred in industrial capitalism, where a deep antagonism has developed between childbearing and infant-care on the one hand and wage work on the other, undermining women's bargaining power in the labour market. This conflict will be examined in the sequel to this study, *Weathering the Storm*.

No community can survive unless the average lifespan of its productive members is sufficient for them to produce offspring, care for them and prepare them to the point where they are able to become fully productive. In the community of producer households there are three generations: children who are not yet producing their own upkeep; the elderly who have ceased producing all of theirs; and the intermediate generation of adults who must produce a sufficient supply of subsistence goods to cover the upkeep of all of them.[35] This lifespan pattern of productive capacity is roughly in symmetry with the maturation of procreative capacity as well. The middle generation commands both elements of labour-power, while children and the aged are incapable of sustaining either of the two basic conditions of life. It is therefore necessary for every class of adult producers to generate continuously a 'subsistence surplus' (in addition to any surplus which may be extracted by non-productive classes) in order to reproduce itself from one generation to the next. The way families manage the balance between producers and consumers within households is essential to their living standards and very often to their survival.

In all societies, households experience difficult and somewhat easier phases of the family cycle, according to the shifting ratio of producers to consumers present within them. The period of maximum childbearing, coming soon after marriage in most societies, is particularly strenuous. Women's reproductive labours are at a peak, which inevitably entails some reduction in other endeavours (though often insufficient for their own health). If mothers are breastfeeding, their nutritional needs are high, while the eldest children may not yet be recovering the costs of their own upkeep. In communities living close to the margin of subsistence, special provision will need to be made through the preparatory processes of mate selection, marriage and household formation to ensure that the conjugal unit is in a position to survive through the subsequent stage of peak drain on its resources. This may involve marital endowments, the prior attainment of full adult occupations and incomes, the support of an extended kin network, and so on. The solutions are varied but the problem is universal. Preparatory provisioning in some form is essential in dealing with the protracted generational turnover of human labour-power. Obviously, the more control couples have over their fertility the more control they will have over their own destiny, in anticipating household composition and building up a savings fund before entering the period of maximum drain.

Conceiving of Family Forms in Modes of Production

Turning our attention to the other side of the intellectual divide, let us consider how to integrate this perspective on the reproduction of labour-power with the study of family forms. Family formation is a ubiquitous feature of human cultures. All known societies structure mating through marriage and place individuals in society through kinship. The universal disposition of human communities to organize demographic reproduction through the medium of family groups does not necessarily mean that family formation is genetically encoded, the end-result of specific biological drives. My argument is the converse: that we are impelled to form families because human reproduction is fraught with problems that are *not* resolved biologically. Since these issues have been discussed above, we can be brief here.

Family formation is best understood as a *social* response to the vulnerability of our natural condition. By conjoining kin groups through marriage, families ensure a minimal level of community support and co-operation in a broad range of environments. The regulation of mating through conjugality stabilizes the relationship between sex and procreation that had become unhinged with the supression of oestrus in the course of hominid development. A persistent libidinal surplus is channelled through marriage and men's exclusive 'conjugal right' secures the social bond of fatherhood, mitigating the explosive uncertainty of paternity. The development of heritable property and paternal obligation furnishes males with an interest in limiting fertility – an interest that females (for their own reasons) had always had. The exhausting process of

22

childbearing is legitimated and sustained in a secure setting wherein resources are pooled and shared out between the sexes. Maintaining households as enduring sites of domestic co-operation, families nurture the young and care for the elderly, forging networks of solidarity between the productive and dependant members of the community. Given the problems associated with the extraordinarily slow pace of human maturation, we must recognize, in particular, the decisive role of family socialization in preparing youth to take their places as productive adults in society.

People make enormous sacrifices to safeguard their families' continuity, honour and living standards; in return, loyal members are entitled to sustenance and protection from the family group. The peculiar nature of this reciprocity distinguishes kinship from other types of human association. While familial bonds are the most intensely personal of all ties, they are not, in the first instance, personally chosen. A marriage partner may be selected, but kinship is a lifelong commitment assigned at birth. Its obligations are neither freely undertaken nor can they be readily repudiated. This involuntary onus is particularly problematic in so far as the individual's reference group is a moving target, with births and deaths, marriages and migration repeatedly altering household composition and reconfiguring kin networks. Furthermore, the obligation to provide for dependant members normally extends beyond the co-resident nucleus to close kin living elsewhere. The circulation of goods and care-giving within kin networks is thus open-ended, multilateral and diffuse; exchange is typically characterized by incommensurate worth, indefinite recompense, transferable onus, multiple 'currencies' and contending claimants. These features tend to blur the calculation of self-interest, suppressing explicit assessments of fair value between spouses and wealth-flows between generations.

Within the domestic circle, individuals still act in self-interested ways, but they are severely constrained by their position in the family and the need to preserve close ties. Reflecting the obligatory nature of family association, spousal allegiance and filial duty normally override questions of equity. The distribution of wealth and power within families is thus prone to imbalance and hierarchy. While dependants are sheltered and sustained, they are also vulnerable to abuse and exploitation by family heads.[36] Complicating the management of these intimate asymmetries is the difficult problem of parenting. Unlike most forms of human association, the parent–child relation is routinely reversed. Nearly everyone who survives to maturity is destined to change places: to move from being a (helpless) child to becoming a (controlling) parent, and then reverting, in old age, to a state of child-like dependency. The intensely personal experience of this inversion (however it is culturally construed and mitigated) must have profound implications for familial relations across the full spectrum of human societies.

While taking due cognizance of these ubiquitous features, it would be an error to try to deploy them in generating a cross-cultural definition of 'the family'. The global variety of family forms is such that for every common denominator postulated by one scholar, another subsequently discovers exceptions.[37] To persist in the search for a universal essence of 'the family' is a futile and idealist exercise. A more adept starting point, from a materialist perspective, is to analyse prevailing family forms in particular societies, relating them to the modes of production in which they flourish. Proceeding in this fashion, our field of study must include all the families of the realm in their full diversity. To discount atypical domestic groups because they fail to conform to the familial mainstream would be to propound a deceptively neat view of history. But if our primary objective is to analyse the development of *predominant* forms, our paramount task must be to explain mass *conformity*, not deviance. Why do the great majority of families in a society share so many features in common? What ensures their similarity with one another and induces new family branches to replicate the forms of their predecessors?

My working hypothesis is that these homologous dynamics originate in the overarching influence of dominant modes of production. Such congruence can never be explicated in purely pragmatic terms, however, based upon the need of all families to secure their members' subsistence. There is also, indispensably, a normative dimension. A mode of production entails a 'way of life' and, as such, is a cultural construct. A family form rises to prominence and sustains its primacy, in part, because it is successfully projected as a kinship ideal, inspiring widespread emulation from most members of the community (who, in their conformity, constitute the mainstream), while exposing transgressors to scorn and marginality. Family reputations are based upon publicly perceived adherence to norms governing the processes of familial reproduction: mate selection, cohabitation, sex, procreation, child-raising, inheritance, and so on. Since a person's behaviour in these areas is typically thought to reflect upon the whole group, members come under enormous pressure to uphold 'the family's good name', to avoid, at all costs, its public disgrace. Compliance is enforced at three principal levels: through the legal codes and institutional powers of Church and state; by means of community vigilance; and through the exercise of domestic authority, primarily by family heads. Most of the time, these forces work in broad congruence; rarely, however, are they completely harmonious. Dissonance between levels typically gives rise to concerted attempts to re-establish an acceptable consistency between rules of familial conduct and community practices.[38]

Treating kinship systems as ideal types, structuralist anthropologists have been preoccupied with questions of kin reckoning, naming practices and general rules of kinship classification, producing a formalist discourse abstracted from the mundane concerns of family subsistence. Declining to indulge in such schemas, social historians often fall prey to the opposite error: in their limitless pursuit of particularity, they eschew theory construction altogether. Justifiably wary of deterministic models which drain the past of contingent variety and fortuitous combination, they neglect to offer any sustained reflection on the conceptual frameworks and causal logics that are inevitably embedded in their work.

The theoretical key to integrating analyses of kinship systems and family economies is to relate the former directly to its substratum, the life-cycle of the domestic group. Kinship codifies prevailing ideals concerning the management of the domestic cycle. In the following chapters, I will focus, therefore, on the crucial processes of transition during the turnover phase of the cycle, when offspring reach adulthood, marry, join or form households, and begin to procreate, while their parents retire and die. Let us review these steps briefly.

(a) *Achieving a livelihood:* How do young people gain regular access to a viable means of production in order to provide for themselves and their dependent children in the future?

(b) *Acquiring household space:* How do young people obtain dwelling space as they come of age? What residence rules and norms of household formation govern this acquisition? Is household formation dependent on property transfer from parents to offspring?

(c) *Getting married:* How do young people become eligible for marriage? Who controls mate selection and marital timing? Is any form of wealth transfer involved in the marriage contract, and if so, what type? What connection, if any, does marriage have to inheritance?

(d) *Bearing and raising children:* Under what circumstances does childbirth become legitimate and couples free to procreate? How is fertility socially regulated, both through marriage and within it? How do families deal with an increasingly burdensome dependency ratio as women pass through their childbearing years?

(e) *Providing for parents:* When children become productive adults and marry, what kind of commitment to their parents do they maintain? Are they obligated to provide and care for them in old age? What role (if any) does inheritance play in structuring relations between the generations, ensuring that commitments are met on both sides?

The ways in which these steps are interrelated is the crux of family structure; it is on this basis that one family type ought to be distinguished from another. The sequence through which people move, from being children to becoming parents themselves, is shaped by the mode of production and regulated by community vigilance; it is also subject to deliberate action by the participants themselves.[39] There is considerable scope here for contention between the generations and the sexes; when shifts in the balance of power become widespread and durable, they foster far-reaching changes in family forms.

In seeking to place the field of family studies within a revised marxist paradigm, untenable abstractions must be avoided. We can never arrive at a transhistorical formula which expresses a general relation of 'the family to the mode of production'; this is as chimerical as searching for a universal essence of 'the family'. Since modes of production operate at several planes of determination, they are best conceived at different levels of abstraction; the same holds for family forms. Under feudalism, for instance, the seigneurial property form fostered a stem family cycle among the peasantry, based on unigeniture in land. But the system developed very differently in Eastern and Western Europe. Consequently, we see divergent forms of the stem cycle evolving: in the East, a common variant was based on early marriage and a patrilocal residence rule; in the West, a weaker stem variant was the norm, based on later marriage and neo-local household formation. At the highest level of abstraction, one might say that feudalism fostered two (or more) dominant family forms. Any principle of determination in such a model appears to be rather weak. Proceeding in a historically grounded fashion, it would be more correct to say that the feudal mode of production had developed in very different ways in Eastern and Western Europe, and that these variants had conditioned the development of distinct family cycles on a regional basis. Once we grant that the mode-of-production concept must itself be deployed at different levels of abstraction, we are free to elaborate family forms at all levels of the model. In this way, the rich variety of family forms displayed in a given society may be fully appreciated without abandoning efforts to discover their related roots and common limits in the property forms of the mode of production within which they arise.

Prevailing modes of production are no more fixed in temporal terms than they are spatially homogeneous. They are deeply marked by their historical predecessors and by the specific conditions of their origins and their roads to power. The capitalist mode of production admits independent two-generation nuclear family households among wage-earners, tending to uproot inheritance, expunge vestiges of prior family forms, and disperse kin relations in the sphere of employment. This sweeping generalization is valid at an epochal level of abstraction, in so far as it can be shown that all capitalist societies exhibit such tendencies sooner or later. But in Western Europe during the early era of industrial capitalism (examined in *Weathering the Storm*), these trends had not become prevalent. We find that proletarian families were often vertically extended; their households regularly contained non-nuclear extras; and family members frequently worked together as labour-teams in mines, mills and workshops. Is the model thus refuted? No. Industrial capitalism was not, at this stage, a mature system whose tendencies had fully developed. In the second half of the nineteenth century, remnants of the first (mixed and transitional) stage were jettisoned: family extension was reduced; households became more private, their composition more strictly nuclear; and employers moved to eliminate family hiring, paying all wages directly to individual workers. In sum, this was a purer stage of capitalism than its predecessor, for family forms as for other structures.

The model we develop of a mode of production is elaborated at its highest level of abstraction from a study of the mature system in periods and places of its most complete extension. From there we move backward and forward in time, tracing the mode's dynamic tendencies through various stages of its ascension and decline, approaching more closely the terrain of history proper, with its rich variety, unevenness and concatenation. This 'return to the concrete' constitutes the acid test of the model in question. However, it can never furnish a direct check on the theory at its highest level of abstraction, since no paradigm can fully reproduce in thought the historical forms whose deep structures it is designed to illuminate.

Yet since I am treating modes of production as immensely influential social structures, and not simply as convenient ways to think about societies, the empirical onus of the theory must be taken seriously. The assertion that modes of production condition the development of family forms ought to be falsifiable in principle. If it could be shown, for example, that the basic structure of family forms did *not* change as the prevailing mode of production was transformed in the passage from feudalism to capitalism, then the proposition advanced above would be seriously vitiated. As I have said, this is precisely what Peter Laslett and his associates in the Cambridge Group for the History of Population and Social Structure have argued: that the Western family was small and nuclear from at least the sixteenth century on, undergoing no basic structural change in the course of the Industrial Revolution.[40] If the Cambridge scholars are right in this, then I am wrong, and the argument that modes of production deeply condition family forms is a dead duck. However, the argument cannot be decisively settled simply by reference to 'certain historical facts'. In large measure, our disagreements hinge on how family forms ought to be conceived.

The Cambridge Group's approach focuses on questions of household composition. In his renowned introduction to *Household and Family in Past Time*, Laslett defined the family as 'those who share the same physical space for the purposes of eating, sleeping, taking rest and leisure, growing up, childrearing and procreating'. He excluded 'kin and affines who live close by, even if they collaborate so closely in the productive work of the family that for economic purposes they are part of it.'[41]

By sharply demarcating the family as a cohabiting group from the larger kin network, the Cambridge Group's approach buttresses the insularity between the discourses of domesticity and kinship. In a critique of the paradigm, Robert Wheaton has insisted that 'this separation of household structure from kinship system can no longer be maintained. ... The boundaries of the "family household" are evidently far more porous than the concept at first suggests. ... In the end, we can understand household structure only within the context of the kinship system.'[42] Separating the family as a cohabiting group from the larger kin network, the Cambridge paradigm tends to reduce families to households.[43] While the displacement has been widely recognized in the past decade, social historians are still inclined to use the terms almost interchangeably.[44] Because a family-cycle approach frames the relation between co-resident groups and highlights the constant formation, fission and dissolution of households, its analysts are generally more attuned to the importance of kin networks extending between households and less likely to perpetuate this conflation.

When Laslett defines families as kin groups that eat and sleep together, he brings their common consumption to the foreground.[45] Their relation to production – the way they make a living – remains firmly in the background. In a family-cycle perspective, consumption, production and demographic reproduction receive a more balanced and integrated treatment. We deal with family forms in direct relation to the life-course, highlighting age transitions and relations between the generations. The Cambridge Group's measure of mean household size amalgamates households in all phases of the family cycle, and thus tends to obscure changes in composition over the course of the cycle. The frequent movement of kin (and non-kin) in and out of households is much easier to perceive from a cyclical standpoint, once the households of a community are grouped and analysed by phase.

Employing Laslett's definition, the Cambridge Group's resident scholars and international associates have focused their empirical quest on a taxonomic exercise: slotting the households of a community into a pre-existing set of categories according to their co-resident composition; adding up the proportions falling into various categories and comparing communities according to the distribution of households in each category.[46] The most notable discovery of this research has been that three-generation households were rare in Western Europe before the Industrial Revolution. The broad dissemination of this finding has served to rectify a pervasive misconception in family history dating right back to Le Play.[47]

From a research standpoint, the primary appeal of the household composition methodology is that it generates standardized measures from census-type records that can be employed for comparative purposes in studies around the world. In a field of scholarship where quantifiable data are scarce, this facility has given the method an enduring popularity. The problem, however, is that the exercise has become much more than a technique for casting a narrow band of light on family structure. The Cambridge classification scheme has become a paradigm, an encompassing way of thinking about family structure, which is blinkered and misleading.[48] In the process, a new set of myths has been born. Perhaps the most tenacious one is that family structure changed very little with the development of industrial capitalism.

The foregoing criticisms of the Cambridge Group's approach have been expounded by family historians ever since its influential collection *Household and Family in Past Time* first appeared in 1972. The superiority of family-cycle perspectives seems generally to have been established in the past decade.[49] This is a welcome trend from a marxist standpoint. Family-cycle perspectives are much more open to the insights and concerns of historical materialism than is the household composition model. There are, however, many different paradigms articulated within the terms of this discourse, nor is there anything approaching consensus on the best framework to adopt in situating the microcosm of family change within the macro-dynamics of societal development.

Many social historians cast their work against the vague backdrop of modernization theory, where the global processes of industrialization, urbanization and cultural modernization are thought to have had certain effects on families, germinating in the urban upper middle class and spreading downwards through the social order. This framework is implicitly based on a cultural-diffusionist assumption: that lower classes and backward regions lag behind their superiors but eventually follow them on the road to modernity and progress. A revisionist current of social historians have rejected the modernization paradigm, placing the protracted process of proletarianization at the centre of its work.[50] Class formation and changes in the family cycle are seen as two facets of a complex but unitary process, involving an intricate transformation in the social relations of goods production and demographic reproduction. My intellectual debt to these historians is considerable, as citations in the following chapters will indicate. Their relationship to marxism is in most cases a loose and ambivalent one. Perhaps this book will persuade scholars seeking alternatives to the modernization paradigm to consider the merits of a reworked mode of production framework in comprehending the development of family forms in the long run.

Patriarchal Power and Family Relations

Family forms may be distinguished from one another in many ways, but the critical factor in the framework I am proposing is the way in which the younger generation attains full househeadship. This raises directly the question of power relations between the generations. The other axis of househead authority is gender-based: the power of husbands over wives. It is the combination of these two dimensions of authority within the intimate nexus of family relations that delineates the distinct character of domestic patriarchy.

The term 'patriarchy' has become very popular in feminist studies, but there is no consensus about its specific meaning nor its status within feminist theory.[51] Furthermore, some feminists have questioned the utility of the term altogether.[52] I shall not enter these debates here, but I should say in passing that I find the term a potentially very useful one, providing we avoid using it in a suprahistorical fashion, as some sort of universal drive for male rule.[53] My own inclination is to specify and delimit the term somewhat, making it bear some explanatory weight, so that its precise use in a discourse may furnish some analytical leverage beyond the labelling and assimilation of all phenomena of male dominance. So I will refer to *domestic* patriarchy only, and leave to one side questions of the term's applicability in designating state forms and male supremacy in public life.[54] The central objective of the analysis is to situate domestic patriarchy as a property relation in the regulation of labour-power's reproduction.

In this text, patriarchy refers to systems of male headship in family households. A great variety of such systems exists; each requires historical specification. Some combination of the following five prerogatives held by husbands and fathers over their wives and children are generally found in patriarchal family systems, with varying strengths and modes of assertion: (a) the right to represent the family group and to speak in its name in the community; (b) effective possession of, entitlement to, and ultimate disposal rights over family property, including income; (c) supervision of the labour of other family members; (d) conjugal rights of sexual access to, and exclusive possession of, one's wife in marriage (hence securing paternity); (e) custodial rights over children, entailing ultimate authority in their upbringing. These prerogatives are normally accompanied by the patriarch's obligation to his wife and children, which reciprocates, and hence reinforces, their obligation to obey him. It is the conscientious discharge of the obligation to care for and protect one's dependants which fully entitles the househead to subsume their interests beneath his own in representing the family as a group. What counts as a 'good father and husband' in a patriarchal context is a head who exercises his prerogatives with some demonstrable sense of responsibility for the well-being of his subordinate kin.

Note that the two dimensions of authority relations within families, along the lines of gender and generation, are integrated in this definition. Michèle Barrett has objected to the term on precisely these grounds: that patriarchy conflates the rule of the father with the dominance of husbands over wives.[55] Far from being a weakness, however, the recognition of the practical fusion of masculine and parental power in the person of the household is the concept's greatest strength. One would not want to lose sight of gender and generation as distinct dimensions of domestic power, nor to maintain that they could never be found apart. Here Barrett's point is well taken. However, if they *are* pervasively fused in reality it is a mistake to disjoin them conceptually, to treat women's oppression in isolation from the rule of the father, and secondarily the mother, over their children.

It is one thing to specify the various prerogatives which typically comprise patriarchal power; it is quite another to explain their sources – this must be done in specific historical contexts. Nevertheless, I want to set out here my basic approach to this complex problem, distinguishing it from others. The issue can be broached by considering possible answers to the question: 'If marriage is an oppressive institution for women, why do the vast majority elect to wed, remain married or remarry?'[56] The answer I prefer is that for most women most of the time the alternatives to marriage are much worse. *Male dominance in marriage is sustained by means of the degradation of alternatives to marriage, and the individuation of women's experience within it.* By this reasoning, whatever improves women's life-opportunities outside marriage, whatever makes it easier for young women to remain single and wives to leave their husbands, will strengthen women's bargaining power within marriage. As the alternatives improve, the threat to leave becomes increasingly plausible (regardless of whether it is explicitly raised), enabling wives who wish to continue to live with their spouses (as most do) to make stronger demands upon them.

The foregoing argument is based on a paradigm of constrained choice. Life-necessities and social compulsions do not eliminate all choice; they force people to select from a limited range of available options. Even slaves must decide how to respond to their masters' commands: what is to be gained from resistance, or alternatively from acquiescence, and at what price? The wife of a brute must decide whether to leave or stay; there are costs and benefits entailed in either course of action. How do people choose between limited alternatives? I am positing a largely rational calculus of relative advantage, entailing inevitable trade-offs between various courses of action. Passivity and habit are treated here as the repeated adoption of a particular course of action; simply to keep on doing what one has done before is to forgo alternatives, consciously or otherwise. But since people's present dispositions are shaped by past experience, the investment of self in reiterated behaviour may make fresh

31

approaches difficult to consider. Both material and ideological dimensions are involved in the consideration of alternatives. No attempt is made to separate them here; the base/superstructure metaphor is rejected for this purpose. The availability of an option is both a matter of practical access to it and its recognition as a possible course of action. If an action is unthinkable, it is not within the range of available options. The costs and benefits of any action also combine material and ideological elements. The consequences of leaving one's husband may be a lower living standard and the condemnation of the community. Both are real costs; both are influential in preserving marriages. Furthermore, the two tend to be reciprocally reinforcing. The poverty which results from being cut off from a household's resources lowers a woman's status in the community; community scorn, in turn, may lead to ostracism and impoverishment.

Choice-theoretic models of this sort are often predicated on an abstract individualism.[57] Two important qualifications will help us to avoid the pitfalls of atomism. First, since people are immersed in the culture in which they make decisions, all forms of calculative rationality are culture-specific. We reject the pragmatist assumption that material circumstances dictate specific courses of action, furnishing the basis for a practical rationality that operates 'beneath' the higher realms of 'culture'.[58] Second, since people live within a web of established social commitments – above all, family bonds – the need to preserve important relationships limits their options.[59] Paradigms of the marketplace, which assume that all participants in the game are free to compete or cut a deal with every other player in pursuing their own interests, are rejected, even in the analysis of capitalism. I assume that most women (like most men) are subsistence-optimizers, interested in their own well-being and prepared to take steps to improve their lot whenever they can do so without taking untenable risks. But they normally do so with the best interests of their children at heart, not on the basis of an individualist interest narrowly conceived. This consideration limits to some degree the exercise of self-interest in relation to their husbands. If women remain in oppressive marriages, if they often bite their tongues and tolerate abuse, it is fundamentally because the alternatives for themselves and their children would appear to be worse: the risks involved in leaving are prohibitive.

In response to the question 'why do most women marry?', two familiar propositions are rejected. The first is that women (and men) are biologically driven to live monogamously and to procreate; they enter marriage to obtain these objectives. There is certainly a virtually universal desire for sex, but the objects of this desire and the social relations of its satisfaction are not biologically predetermined. Similarly, I am prepared to grant that there is a near-universal desire to procreate, but the provision of legitimate opportunities for childraising within marriage, and their legal prohibition, economic precariousness and cultural debasement out of wedlock, are the result of social structure, not biology.

A second approach accounts for women's wish to marry and remain in oppressive marriages primarily in ideological terms. In a patriarchal world, most women's subjectivity is formed in such a way as to render them victims of false consciousness. Pervasively socialized to subservience, they become unable to perceive and to act in their own best interests. Theories of false consciousness have ill-served marxists in explaining the accommodation of workers to capitalism; they are equally pernicious in accounting for the accommodation of women to patriarchy. The problem with such theories is that they postulate 'true' interests as being unitary and straightforward (as in 'you have nothing to lose but your chains'), and consequently must propose a lack of correspondence between people's consciousness and their 'genuine' (i.e., revolutionary) interests. The source of the dominant ideology is therefore held to be extrinsic to the situation, and its appeal a chimera. If subordinates respond conservatively, it is because they were brainwashed or misled and their authentic interests were betrayed. An unwillingness to face squarely the awkward fact that the self-interest of the oppressed is not unilaterally revolutionary leads to the substitution of an utterly idealist explanation for acquiescence or prudence.

The sounder materialist premiss is to postulate diverse strategies in the furtherance of interests and a mix of ideologies generated in reference to them. What differentiates complaisant from combative strategies? One key variable is the time horizon: are objectives considered and alternatives weighed in the short run or the long? A second critical factor is whether the individual or the group constitutes the basis of intended action. Acting as individuals in the short term, the oppressed often have more to gain from pleasing their masters than from antagonizing them. On the other hand, collective resistance may win concessions over time, furnishing rational incentives for struggle. There is no a priori reason why the calculus of relative advantage will consistently favour one or the other of these courses of action; it will depend upon the prevailing interpretation of past experience, the capacity for collective action, and the present correlation of forces.

Due to their vulnerability, subordinates usually have an immediate stake in preserving the relationship with their oppressor. In an ultimate sense, they need their master's subjugation like they need a hole in the head; but life rarely presents such ultimate, revolutionary opportunities. Normally, the risks of being punished, cut loose and discarded are severe: the hazards, that is, of slaves being sold, proletarians fired, and wives deserted or divorced. Only by considering each partner's alternatives outside the relationship can one appreciate the paradox: that he who benefits most from a relationship normally has less to lose from its severance than she who is oppressed within it.[60] It may further a wife's immediate interests to be acquiescent to her husband and to serve him well if her actions elicit better treatment from him. Her behaviour may be calculated, rational and self-interested; it need not be predicated upon masochism, self-debasement or a wholly mystified identification with the master's viewpoint. As long as the prospects for upending a subservient relationship are remote and the likely consequences of quitting it severe, a modicum of acquiescence, avoiding provocation in order to preserve the peace, will be the preferred and rational course of most subordinates most of the time. This does not imply that women are necessarily content with their lot in life and are unwilling to confront husbands, seeking a better deal. Forms of resistance and bargaining, the negotiation of explicit pacts and implicit understandings, are a normal and necessary part of married life. Vast disparities of power do not preclude reciprocity between spouses; nor does oppression prevent the development of compassion, affection and attachment.[61]

Among subordinate groups, dominant ideologies refer to the positive incentives which await individual compliance, celebrating the just rewards of obedient slaves, diligent workers and dutiful wives. Radicals may disparage such meagre rewards as self-defeating 'crumbs from the master's table', but to the hungry they are none the less food. It is arrogant to disdain the cruel choices which the relatively powerless are compelled to make and to live with in the name of higher forms of struggle which are simply not available to subordinates under normal (non-revolutionary) circumstances. Social hierarchies run into difficulty only when subordinates have more to gain and less to lose by collective contestation than by placating the powerful and bargaining individually for a better deal under the existing rules of the game. This is why the alternatives to marriage available in any given historical period are of such importance in setting the contours of spousal power relations. As long as these alternatives are legally limited, economically inferior and culturally debased, individual women have every interest in seeking mates and remaining in oppressive marriages.

In daily life, the terms of spousal power are not so starkly posed. The question women face is not whether to leave or stay on, but rather how to make the best of their immediate situations, obtaining subsistence, stability and a measure of human dignity. The thesis on spousal power proposed above may now be extended to daily life: *the strength women can exert in relations with their husbands is crucially dependent upon the character of their relations with one another.* Male dominance within marriage is dependent upon the individuation of women's experience, their separate subordination to particular men, their relative isolation from – and competition with – other women. Conversely, the forging of solidarity and a sense of community among women buttresses their marital bargaining power. In discussions with other women, wives share their experience of marriage and learn how their own partnership stands in

34

relation to others in the community. This permits them to 'speak bitterness' to one another, to 'spread the word' on particularly bad husbands and bring some community pressure to bear, mitigating the worst excesses of patriarchal power. Women's (and men's) community networks should be included in family studies wherever the historical materials allow. Recognizing their importance, feminist scholars have sought to illuminate the ways in which women sustain social networks to cope with the demands of daily life, building supportive communities to counter male aggression in a vast array of societies.[62] Informal cultures of solidarity and solace, while critical to the bargaining power of women within marriage, do not normally contest the entrenched prerogatives of patriarchs, only their most abusive exercise. To condemn a brutal husband is to advocate better treatment, reinforcing the established model of a good husband, a kind and compassionate master. And a good husband deserves a good wife – one who is cheerful and industrious, who serves and obeys him. In the absence of a women's movement, female friendship and support networks do not contest the basic terms of marriage and patriarchal power *per se;* they mitigate its worst excesses, furnishing assistance in coping with life and living with particular men. This is not to denigrate the importance of community networks for women, merely to insist that they are not revolutionary unless linked to an independent women's movement for change.

Radical feminists have correctly highlighted the role of rape, wife-battering and physical intimidation in the maintenance of male dominance. Yet they exaggerate the importance of violence and underestimate the discredit that the grossest forms of brutality bring to the ideology of male supremacy, which is not normally legitimated by 'might makes right' arguments. Concomitantly, they tend to ignore the degree to which masculine civility, beneficence and protectiveness anchor male dominance, precisely because these dispositions embody masculine ideals and tend to elicit positive co-operation from wives who feel that they are fortunate to have considerate husbands who do not beat them.[63] Any form of rule that is preserved through fear alone is inherently unstable, and male dominance has shown itself to be rather resilient over the centuries. Of course, the formula for maintaining male supremacy (or any other form of enduring social power) is through a judicious combination of carrot and stick, often wielded by the same master. The two faces of patriarchy are complementary in practice, even though they generate ideological contradictions.

Are all family forms throughout history patriarchal? Many radical feminists seem convinced that they are, corroborating, paradoxically, an assessment of history and human nature which has traditionally been propounded by the most androcentric of anthropologists.[64] However, the anthropological evidence on foraging peoples indicates a frequent (but by no means uniform) pattern of rough parity between the sexes, with only slight and mild political advantages accruing to men.[65] Since these peoples are the closest twentieth-century ancestors of Stone Age bands, there are grounds for suggesting that the record of systematic male dominance may well be a recent one. On the other hand, modern studies do not sustain Engels's belief that the origin of women's subordination lay in the rise of class-state formations. Some pre-class societies exhibit strong and persistent patterns of male dominance in married life and community politics.[66] Anthropological research lends no support either to the orthodox marxist position, stemming from Engels, nor to its opposite, which posits a universal pattern of male dominance. Variation in gender relations in pre-class societies may be difficult to explain at present, but the evidence of considerable variation is clear.[67] If class and state formation did not inaugurate women's oppression, they certainly rendered it pervasive, legal and systematic. Wherever households became a repository of private property in the means of production, conjugal relations tended to become patriarchal.[68] The material stakes in assuring paternity rose; controlling women's sexuality and fecundity was no longer simply a demographic question but became a matter of immediate political concern to property-owners. Clear male householdship and political alliances thus tended to arise when this combination of factors was present. Agnatic marriage and inheritance rules followed, reproducing the advantages of male householders from one generation to the next.

The new family history of the past two decades has been an extremely positive development, but one of its gravest weaknesses remains the failure of most scholars to take seriously the question of power within families. Householdship is a familiar term in the literature, but it is generally addressed in order to identify household types or describe family forms. The prerogatives of householders – the causes and consequences of their power – are rarely examined, much less explained. Either patriarchal authority is taken for granted and hence naturalized, or it is presumed to have disappeared with the advent of companionate marriage in the modern era. Feminist scholars, by contrast, have raised the question of patriarchal power and sought answers in various directions. When family historians remain blind or indifferent to this issue and impervious to feminist insights in addressing it, their own scholarship is correspondingly impoverished. The question of patriarchy – its persistence and change – must now be placed on the agenda of family studies, both historical and contemporary.

2

Peasant Family Forms in the Feudal Mode of Production

The twin figures of the peasant tilling the soil and the landlord appropriating the agrarian surplus are familiar enough in a vast range of societies, past and present. Unfortunately, we still lack a satisfactory typology of peasant–landlord relations of agricultural production in the historical materialist tradition. We can begin, however, by distinguishing feudalism's property form in land from others. On the one hand, the landholding nobility of medieval Europe (and feudal Japan) differed from the landed ruling classes of the ancient Islamic states and the Chinese dynasties by their personal possession of landed estates, and the absence of such a private property form in the latter cases.[1] On the other hand, the conditional nature of the feudal nobility's landholding, with benefice tied to vassalage, clearly distinguished the manorial property form under feudalism from the absolute and freely alienable private property of either the anterior slave mode of production in Antiquity, or the capitalist mode of production which succeeded feudalism in Europe.

Pursuing the guiding thread of this delineation, I will advance a preliminary definition of the feudal mode of production in order to frame the ensuing discussion. In agricultural formations where feudalism predominated, two distinct social relations were found in combination, based on a conditional form of private property in land: a relation of state *within* the aristocracy, and a relation of exploitation *between* the landed aristocracy and the class of dependent peasant cultivators.[2] In the upper register, one finds a fief system. A suzerain presided over a domain of parcellized sovereignty, wherein lords of every rank were granted fiefs in trust (usually land) in return for a solemn pledge to perform loyal state service (usually military) to one's overlord, and ultimately to the suzerain. While ideologically the vassal received a fief in recognition of his service, practically speaking he was compelled to service because he held a fief. What is critical, however, regardless of their symbolic relation, is that vassalage and benefice were fused in this scalar property form, which cohered a multitiered ruling class based on the land and constituted its state power.

In the lower register, the seigneurial system bound dependent peasant cultivators to the land and to their lords in a relation of political dominion and economic exploitation. In return for effective possession of a holding, peasants were obliged to pay the lord's agents a set of dues, taxes and rents, fixed by custom and adjudicated in manor court, the local level of the feudal state. These exactions were levied not only against the land and its consumable produce but also against the persons of the peasant household, constricting their ability to dispose of their time, labour-power, possessions and offspring as they saw fit.[3] Land and household members were thus bound together through the basic relation of feudal exploitation, which was more than a bundle of rents. It was also, indispensably, a relation of personal servility, which the peasants were not free to evade or quit with impunity. All their customary rights on the land were predicated on maintaining an acceptability to their lords: 'That acceptance was the crucial fact: it, and it alone, constituted "title".'[4] Furthermore, since all family members of the household shared the servile status of the tenant head and were burdened by the same set of obligations, peasant dependency entailed 'the rigorous subjection of the family as well as the individual'.[5]

Various forms of vassalage, benefice and landlordism can readily be found in history, but their full synthetic unity appears only in medieval Europe and feudal Japan.[6] It was the scalar form of conditional property, structuring a pyramid of parcellized sovereignty over agricultural land, which fused the two registers of the feudal mode of production, lending medieval social formations (which were ramshackle constructions at best) a minimal internal coherence. In recognition of both tiers of this ensemble, it would perhaps be more correct to designate this 'the feudal–seigneurial mode of production'. In the ensuing discussion, 'feudal' should be taken as an abbreviation of 'feudal–seigneurial' in reference to the mode of production as a whole.

The family form of the household constituted the basic cell structure of feudal relations of production for the class of dependent peasant cultivators. Through this unit, family members secured access to the means of production and subsistence. Inheritance for peasants did not normally extend beyond the next of kin, and an eligible heir had to be produced on each holding or there was a risk of reversion to the lord. The feudal mode of production was thus characterized by a strong linkage of landholding to marriage and marriage to procreation.[7] Those without land could not easily marry, and those with land had to marry and produce offspring to keep the holding productive and in the family. Only legitimate offspring (i.e., those sanctified by wedlock) could succeed to a holding. The timing of marriage was normally dependent on entry to a holding, and marriage was the principal social regulator of fertility. The land-poor therefore tended to marry later than well-established peasants, and to raise fewer children. The poorest stratum did not reproduce their own numbers in most periods. The population grew by means of a molecular process of downward mobility engendered within peasant families. Those young adults who were not favoured by inheritance and lost out in the scramble for established village holdings became the mass labour force of the system's extensive growth, moving to the periphery and clearing new land.

Women's foremost conjugal duty was to bear legitimate offspring, both to work the holding from an early age and to inherit it eventually. A wife had to produce an heir in order to qualify for lifelong support from the holding she joined in marriage in the event that her husband predeceased her. Her spouse and the lord shared an interest in ensuring that the holding was fully supplied with a family-based labour force, able to pay its dues and furnished with an eligible heir when the time came to pass it on. Women were therefore valued, above all, for their procreative capacities by the male householders of both classes.[8] Fertility rituals persisted in peasant communities throughout the Middle Ages, exorcizing 'the ever-potent evil: the sterility of the marriage bed'.[9]

Every mode of production based on private property, in whatever form, requires a regular and legitimated means of intergenerational property transfer intimately aligned with its basic relations of production. At the dawn of the Middle Ages, many regions of Europe had strong traditions of partible inheritance. In the conquest of seigneurial domain (not in regions remaining peripheral to noble jurisdiction) these traditions gradually gave way before an assertion of impartibility: the right of the lord, the tenant head and his designated heir to keep the main arable holding intact, while compensating non-heir siblings for their *de facto* subordination.

It is difficult to discern the effects of this alteration on peasant family structures in the Middle Ages. Much of the argument of this chapter is based on a reading of the shadows, supplemented by retrospective inference in light of better known early modern family forms. The account is therefore inevitably subject to doubt and qualification, and to the sort of 'regional exceptionalism' which predictably ambushes those who dare to utter sweeping generalizations concerning European feudalism. The early modern evidence which social historians have amassed on peasant family forms and village demography is far more plentiful than, and of superior quality to, that available for the Middle Ages. While striving always to consult whatever medieval studies were pertinent to the problem at hand and to accord them due weight, I have not refrained from drawing extensively on early modern sources, projecting them 'backwards' in time. While this procedure is obviously not without difficulties, the question is whether it is tenable at all. It would not be in a work of social history, where temporality is decisive, but this is a work of historical sociology, which is a different matter. This does not entitle one to abuse historical materials by ignoring their context, but it does mean that they need to be organized differently. The object of study here is peasant family forms in the feudal–seigneurial mode of production. This mode is not temporally confined to the Middle Ages, but persists in many of its land-based agrarian features right down to the collapse of the *ancien régime*.[10] Early modern sources are relevant wherever they illuminate feudal structures which are not yet superseded. Optimally, a dominant mode of production is studied in its prime, when its social relations are mature, fully extended, and not yet heavily imbricated with its successor mode(s). For feudalism, this is the high Middle Ages. The problem then is how to handle the tension of temporal discrepancy between the object of study, ideally conceived in its medieval prime, and the richest empirical sources, drawn from the early modern era, when feudalism had lost its overarching dominance and was undergoing deep permutations. Every effort has been made to ascertain the medieval origins of patterns which are elaborated in detail by reference to early modern studies. Where origins could not be established (in the case of late marriage and rural domestic service, for example) I have left their discussion to the next chapter.

Among the aristocracy, a supraregional class, matters were somewhat clearer. The integrity of landed estates was assured through a realignment of kinship structures which became evident across Europe in the twelfth century. Several scholars have noted this shift to what might be termed conjugal patri-line.[11] Under feudalism, the form of househeadship was patriarchal and the mode of land transfer was patrilineal; their combination formed a nexus of male power in the family households of both the aristocracy and the peasantry. In peasant households, the authority of husbands and fathers over wives and children was based on their status as tenants, managers of family lands held at the will of their lords. In moving from her natal to affinal family, a woman thus passed directly from the custody of her father to that of her husband, regardless of whether she inherited land or just a dowry of chattel wealth. In order to maintain family continuity, it was essential that women be entitled to inherit holdings when appropriate men were not available; but when they did so their tenures were normally brief. Patriarchal power was manifest in both classes in the persistent drive to install married men as tenants, minimizing landholding among women. When daughters inherited land in lieu of sons, their husbands were recognized by lords as tenant heads in charge of managing family lands. When husbands died and widows were left with estates, they were immediately pressed to turn them over to heirs or alternately to remarry. In either case, family land was placed back in the hands of men as soon as possible.[12]

Kinship was reckoned bilaterally in feudal Europe. If unilineal descent groups had *ever* been prevalent among the Germanic peoples, they had long since disintegrated by the time of the mass migrations in the fifth and sixth centuries AD.[13] By the early Middle Ages marriage was exogamic, with few signs of cross-cousin unions, and the kindred were diffuse, overlapping, ego-centred networks, radiating laterally from the conjugal pair through the natal families of both partners. In manorial zones, the kindred were not property-holding entities and performed no corporate functions apart from the persisting solidarity of the feud. Yet they were networks of considerable vigour, sustaining diverse forms of co-operation and mutual support – work exchanges, the swapping of tools, lending, vouching, pledging, and so on. Since lords and peasant communities encouraged marriage within the local community, kin networks grew dense in long-standing settlements.

But despite the vitality of collateral ties, the dominant axis of kinship organization was intergenerational, reflecting the supreme importance of land inheritance passing down through the male line. Conjugal patriline in land (the major means of production) was a linchpin of the feudal mode of production.[14] While chattel property was dispensed to daughters as well as to sons, the main land parcel was not normally divided equitably. Every effort was made to preserve it in one functional piece and to pass it through the male line to a designated heir or heirs. The offspring's inheritance rights were normally secure against the subsidiary claims of the father's siblings; this applied to daughters as well as sons. Such conjugal primacy in inheritance accorded with the lord's interest in retaining control of land, and not permitting obligations to be lightened through a change in the status of tenant heads.[15] The generalizations of the foregoing account should be treated cautiously. Bear in mind that a woman in the Middle Ages had to give birth to four children to secure a 60 per cent chance of furnishing a son who would survive his father and be in a position to take over the holding. Roughly 20 per cent of fathers would have no children alive when they passed away, and another 20 per cent no sons.[16] Under these circumstances, all rules of inheritance required a pragmatic flexibility in order to prove viable in the long run.

Two of the seigneurs' vital prerogatives placed limits on the reproduction of peasant family forms from one generation to the next.[17] Through merchet (a fee for seigneurial consent to the marriage of villein daughters) lords normally enforced a loose endogamy within their estates, preserving their future labour force intact. The marital pool of villein tenants was thus confined for the most part to those who were subjects of the same lord. Secondly, through heriot, a succession duty of sorts, lords could normally prevent their dependants from passing on productive wealth to anyone who was not an active member of the family. Married daughters, living elsewhere, were usually excluded. On manors which were heavily dependent on the labour services of villein tenants, the lords took a particular interest in regulating the process of land devolution, marriage and procreation, in order to ensure that peasant families would be able to meet their full labour obligations in the future.[18]

Inheritance laws and customs varied widely from one region to the next across medieval Europe. Despite this undoubted variety, the overriding objective of lords and peasant heads alike was well-nigh universal: to prevent subdivision of the main heritable land parcel so that it might be passed on to the next generation as a viable holding, one capable of supporting a family. They were not invariably successful in achieving this, but it was nevertheless their objective, setting the context for a pervasive behavioural norm against which demographic pressures toward land fragmentation operated in the long term. With due regard for regional diversity, I shall propose that the predominant peasant family form fostered by feudal land devolution was of the stem type: a designated heir married into the main holding, compensated his non-heir siblings if they wished to marry and leave, raised a family and ran the farm upon the retirement or death of his parents. These households were formed in a virilocal way – broadly defined – where the heir and his bride came to reside on his family's holding (if not actually under his parents' roof). Those siblings who departed and did not manage to marry into an established holding generally formed nuclear families if they married at all (a great many did not); their residence norm was neo-local. This dispossessed and downwardly mobile stream of young adults constituted a continuous by-product of demographic growth within the seigneurial system. In short: among the villein class, stem families tended to form on the established arable, while nuclear families set up on marginal land around the periphery of villages or took off to re-establish themselves in new settlements.

Within family cycles of the stem type, the crucial variable was the timing and modality of househead transfer from the elder peasant patriarch to his son (assuming that the father was still living when the heir came of age). In Eastern Europe, and in much of the Western Mediterranean as well, the heir and his bride customarily moved into his father's household, while the old man remained in full and active control of the farm. In this transition, the assumption of househeadship by the younger generation did not occur at marriage, but at the death of the senior patriarch on site. This is the pattern which, from Le Play on, has been classically associated with the stem family; I shall term it the *strong-stem variant*.[19]

In most of the seigneurial zones of Northwestern and Central Europe, however, the heir's marriage normally entailed his assumption of househeadship, taking over the daily management of the family lands and being recognized by the lord and the village community as the new tenant head. Either the heir had to wait to wed until his father died, or the latter retired, making way for his son's full tenancy. Demographic realities – and the strong resistance of peasant patriarchs to retiring – made the latter a minority arrangement, though by no means rare. Widows, on the other hand, usually lacked the power to postpone the marriage of heirs in order to retain househeadship; they were constrained to retire or remarry, whether they wished to or not. Regardless of who remained alive when the son married and took over the holding, the basic form of unigeniture was the same. I shall term it the *weak-stem variant*. Under succession arrangements of this type, the two adult generations tended to live in separate residences on the same manse, so that co-residence, narrowly defined, remained simple and nuclear throughout the cycle. (The significance of narrow and broad definitions of residence norms will be discussed in a later section of this chapter.)

What evidence indicates that such a family cycle was prevalent among villein tenants in Western Europe in the Middle Ages?[20] Legal codes, manor court rolls, and wills reveal the widespread use of retirement contracts, primarily for widows, which suggest attempts to regulate such an arrangement, ensuring in particular that heirs discharged their obligations to their mothers and siblings.[21] The provision of a detached residence for an elderly couple, or a separate room for a widow, often with its own entrance, were frequently stipulated in such contracts.[22] Given the reluctance of senior peasant patriarchs to retire, it is probable that the great majority of these arrangements were established at their deaths. In English common law, a dower right normally entailed the provision of separate quarters for widows. Widows and heirs apparently preferred this arrangement to the alternative of residing together.[23] Other types of evidence point in the same direction. Site excavations and manor censuses reveal a frequent pattern of two or more farmhouses per manse, indicating the preservation of unitary holdings in conjunction with separate conjugal residence.[24] Residential subdivision might account in part for very low levels of three-generation households on customary lands where villein holdings were not normally divided through inheritance.

This, then, was the basic form of the stem family cycle prevalent among dependent peasants in the manorialized zones of Northwestern Europe. Max Weber thought that it arose as 'a compromise based on local decentralization without partition.'[25] He saw it as an accommodation between the extended kindred and its family nuclei; I think it is more correctly perceived as a compromise between parents and their children appearing as the corporate prerogatives of the kindred dissipated. Let us now turn to survey the origins of peasant family forms in the transition from Roman Antiquity to the early Middle Ages, before resuming our discussion of the seigneurial order in more detail.

Origins of Feudal Land Inheritance and Peasant Family Forms

The feudal–seigneurial mode of production coalesced in a centuries-long gestation, following the interspersion, collision and collapse of two vast and variegated social formations – the Roman West and the Germanic federations.[26] The social relations of the early medieval peasantry arose as a synthesis of mutated elements from both antecedents. An adequate summary of this transition (beginning with the decline of slavery in the later Roman Empire and culminating in the generalization of the manorial infrastructure in the Carolingian era) cannot possibly be attempted here. I seek merely to highlight certain features of the metamorphosis occurring on both sides, in order to indicate the close association between class relations, population trends and family forms in the protracted process of feudal genesis.

The transition from Antiquity to feudalism remains an obscure chapter in European history, despite considerable advances in historical knowledge secured in the past three decades, primarily by means of the rapid expansion and technical refinement of archaeological fieldwork.[27] While furnishing dramatic new insights into the material culture of peasant households, the excavation of early medieval settlements sheds no direct light on their familial relations and illuminates even less the contours of extended kinship forms in this tumultuous era. Our primary sources on kin relations remain the same as they have traditionally been in the historiography of 'the Dark Ages': a smattering of law codes from the Roman Empire and the barbarian successor states, and the Latin texts of a handful of authors. Consequently, it is more than usually necessary to emphasize the uneven and patchwork nature of the following account, particularly as it pertains to the Germanic component of the feudal amalgam, where the evidentiary base is scant indeed.

Developments in the Late Roman Empire

In its prime, the Roman Empire had been based on a combination of agricultural modes of production, with a slave labour force at its heart working the great estates of central and southern Italy and Sicily. This force had been built up in the Republican era by means of the massive importation of bondmen, acquired by taking prisoners in the course of military conquest and selectively enslaving peoples on the Empire's expanding periphery.[28] The encouragement of childbearing among the slaves of rural Italy was by no means rare, but the population in bondage failed to reproduce itself. High mortality rates were a major cause of this dearth, but Roman slaves also manifested extraordinarily low fertility. Marriage between slaves was illegal, and so long as replacements were plentiful, masters had no strong incentive to foster enduring conjugal relations among common field slaves.

Since many more males than females were enslaved, there was a persistent shortage of the latter. The sex ratio of urban slaves has been estimated in one study as three males to every two females, and in another, as two males to every female.[29] While this is a staggering imbalance, it is probable that the rural ratio was more severely skewed. Family formation among agricultural slaves was not unknown, but the sex ratio in itself meant that a majority of bondmen would not have had the opportunity to form enduring unions and create families. Through the widespread manumission of older slaves as their labour-power declined, masters sought to keep the dependency ratio low, evading the costs of keeping the elderly alive. Continuous restocking from abroad was necessary to maintain the labour force at strength. Italian slavery in the Republican era was an import-replacement regime by default, if not as a matter of conscious Senatorial policy. This does not imply that slave-breeding was rare, merely that it was insufficient, given very high death rates, to replace the servile labour force indigenously over time.

After the territorial expansion of the Empire ceased (with Trajan's conquest of Dacia in AD 106), the Roman legions were thrown increasingly on to the defensive. The Principate turned its military energies to repulsing barbarian incursions along the Rhine–Danube frontier. As the supply of enslaved youth from the hinterlands ebbed, slave prices rose. In the face of persistent shortages, with no prospects of obtaining alternative sources, the aristocracy made a belated attempt to convert to a self-sustaining regime of indigenous reproduction.[30] Successive emperors decreed subsidies and tax breaks for the owners of slave progeny: 'Slave owners and jurists began, in the second century if not earlier, to respect … family relationship[s] and to see slave families as entities which should be left undisturbed insofar as possible.'[31] Owners were initially exhorted to avoid breaking up families through sale or inheritance; by the late fourth century, it became illegal to do so.[32] The overall demographic effect of this effort is unclear, but it was probably modest. The economic impact of the conversion was almost certainly negative, as de Ste Croix has argued.[33] Concerted moves to even the sex ratio by permitting adult women to devote a considerable part of their energies to repeated childbirth and infant nurture must have detracted from the productivity of slave labour-power and the profitability of deploying it.

Did diminishing supplies and declining rates of slave exploitation constitute a formidable problem for the Roman West? Should this be taken as a decisive factor in the Empire's demise? A. H. M. Jones and G. E. M. de Ste Croix have argued in the affirmative; M. I. Finley and Peter Garnsey are sceptical.[34] The answer must hinge in large part on the alternatives to slave labour available for the cultivation of large estates: the indigenous peasantries of Italy, Gaul and Spain (to be discussed in a moment). What *is* clear is that the traditional mode of production on the *latifundia* – ganged labour under intensive supervision, subsisting on rations and domiciled in barracks – proved increasingly unprofitable. Gradually, it was abandoned and estates were sectored in two. While the home farm continued to be worked by domestic slaves, field slaves were granted small plots from which they were expected to subsist while surren-

deing a portion of the crop. Accompanying the elevation in status which occurred with the ceding of direct access to the means of subsistence was the
dissolution of slave barracks – the notorious *ergastula*.[35] *Servi casati* (literally,
hutted slaves) were able to form families, put their children to work on their
own land and transfer allotments to them upon decease. Labour scarcity was
'the practical reason which everywhere favoured heredity'.[36] Yet the familial
autonomy of the *servi casati* was extremely limited:

> Slaves fortunate enough to be given plots of their own were obliged to spend
> one out of every two or three days inside the dominial court doing whatever
> they were ordered to do; on those days they took their meals in the refectory
> and were thus reincorporated into the master's family. Their women were
> obliged to perform communal labor with the other women of the estate. The
> master took children from their huts as needed to replenish the ranks of his
> full-time servants.[37]

While never being recognized in Roman law, the domicile and familial rights
of slaves gradually began to be conceded *de facto* on large estates, under the
burgeoning influence of the Christian Church.[38] When this bundle of rights
became customary, the *servi casati* had achieved the status of serfs.[39]

Outside Italy and Spain, peasant cultivators possessing hereditary land were
the mainstays of agriculture throughout the Roman Empire, while slaves were
primarily employed as domestics in aristocratic households. Peasant families
were engaged in a broad range of class relations, from freehold ownership to
servile dependency. Across the full breadth of this spectrum, their position
gradually deteriorated from the second century AD on; an increasing proportion of them were enserfed.[40] In the last two centuries of the Western Empire,
ex-slaves and tenant farmers gradually converged. 'What difference can be
understood between slaves and *adscripticii*' (peasants bound to the land), Justinian asked rhetorically in the sixth century, 'when both are placed in their
master's power and he can manumit a slave and alienate an *adscripticius* with the
land?'[41] In this blending, 'the major question was that of domiciling: once
genuine independence of the hut had been acquired [by ex-slaves], fusion with
free *coloni* or tenants followed.'[42] Significant changes in the documentary records of the early Middle Ages indicate a general recognition of family rights
throughout the zones of settled agriculture across Western Europe. In contrast
with the Greek and Roman censuses of the Ancient World, the *mansus servilis*
of the peasant was now clearly distinguished from the *mansus indominicatus* of
the lord.[43]

What, then, of Roman marriage and family forms? Bear in mind that the
evidence upon which the following summary is based is largely drawn from
Roman law and aristocratic custom; very little is known about the families of
the lower classes. Marriages between slaves, freedmen and freeborn persons

were illegal and their progeny illegitimate, though cohabitation between those of different legal status was not rare. On the other hand, it was perfectly legal to marry one's cousin and such a union was not stigmatized, but there is no evidence that cousin marriages were common.[44]

Among Roman citizens eligible to wed, the legal process was remarkably casual; cohabitation, plus 'marital intention and regard', constituted marriage. The dissolution of a marriage was equally relaxed, and became easier over time. A simple notification of intention to divorce by either partner sufficed. No cause was required, nor was there much concern to establish blame.[45] Rates of divorce and remarriage appear to have been high, rising considerably from the late third century BC on. Though legally even-handed, the practical consequences of seeking divorce were far more difficult for women, who had to secure economic support from their fathers to proceed.[46] The legal powers of the paterfamilias were almost absolute. His wife's only recourse in law was to leave him. As for the marriage of offspring in his *potestas,* it was his right to compel them to divorce until the second century AD. There is no evidence, however, that the prerogative was widely exercised.

Amongst the propertied classes, first marriages were typically arranged by fathers; mothers might be consulted, but it was clearly a father's right and duty to find an appropriate man for his daughter, making a *digna condicio,* a suitable match. The principals had to consent to the union, but the legal grounds of a daughter's objection were slight: having to establish the man's moral turpitude. Her capacity to play an active role in courtship and mate selection was extremely limited. In contrast to medieval customs, a betrothal promise (the *sponsio*) was given *on behalf of* a young woman, not *by* her. It was normal for a son to take the initiative in arranging his marriage even though he had no more legal right to do so than his sister. The minimum legal age for marriage was twelve for females, fourteen for males, and first marriages were entered early. Half the females whose age is recorded on inscriptions were married by the age of fifteen. It was considered ideal for first marriage to follow soon after menarche. Young men, on the other hand, were expected to wait a year or two after assuming the white toga of full manhood.[47] Consequently, there was an age gap between spouses of perhaps five to seven years. Among the lower classes in Rome, it appears that women were older at marriage – most were in their late teens – and the age gap was somewhat less.

A dowry from the bride's natal estate would normally accompany her into marriage. The law did not require this, but the family head was under a moral obligation to provide one, and dotal exchange was practically universal among the propertied classes. The fund was a very substantial sum during the Principate, but not nearly so onerous as it would later become in medieval and early modern Europe.[48] It seems to have had a double purpose. In the first place, income and other benefits from the dowry's use helped to defray the wife's maintenance costs; in this sense, the gift was designed to cushion the husband's *onera matrimonii*. Consistent with this purpose, he owned it for the duration of the marriage and could manipulate it as an integral part of his estate. But secondly (in potential conflict with the first objective), the dowry fund was available for the woman's independent support when the marriage ended through divorce or her husband's death. In the former case, ex-wives could sue for its return and would normally obtain its full value, minus deductions for the custody costs of the couple's children, who usually remained with their father. In most cases, binding pacts were made between patriarchs at the time of marriage, specifying the dowry's disposition when the union was termi-nated.

The legal form of marriage had major implications for dowry and inherit-ance. In the early Republic, most marriages were contracted *cum manu*. Brides were legally transferred from their fathers' *potestas* to that of their husbands, where, except for the right to divorce, they had the same legal standing as children. In leaving the natal household, they severed all legal connection to it; dowries represented their final claims upon the paternal estate. By the late Republic, and increasingly in the Imperial era, most marriages were contracted *sine manu*. In this arrangement, a woman did not leave her father's *potestas*. While joining her husband's household, she never became a legal member of his *familia,* thus limiting his dominion over her. Furthermore, when her father died or emancipated her, she was entitled to own property.[49] This streng-thened her right to the return of her dowry in the event of divorce and enabled her to lay further claim to a share of her natal estate, since she retained membership in her father's *potestas*. The rise of *sine manu* marriage registered a dramatic weakening of the conjugal bond. Not surprisingly, divorce rates climbed concomitantly. Amongst the aristocracy, serial marriage became the norm. It is not clear whether the same shift occurred amongst the lower classes of Roman citizens.

The rule of intestate succession in Roman Antiquity was firmly partible. All family members who remained part of a man's *potestas* at the time of his death were held to be *sui heredes*, eligible to inherit – wives [*cum manu*] and daught-ers, as well as sons. To avoid the fragmentation of his estate, a man could write a will in which some of his children were disinherited. Sons had to be men-tioned explicitly to be renounced, whereas daughters could be denied shares by omission.[50] In practical terms, the partible sentiment reflected in the intes-tate law of equal shares meant that no one *sui heredes* ought to be forgotten, but that a daughter's share could take the form of her dowry. Since disinherit-ing sons was a messy business, it was preferable not to have too many. A strong desire to avoid the risks of patrimonial fragmentation probably motivated a concerted effort to limit births in marriage. There is plentiful evidence that a wide variety of contraceptive methods were practised, but it is impossible to estimate with any accuracy how effective they were.[51]

While slave marriages were not recognized in law, they were widely considered by masters and Roman citizens at large to be a normal occurrence, and were permitted with increasing frequency under the Principate. Progeny were legally reckoned *in utero* and paternity was unacknowledged, but in enduring unions fatherhood seems to have been socially recognized by owners and fellow slaves.[52] The servile family was discussed in terms which distinguished it from the master's family within his household. Sepulchral inscriptions reveal that slaves themselves referred to their deceased loved ones as wife (*uxor*) and husband (*maritus*), and employed the same terms as the upper classes for other kin relations.[53] Our knowledge of slave family life is limited to urban slaves, overwhelmingly from the huge *familiae* of the Senatorial elite; by comparison, conjugal formation and fertility among rural slaves must have been severely stunted. Since slave families were formed inside the extended households of their owners, the size of those households largely determined the possibilities for finding a mate and cohabiting. In this regard, information from elite households is obviously atypical; the number of slaves attached to an average household would have been small. This fact alone would have sharply restricted family formation among slaves.

Masters generally recognized that family formation among the servile population would contribute to the stability and morale of their labour force and were thus favourably disposed to it. Couples were often permitted to sleep together, and when children arrived, small alcoves were provided for a huddled co-residence. Yet since masters did not go to great lengths to facilitate slave unions or to keep families together, they were extremely vulnerable to arbitrary severance through sale or bequest. Papyrological evidence from Roman Egypt provides extensive information on slave sales from the first to the fourth century. The vast bulk of sales were of individuals, exchanged from the age of four on. There are a few recorded instances of mothers and young children being sold as a unit, but none of a husband and wife, nor of a couple and their offspring.[54] Many sales entailed forced transfer over considerable distance, indicating that family dissolution was permanent and the chances of visiting one's spouse or children were slim. Though records from other regions of the Roman Empire are much sparser, they portray an essentially similar picture. Whenever commercial interests dictated, owners treated the family bonds of their *instrumentum vocale* with cruel indifference. The only mitigating factor in this grim situation was the opportunities entailed in manumission, which was common. Provided both spouses could secure their release, they could live out their twilight years together with a security from peremptory severance that they had never known. The manumission of one or more family members remained, however, entirely at the whim of the owner.

On the evidence of funerary inscriptions, Brent Shaw and Richard Saller maintain that the nuclear family prevailed among urban classes in the Roman West.[55] They draw this conclusion after finding that the overwhelming majority of individuals named on 25,000 tombstones of civilians of every social class were members of the immediate family – spouses, parents, children and siblings of the deceased. Very few other kin were mentioned. On these grounds, Shaw and Saller are prepared to extend the nuclear family continuity thesis, advanced by Laslett and the Cambridge Group for the early modern era, right back to Antiquity. Is the inference warranted on the basis of their (undoubtedly valuable) evidence? I think not. Funerary inscriptions were remembrances of the dead by their closest kin. It is difficult to conceive of an extended family form where the same relations would not be preponderant in a comparable register of emotional devotion. In societies where unilineal descent groups prevail, for example, avuncular relations are often pivotal for specific jural purposes, but anthropologists do not find that such ties become primary emotional bonds, closer than attachments to one's nuclear kin, except in unusual cases of prolonged co-residence. The co-residence of nuclear kin thus receives an indirect confirmation from the inscriptions, but unfortunately firmer evidence does not exist for classes beneath the tiny Senatorial elite. Statistics on co-resident composition, abstracted from the family cycle, do little to distinguish prevailing family forms from one another, since two-generation co-residence in pre-industrial societies is strongly predicted by demographic probabilities.

The Germanic Peoples in Transition

The Germanic tribes, ranging along the northern periphery of the Western Empire from the Rhine and Danube valleys to the North Sea and the Baltic, had had extensive contact with the inhabitants of the Roman world long before the incursions of the late fourth and fifth centuries that sealed the Empire's fate. By the fourth century, the imperial garrisons guarding the northern boundaries were manned by Teutonic mercenaries whose relatives camped within the walls; their leaders held many of the highest posts in the army. We have no clear picture of the Germanic peoples prior to extensive contact with Latin civilization; what we do know of pre-Roman periods is wholly derived from archaeology. Literary evidence begins with the accounts of Julius Caesar (writing in the first century BC) and Tacitus (at the end of the first century AD). These sources (the latter much superior) must be employed with great caution.[56] Viewing the 'barbarians' (literally, 'the strangers') through Latin eyes, they wrote partly to comment, by way of contrast, on Roman culture.

By Caesar's time, the Germanic federations had left their nomadic, pastoral roots far behind. Since their social formations were extremely varied, generalization is difficult, but archaeological evidence indicates that most had become lightly settled agriculturalists by the pre-Roman Iron Age (1200–700 BC). They lived in widely scattered farmsteads, hamlet clusters and small villages, 'islands of light soils ... in a green sea of woods and waste' where they combined the raising of cattle, sheep and goats with the cultivation of barley, oats, corn and wheat.[57] In pre-Roman times, theirs was an extensive agriculture organized around stock-raising; a form of semi-sedentary pastoralism wherein cereal crops appear to have played a secondary but indispensable role. They practised slash-and-burn agriculture using scratch ploughs on impermanent fields, lacking regular layouts, crop rotation and systematic soil restoration. But in the first four centuries AD, there was a major expansion of settlements beyond loess soils, field layouts become more regular, wood ploughs more substantial and sophisticated, capable of cutting deeper furrows on light clays and intermediate loams, and there are even indications at one site of primitive forms of soil restoration.[58] We must avoid exaggerating this development; as a transition to heavy plough agriculture and permanent settlement, the process was evidently incomplete. Soil restoration could not have been widespread, since archaeological evidence indicates shifting cultivation, long fallow, two-course cropping, and repeated rearrangement of huts and field boundaries, the mark of semi-permanent villages.[59] In some settlements, craftsmen smelted iron in shaft and domed furnaces as advanced as those of their Roman counterparts. But since only a minority of cultivators employed iron plough blades, and there was evidently a general scarcity of iron, it appears that their forges were not as numerous, intensely worked or highly organized as Roman ironworks. In many respects (such as level of urbanization or the development of literary culture) the Germanic societies lagged light years behind the Roman West. Yet recent archaeological evidence compels a revision of prior assumptions of a vast technological gap between these two civilizations on the eve of the migrations. As the productive capacity of the Roman economy stagnated, Germania forged ahead. 'The first four centuries AD were a time in which the great technological backlog of Northern Europe in the Iron Age was largely eradicated.'[60]

What, then, of the kinship forms of the Germanic peoples? By the time the Sippe (the Germanic kindred network) appears in historical texts, it is already a structure in decline.[61] In the barbarian successor states, the political functions of the kindred – providing for territorial defense, domestic security and dispute settlement – were beginning to be replaced by the dependency of peasants upon local landlords and the extension of the latter's authority. The character of the pre-migration Germanic kin system is thus difficult to discern and a matter of considerable controversy.

Previous views of the Sippe as a clan or lineage (a unilineal descent group) have been widely discredited, but modern scholars are far from being able to compose an empirically convincing alternative. An earlier generation of historians, with few exceptions, had assumed that corporate groups could be formed only by unilineal descent reckoning; the functions of such groups were held to be largely determined by their structure, formally conceived.[62] Finding evidence in Germanic legal codes and Roman literary accounts for the pervasive practice of blood-feud and for territorial domains named after ancestors, historians concluded that unilineal descent groups must have been predominant amongst the Teutonic tribes, since bilateral kindreds presumably could not exercise these functions. The pivotal question thus became: were the clans matrilineal or patrilineal? Evidence could be adduced for either position, so this became a major bone of contention. Some historians have sought to resolve the difficulty by positing a changeover from the former to the latter in the development of these societies from primitive-communal to private-agricultural modes of production.[63]

The original inference (from function to structure) made by all parties to the dispute has subsequently been shown to be schematic and unwarranted. 'Corporate functions carried on by extensive groups are in themselves no argument for unilineal structure.'[64] How, then, to proceed? Goody's advice is cogent: 'the question is not to define patrilineal as against bilateral societies or kinship systems, but to discover whether groups or groupings of such and such a kind were recognized or utilized by the actors.'[65] This is the way I have endeavoured to proceed below, identifying the operative kin network involved in a particular type of action, and then composing a picture of the overall kinship structure by relating these diverse elements to one another.

Kin reckoning was clearly bilateral, and it appears that descent groups, territorially circumscribed with fluctuating memberships, were also formed through cognatic ties. In such an arrangement, where people trace their ancestry to more than one descent group, inheritance practices and residence norms are critical in defining group membership. Among the Germanic peoples, the cognatic group was normally biased in a patrilineal direction. That is to say, the group was constituted by kinfolk who traced their descent through both lines, but male ancestry was primary in the group's internal hierarchy.[66]

Both Caesar and Tacitus depict the kindred allocating arable land to individual families annually. By the first century AD, the latter informs us, this was done 'according to rank'; evidently the kindred group was increasingly strained by the processes of class differentiation. In Todd's judgement, 'by the time Tacitus wrote, private ownership of farm land was already becoming accepted among the Germans.'[67] This is undoubtedly true, but it still leaves unanswered the question addressed by Caesar and Tacitus of the allocative mechanism of land distribution. The decisive factor here is the extent of soil restoration and crop rotation, agricultural practices that promote the longevity of fields and surrounding settlement sites. If fields are not regularly replenished and are consequently impermanent, then some means of annual (or perhaps longer) reallocation would have been vested in a community's leadership within a given domain, most probably in the kindred group. In such circumstances, the kindred probably retained corporate powers that checked the domestic authority of househeads – scuttling property transactions or meddling in arranged marriages, for example. If, on the other hand, agricultural techniques had advanced sufficiently to foster permanent settlements, land parcels could be held in perpetuity by individual families, and new lands entering cultivation for the first time could be treated as supplementary acquests to the core arable. In those barbarian successor states where manorialization succeeded in establishing the permanence of land in cultivation, family groups held land, not the Sippe. In most cases, family holdings were passed from father to sons; only in the absence of eligible sons would daughters inherit. Normally, sons would marry in and daughters would depart to live with their husbands' kindred. In Visigothic law, daughters were placed on an equal footing with sons, but this appears to be exceptional; the agnatic bias of most Germanic and Frankish law codes is explicit.[68] Lastly, if there were no offspring, the siblings of the deceased might take up the land.

Before widespread manorialization and the emergence of a standardized family holding in the ninth and tenth centuries, partible traditions prevailed across most of Northwestern Europe: all sons were entitled to marry in, raise families and subsist from the land of their fathers. In Anglo-Saxon England, where the primogeniture privilege was already emerging, the first son acquired the parental home; continental traditions appear more even-handed. The fissiparous potential of partible customs was held in check by the larger kin group, whose elder leaders enforced a strong tradition of joint management of farmsteads between brothers. Co-parcenary inheritance may well have involved the establishment of separate residences (as Thomas Charles-Edwards argues was the norm in Anglo-Saxon England), but it was unlikely to have entailed the division of the parental holding.[69]

The kindred group, whose membership was in a constant state of flux, probably did not exceed fifty households.[70] Yet whenever they were densely settled in a district, the group had a definite presence there. This took the form of a domain (a *villa* or *fundus*), an extensive ensemble of 'arable, vine and orchard, undivided pasture, forest and waste, of demesne and dependent tenancies'.[71] With the intensification of plough agriculture, the domain was internally subdivided and conjugal families became more sharply distinguished from the larger kindred; but the group none the less maintained its external boundaries and genealogical identity.[72] Alienation of the kindred's land to outsiders was generally prohibited, strangers migrating to new lands were expected to declare their kindred, and settlements bore the name of their reputed ancestral owners.[73] Leading members of the group appear to have met periodically to plan and co-ordinate grazing and land-clearing initiatives. In this sense, 'the

Germanic Sippe ... exerted a kind of overlordship over its territory, held some residual rights to the land of its members, kept the peace and adjudicated disputes among them.'[74]

The broader kin network furnished an elementary form of security for unarmed rural folk in an age of social turmoil and marauding depredation. It served a variety of purposes, supplementing the solidarity of the immediate family group and filling in for next of kin when families broke down: 'The kindred gave support and standing, fed a man if he were in prison, took on responsibility for the baptism of infants, looked after orphans, guarded the insane and the deaf-and-dumb, and curbed evil-doers.'[75] It was the last of these supports that emerges most clearly in legal codes and contemporary narratives. The blood-feud, 'the most undoubtedly Germanic of all barbarian institutions', was the normal way of settling differences arising from homicide, wounding, rape, theft, cattle-rustling and treachery. Grievous assaults were treated as attacks upon the victims' kindred; the latter were obliged to seek retribution through reciprocated violence, negotiated compensation, or both.[76] Mirroring this mobilization, the assailant's kindred were liable to suffer blows of retributive vengeance, or to muster compensatory funds (the *wergeld*) in order to pay up and settle the dispute. On both sides, the range of kindred summoned to action and obliged to heed the call was bilateral, generally restricted to close kin and to those residing in the vicinity. The bilateral nature of the kindred must have served to limit the extension of vendettas in time and space, since many potential participants would have found themselves with a foot in both camps, harbouring, on that account, an acute interest in settling outstanding scores peacefully and suppressing further rounds of bloodshed.[77]

An array of governing forces in the emerging feudal order – the Church, Royal courts and the formative organs of manorial authority – sought to restrict the blood-feud, enforcing compensation and deterring prolonged bloodshed. It was hoped that Christian marriages would forge alliances between kin groups and thus prevent feuding.[78] The Church also established confession as a religious rite, with serious sins meriting public penance. Castigation in full view of the community was designed to shame perpetrators and extract symbolic retribution, restoring the victim's honour without requiring private vengeance. In communities where the Church was strongly established, the local priest was able to induce parishioners to bring most of their grievances to him. Even so, 'the feud yet lived for centuries in Western Europe without frontal attack and without stigma.'[79] 'The Middle Ages, from beginning to end, lived under the sign of private vengeance.'[80] The persistence of kin-based vendettas and compensatory settlements is salient, indicating the weakness of the medieval Church and state at the local level, particularly in areas that were ethnically and geographically remote from the king and his central bureaucracy.

But it is misleading to infer from the persistence of the feud that the early Middle Ages was an era of general lawlessness. The ensemble of Royal courts constituted a widely recognized public authority, adjudicating disputes in all the barbarian successor states. Aggrieved parties were often keen to take opponents to court in order to mobilize community support and resolve the conflict, avoiding further reprisals.[81] There are documented cases of peasants travelling 120 kilometres to seek a hearing in Royal courts. Given their litigious disposition, why did the feud persist? In the first place, courts were nonexistent in many areas and the unfree did not generally have access to them. Yet even where aggrieved parties could obtain court hearings, they frequently opted to pursue feud vengeance and customary settlement. The kin group provided a direct, informal and 'horizontal' recourse, which was often preferable to entrusting one's fate to lords and court personnel. In conflicts with social superiors, the chances of obtaining redress in court were almost nil. There seems to have been a *de facto* division between civil disputes (over land claims, for example) and criminal matters (such as assault or homicide). Kin-based vengeance was more likely in the latter case. 'Moral' transgressions (various forms of sexual misconduct, for example) were increasingly taken up by Church courts, but their functioning presence at the parish level was extremely patchy before the late Middle Ages.

The patriarchal prerogatives of husbands as househeads over their wives and children were clearly reinforced in the legal codes of the barbarian states. Men of the elite were free to take several wives, while severely punishing those suspected of adultery. It is impossible to gauge the extent of polygyny among the Germans, but if it was common it may well have fostered the tendency to trace relations through the female line for certain purposes, in order to differentiate the status of a man's progeny. Female chastity at marriage was highly valued and fathers strictly controlled their daughters' nuptials, conveying their 'right of protection' to the groom in the wedding ceremony. Despite paternal surveillance, the abduction of young single women for clandestine marriage was sufficiently common to elicit repeated condemnations by Church authorities and measures of legal redress.[82]

Among the dependent peasantry, women's position relative to men was undoubtedly stronger. Monogamy was the norm, and single women had more say in mate selection.[83] Evidently, they tended to marry somewhat later than their Roman counterparts, probably in their early twenties, without the pronounced age gap between spouses that placed teenage girls so firmly under the control of their adult husbands in Roman Italy.[84] When Florence and its surrounding countryside are compared with England in the fifteenth century the same disparities are evident, although in both areas the average age at marriage had increased by two or three years. The persistence of this regional difference is significant, since late marriage and a small age gap are defining characteristics of the globally unique 'Western European marriage pattern' to be discussed at length in the next chapter.

Germanic women engaged in a wide range of productive labours around the household, harvesting and preparing cereals, fashioning cutlery and baking ceramic ware over open fires, spinning and weaving wool on small looms; while men dominated the higher-status activities of tending the herd and iron forging.[85] Yet in so far as women bartered the products of their own labour and worked co-operatively in a supradomestic capacity in all-female work-teams, they appear to have achieved a basis of autonomy and power in the community not enjoyed by their upper-class sisters.[86] Tacitus comments that German men 'believe that there resides in women an element of holiness and a gift of prophecy; and so they do not scorn to ask their advice, or lightly disregard their replies.'[87] However, the position of rural women probably deteriorated as a primarily pastoral economy gave way before the adoption of heavier plough agriculture, the parcellization of arable land, the settlement of communities of growing density, and the emergence of increasingly autonomous conjugal family groups. Such a decline is widespread in the transition to heavy plough agriculture.[88] In Wemple's view, Western Europe was no exception: 'the settlement of the Germanic tribes was accompanied by the domestication of their wives.'[89]

Feudal Synthesis in the Early Middle Ages

Hard hit by plague and suffering declining birthrates, the populations of Italy and Gaul stagnated in the late Imperial era, contracting from the third century on. As rents and taxes skyrocketed, one hectare in five of the established arable of the Western Empire was abandoned.[90] In the meantime, the Germanic peoples grew apace. The widening disparity generated cumulative migratory pressures, as cleared land filled to overflowing across the Northern plain while vast stretches of Mediterranean *latifundia* went to pasture. In search of land, the Ostrogoths spread eastward beyond the Don, provoking a violent eruption from the Huns of the Volga steppe who counterthrust westward in 372, driving all the way to the Danube, delivering crushing blows to the Goth federations.[91] The latter, in turn, sought sanctuary across the Roman frontier, thus inaugurating a complex chain-reaction of migration and resettlement that has been dubbed 'the Invasions'. The term may be accurate in reference to the bellicose horsemen of the Huns, Alans and Vandals, but it is misleading when applied to the Germanic itinerants. Their forays were not military blitzkriegs culminating in hostile takeovers. Initially they were rather tentative movements of relatively small forces, lightly armed and looking for land. They encountered little Roman resistance: their demands for land were met so generously that ransacking excursions were exceptional and the takeover was largely pacific.

Yet the severity of social dislocation in the wake of the Western Empire's terminal prostration in the late fifth century should not be minimized. The regression of the ensuing century was staggering. Consider four major reverses:

- The breakdown of centralized state authority and administration. In consequence, road maintenance and transport safety suffered; minting and monetary control collapsed, and the fiscal capacity to extract taxes was temporarily lost. With a sharp rise in lawless marauding, the personal security of unarmed commoners deteriorated.

- The disorganization of agriculture, with field systems disrupted and regular crop rotations suspended. Rural communities became increasingly unsettled, their inhabitants more transient, and many sites were abandoned. Archaeological evidence reveals the surprising impermanence of village land use and the repeated shuffling of farm buildings.[92]

- A shrivelling of urban life (the parasitic fluorescence of Roman civilization) as inhabitants fled to the countryside in response to widespread disorder, rampant pandemics, dwindling trade and the disruption of food provisioning.

- Perhaps three souls in ten were lost across Western Europe from 542, when plague struck, until the downward spiral bottomed out sometime in the seventh century.[93]

The severity of the demographic collapse furnishes a useful index of the overall retrogression. Why was the population loss so grievous? The migrations themselves would appear to be implicated. Before the Western Empire's dissolution, intensive contact between Roman and Germanic peoples had been confined mainly to elites. When itinerant masses began to commingle, living as close neighbours and intermarrying, disparate ethnic groups were exposed to the ravages of alien diseases for which they lacked effective antibody defence.

From the nadir in the middle decades of the seventh century, the peoples of Western Europe staged a recovery, their numbers growing slowly at first, then quickening in the latter decades of the tenth century. The most remarkable aspect of this growth phase was its longevity. There were no deep or long-term contractions in the expansive trend until the fourteenth century. Over six and a half centuries, the population of Western Europe probably quadrupled.[94] Underlying this buoyancy was the subsidence of the plague and the lengthening of life. More favourable conditions for marriage and childcare contributed to rising fertility and reduced infant mortality. The gradual convergence of the class relations of ex-slaves and formerly independent peasants had positive demographic effects: 'When peasant status [became] more uniform ... matrimonial segregation soon disappeared between two groups within the peasantry who, until recently, were kept apart by legal criteria of ancient slavery.'[95] The demographic consequence of the consolidation of family rights among a large part of the agrarian toilers was considerable, if ultimately impossible to measure. Duby writes:

> The most profound repercussions on the growth of population and productivity arose from the development of unfree status. As long as young men and women remained members of a gang of household slaves in a master's dwelling, without legal possession of goods, homes or even their own bodies ... a whole section of the rural population languished in conditions most unfavourable for human reproduction. Children exposed to the dangers of childbirth and infancy in slave gangs had least chance of survival. When masters gradually allowed such gangs to disperse and decided to settle their slaves as couples on farms managed by themselves, not only did they stimulate the productive capacities of these workers; they placed them in a much better position to beget children and bring them up into the adult world.[96]

The population build-up of these centuries was gradual, halting and unevenly spread. By the year 1000, vast stretches of Northwestern Europe were still empty. Perhaps four-fifths of England was covered in forest, marsh and waste, and an estimated three-quarters of the land mass of modern-day France had almost no human inhabitants.[97] Only the most fertile regions, such as Île de France and Southern Flanders, were densely populated with sizeable villages within easy travelling distance of one another. In zones of this type, on flat plains and gently rolling river basins, growth was substantial from the seventh through the tenth century, with many villages doubling or trebling in size.

Economic dynamism and population growth were accompanied by a dramatic increase in class stratification and the crystallization of a ruling class–state nexus. The old barbarian governing structure of chiefs and council assemblies based on kindred groups was submerged in the post-migration states and replaced by warrior-autocrats who assembled military retinues and ruled through them. These retinues, furnishing the basis of a nascent aristocracy, cut across kindred authority; they were divorced from agricultural production and maintained through tenant dues from lands granted by kings and by the bounty of military conquest.[98]

The structure of landholding in the Roman West was deeply shaken by the barbarian takeovers, yet great estates persisted in England, Gaul and Germania. While many were comprised of dispersed small-scale holdings, most were at least partly concentrated and centrally administered, with head manors supervised by on-site lords and their appointees.[99] Only a small minority of villas were still organized along classical Roman lines. In a survey of seven polyptychs drawn up in the ninth century, 7 per cent (of 275 discrete manors) were comprised wholly of demesne land worked by a slave labour force attached directly to the master's household. Two-thirds of all manors already had a bipartite structure (characteristically feudal) combining a home farm with tenant holdings.[100] With the gradual liquidation of the servile domestic retinues that had formerly worked demesne fields, lords required their dependent tenants to divert more time and energy from their own plots to toil for two or three days a week on the home farm.[101] As labour services increased, dues also hardened; farm product rents, usually expressed in proportional terms for the *coloni* of the Roman West, were increasingly set in absolute quantities, invariant with harvest yields.

The enserfment of formerly free peasants proceeded on several fronts. The consolidation of lordship over established estates gave rise to an extension of manorial domain over adjacent villages, hamlets and scattered farmsteads that had heretofore passed down from one generation to the next on the basis of *de facto* squatters' rights. The inhabitants of such outlying settlements had been operating beneath the remote and loosely construed overlordship of kings and regional magnates. But with the spread of benefice, lordship was localized. A central facet of this expansion was the prodigious growth of the monastic orders in the sixth through the tenth centuries, appropriating vast chunks of the European countryside.[102] Ecclesiastical manors were normally well administered and technologically advanced. Their labour forces, however, were no better off than those of secular estates: the great majority of their tenants were unfree. While lords imposed themselves upon peasants, the utterly destitute, lacking any means of support, commended themselves to lords, relieved to become their dependants in return for land and a modicum of protection from tax collectors, marauding bands, and the private armies of feuding notables.[103]

Many scholars have noted the close association between the consolidation of lordship in the Carolingian era and the truncation of the kindred's range and power.[104] While this correlation seems generally valid, it is none the less imprecise. Two misconceptions may result. First, the causal relation is conventionally presumed to flow *from* ascending lordship *to* the kindred's enervation, but a good case can be made for the reverse, altering the account in significant ways. In the latter version, the erosion of certain functions of the kindred is induced by causally prior changes in the mode of agricultural production, which in turn pave the way for the extension of lordship. This thesis is particularly persuasive in so far as the shift in the control of arable land from the kindred to the on-site family is not unique to Europe; it appears to have been typical of the global transition from horticulture to plough agriculture.[105]

Fundamental functions of the Germanic Sippe – allocating land and defining community domain − were irreparably breached in the transition from scratch plough agriculture and impermanent settlement to heavier iron plough cultivation and fixed site development. As the kindred ceased to be a sufficient basis of collective settlement, agricultural co-ordination and land management, the resulting vacuum encouraged the mass commendation of communities of free cultivators into the thrall of the emergent seigneurial class.[106] Within the landholding elite, a parallel shift from a ramified, ancestrally based kin ensemble to a more streamlined estate lineage may also have paved the way for the rise of the military retinue, cutting across ancient kin ties.[107]

Conventional wisdom tends to foster an exaggerated image of the kindred in terminal decline, of a dying institution overwhelmed by the inexorable and deeply antagonistic forces of lordship. In reality, 'kinship remained immensely strong in daily life.'[108] Certainly, kin extension was truncated and realigned within the field of seigneurial jurisdiction; in the event of conflict between the two systems of loyalty, kinship was subordinated. But we should not overestimate their antagonism. Kin solidarity persisted throughout the feudal epoch as a profound and necessary complement to the class bonds of loyalty and service. (This point will be elaborated in the next section.) If we envision a complete atrophy of kin bonds extending between domestic groups, 'the conjugal family' emerges from the early medieval mists standing on its own. Alan Macfarlane has painted such a picture for medieval England, but his argument has been widely criticized by historians.[109] If the solitary nuclear family thesis is somewhat misleading for England, it is sharply at odds with evidence from the continent, where extended kin bonds were common in long-standing village communities.

Kinship and Feudal Class Relations

The importance of conjugal patriline in feudal reproduction has often been obscured by an excessive preoccupation with the fief as an ideal juridical relation. The ideology of benefice, fealty and vassalage had no place for principles of kinship obligation and inheritance rights. In theory, all land belonged to the suzerain, who granted it to his barons, who subdivided it in turn, granting parcels to lesser nobles and so on through an elaborate chain of subinfeudation, until lords of local manors finally admitted peasant tenants, the direct producers. This hierarchy was based on relations of reciprocal obligation between subordinates and superiors which were not kin-based.

Since fiefs were ostensibly held in trust, on the basis of sacred bonds of personal obligation pledged for life, they were logically terminated at the time of the subordinate's death. In the Carolingian Empire, the fief could not be transferred legally as an inheritance; another oath of personal homage and fealty was required.[110] Formally, there was no guarantee that the vassal's designated offspring would regain it; that was entirely at the discretion of his lord. For the majority of servile peasants, as well, customary tenure rights of land inheritance were not legally enshrined. Before the twelfth century a family's holdings, in theory, were revocable at regular intervals or at the death of the head. The feudal relations of fief and lordship thus formally subverted kinship as a social relation of property management and devolution. In reality, however, kinship held its place and became pivotal in property management, while feudal relations between subordinates and superiors sealed the juridico-political relations of state.[111] Significantly, feudal relations were themselves depicted in familial terms; the granting of a fief, for example, was accompanied by symbolic gestures which duplicated the rites of adoption.[112]

The principle of fief reversion upon the vassal's decease was never firmly established in the formative stages of feudal state formation in the Carolingian era. At the dissolution of the Empire, the fief in practice became the vassal's secure patrimony across Western Europe.[113] The shift to perpetuity in fief granting was roughly paralleled by a growing acceptance among the nobility of the principle of heritability in peasant tenure. As Fourquin has commented: 'Even more than in the case of fiefs, bargains between the lord and the heirs led to recognition of an hereditary right, which, as one might expect, was followed by recognition in hereditary law.'[114]

By the thirteenth century, the right of *retrait lignager* – to retain property in the family line – was the rule, and limited-term leases were the exception, for established villein holdings on most estates. Seigneurs who tried to abrogate this customary prerogative in the name of their own legal rights were likely to meet stiff resistance from the village community:

A landed proprietor might be hoping to conserve his estates by concluding contracts for a limited term. But when a lease expired he was in for trouble if he refused to renew it in favour of the former tenant, and on almost the same conditions. Even worse trouble was in store for the new tenant, if such could be found: he was usually a stranger to the village, since the natives neither wished nor dared to play the part of 'interloper'. Both landlord and tenant were likely to pay dearly for their infringement of what the peasant community regarded as their rights: whether it was boycott, theft, murder, 'fire and sword', no punishment was considered too great. Nor was this the limit of popular demands; leaseholders claimed the privilege of first refusal when their property was being sold, and even farmworkers considered themselves permanent, with a hereditary right to their positions as 'harvesters, threshers, shepherds, woodsmen'.[115]

Lords retained ultimate control over the composition of their labour force by screening and selecting new tenants. Yet within the constraints of manorial courts and local custom, peasant heads, villein and free, could manage property transmission – designating heirs, determining dotal portions and planning for retirement – in pursuit of their own objectives. The seigneurs' standard levies on marriage and inheritance were fastened on to the customary prerogatives of peasant family transmission as parasitic impositions which extracted producer wealth and framed options without ever negating the basic right of familial heritability. Everywhere under feudalism, servile obligation in return for land tenure was depersonalized and placed on a class footing, as the dues of one family household to another: 'The bond of fealty tended to unite not so much two individuals as two families, one of them pledged to exercise authority, the other to submit to it.'[116]

While the arbitrary *personal* power of overlords was undoubtedly restricted by the triumph of heritable patrimony, the *class* power of the aristocracy was solidified. In the first place, family heritability helped to settle peasants on the land, providing the security of tenure necessary to convince the mass of cultivators (and especially the youth) to stay put and endure lean seasons and exorbitant rents. Secondly, the principle of heritability applied not only to land tenure but also to the person of the tenant. In this way, servile status was naturalized; heirs were automatically accountable for their fathers' debts and obligations, and enserfment was organically reproduced – serfs gave birth to serfs. Thirdly, the tradition of inheritance within the family furnished a powerful check to the commercial alienation of land, and thereby handed the lords a point of juridical principle, with strong support among the peasantry, which facilitated their efforts to retain control of their properties and prevent them from being broken up, with jurisdiction dissipated.

The transmission of land within and between village communities ran primarily along familial lines in the feudal epoch: 'Family land was much more attractive [to peasants] than non-family land because it was cheaper, it gave better title, and [in the event of marriage to an outsider] it facilitated the absorption of the immigrant into the local community.'[117] Manorial courts generally upheld the right of heirs against the claims of lessees. Leasehold agreements were deemed to expire upon the lessor's decease, and original holdings were routinely reassembled for inheritance. In most cases, villein land could not be sold without the express permission of the prospective heir given in court session. In some areas, descendants retained the right to buy back family land that had fallen into the hands of non-kin for twenty years.[118] The principle of family heritability, far from subtending feudal class relations on the land, underpinned them. Conjugal patriline and patriarchal househeadship became pillars of the feudal ensemble, at the base of its structure of reproduction.

The Emergence of the Manse and Impartible Inheritance

With the expansion and consolidation of manorial authority, a more intensive common-field agriculture was established in the larger village settlements, with short strip furlongs in open fields, communally regulated crop rotation, seasonal grazing on the stubble, and deeper plough cultivation extending on to heavier soils. By the tenth century these general features had appeared along the Rhine, in Franconia, Hesse, Dijonnais, Artois and the Paris basin: 'Seignorial lordship prevailed in all the common-field regions of Europe.'[119] Ancient settlements were reorganized and newly established ones were laid out in regular forms from their inception. Central to this process was the emergence of the manse, the standard peasant holding, an ordered combination of fields (or strips in open fields), messuage, and dwelling space sufficient to support a family.[120]

It is clear from documents of the time that the concept of the *mansus* (*huba* or *hide*) was inextricably fused with the family. 'For the Venerable Bede, the hide was "the land of the family"; in the records of Germania, the *huba* was "the place of the residence of a family", or more simply the *familia*.'[121] The layout and size of the manse varied considerably from place to place, according to the ecology of the area and the type of agricultural production prevailing there. Despite this heterogeneity, the overall trend was clear: arable acreage was standardized according to the area a plough team could cultivate in a normal planting season. The manse as a whole, the secure possession of a family, became increasingly indivisible by inheritance. Concomitantly, the distinction between the manse and acquests was deepened. Allodial lands, often haphazardly arranged around the fringes of a village's main fields, were readily swapped. They could be acquired during the lifetime of one generation and distributed in partible fashion to the next, compensating children excluded upon marriage from the main manse. A fuller discussion of this 'compensatory impartible' inheritance system (as I have dubbed it) appears later in this chapter.

At the collapse of the Roman West, 'the ordinary rules of succession ... in the greater part of Europe favoured the equality of heirs [i.e., sons] of the same degree.'[122] Where feudal relations predominated and seigneurial authority held sway, equal access between sons was gradually replaced by the designation of a single heir to marry in and take over the family manse, while the other children were compensated as they wed with acquests, chattels and cash sums. Partible customs were more likely to persist on the periphery of feudal Europe, in thinly populated hilly areas beyond seigneurial grasp, where pastoralism prevailed and there was not great pressure on the land.[123] Much of the range in inheritance customs and family forms, so notable across medieval Western Europe, was thus a variation between feudal zones and peripheral hinterlands lying outside the seigneurial infrastructure of the feudal mode of production. Variation between the different manorial regions was less marked; indeed, I am arguing that a minimal impartibility on villein holdings was characteristic of seigneurial lands – if not invariably *de jure*, then at least *de facto*.

The conversion from equal access to impartibility, with secondary siblings

63

excluded, seems not to have been adopted by peasants on their own but to have arisen in compliance with seigneurial pressure.[124] The lords had compelling reasons for discouraging land subdivision. They wished to maintain the economic viability of the arable parcels within their domain; simplify the collection and reduce the evasion of dues; obtain labour-services on the demesne performed with beasts of burden, instead of with men on foot (as was usually the case with smallholders); prevent the transfer of land to the Church with the entry of tenants' offspring into monastic orders; and control commercial land exchange, which might weaken tenure claims within their domain. If peasant househeads had perceived the seigneurial drive for impartibility as an affront to their basic testamentary rights, the principle would have been difficult to establish. As it was, the break with strict egalitarian customs proceeded smoothly, because the patriarchs of both classes (while differing sharply over other aspects of inheritance) were keen to preserve the viability of family holdings.

While the shift to manse indivisibility finally crystallized the compensatory impartible form of peasant inheritance in Western Europe, let us not lose sight of elements of continuity in the resulting configuration, stemming from homologous features in the kinship and property forms of the Germanic and Roman precursors. Both inheritance systems had been formally partible, yet with sufficient flexibility to avoid the uncontrolled subdivision of family arable. Both opted to designate sons as heirs, compensating daughters with dotal prestations. Yet because they favoured transmission to offspring over and against the claims of collateral kin, both installed daughters in lieu of sons. Early medieval marriage customs melded elements from each side into a distinctly feudal synthesis. Roman and Germanic nuptial patterns were vigorously exogamous, with cousin marriage being a rarity. In both cases, the bride entered the union with assets from her father's estate and was greeted by the groom with gifts and subsistence undertakings.[125]

The essential difference in dotal customs was that the dowry was primary in Roman nuptials, whereas the husband's gift to the bride took precedence in Germanic societies. The latter prevailed initially in the early medieval states, 'yet within five centuries of its demise, the dowry had begun to re-emerge' in Western Europe, and by the height of the Middle Ages, with the imprimatur of the Christian Church, the dowry (or dot) was clearly dominant once again.[126] The medieval dower – the wife's right to support from her husband's estate – appears then as a subordinate counter-gift, probably of Germanic origin. The dower did not take the form of a bride-price paid to the bride's kin; it was the wife's own due. The Germanic peoples had had a similar prestation, termed the morning gift [*Morgengabe*], offered traditionally on the morning after the wedding night in return for the bride's gift of her virginity. By the ninth and tenth centuries, her marital claim on the dowered portion of her husband's estate had apparently grown much stronger throughout the Western Mediterranean, subordinating the claims of her husband's blood kin for as long as she lived.[127] Furthermore, in a sure sign of conjugal ascendancy, the subsistence rights of widows began to be upheld consistently against the demands of impetuous heirs. 'The widow's [dower] rights seem to have been by far the most durable and firmly established of all inheritance customs.'[128]

While a woman clearly gained power, through the dower, in relation to her husband's kin, she simultaneously lost power, via the dowry, in her own kin group. The dowry was her part of the natal estate; its acquisition normally blocked her from making any further claim upon her parents' patrimony. Despite regional variations, what is none the less striking is the generalized emergence of this particular marital exchange configuration (the dot and the dower combined, with the former dominant), across Western Europe among peoples of diverse origins and histories. It suggests that these practices were not incidental to the formation of the larger seigneurial ensemble, and particularly to its characteristic, compensatory impartible, mode of land devolution.

The Influence of the Church

What impact did the spread of Christendom across the Roman West have on family forms? Due to the enormous influence of the Gospel accounts of Jesus's life and teachings upon the development of Christianity, it seems appropriate to begin with a brief look at the biblical texts. Here we are in for a surprise. In the modern world, Christian churches of every denomination have a well-deserved reputation as implacable champions of the family in its traditional form. Upon a careful reading of the Gospels, however, we find that Christ's life and teachings do not present the family as a group specially blessed by God or worthy of abiding Christian devotion. On the contrary, Jesus of Nazareth is portrayed as rejecting his own family and counselling his followers to do likewise, freeing themselves to follow him in doing God's work.

Christ was ostensibly born of a virgin; his earthly parents sink into obscurity after the nativity story. The only Gospel tale of his childhood is Luke's account of Jesus as a twelve-year-old slipping away from his parents on a trip to Jerusalem. Discovering his absence from their party on the way home, Joseph and Mary return to the city to find him in earnest discussion with the temple elders. After conveying their anxiety, Mary asks her son why he left without informing them. Jesus replies with questions: Why had they bothered to return to fetch him? Did they not know that he must be about his father's business?[129] Here is an early portent of his future disposition: shunning his family to pursue a self-proclaimed mission.

As an adult, Jesus appears to have been severely alienated from his family. Three of the Gospels recount a story of his mother and brothers approaching a crowd that Jesus was addressing and asking to meet him. Informed by a disciple of their presence, he refuses to see them, effectively disowning his earthly family. He asks rhetorically: 'Who is my mother and who are my brothers? Whoever does the will of my Father in Heaven is my brother and sister and mother.'[130] Jesus speaks here, as he does many times, of the congregation of the faithful as his real kindred. He surrounds himself with twelve disciples, an all-male group who constitute a surrogate family. Most seem to be bachelors; none is portrayed as a devoted family man. As the married Peter remarks: 'We have left our homes and followed you.'[131] Being a member of his entourage, constantly on the move from place to place, was probably incompatible with stable family life.

Jesus's estrangement from his family was apparently reciprocated. In the Gospel of John, we find that his brothers did not believe in his divinity, and Christ remarks that 'a prophet is not without honour except in his own country, among his own relatives, and in his own house.'[132] In the Gospel accounts, Jesus's personal alienation seems to have coloured his attitude to the familial bonds of his followers. As he recruits a disciple, the man asks him if he may first go home to bid farewell to members of his family who are mourning his father's death, assisting them in the burial. Jesus interprets the request as faltering commitment, exhorting him: 'Follow Me, and let the dead bury their own dead.'[133] This callous instruction, referring to the man's living kin as if they were irredeemably alien, stands in marked contrast to Jesus's counsel of compassion in dealing with friends and strangers.

Jesus is frequently reported to have urged the devout to resist family pressure in pursuing their new life-mission. This is not surprising, since the close kin of his followers were frequently hostile to their Christian vocation. The problem of the Gospel accounts for Christianity as a familial faith is that Jesus speaks of the two commitments as *inherently opposed,* regardless of the attitude of kin:

> Do not think that I came to bring peace on earth. I did not come to bring peace but a sword. For I have come to 'set a man against his father, a daughter against her mother, and a daughter-in-law against her mother-in-law'. And 'a man's foes will be those of his own household'. He who loves his father and mother more than Me is not worthy of Me. And he who loves his son or daughter more than Me is not worthy of Me. And he who does not take up his cross and follow Me is not worthy of Me.[134]

Jesus reportedly interprets the commandment to honour one's father and mother as an injunction to obey God the Father, giving short shrift to earthly parents: 'Do not call anyone on earth your father; for One is your Father, He who is in Heaven.'[135] While instructing the devoted to love their neighbours and turn the other cheek to enemies, his response to family conflict is singularly harsh: 'If anyone comes to me and does not hate his father and his mother, wife and children, brothers and sisters, yes and his own life also, he cannot be My disciple.'[136] Many of his followers must have been deeply pained by the familial estrangement required by devotion to Christ. In consolation, he is quoted as assuring them: 'Everyone who has left houses or brothers or sisters or father or mother or wife for My name's sake, shall receive a hundredfold, and inherit everlasting life.'[137]

The Gospels do not recount that the bachelor from Nazareth said very much at all about conjugality, but what he does say is derogatory. In a sharp break with Jewish tradition, he condemns divorce outright and disapproves of marriage to a divorced woman; that too is a form of adultery.[138] In a passage that was to have profound ramifications for Christian attitudes, Matthew reports that Jesus challenged the devout to eschew marriage in favour of a life of celibacy 'for the Kingdom of Heaven's sake. He who is able to accept it, let him accept it.' The Gospel of Luke cites Jesus remarking that 'the sons of this age marry and are given in marriage. But those who are counted worthy to attain that age, and the resurrection from the dead, neither marry nor are given in marriage.'[139] As this excerpt suggests, Jesus's advocacy of celibacy seems to have been motivated by his sense that the end of the world was at hand, and that his followers needed to prepare themselves for the new age. On the cross, he predicts that 'the days are coming in which they will say, "Blessed are the barren, the wombs that never bore, and the breasts which never nursed".'[140]

One might justly ask whether the Gospels present an accurate picture of Jesus's relations with his own family or a balanced sampling of his advice to followers on marriage and familial obligation.[141] That question, however, is not germane to our inquiry. My argument is simply that the Gospels fairly reflect the collective memory that early Christian communities had of their Messiah. Significantly, most sects seem to have followed in the Master's footsteps. They moved about in loosely formed groups, essentially homeless, refusing all bodily comforts including sexual companionship in marriage. Convinced that the Second Coming was imminent, they sought to purify themselves through rigorous fasting and sexual abstinence, and to save souls for Christ by means of conversion and adult baptism. By and large, the roving evangelists of the early Church set their sights on an extroverted ministry in which a stay-at-home devotion to kin was at best a time-consuming diversion and frequently a disqualifying commitment. Placing their paramount human loyalty in the congregation of adherents, they embraced familial bonds only when these could be readily maintained within the community of believers. The early devotees had 'very little to say in praise of marriage', while their esteem for celibacy 'became a distinguishing feature of Christian life'.[142] Procreative continuity was disdained as a 'false paternity'; the true path to perpetuity was through spiritual devotion in preparation for the new age. From this perspective, marriage was an earthly distraction, the sign of a divided heart. As Paul advised his followers at Corinth: 'He who is unmarried cares for the things that belong to the Lord – how he may please the Lord. But he who is married cares about the things of the world – how he may please his wife.'[143] Paul singled out sexual seduction as the main reason for distraction. Reiterating Jesus's advice, he urged Christians to practise abstinence, 'for the time is short'.[144] Moderates sought to temper this stringent counsel, but in the apostolic Church the anti-familial perspective of the radicals predominated. In the fourth century, for example, the renowned Bishop Gregory of Nyssa still taught that 'marriage is the first thing to be left behind; it is the first station, as it were, for our departure to Christ.'[145]

After the conversion of Constantine (AD 313), Christianity ceased to be the religion of marginal and persecuted minorities. In the next three centuries, the new faith emerged as the compulsory creed of European society as a whole. Having made its peace with secular elites, the Augustinian Church deployed the coercive power of the Imperial state to wipe out heresy, stifle sectarianism, and forge the unity of Latin Christendom under the bishop of Rome. Since Christ's return was no longer felt to be imminent, the temporal horizon of the earthbound Church was correspondingly lengthened. Demographic expansion and social class stability became paramount concerns for sovereigns and bishops alike. The Church's institutional growth was dependent upon the accumulation of wealth and new members; an ascetic and celibate priesthood could supply neither. The Church of the whole society required a positive doctrine of familial relations for its burgeoning lay membership that the Gospels manifestly failed to provide. Essentially, this was ensured through the development of the sacraments – above all, marriage and baptism – which conferred divine favour upon approved forms of familial relations, while shielding the devout from evil spirits.

As the faith spread and local parishes mushroomed, Christian communities became culturally mainstream, residentially settled and universalist. In the process, the original antagonism between devotion to congregation and devotion to kindred was superseded. In stark contrast to the desert bands and wandering sects, the urban communities of the 'Great Church' sought to reconcile Christian witness with family devotion. The secondary Pauline texts (considered by most modern scholars to be forgeries written after Paul's death) laid the groundwork for a vigorous counterattack against the radicalism of the early Church. In these texts (principally I and II Timothy and Ephesians) Paul's message was tamed; the militant preacher appeared as 'a patron saint of domestic life'.[146] Moderates could cite a passage in the letter to the Ephesians, for example, which directly countered Paul's derogation of marriage. Wives were instructed to submit to their husbands 'as to the Lord', while husbands were to love their wives, to nourish and cherish them 'as their own bodies, just as the

Lord does the Church. ... And the two shall become one flesh.' In contrast
with the Gospel accounts, conjugality is here treated as the blessed outcome of
Christian fellowship. Marriage is held to be natural for Christians because 'we
are members of His body, of His flesh and His Bones'.[147] As congregations
began to swell with the offspring of Christian unions, the procreative purpose
of marriage was heralded.

The early medieval Church exhibited an ambivalence towards marriage
that would mark its disposition throughout the Middle Ages. The root of
clerical distrust was not marriage *per se;* from St Augustine on, the moderate
mainstream of Christian theology considered marriage to be blessed by God.
The sticking point was the vexatious idea that conjugality entailed sexual licence. The clerical elite remained adamantly opposed to the pursuit of sexual
pleasure in the absence of procreative intent, yet it was clear that the sexual
appetites of most people far exceeded the biological needs of reproduction.
This libidinal surfeit, arising from the suppression of oestrus, distinguished humans from 'lesser' mammals. Seemingly in recognition of this fact, marriage
had been justified by Christian theologians (initially by Paul) as the necessary
vehicle of irrepressible concupiscence, serving as 'a remedy against sin, to
avoid fornication'.[148] But the Church could never reconcile the *Homo sapiens*
libido with the belief that humans had been created in God's image, according
to His plan. The discrepancy was resolved through the Augustinian version of
original sin, where indomitable sexual desire was taken to be both the proof
of, and the penalty for, Adam's fall.[149] In so far as the Church's conjugal doctrine remained narrowly fixated on the channelling of sexual desire, the veneration of celibacy inevitably cast marriage in a poor light.

What Christianity needed was an uplifting rationale for marriage, one
which focused on the spousal relationship while de-emphasizing its sexual aspect. In the first decades of the fifth century, St Augustine argued that the
virtue of Christian marriage was to be found in lifelong companionship. He
advanced a model of Christian marriage fashioned after the original human
couple, Adam and Eve, whom he envisioned strolling arm in arm through the
Garden of Eden sharing the forbidden fruit out of friendship, not through
Eve's erotic enticement.[150] Conjugal companionship was naturally heterosexual
so as to produce progeny, but this was the only legitimate purpose of sex.
Devout couples would minimize sexual contact so as not to degrade the companionate purpose of the union, strictly observing the rule of abstinence on the
Sabbath, throughout Lent, and on other holy days.[151] While maintaining the
early Christian distrust of conjugal sexuality, Augustine none the less furnished
a spiritually honourable motive for marriage. The conjugal pair and their offspring were now conceived as the basic cell structure of Church and state in
their combined lay edifice, integrating society from top to bottom.

Yet Augustine's positive conjugal doctrine did not go so far as to place the congregation of families on a par with those who repudiated sex in order to draw closer to God. The monk Jovinian had argued for such equality, taking issue with the self-righteous sanctimony of celibate devotees. He criticized the anti-sexual rantings of Jerome, who had written (advising his sister to remain celibate): 'Learn from me a holy arrogance: know that you are better than they are!' Jerome denounced Jovinian's position as dangerous heresy, and the monk (himself celibate) was summarily excommunicated.[152] As the clerical elite struggled to enforce celibacy throughout the ranks of the priesthood, sexual renunciation became a pivotal justification for the powers invested in the clergy in mediating the laity's relationship with God. Eusebius explained:

> Two ways of life were thus given by the Lord to His Church. The one is above nature, and beyond common human living; it admits not marriage, child-bearing, property nor the possession of wealth. ... Like some celestial beings, these gaze down upon human life, performing the duty of a priesthood to Almighty God for the whole race ...

> And the more humble, more human way prompts men to join in pure nuptials, and to produce children, to undertake government, to give orders to soldiers fighting for right; it allows them to have minds for farming, for trade and for the other more secular interests as well as for religion.[153]

True to the distrust of its founder, the Western Church in the first millennium of its existence played a subsidiary role in the regulation of marriage. Local family customs and civil law set the permissible limits of mate selection and determined the legality of disputed unions. The wedding itself was a secular rite conducted as an exchange between families. After the ceremony, a priest might be invited to bless the marriage bed, thus ratifying an already established union. The failure uniformly to provide a special church service where the couple's lifelong commitment to one another could be blessed reflected the clergy's lingering ambivalence concerning marriage as a sacrament, consecrating a wholly honourable Christian vocation.

In the eleventh and twelfth centuries, Church authorities moved decisively to rectify past negligence. They undertook three related initiatives which effectively placed marriage firmly under the bishop's jurisdiction, loosening the grip of parents on mate selection.[154] First, with Gratian's *Decretum* of 1140, canonists determined that the essential prerequisite of a legal union was the consent of the principals (recalling Roman law, and inspired by the rediscovery of its texts). Any marriage imposed by parents or others against the express wishes of the individuals concerned was deemed invalid. The subsequent coital consummation of the union ratified express consent and made it legally binding. Second, Church authorities became increasingly insistent that the only proper entry to marriage was through public solemnization in a church ceremony. This was achieved by refashioning the nuptial ritual so that the couple came before the parish community at the church door, where the priest presided over an exchange of vows, rings, and the bride's endowment. The wedding party then proceeded into the church for a special Mass and blessing (signifying the full acceptance of marriage as a sacrament by the Councils of Florence and Trent).[155] Third, as canonists articulated an increasingly elaborate set of impediments to marriage, the Church deemed it necessary to go beyond obtaining the couple's avowed assent to marry in order to inquire more thoroughly as to whether they were eligible to wed. To this end, the system of banns was instituted in the thirteenth century; impending nuptials were announced at Mass for several consecutive weeks, soliciting public objection to their validity. This form of matrimonial invigilation was supplemented by confessionals and Church courts empowered to mete out public penance for sins against marriage, such as fornication and adultery. The medieval Church thus developed a formidable set of proceedings for disseminating its rules on marriage and ensuring compliance with them.

The extension of the Church's regulative grasp over marriage had a number of far-reaching effects on medieval family forms. The deepening involvement of priests in the nuptials of Christian adherents, and the subsequent standardization of the liturgy, tended to homogenize marital norms across Western Europe.[156] By refusing to recognize unions that lacked the publicly stated and witnessed consent of the principals, Church authorities tempered the unilateral power of the elder generation in arranging their children's marriages without regard to the latter's wishes. The Church extended the incest taboo (firmly established among the Germanic peoples) to kin of the fourth degree; the campaign against cousin marriage buttressed the conjugal bond against collateral ties. A firm insistence on monogamy gradually rid Western Europe of polygamous vestiges; bigamy became a capital offence. While elite men still took mistresses, these women could never become their wives, nor were the progeny of such liaisons considered legitimate heirs. The repression of concubinage and marriage by abduction fortified the social construction of paternity, strengthening the claim of 'legitimate' offspring to inherit the patrimony. While buttressing patrilineal inheritance, the Church's exogamic intervention (against cousin marriage and unions with affines) cut down the field of eligible partners, complicating mate selection and the transmission of family holdings between generations. The Church thus enhanced its opportunities for acquiring land through wills and deathbed bequests. By discouraging remarriage, the clergy fostered an 'order of widows' in long-standing congregations. While in poor communities widows looked to the parish for alms, in rich congregations bequests from widows became a crucial source of revenue for Church coffers.[157] Ecclesiastical concern with the morality of family life was thus happily aligned with the Church's material interests as it became Europe's greatest landlord, possessing perhaps a quarter of the wealth of Western Europe by the eleventh century.

Concomitant with its takeover of marriage, the Church instigated a cultural counter-revolution in sexual mores that has had profound and lasting effects upon Western civilization. A wide variety of erotic dispositions and sexual practices that had flourished in the late Roman Empire were driven underground. In the wake of Jerome and Augustine, the early medieval Church became increasingly hostile towards bisexuality, homosexuality, the sexual adventures of young men before marriage, common-law cohabitation, concubinage and consensual divorce – practices that had achieved broad acceptance among elites in the Roman West.[158] In Roman culture, a vigorous sexual appetite was natural, a healthy form of life-energy; the objective was to manage it in a dignified manner. Christian theology broke radically with this conception, treating involuntary sexual desire as a curse, a corrupting weakness of the flesh, a sure sign of original sin. As Clement of Alexandria had commented in the second century, 'Our ideal is not to experience desire at all'.[159]

Faithful to the ascetic outlook of the early Christians, the medieval Church condemned recreational sex within marriage as wanton lust. Husbands were advised to forget the sexual games of their youth when approaching the marriage bed; men who cherished their wives too ardently were on a moral par with adulterers.[160] The Church decreed that couples must refrain from sex on a wide variety of holy days, and during menstruation, pregnancy and breastfeeding. And since the wish to bear children was the only legitimate motive for sex, any action intended to avert conception was held to transgress natural and divine law. Contraception, withdrawal, and coitus with the man lying beneath his wife (in the hope that gravity would prevent the seed's implantation) were all condemned as abominable sins.[161] The demographic impact of these coital strictures is a matter of conjecture. While lay adherence to the clergy's contraceptive prohibitions would tend to raise the birthrate, injunctions to abstinence would have had the opposite effect. Furthermore, it is difficult to estimate, even roughly, the degree to which the Christian masses conformed to the Church's decrees in sexual matters, although we do know that Church authorities strove mightily to obtain their compliance. In the penitential handbooks, priests were instructed to inquire in the confessional as to whether parishioners were observing all sexual proscriptions and to impose penance on transgressors.[162]

While Church leaders were prepared to specify in detail the legitimate scope of sexual comportment, they effectively denied married Christians the right to decide such matters for themselves. From Gratian on, canonists ruled that the coital consummation of marriage gave rise to a 'marital debt': the obligation to accede to the sexual overtures of one's spouse upon request.[163] In the light of the clergy's deep fear of the destructive power of libidinal impulse, the perversity of this ruling is manifest. While individuals were warned to keep a tight rein on their own sexual desires lest they be consumed with lust, they were required to respond positively to their spouse's desires at all times.

In doctrinal terms, the obligation to perform sex on demand was incumbent upon both spouses; yet there can be no doubt that women suffered disproportionately from this injunction (above all, because they bore the burden of conception). For Christian theologians, women did not naturally possess sexual desire, though since Eve they had been easily led astray by lascivious men. The Church nevertheless implicitly recognized women's sexuality. Ecclesiastical art was replete with images of lust personified by women, and manuals for confessors instructed them to question women in detail on the use of contraceptives, masturbation with the aid of phallus-like objects, lesbianism and bestiality. The author of one such manual believed that 'sexual sins' of this sort were likely to be committed by many ordinary women attending confession.[164]

The Church's conjugal strictures were not all negative. The suppression of polygamy, concubinage and nuptial kidnapping furnished some security for women within the confines of Christian marriage. Yet the darker side of clerical enforcement was manifest in the perpetuation of a masculine bias on adultery and remarriage, bringing the sexist double standards of Greek and Roman Antiquity forward into a new era. Doctrinally, extramarital liaisons were serious sins for either sex, but in practice women bore the brunt of ecclesiastical repression.[165] Wrapping the double standard in a cloak of piety, the Church rendered an inestimable service to landholding patriarchs, lords and peasants alike, propounding 'a code of sexual purity which assisted the stricter subjection of the married woman ... as the vessel through which transmission of the patrimony was achieved'.[166] Since indubitable fatherhood was a prerequisite of a stable inheritance system, wives had the subversive capacity to arouse suspicion as to the paternity of their children. As the redoubtable Doctor Johnson warned, women's marital fidelity 'was of the utmost importance, as all property depends on it. We hang a thief for stealing sheep, but the unchastity of a woman transfers the sheep and farm and all from the right owner.'[167] The moral sanction of the Church was a more effective restraint than all the chastity belts in Christendom, making it treacherous for women to stray from the marriage bed and perilous to disclose it publicly. Agnatic property transmission was also naturalized by the belief that human procreation was the result of the male seed implanted in the nurturing soil of the female womb, thus denying women's genetic contribution to new life. The Virgin Birth of 'God's only begotten Son' sustained a 'monogenetic' notion of paternity, though the belief did not originate with – nor was it unique to – Christianity.[168]

In the early modern era (perhaps earlier) the peasants of Western Europe developed a unique marriage pattern, where women delayed nuptials until their mid twenties and at least one in ten never married. Due to the central importance of this nuptial regime in restricting fertility, I shall examine the socioeconomic conditions fostering its development in the next chapter. At this point, it will suffice to consider whether the installation of Christian conjugal norms and sexual repression in the Middle Ages was a formative impulse in the development of the Western European marriage pattern. It seems probable that it was, for several reasons.

First, and most obviously, the Church exercised a considerable moral influence in inhibiting premarital sex. It was the parents' duty to keep their children from fornicating; those who failed to do so would be held responsible on Judgement Day.[169] If young people had been free to copulate prior to troth-plight without suffering serious consequences, nuptial delay would not have checked fertility to the extent that it did. The Church's influence in *delaying* marriage was inadvertent. Christian texts proposed early marriage 'as an antidote to youthful spirits and the hideous sin of premarital sex', and Church leaders warned repeatedly that late marriage promoted prostitution.[170] Regardless of intent, however, several regulations do seem to have fostered nuptial postponement. The prohibition on divorce provided a heavy dose of sobriety in contemplating a prospective partner for life, thus raising the betrothal stakes. By discouraging widows from remarrying, priests slowed the overall rate of marriage considerably in a world of high adult mortality. When the Church's stricture against cousin marriage was combined with the lords' drive to confine coupling to the manorial community, the result was a severely circumscribed pool of eligibles from which to choose a mate. The clergy's insistence on the consent of the principals for a church-sanctioned union strengthened the younger generation's capacity to resist matches sought by parents or guardians. In so far as the Church also condemned elopement and clandestine marriage in the absence of parental consent, the net effect was to foster a complex, multilateral decision-making process, prone to deferral and stalemate. I shall discuss this matrix at greater length in the next chapter.

As for the relatively high proportion *never* marrying (the second often neglected prong of the Western European pattern), there is a strong case to be made for deliberate Christian intervention. As we have seen, Church leaders, from Jesus on, had preferred celibacy to marriage as a life-alternative for devout Christians who were seriously striving for perfection. Continence allowed both sexes to 'hold themselves free for God and Christ'.[171] Female virgins in particular were exalted figures in Christian hagiography; many became saints revered by the masses. 'For a Christian girl, therefore, "marriage to Christ" was not such a daunting prospect compared with a marriage ... to an older Christian husband.'[172] With the effective enforcement of clerical celibacy in the twelfth and thirteenth centuries, great numbers of men were removed from the marital pool. Additionally, through the development of the religious

Orders (beginning with the Order of St Benedict in the Carolingian era), the Church invested vast amounts of spiritual energy and material wealth in providing alternatives to marriage, assiduously recruiting young men and women and regulating their lives in separated, celibate communities.

The pressure on young adults to 'marry the Church' did not stem solely from clerics. 'Disgust at the recollection or prospect of marriage seems to have played a very large part in recommending the monastic life to women.'[173] Aristocratic parents with large families were inclined to encourage one or two children to enlist in Christ's service to ease their inheritance bind, alleviate sibling conflict, and avoid the perils of premarital pregnancy (as the Church stiffened its opposition to abortion and infant abandonment). But most importantly, to 'give a child unto the Lord's service' would please Him, assuring divine favour for parents facing death. While the immediate demographic effect of the enforcement of clerical celibacy and the growth of the monastic Orders was probably slight, the broader impact of their example, in making it respectable to repudiate marriage, must have been a major factor (while by no means a sufficient cause) in the development of non-universal marriage.

The rite of baptism underwent a correlated transformation in the passage from late Antiquity to the Middle Ages. In the apostolic Church, baptism had been reserved for adults who approached the Church seeking to become members. According to the New Testament, individuals had to believe in Christ and repent of their sins to qualify for Church membership. In practical terms, this meant that supplicants required the sponsorship of a member in good standing of the parish community they sought to join. Adult baptism was a non-family rite. In the universalist spirit of Paul's letter to the Galatians, baptism effaced those socially ascribed distinctions of birth that families bequeathed to their members: 'For as many of you who were baptized into Christ ... there is neither Jew nor Greek, there is neither slave nor free, there is neither male nor female; for you are all one in Christ Jesus.'[174]

As the Church gained millions of new adherents in the initial phase of sweeping expansion across the West from the fourth through the sixth century, the need arose to welcome the progeny of Christian marriages into the Lord's communion. Under the doctrine of original sin, it was imperative that infants be baptized so that their souls would not suffer eternal damnation if they perished before becoming members of the Church. (Bear in mind that almost half would die before reaching puberty.) Infant baptism addressed these concerns. The automatic baptism of the progeny of Christian couples recalled the Old Testament covenant between God and His chosen people, breaking radically with the New Testament concept of the self-willed conversion of individuals to the faith regardless of their parentage. 'Baptism was as involuntary as birth and it carried with it obligations as binding and permanent as birth into a modern state, with the further provision that the obligation attached to baptism could in no circumstances be renounced.' For to repudiate one's faith was to commit heresy, which merited not only excommunication but also death (as Thomas Aquinas had decreed).[175] The shift from adult to infant baptism thus marked the transformation of the Church from a community of willing believers frequently persecuted for espousing their beliefs into a universal society based on mandatory adherence with a proclivity for persecuting heretics.

As a sacramental ritual, baptism celebrated a second, spiritual, birth. In a preliminary rite at the door of the church, 'the priest called on the redemptive power bequeathed by Christ to his Church to expel the Devil from a child, shattering the grasp he had acquired over men at the Fall and maintained generation after generation.'[176] Thus exorcized, the baby was carried inside the church, anointed, and passed from the priest to the designated godfather who, in raising the infant from the holy font (as a midwife would from the mother's womb), became the Church's sponsor of the child's spiritual voyage through life. Redolent with patriarchal symbolism, this rite removed birth from the corporeal realm of the mother's labour in the community of female assistants.[177] Before God the Father, in the name of His only begotten Son, the priest gave the child a name and a beginning, saving his or her soul from eternal damnation. Baptism thus overcame a spiritual deficit which the birth mother and her midwife had been powerless to remedy.

Infant baptism spread rapidly throughout Latin Christendom, fostering a specifically Christian form of kinship in which godparents were related (as in marriage) not just to the child, but to the entire natal family. The fact that the Church's exogamic provisions were very generally extended to godfamilies, barring sexual relations between spiritual kin, indicates how seriously these new relations were taken. As Joseph Lynch has commented (in a definitive study of the subject), 'co-parenthood emerged by the sixth century as the heart of a system of personal alliances among adults ... used at all levels of Frankish society.'[178] From the clergy's standpoint, Christian kinship set a spiritual standard against which natural kinship could be judged, furnishing an opening for priests to press their influence in the dense thickets of pagan kinship customs.

Although parents were excluded from the ritual itself, they welcomed the infant's protection from evil spirits and the safety-net provided by godparenthood in a world of high mortality. As appointed guardians, godparents were expected to take an active interest in their godchildren's well-being, to teach them the Creed and the Lord's Prayer, encourage them to do good works and confess their sins. This kin-like bond was fostered during the child's maturation through visits, gifts and various forms of support. If parents died or were incapacitated when their offspring were young, godparents were obliged to take the children in or secure their placement with natural kin. The youthful recipients of this attention were expected, in turn, to treat their godparents with respect and affection.

The impact of clerical intervention on the laity's familial norms was undoubtedly far-reaching, but it was mediated by the vast cultural remove between the stipulations of bishops, inscribed in Latin, and their vernacular reception amongst the lay *illiterati*. The breadth of the chasm was reflected in frequent complaints by medieval canonists concerning the people's widespread ignorance of – and indifference to – Church law. Conversion of the masses did not eradicate pagan beliefs root and branch, but reworked them in a new synthesis. In most cases, the indoctrination of adherents in 'popular Christianity' was selective, avoiding direct confrontation with pre-Christian customs.[179] The breach with polytheism was softened and blurred by the formulation of the Trinity and the vision of a panoply of saints flanking the Lord in heaven.

One of the principal attractions of Christianity had always been the Gospel stories of Jesus performing miracles. The medieval Church elaborated upon this fantastic legacy, offering rites to ward off evil spirits beyond anything the heathen could muster. Routinely, priests performed rituals that were essentially pagan in origin and inspiration; they conducted fertility rites over fields and marriage beds, and led bereaved families in graveside communion with their deceased kin. Congregations resurrected 'a horde of popular superstitions': mystical cults, shrines of the saints, exorcism, conjuring and divination. Cathedrals became repositories for an inventive array of supernatural objects which attracted pilgrims and donors from far and wide.[180]

In the delicate area of family life and marital custom, the Church was typically amenable. Clerical campaigns against deviant conjugal patterns (such as polygamy and concubinage) were certainly bold; but among subordinate social classes these practices were uncommon, and among elites their suppression was gradual and selective. Bringing its weight to bear over several centuries, the Church succeeded in reforming aristocratic marital customs without engendering a deep reorientation in mass norms. In papal decrees, the Church refused to recognize marriage among kin to the seventh degree; at the level of the parish, the ban merely extended to cousins. Clerical insistence on the consent of the principals did temper parentally arranged marriage, but this canon was not accorded a radical interpretation that would have challenged the right of fathers to propose and veto a match. In sum, the Church's influence in shaping family forms was profound, but Christian norms were usually blended with other forces rather than radically displacing them.

Having briefly reconnoitred the precursor formations of the feudal amalgam in their early medieval coalescence, we return now to our central subject, undertaking a more detailed examination of peasant family forms within the feudal–seigneurial mode of production.

The Manor, the Village and the Peasant Holding

Eighty to 90 per cent of the population of medieval Europe was engaged in arable and pastoral farming; the majority of rural households combined the two. While cities played a dynamic role within feudal formations, our focus is on the mode of production, overwhelmingly agricultural. The techno-structure of European feudalism, while not exclusive to this mode of production, was nevertheless typical of it: wood or iron plough cultivation with draught animals on mixed arable, in conjunction with grazing pasture on adjacent lands for domesticated mixed-species animal herds. In this combination, agriculture (on private holdings) was structurally dominant over animal husbandry (on commons) in terms of nutritional output and noble revenue.[181] Within a manorial economy, the predominance of cereal production had its ecological limits, since pasturage serviced the arable. Effective tillage required a good stock of sturdy draught animals, and a large herd was needed on the fallow to restore leached soil with natural fertilizer. The tight interdependence of the two activities (associated normally by their spatial interlacing) was a hallmark of feudal agriculture across Europe. Their eventual disengagement in the early modern era would open the door to cash-crop specialization and capitalist agriculture.

The corporate framework of feudal production was the lord's manor, normally organized bilaterally: (a) the demesne, the lord's home farm, was worked by his own servants (the *famuli*) in combination with labour services exacted from the lord's subject peasants; (b) strips or plots were leased to tenants paying rent. Seigneurial revenues were thus doubly derived; the servile populace working the land and serving the lord's household was also bilaterally organized and hence divided. Variation in manor organization was considerable.[182] Many ecclesiastical Orders ran huge estates as demesne manors, where separate peasant leaseholds were non-existent or entirely peripheral. At the other extreme, the manors of absentee lords often devolved entirely into peasant plots, so that noble income was derived wholly from rent in various forms.

Within the manorial framework, the labour force of dependent peasant cultivators lived in villages. There might be one or several villages attached to a manor; less frequently, a village community would be divided between two manors. Medieval villages averaged perhaps 500 to 700 souls, grouped in slightly more than a hundred households. More than a cluster of dwellings, they were functioning communities of co-operative endeavour in production, consumption and demographic reproduction. Peasant subsistence was based on the working up of food, clothing and shelter for local use. While there was normally a good deal of barter and exchange between households, communities as a whole strove for self-sufficiency in basic amenities. This was not merely a cultural preference, as manifest in a marked suspicion of strangers.

The vigilant preservation of local self-reliance was frequently a matter of survival for dependent peasants, since the seigneurial mode of exploitation drained them of disposable income, while grain prices fluctuated widely from harvest to harvest. (The price of no other commodity group oscillated to the same degree.) It was dangerous for households to count on being able to meet their basic needs through the cash nexus of the marketplace.[183]

How should we characterize relations between co-resident families in medieval villages? The peasant household was based on a discrete holding and its members were profoundly affected by that individuation. The holding was reasonably secure; its tenure was a conditional possession in law, not an outright ownership, yet the peasants nevertheless felt that they had their own family property, which in every sense but ownership they did. Their household was not a business in a commercial, profit-oriented, sense; but it was certainly an independent enterprise whose members' lives depended on its success.

It would be wrong to exaggerate the peasant household's atomization under feudalism, however, as Macfarlane has done.[184] In strictly pastoral settlements, households were quite autonomous, yet most arable villages were communities of co-operative endeavour and practical interdependence. Villages were legal entities, able to borrow money, raise taxes, pass and police bylaws. Village assemblies, ancient forms of local government that coexisted with seigneurial authority, were still functioning across much of Europe in the sixteenth and seventeenth centuries. They played a vital role in the collective management of the village commons. Where every household's animals grazed in a herd, there were compelling grounds for regular co-operation between househeads, villein and free alike. Hedges had to be tended to keep everyone's cattle off the open fields, and herdsmen hired and supervised. If there was an insufficient supply of grazing stubble, wasteland and meadow, everyone's livestock suffered; and if the cattle or sheep invaded the arable, the crops of all were jeopardized.[185]

Unlike farms under capitalism, the peasants' arable in an open field village lay staked out side by side without interior barriers, as strip furlongs in outlying fields. The selection of spring and autumn crops and the fields to lie fallow and be opened up for grazing was normally determined collectively, in periodic village assemblies. Informally as well, co-operation was imperative. Poor and even middling households who lacked sufficient draught animals to comprise a plough team had to pool animals and harness a common team, working out equitable arrangements according to their respective contributions to the team's assembly. Women's domestic manufacture was also predicated on swap arrangements, informal loans, borrowing of tools and raw materials, and joint production between neighbours based on a similar type of barter and verbal covenant: 'Every day they would go to borrow a cooking utensil from one woman neighbour, to ask advice of another, and they would gossip on the doorsteps of their houses, or meet in those traditional meeting places of womenfolk – the well and the washing place.'[186]

The dwellings of common folk were not defined as a domain of clear-cut privacy in the way modern homes are. There was nowhere for families to hide. Physically, the huddled skein of huts in a large village was not conducive to social segmentation; pathways cut through yards, doorways were open, and the walls of dwellings were insubstantial. Socially, the barriers of familial privacy were frequently transgressed. Servants and farm labourers frequently lived under the same roof as the peasant families they worked for; they could not invariably be expected to keep their mouths shut. To prosecute cases of sexual misconduct, Church courts invited evidence gained by snooping, thus validating the Peeping Tom. Priests were instructed to probe into the most intimate details of their parishioners' sex lives in confessionals. All sins laid bare by these inquisitions were to be expiated through penance, with serious offences requiring public debasement (although by the late Middle Ages minor penitentials had been privatized).[187] The informal institutions of moral conformity joined the Church in rendering residential privacy tenuous. Indignant villagers publicly ridiculed couples whose conjugal relations were found to be in flagrant breach of community norms; the cuckold, the 'scold', the 'henpecked' husband (who failed to assert his patriarchal authority) and the chronic wife-beater (who abused his) were the favourite targets of shaming rituals. Significantly, neighbours who had permitted such deviance to persist without taking steps to expose the culprits were often implicated in these dramas of collective righteousness and personal humiliation.[188]

After considering plentiful evidence of the community's barrage on familial privacy, many historians have concluded that 'there was no such thing as private life', and that 'the separation of life into public and private was unknown'.[189] These dismissals seem to stem from implicit comparisons with standards of domestic privacy achieved within modern capitalism, based upon an absolute form of private property; as such, they give rise to misconceptions. In a feudal society based on conditional private property and fragmented public power, the boundary between private and public domains was not sharply delineated, but fostered a murky overlapped zone where custom and appearance held sway in cueing social practice. Privacy was not conceived as an inalienable right, but was felt to be conditional upon the maintenance of an acceptable face to the community at large. Families that were able to maintain a respectable demeanour were accorded a modicum of privacy. For the sake of community peace, they were entitled to the benefit of the doubt; a slight *faux pas* was graciously overlooked. But to preserve the fragile membrane of public discretion which inhibited snooping and deflected malicious gossip, families had to maintain an upstanding reputation in the community. One serious scandal could open the floodgates of communal prurience and rectitude.

Most discussions of private and public 'space' fail to distinguish between the territory and jurisdiction (since in a capitalist context the two are normally coincident). We have seen that under feudalism the delineation of residential *space* was flexible and imprecise, the boundary extremely porous, and privacy conditional. Yet as a sphere of *authority,* the household was unambiguously the domain of the family head: he was in charge, or at least he ought to be. The charivari rituals which exposed cuckolded or henpecked husbands to public ridicule were certainly an invasion of family privacy; but at the same time, they were a vigorous defence of patriarchal prerogative. They reminded husbands of their duty to maintain the public face of conjugal authority by humiliating those who had failed to do so.

In the absence of a culture of domestic privatism, family members alternated through the day between family and neighbourly groups and activities; they regularly dined with, and slept in the same bed as, their servants. Flandrin cites an observer of a late-sixteenth-century French pastoral village who recalled:

> It is rare for a family to spend the winter alone and isolated in its cow-shed; neighbouring families assembled together spontaneously and chose for the purpose the biggest and warmest cow-shed. In the morning, after the soup, everyone hastens to join the group: they sit in a circle on benches, they chatter, they laugh, they complain about the taxes and the tax-collectors, they repeat the gossip that is circulating about the girls and young men, or they just sit and meditate. At five o'clock they part company to go and have their meal, then they return and continue chatting for a while, then each one returns to his own home to sleep.[190]

Neighbourhood relations often assumed reciprocal obligations of a character that we would associate, in a modern capitalist context, with next of kin, particularly on such critical occasions as confinements, baptisms and funerals.[191]

How dense were kin relations between household groups in medieval villages? Most studies of English parishes indicate surprisingly few kin ties. In Homans's terms, 'family and village tended to be two bodies different in kind'. In Kirkby Lonsdale, an upland northern community in England, Macfarlane found almost no kin links between households.[192] Terling, Essex, in the seventeenth century also displayed a low density; fewer than half the householders had kin in the parish, and most of them had only one kin tie.[193] Bennett, by contrast, conducting a network analysis, found very extensive kin links between households in late medieval Northamptonshire, mostly along cognate lines, but supplemented by less intense affine contacts.[194] In the freehold zones of East Anglia and Kent, kin-based communities, holding land jointly, appear in some areas in the early Middle Ages.[195] Clear differences appear between the various strata of the thirteenth-century Suffolk community of Redgrave. Those in the middle, holding between two and ten acres of land, 'were the most likely to seek economic viability by the development of strong and repeated links with neighbours and kin of similar social and economic status. High ego-centric network densities particularly at the level of the *tenementum* were a characteristic highly specific to this group.'[196] The basic reason for low kin density in most seigneurial regions of medieval England appears to lie with a marriage norm of village exogamy. In the Spalding manors of Moulton and Weston in late-thirteenth-century Lincolnshire, a majority of villein women married outside the manor; and in three Cambridge manors in the early fourteenth century, almost half the recorded marriages were 'extra-homaquim'. The same pattern holds true on the manors of the bishopric of Worcester.[197]

The picture on the continent is very different. Flandrin, reporting on studies of French villages in the early modern era, finds a norm of parish endogamy in many villages, with the proportion marrying within the parish ranging from a low of 31 per cent to a high of 93 per cent, with most in the 70 per cent range. Kin density among the households of many villages was such that 'it is as though the concept of kinship were founded on the fact of belonging to the village community more than on ties of blood and affinity.'[198] In communities of this sort, parish endogamy must have repeatedly breached the Church's strictures against cousin marriage.[199]

What sense can be made of regional variations in the density and type of relations between households in medieval villages? As a general rule, it appears that zones of predominant freeholding tended to foster compact holdings, commercial relations between households, a wide disparity of wealth, more nuclear families, village exogamy and migration, and a relatively weak or absent manorial court. Here were grounds for a sturdy competitive sense of household individualism. Zones of predominant villein holding, however (feudal zones in the strict sense), were more likely to be based on open fields, co-operative relations between households, fixed landholdings with a majority of moderate size, stem families and compound co-resident groups, a higher rate of village endogamy, restricted migration, and a strong manorial jurisdiction. In these regions, household atomism was powerfully curtailed by collective relations. Because of this variation, it is difficult to generalize about relations between households, beyond eschewing a one-sided stress on either household atomism or village communalism. Both are stereotypes, fuelled by an ideological tempest in a teapot; neither extreme is at all representative of the great majority of medieval villages in Western Europe.[200]

The Division of Labour between Spouses

The irreducible cellular unit of the feudal mode of production was not the lord's demesne but the peasant holding – the family's dwelling complex and fields. To an extent that today seems extraordinary, the peasants' universe revolved around the opportunities and problems besetting their households. And no wonder. Goods production, subsistence consumption, and the reproduction of their labour-power were all carried out through the same unit. Ladurie comments on the primordial importance of 'the *domus*' in his vivid depiction of the village of Montaillou in southern France in the thirteenth century. His remarks seem applicable to the peasant household more generally under feudalism:

> The best way to understand Montaillou is to ... go straight to the basic cell which, multiplied a few dozen times, went to make up a village. This basic cell was none other than the peasant family, embodied in the permanence of a house, and in the daily life of a group co-resident under the same roof. ... The term *familia* ... never crosses the lips of the inhabitants of Montaillou themselves, for whom the family of flesh and blood and the house of wood, stone or daub were one and the same thing.[201]

The bulk of the labour-power required to work the holding year-round was supplied by the family's own members, who functioned as a labour team. The primary division of labour was gender-based, pivoting around an outer economy of arable fields and pasture, managed by the househead, versus an inner economy of the dwelling place and its adjacent buildings and yard-space (the messuage), managed by his wife.[202] Peasant inheritance norms buttressed this sense of natural spheres – the place of men on the land and women in the house and its immediate surround – for land was passed down from fathers to sons, while daughters were compensated via dowries with chattels, usually livestock and household property.[203] By the age of eight, children were part of the household's labour team, and by ten to twelve were probably offsetting the costs of their own upkeep on reasonably productive holdings. Young boys accompanied their fathers and girls their mothers on their rounds as they worked, learning their parents' skills by regular observation and graduated responsibility. The basic division of labour between the sexes was thus inculcated at an early age through an informal apprenticeship to parents of the same sex.

Househeads did the ploughing, ditching, hedging and reaping, looked after the herd, built field shelters and repaired agricultural implements. They jointly administered the village commons and remote pasture, allocating grazing access and supervising shepherds. Individually and collectively, men thus directly managed the major means of production in the village.

The inner economy of the messuage – the house and its adjoining farmyard and garden – was the wife's domain, where she forged a realm of autonomy and self-confident competence.[204] Here she directed the work of servants and children, as well as exerting her own labour-power. Much of her work was devoted to supplementing a staple diet of cereal grains with milk, beer, vegetables, eggs and poultry, as well as gathering nuts, wild fruit, herbs and firewood. Wives and daughters also supplied most of the family's clothing, through sheep-shearing, wool-combing, spinning and weaving. Spinning and weaving were typically done in the company of other women in the evening hours, at a time when men's workday was complete.[205] While men worked from sunrise to dusk, women toiled even longer hours, rising before dawn to prepare breakfast and working after dinner in the evenings. Men's work displayed a greater variation in intensity, depending on the season and the weather; women's work was more continuous year-round.[206]

Peasant women were domestic generalists, combining a great variety of tasks; but one should not imagine that each housewife performed the full range of labours mentioned above. Barter arrangements among the women of a village, plus exchange with local commodity producers (bakers and brewers, for example) fostered a surprising degree of interhousehold specialization in the division of female labour, particularly in the area of food production.[207] Since both sexes tended to barter or sell the produce of their own sphere, women regularly managed commercial transactions in the market for vegetables, poultry, dairy products and cloth, handling their own money supply. Commodity production was not separated off from the rest of women's work in and around the house, as it would be under capitalism.

There was necessarily a pragmatic flexibility built into the peasant family's division of labour.[208] At harvest time, everyone aged six and over could be expected to work long hours in the fields, leaving other tasks in abeyance until the crop was in. When field work was slack, husbands as well as wives worked around the yard and engaged in a variety of domestic manufactures and dwelling improvements. Yet it was much more common for women to lend a hand in men's work than vice versa, and this flexibility and seasonal fluctuation did not efface a clear demarcation in the marital division of labour.[209] Whenever a wife worked alongside her husband in the fields (planting, weeding, gleaning, binding, winnowing or thatching), she 'helped out' in his domain and laboured under his direction. Even when they toiled in proximity, men and women generally did different things: in the fields, women led the draught team, men guided the plough; in the house, women made cloth and men made furniture.

Reinforcing the sexual segregation of spheres were the requirements of labour service on the lord's demesne, where many field tasks were stipulated as men's work, and wives were regularly exempted as a matter of seigneurial policy.[210] The delineation of gendered spheres had major implications for village social life: beyond the family, peer groups and friendship networks were primarily homosocial.[211] Furthermore, women were excluded from the political offices and regulatory bodies of the village: 'women were not the heads of tithings; they did not sit on local juries; nor did they fill the office of constable or reeve.'[212]

The tasks that we associate with the household today – housework and childcare – were typically women's work under feudalism as well. But here they were combined with domestic manufacture, constituting a secondary component of women's total workload, consuming much less time than they do in a modern context. Housecleaning could not have taken up much of a woman's time. Peasant huts typically combined a stable at one end of the building and domestic space for humans at the other; their crude interior partitioning did not suffice to keep the two species apart. They were rudimentary dwellings in every sense, fashioned from locally available materials: stone and daub (clay or mud) walls, with thatched roofs and stone or earthen floors. The hearth stood at the centre of the hut, equipped with a hook, a pot, and a few simple wood and clay implements. Furnishings were sparse: a trunk, benches along the wall, perhaps a wooden stool or two around the fire. 'Wind, rain, small animals, and every sort of parasite – creeping, scratching, jumping – came in all the time.'[213] Keeping the place clean and tidy was a losing battle; women evidently did not spend much time trying.

Mothers spent far less time caring for young children in the Middle Ages than they do today. In the first place, it was not their exclusive concern; they shared the work with hired sitters, older siblings (often still children themselves), grandmothers, and maidservants.[214] Secondly, childcare did not force the withdrawal of mothers from goods production as it so often has under capitalism; infants were transported around the yard and to the fields, so that mothers could continue to work.[215] Toddlers were sometimes left unattended, though parents were reluctant to do this, and the practice met with community disapproval.[216] Some scholars have interpreted evidence of such inattention as reflecting a callous indifference to children.[217] But this seems most unlikely; peasant women normally nursed their infants for at least two years, hardly indicative of a lack of early bonding. Babies were swaddled as a security measure when mothers were otherwise occupied, but the confinement was not continuous, and infants were permitted to crawl around while adults kept an eye on them.[218] The primary reason that childcare consumed less of a mother's time must have been the constant press of other responsibilities and the availability of alternative minders, not a general absence of maternal feeling. This said, there is little doubt that medieval peasants – women and men alike – would have found the modern mystique of mothering, and our obsession with correct childrearing practices, strange indeed. As Chaytor and Lewis have remarked:

'A woman's reputation was at stake as a child-breeder, not a child-rearer.'[219]

Women who are exclusively housewives today, lacking their own wage income, are in a far more dependent position than peasant housewives were. The domestic labour of medieval peasant women was not divorced from goods production, nor from money-generating commodity production. They thus appeared, in a straightforward sense, as indispensable members of family production teams with their own sphere of competence and jurisdiction. One of the reasons for the strong linkage of landholding to marriage in peasant communities was the widespread recognition that a man could not manage a holding productively without a wife as his full-time co-worker. If a young man inherited land upon reaching the age of majority, he would normally marry shortly after taking up the tenancy. And whenever wives died, widowers were quick to remarry – much quicker than widows in most cases. The importance of peasant women's undeniable contribution to production in the medieval era was clearly recognized by husbands in wills, where by all accounts they were unstintingly generous, often expressing unabashed gratitude to their spouses for years of service to the family.[220]

Many historians have characterized the peasant household as a co-managed unit, with the wife an equal partner, noting that she was in a position to inherit holdings and her husband's testamentary power.[221] Some feminists, apparently in search of a pre-capitalist golden age for women, are determinedly upbeat about women's power under feudalism. JoAnn McNamara and Suzanne Wemple, for example, write: 'Endowed with their own property and rights of inheritance, secure in their marital status, women were equipped to act with power and decision in the fluid society of the first feudal age.'[222] Kathleen Casey, referring to the fifteenth century, verges on the euphoric:

> Late medieval women were exceptionally favoured. They had room for manoeuvre within a mixed or ambivalent kin set; within a set of religious values that were androgynous or even asexual as often as they were misogynist and anti-sexual; and within an unsystematic mosaic of customary law. Private stipulations permitted ... informal equality under formal inequality.[223]

It is certainly important to note the pervasive discrepancy between women's formal subjugation and their real strength.[224] Legally, women were permanent minors, placed in the care and under the personal authority of men – first their fathers, then their older brothers (when fathers died), and finally their husbands. In common law, they could be 'disciplined' (i.e., beaten) for disobedience by husbands as well as fathers.[225] The community face of patriarchy was largely pacific; in public places, a good woman refrained from arguing with her husband and a considerate man would decline to reprimand his wife loudly. At home, women were less likely to defer and men to restrain their anger at being crossed.

The peasant household was a deeply co-operative endeavour, and women were vital to its daily management; their indispensability furnished wives with some bargaining power. Yet the peasant marriage was hardly an egalitarian partnership. Middleton's assessment is much more sober, and undoubtedly more accurate: '[The medieval peasant wife was] the subordinated partner in a co-tenancy where the conjugal property had been placed under the guardianship and control of her husband.'[226] The problem in inferring a rough parity between husband and wife, stemming from her strong role in goods production and village exchange, is that the other half of the conjugal relation is ignored: the land/marriage/fertility nexus. Fathers presided over marriage as part of the inheritance system, and husbands were recognized as tenants, property-owners and householders. The determinant role of women married to landholders was to furnish them with legitimate offspring – above all, heirs. We shall examine this side of conjugal relations more closely in a later section of this chapter.

We have thus a version of 'companionate marriage' where the husband presides. Modern minds are inclined to balk at the combination. With a feminist sensibility, we would like to believe that the abiding emotional bonds of love, affection and respect which we associate with companionate marriage can flourish only between persons who at least strive to exercise parity in their relationship. But this is to misread historical realities through the prism of modern ideology. The conjugal values of the time embodied the duality without contradiction; they had no difficulty idealizing a patriarchal partnership. Early modern moralists, the authors of countless advice manuals on marriage, insisted that the man ruled the roost but that he ought to include his wife in its governance; she was to obey him, but he must consult her. In the words of William Gouge, 'He is the highest in the family and hath ... authority over all. [Yet their relationship was] the nearest to equality that may be ... wherein man and wife are after a sort even fellows and partners.'[227]

Peasant Stratification

In class-divided modes of production, the families of labouring classes are hierarchically stratified in ways which inhibit, but do not eliminate, their members' capacity for solidarity and collective action. Peasant families under feudalism were stratified primarily by the size of their holdings but also by the nature of their class dependency. The disparity of arable acreage between large- and smallholders in medieval villages could reach ratios of twenty to one, with a normal ratio of four or five to one.[228] Peasant stratification was also based on grazing and usage rights on common lands and open fields: these could vary from full access to exclusion, depending on the status of the household's tenure and the family's capacity to pay entry fees. And access to land is useless unless one can productively work it. There was an enormous difference between those who cultivated the land by hand implement (a pauperized minority), a draught animal or two (many smallholders), or a properly harnessed plough-team (middle- and largeholders).

Despite this disparity, the distribution of land was unimodal, displaying a 'normal' curve, skewed somewhat towards the landless end of the spectrum. The majority of customary holdings were of a fairly standard size, geared to optimize the productivity of a family labour team.[229] They could not normally be broken up for sale, and multiple tenancies were generally forbidden. In the early modern era, middle-sized holdings declined and the peasantry polarized as its internal antagonisms erupted, destroying its cohesion as a class. (This process will be examined in the next chapter.) But in the Middle Ages, families that worked customary holdings of a standard size constituted a centre of social gravity in the village, inhibiting the competitive fragmentation of the peasantry.

Peasant families were also differentiated by the personal status of the house-head and the conditions of family tenure.[230] Allowing for regional variation, the core of the middling peasantry were generally of servile status, rendering the bulk of the lord's surplus labour on his demesne. Freeholders (who possessed a minority of peasant-held land in the Middle Ages) were normally concentrated at the top and bottom of the heap.[231] The legal difference between the prerogatives of serfs and freeholders was vast:

> In theory the villein's land and his livestock belonged to his lord and could not be alienated without his consent. A villein could not change his place of residence or give away his daughter in marriage without the lord's permission. He was not permitted to sue his lord in the King's Courts; his right to enter into agreement concerning his goods and property, to bequeath or inherit land and livestock, were in various ways limited to a lord's rights over his person and property.[232]

By contrast, the freeholder was legally entitled to move away, to arrange a son's or daughter's marriage without the lord's permission, to buy and sell livestock and land, and to sue or be sued in national courts.

In practice, the prerogatives and obligations of villeins and freeholders were not as disparate as they appear in law. The vast majority of peasants stood on the murky middle ground of customary rights. Fines for manorial transgressions were *de facto* licence fees rather than juridical deterrents to felony. The freeholder would normally be exempted from some but by no means all these levies. The decisive difference between free and villein was that the former paid their rents in money or in kind, and were exempt from the labour services which the latter were compelled to render. In addition, rents tended to be heavier on villein land, so that unfree families required more land than freeholders to generate a comparable standard of living.[233]

In the upper echelons of the peasantry stood a set of secure tenants who had frequently benefited from their lords' needs for ready cash to purchase their liberty. Their families were able to acquire property through purchase or lease, hire poor freeholders to supplement their labour force, and sell their surplus produce at a profit. Rich peasants might also set up mini-manors by leasing out land to poor villagers. By embarking on concerted programmes of land acquisition they were able to offset the friable consequences of inheritance, thus negotiating the devolutionary transition which often pauperized smallholders.

The relationship of flourishing husbandmen to destitute cottagers was fraught with tension, yet there was an undeniable symbiosis between the two strata.[234] Husbandmen required extra hands at harvest time, and cottagers needed to supplement the produce of their own tiny plots by working for others. The transfer of labour-power from poor to more prosperous holdings (later institutionalized in the system of domestic service) was typical of feudal villages.[235] The cottagers' means of subsistence were mixed. On the one hand, they appeared in the guise of pre-feudal gatherers, hunters and horticulturalists. On the other, they were compelled to sell their labour-power to survive, and in this they anticipated a modern proletariat. In the context of the medieval village, however, they were neither foragers nor wage labourers. They lived as an integral underclass of peasant smallholders, shifting in and out of the manor's labour force and forming what David Levine has termed a 'cottage economy'.[236]

The juridical freedom of smallholders was synonymous with the constant insecurity of their livelihood. With nothing much to inherit, their offspring stocked the village fringe, living in wretched shacks on tiny patches of commons waste devoid of appurtenance. Their residential rights were tenuous, asserted by the customary claims of the squatter. When pressure mounted on an overburdened commons, they could easily find themselves targeted for harassment by the village's 'better sort'. One rung beneath this 'residence threshold' (as Goubert has termed it), the vagrant poor would 'encamp in the countryside, away from the villages, on the fringes of *terroirs,* putting up flimsy huts, using natural caves, or allowed to live in some tumbledown building if they could be of service as labourers, ditchers, hedgers, basket-makers, knife-grinders, clog-makers, charcoal-burners or rag-pickers.'[237] Residential patterns thus served both to register and to reinforce the marginal position of this underclass in production.[238]

While medieval peasants were predominantly subsistence generalists, they did harbour a small number of specialist craftsmen within their ranks. The basic tools of production on the farmstead were fashioned by ironsmiths, carpenters, masons, thatchers, tilers and potters. In densely populated regions, these craftsmen enjoyed enough work to set up shop and reside permanently in a single village, enjoying a living standard that placed them in the upper echelons of the village community. To ply their trades in sparser areas, they had to move from village to village. Rarely, however, were they completely divorced from the land; most owned a small plot of arable, where they grew the bulk of their food. Even those of a lower rank than the skilled trades listed above – miners, smelters, charcoal-burners and glaziers – seldom worked year-round at these jobs. They continued to live as peasants, holding small plots and working the land. While craft specialists in possession of their own means of production were almost invariably men, women were sometimes hired on a seasonal or day-labour basis as thatchers, ditchers and sheep-shearers.[239]

Disparity in peasant wealth generated considerable variation in household size and composition. The yeoman stratum tended to form larger co-resident groups than did smallholders. Prosperous parents were able to maintain their children on-site through their adolescent years; they were also more likely to have servants living with them, either in the same dwelling or in adjoining quarters. Since richer families could acquire additional land locally, their off-spring were more likely to take up residence in the village upon marriage. The sons and daughters of cottagers were more often forced to leave, seeking their livelihoods elsewhere. Local kin networks were thus thicker in the top half of the community than at the bottom. A marked propensity to marital homo-gamy, fostered by the 'levelling' pressures of dotal bargaining, tended to repro-duce the wealth and status gradations of the peasantry from generation to generation.

There was a great deal of transit back and forth between neighbouring vil-lages in medieval Europe, much of it temporary. Mobility varied, of course, with the availability of land. When land was tight, tenant families stayed put. In Kibworth, Howell found that 'no family left the village or ceased to hold some land between 1280 and 1340 and only five families entered the manor.' In the wake of the Black Death, however, many families voluntarily left the village, presumably in search of greener pastures.[240] But even when families clung tenaciously to their holdings, as they normally did, their individual members were often itinerant.[241] Young adults were frequently on the move, leaving home in search of temporary work or a small piece of land to set up a household. While all members of the village community might have occasion to move, especially in times of family crisis, the most mobile strata were those at the top and bottom of the peasant hierarchy. Prosperous tenants were in-clined to buy or lease land in other villages; their siblings or offspring might then take up residence there. Down below, hunger and insecurity often sent poor cottagers packing. Itinerant journeymen and day labourers pursued seaso-nal work, depending on the vagaries of the weather. Paupers, vagabonds and scavengers tramped back roads and country lanes in search of their next meal.

The Mode of Seigneurial Exploitation and the Reproduction Cycle of Labour-Power

Agriculturalists in all modes of production must manage the changing relation of hands to mouths through the various stages of the family cycle. Their households must also cope with a seasonal labour cycle which brings sharp fluctuations in the need for labour-power: from harvest peaks when the family's own members are insufficient, to winter troughs when there is not enough work to keep the core residents productively occupied. Unpredictable weather variations complicate matters, particularly during the most draining phase of the family cycle when young children are not yet recovering the costs of their upkeep. These vicissitudes, universal to agriculturalists, are exacerbated under feudalism by the inflexibility of the seigneurial mode of exploitation.

The lords' extraction of a surplus from peasant households assumed a great diversity of forms – rents, fees, fines, levies and taxes.[242] This bundle of exactions was paid in labour service, produce or cash, often all three combined. Despite the bewildering array of dues, the basic distribution of the agrarian product between lords and peasants was starkly transparent. The critical factor in the feudal mode of exploitation was the way this division was effected. It was not a sharecropping arrangement, whereby lords creamed off a proportion of variable agrarian yields. Rather, most of the lord's exactions were fixed; they were set before, and levied independently of, the harvest. Peasant households thus bore the direct brunt of variations in yield from one harvest to the next. They toiled in order to retain whatever was left over *after* their rents, dues and fines had been paid.[243] This, then, placed the peasants directly at the mercy of nature's vagaries. In years of bountiful harvests, a family's diligence would be rewarded: after paying off the lord and meeting other obligations in the village, there might be enough left over to raise its living standards, improve its livestock or agricultural implements, prepare a daughter's dowry or lease another strip of land. In lean years, especially after a succession of crop failures, the lord's exactions would deplete the family's meagre reserves and sink it into debt, forcing househeads to sell off livestock and land. The poorest families would be driven to landless penury and dangerous desperation.

The Achilles heel of the feudal mode of production lay here, in the mechanism of peasant exploitation, which was indifferent to the capacity of the exploited to pay. So long as land of good quality was available in the vicinity, the seigneurial regime had a safety valve: those unfortunates who lost their grip on the bottom rungs of the tenure ladder were able to re-establish themselves on newly cleared land. The lord's thirst for extra revenue was thus satiated by broadening the base of the dues-paying pyramid. Once population growth exceeded the limits of available land, the latent contradictions of the system became manifest. Overcrowding strengthened the lord's hand, since there was nowhere else for tenants to go. The ratchet-like mechanism of feudal exploi-tation raised the rate of surplus extraction through buoyant years, and then bled peasants white in lean years, draining their savings, deteriorating the pro-ductivity of their land, sapping their labour-power to the point of exhaustion, and ultimately provoking a mortality crisis. Lords often discovered that they had a full-blown crisis on their hands after the destructive wave had already broken. The first sign might be a sharp fall in labour productivity on the demesne, followed by rapid accumulation of peasant debt, refusals to pay, land desertion, and finally a mortality crisis and a net drop in village population. The charity and insurance programmes of the Church and nobility were de-signed to alleviate such crises, head off revolts and prevent the poorest layer of the peasantry from fleeing. Often, they were too little too late.

The seigneurial mode of exploitation ensured that money wealth was regu-larly drained from the peasant economy.[244] The rural masses were largely sep-arated from the benefits of urban–rural commodity trade, the bulk of which went on over their heads. Consequently, the investment imperative of peasant households was conservative and labour-intensive. The weather could not be foretold, and the lords' exactions forced them to play it safe and not to tempt nature's fickle fate. Peasant planting strategies tended to be conservative, diver-sifying subsistence crops to insure against crop failure. The only flexible re-source peasant families could bring to bear to improve their lot (or merely to keep from sliding backwards) was their own members' labour-power. Theirs was a subsistence rationale, not a market-oriented one. Even when they sold their grain on the market (as increasingly they did in the late Middle Ages), they tended to gear the volume sold to cover their money rent and necessary expenses, not in positive response to price fluctuations. Falling prices would induce peasants to increase sowings and sales, while rising prices and good yields would relieve the pressure, convincing them to ease off.[245]

Given the precarious nature of yield variation, the implacable tendency of peasant households to intensify the exertion of their members' labour-power was a rational response to the form of the lord's exploitation. Labour services on the demesne placed especially onerous demands on their labour supply. Since family labour was usually cheaper than hired labour, the family on a moderate or large holding was under persistent pressure to enlarge its numbers. Given high and unpredictable mortality rates, couples sought to beget suffi-cient children to be sure of having a healthy male heir when the time came to pass on the holding. But this expansive logic ran smack-up against the counter-pressure to check fertility in order to simplify property transfer and keep the basic means of production intact. On a decent-sized holding, a large number of children would have been welcomed as a present labour force; as eventual claimants on the household's wealth, however, they were not. The bind was exacerbated by the unpredictable consequences of mortality, which induced a chronic tendency to 'overinsure' against the failure of male heirs.[246] The upshot was that the daily and the generational cycle of labour-power's reproduction were antagonized – caught within a larger contradiction.

On smaller and less productive holdings, an increase in family labour supply was not always a good investment. For these families, unevenness in seasonal labour demand would often render children in their teens and early twenties, who might otherwise have been an asset, a net drain. Their value at harvest time simply could not offset the long winter months of relative idleness. Furthermore, if they remained at home there was no opportunity for the offspring of smallholders and cottagers to accumulate their own funds in preparation for marriage and household formation. For this reason, both generations had an interest in sending youth out to work, where they could earn their own keep and accumulate modest savings for the future. Regardless of the specific inheritance customs of a region, the children of cottagers and smallholders became a 'surplus' population, victims of the way seigneurial extraction squeezed the reproduction cycle of land-poor households. An extensive pattern of family settlement generated by this cycle became evident as soon as social historians moved beyond the village monograph to study clusters of villages and hamlets in a regional perspective. From a 'home-base' village where a prosperous group of relatives resided on well-established holdings, the subordinated children of the younger generation spread out, taking up marginal holdings in neighbouring settlements. The downward mobility of 'overflow' family branches was clearly manifest in the size and precariousness of their holdings, in contrast to those who inherited land in the village of their birth.[247]

'Overpopulation' was endemic to the feudal mode of production, not because of the natural profligacy of the rural poor (who, in fact, had lower reproduction rates than prosperous peasants) but because of the conflict which feudalism engendered in the peasants' reproduction cycle.[248] In the face of this bind, househeads strove to keep three key variables in alignment: land, labour-power and the timing of pre-mortem inheritance. The obvious way to attenuate the problem of 'extra' offspring was to acquire more land (through purchase or clearing efforts). Many wealthier househeads were able to do this in buoyant years, before offspring came of age and parents retired or died. They were then in a position to settle non-heirs on acquired lands while keeping the main holding intact. A second alternative when there were few children was to move away from a strictly familial labour team and take in servants, or hire seasonal day labourers, especially in the early years of the family cycle when one's own children were too young to make much of a contribution to farm production. Once again, this was a viable strategy for the upper strata of the peasantry, but most poorer households simply could not afford it. A third strategy was to delay the marriages of one's offspring, often by sending them out as young adults to service in another's household, where their wages could be accumulated in a fund for their eventual marriage settle-ments. This was an alternative which poorer househeads could pursue. Do-mestic service for young single adults (from fifteen to thirty years) became commonplace throughout Western Europe in the early modern era, though its prevalence in the Middle Ages is unclear.

While the first strategy adjusted land to the changing size and composition of the family labour team, the second and third alternatives inverted the equa-tion, tailoring the household labour force to available land and its uses. The consequences of these strategies were sharply contrasted. The drive to acquire more land, in evidence throughout the medieval epoch, pushed a stream of pauperized young adults, losers in the scramble for holdings in their native villages, out on to the fringes of settlements on poorer land. This was the main demo-economic growth dynamic of the high Middle Ages, which eventually overran the ecology of its own resource base in the fourteenth century.[249] We shall review the basic features of this crisis at the end of this chapter.

The second and third strategies of peasant househeads – to hire servants in the initial phase of the family cycle, and then to send some of the children out to service later on – were generally pursued in combination, when land was tight and the first avenue was practically blocked. The aggregate effect was to absorb young people locally in domestic service and inhibit their capacity to marry, thus delaying procreation and rendering an extraordinarily large portion of them celibate for life. When this pattern became prevalent across Western Europe, the equilibration of land with labour-power was primarily effected by means of a 'nuptial valve': land scarcity indirectly pushed the age of marriage up, the incidence of marriage down, and thus shortened the normal fertility span, adjusting it – roughly and in a delayed fashion – to available places on the land and alternative livelihoods.

When did this distinctive Western European marriage pattern first develop? The answer is not yet clear. Levine has speculated that it may have originated in late Antiquity with barbarian demography, recalling Tacitus' reference to Germanic women being 'not hurried into marriage [and] as old and as full-grown as the men [who were] slow to mate'.[250] A shard of corroboration is found in a ninth-century survey of the Church of St Victor of Marseille, where there was very little age difference between spouses, and both appear to have married in their mid to late twenties. But other medieval sources, primar-ily of a literary and legal character, indicate a young age at first marriage for women – not long after puberty.[251] The problem is that most of this evidence refers to elites; peasants almost certainly married later: how much later is the question. In lieu of further substantiation, it seems doubtful that late marriage prevailed in the age of great expansion from AD 1000 to 1250, when mass colonizing movements out on to new arable were probably of sufficient scope to foster marriage and household formation at an early age. It seems most unlikely that an average annual growth rate of about one-quarter per cent could have been sustained for three centuries (given quite high rates of medieval mortality) if women were delaying childbearing until their mid to late twenties. The other facet of the 'nuptial valve' is a relatively large portion of the population never marrying. We know that the monastic Orders grew massively throughout the early and high Middle Ages by means of the recruitment of young women who would remain single and celibate for life. It may be reasonable to infer that the proportion of the population not involved in childbearing was rising during these centuries.

The period when one might first expect marital delay to become widespread is the century of stagnation and land scarcity leading up to the Black Death. Smith and Hallam have made a preliminary case for the prevalence of late and non-universal marriage in England before the plague.[252] Evidence for the rest of Northwestern Europe before the sixteenth century is scanty. Women in the Middle Ages appear to have married early in Mediterranean Europe, while most men wed in their late twenties.[253] Outside England, the Western European marriage pattern probably was not consolidated in the Middle Ages.

But here we must make a distinction between late marriage and the nuptial valve. When women's mean age at marriage shifts over time in sensitive response to economic opportunity, then the regulative action unique to this marital regime is operative, even if its restrictive impact has not yet been fully achieved. There *is* some evidence that nuptial equilibration was already working, albeit feebly, in the thirteenth and fourteenth centuries: 'The sensitivity of household size and structure to long-term demographic and economic trends argues strongly that population dynamics in medieval society was already at least partially functioning as a self-regulating or homeostatic system.'[254] The micro-genesis of this system is not hard to fathom: it was readily apparent to peasant heads that limiting the number of progeny enhanced their families' fortunes, making it easier to keep the holding intact. A large brood would almost certainly entail downward mobility for most children. Anything that could limit fertility to a maximum of three or four children would improve the chances of prosperity; the delay of childbearing, when coupled with the delay of weaning (thus lengthening intervals between births), would do it. I am not suggesting that peasants considered these matters in the way that modern couples discuss how many children they wish to have: whenever late marriage and prolonged suckling customs developed, they undoubtedly arose in a culturally immersed way. But the consequences of various childbirth schedules for the subsequent operation of inheritance strategies were not lost on peasants, who welcomed male infants and first births with jubilation, while greeting girls, and boys who came much later, as a calamity.[255]

Peasant Inheritance Customs and Strategies

There was a great range of inheritance customs in Western Europe, varying both between regions and within them: generalization is problematic. The critical distinction in legal codes was between partible and impartible inheritance. For purposes of initial clarification, we can construct two polar inheritance models and project their demographic consequences as ideal-types.[256] In a system of impartible inheritance (associated with open field cultivation, relative land scarcity and heavy seigneurial authority), there is a fixed number of openings on the land, marriage is delayed, a large proportion of non-heirs remain single or emigrate (village population growth is therefore slow), and a stem family structure prevails. Under a partible rule (associated with easier land access, freeholding and non-agricultural by-employments), land tends to fragment, marriage is facilitated, nuclear families form and multiply on separate plots, and emigration is reduced, resulting in a pattern of quicker population growth and eventual overcrowding on the land.

Due to the prevalence of pre-mortem disposition, the formal differences between partible and impartible legal codes did not, in reality, generate two opposing inheritance systems. As we shall see, there were many ways to circumvent equal shares in a partible region and to compensate non-heir children with small land parcels in an impartible region. In practice, neither system was prevalent as a pure type.[257] In most regions some sort of trade-off was worked out between them.[258] Consequently, we should not be surprised to find that studies contrasting partible with impartible villages often discover few significant differences in their basic demographic features and land/population ratios.[259] Such a finding does not negate the role of inheritance customs in shaping family forms; but it does suggest that the two models are ideal-types, while class and patriarchal interests dictated an intermediate course. Rather than classifying inheritance systems in formal terms as partible or impartible, it would be preferable to distinguish different types according to their capacity to regulate the rate of marriage and household formation in response to the socio-economic opportunities available in the community. 'Tight' systems tend to block nuptials by limiting the number of places on the land, enforcing a threshold beneath which one dare not proceed to marriage, and inhibiting circumvention by means of the development of alternative livelihoods in the local area. A 'loose' system flexibly adapts places to the stream of youth reaching marriageable age. In these terms, the diverse regions of Northwestern Europe were inclined to be on the 'tight' side, adjusting marriage rates, household formation (and, indirectly, fertility) to available places on the land.

As noted, the normal practice of the medieval peasantry was to keep the ancestral holding intact and to compensate offspring excluded from the core tenement as generously as possible by means of an ancillary land grant, chattel wealth or a money settlement.[260] This is what I have termed a compensatory impartible inheritance regime, characteristic of the feudal-seigneurial mode of production.[261] This form of inheritance was substructured by the seigneurial property form, which typically fostered a segmentation of village arable between villein tenements and allodial fields. Specific arable strips were tied by manorial custom to discrete messuages within the village proper; this ensemble comprised the manse. The entire parcel, with concomitant use rights in commons, constituted a family's holding and was not normally permanently alienable or divisible, thus expressing and perpetuating the impartible side of the inheritance regime. In addition to the core of customary tenements, freehold lands were cleared in and around villages. These fields could be more readily divided, recombined and transferred within and between families by lease, sale or bequest. As supplementary resources, they permitted families to adapt land flexibly to available labour-power in passing through the various phases of the domestic cycle. Furthermore, in devolving the patrimony parents could use acquired strips to compensate secondary children, ensuring their continued residence within the village community after marriage. Providing the crucial distinction between ancestral holdings and acquests was maintained, the development of a land market in the latter facilitated the inheritance process.

The inheritance customs of European peasants are often described as 'egalitarian' and 'partible', but such terms, with their modern connotations, are misleading. In the first place, one must recognize that the customary sense of equal shares had a rather different meaning among pastoralists and cultivators. In pastoral communities, equality in land meant equal access for one's herd, not subdivision into small fields. This egalitarianism (which was typically an equality of sons only) was not then a *distributional* value (equal shares of a divided pie) but a *collective familial principle* that legitimate sons had an inalienable right to attain life-support from the land of their fathers.[262]

In grain-growing regions, the principle of familial access was also strong. In fourteenth-century Halesowen, 'there is clear evidence in the court rolls ... that the villagers regarded their farms as belonging to the family as a whole in the sense that every member of the conjugal family had a claim to be supported by it.'[263] When sons grew up and were ready to marry, what could such a principle mean? If strictly implemented, the egalitarian partition of land between sons would bankrupt a family farm in a few generations. Yet even where partibility prevailed in law and local custom, freehold land made it possible to circumvent the friable consequence of formally partible customs. There were many ways to avoid subdivision. In the majority of cases, two or more sons did not survive their father's death, so the problem would not arise. If there were two or more sons, one could often be dissuaded from returning to claim his portion; or alternately, he might sell his share to the designated heir and depart. Formally, all sons might hold jointly, while in practice only one worked the land. The value of land was often set absurdly low to fix an affordable rate of non-heir compensation. In the Swedish province of Gotland, 'the peasant adroitly side-stepped the inheritance laws [prohibiting exclusion] by selling the farm to one of his children, usually the eldest son, for a nominal sum far below the actual market value.'[264] Marriage strategies could often counteract partible customs. The timing of nuptials was of critical importance in this regard. A preferred son would be granted most of the patrimony at marriage, while his siblings would have to settle for chattels or small plots when their turns came. If the family had been able to acquire extra lands and use rights during the househead's tenure, these ancillary parcels could be distributed to secondary children. In the worst of cases, space for a dwelling and garden might be carved out at the uncleared margin of the main holding to keep secondary siblings in the vicinity and furnish a roof over their heads.[265]

The other way to avoid subdivision was to pass the holding jointly to surviving sons who would marry in and either share a hearth or establish separate residences. The practice was common in medieval Italy and Mediterranean France. Bloch has proposed that co-parcenary customs were widespread among medieval peasants across Western Europe, but this is a dubious generalization, particularly for the northern parts of the continent.[266] In view of the early modern evidence, one would be surprised to find that joint inheritance was common in medieval England, for example; yet Harvey has speculated along these lines for the twelfth century, in an era prior to routine land survey, field measurement and the deeding of customary holdings.[267] Throughout Western Europe, co-parcenary customs and joint families were most commonly found in pastoral uplands, in zones of sparse settlement where stockraising was primary. In the nucleated villages of the plains, however, where heavy plough agriculture predominated, the designation of a primary heir seems to have been the main way to avoid the subdivision of family holdings.

The need to allocate portions to departing siblings could make it extremely difficult for the heir to maintain the family holding as a viable enterprise. Yet the overriding purpose of these settlements was to ease the bitter pill of exclusion, and thus to safeguard the holding's integrity, not to jeopardize it. We ought to treat non-heir compensation and family tenure impartibility as complementary principles in a genuine, if awkward, synthesis, not simply as antagonistic objectives stuck together as a compromise. In a system of absolute private property, unigeniture certainly renders these two principles irreconcilable. But in the conditional form of feudal property, with parcelled sovereignty, one party's claim was typically dependent upon the proper discharge of specified obligations to another. The principle of non-heir compensation was more than a vestige of ancient partible customs, constituting (in Goody's terms) 'diverging devolution'. Under feudalism it became a one-time pre-mortem settlement in the service of land integrity. As Goody himself has recognized, 'no person could receive both gifts ... dowry and inheritance [at death] were alternative not cumulative.'[268]

In practice, the twin objectives of compensating non-heirs and retaining the holding intact were often mutually destructive. The critical variable in this regard was how much wealth a family could dispose of. For the upper stratum of the peasantry, the bind was manageable. The settlement portions could be paid to departing siblings before or after a father's death without dividing or debilitating the main holding. Poor families were not so fortunate. The compensation of secondary siblings might easily plunge the family tenure into debt, jeopardizing its retention. Many smallholdings were whittled down around the edges or forfeited in penury. In a period of population growth, the impartible objective slowed but could never halt the inexorable morcellement of peasant land in the long run. This tendency was endemic to the way in which the seigneurial mode of exploitation structured the equilibration of labour-power and land.

Smallholdings and cottage plots typically would not support a family. But if supplementary income could be gained (with parents or elder siblings lending a hand), newly married couples could often make a go of it. Cash dowries or settlements could be used to buy land locally if any was available. The objective of keeping one's children in the local area might thus be realized, if not in the parents' village, then in a neighbouring village or hamlet. Do not underestimate the capacity of peasant heads, even in a land-tight period, to find some way to place a small patch of soil beneath the feet of their non-heir sons and brothers. In impartible Halesowen at a time of acute land shortage, almost half the families with two or more sons over twelve were successful in settling more than one son in the village, and 60 per cent of young landholders furnished a sibling with land.[269]

Manorial court rolls indicate that there was an active market in freehold land in the Middle Ages. Such evidence has often been taken to signify the declining importance of family inheritance among dependent peasant cultivators, yet several historians have argued persuasively that medieval land markets generally buttressed familial land management and heritability.[270] 'Small pieces of free land were shunted from family to family via non-inheriting children so that the principal family holding could pass from generation to generation intact.'[271] Howell points out that the frequency of permanent alienation by sale can easily be overestimated in a face-value reading of court rolls; a considerable portion of recorded transfers, when traced over time, turn out to be lease arrangements, not sales. Leased fields were routinely acquired and shed as families moved through the phases of the family cycle, reverting to their original tenants for inheritance purposes.[272] Blanchard comments on the strength of reversionary rights retained in the collective memory of late medieval villagers

99

in Somerset and Derbyshire: 'In spite of the passage of land through three or four non-family hands, there was a marked tendency for it ultimately to revert into the possession of either the original family who had alienated it or their "successor" in the land market.'[273]

In a formal reading of court records and legal codes, regional customs often appear to dictate the course of wealth transmission between the generations; in practice, peasants enjoyed a margin of leeway. Royal decrees and manorial injunctions were designed to deal with cases of sudden and premature death, where the househead's wishes with regard to the patrimony were not known. Such *pro forma* stipulations did not seriously constrain the options available to living househeads, particularly males. In contrast with the nobility, peasant inheritance practices were pragmatic and present-centred. Written wills played a minor role, due to the prevalence of pre-mortem inheritance and to the high proportion of peasants who died intestate.[274] While aristocrats generally adhered to principles such as primogeniture quite strictly, planning far in advance precisely how the steps of devolution would unfold, peasant heads could not afford to fulfil such codes to the letter.[275] Whereas formal inheritance rules selected an heir 'automatically', according to a person's sex and birth-order and regardless of their fidelity and competence, the 'hearth heir' custom provided peasant househeads with the latitude to choose a successor on his merits. Senior patriarchs were likely to give the nod to a younger son who had remained loyally at home and was currently working on-site, as against a departed elder son whose whereabouts were uncertain or whose life-circumstances were dubious.

A marriage was generally arranged 'when the time came'; rarely was it set up years in advance when the children were still very young, as noblemen tended to do. The nature of the allotment for non-heir sons and the size of daughters' dowries were much more likely to be determined by the ability to pay than by formal guidelines, to which ritual obeisance was nevertheless paid. Peasants preferred not to flout the rules, but they were often prepared to bend them for situational advantage.[276] Above all, it was necessary to reward the willingness of children to remain dutifully at home as members of the family labour team. In this way, peasants displayed what Flandrin has called a 'household spirit', in contrast to the nobility's 'lineal' or 'house spirit':

> The family was the household formed, at a particular moment, by the parents and those children who were still living with them. Only those children had a share in the inheritance at the moment of the dissolution of the community, the separately endowed children, who had set up house elsewhere, being excluded from it.[277]

Peasant househeads managed the conflict between their households' present labour needs and the devolution of the patrimony by delaying the latter as long as possible, retaining the labour-power of single children on-site well into their twenties, or sending them out as servants so that they might make a contribution to their own settlements. Elderly peasants appeared extremely reluctant to retire; their maxim was to 'keep your clothes on until you go to sleep'.[278] Paternal deferral threw the contradiction on to the shoulders of the younger generation, as they, in turn, would shift it on to their offspring. Such delay was bound to foster tensions in the household, as children were forced to bide their time, or go into service waiting their father out until his eventual disposition became clear.[279] In the words of French peasants, he was 'le père qui vit trop'. In the meantime, his children represented (and often consciously asserted) competing claims against a very modest account. Even a designated heir might grow frustrated as the years passed on; he might finally acquire effective possession of the holding in his mid twenties, only to be saddled with the obligation to compensate his younger siblings as they departed.

Many historians have noted the prevalence of pre-mortem property transfer in medieval and early modern Europe.[280] Does this contradict the assertion that patriarchs tended to cling to the reins of domestic power until death? I do not think so. It is one thing to begin the devolutionary process and quite another to complete it, surrendering househeadship. The father's death usually hastened the transfer but did not inaugurate it. In Terling, Essex, in the late sixteenth and seventeenth centuries, 58 per cent of grooms' fathers and 42 per cent of brides' fathers were dead at the time of their offspring's weddings.[281] Razi estimated that 50 per cent of children were too young to marry and hold land when their fathers died in early-fourteenth-century Halesowen.[282] The father's dilemma was thus starkly apparent. He might wish to delay the process of devolution: to stay in control, keep his options open and accumulate the wealth necessary to settle his offspring. But the longer he delayed getting started, the more likely it was that he would never see the process through to completion. Secondly, pre-mortem inheritance is generally taken to refer to the senior generation, not simply to the head. Married women usually outlived their husbands, and property devolution tended to accelerate with the latter's decease, since widows lacked the power their husbands had possessed to delay the process. With fathers in the grave, impatient heirs often found the lord to be a tactical ally, since he was interested in replacing elderly female householders with young and vigorous males. The origin of pre-mortem inheritance and the retirement contract probably lies here, in the seigneurial drive to replace the elderly, moving the younger generation into full tenancy.[283]

The laws and customs of property devolution prevalent in a given region limited but did not dictate the testamentary course a househead could pursue. A father had choices to make and room for manoeuvre, and his children knew it. There was a price to be paid for such pragmatism. Owing to the weakness of birth-order succession rules, the essentially arbitrary nature of the peasant patriarch's actions could not be masked. It is one thing to have one's destiny determined by unfair rules; it is quite another to be subject to the personal judgement of one's father. Any exculpatory appeal he might make to custom in seeking to justify his decisions was bound to ring hollow in his children's ears. They were undoubtedly as aware of his options as he was, being in the unfortunate position of having to compete with one another in seeking to influence the sequential allocation of scarce resources. The greater his discretionary latitude, the keener they would be to court his favour in what was likely to be the key determination of their futures. Step by fateful step, a father's intentions and biases were revealed: the naming of the primary heir; the arrangement of sibling marriages; the determination of dotal portions; the disposal of supplementary lands among secondary sons; the drafting of a will. This was a deadly serious game of family politics.[284] Parents worried about the perception of inequitable dispensation. A widow wrote to her counterpart: 'I have to purvey for more of my childer than him, of which some be of that age, that they can tell me well enough that I deal not evenly with them to give John Paston so large and them so little.'[285]

Regardless of the ideology of equal shares, the actual portions were highly unequal; there were bound to be winners and losers in this zero-sum game. The build-up of tensions within families, in the turnover phase of the cycle when parental decisions were being made, must frequently have been explosive. A daughter who had delayed marrying, for example, under the reasonable assumption that her dotal portion would rise over time, might find that the reward for her patience was a depleted allowance due to the unexpectedly large portion allotted to her older sister who 'married up'. Sibling conflicts over inheritance often ended up in court, and occasionally led to violence.[286] A certain defensive flexibility in acquiring and shedding extra land through the secondary market was undoubtedly critical in defusing sibling rivalries.[287]

The more sharply an inheritance regime differentiates the fortunes of children, favouring some and practically divesting others, the more deeply it antagonizes the sibling group. And the more leeway an inheritance regime provides fathers in the exercise of peremptory allocation, the more it induces children to compete for their favour in an atmosphere of explosive uncertainty. By these criteria, an impartible and flexible (or relatively anomic) regime maximizes the potential of sibling rivalry, and the estrangement of those who lose out in the inheritance lottery. This is the combination that was prevalent across Northwestern Europe.

I am not suggesting that there was no room for co-operation between siblings in the course of devolution. Once fathers were in their graves, the compensatory side of the process might furnish the opportunity for magnanimity on the part of a recently married heir, who might redeploy the chattel wealth of his bride's dowry to enhance his siblings' shares. Alternatively, the disenfranchised might jointly pursue various legal avenues of recuperation. Given a measure of family loyalty and some land to spare, some sort of reconciliation could usually be worked out. Wherever subsistence resources were scarce, however, the choices of subordinated siblings were rather unpalatable: either to stay at home and remain celibate, working for one's brother and living under his authority; or to leave – going into domestic service, entering a monastery, joining the king's army, or accepting a tiny plot on the fringe of the village. Relatively few siblings in their twenties appear to have remained at home once their brothers had taken over the household. Relations were bound to deteriorate at this point; both heirs and their siblings might precipitate the latter's departure.[288] Such pressures probably furnished a powerful motive for the spread of service in husbandry, as the land situation tightened across Northwestern and Central Europe in the sixteenth and seventeenth centuries. Entering domestic service was a convenient way out for those who were in no position to marry. To the relief of both parents and children, one presumes, rural youth could leave their parents' homes to work elsewhere, enhancing their own settlement portions in the years immediately prior to marriage.

So strong is the regional correlation of *inter vivos* inheritance with domestic service that one may postulate a causal connection: domestic service for single youth was a necessary adjunct to an inheritance system of unigeniture where the transfer of patriarchal authority generally coincided with the eldest son's marriage. The continued co-residence of married and single siblings appears to be possible only where strong patriarchal control remains in the hands of the elder generation, as was the case in many regions of Eastern and Mediterranean Europe. (Domestic service will be more fully discussed in the next chapter.)

Marriage as a Facet of Property Devolution

By its very nature, marriage is a dual union. On the one hand, it is a coupling of two individuals who go on to create a new family; on the other, it is the joining in kinship of two established families. The relative weight of the interpersonal and interfamilial facets of mate selection and marriage varies greatly, of course, both between societies and within them. We can conceive of this variance on a continuum, ranging from cultures where most marriages take place under the impetus and direction of the individuals, to others where they are normally arranged by parents and community elders. It would be a mistake, however, to split the continuum into polar models, creating an absolute dichotomy between societies of insouciant romance and others of parental dictatorship.[289] Regardless of conjugal law and symbolic formalities, in *no* culture can the express wishes of the other generation be defied with impunity.

The other critical variable in the process of mate selection is the position (and width) of the 'decision window'. In some societies, prospective partners are ceremonially joined as husband and wife before being introduced to one another. In these cultures, post-nuptial escape-hatches must be permitted for non-consummation and other 'worst-case scenarios', through an initial phase of conjugal probation, the acceptable return of brides to their parents' home, provisions for annulment or divorce, and so on. These measures are necessitated by the absence of pre-nuptial contact and assent between the principals. Medieval Christendom, on the other hand, provided individuals with a betrothal veto, while also insisting that the free exchange of marriage vows entailed a once-in-a-lifetime choice ('till death do us part') by prohibiting divorce and inhibiting remarriage.

Wherever the younger generation gains access to the means of production primarily via inheritance, marriage typically constitutes a decisive moment in the process of property devolution. In these cases, the dimension of familial alliance is bound to loom large. This was certainly true for the dependent cultivators of feudal Europe. In addition, women could inherit land, 'the positive control of marriage arrangements ... [being] stricter where property is transmitted to women'.[290] Whatever else they were, peasant marriages were property transactions between families. Too much was at stake to allow children to dictate the timing or the terms of the match. And although the clergy insisted on the explicit consent of the principals for a valid union, thus tempering parental power, the Church also promoted marriage as an alliance, 'the pre-eminent method of bringing peace and reconciliation to the feuds of families and parties, the wars of princes, and the lawsuits of peasants'.[291]

The act of marriage normally entailed a daughter's departure from her family's household and her entry into her husband's household. Each step was accompanied by a prestation. In departing, she received a dot, her portion of her family's wealth. On the church steps, signalling her entry into her husband's household, she received his dower, a pledge to support her for life so long as they remained legally married. In the (likely) event that he predeceased her, she was guaranteed a subsistence allotment from his estate for life or until she remarried (provided they were still married at the time of his death). The heir was legally required to furnish this as a condition of his own inheritance.

This particular dotal exchange – the dot and the dower combined – became an integral part of the compensatory impartible inheritance regime on the manorial lands of medieval Europe. In peasant families, the dot normally represented a daughter's first and last share: a once-only settlement which effectively debarred her from returning to lay subsequent claim upon her natal estate at the time of its final settlement. This exclusion was a key factor in ensuring the integrity of the family holding as it passed into the heir's hands.

The dower, on the other hand, guaranteed her integration into her husband's estate.[292] Here her subsistence rights were secured against the claims of her husband's siblings, and she had legal recourse against any failure of the heir to provide these goods after her husband's death. In common law, the dower was normally a one-third share of the family estate, but among peasants it was more often a use right, ensuring access to the means of subsistence for life or until remarriage. She was not entitled to alienate her share commercially. The dower's discharge did not entail subdivision of the main holding, though it might constitute a considerable drain on it. It acted as a compensation, mitigating a daughter's dotal alienation and obviating the need for a widow to turn back to her natal family for support. In this way, the dower bolstered land integrity in the main holding of both families.

Many scholars (Goody most recently) have heralded the dot's emergence as a triumph for women's rights, entailing the overthrow of patriline in favour of bilateral devolution. There was undoubtedly a clear advance in the movement from bridewealth to dowry; in the former women were the *subjects* of settlements carried on among men; in the latter they were the *recipients* of settlements.[293] But we have reason nevertheless to be sceptical about how far dotal exchange worked in women's favour. In the first place, dowries generally did not include substantial land portions, certainly not among the peasantry; they were normally comprised of movable wealth: household furnishings, livestock and cash.[294] In agricultural economies, 'chattel interests' cannot be considered the equivalent of 'real estate'; hers was far from being an equal share of the family property. Second, as mentioned, the dot was normally granted on the basis of her renunciation of all further claims upon her family's lands so long as they were in active and proper use by the heir. Dotal exclusion was by no means universal or irreversible in the Middle Ages (we shall examine some exceptions in a moment); but it was nevertheless the usual practice, to women's enormous detriment. Third, we should not be deceived by the appearance of the dot as a gift from her parents. In peasant households, her own labour contribution to its accumulation was likely to be considerable; the poorer her family was, and the older she was at marriage, the greater her own contribution was likely to be. Furthermore, while the dowry normally comprised the lion's share of her portion, it was not the only source. Friends, neighbours, charities and employers might also donate goods or cash funds to supplement her share.[295] Fourth, more or less immediately upon its receipt, her dotal portion became part of her husband's holding, where its benefits were shared. As Blackstone, the English jurist, noted: 'the marriage transfers the bride's chattels to the husband'. Her portion became, in effect, a sunk investment.[296] In some states she was entitled to its restoration in the event of a marital breakdown where she was held to be blameless, but among peasant households without much surplus, this formal right frequently could not be

exercised. Finally, the actual transmission of the dot and the dower was temporally staggered. While both were set up at marriage, the dot was immediately invested in the farm, while the dower was only a promise until a husband
died. Perhaps a third of wives would die before their husbands, and most of
the rest could not expect to receive in subsistence anything approaching what
they had contributed in the first place. The security of the dower was welcome, but as a return on a woman's investment it was a very poor deal indeed.
For all these reasons, women's dotal rights in medieval Europe, certainly
among the peasantry, were not all that Goody makes them out to be.[297]

Dotal exclusion was not universal, however, and did not appear as absolute
in common law. Ancient partible traditions were used in some regions to
uphold an endowed woman's right to return her dotal portion to the family
pool upon her parents' decease, restoring her inheritance entitlement in the
process.[298] It is difficult to sort out precisely when and where endowed women
could return to claim. It appears that exceptions were made to the general rule
of dotal renunciation when (for whatever reason) the designated heir was non-
existent, absent, incapacitated or in default, and thus unable to run the holding
as a productive dues-paying enterprise. In these instances, a daughter's claim
might be re-established, in order to keep a holding in the family and forestall
its transfer to other tenants. In such circumstances, her claim would also be
honoured against those of collateral kin.[299]

In about one household in five where only girls survived, one daughter's
dowry would include the holding; instead of departing, she would marry in.
The normal flow of women away from the land of their birth was reversed in
these cases, and males entered the holding of their brides' families. In these
cases, the principles of agnatic inheritance and patrilocality were temporarily
suspended, but by no means negated, as Goody suggests.[300] Daughters were
thus heirs of last resort, filling in missing links in the chain of male succession.
Since heiresses safeguarded the principle of family heritability, peasants felt that
second-best heirs were preferable to none. In most cases, lords did not dissent;
yet male succession was routinely resumed in the next generation. The demographic wheel of fortune thus permitted a minority of women to get a toe in
the door of patriline, but by the law of averages their daughters would find it
shut in their faces once again. Patriarchal authority and the traditional division
of labour between spouses were not overturned, or even significantly altered,
by virtue of the temporary inversion of patrilineal succession. Incoming husbands became househeads, managed the fields, and represented the family in
village affairs.

Lords were inclined to be much more interventionist when heiresses married, insisting on their right to approve or veto the match, since the prospective entrant was slated to become a new tenant. Any father of an heiress who
proceeded without obtaining the lord's permission risked being ousted from

his lands. For the villein heiress without a father, 'it is her husband who is the central figure. He acts as the payer of the merchet and the entry fine for the girl and her land; he is accepted as the tenant responsible to the lord.'[301] Heiresses were also marginalized in relations between fathers and future husbands, as the following contract indicates: 'Hugh Coverer, marrying Emma Lord, and taking over her father Richard's land ... [undertakes to] keep said Richard in board as well as he [Hugh] keeps himself.'[302] This is clearly an agreement between two men conducted over the woman's head, transferring patriarchal authority (with the attendant obligation to provide) from one generation to the next.

Within a virilocal system, those who married away from their natal estate (mostly women) experienced a clear break in the family cycle, which heirs (mostly men) did not. The consequence of this difference can best be appreciated through an analysis of the kin and neighbourly support networks of men and women, as Judith Bennett has done in the medieval village of Brigstock, Northamptonshire.[303] She found that men's original kin networks were retained through marriage and then extended to affinal kin, while women's contacts with their own kin were disrupted and curtailed. As they moved away at marriage, brides had to rebuild support networks within their husbands' kin group. While kin descent was reckoned bilaterally, through her line as well as his, this did not alter the fact that she left her family's land and support network, while he assumed a leading role in his.

The full sexist discrimination of the inheritance system stood revealed at the moment of birth much more so than at the time of marriage. As an old French proverb put it: 'When a girl is born, one of the main beams comes falling down.'[304] This sense of ill-fortune reflected the fact that the cost/benefit equation for male and female children was drastically imbalanced: male heirs married in and attracted value, daughters married out and alienated value. 'Marry your sons when you will and your daughters when you can' went the traditional adage. This asymmetry may well have led to selective infant mortality by sex, with higher rates of infanticide, abandonment and neglect for females, particularly in periods when land was scarce. While some family historians remain sceptical, the evidence of neglect and inferior treatment of baby girls is strong.[305] In the Florentine *catasto* of 1427, Herlihy and Klapisch-Zuber found six males for every five females below the age of fifteen. While some of this imbalance might be attributable to reporting and registration biases, they conclude that the Tuscan population was 'incontrovertibly ... marked by a true deficit of females'.[306] Sex-selective infant abandonment and neglect were almost certainly a major factor in generating the imbalance. Both wealthy parents and foundling hospitals (receiving mostly the infants of the poor) were more likely to place baby girls with distant wet-nurses, where their chances of survival were slim. Herlihy and Klapisch-Zuber speculate that 'the hospitals were responding to pleas of the parents who spoke out more often for their male babies than their females. Perhaps they recognized that girls, who would require a dowry, cost more than boys.'[307]

Beyond the question of differential infanticide, a dotal marriage system with patriline in land was bound to affect the way in which male and female infants were welcomed into the world and raised as children. 'The birth of a male baby was greeted by gunshots and rejoicing. If a girl was born, the father feels cruel disappointment. He is almost humiliated.'[308] In fifteenth-century Tuscany, girls were sent into service much more often than boys, 'testimony of the fragility of their roots in the family. ... The serving girls sought above all to amass a dowry. ... Young boys in service ... remained more closely linked to the paternal hearth. ... [They] continued to be heirs to the paternal wealth.'[309]

Mate Selection, Betrothal and Wedding Rituals

All those with a major stake in marital negotiation endeavoured to make their influence felt. The primary interest of lords in the marriages of their subjects was to retain control over land tenure and the distribution of chattel wealth. They insisted on being informed in advance when villeins were preparing to marry their children. In most cases seigneurial assent was a routine matter, and the Church decreed that lords could not prevent a valid marriage. But where substantial holdings were to be transferred, in the marriages of widows and heiresses, for example, they were liable to take a more active interest.[310] The merchet registered the lords' power to regulate not the marriage *per se* but the property transactions associated with it. In practice, it was a licence fee paid by villein househeads to give their daughters in marriage. Since the levy was normally calculated as a certain percentage of the dowry, it varied widely across the spectrum of peasant wealth. In smallholding and landless families, the sum was often mustered by brides themselves.[311] Of all dues, villeins found the merchet especially noxious, symbolizing their unfreedom. In medieval Halesowen, 30 per cent of fines recorded on the court rolls were issued for evasion of merchet, through the concealment of nuptials or the misrepresentation of dowry inventory.[312] Since an extraordinarily stiff fine was levied against brides who alienated dowry wealth by marrying off the manor, the merchet tended to foster local endogamy. When the Church's rules against unions with kin to the fourth degree were combined with pressure for manorial endogamy, the pool of eligible marriage partners was severely circumscribed. If both strictures had been rigorously upheld in villages thick with kin ties, virtually the entire population of young single adults would have been ruled off limits. In reality, neither interdiction was strictly enforced, save in cases where an impending union was deemed objectionable by the community's 'better sort'.

In the legal codes of most early medieval states, a woman could be given away at marriage against her will, although nuptial coercion was prohibited in Anglo-Saxon England from the sixth century. But the practice was deplored by jurists everywhere, and it was customary for women to consent to betrothal.[313] Once the Church's jurisdiction in marriage was consolidated in the twelfth century, all valid marriages required the partners' own consent.[314] Under strict canonical interpretation, a couple was joined in marriage as soon as they recognized one another unconditionally as husband and wife, speaking in the present tense. Since their vows were held to consecrate the marriage before God, the contract required neither third-party witness nor religious solemnization. In the event of an irreconcilable conflict with parents or guardians, Church courts generally sided with the couple.[315]

In its radical form, the canon of individual consent was profoundly at odds with popular custom and the Church's own interests; as such, it was inherently unworkable. In the first place, the doctrine licensed clandestine unions, with parents being cut out of the picture entirely. The legality of this exclusion was an anathema in landholding communities. Second, in so far as betrothal vows were taken to constitute a real marriage, the church wedding became a hollow formality; the exchange of vows before the priest simply ratified a prior contract. Third, private unions prevented priests from ascertaining beforehand the marital eligibility of the principals, thus making it almost impossible to enforce the Church's strictures. Fourth, the legitimacy of the contract broke down in the face of contested spousals, since without witnesses, Church courts had no way of determining what vows, if any, had been exchanged.

Given these deficiencies, ecclesiastical authorities moved in the twelfth and thirteenth centuries to moderate the doctrine, requiring the reading of the banns and solemnization in church before a marriage could be considered valid. These amendments served to reconcile Church doctrine with community practice. Henceforth, betrothal vows were treated as a declaration of intent to proceed promptly to an open marriage in the parish. While appellants might still argue in Church courts that an exchange of vows in the present tense constituted a legal marriage, the prevailing parish interpretation was that betrothal promises were no longer considered sufficient to make a union. In moderating the doctrine of consent, the clergy, in effect, returned ceremonies of handfasting and spousals to the lay community whence they came. Rites of trothplight still troubled Church authorities, though they refrained from attacking them openly. Conflict with entrenched community norms was averted by placing an ecclesiastical imprimatur on spousal rituals, attempting to imbue them with religious significance. The Church's adaptation was only a partial success. The ritual retained its secular character, conducted in a plebeian setting, often without a priest present.[316]

The clergy's principal strategy in moving to stabilize its nuptial intervention was to place a heightened emphasis on the importance of the church service and the wedding liturgy. The regularization of the banns served this end. Proclaimed by the priest on three consecutive Sundays, the banns invited community objection to proposed marriages on the grounds of canonical law. They spread awareness of the Church's conjugal stipulations and induced people to articulate their concerns about a particular match in the light of ecclesiastical precepts. There were three main grounds for challenging the validity of an impending union: (a) the identification of kin ties between the principals (hypothetically to the fourth degree); (b) evidence of previous 'sexual misconduct' (particularly by the woman with someone other than the groom-to-be); and (c) the claims of others to be married or betrothed to either party. Whether such 'lets or impediments' were publicly aired had rather more to do with prevailing community norms and family reputations than with the formal strictures of canonical law.

The Church's purpose in insisting on individual consent was to prevent parental coercion, not to displace the older generation's influence entirely. The clergy had no desire to supplant arranged marriages with love-matches. They warned children that it was a mortal sin to disobey their parents, and their sermons and synods decried clandestine marriages contracted without parental approval.[317] 'Unless the bride is given by the parents', declared Pope Evaristus, 'the marriage is not legitimate.'[318] Furthermore, French and German laws backed parents, entitling them to disinherit children who married against their express wishes.[319] Even where the prerogative of the parents was not protected in law (as in England), their approval was none the less essential for a viable match, especially one involving substantial property exchange.[320] There were great dangers in pursuing clandestine courtship. Parents insisted on being informed of courting initiatives in the early stages in order to exercise their own judgement and assess the property side of the match. If the young couple handed their parents a *fait accompli,* dotal portions could be slashed and promises of inheritance withdrawn. The threat of disinheritance was probably sufficient to keep all but the most impetuous offspring from eloping or proceeding to nuptials without permission. Conversely, we must also recognize that there were real limits to parental pressure in the event that either individual was adamantly opposed. In the first place, the priest would ask them publicly if they consented, and the slightest murmur of dissent was bound to create a scandal. Even if this hurdle were cleared under the intimidating gaze of a parent, there was a great risk that the union might subsequently remain unconsummated, threatening the marriage with annulment, the return of the dowry, and community disgrace for both families.

In short, no one could proceed legitimately over the strong objection of others; any one of the four parties could effectively scuttle the match. Tales of woe, widely circulated, served to warn the intemperate of either generation of the disastrous consequences of proceeding unilaterally in these matters. The protocol of multilateral consent did not mean, however, that everyone was necessarily pleased with the match; occasionally, such displeasure could induce pre-emptive action. In the face of objections, some lovers eloped and married clandestinely; at the other extreme, threats by parents sometimes persuaded the reluctant to wed. And yet, as the Church became increasingly committed to obtaining the consent of all four parties, a minimal level of agreement appears to have been achieved in the great majority of cases.

While historians agree that both generations normally possessed at least the defensive power of veto in marital negotiation, controversy has centred on which generation held instrumental power to propose a match and set a date for nuptials. Scholars examining the medieval peasantry are inclined to emphasize the senior generation's prerogatives. Homans put the inaugural shoe on the parental foot in medieval England, while recognizing that 'good fathers cannot have wholly disregarded their children's inclinations'. Hanawalt's more recent survey concurs, where both families were substantial landholders. Macfarlane (while leaning in the children's direction) notes that the norm for the 'middling ranks seems to have been for parents to advise the children and to suggest a range of possible partners, delimiting a field of eligibles and making sure that passion did not lead children to "throw themselves away", "ruin themselves", or in any way cross those invisible status lines which were so important.'[321] In early modern France, both Flandrin and Goubert see primary power resting with senior patriarchs, while acknowledging the real limits of their powers. Surveying early modern England, on the other hand, Macfarlane, Wrightson and Gillis all emphasize the initiative of the younger generation, though by no means ignoring parental influence.[322]

I would speculate that the influence of the younger generation increased over time as the age of marriage rose. Indicative of this shift, there appears to have been an inversion in the customary sequence of parental bargaining and intense courtship, as the Church deepened its involvement in nuptial regulation. In Anglo-Saxon England, the first step in matchmaking had been to obtain the consent of the bride's kin; then the groom's kin offered her family a number of sureties (called *weds*) which guaranteed her future maintenance and protection. Only after agreement had been reached on these conditions were the couple's hands joined and vows exchanged.[323] By the early modern era, the ceremony at the church door had symbolically reversed these steps: couples exchanged vows and then he pledged her dower. In the course of this evolution, there would probably have been an intricate dialectic between a shifting balance of generational power and the gradual emergence of the late marriage norm. It is one thing for a father to 'marry off' his teenage daughter; this occurs in many cultures. It is quite another matter for him to line up a match for a daughter in her mid twenties who had lived away from home for several years. If this surmise is correct, then the medieval norm might be characterized as one of parental initiative predicated on the consent of the children, whereas the early modern pattern evolved towards a regime of genuine equipoise, where neither generation could proceed very far without securing the agreement of the other. Any decision-making matrix of four players where everyone possesses veto power is prone to blockage and strategic deferral. In the next chapter, I shall argue that this grid furnished the easily stalemated micro-context of delayed marriage in Western Europe.

The need for multilateral agreement does not imply equal power in matchmaking. The initiative in seeking out a prospective partner and making proposals lay very much with the men of either generation. The male suitor would commonly approach his prospective mate's father and ask for permission to court his daughter. Because of the status difference between a young man and an older househead, and the extreme delicacy of a potential refusal, this request was often conveyed through an intermediary, popularly known as a 'marriage broker' or a 'matchmaker', chosen by the young man. If the approach was well received, he would inform his own parents and begin to court the woman formally. We may suspect that a good deal of informal courting had normally preceded the initial consent of fathers, but we would be unwise to project our own preconceptions too far in this regard. Courtship was a public and highly ritualized affair with an elaborate set of incremental steps, each one requiring a positive (but measured) response before the next could be undertaken.[324] Far from facilitating insouciant coupling, village youth acted collectively at festivals, fairs and dances to invigilate the process, discouraging 'unsuitable' matches and seeking to stem the subtraction of eligible mates from a limited source. Charivari rituals revealed the intensity of competitive jealousy and collective defence of the bachelor pool.[325] We should not assume that the process of getting acquainted, discussing various interests, flirting and clarifying mutual attraction could normally have proceeded very far before it was necessary to formalize the relationship and seek parental approval.

Once the courtship was approved by both sets of parents, the respective househeads got down to serious bargaining. As far as the heir's father was concerned, the critical factor was to safeguard the holding; the destiny of his son was perceived within that context. A match would be seen as honourable if it enhanced the holding; as tainted or even disgraceful if it jeopardized the patrimony. The necessary correlation of dowry with holding size substructured the process of mate selection, promoting matches between the children of families of roughly equal wealth and status while rendering other couplings impractical, precluding family support for them.[326] The localized nature of courtship rituals, carefully supervised in the community, ensured that young adults were linked with others of the 'proper' social standing: 'Marriages of this kind meant that people knew the families with whom marriage was planned and could keep a watchful eye on the arrangements concerning the patrimony.'[327] Parental controls on courtship and marriage tended to be relaxed in communities with a low level of vertical stratification, and conversely, to be tightened whenever class cleavages widened, particularly with the growth of a landless proletariat.[328] In short, supervised courtship and the exigencies of marital bargaining fostered a high incidence of class endogamy amongst Western European peasants. Segalen found the pattern so prevalent in France that she deemed it 'the rule of homogamy'.[329]

Among the nobility, matrimonial bargaining might be initiated when children were very young and drag on for years; peasant patriarchs, by contrast, were inclined to postpone negotiations as long as possible and were reluctant to proceed before the couple indicated a mutual marital interest. Once negotiations had been entered, they were usually brought to a quick conclusion. The successful completion of an agreement between family heads was generally marked by a celebration of betrothal, where the consent of the principals and the support of their parents were proudly displayed. Before the official betrothal, most couples would probably have pledged themselves to one another in more private and informal circumstances; the public ceremony served to place their marital intent before the entire community. With all these prerequisites in place, families were urged to schedule the proclamation of the banns within a few weeks. The period of formal betrothal was thus over in one to three months. The entire courtship, from the first indications of interest to the wedding finale, would normally have been completed in six months to two years. The last stage of formal betrothal was thus a relatively brief phase of the process.[330]

Through the modern prism of true-love ideology, the pragmatic side of peasant marital bargaining appears extremely crass, inviting the conclusion that love played no part. Is it fair to say that intangibles of the heart assumed little or no importance in mate selection? Many historians have thought so, perceiving a notable absence of affection and emotional intimacy between spouses.[331] Traditional proverbs are often cited to validate this assessment. 'Never trust a starry night or a nice arse. ... A pretty girl will never make you rich. ... Look at the girl at the kneading trough and not at the ring dance.' Rustic maxims of this sort were certainly commonplace, but most took the form of gerontic admonition (as these do), warning young people against erotic enticement or romantic impetuosity. As such, they furnish indirect evidence of the powerful temptations of a starry night or a ring dance. Traditional peasant 'courtship by blows' in France – thumping backs, swatting the knee or shoulder, spitting in one another's mouths, squeezing hands with knuckle-cracking pressure (in direct proportion to the intensity of attraction) – seem strange by modern standards, but were unmistakably rituals of affectionate display. The Church courts

113

of England, dating back to the fourteenth century, record the testimony of peasant youth who sought to break off relationships with suitors because they could not find it´in their hearts to love them, or because they had fallen in love with another.[332]

Merely because we find it difficult to acknowledge the considerable role that material interests play in mate selection today, we should not conclude that people's explicit recognition of such factors in the past signifies the absence of emotional attraction on their part. We should eschew the temptation, based on the modern ideology of romantic love, to counterpose economic interest and hard-headed bargaining to factors such as personal charm, beauty and sex appeal. Then, as now, mate selection involved a complex mix of drives and considerations. The prevailing blend undoubtedly shifted in the transition to capitalism; but there is no warrant for conceiving of traditional and modern courtship as diametric opposites – the former predicated on 'material interest', while 'love reigns supreme' in the latter.[333] It appears that the change in prevailing ideology has in this case been much greater than the shift in mass practice.

In a society that did not ritualize puberty, marriage marked the great watershed between youth and adulthood, with betrothal constituting the principal rite of passage for both sexes. The ritual of 'spousal' or 'handfasting' placed the couple in a transitional state, no longer single but not yet married. The successful culmination of betrothal in nuptials elevated men to the position of househeads and women to the status of men's helpmates and legitimate childbearers.[334] Trothplight was normally a public ritual, with witnesses for each of the principals present. Private and informal betrothal remained legal, but was none the less suspect; the union attained its validity by going public.

In a society where divorce was prohibited, the betrothal period provided a vital, if brief, opportunity to intensify the relationship while still being able to call the marriage off. While the great majority of those who were betrothed did go on to wed, the spousal pledge was in most cases revocable so long as there was no sign of bridal pregnancy.[335] Legal action for breach of promise was admissible in Church courts, but judges finding in the accuser's favour were more likely to assess compensatory fines and require defaulters to do penance than to force a union. The betrothal period thus represented a brief test of the viability of the match. The wedding was liable to be called off whenever: (a) the property side of the contract fell through; (b) there was an undue delay in proceeding to set a date and publish the banns, creating an impression of stalling; (c) the banns turned up a telling objection from the community; or (d) serious evidence of personal incompatibility arose:[336] 'Many young people appear to have taken advantage of this recognized trial period to test the relationship not only between themselves, but with family, peers, and the wider community.'[337]

The degree of intimacy that betrothed couples were legitimately permitted to enjoy varied widely.[338] In some communities espousal merely sanctioned an acceleration of supervised courting, while in others it authorized cohabitation in the groom's household. In Mediterranean Europe, where a high value was placed upon the bride's chastity, courting was tightly controlled right up until the wedding. In Northwestern Europe, by contrast, courting surveillance was relaxed as soon as betrothal was publicly celebrated, and couples were normally extended the privilege of night visiting, during which physical intimacy was permitted. In England, witnesses in Church courts testified that

> a good deal of kissing and cuddling went on, often in private or semi-private, and couples sometimes spent whole nights together, perhaps before the fire in the hall of the house where the woman lived with her parents or employers, in an inn or alehouse, or (in summer) in the open air.[339]

This is not to suggest that the stalwarts of village respectability endorsed pre-nuptial intercourse. However, the nocturnal privacy customarily ceded to the betrothed made it difficult to inhibit sexual intimacy at whatever level a couple might desire. Church authorities did not approve of pre-nuptial sex, but in most periods they made little effort to repress it. At other times, however, Church courts cracked down, imposing stiff fines and public penance on evidence of premarital fornication.[340] Despite these variations, all Western European cultures distinguished between preliminary phases of courtship and a subsequent stage of formal betrothal; greater intimacy was permitted during the latter stage.

It has been estimated that in early modern England roughly one bride in four was pregnant when she wed.[341] It seems reasonable to infer that a much higher proportion of women, at least half, were no longer virgins at marriage. Since betrothed couples had made a publicly recognized marital vow, their coital union bent, but did not fundamentally breach, the Augustinian doctrine that the sacred purpose of all natural sex was procreation within marriage. Pre-nuptial sex tested fertility, and pregnancy positively demonstrated procreative capacity, while obligating the betrothed to wed promptly. The benefit of securing this valuable information (thereby eliminating one of the great intangibles of marriage bargaining) must have operated as a silent counterweight to the moral wrath of the Church in a society where such importance was placed on the preservation of the family bloodline. While the Church maintained its disapproval, the parish priest who presided at weddings was inclined to look the other way.[342] In the time-honoured tradition of Catholicism, all sins were forgiven while a uniform standard of moral conduct was nevertheless upheld.

Given the commonplace nature of 'premarital sex', it is tempting to conclude that the sexual mores of medieval and early modern villagers were remarkably permissive. Such an inference would be unwarranted, conflating premarital with betrothal sex. There is no evidence that many single people were sexually active before trothplight; nor is this surprising, since fornication was strictly proscribed. Far from being libertarian, the sexual norms of most Western European communities were highly repressive. As the system of late marriage spread, youth remained celibate for ten years, on average, from puberty to trothplight. Such a regime could never have been imposed had peasant communities and Church courts lacked the capacity to deter the vast majority of single adults from engaging in intercourse before pledging solemnly to wed.

On the day of the big wedding, the church service played a minor part in the proceedings. Festivities began in the morning and carried on into the night, combining rites of separation and inauguration.[343] Several rituals (all with regional variations, but expressing the same themes) were specifically designed to assuage feelings of envy and jealousy on the part of unmarried siblings, whose own marital fortunes were directly affected by the present contract. Parental loss and the transfer of patriarchal power were recognized in pre-service rituals, where the groom came to the bride's house and stole her away without the father's consent and against his will. The kiss exchanged by the bride and groom during the mass or at the church door symbolized the joining, in peace, of two individuals *and* their families.[344] Several symbolic gestures in the wedding ceremony depicted the wife's willing submission to her husband's authority. The bride, for example, 'kneels on the first step of the altar and places a fold of her dress beneath the knee of the husband she has just married'.[345] Her recited vows differed chiefly from the groom's in the pledge of obedience ('to honour and obey') and a promise of sexual access: 'for better for wors, for richer for pourer, in sicknesse and in hele, *to be bonere and boxom, in bedde and atte bord,* tyll dethe vs departhe'.[346]

At the close of the service, the newlyweds were presented with a series of obstacles to surmount. They might be locked in the church, 'chained' in the churchyard, blocked at the gate or accosted on the road, so that 'the bridegroom has again and again to pay his footing as a husband'.[347] For her part, the bride often had to perform an initiation rite, such as spinning some yarn with a distaff she had been given, 'to demonstrate her qualities as a housewife':

> The woman established her mistress-ship not only by taking possession of those symbols of household authority – fire tongs, brooms, keys – but by relinquishing her maidenhood symbolized by her garter. ... [T]he investiture of broom and tongs suggests a limited jurisdiction. The same was true of the festive consumption, which was organized and served by the men, further defining the degree to which the household was still the male domain.[348]

Widows and the Family Cycle

Having survived to the age of twenty, medieval peasants could expect to live only another twenty to twenty-five years.[349] It was therefore a frequent occurrence for married people of both sexes to be widowed during their reproductive years. Remarriage was commonplace; in a quarter of all marriages at least one partner had been previously wed. In two out of three cases, wives outlived their husbands, so landholding widows were by no means rare in the Middle Ages. In one English estate survey, one-seventh of the tenants were widows; in another, 55 per cent of all land-inheritance transfers went to widows: 'We must not picture the widow in the late Medieval village as a poor cottager or smallholder on the edge of village community, but as frequently the tenant of a full holding, living an active life near the centre of things.'[350] In the fifteenth-century *catasto* of Florence, over 15 per cent of all households were headed by women, almost all widows.[351] Since most male tenants made their wives executors of their estates, widow tenants were legally entitled to enter contracts in their own names, arrange their children's marriages, and decide on their own remarriage.[352] In Montaillou, 'a young wife oppressed by an older husband eventually became an elderly mother venerated and respected by her male children.'[353] If, on the other hand, the family was propertyless, she inherited nothing but trouble: 'The [landless] widow in Tuscan society was often solitary and usually ignored. ... She often passed her final days in poverty.'[354]

The key to the peasant widow's claim on the family estate was the dower which her husband pledged to her at the church door. It varied widely, depending on the inheritance customs within which it was couched. Minimally, the dower was a subsistence provision guaranteed until a wife's death or remarriage, charged against the new tenant, whoever he was.[355] However, in impartible regions she could often take over the entire holding. She paid no entry fee for assuming househeadship, an implicit recognition by the lord of her co-tenancy in the original holding.[356]

Either in addition to dower rights or in lieu of them, men often had wills and retirement contracts drawn up which reflected great concern for the future well-being of their wives. These documents specify in minute detail the obligations of the children, and especially the prime heir, to support their mother for as long as she lived and remained a widow.[357] If her son did not uphold the contract, he risked forfeiting the estate until her death. In return, her principal duty was to complete the upbringing and 'putting forth' of the children.[358]

Widows played a vital role in family property devolution, passing land to heirs when they married or reached the age of majority. If a widow's own children were dead or living elsewhere, she could still use the holding's value to strike a deal with an unrelated lessee, who undertook to provide her with specified subsistence goods in return for access to the land. The details of such pacts closely resembled retirement contracts with next of kin. Whatever form the dower took, the crucial variable in practical terms was whether she was entitled to hold on to it until death or was forced to forfeit it when her children came of age or she remarried. This too varied widely, becoming a bone of contention between widows and heirs in manor courts.[359] If the widow retained some assets to take into a second marriage, they were likely to take the form of a restoration of the original dowry of her first marriage; seldom was she permitted to subtract family land from her children's inheritance.

Since landholding was the touchstone of social status under feudalism, widows who were full tenants were indeed in positions of remarkable power for women. Yet for most, this was bound to be a transient experience. Given the strong patriarchal bias against women holding land, female tenants came under intense pressure to dispense with estates. In rare circumstances they were able to retain effective control of family lands for the rest of their lives, replicating the peasant patriarch's capacity to resist pressures to retire. But normally, within a year or two of their husbands' death, widows would be forced to choose between two basic options: either to transfer family holdings to designated sons, or to remarry and place them in the care of second husbands.[360] Both courses of action reinstalled men as full householders and diminished women's domestic authority accordingly. The acts of marrying widows and entering their property were so routinely combined as to become a singular transaction in manor court records, completed with the payment of an entry fee.[361]

In considering their options, widows were typically pushed in different directions by lords, their own children, and the village community. Lords pressed remarriage on villein widows, particularly if they were unable to keep their holdings fully cultivated and meet the obligations of tenancy.[362] Before the Magna Carta (1217), English lords had the legal right to order villein widows to remarry by a specified date, or pay a stiff fine. Bennett and Raftis cite cases where lords did not hesitate to force remarriage upon widows.[363] However, the latter could often pay a fine to postpone the date of remarriage, and if they were freeholders, lords could not force them to remarry.[364] On the estates of Westminster Abbey, widows customarily held their deceased spouses' tenancies for a year and a day, and were then compelled to choose between exercising their dower option or becoming full tenants. If they chose the latter course, they had to remarry without delay; in the event that they were unable to find marital partners, the manor court chose for them.[365]

While lords were generally keen for widowed tenants to remarry, they also insisted that they choose a suitable partner. It was the lords' prerogative to accept or veto new tenants, and prospective husbands, as men, were considered to be new tenants.[366] Men seeking a widow's hand would purchase the lord's assent. The fee for gaining his permission was normally very steep, far higher than the rate for first marriage, making it prohibitive for all but the wealthiest peasant bachelors.[367] The difference in fees between first and second marriages reflected the lords' clear right to seize and regrant widows' lands upon remarriage. It was, in effect, the price exacted for waiving the seigneurial right to confiscate the holding.[368]

Against lords pressing for remarriage, peasant offspring often wanted their mothers to remain widowed out of respect for their father and (perhaps more importantly) in order to facilitate the property's succession to themselves.[369] The blunt counsel or silent suasion of children as they reached marriageable age was a very different kind of pressure from that exerted by lords, but it could be just as constraining. If a woman wished to remain single, she was wise to proceed promptly with devolution. Once the transfer was complete, the woman 'went her way', as wills and old law codes phrased it.[370] Yet she was none the less well protected in law and custom against the heir's failure to ensure her ongoing subsistence.

The village community exerted its own pressure on widows – generally against remarriage and thus on the side of heirs. Particularly if they were not yet old or senile, widows were culturally threatening figures in the medieval village – sexually experienced independent women, householders and executrices of estates: 'The older women ... who had accumulated information over the years had considerable power to use what they knew, either to damage a reputation or to influence the decision of the men of the household.'[371] The young single women of the village, with no immediate prospects of becoming landholders themselves, resented unfair competition for a limited pool of bachelors. Pointed charivari rituals by village youth express such resentment.[372] The intimidation appears to have been successful. Widows took twice as long to remarry as widowers, and they were much less likely than men to remarry at all.[373]

In the absence of community pressure, how many widows would have remained single as a matter of personal preference? It is conceivable that the difference between the sexes in rates of remarriage simply reflects the sturdy independence of mature women from men. This possibility prevents us from simply assuming that the disparity is a measure of gender oppression, the product of a double standard. Yet given the pervasive vulnerability of single women at any age, I am inclined to favour the latter interpretation. It seems more likely that the marital deferral of widows was engendered by various forms of community pressure against 'hasty' remarriage, a stigma and a duress that men did not face.[374] The sexual double standard was probably a factor here as well. In Mediterranean Europe, where the taboo against premarital sex was strong, the rate of widow remarriage was extremely low; in North-western Europe, by contrast, most widows remarried.[375] The convictions of the priesthood could be influential as well. A Danish priest remarked: 'Marriage between old widows and young servants I feel to be almost sodomy and therefore try to stop it as much as possible.'[376] The one option that widows did not have was to take lovers without remarrying: 'Widows had to be chaste. Even freewomen lost their halves or thirds if they fornicated. In hundreds of medieval charters widows disposed of their lands *in libera et pura viduitate mea* ("in my free and pure widowhood") and the purity was a condition of the freedom.'[377]

In conjunction with community constraints, there were underlying structural factors that affected a woman's prospects of remarrying. The tighter the land market, the more attractive landholding widows became as marriage partners.[378] And in regions where they retained dower rights in the land of their first marriage, widows were very much in demand. If, however, local customs and manorial law stipulated that they were forced to relinquish their dower rights in order to remarry, a much higher proportion remained single.[379]

Regardless of the particular course they chose, however, peasant widows could count on being relatively secure in the basic means of subsistence, providing they could ensure that their holdings were fully worked.[380] The contrast with proletarian widows, holding nothing substantial to bequeath, could not be sharper. Under capitalism, young working-class women are in a better position than their medieval peasant sisters, with extra-domestic employment opportunities, less parental influence in mate selection, and a wider field of matrimonial choice. In old age, however, just when many women in the Middle Ages gained leverage, modern proletarian women lose all social power. Sinking into poverty, they are left to live out their lives on inflation-shrunk pensions. Many would doubtless envy the attention from their children and the security of the retirement contracts that their sisters of an earlier epoch obtained, to say nothing of the latter's prominence in community life.

The stark difference between the position of elderly parents, and widows in particular, under feudalism and capitalism serves to highlight the profound structural difference between the stem and nuclear family cycles which are characteristic of the two modes. The key difference here is not the co-residence pattern *per se,* but property rights in the means of production. For even though peasant children married and lived apart, they were still deeply dependent upon their parents' goodwill to remain eligible for succession to the family holding. An important (property) element of the domestic cycle *continued until the death of both parents.* This element is absent in the working class under capitalism, where the domestic cycle is severed after children leave home, marry, and set up their own households. The difference between the two family cycles lies in the modalities of their generational renewal.

Household Composition and Divergent Family Cycles

It seems as if every undergraduate who has enrolled in a social history course in the past fifteen years has learned that 'contrary to popular mythology, the Western family in the past was small and nuclear'. Thus spake the professoriate in unison, referring inquisitive students to Peter Laslett's tables in *Household and Family in Past Time,* which apparently prove the point beyond a shadow of a doubt. What do these famous tables show? In the first place, they are not about families but about household composition, from which family structure is *inferred.* Since Laslett defines the family as a co-resident group, the discrepancy does not trouble him; he employs 'family' and 'household' almost interchangeably. Such conflation should, however, trouble family historians. Laslett and his associates found that the mean household size of 100 communities in early modern England was 4.75 persons. This was smaller than expected, so they called it 'small', and this diminutive has subsequently been repeated so frequently that it has become a truism: our ancestors lived in small groups, as we do today. But did they? By fixating on mean household size, the Cambridge paradigm disregards the elementary fact that more people live in large households than in small ones. Given this asymmetry, the average size of households is a deceptive index; the more illuminating measure is the proportion of the population living in households of a certain size. In fact (as Laslett himself acknowledged), when the average size of households was 4.75 persons, *53 per cent of the population lived in households of six or more people.*[381] Could households of six or more people not be described as 'moderately large'? In relation to modern households, does it make any sense to term them 'small'?

We turn now to the more complex issue of the relationship between family structure and household composition. In Northwestern Europe (in contrast to central and southern France and Italy), the great majority of early modern households appear to have been 'simple' – comprised of a married couple, their children, and perhaps a lodger or servant. Parents of the couple were infrequently found living in the same dwelling space. The evidence for medieval households is much sparser, but it indicates a similar configuration. Most historians, following Laslett's lead, have insisted on terming this co-residence pattern a nuclear family formed by a neo-local marriage pattern.[382] It follows that the nuclear family prevailed then as it does now, with no great change in the intervening period. The problem with this approach is that it reduces family structure to household co-residence, narrowly conceived, ignoring significant variance in the family cycle. The result is a tendency to equate a centripetal peasant family cycle based on land inheritance with a centrifugal proletarian cycle based on the independent acquisition of employment, accommodation and marriage partners by the younger generation. I shall address the continuity thesis more fully in the next chapter. Here I merely wish to reconcile the finding of a simple household composition with my designation of a (weak-) stem family cycle prevailing in Northwestern Europe.

There are three reasons why the form of the family cycle cannot be directly inferred from a one-time reading of co-resident composition. In the first place, the stem phase of the family cycle is bound to be missed entirely in a large minority of cases, due to the death of the parents before the marriage of the heir.[383] The formation of a high proportion of vertically extended households in such a community (where a married couple lives with one or more elderly parents) is thus demographically precluded. In the rest, the phase of stem co-residence is likely to be very brief, particularly when age of first marriage is late. Through a simulation exercise, Wachter, Hammel and Laslett have attempted to demonstrate that the extremely low incidence of households of the stem type in the reconstituted communities of early modern England fell far short of the frequency that would be demographically attainable if both adult generations had seized every opportunity to live together.[384] They have argued, in other words, that there was a strong preference for neo-locality and a cultural aversion to living together after marriage. I have recognized this preference in the designation of a *weak*-stem variant, while holding open the question of the prevalence of weak- versus strong-stem variants in various regions of Northwestern Europe. Steven Ruggles has recently subjected Wachter, Hammel and Laslett's simulation model to a penetrating critique.[385] Under an alternative model, he calculates that the demographic constraint on stem co-residence was much greater than Wachter, Hammel and Laslett had postulated, and in fact that two-thirds to three-quarters of those who could have lived in vertically extended households actually did so.[386] This is a surprising finding (not least to its author, 'who was weaned on Peter Laslett's *The World We Have Lost* and wholeheartedly believed that the preindustrial English preferred to live in nuclear families'). If his model stands the test of scholarly scrutiny, then the stem family ideal will be shown to have been much more pervasive than has been heretofore supposed, corroborating my basic argument.[387]

The second reason why the form of the family cycle cannot be directly inferred from co-resident composition is that in cases where an elderly widow (or widower) is living with a married offspring, the family form is indeterminate unless the household is known. It may be that the son has married into his parent's household (in which case this is a stem form), or it may as easily be that the widow has gone to live with her son and daughter-in-law in a household that they had established independently (in which case this is an nuclear form, residentially augmented). The former situation was relatively common among early modern peasants, the latter arrangement common among nineteenth-century proletarians. Neither form can be inferred from household composition data by itself, where the head of the household has not been clearly designated (as is often the case).

Thirdly, a stem family cycle can occur where heirs marry into unified holdings and establish separate living quarters from their parents. In a census tabulation of such a community (where households are defined as cohabiting units) no vertically extended households would appear. Would we then be entitled to conclude, as Laslett has, that the stem family is a myth in historic communities where this arrangement was common?[388] To the contrary: if the productive base of the two households is unified; if they jointly subsist and pay dues from the same land; if they keep it in the family by passing it on from father to son; if youth's destiny is bound up with land inheritance, then I would argue that there is nothing essentially nuclear about their family structure at all. Certainly, due to separate quarters, this is closer to a nuclear form than the classical (strong-) stem family is. But these two stem variants have much more in common with one another than either has with the nuclear family, where the younger generation goes out, achieves its own livelihood, marries on its own and forms independent households.

Because of the propensity of Western European peasants to establish separate residences from their parents upon marriage, they are taken by family historians to exhibit a neo-local residence norm.[389] The term, however, is a slippery one. Four aspects of residential locality must be distinguished: (a) coresidence 'under one roof' in the same dwelling space; (b) taking up residence on the property of; (c) living in the community or neighbourhood of; and (d) establishing and funding the household. Anthropologists normally speak of virilocal (or patrilocal) communities where it is customary to take up residence on the property of the groom's parents or in their immediate vicinity. These residential patterns are more common cross-culturally than dwelling coresidence. Under a standard anthropological definition, the peasants of Western Europe exhibited a virilocal norm.[390] Family historians, following Laslett, have used the term in its most restrictive sense (i.e., in the parents' house), thus characterizing the prevailing pattern as neo-local and the resulting family form as nuclear.

Behind the terminological difference lurks a theoretical divergence between two paradigms: one foregrounding household composition, the other the family cycle. From the cyclical standpoint, the key question is the modality of inter-generational turnover. This is why I prefer the broader anthropological definition of household formation norms, pivoting around the transmission of productive property in the course of this turnover: a continuous cycle is virilocal (or uxorilocal), a discontinuous cycle is neo-local. Within this framework, the question of dwelling space – two living quarters or one – is by no means inconsequential. It has vital implications for the transfer of patriarchal authority from father to son, wherever fathers live to see designated heirs come of age.[391] This is why I have taken care to distinguish between strong and weak variants of the stem form, based on the capacity of fathers to persuade or

123

compel their sons to marry into the household while the senior patriarch maintains his househeadship and control of the family enterprise.[392] Heirs undoubtedly wished their fathers to retire, so that they could get married, take over the holding and finally become full adults. But as we have seen, peasant patriarchs were extremely reluctant to step aside. In the face of this intransigence, most sons in Northwestern Europe apparently preferred to wait rather than to marry into their father's household while he remained in charge. Their own insistence on full headship may well have been a factor in delaying their marriages.[393] When fathers died, heirs were finally free to marry into holdings while mothers retained their own households.

When old men lingered on, a separate residence might be a satisfactory compromise. It would expedite the heir's marriage, permitting him to establish a household even if he could not yet take over the full management of the holding. While his father's presence as senior male tenant and long-time head would undoubtedly detract from his own patriarchal authority, this overshadowing was bound to seem less noxious at a distance. Living in separate quarters, being served by his wife at his own table, at least permitted him to feel that he was master of his own house. Even if it was a little house on someone else's land, he could still be his own man: a self-respecting househead.[394]

The form of the family cycle has a major bearing on the destinies of future generations. In the stem cycle, where two or more sons reached adulthood, the designation of a single heir generated a wrenching split in the younger generation. Some would fall heir to, or marry into, viable tenures; others would be pushed out on to the margins to eke out an existence on tiny plots, as cottagers with huts and gardens. The transition from natal to procreative family was thus radically dissimilar for those who remained and those who left. I have registered this divergence through the designation of the *stem* cycle in the former case, and the *nuclear* cycle in the latter. The stem form is structurally dominant in the feudal mode of production, giving rise to the nuclear form as an extrusion from its own reproduction cycle. Thus far we have been primarily concerned to analyse the former; let us turn now to examine the latter briefly.

For village youth who lost out in the familial allocation of choice land, their fortunes lay elsewhere. They went in a myriad of directions. Many left the home parish for good, becoming itinerant farm labourers and journeymen. Their livelihood was now basically proletarian: they subsisted in the main from wages, though they did not constitute a working class in the modern sense. The family cycles of the landless were outward bound. Young farm labourers were no longer dependent upon their parents, nor upon a long-term lease with a lord to secure their future livelihood. Dowries and settlements were small or non-existent and played a neglible part in courtship and matchmaking. The capacity of parents to steer the proceedings was correspondingly reduced. Among the land-poor, daughters often paid their own merchets, obtaining open licences that left them free to marry whomsoever they wished within a certain period.[395]

Such arrangements did not mean that it was easier to marry. Once the heir had taken over the holding, his unmarried siblings had to work for him and submit to his domestic authority. Sibling rivalry frequently became intolerable in these circumstances; the great majority preferred to take their chances and leave.[396] For the offspring of smallholders, this was a venture into utter penury. It took more time to accumulate sufficient funds to wed. Consequently, the village poor had lower rates of marriage than prosperous peasants.[397] In addition to economic constraints, there were often political barriers to marriage. Parish officers and manorial courts often refused to legitimate conjugal unions among the landless, fearing that poor couples and their children would become a permanent charge against parish coffers: 'The medieval establishment disapproved of the fringe-dwellers and did all that it could to prevent their undue multiplication.'[398] Clandestine marriages were most frequent among the village poor.

The households of poor cottagers were organized very differently from those of well-established landholders, with 'members travelling daily from the house which served primarily as a base of operations to work as day labourers or for longer periods away from the household as servants.'[399] The creation of stable household space where a young married couple could cohabit was extremely difficult. Farm labourers normally lived in shacks on the employers' land, but since their employment was seasonal and irregular, they could not count on being able to remain in such quarters year-round. Consequently, their incentive to invest any energy or resources in fixing them up was practically nil. At best they might take up semi-permanent residence in one-room shacks on tiny plots of peripheral land remote from the core of village settlement and collective security. There they supplemented their meagre wages with extensive gardening and poaching in nearby fen and stream. Given the difficulty of marrying, the insecurity of seasonal employment and the problems of stabilizing household space for durable cohabitation, it is not surprising that the underclass of land-poor labourers displayed lower reproduction rates than settled peasants. In Halesowen, before the Black Death, poor couples bore an average of 1.8 children, a negative reproduction rate, while prosperous couples had 5.1.[400] (It was not until the eighteenth century that this demographic equation turned, and the rural proletariat began to grow dramatically by means of the self-expansion of its own ranks.)

The process of family formation among land-poor labourers and cottagers thus stands in stark contrast to that of the settled peasantry. Among the former, we see a discontinuous (or neo-local) transition: youth leave home, seek their own livelihoods, court in a less regulated fashion, and marry without the benefit or discipline of land settlement and dotal exchange, largely outside the context of arranged marriage, though by no means beyond the imprecations of the village's 'better sort'. For their part, parents could not count on their landless offspring supporting them in old age, nor did they have an effective way of enforcing retirement contracts where they existed. They probably considered themselves fortunate to know the whereabouts of their children, and to see them once again after a long absence before they died. 'Entire families thus dispersed at the death of a father: the widow to Florence, the girl to a market town, the boy to the household of a neighbouring peasant.'[401] Contrast this dispersal with a landholding family, where the father's death triggered a centripetal response, with the reassembly of leased land, children returning to claim, and the heir marrying in and taking over the holding.

From Overextension to Crisis

We have seen how the generational reproduction of peasant families fostered a powerful drive to acquire more land. From the peasants' standpoint, this was the best way to compensate secondary heirs while keeping the family's original holding intact, reducing family tension by alleviating the inheritance bind. The lords had their own reasons for sponsoring land-clearing initiatives. The way to raise revenues without raising the rate of exploitation on existing holdings was to expand the base of dues-paying holdings. Thus, the micro-dynamics of the manorial system thrust strongly outward on to newly cleared land. It remains only to sketch the global effects of this extensive pattern of land cultivation on the long-term viability of the feudal social formation in the high Middle Ages.

In the prolonged period of growth from the late tenth through the late thirteenth century, the population of Western Europe probably doubled, building up on the best arable and spreading out on to increasingly marginal land. This was an extraordinarily vigorous and protracted growth for a pre-industrial population, still subject to withering mortality crises; it averaged about one-quarter per cent per annum over the course of three hundred years.[402] Part of this expansion was absorbed on the existing arable, sustained by means of a considerable rise in tilling productivity and grain yield on steadily shrinking holdings. Agricultural productivity made substantial progress on the more advanced manors through the high Middle Ages. Duby has estimated a rise in harvest/seed ratio from 2.5:1 to 4:1 from the ninth to the thirteenth century.[403] After allocating seed to the next crop, such an improvement would have about doubled grain available for human consumption. Duby may well have overestimated the advance, as Van Bath has argued, but substantial agricultural progress was undoubtedly made in these centuries, marked by a series of technical innovations: the iron plough for deeper tilling, the horseshoe and stiff harness for equine traction, the watermill for mechanical power, the growth of nitrogen–fixing legumes and, most importantly, the pervasive adoption of the three–field crop rotation for soil restoration.[404]

Much of the population increase was sustained on newly cleared land.[405] Some of this was achieved by extending fields into waste and woodland in the immediate vicinity of villages. Yet the greatest gains for new settlement were not made locally, but came through massive colonization efforts.[406] Vast forests were cleared and marshes drained, as interiors and coastlands were claimed for settlement in England, France, the Rhineland, northern Italy and western Germany. On an even more ambitious scale, whole new arable regions were forged through colonizing mobilizations staged by monastic Orders and monarchs: the mass migrations of the Germans east of the Elbe; the damming and dyking of the North Sea organized by the Count of Flanders and the Dutch monarchy; the military reconquest of Islamic Iberia, followed by Spanish settlement.[407] In these institutionally sponsored projects, land reclamation was most often the work of landless labourers, attracted by offers of light rent and the absence of servile obligations. As a result of the demographic tendency described earlier – to build up and shed surplus populations from core manorial holdings – there was a continuous stream of dispossessed (hence downwardly mobile) young adults dispersing to remote regions, clearing land and striving to re-establish themselves as smallholders. Kin networks were fractured and thinned out through colonizing exodus; for migrants, 'the influence of kin was relatively low and the independence of the conjugal unit was relatively high'.[408]

Concomitant with the expansion of the total area under the plough, the average size of holdings dropped, swelling the proportion of tenements which could no longer support a family. From the ninth to the thirteenth century, the average English holding shrank from roughly 100 acres to 20 or 30. By the thirteenth century, most holdings in England and France were less than the four to six hectares necessary to sustain a household of four or five people, and average yield per hectare was stagnant. In central Germany and the Rhine-Moselle district, farms were so fragmented that failed harvests brought many families to the brink of starvation. Inevitably, then, the size of the labour team working each plot would have shrunk as well, though with technological improvements, not by the same proportion as average holding size. Since it is doubtful that peasant families had more supplementary labourers attached to their households in the ninth than in the thirteenth century (in contrast to lords), it is reasonable to assume that the average peasant family size and co-resident extension was reduced considerably through these centuries: 'The main effect of agricultural expansion was to lower the obstacles to the segmentation of family groupings and to enable a greater number of individuals to survive, in circumstances as straitened as those of their forebears.'[409]

Pressure on the land gradually took its toll in ways which were not immediately apparent. Given the primacy of grain production in the feudal economy, pasturage was converted into arable as a path of least resistance in land
reclamation; this shifted the ecological balance of animal husbandry and farming. With reduced quantities of manure being dropped on the arable, its nutrient depletion was accelerated. The dearth of fodder weakened draught
animals and impaired their ploughing stamina, contributing to inefficient land
use. Forest cutbacks in hilly regions exacerbated erosion, exposing thin soils
which had brief lifespans as viable grain producers. Floods and dust storms
became more frequent. New land coming under the plough for the first time
could no longer offset the exhaustion of old lands depleted through centuries
of use. As hinterland expansion proceeded, ancient arable had to be withdrawn
from cultivation.[410]

In these circumstances, the ranks of the landless poor swelled as a mass
underclass, increasingly divorced from productive property and viable livelihood. Their underemployment represented a massive squandering of labour-
power and a wasteful drain on parish resources, particularly through the winter
months. This population became enfeebled, morbid, and vulnerable as a
human host for pestilence. Pauperization and swelling landlessness thus invited
pandemic devastation. Should we adopt a Malthusian perspective, and cite this
underclass as the source of overpopulation on the land?[411] The evidence will
not warrant it. As noted, there was a positive correlation throughout the feudal
epoch between the wealth of peasant holdings and the size of family groups
resident on them. Smallholders and the landless poor tended to marry later, die
younger and have smaller families than wealthier peasants. In periods of land
scarcity, economic stagnation and fragmentation of holdings (such as the century preceding the Black Death) the landless poor did not generally reproduce
their own numbers. The swelling of their ranks came entirely from above. It
might occur in apparently 'opposite' ways. In impartible zones, the systematic
exclusion of non-heir offspring from the holdings of their parents precipitated
their descent into the ranks of cottagers and landless migrant labourers. Conversely, in areas where land was more readily subdivided, the same essential
result would occur, as the average size of holdings shrank and a class of land-
poor cottagers piled up at the bottom of the village pyramid, with each stratum pressing on the resources of those beneath it. In land-tight Halesowen in
the first decades of the fourteenth century:

> The rich, and to a lesser extent the middling villagers ... married younger, lived
> longer and had more children. ... [They] settled their younger children on the
> lands which were previously occupied by their poorer neighbours. ... Many
> families of small means died out and their holdings were taken up by new tenants.

Others had to sell or to sub-let their lands in order to buy food to remit debts and to pay rents, fines and amercements. ... When the peasants in the upper stratum of village society could not expand horizontally, since the reserves of reclaimable land were giving out, they had to expand vertically in order to settle their surplus children. This they did by 'colonizing' lands held by the poorer and weaker members of the community whom unfavourable economic conditions pushed either up to heaven or out from their holdings and often from the village altogether.[412]

The overexploitation of the peasantry by the landed aristocracy in conditions of stagnant productivity resulted in an overexploitation of the land by the peasant producers, which eventually became subject to an ecological law of diminishing returns. The demographic and ecological balance on the land, precariously established in the preceding centuries of expansion, was now upset and reacted ultimately to drag down the rate of seigneurial exploitation. By the late thirteenth and early fourteenth century, noble incomes were stagnant or slumping all across Western Europe. This, in turn, precipitated an unprecedented wave of warfare among rival knights, as noble households tried to recoup their losses in marauding ventures.[413] Economic and demographic growth now stalled; the warning signals were everywhere. A climatic shift in 1315–17 (a string of unusually wet winters and cool, rainy summers) led to major harvest failures, triggering widespread famine. From then on, a series of subsistence and mortality crises unfolded with increasing frequency.

Intruding into this gathering feudal storm from outside Europe, the lethal scourge of the Black Death delivered a devastating blow to the already weakened peasant masses, wiping out about a quarter of the population of Western Europe in four years (1347–51). By 1400, a series of subsequent epidemic waves had pushed the mass carnage to an estimated two-fifths; among smallholders and cottagers, the proportion must have risen above half.[414] Normally under feudalism, demographic recovery followed fairly quickly on the heels of mortality crises, but the repercussions of this devastation were such that enduring population growth did not resume across Europe for a century. The general crisis of the fourteenth and fifteenth centuries marked the beginning of the end of feudalism in Western Europe.

Most economic historians are agreed that by the early fourteenth century, Western Europe was in the throes of a Malthusian crisis.[415] The symptoms of an overpopulated society were evident: the fragmentation of peasant holdings beneath the minimum threshold of subsistence viability for an average family group, diminishing returns to increasingly marginal land, rising grain prices and widespread malnutrition. Well before the Black Death struck, population growth had ground to a halt and was contracting in some of the densest areas. While the plague did not originate in Europe, and would have wreaked havoc regardless of the population density and the standard of living prevailing at the time, the anaemic, malnourished condition of the impoverished masses arguably sapped the population's recuperative capacities.

Can we agree with this aspect of the Malthusian interpretation? Was Western Europe 'overpopulated' by the early fourteenth century? Provided this condition is understood as the outcome of social structure, and not of an absolute conflict between profligate breeding and the limits of nature's resources, the term is apposite. We must insist that the demographic impasse was *feudalism's,* involving a grossly wasteful and unproductive allocation of the surplus product by the ruling class, and (intimately related) an extensive mode of growth, with cumulative obstacles to progress in intensive agriculture. The problem with the Malthusian interpretation is the way it naturalizes this impasse, by postulating an ecological limit on raising the level of grain yield per hectare on prime arable. This barrier is invoked on the basis of poorly specified impediments to technical innovation having to do with the conservative nature of peasants and their hidebound cropping practices. In a wide-ranging comparative survey, Ester Boserup has shown that population build-up, resulting in pressure on available resources, has often catalysed agricultural intensification, increasing labour inputs on established arable and inducing experiments with new planting strategies.[416] She attributes a string of major productivity breakthroughs in the history of agriculture to the stimulus of population build-up. While her argument has been faulted for being reductive and monocausal, its core proposition has drawn widespread assent from agricultural historians. More often than not, demographic pressure *does* galvanize technical innovation and labour intensification in agriculture, raising yields per hectare. This causal sequence appears to have been a central dynamic in the progressive shift from hoe to plough agriculture in prehistoric Europe. Why was the crisis of the early fourteenth century not resolved in this fashion?

There seem to be two possible answers to this question. The first is to argue that it takes time in a high-pressure situation before innovative intensification spreads sufficiently to overcome the impasse; the lethal tidal wave of the Black Death crashed over Europe before this adjustment had had time to develop and spread, terminating at a stroke the conditions of population pressure that foster such innovation. The trouble with this line of reasoning is that there is no evidence from the most densely settled regions of the European countryside that any sort of a breakthrough in intensive agriculture was occurring in the pre-plague period, after a full century of deepening stagnation.[417] It therefore seems utterly conjectural to propose that a Boserupian resolution of the Malthusian squeeze was in the offing but cut short by the exogenous holocaust of the Black Death. The superior hypothesis is to argue that a set of impediments to successful agricultural intensification had gradually accumulated in the seigneurial system, counteracting the potentially stimulative impact of demographic pressure on agriculture. In fact, demographic pressures had produced the opposite effect – falling yields on prime arable due to nutrient depletion, and a growing imbalance between grain growing and stockraising. Protracted crisis was by no means the *inevitable* outcome of population build-up under feudalism. But it must be seen as the *most likely* result, given the mass squandering of wealth at the top of the class structure and surplus labour at the bottom, and the chronic weakness of the system in bringing the two together in intensive agriculture.

3

Population and Changing Family Forms in the Transition from Feudalism to Capitalism

PART I: LATE MEDIEVAL CRISIS AND THE ORIGINS OF THE WESTERN EUROPEAN MARRIAGE PATTERN

The terminology of 'the early modern period', so congenial to the discourse of modernization theory, has enjoyed a very popular, if vague (and hence arbitrary) existence in the historiography of Europe. Does it have any merit from a historical materialist standpoint? It does, providing we extract it from the modernization paradigm and assign it a more precise and theoretically substantial role: to designate the transitional period from the onset of feudalism's demise through to capitalism's eventual consolidation as a dominant mode of production. These demarcations should be sought in changes in the social relations of exploitation in each mode. The early modern period is thus inaugurated with the widespread commutation of dues (the replacement of labour services by produce and money rents) and the concomitant decline in demesne agriculture in the late fourteenth and fifteenth centuries. This marks the beginning of the end for the feudal–seigneurial mode of production in Western Europe, though components of this structure persist on the land until the final collapse of the *ancien régime*. The transitional period draws to a close with capitalism's industrial consolidation as a mode of production: the generalization of capitalist manufacture in the late eighteenth and early nineteenth centuries.

During the early modern period of roughly four centuries (to focus only on the leading edge of change) no mode of production dominated simultaneously at all levels of the social formations of Western Europe. This is what characterizes it as a transitional era. To be very schematic about it: the first half of the early modern period is taken up with the decline of feudalism (in this account, with the disintegration of the peasantry as a social class), while the latter half is primarily concerned with the rise of capitalism (with the formation of the proletariat). The chapter has been divided along these lines.

But the important thing conceptually is to recognize the profoundly intertwined nature of feudal disintegration and capitalist genesis, to avoid thinking in terms of their spatial and temporal separation throughout the early modern period. It is only when modes of production clearly predominate, at the summit of their consolidated power, that it is appropriate to work with a 'pure' model of a given mode, operating under the impetus of its own reproduction through time. In a transitional era we must stay rather closer to the ground, paying close attention to sequence and temporality in order to discern the interlaced strands of the two modes of production as they commingle in reality. Consequently, the organization of this chapter is more tightly chronological than that of the last, taking up thematic issues as they first arise within the period under discussion.

The genesis of a mode of production is often conceived in terms of the birth metaphor, with capitalism growing 'in the womb' of feudalism, and finally issuing forth after a period of gestation, presumably as a perfectly formed miniature of its adult self, complete with ten fingers and ten toes. Marxists, from Marx on, have unfortunately been fond of the birth image; but when it dominates our thinking, the search for the wellsprings of 'nascent' capitalism becomes misguided and confused. We tend to scan backwards, searching for the capital–wage labour relation 'in embryo', as it will later appear. Presumably, the sperm of free capital fuses with the proletarian egg, and this is the magic moment when the capitalist mode of production is conceived. But capitalism does not develop in this way. Merchant and banking capital predate capitalism as a mode of production, as do rudimentary forms of wage labour. These forms of capital and wage labour develop apart from one another in most cases. On a general and decisive scale, the engagement of wage labour with capital in the sphere of industrial production occurs at the very end of the early modern drama – in the final act, as it were. Since the 'birth' of capitalism occurs long before the capitalist mode of production is finally 'conceived', the entire metaphor is misleading.

New social classes and family forms are not built in a day, nor do they change everywhere all at once. This is to state the obvious, yet periodization schemas can easily founder on the rocks of this convolution. Within Western Europe, the tempo of proletarianization was highly uneven, its routes several and diverse. Consequently, one should avoid postulating overly dichotomous before/after turning points, focusing exclusively on the leading edge of change and assuming that the steps of the vanguard are retraced by those who come after. In a periodization exercise of this sort, it will suffice to identify conjunctures of initial genesis and final consolidation, while resting content, in between, to note the general trend-lines of change, delineating stages of development, broadly conceived. Our perspective on infrastructural transformation is to situate changing family forms within shifting class relations: the demise of inheritance-based stem family forms within the disintegration of the peasantry (Part I); the forging of independent nuclear family forms within the process of proletarian formation (Part II); the population boom and the takeoff into industrial capitalism (Part III). Since proletarianization is overwhelmingly a rural phenomenon in the early modern period, our attention throughout this chapter will remain centred on the primary producer classes who live and labour in the countryside.

While the changes in class and family formation which I seek to sketch out here unfold relatively slowly, displaying hybrid admixtures and unstable amalgams in progressing from one stage to the next, it would be a mistake, on that account, to infer that we were investigating an evolutionary development, where one would wish to stress elements of continuity over those of change. Many family historians of the early modern era, centring on the Cambridge Group but by no means confined to it, hold that the history of 'the' Western family is, in most significant respects, one of remarkable homeostasis – a veritable island of domestic perdurance in a sea of economic change and political turbulence. I take strong exception to this view. In arguing the case for revolutionary change, I shall try to avoid simply reversing the conservative optic, obscuring in the process those aspects of continuity which the Cambridge Group have emphasized: the relative stability in mean household size and nuclear co-residence over the centuries.[1] But I should say at the outset that these are not, in my view, the most important dimensions of family structure or familial experience; the organization of the family cycle is. The early modern transition from peasant to proletarian family cycle and procreative regime constitutes a revolution in the history of family forms – a development as vital in the making of the modern world as any other facet of its creation.

If the process of proletarian family formation is relatively gradual, lacking sharp turning points, why term it revolutionary? This characterization should not hinge on the pace of change so much as on evidence of irreversible disjunction – of disintegration, release and genesis in passing from one mode of production to another. The modern nuclear family cycle is genuinely novel. Incorporating many elements of its predecessors, it none the less fashions them anew. In this sense, the transition may be termed revolutionary, involving qualitative changes in both the organization of the family cycle and the mode of patriarchal dominance. The purpose of this chapter is to trace out key features of this transformation in Western Europe and to situate them in the broader demographic and economic context of the transition from feudalism to capitalism.[2]

The context is conceived in terms of a long wave, based in the agrarian–seigneurial infrastructure. I have organized the chapter so that it is configured by the crests and troughs of this overarching pattern: (a) 1347–1450, the late medieval depression; (b) 1450–1600, the boom of the 'long' sixteenth century; (c) 1600–1750, seventeenth-century crisis and lingering stagnation; (d) 1750 on, the takeoff into industrial capitalism. At each stage, I endeavour to discern the demographic components of the secular shift which inaugurated a new phase in the cycle, and the changes in class relations and family forms which stabilized and perpetuated the new reproductive regime.

The presentation of four stages is certainly a useful heuristic device, bringing a semblance of order to an otherwise bewildering array of trends and cross-currents; but it is more than a convenient concept imposed on an intractable reality. The long agrarian wave is a prime mover in Western Europe in the early modern era, integrating diverse regions in a continental economy.[3] Its action does not efface regional variety and distinction, but modulates regionally specific tempos of growth and stagnation with an overarching rhythm of development. Continental integration, by means of the long wave, makes the generalizations of this chapter possible. (Whether I have discerned them clearly or described them adequately is of course another matter.)

The Shifting Balance of Power in the Wake of the Black Death

The feudal–seigneurial mode of production had stalled for half a century and was teetering on the brink of a subsistence crisis when the peoples of Europe were devastated by the Black Death. The plague entered Europe in October 1347 by means of infected crews travelling on ships from the Crimea and lodging in Mediterranean ports. The lethal bacillus was then disseminated with alarming speed, transported across or around the Alps to strike Paris in six months and southwest England by December; the whole of England was engulfed in a matter of months.[4]

Mortality crises in medieval villages were normally followed by growth spurts, which restored lost numbers in a generation. Vacant places on the land were eagerly taken up, the pace of nuptiality and household formation quickened, and fertility rates rebounded rapidly from their traumatic suppression in the midst of sudden, but usually very brief, plague onslaughts. There is evidence of such resilience even in the immediate aftermath of the Black Death, but subsequent pandemic outbreaks repeatedly aborted promising recoveries.[5] The plague abated towards the end of the century but lay dormant as an ominous force, erupting sporadically in the fifteenth century, usually on a localized scale.[6] While these later scourges killed fewer people, their long-term effects were more debilitating than the Black Death itself. They attacked primarily infants and children who had been born after the first infestation had subsided and therefore lacked the immune systems developed by its survivors. Such a selective mortality pattern drastically depleted specific age cohorts, who then passed through their own reproductive years generating an-other 'hollow' cohort.[7]

Sustained population growth across Western Europe did not resume for a century. The liftoff in the second half of the fifteenth century rose from a nadir of perhaps two-thirds of the early-fourteenth-century plateau.[8] But the dam-age was unevenly spread; England and France were particularly hard hit. The former suffered a decline of perhaps 50 to 60 per cent from 1348 to 1450, while the latter's loss has been estimated at almost one-half.[9] Empirical studies of specific regions, as opposed to educated guesses on a country-wide basis, often present an even bleaker picture. In France, the net loss in East Nor-mandy was about 70 per cent, in Haute Provence 64 per cent, and in the Paris Basin 50 per cent, conservatively estimated.[10] Contractions in northern Italy were of similar magnitude: 70 per cent in the Prato area, 65 per cent in and around Florence, and 63 per cent in rural Pistoia.[11] This staggering depopula-tion induced a deep and prolonged depression in agricultural production, as demand for foodstuffs collapsed, international trade contracted, cereal prices slumped, labour-power suddenly became scarce, real wages rose, and seigneu-rial revenues all but dried up. Out of the depths of a classically feudal crisis, the stage was being set for the transition to capitalism.

It appears at first glance as if one were viewing a medieval movie run in reverse, undoing the population build-up and extension on to newly cleared land of the last three centuries. Wherever the plague struck, the survivors retreated from marshy moors, saline coastlands, mountainside and fen, re-grouping on the best arable in older, larger and more securely established settlements. Plague epidemics sliced through states extremely unevenly: some regions escaped almost unscathed, while others were devastated. In the most severely ravaged areas, outlying hamlets and smaller villages were deserted en-tirely.[12] Germany lost a quarter of its village settlements, mostly in arable re-gions, while in England perhaps one village in fifteen disappeared; in France and the Netherlands, by contrast, few villages were entirely abandoned. Des-pite this unevenness, the regrouping of the remaining population in larger villages and towns, and the elimination of many small hamlet clusters, was 'part and parcel of an all-European pattern of *Wustungen*' (lost villages), whose net effect was to concentrate rural population settlement.[13] *Wustungen* also entailed mass migration to the cities in response to employment opportunities and rising urban wages, but this resulted in very little net urbanization. The plague pandemics of the late medieval era had struck down a higher propor-tion of city-dwellers than country folk.[14] Migrations of this period did not do much more than restore the pre-existing rural/urban balance, since a very high proportion of the newcomers died without leaving surviving offspring. In Northwestern Europe, it is estimated that a mere 7 per cent of the population lived in cities of over 10,000 people in 1500.[15]

The movement away from marginal lands and barren soil, forsaking fields which had been cleared with tenacious devotion in the previous century, was not a reversion to the medieval status quo ante in any essential sense. Most significantly, the balance of class power on the land turned decisively in favour of the peasantry. In the twelfth and early thirteenth centuries, land had been extremely tight, labour abundant, and prospective tenants plentiful. This had enabled lords to dictate the terms of tenancy: to raise rents, enforce services, control inheritance and other land transfers, and oust recalcitrant or indebted tenants, replacing them readily. By holding out the constant threat of eviction before the village community, lords upheld manorial discipline. The Black Death and its subsequent plague outbreaks transformed this basic equation on the land, rendering labour scarce and arable land abundant. The peasants were not slow to seize the initiative. In the latter decades of the fourteenth century a wave of insurgency swept across Western Europe, culminating in regional uprisings: the Paris Basin Jacquerie of 1358, the Tuchin movement in central France (1363–84), the urban-based insurrections in Tuscany and Umbria in the 1360s and 1370s, the English rising of 1381, the Catalan revolts of the late fourteenth century.[16] Such regionally co-ordinated revolts, headed by a mixture of rural rebels and urban heretics, made demands both against the Crown (to rescind new taxes) and against local lords (in response to seigneurial reaction). These were flashpoints of conflict cresting above a flood-tide of peasant rebellion welling up at village level.[17]

The pattern of retreat from precarious villages revealed not only a desperate flight from plague infestation and a search for greener pastures in an ecological sense, but also a defiant repudiation of the worst landlords in favour of their more adaptable brethren who demonstrated a willingness to lighten rents and forgo the most noxious dues of servile tenure.[18] On a local scale, resistance could take many forms: rent strikes; withdrawal of labour services; refusal to pay amercements or to heed manorial injunctions to repair dilapidated buildings, torn-down fences and clogged ditches; rejection of orders to take up vacant land under the old servile terms; and intimidation of Royal tax collectors.[19] Such defiance spread like wildfire in the last decades of the fourteenth century.

In the immediate aftermath of the Black Death, many lords spurned demands for the conversion of villein holdings and the abandonment of servile dues, and instead tried to crack down on delinquent tenants. Their immediate response to the tenant losses of the Black Death, and to the lost revenue which it entailed, was to tighten the screws of seigneurial exaction. Monarchs and princes came to their defence with a spate of draconian decrees designed to repress vagabondage, pin labourers down and fix wages.[20] But subsequent plague outbreaks in the 1360s and 1370s left vast stretches of arable lying fallow. The lords' position had been weakened drastically. Seigneurial repression was largely unenforceable. At the local level, lords who clung to the full array of customary exactions found themselves with deserted holdings. Freeholders took off readily, and even serfs, supposedly bound for life to their lords' land, began to leave without permission in search of better soil, lighter rents and more accommodating lords. They deserted with impunity for the most part, paying no exit fees and taking domestic chattels and animals which belonged legally to the lord. On the ecclesiastical manor of Worcester in the 1450s, courts suddenly stopped recording the movements of serfs who had left the manor; evidently, 'the authorities realized the futility of attempting to secure their return'.[21] With this concession, the distinction between servile and free tenants faded, despite later attempts to reimpose serfdom. 'When manorial lords in the sixteenth century claimed their tenants were villeins by blood, we see either isolated pockets of continuing archaic custom or else deliberate attempts to resurrect a legal concept that was in practice long dead.'[22]

In the face of unprecedented peasant mobility, the class discipline of the lords crumbled. No longer did they refuse entry to vagrant serfs or return them to their masters; now they bid competitively against one another to persuade newcomers to take up vacant holdings.[23] To salvage overgrown arable before it permanently deteriorated, lords waived most labour services and lightened rents and heriots, thus inadvertently encouraging the very mobility they deplored. Across great stretches of manorial land in Western Europe, the maintenance of the most burdensome labour service, regular work on the demesne, became untenable. The seigneurial reduction of labour services in favour of money rents had crept forward in many areas in the twelfth and early thirteenth centuries, mostly due to the lords' desire to monetize their incomes directly without having to sell the agrarian surplus. But in the latter decades of the fourteenth century and in the first half of the fifteenth, the shift was abruptly accelerated under a far more urgent imperative: to induce tenants to take up vacant holdings in the midst of widespread peasant insurgency, where the nobility was very much on the defensive. The scope of the forfeiture of labour services was unprecedented, if uneven. Regardless of subsequent retrenchments (which were often very substantial), the full seigneurial yoke could never be reimposed on the Western European peasantry.

In forcing the relinquishment of labour services and the leasing of demesne land, peasants triggered a far-reaching mutation of the relationship between manor and village. The erosion of commons lessened the necessity for the communal regulation of crops and stock. While open fields were retained in most regions, strips within them were now swapped in such a way as to obviate the need for collective rotations. 'Everyone was anxious to group their lands together, for their fields to be near their farmsteads.'[24] With the expansion of large holdings and the demise of labour service, the demand for day labour rose and hiring became the pre-eminent contractual relationship of the local economy. High tenant turnover, increased mobility between villages, and the rise of absentee landholding loosened the bond between manor and village. As peasants paid out more in cash and less in labour service, their need for monetary income increased. Turning to merchants and town markets to sell their produce, they deepened their dependence on extra-regional trade. Manorial autonomy declined sharply.

Did the commutation of dues and the leasing of demesne land end lordship in Western Europe? Did this decisive alteration in the seigneurial mode of exploitation finish off feudalism in the process? Many historians have answered in the affirmative, restricting the terminology of feudalism to the Middle Ages and depicting the early modern era as an age of merchant capitalism. Marxists, more concerned with transformation in the prevailing mode of production than with the growth of market exchange per se, have correctly dissented from this view.

The *form* of rent had changed; the importance of this alteration should not be slighted. But the peasant–landlord *axis* of surplus extraction and class conflict persisted. The decline of serfdom did not leave peasants free from seigneurial discipline and constraint, though it certainly weakened the sinews of their oppression, enabling them to forge more autonomous village communities.[25] Despite undoubted alterations in tenure forms, the typical unit of peasant production was still the customary holding worked by a family labour team. The limited incentive structure of peasant production was not transformed. The primary orientation of peasant households in most regions of Western Europe remained a subsistence-based one, selling in order to purchase necessities in the never-ending struggle to make ends meet. Agricultural technology, embedded in the web of peasant-landlord relations, was not revolutionized by means of the commutation of dues. Until the mid eighteenth century, its progress was modest, unremarkable by medieval standards. The motor force of economic growth was still the productivity of agriculture: the primary growth dynamic of the system remained extensive until the end of the *ancien régime*. The long cycles generated in the early modern era (the 1450–1600 boom and the 1600–1740 depression) were feudal-agrarian in nature. Their characteristic price and wage movements were quite unlike the subsequent long waves of industrial capitalism, which finally achieved pre-eminence in the nineteenth century. Before 1750, early modern vital rates appear to have fluctuated within the same basic parameters as in the Middle Ages; the pace of population growth in the long term was of a similar order of magnitude.[26] In sum, the seigneurial ensemble – increasingly imbricated with capitalist relations as it declined and unravelled – persisted on the land, framing peasant–landlord relations down to the end of the *ancien régime*.[27]

Continuity and Change in Peasant Stratification

In relinquishing labour services, lords faced a dire scarcity of labour on de-mesne land. Hypothetically, their fields might have been kept in production by mass enslavement or the employment of free wage labour. Neither option was a viable one in Western Europe in the fifteenth century. The *famuli,* unfree domestic servants attached to the lords' households, were numerous in the early Middle Ages but had now all but disappeared. The peasantry was not about to tolerate mass enslavement. The customary rights, settlement density and community autonomy of peasant villages were too great, and the freehol-ders' ranks too numerous, to countenance such a massive regression. As for the proletarian option, the availability of vacant tenancies on fertile arable reab-sorbed the bulk of the cottar underclass, making day labourers scarce and prohibitively expensive, especially for cash-strapped seigneurs. Another alter-native was sharecropping, but this too suffered from the ready availability of arable and the sudden paucity of landless labourers. It was not a viable alterna-tive in most of Northwestern Europe, though it spread in Mediterranean areas, particularly in Italy, where its use predated the plague.[28] In the sharecropping zones (the Mezzadria), propertyless labourers remained plentiful in the fif-teenth century, and were attracted by the lords' initial provision of agricultural capital.

In most regions, the seigneurs' only recourse was to lease out demesne land on easy terms to their most productive tenants. Well-off peasants acquired substantial holdings in this way. The leasing of demesne land thus exacerbated the social inequality of the village community, providing a major impetus to the emergence of a distinct yeoman class whose favoured offspring would eventually become commercial tenant farmers employing labourers. The pri-mary impediment to more rapid accumulation by this stratum in the late four-teenth and early fifteenth centuries was the limitation imposed by a family-based labour team. Since wage labour was so expensive, only the weal-thiest and most successful market-oriented farmers could afford to employ day labourers for anything more than short-term contracts in peak season.[29]

In addition to land, lords leased or sold outright to local craftsmen other means of production – kilns, ovens, mills, wine presses, breweries and so on. With this shift, artisans who had formerly been the lords' men emerged as commodity producers in their own right. Fees for service and prices for home-grown produce replaced compulsory services in the village economy. The depleted ranks of the cottar underclass could not capitalize on the leasing of demesne land and the growth of the land market. They lacked the resources to buy up large land parcels, even at bargain prices, or to switch and specialize their crop mix in response to shifting commodity markets, as grain prices plummeted.

Yet by the Darwinian logic of feudal crisis, the smallholders who did survive made substantial gains in the century after the Black Death. In the first place, their productivity rose when they worked for themselves, as they abandoned barren land to take up holdings on richer arable and pasture. Modest land parcels came very cheap in this era; entry fines were nominal or waived outright, and rents declined. Mobility was relatively easy (which gave the poor a novel element of choice in the land they worked) and many smallholders succeeded in working themselves up into the ranks of the middle peasantry. Secondly, wages rose against the slumping price of food staples, roughly doubling in real terms, as labour scarcity compelled employers to bid up the price of labour-power. The land-poor had traditionally relied on supplementing their own produce with wage income (in kind or cash); the fifteenth century improved their lot dramatically in this regard. Thirdly, the dependency ratio of surviving peasants was substantially improved after the plague, 'that holocaust of the undernourished', which swept away the weakest sections of the population – infants, the elderly, the sick and the landless poor – in much greater numbers than more robust groups.[30]

While family continuity was jeopardized by horrendous mortality crises, the survivors found that the inheritance bind had been relaxed, and children could be placed fairly easily on the land as they approached marriage age. The downward mobility of non-heirs, typical in the previous century, was now reduced to a trickle, more often the result of multiple deaths in families than lack of access to good land. The proportion of landless cottars and smallholders in the peasant population declined quite substantially from pre-plague levels.[31] While the living standards and acreage of cottars and smallholders appear to have improved in the century following the Black Death, the gap between them and the upper stratum of the peasantry was not closed and may well have widened, owing to the rapid land accumulation of the latter. Still, this was not an era of social polarization on the land; it appears, rather, as the last golden age of a solid middle peasant majority, fully deploying family labour without relying on hired hands.[32] The process of polarization, which would see the erosion of intermediate strata and the proletarianization of smallholders, lay in the future.

One response of lords and gentry to vacant arable and scarce labour was to convert to forms of agriculture which were less labour-intensive, such as animal husbandry, which had been increasingly sacrificed in the preceding century. The balance between grain-growing and grazing now swung back the other way, as vast tracts of noble land across Northwestern Europe, especially in England, were allowed to grow over, and herds were bred to replenish stock. Once again, this was not a simple reversion to the medieval status quo. The formerly tight interlacing of mixed arable and commons pasture, typical of feudal agriculture, was now loosened. Sheep farming for wool sale (much of it an export market) developed as a monoculture in the fifteenth century, with the drastic contraction of arable in whole regions. The door to capitalist agriculture, based on regional cash-crop specialization, was thus unlocked. It would take another two centuries to wedge it wide open.

Tenure Shifts and Inheritance Forms

By the latter half of the fifteenth century, the manorial form had undergone profound mutation. With the break-up of demesne agriculture, manors ceased to have a bilateral character. Absentee lordship became widespread as noble households withdrew from direct participation in managing their estates. With the decline of personal servility, the seigneurial authority of manor courts was weakened. Many met less frequently and some lapsed altogether. While most continued to meet and adjudicate disputes within the village community, they increasingly ceded legal power to Royal courts, as aggrieved peasants gained access to the lowest tier of the latter to appeal manorial fiat.

Changes in rent and tenure forms were integral to this mutation. In England and the Low Countries, labour services were replaced for the most part by cash rents, while in France, Spain and Germany, produce rents were the more common substitute. While the variation is significant, the general direction of change was almost everywhere towards the monetization of appropriated surplus. The collection of money rents as a rising proportion of all dues increased the degree to which peasant households were forced to produce for the market, even if the vast majority remained subsistence-oriented, selling to meet expenses, not primarily to make a profit. Tenure forms underwent a concomitant evolution, through a bewildering array of regional variations which cannot distract us here. Once again, the overall direction of the transformation is tolerably clear.

In the feudal property form of parcellized sovereignty, the class relationship between the owners and possessors of land was framed by manorial custom as an intricate web of conditional prerogatives. Dependent peasants possessed land at the will of their lords. But in recognizing their tenants, lords extended to them a set of rights and protections which stabilized the relationship of dependency according to the customs of the manor, to be adjudicated on an ongoing basis and hence continuously redefined in court proceedings. The web of dependent tenancy and manorial custom was not removed with the forfeiture of labour services, but its corners were certainly lifted. The shift in class forces on the land helped to dispel a great deal of the feudal fog. The rise of the Absolutist State, the extension of its legal jurisdiction and powers of taxation, subverted manorial authority, sundering the economic and political relations of class domination which had heretofore been fused at the local

143

level.[33] This double blow, from peasant resistance and monarchial centralization, unsettled landlord–tenant relations. Their restabilization became the primary concern of the aristocracy generally, and Royal jurists in particular.

The judicial appeal to manorial custom was gradually replaced by written
deed and formal survey; tenure in perpetuity declined before more limited
leasehold contracts. The prerogatives of owners in disposing of land (mostly
lords and local gentry, but also peasant freeholders) were rendered less conditional; property rights became increasingly clearcut with the renaissance of
Roman jurisprudence.[34] These changes proceeded slowly and unevenly; we
should not overestimate the pace of transformation. In early Tudor England,
where the conversion went the furthest,

> the concept of absolute ownership of land was quite foreign to the common
> law and to all but a few very avant-garde law writers. No one but the Crown
> enjoyed full proprietary rights: everyone else held, by some sort of conditional
> tenure, of some superior lord – ultimately, and sometimes directly, of the Crown.
> ... The manor was still in 1500 and for a long time to come, the key to, and
> the essential unit of, landownership.[35]

On the continent, freeholders were still a minority of peasants. The gradual
shift from servile and conditional landholding to more contractual and absolute
forms had potentially far-reaching effects on the inheritance rights of peasant
families, but would have major repercussions for inheritance *practices* only
when the land filled up in the sixteenth century. Until that time, the primary
concern of lords and peasant householders alike was merely to find an heir – any
heir – to take up family holdings.[36]

With the population losses of the Black Death and recurring plague outbreaks, the continuity of family inheritance on the land was shattered. Among
the peasants of Languedoc, 'a large number of families and even entire lineages
disintegrated altogether.'[37] The consensus on this point among the historians of
diverse regions is virtually unanimous: however it is measured, the proportion
of holdings transmitted *within* families plummeted sharply.[38] In Kibworth Harcourt – to consider just one example – no family had left the village or ceased
to hold land in it from 1280 to 1340; fifty years later, only sixteen families had
resided in the village for more than a few years.[39]

Family heritability was severely disrupted for two essential reasons. The
extraordinary mortality rates of those dark decades were obviously a factor;
studies point consistently to the death of filial heirs. In Coltishall, Norfolk, for
example, the proportion of tenants survived by at least one son declined from
a pre-plague level of 69 per cent to 47 per cent in the last half of the fourteenth century.[40] But the more critical variable, in my view, was intergenerational mobility, due to the widespread availability of cheap land. Children
coming of age were no longer constrained to bide their time at home awaiting

144

their inheritance portions.[41] They could set out on their own more readily, working as a servant or day labourer for a time, and saving up to buy land.[42] The very premiss on which the medieval inheritance system had operated – that inheritance was by far the best means of acquiring land, while alternative livelihoods were scarce – was now nullified, and was to remain so for over a century. There was plenty of good land that could be acquired quite cheaply without waiting for a father to retire or die; wages were up as well, and labour-power was very much in demand. Much of the mobility which was so pervasive in the late fourteenth and fifteenth centuries appears as the flight of children away from family land and the oppressive authority of lords and peasant fathers alike.

The eclipse of family heritability can be laid squarely at the feet of the younger generation; there is certainly no evidence that lords or peasant elders wished to dispense with the principle. The lords were busy trying to turn the ancient villein right to inherit customary holdings into an *obligation* to do so. They made strenuous efforts to track down the offspring of abandoned tenancies and, failing that, to notify collateral kin and solicit their entry.[43] Whenever vacant holdings were desirable and their tenure terms were not too burdensome, kin could usually be found to fill in for missing heirs and preserve customary tenements in the extended family for a number of years until orphaned children came of age.[44] That there was not an even greater disruption of generational continuity on family lands in this era was largely due to the density and vitality of kin ties extending between households in the local area.

Peasant patriarchs can hardly have viewed the desertion of eligible heirs with equanimity, since their own security in old age, and that of their wives, depended on the arrangements they could make with married children inheriting portions and residing locally. Such arrangements were evidently more difficult to secure in the fifteenth century than they had been formerly. Dyer found only nine retirement arrangements in 1,300 court records in a number of West Midland villages from the late fourteenth through to the early sixteenth centuries, such contracts had been commonplace in medieval England:

> It is understandable that young would-be tenants should avoid taking on holdings encumbered with the expensive and inconvenient obligation to maintain an old couple. The result can be seen in references to aged tenants struggling to keep their lands going and eventually giving up in destitution.[45]

The elderly often compensated for their children's absence or dereliction by contracting with single persons to maintain them while working their land.[46]

With customary holdings passing out of family hands, was the parcel being taken over intact by another family or broken up? Obviously the consequences of integral takeover were not nearly so serious for the principle of family heritability as dispersal would be. Rights of reversion, for example, could be

145

maintained in the first case but not in the second. Ian Blanchard found at Baslow, Derbyshire, that thirteen of twenty-two holdings in 1520 had retained their form throughout the previous 165 years, and another five had existed for 120 to 150 years.[47] The same impression – of remarkable persistence in tenement structure while families came and went – may be seen in Kibworth Harcourt, where Howell has assembled a series of maps dating from 1086 to 1780.[48] In Kibworth, as in Baslow, there is no major disruption in the morphology of village land from 1340 to 1484, though the configuration of buildings alters somewhat owing to certain holdings falling temporarily vacant and being taken over and consolidated as part of multiple tenures.

In speaking of a complete disruption in 'family tenure', one must take care to distinguish between families and holdings. The discontinuity was in the former, not the latter. Even then, it is easy to exaggerate. The reduction in family transfer has generally been estimated by means of surnames. In Halesowen, where Razi was able to reconstitute more extended family networks, he found that collateral kin, with different surnames, were often taking up holdings where offspring were unavailable.[49] As well as a shift in land transfer from families to unrelated others in the late medieval period, there was also a conjunctural trend *within* families from the cognate line to collateral kin.

While the *practice* of family land transmission was sharply curtailed in the late medieval era, the *principle* was preserved as a *desideratum* by seigneurs and peasant household heads alike. The situation was a transient one, resulting from the unusual availability of cheap land. As soon as the population began to grow once again on a sustained basis and vacant holdings were taken up, familial inheritance of customary land was re-established as a compelling practical reality. We shall examine this recuperation in a moment.

How did peasant families respond to a population loss of this magnitude and to a sharp reversal of the traditional land/labour-power ratio? One must bear in mind the unevenness of plague mortality, not only from region to region but from house to house.[50] There also tended to be far less change in the number of households than in their average size. Co-resident flexibility was a domestic shock absorber, permitting families to adapt to the trauma of plague loss.[51] In these circumstances, the disruption of family life and inheritance transmission was less than the aggregate loss might suggest at first glance. While familial continuity was certainly disrupted, with families scrambling to make short-term adjustments, traditional practices could usually be resumed when the land market tightened once again.

What accounts for the retention of traditional inheritance customs through a conjuncture in which they were bypassed by the majority of village youth? The paradoxical effect of the elimination of potential heirs was that it tended to reinforce patrilineal norms. The comparative ease in acquiring extra land relaxed the compensatory imperative, making it easier to avoid the subdivision of customary holdings. There are many reasons why the average size of hold-ings would tend to increase in this period (above all, leasing out of demesne land), but it appears likely that an effective enforcement of impartible norms was one factor.[52]

The divergent trajectories of family dynamics in southern France and Eng-land is striking (reinforcing the notion of an enduring regional difference in family forms between Mediterranean and Northwestern Europe). Safeguarding land integrity in southern France meant retaining family members on-site, extending the co-resident group through marriage, under the authority of the senior patriarch. In England, subdivision was prevented by the designation of a single heir and the exit of his siblings as they came of age. In Languedoc, Ladurie portrays 'the astonishing reinforcement of institutions of lineage in the period 1350–1500', a recrudescence of the ancient *frérèches*.

> The reaction of the surviving families … [was to] close ranks and reconstitute the solidarity of the lineage. … In fifteenth-century Languedoc there was a move to substitute the extended patriarchal family for the nuclear family, to reconstitute the 'great household' of archaic rural societies.[53]

The power of the elder patriarch over his co-resident children was streng-thened substantially:

> They lived under the same roof, eating and drinking the same bread and the same wine. There was a sole money box, and the patriarch retained the keys. Without the express consent of the parent, the married son did not have the right to more than five sous for himself. … The veritable master of the wife's dowry … was the husband's father. It was he who received and disposed of it. Among the extended family groups that allied themselves to one another through marriage, the dowries passed from father to father.[54]

The historians of English villages portray a very different – in some ways diametrically opposed – evolution of family forms in the late medieval era. They find some shrinkage in the size of the household unit, resulting from an increasing flow of young adults leaving home and attaining their own land, registering a loss of patriarchal power over the occupational and marital des-tinies of the younger generation.[55] As the land refilled, however, fathers re-gained their authority, owing to the low level of proletarianization prior to the sixteenth century.

> The increase in the amount of land available for temporary alienation posed a threat to paternal authority, but the low level of industrial activity in all the Derbyshire villages save Barlow prevented its materialization. … The tendency towards nuclear household formation amongst stem or extended families was all but extinguished.[56]

Land Availability and Inheritance Norms

Since peasant family heritability waxes and wanes according to the availability of arable land, it is useful to look more closely at this factor. Neo-Malthusian analysts such as Postan and Ladurie are prone to underestimate the dynamism of agrarian productivity in response to growing population density, and therefore tend to treat the barrier of overpopulation in excessively absolute and natural terms.[57] This misconception stems from a reduction of the complex variable of land availability to its ecological limit-condition, experienced as a ratio of population to potentially arable land at a given level of agricultural technology.

Marxists, stressing the dynamism of productive forces and the real constraints of the prevailing social relations of production, have rightly rejected the naturalist rendering of an inflexible ceiling on population size.[58] In so doing, however, they have inadequately conceived the variable of land availability within the feudal mode of production. Yet it is a crucial factor in all agricultural formations, and quite compatible with class analysis, providing one conceives of a given mode of production as being deeply immersed *in* a natural environment, and not perched *on top of* it. Four major components determine the overall availability of land in a social formation where class and commodity relations have attained prominence: (a) an ecological limit-condition, given by natural geography and climate, modified by the prevailing modes of tillage and soil restoration; (b) a class determination of accessibility, based on prevailing property relations and the productive resources that the households of various classes command; (c) the prevailing form of inheritance and nuptial prestation, shaping the transmission of land between generations within classes; and (d) the character of the land market.

The radical alteration of land availability in the late fourteenth century was the result of shifts in the first two factors above: a contraction of land in use following a massive population loss, leaving good-quality land available; and a shift in the class relation of forces and the mode of seigneurial exploitation. This involved the relinquishing of labour services and the leasing of demesne fields; the conversion of some customary holdings to leasehold, making a great deal of land available for acquisition on the market above and beyond that made vacant by extraordinary mortality; and the regrouping of arable in more contiguous parcels.

These demographic and class shifts disrupted family continuity in land, loosening the anchorage of the peasant family cycle in the transmission of customary holdings from fathers to sons. The extension of the land market in the late medieval era occurred in response to these changes, and was not itself a major factor in determining them. As we saw in the case of the land market in the high Middle Ages, the pervasive exchange of small freehold parcels need not undermine family devolution but may well buttress it, enabling families to acquire and dispense with land as needed in different phases of the family cycle, obtaining extra plots to compensate secondary heirs. By the late fourteenth century and throughout the fifteenth, this market had been extended. It included much larger land parcels and allowed for the acquisition of multiple holdings, while entry fees had been reduced and rents lightened. The price of good quality arable was low, and there were fewer legal and customary impediments to purchasing it.

In these circumstances, surviving offspring could acquire land, or alternative livelihoods on the land, without having to wait for the devolution of the family patrimony. Fathers inevitably lost their power to dictate their sons' future course. 'Where the cash nexus existed, sons in agricultural families could enjoy an existence independent of their fathers' control ... providing for their own sustenance and establishing their own household.'[59] The land market itself did not engender these circumstances; it mediated and realized them. The distributional dynamic of this market was not polarizing in the late medieval era, as it was later to become. Middle-sized tenants, by and large, strengthened their positions over time, and the overall distribution of land within the peasantry remained unimodal; the core of customary holdings held firm. In short, this was not a *primary* land market, subverting the familial and community cohesion of the peasantry as a class.

When the underlying ecological and property conditions stabilized in the latter half of the fifteenth century and sustained population growth was finally renewed, family heritability was gradually restored to full strength once again. In England, hereditary copyhold became the normal form of customary tenure, with succession to the holding secured for future generations. Land itself was surveyed, staked and mapped much more clearly in the sixteenth century, and there was an increasing reliance on written wills drafted in detail to clarify and implement the intent of the legator. These developments made land transmission by inheritance more precise and secure. The sixteenth century saw a marked increase in land transfer within families as a proportion of all transfers. In fifteenth-century Languedoc, well over half of the taxpayers disappeared from one tax list to the next, leaving no trace of their names; in the sixteenth century, this had been cut to a quarter.[60] In six West Midland manors, land transfers within families at death rose from 45 per cent in the fifteenth century to 67 per cent after 1500.[61]

The refilling of places on the land raised the value of family holdings in the eyes of young adults reaching their majority, as the prospect of acquiring other land declined. The security of elderly tenants improved once again, as designated heirs were obliged to make very substantial commitments to their parents' upkeep to retain their favour.[62] The traditional right to return to claim, and the associated right of reversion (reassembling leased land for inheritance) were vigorously reasserted in the sixteenth century. Yet they were not easily re-established, since they ran against the rising tide of absolute property rights and the conception of land as a permanently alienable commodity like any other. The result was considerable contention on inheritance rights in both manor and Royal courts. One response to this insecurity was to withdraw all customary portions from the land market:

> Henceforth family land would not enter the market. It would be used by fathers to manipulate their children with promises of inheritance. Their objectives remained the same – to ensure the maintenance of their sustenance through the phases of their life-cycle – only now the arrangements to achieve this were internalized within the family rather than externalized through the market ... reflecting the [re]concentration of power in the hands of the family patriarch.[63]

Origins of the Western European Late Marriage System

Durable population growth did not resume across Western Europe until the middle decades of the fifteenth century. In view of the quick rebound which medieval and early modern villages typically achieved, why was the late medieval recovery so long in coming? If (as seems clear) the plague pandemics that followed the Black Death struck down infants and children in inordinate numbers, these 'hollow' age cohorts would in turn produce smaller cohorts, even though the fertility rate of married women did not decline. Does the age-biased nature of the mortality pattern fully explain the long delay before recuperation got under way?[64] Many scholars are sceptical, particularly concerning the latter half of this depression. While the sharp, short declines so much in evidence in the late medieval era were clearly plague-induced, epidemic mortality cannot explain the pattern in the intervening years when the plague was dormant, yet the population remained stagnant or even contracted slightly. These phases of lingering depression suggest that fertility was being curtailed on a mass scale. Many historians have speculated that mortality crises seared their traumatic 'lessons' into the consciousness of the survivors, to limit their numbers and avoid land subdivision.[65] This hypothesis sees a behavioural change placing a long-term check on birth rates and thus accounting, in part, for delayed recovery. There are two ways such a curtailment might have operated: by prolonging birth intervals within marriage and/or by raising the threshold to marriage. Let us consider each factor in turn.

Several historians have postulated a sharp rise in fertility control (contraception, abortion and infanticide) in response to plague trauma. Lacking hard evidence, the argument proceeds by plausible inference.[66] We do know that at this time Church authorities castigated husbands who engaged in non-procreative sex acts which were 'against nature and against the proper mode of matrimony'. They feared that sodomy (homosexual and heterosexual) was widespread, and decried the use of coitus interruptus.[67] The Franciscan Alvarus Pelagius indicted husbands who 'often abstain from knowing their own wives lest children should be born, fearing that they could not bring up so many, under pretext of poverty'.[68] Ecclesiastical venom was aimed especially at women 'who arrange that they cannot conceive; and if they have conceived, they destroy them in the body. You ... are more evil than are murderers.' Such women were blamed for the calamitous population losses of the era: 'O cursed by God, when will you do penance? Do you not see that you, like the sodomite, are the cause for the shrinkage of the world?'[69] This was a sinister accusation in a world where almost everyone believed that God punished communities by plague or famine for the sins of their members. The prosecutors of witches, incited by the notorious *Malleus Maleficarium* published under papal imprimatur in 1487, peppered their indictments against women (85 per cent of the accused) with charges that they were suppressing fertility (slaying infants in the womb, roasting first-born males, robbing men of their 'vital members', and so on). The Bull of Pope Innocent VIII accused witches of hindering women's conception and debilitating men's coital capacity. As Nancy Folbre has remarked, 'the relationship between the assertion of female control over reproduction and the persecution of witches seems more than coincidental.'[70] Clearly Church authorities detected clandestine forms of fertility regulation sustained by informal women's networks, and sought to eradicate them.

Were these informal community measures pursued in the fifteenth century with greater vigour than they had been in the pre-plague epoch? We have no way of directly knowing. But it seems reasonable to infer that they probably were, if one is prepared to grant that marital fertility was amenable to deliberate restriction (by prolonging birth intervals) and therefore that reproductive couples, or women acting on their own initiative, could respond to mounting disincentives for bearing and raising large families.[71] While wages were generally high in this period, the demand for family labour on most peasant holdings was limited, with slumping grain prices, slack markets for agrarian products, and the former burdens of labour service greatly curtailed. The prospective contribution of child labour to the natal family was probably negligible, particularly since youth had easy access to non-inherited land and wage incomes, and were therefore no longer constrained to remain faithfully at home to await their portions. These opportunities – to make a living beyond the purview of one's parents' guidance and independently of their resources – eroded the obligation to provide for them in old age. This too would weaken the incentive to childbearing. The extent of women's capacity to reduce childbearing

151

and shape their own reproductive careers is extremely difficult to estimate, as is the demographic impact of the Church's vicious repression of all such attempts. In any case, it is doubtful that fertility control *per se* was the primary factor in an overall decline in the birth rate (if indeed such a decline occurred).

It is very probable that most of the restriction was generated through a move towards the Western European marriage pattern, as it has come to be called. John Hajnal first identified what he dubbed the European marriage pattern, characterized by late (an average female age of twenty-three or over) and non-universal (less than 90 per cent) marriage.[72] It is more accurately termed Western European; Hajnal detected it west of a notional line from Trieste to Leningrad. To the East, marriage occurred somewhat earlier and was more universal. Subsequent research has amply confirmed his findings for the seventeenth century and later; but it is not yet clear when, and under what circumstances, the pattern first arose.

My guess is that it appeared in the aftermath of the Black Death – precisely when, by Malthusian reasoning, one might least expect to find it. In that conjuncture, peasant communities in the West developed a more stringent application of the impartibility rule in devolving the patrimony, a greater inclination to postpone marriage until sufficient resources had been marshalled, and a stricter prohibition on bearing children out of wedlock.[73] Raising the minimal threshold of marriage, these changes prevented post-plague fertility rates from spurting upwards as they did in the wake of less severe demographic crises.

At present, this must be considered a working hypothesis. (The available evidence for it will be considered below.) However counter-intuitive the argument seems by neo-Malthusian standards, it is worth taking seriously in the light of the better documented response of Irish peasants to the Famine of 1845–50. Land impartibility became the rule thereafter in most regions of rural Ireland. The average age at first marriage rose an astounding seven to eight years in the century from 1820 to 1920, while the celibacy rate doubled. Fertility rates never returned to their pre-Famine levels.[74] In Ireland as well, the quick demographic rebound in the aftermath of a mortality crisis failed to materialize.[75] Granted, mass emigration explains most of the further depopulation of Ireland in the wake of the Famine, just as subsequent plague outbreaks after the Black Death probably account for most of the continued contraction in late medieval Europe. But one doubts, in each case, whether these factors can explain it all. Was there not also a suppression of fertility via a declining incentive to marry and a tightening of impartible rules on customary holdings? The thesis has typically been formulated as an instinctive recoiling from the consequences of past improvidence, relying inordinately on a psychological response to the collective memory of plague trauma to account for fertility restriction. There is evidence that people *did* construe such lessons from the devastation.[76] This is not idle speculation. What is idealist is to imply that these beliefs were sufficient by themselves to generate a massive restriction of marriage in the absence of material changes in the conditions of household formation that might enable such beliefs to influence nuptial decision-making in demographically significant ways. We ought to relate this new-found prudence to changes in the mode of seigneurial exploitation and a shift in the balance of class power, as neo-Malthusian analysts have largely failed to do.

Different marriage patterns are bound up with divergent norms of household formation, co-residence and intergenerational wealth transfer. While in the West, neo-locality (in the narrow sense) and the weak-stem family form prevailed; in the East, patrilocality was customary in many regions, and strong stem and joint family forms were prevalent, giving rise to larger compound households with extended co-residence and co-operative production. The East/West difference in marital norms and family forms seems to be related to the differentiation in prevailing modes of seigneurial exploitation, originating in the generalized crisis of the feudal order in the fourteenth century. Labour services on the lord's demesne were intensified in Eastern Europe, while they were replaced by product and money rents in the West. These divergent trends appear to have fostered different patterns of land/labour-power equilibration. In the East, land tended to be redistributed around cyclical fluctuations in the size and dependency ratio of the co-resident family group; the integrity of holdings was safeguarded through the vertical extension of this group. In the West, land integrity was maintained through the delay and deterrence of marriage, and the labour-power of youth was redistributed between farmsteads through the institution of domestic service.[77] The late marriage system may have been coincident originally with a distinctive manorial infrastructure, comprised of the three-field strip system and nucleated village settlement, coupled with a strong tendency to local endogamy. Mitterauer and Sieder posit that 'extensive changes in the agrarian structure brought about by the colonizing movement of the High Middle Ages were confined precisely to those areas in which the European marriage pattern and corresponding family forms developed.'[78]

In the feudal system, as explained in the last chapter, landholding was tied to marriage. Lords were extremely reluctant to permit single people of either sex to take up tenancies while remaining single, or to retain them without remarrying if widowed. Although the size of merchet fines often made it more difficult to marry, the net effect of seigneurial influence was to hasten marriage and remarriage by driving to increase the number of places on the land, making marital status a condition of landholding and forcing senior tenants into early retirement, thus clearing the way for the marriage and entry of heirs. The underlying economic rationale for this seigneurial pressure was to ensure a full contribution from each tenant family to demesne agriculture and to broaden the productive base against which rents were drawn.

As the lords relinquished labour services and leased out demesne land, they dissipated their own drive and capacity to harness directly the younger generation's labour-power. This slackening was in marked contrast with Eastern Europe, where the extension of demesne cultivation intensified their interest in doing so. In the West, the seigneurial bond between landholding and marriage was loosened. The pressure on widows to remarry was eased, merchet fines declined, and young single men could often acquire land without marrying immediately. As the interference of lords in the marital affairs of their tenants was reduced, peasants became less servile and their village communities more autonomous.

Under this hypothesis, the origin of the Western European marriage system, holding fertility in check, lay in a twofold alteration which came about in the aftermath of the Black Death: a relaxation of the seigneurial union of landholding with marriage, and a concomitant tightening of the peasants' own community and familial rules governing the minimum requisites of marriage. The first factor raised the proportion of tenancies held by single and widowed people. The second factor intensified community pressure *not* to marry until a stable livelihood· had been achieved, augmenting the effect of the first. In a land-tight period, betrothal and premarital pregnancy were often used by impatient young people to provoke parental retirement and acquire a holding. In a situation where other land was readily available, the same impatience to get started as an adult producer now served as a rationale for *delaying* marriage. With a great deal of land available outside family inheritance, lords were inclined to ease the entry stipulations on family tenures, and parents felt compelled to offer settlements to unmarried children as soon as they reached the age of majority to ensure that they stuck around and remained committed to caring for their parents in old age. At the same time, the peasant community raised the minimum requisites of marriage, insisting that larger land parcels be assembled before assenting to a match. This was the prudent 'lesson' of the past calamities. The upshot of these changes was a trend to marital delay.

Standard neo-Malthusian reasoning predicts the opposite shift: an eased availability of land ought to induce earlier and more universal marriage, since there are places on the land that need filling. But this causal relation holds only if the normative link between landholding and marriage is not disturbed. In this particular conjuncture it *was* altered, with the paradoxical result that abundant land removed the younger generation's incentive to press for early marriage at the same time as it gave them more bargaining power in relation to their parents and lords. In this way, the incentive structure of marriage was conjuncturally tilted against early nuptials.

The foregoing is conjecture; what evidence can be mustered in its defence? In the aftermath of the Black Death, what happened to the mean age of women at first marriage?[79]   At this point, we have evidence only for the diametric 'corners' of Western Europe, Italy and England. In the late Middle Ages, men and women in Mediterranean Europe exhibited a marked disparity in mean marriage age. A number of studies, urban and rural, have found males marrying in their mid to late twenties, while females wed in their teens.[80] Women's ages were thus clearly outside the 'Western European marriage pattern'. Yet in Tuscany, Herlihy and Klapisch-Zuber found that the age of females at first marriage *rose* from 15.3 in the Prato countryside in 1372 to 19.5 a century later in a period of demographic recovery. In the city of Prato an even greater climb occurred: from 16.3 to 21.1 over the same period. A similar rise took place in Florence and the surrounding area: 'This delay in contracting a first marriage would tend to slow the formation of new families, [and] dampen the birth rate.'[81] Clearly, there was movement towards the late marriage system in fourteenth-century Italy, though it is uncertain when this distinctive nuptial regime was eventually consolidated. The rise in marriage age in Italy was evidently associated with an increase in dowry values in the same period: 'The difficulties of dowering a daughter preoccupied family heads.'[82] Dante had occasion to lament the passing of an age when:

> A daughter's birth did not yet fill
> A father's heart with fear
> For age and dowry had not yet fled
> To opposite extremes.[83]

In England, the medieval marriage pattern already looks 'European': in Rutland in 1377 and in Gloucestershire in 1381, a surprisingly low proportion of the population was married.[84] (It is difficult to believe that the proportion could have been any lower before the Black Death.) Hajnal had originally discounted the possibility that delayed and non-universal marriage could have arisen in medieval England, based on his reading of the Poll Tax rolls of 1377, which seemed to suggest that virtually the entire adult population was married. But Smith has recently reworked this source, with a heightened awareness of its limitations, and has convincingly refuted Hajnal's inference.[85] The best available source for late medieval England is the records of the Spalding Priory from five manors in the Lincolnshire Fenland, investigated by Hallam. He found a strong pattern of late marriage throughout the period for all five manors, estimating the mean age in two different ways. But his most significant and surprising finding was that the mean age of women at first marriage rose in four out of five manors: from twenty-four before the Black Death to twenty-seven in the century after.[86] Other estimates on English villages present a mixed picture. Razi calculates that the post-plague marriage age in Halesowen declined substantially for both men and women.[87] This is the only local study I have found which weighs against the hypothesis under consideration. Howell, in Kibworth Harcourt, found 'no very noticeable fall in marriage age' for men after the Black Death – it remained about twenty-five.[88] (Unfortunately, records did not permit her to gauge the demographically more relevant female age.) Finally, Campbell detected corroborating evidence in Coltishall for 'a demographic lurch in the late fourteenth and fifteenth century', reducing fertility through later and less frequent marriage.[89] Additional confirmation for England is found in Gottfried's large sample of wills from 1430 to 1480. While the sample is drawn from the propertied classes (those in a position to leave a will) it included many people of modest means, rural and urban. A remarkable 24 per cent of all males died unmarried, and 49 per cent of those who married died without a male heir. Fifty-four per cent left no children, while only 18 per cent had at least one child of each sex to succeed them. While the sample undoubtedly reflects very high levels of infant and child mortality, it also indicates the prevalence of delayed and non-universal marriage, which would curtail fertility very substantially.[90] These findings, while still preliminary, indicate that the distinctive Western European marriage pattern originated, in England at least, in the wake of the plague pandemic.

Regardless of when the emergence of the Western European marriage pattern is dated, one is bound to return to the late medieval period as a watershed. If the pattern is ultimately found to be medieval, then we would need to explain how it survived the catastrophic decline of the Black Death, and was subsequently revived as the land refilled in the sixteenth century. If, on the other hand, the system was not widespread in the high Middle Ages, then perhaps it was established, as suggested here, in the century 1350–1450, in response to plague devastation and the commutation of dues. Or, considering the final alternative, if the nuptial valve was established across Western Europe in the sixteenth and seventeenth centuries (when evidence for it first becomes indubitable), questions are raised about the difference between medieval and early modern social structures. Why did the latter, and not the former, generate the late and non-universal marriage pattern under land-tight conditions? Is not the difference attributable to changes in the seigneurial infrastructure in the intervening, late medieval, period? Whether or not the particular hypothesis I have proposed is sustained, the larger issue remains: what happened in the late medieval crisis which set the stage for the (original or subsequent) development of the high-threshold marital regime, distinguishing family reproduction in early modern Western Europe from every other pre-industrial formation known in history? The question is of interest well beyond the ranks of family historians. For this homeostatic fertility regime, at first through its blockage and later in its rupture, played a catalytic role in the 'primitive accumulation of proletarian labour-power', a prerequisite to industrial capitalism's ascent. We shall explore this second watershed, the bursting of the nuptial valve, in the final section of this chapter.

Demographic Recovery: 1450–1600

After a number of aborted spurts, the population of Western Europe finally resumed sustained growth in the 1450s. The generality of the recovery is striking: by 1500, numbers were on the rise in every major region. Yet the turning point was staggered, as one would expect. German growth resumed early in the fifteenth century, and had made up most of the previous century's one-third loss by 1500.[91] In England, periodic advances were thrown back sharply by recurrent plague outbreaks, and durable expansion did not resume until the last quarter of the fifteenth century.[92] Such unevenness was manifest within countries as well. In the Paris Basin, a relatively shallow decline was followed by a modest growth, perhaps 50 per cent between 1450 and 1560. In Provence, where the depression had been deeper, the recovery really got rolling in the 1470s and had trebled the number of households by 1540. In Normandy as well, severe losses were followed by a spectacular rebound, with growth of 70 per cent in just forty years.[93]

The rate of European demographic expansion in the 'long' sixteenth century is impressive by pre-industrial standards, especially since 'not a year passed without various cities or entire regions of Europe suffering badly from some epidemic.'[94] In France, Germany, England, the Netherlands and Norway numbers swelled at an average rate of 0.4 to 0.6 per cent per annum for eight to ten decades in a row. At this pace, populations double in one hundred and twenty to one hundred and fifty years. Some regions grew even faster: Holland, Sicily and Castille doubled in less than a century. On the continent, pre-plague ceilings of the fourteenth century were surpassed in most regions at some point in the middle decades of the sixteenth. Population growth tended to slow thereafter.[95] It appears that the English were slower to restore lost numbers than people in most regions of continental Western Europe; they probably did not exceed their pre-plague peak until the early seventeenth century.[96]

What triggered the fifteenth-century turnaround and then sustained rapid growth for a century or more: declining mortality, rising fertility, or some combination of the two? There is insufficient evidence to answer with assurance. The best guess is that improving life expectancy was the initial catalyst, but that the recovery was sustained and generalized through the sixteenth century by means of a rising, and then persistently high, birth rate. (Undoubtedly the respective contributions of mortality and fertility changes varied from place to place. Here as elsewhere, a summary estimate of the prevailing trend is presented.) Contemporaries most often attributed renewal to a respite from war and pestilence. With the end of the Hundred Years War and bloody conflict in southwest Germany in 1453, there was a brief lull in military and civil strife in Western Europe. This ebb was no doubt a factor, but probably a minor one, prolonging life in regions formerly ravaged by military campaigns and armies of occupation. In the century of most rapid overall population advance, 1470 to 1570, subsistence crises remained severe; there appears to have been no let-up on this front. In addition to numerous local crises, the years 1481–82, 1527–31, and 1556–57 were years of consecutive harvest failures; grain prices skyrocketed across the continent.[97]

Death by starvation was rare in the famines of early modern Europe. But chronic hunger and malnutrition took their toll on the poor, sapping their stamina, depressing the productivity of their labour, weakening their resistance to disease and suppressing fertility. While millions lived in abject poverty at all times in the early modern era, the fifteenth century was one of the best periods for the labouring poor. Wages were buoyant, land and food relatively cheap. It is probable that improved living standards (diet and shelter) contributed to a decline in death, particularly infant and child mortality. Epidemics still took their toll. Losses of a fifth to a third in one year were commonplace in cities, appearing horribly reminiscent of the Black Death. But such flare-ups were now localized, or at worst spread unevenly across a region. The continental sweep of the Black Death's first scourge never recurred. This difference may well have played a major role in prolonging life, unleashing the forces of demographic recovery in the sixteenth-century boom.

What happened to birth rates in the 1450–1550 recovery? The evidence is scant; the earliest continuous parish registers suitable for family reconstitution begin around 1540. In the preceding century we are reduced to weaker forms of evidence, coupled with deduction and educated guesswork. Gottfried's study of wills indicates that the English population was maintaining itself in the 1470s for the first time in the fifteenth century owing to a rising number of children per family. In the 1480s the proportion of his sample who married also rose, which would tend to lift the birth rate.[98]

Why would fertility rise in these decades? Heilleiner has postulated 'a certain weakening of the "prudential restraints" among wage-earning classes' by the early sixteenth century, with the bypassing of guild labour control in towns and the growth of casual wage labour, urban and rural. Some loosening of paternalist supervision of employers over the private lives of their workers would probably have raised the proportion of married people and lowered the average age of marriage. An English statute of 1555 complains of 'over-hasty marriages and over-soon setting up of households by the young folke of the city'.[99] From the mid sixteenth century when parish register materials begin, birth rates are already very high. In East Normandy, 'the factor chiefly responsible for [population] growth seems to have been the age of marriage, which was still low with the median age of 21–22 for women.'[100] In Holland, Jan de Vries discerned a similar pattern during a strong growth phase in the early seventeenth century. Finding evidence of high and rising mortality, he concluded that population increase could only have been due to an even higher birth rate, climbing more rapidly.[101] Dyer has reasoned along the same lines for England in the early sixteenth century. He builds a strong case that mortality must have worsened from 1450 to 1525. Vigorous growth throughout this period would therefore have been due to rising and high fertility.[102] From 1541 on, we are on firmer ground, thanks to the magisterial reconstruction of English population history by Wrigley and Schofield. In the second half of the sixteenth century, in a phase of rapid but decelerating growth, both fertility and mortality changes contributed substantially to fluctuations in the intrinsic growth rate.[103] If these patterns are indicative of growth dynamics on the continent, then buoyant fertility, through relatively easy marriage, made a substantial contribution to Western European demographic advance in this era.

Economic Recovery and Deteriorating Wages: 1450–1600

The population of Western Europe almost doubled between 1450 and 1600.[104] How was this remarkable expansion sustained? Agricultural productivity improved somewhat, particularly during the period 1450–1500. This was more as a result of enclosure, the consolidation of holdings, and a better balance between stockraising and grain-growing than by technological innovation. The advance permitted a slight urbanization; the proportion of city-dwellers in Northwestern Europe rose from an estimated 6.6 to 8.2 per cent over the course of the sixteenth century, and in Central Europe from 3.7 to 5.0 per cent.[105] While this entailed a modest reduction in the proportion of socially necessary labour time devoted to food production, agricultural efficiency did not improve sufficiently to sustain indigenous urban growth. Deaths exceeded births among city residents throughout the period. Without this persistent urban drain, population expansion would have been much greater.

If the source of growth was entirely rural, its axis remained primarily extensive: a vast move out on to sparsely settled land. It was reminiscent of the medieval boom in many ways: colonization east of the Elbe, new dyking advances against the North Sea, molecular migration upland from densely inhabited plains, the reconversion of pasture to arable, the draining of swamps, the tillage of waste; and everywhere, deforestation.[106] Yet the excursion pushed further than the great wave of 950 to 1300, particularly in its massive assault on the woods. Vast stretches of forest were cleared in the quest for more arable, but also to obtain wood for fuel and building materials.[107] The Crown and owners of great estates place increasingly stiff curbs on cutting and even on gathering. Restricted access to woodlands, treated formerly as commons, eliminated a vital means of supplementing subsistence for the swelling ranks of the land-poor, thus stimulating proletarianization.

The sixteenth century has been dubbed the age of 'price revolution'. By modern capitalist standards the inflation of that era appears rather tame, yet it was completely unprecedented at the time. The leader of the upward trend was grain, soaring in value as the century wore on. Between 1500 and 1600, its price rose 500 per cent in England, 379 per cent in Belgium, 651 per cent in France, 318 per cent in the Netherlands and 255 per cent in Germany.[108] The factor behind this trend was stagnant agricultural productivity in the face of swelling demand. Consider the latter factor first. Grain was the one commodity the masses could not do without. People continued to buy bread even when prices skyrocketed, cutting back on other less essential commodities. The rise in population clearly bolstered demand for grain; this was coupled with an increasing proportion of the population divorced from their own land, and therefore needing to purchase food staples. Throughout the sixteen century demand for grain, growing exponentially, outstripped supply; prices rose accordingly.

This relative shortage persisted for over a century, indicating that agricultural productivity had stagnated, running up against the old impasse of diminishing returns on increasingly marginal land. Otherwise, increasing investment in arable (more intensive weeding, tilling, new crop rotations and massive clearing efforts) would soon have boosted harvest yields to levels sufficient to have ended scarcity and punctured price inflation in a decade or two. The fact that this did *not* occur is a clear indication that the underlying block lay in the still essentially feudal disjunction between surplus expenditure and productive reinvestment, a failure which was exacerbated by the rapidity of demand expansion. The agricultural–industrial price ratio is a revealing measure of the underlying problem. Between 1500 and 1640, agricultural prices in England rose 2.3 times against industrial prices, and the ratio continued to deteriorate until 1730.[109] As the sixteenth century wore on, all the familiar symptoms of overextended feudal agriculture reappeared: a curtailment of animal husbandry in favour of arable expansion, insufficient manure, poor stockfeeding, resulting in a deterioration in ploughing stamina, the tilling of marginal soils and their subsequent erosion.

Land rents in the sixteenth century generally followed grain prices upward after some delay. The duration of the lag and the extent of the rise varied greatly, depending on the strength of customary tenure and the peasants' capacity to resist the circumvention of fixed dues by lords eager to cream off producer profit from the agrarian windfall. Where peasants were relatively weak – as on estates in the south of England, for example – rents nearly quadrupled from 1520 to 1580. In Eiderstedt, Germany, rents tripled over roughly the same period. In Languedoc, by contrast, well-entrenched peasant producers kept the bulk of the cereal price rise, as land rent rose only slightly from 1500 to 1560. In East Normandy as well, peasant resistance prevailed and a modest rise in nominal rents lagged far behind price inflation.[110] The entry fine was the one levy which the lords managed to extricate from the customary bundle of fixed dues. They hiked this charge steeply almost everywhere in the sixteenth century. As the rural population swelled, choice arable became scarce; country gentlemen, urban merchants and prosperous yeomen bid up its price in a hectic scramble for land.

While money wages rose slightly in the sixteenth century, their value declined severely in relation to the cost of grain and other foodstuffs which comprised about two-thirds of a wage-earning family's budget. Several continuous wage series have been assembled by historians and then set against the prices of various subsistence commodities to devise a rough measure of trends in real wages and hence proletarian living standards. While one would not wish to rely too heavily on any single series, their consistency across Western Europe is remarkable, and the overall picture is compelling. In Languedoc, Ladurie estimates that a 'grain wage' lost half its value between 1480–1500 and 1585–1600. In Lyon, on the basis of excellent records, the buying power of a 'wheat wage' dropped to half its original value between 1500 and 1597. A Modena 'bread wage' was devalued 50 per cent between 1530 and 1590, while a Florence wage slumped 60 per cent between 1520 and 1600. In Vienna, wages lost more than half their value against a standard basket of goods between 1510 and 1590; in Valencia, a similar decline occurred between 1500 and 1600. In southern England, a builder's wage fell to half its original value against a bundle of subsistence commodities between 1500–1509 and 1610–19.[111]

In the face of a prolonged labour glut, women's wages declined even further than men's, just as they had risen further in the preceding century in conditions of labour scarcity.[112] Since money wages were supplemented in the sixteenth century by payments in kind and domestic production, the decline in monetary equivalents cited above was probably somewhat attenuated. The deterioration of living standards was not quite as severe as the drop in real wages. When one considers, however, that the labouring poor had not been very far above the subsistence floor in 1500, the subsequent decline is awful to contemplate. The underlying cause is readily apparent: a deteriorating ratio of land to labour-power, swelling the ranks of the nearly landless, driving real wages down as the village poor became increasingly dependent on wage income to stay alive.

Peasant Polarization

In the course of the sixteenth century, village communities across Western Europe began to polarize, a process which would persist and deepen right through the nineteenth century. The trend was uneven; it began in arable regions, while pastoral districts were much slower to change. Whenever the pull of markets for agrarian commodities was strong, polarization proceeded apace; in remote regions, the dynamic was weaker and delayed. Despite such unevenness and variation (which was not effaced over time) the erosion of the formerly solid middle ranks of the peasantry was none the less a general phenomenon of the sixteenth and seventeenth centuries. In Languedoc,

> the medium-sized holding was literally ground to pieces ... the economic boom of the sixteenth century ... split the peasantry. A small group of *coqs de village* were growing rich from the exploitation and extension of their estates, but the peasant masses were sinking deep into poverty as a result of the subdivision of holdings.[113]

A similar polarization had taken place by 1660 in Picardy, a corn-growing plateau north of Beauvaisis:

> At the social peak was the large farmer, flanked by five or six laboureurs, down below was the wretched mass of manoevriers, between them nothing. ... Crushed by debt, the small peasants had to give up a large part of their land to their creditors.[114]

In England, the arable parish of Chippenham, Cambridgeshire, was transformed between 1560 and 1636:

> The larger copyholds of two yardlands and upwards were not affected; nor were the minute holdings of less than six acres. ... But the middle range of sixteenth century holdings, from a half yardland to one and a half yardlands, with one single exception, had disappeared completely.[115]

In Kibworth Harcourt,

> the small twelve acre holding had virtually disappeared by the seventeenth century. In its place we find on the one hand relatively prosperous holdings of over thirty acres, and on the other, a number of skilled craftsmen, carriers and tradesmen with little or no agricultural land.[116]

The same polarization eroded the ranks of the peasantry in rural Saxony. In 1550, 74 per cent of villagers were peasants, and 7 per cent cottagers; by 1750, only 39 per cent remained peasants, while the proportion of cottagers had swelled to 48 per cent.[117]

The precipitating factor in land loss was generally a string of bad harvests, plunging smallholders into debt from which they could not recover. Many gave up family farms and a life's work and stole away. Estate records are replete with brief matter-of-fact epigraphs to human tragedy: 'carried off his goods by night', 'dead insolvent', 'went off in debt and left his corn', 'ran away in debt to be a soldier'. The burden of bankruptcy on widows must have been crushing: 'There is nothing to be had: the man is dead and his wife and children are maintained by the parish.'[118] If mounting debt was the symptom, and harvest misfortune the final straw, what were the underlying causes of dispossession? Was the sixteenth-century land-jam essentially similar to a medieval squeeze, or were there novel features in the situation?

The model of the feudal mode of production developed in the last chapter predicted the build-up of a mass of cottagers at the base of the village hierarchy towards the end of a long wave of growth. Land was tight, the returns to new clearances were diminishing, and agricultural productivity was stagnant or in decline. The medieval countryside had experienced a swelling of nearly landless paupers in the thirteenth and early fourteenth centuries, as the feudal formation stalled and then plunged into crisis. Could not the early modern development be explained in essentially the same terms as its predecessor: as a consequence of overpopulation, an ecological law of diminishing returns to new arable and a fragmentation of established holdings, as Ladurie explained it in *The Peasants of Languedoc*? These factors were certainly in play, and I have endeavoured to give them their due. But they were combined with novel contradictions which gave the sixteenth-century boom and the seventeenth-century impasse their own distinctly capitalist impulsions.

There were two crucial differences. Medieval demand for hired hands in agriculture was never sufficient to forge a rural proletariat out of the swelling ranks of landless paupers; early modern demand was. Secondly, the thick middle ranks of the peasantry held firm in the medieval crunch; in the early modern land squeeze they disintegrated. These differences were intimately related. Medieval congestion produced a 'squeeze-down', broadening the base of the village pyramid. The early modern compression generated polarization, an increasingly bimodal land distribution, and the proletarianization of those who lost out in the scramble for scarce land. What had happened in the intervening period to alter the dynamics of peasant differentiation?

Contrast the fifteenth and sixteenth centuries in this regard. The leasing of demesne land in the fifteenth century gave the most prosperous peasant families an opportunity to become very substantial farmers, with holdings over one hundred acres. But as we have seen, the emergence of a distinct yeoman stratum did not immediately give rise to social polarization, rural proletarianization and the gradual demise of the middle peasantry. Land was still plentiful and yeomen could accumulate large tenancies without encroaching directly on smallholders or marginalizing them. Yeomen had limited market opportunities to exploit their advantage, since hired labour was relatively expensive and agricultural prices were chronically depressed. This combination deterred cash-crop specialization and farming on a grand scale, favouring the self-sufficient family-based team working a more modest holding. But in the sixteenth century, the market equation turned: grain prices climbed steadily, while real wages declined. The combination of cheap labour and high grain prices had also been prevalent in the thirteenth century, but the yoke of labour service had effectively prevented the upper peasantry from taking full advantage of the situation. With the commutation of dues and the conversion to money rents, agricultural income was separated from rent revenue. When peasants marketed the entire surplus product of their holdings and were no longer required to hand it over to the lord's agent or to divert their labour-power to farm the lord's demesne, rent ceased to represent the *direct* realization of the surplus product. The seigneurial levy was now mediated by the market, constituting a *post hoc* subtraction from revenues generated through the sale of the crop by peasant households. Producer profit put in a timid appearance, standing in the shadow of seigneurial rent.

Cereal prices were notoriously volatile in the early modern era, while rents remained sticky. The market demand for land and its going price were reasonably sensitive to the fluctuation of crop prices. Entry and renewal fees could thus be altered to reflect a rise in agrarian prices, but the rest of the rent bundle was fixed by custom on most holdings. The lords were thus caught in a contradiction between tenure structures which tended to fix rents, and a monetary form of surplus appropriation which opened the door to market vagaries and the subdivision of surplus value by means of the separation of profit from rent.

Whenever rents lagged behind a rise in cereal prices, as they frequently did in the sixteenth century, the yeomen (and gentry) who were in a position to sow a large crop and bring a good harvest to market could reap a cash windfall. The largest holders thus benefited out of all proportion to the size of their holdings. Rents would rise in turn to tap this new-found wealth, as entry prices were bid up and seigneurial exactions reimposed. These countermoves caught small- and middleholders in a squeeze. They had not profited much, if at all, from rising grain prices; their crops were mixed, grain surpluses were meagre, and they had sold in the market primarily to meet cash expenses. But they had to pay for the profits of their more prosperous neighbours, as rents chased agrarian profits in an upward spiral.

This is the market side of the equation; now consider its production foundation. Cash reserves enabled well-placed yeomen to take on servants and hire day labourers to meet the labour requirements of enlarged holdings. Since wages sank in the sixteenth century relative to grain prices, per unit labour costs decreased and hired labour became a real bargain. The optimal size of a holding rose. In the medieval context, very large holdings relying on hired hands were generally less efficient than either demesne farms utilizing coerced labour or middle-sized plots worked by peasant families.[119] But in a more market-oriented early modern context, where labour service had been relinquished, strips consolidated, and cash crops specialized to some degree, large holdings became more efficient. The economy of scale had changed. As long as cereal prices rose faster than rents and wages, the larger the holding the better. This was the context in which consolidation of large holdings proceeded at the direct expense of middle- and smallholders.

What were the consequences of this polarization for the class structure of the early modern countryside? There had been vertical antagonisms in medieval villages, based on the petty exploitation of the cottar underclass by the most prosperous peasant households. But the thick layer of households of intermediate size and wealth contained the conflict, cohering the peasantry as a social class. When this stratum was pulled apart, the village community's centre of gravity disappeared, and centrifugal forces were unleashed. The polarization of the village community was both reflected and reinforced through marriage patterns of class endogamy.[120] 'A marriage alliance [between proletarians and well-to-do peasants] was considered most improper, and landowning parents took great pains to prevent their children from making "unsuitable contacts".'[121]

The feudal peasantry began to disintegrate, differentiated by new class interests and alignments. Its upper stratum became increasingly prosperous commercial farmers; their material interests and outlook were gradually allied with the gentry. Both were keen to accumulate land, consolidate holdings, exploit the commons with large herds, or privatize them in a shift away from mixed arable towards cash-crop specialization. Subsistence-based peasants of modest means and poor cottagers tended to resist the practical steps necessary to reorganize agriculture along capitalist lines. They opposed large-scale enclosures by lords and yeomen, insisted on the right of familial reversion against the contractual prerogative of permanent land alienation, defended communal rights and sought to enforce stints limiting the size of herds on commons pasture.

The early modern transition thus engendered complex new alignments of class forces on the land. Conflict within the village community, formerly contained, now broke open. This strife arose within the larger arena of class struggle, where alignments up above (between the Crown, great landlords, upstart gentry and the rising bourgeoisie) were fluid and shifting. This double axis of class forces – a struggle within a struggle – determined, in large measure, the pace of capitalist reorganization in agriculture. If the yeoman stratum (either as freeholders or tenants) received decisive support for engrossment from a prevailing constellation of ruling forces, it could defeat the subsistence-based peasantry, break up the middle core of the feudal village, and drive forward to land concentration and cash-crop specialization. The real success stories in this regard were the Low Countries early in the period, and England from 1520 to 1670. If, however, the peasantry were able to garner support from above for the preservation of customary holdings, communal use rights and unfenced arable, the emergent yeomanry were held in check, unable to effect a transition to capitalist agriculture. Mediterranean Europe, by and large, exhibited this restraint, retreating from the brink of the traverse in the seventeenth-century crisis.[122]

PART II: PROLETARIANIZATION AND CHANGING FAMILY FORMS

From the sixteenth century onwards, the process of proletarian formation – the making of the modern working class – takes centre-stage in this account. Roughly 88 per cent of the total growth of the European population between 1500 and 1800 was comprised of the expansion of those dependent (in whole or in part) on wage income for their subsistence.[123] 'Proletarianization is the single most far-reaching change that has occurred in the Western world'; 'the essential link between the large-scale processes of capitalist development and the lives of ordinary people.'[124] It is a fundamental oversight to embark on a study of early modern family forms without clarifying the main features of proletarianization in the societies under investigation. Yet this is what the Cambridge Group have done, soldiering on in the vapid mists of modernization theory. Before resuming my own account, it is essential to discuss a number of related issues concerning this concept, and the historical realities to which it refers.

There are two facets to the proletarian condition. The first is the *need* to secure income, via the wage, in order to obtain the means of subsistence. The second is the *labour* one performs for an employer to achieve the first. Note four points concerning the relation between these two facets:

1. The need is the consistent precondition of wage labour; people do not normally bother to work for employers if they do not require wage income to subsist.

2. Since it is the employers' prerogative to hire, the need for wage income and the resulting search for employment is insufficient to secure a job. Furthermore, the need persists – indeed, it usually intensifies – in the face of the failure to obtain work.

Proletarianization is thus a twofold process. The negative side is the rising insufficiency of alternative means of securing subsistence, and therefore the increasing need to obtain wage work. The positive side is the attainment of enough work to meet the need. Since the first cannot secure the second, negative proletarianization can proceed far in advance of the demand for wage labour, and hence be accompanied by mass unemployment and under-employment. The importance of the negative/positive distinction for demographic developments will become clear when proletarianization in the seventeenth century is contrasted with that in the eighteenth and nine-teenth centuries.

3. While the need for subsistence persists in the absence of employment, the converse is not true. Excess labour supply does not elicit increased demand in the same proportion. From 1550 on, the supply of proletarian labour chronically exceeded employer demand.[125] This condition was fundamental to capital accumulation in the early modern era.

4. As we move from a consideration of subsistence needs to the performance of wage labour, our unit of analysis shifts. Needs are manifest at the level of the domestic *group*. The household supplies a particular mix of its mem-bers' labour power to employers, and lives as a co-resident group on the total income received in return. Yet in the labour market and the work-place, workers' domestic circumstances are systematically ignored. Normal-ly they are hired and fired *as individuals,* receiving the wage as a personal payment.

While discussing the wage relation at great length, marxists have largely failed to come to terms with the asymmetric connection between the subsist-ence and production facets of this relation. In orthodox accounts, the individ-ual wage-earner is taken for granted as the point of departure. 'The worker' is assumed to be male and the family's sole breadwinner, though this presump-tion generally remains implicit, the household being entirely peripheral to the field of interest. Such tunnel vision, fixated on men's labour at 'the point of production', ignores the unpaid domestic labour of proletarian subsistence, overwhelmingly women's work. This myopia inadvertently reinforces the fetishism of the wage form, which appears as a personal payment for labour performed in the workplace, rather than as a fund for the domestic reproduc-tion of the household's labour-power. The theoretical point is that the house-hold, not the individual wage-earner, must be the primary unit of analysis in an adequate account of the proletarian condition.

What engenders the proletarian response of seeking wage labour? The con-ventional marxist answer is that people will become (and remain) proletarians only when they are utterly dispossessed and have nothing else to sell but their labour-power.[126] This definition excludes *semi*-proletarian households from our purview. It would be more correct to say that households will offer their members' labour-power in return for wages when alternative livelihoods are insufficient to meet their basic needs. They may or may not be devoid of productive property when this need arises. In Western Europe, peasant expropriation unfolded gradually and unevenly over time; most early proletarians were already resorting to supplementary employment before they had completely lost their places on the land. There were several ways to gain a minimal livelihood in the early modern era, involving the land-poor masses in a variety of production relations with employers and merchants. Most households took up a combination of means, interspersing them strategically over the course of the year. We cannot validly speak of proletarianization as a once-and-for-all transition.

The course of proletarian formation is deeply conditioned by people's pre-existing relations of production. Since there is no common pre-capitalist genesis in world history, there can be no globally relevant scenario of proletarianization. Proletarianization has entailed upward mobility for ex-slaves and serfs, and descent for producers of formerly independent means. The process has raised and lowered people's living standards. Wage labour has been welcomed, eagerly pursued, and considered a high-status livelihood in the community; and it has (more often) been shunned, resisted, and reluctantly taken up, initially only by the poorest households of a community. There are a myriad of routes to full proletarian engagement with capital, and a broad variety of cultural meanings associated with them. An adequate theoretical framework for comprehending proletarianization must allow for its full historical diversity. Finally, to understand proletarian formation, we must try to ascertain in what proportions the swelling ranks of the proletariat are comprised of (a) incomers from adjacent classes, the children of peasants for example; and (b) the self-expansion of proletarian families by means of an excess of births over deaths. The particular mix of these sources has major implications for the dynamics of proletarianization. We shall assess this question below, looking at Charles Tilly's pathbreaking work on the components of proletarian expansion.[127]

The common denominator of the proletarian condition is need-induced necessity to seek wage labour in order to attain the means of subsistence for oneself and one's dependants. Upon the rock of necessity, people are forced to choose. Wherever jobs are available, they will seek wage work when no better way of securing the means of subsistence is at hand and non-proletarian alternatives are worse. To form a proletariat, the 'better ways' (a viable holding, a workshop, or a trade) must be placed out of reach. Marx was perfectly correct to emphasize the removal of these options from the grasp of the great mass of labourers through political exclusion and economic displacement. But what of 'worse ways'? Employment will be 'freely' sought whenever non-proletarian alternatives entail a lower living standard; a more demeaning status; more stress, exhaustion and hazard; closer supervision; less independence and leisure-time. At every level of economic development, cultural values are blended with a concern to improve material living standards. But among the poor, in contrast with the rich, the calculus of relative advantage often entails making cruel trade-offs between requisites of well-being. Domestic producers in the early modern era cherished their independence. They were prepared to accept somewhat lower living standards in the struggle to preserve small-scale means of production which were barely viable.[128]

Short of starvation (though within the realm of constant hunger), there were marginal ways for the propertyless to keep body and soul together without resorting to wage labour. They might try poaching, begging, street vending, poor relief or a stay in the workhouse. But these alternatives were widely considered, not just by the prosperous but by the destitute as well, to be inferior to a job, almost any job. They virtually precluded stable family life and household maintenance. The manipulation of 'subproletarian' alternatives by state authorities shaped the supply of proletarian labour-power, as did the displacement of clearly superior alternatives. The work of Lis and Soly has been exemplary in illuminating the underside of proletarian formation in the early modern era.[129]

One can place the proletarian populace on a continuum, based on the extent of a household's reliance on wage income to secure the means of subsistence. For expository purposes, however, it is convenient to break the continuum somewhat arbitrarily by defining two household types: in a semi-proletarian household, wage income is combined with other means of subsistence and both make indispensable contributions to household maintenance; a fully proletarian household has no other way to put bread on the table, and so relies almost entirely on wage income to secure the means of subsistence. Normally, the extent of a household's wage dependency (the negative condition) will be matched with a typical employment pattern (the positive side), so I have utilized both facets of the proletarian condition in identifying their typical features. These are outlined below for fully proletarian households, and their converse suggests a semi-proletarian form:

(a) In a fully proletarian household, at least one of the members is employed year-round.

(b) Full proletarians are hired and fired as individuals, not as subcontracted members of a group. All wages are paid directly to hired workers.

(c) The wage is completely monetary and paid out regularly at short (one- or two-week) intervals. Workers receive nothing else in exchange for their labour-power.

(d) Wage labour is regularized as shiftwork, established and policed according to clock time.

(e) There is a complete separation of the employer's workplace from the space and property of the employees' households.

(f) Workers are free from employer supervision in their lives off the job and away from his premises.

(g) All provisions necessary for subsistence are obtainable in local markets at prices within reach of the households of regularly employed wage-earners.

(h) Domestic labour is reduced to obtaining consumer goods in the market and converting them into consumables. No form of goods production occurs in fully proletarian households.

(i) The private costs of raising the next generation are funded by wage income.

Proletarianization took place over centuries in Western Europe. The process got under way on a mass scale in the sixteenth century and was by no means completed at the close of the nineteenth. In the 1860s and 1870s, for example, it was still common to find semi-proletarian arrangements: wages taken partly in kind, putting out, family hiring, subcontracting and various forms of subsidiary domestic production. Since proletarianization advanced by fits and starts in a highly uneven fashion, there is no single sequence of change in the above-mentioned elements that might capture the experience of most working-class households.

The need for wage income may arise suddenly, marked by a precipitating event or rapid sequence of events: a string of disastrous harvests, quickly mounting debt, eviction or desertion of a holding, followed by a desperate search for replacement income.[130] The need may also arise more gradually, entailing no sudden rupture with a non-proletarian trade, occupation or enterprise. A smallholder has his rent hiked, loses a son to the army and his daughter gets married. In response, he hires out a chunk of his land and increases the household's labour-power offered to a wealthy landholder in the village by bringing his second son along at harvest time. His wife takes in piecework supplied by a merchant to help pay the rent. Incremental proletarianization is potentially reversible. The first son returns, the leased parcel is taken back, cereal prices rise and the family's own land is no longer a net liability. Nor is it uncommon, in a period of substantial proletarian growth, that a minority of households manage to 'swim against the tide', repossessing what had formerly been lost, regaining the viability of independent livelihoods and curtailing wage labour. The course of proletarianization is much more chequered at the level of individual households and parent–child permutations than it is when viewed at an aggregate level, where 'net result' is the index of change. The problem is analogous to studying migration flows. A net migration of 1,000 people a year may turn out to be a movement of 1,100 in and 100 out, or it may be 3,000 in and 2,000 out. Obviously these are very different patterns, and the disparity has major social implications. In working with historical source materials, it may be difficult to tell them apart, yet it is certain that the difference will be invisible if one does not look for it.

With due regard for the unevenness of proletarianization across Western Europe, can any generalizations be made concerning the overall pattern? It is my impression (sure to be contradicted by numerous exceptions) that the course of Western European proletarianization between 1500 and 1750 was:

(a) Mostly comprised of semi-proletarian progressions. Households maintained some land, but required supplementary wage income to subsist.

(b) Incremental economic displacement was the rule; expropriation at a stroke was exceptional.

(c) With mixed livelihoods the norm, the bulk of wage-earning households were generalists, surviving through 'an economy of makeshifts'.[131]

(d) Since most work was seasonal, the labouring poor relied on combining employments, which they alternated and meshed with one another through the year. Specialization came later, in the 1750–1900 period.

(e) While the main movement was off the land into the proletarian ranks, there was a good deal of 'eddy flow' back to the land and into independent trades, though this declined over time, becoming much more unidirectional in the latter half of the eighteenth century.

(f) Despite traffic back and forth, the net result was remarkably continuous. At no time from 1500 on did the ranks of the wage-earning populace stop growing. Not only did numbers increase absolutely, but the proletariat expanded relative to the total population in all periods, though the tempo was uneven.

(g) Immigration from other classes supplied most of the early growth, while self-expansion became predominant in the eighteenth century. In England at least, influx became relatively insignificant in the nineteenth century, as the proletariat grew exponentially through an excess of births over deaths.

(h) The rising need for wage income ran far in advance of available employment throughout the early modern era. Most proletarian households were underemployed, especially during slack winter months. In the transition to industrial capitalism, chronic labour surplus and depressed wages were essential preconditions of capital accumulation.

Proletarianization and Capital Accumulation

It is often assumed that the momentum of capital accumulation, once under way, drives proletarianization inexorably through to conclusion. In reality, the process is more contingent, as Immanuel Wallerstein has noted with regard to the peripheral formations in the world capitalist economy.[132] There are obstacles to full proletarianization within the fields of both capital and labour: let us consider each in turn. Under certain circumstances, maximizing the rate of exploitation entails halting proletarianization halfway, so that wages may remain very low and the costs of reproducing a new generation of producers may be partially funded within another, subordinate, mode of production:

> Competition permits the capitalist to deduct from the price of labour power that which the family earns from its own little garden or field. The workers are compelled to accept any price offered to them, because otherwise they would get nothing at all and they could not live from the products of their agriculture alone, and because, on the other hand, it is just this agriculture and landownership which chains them to the spot and prevents them from looking around for other employment. ... The whole profit is derived from a deduction from normal wages.[133]

Such semi-proletarian arrangements were commonplace in early modern Europe, just as they have been in Third World countries in this century. They can be extremely profitable, provided employers have ready markets for their products elsewhere and are not dependent on generating effective demand for consumer goods within the communities of their present labour force. In the phase of 'primitive accumulation', as Marx termed it, capitalists drew 'fresh blood' from the countryside, freely replacing urban veterans worn out from overwork at an early age in mines, mills and sweatshops. Employers relied, in other words, on externalizing the generational replacement costs of labour-power, continuing to extract wealth from subordinate modes of production while undermining their viability in the long run.

There is, ultimately, a limit to this form of extensive accumulation, which thrives by maintaining a separation between the reproduction cycles of labour-power and capital. In order to deepen capital accumulation, it becomes necessary to integrate the fields of production and exchange by raising real wages and hence the effective demand of proletarian households, so that they comprise an ever-growing sector of the market for consumer goods. However, once the process of extensive capital accumulation has been well entrenched, employers may find it difficult to wean themselves from a dependency on cheap labour in order to go over to a more capital-intensive investment pattern. Real wages must be raised and the subsistence costs of the future labour force included in the employers' wage fund. All this must of course be achieved without provoking a sustained rise in per unit labour costs which would undermine the rate of exploitation, the average rate of profit, and the pace of capital accumulation. The only way this hump can be traversed is by effecting a sustained rise in labour productivity, generally on the basis of capitalist reorganization and sustained technological progress.

In the early modern period, capital accumulation in Western Europe was predominantly extensive. Until the mid eighteenth century, wage income constituted a fairly small fraction of effective demand in the marketplace. While this portion grew considerably as the proletariat multiplied and deepened its reliance on wage income, it was mostly met by local enterprises – farms and workshops – which were small-scale and undercapitalized. Until the close of the early modern era, wage income as effective demand did not furnish a major stimulus to the concentration and centralization of capital. Capital reaped continuous profits from semi-proletarian arrangements, developing a vested interest in their maintenance, which was subsequently difficult to surmount in the eighteenth and nineteenth centuries.[134]

There were obstacles to full proletarianization on the supply side of the labour market as well. Early proletarian households were drawn overwhelmingly from the poorest ranks of society. They were losers in the cruel competition for respectable trades and scarce places on the land. The opportunity to pick up occcasional work was welcomed, but poor families sought to limit their reliance on wage labour, above all because early modern wages were notoriously insecure. The demand for labourers operated on a seasonal, episodic, and task-oriented schedule, and there were many more seeking work than there were jobs. Far from being viewed as an upward route to independence and security (as the phrase 'free labour' suggests), wage labour was seen as a downward path to abject dependency and vulnerability.[135] While there was nothing wrong with moving in and out of the labour market, it was a horrible fate to become permanently attached to it. Few could do so even if they had wanted to: steady year-round jobs were scarce. It was therefore normally impossible to stabilize a household on wage income alone. The more

reliant the poor were on wage income, the more peripatetic was their existence; they moved on from job to job and place to place, eking out a bare
subsistence with no capacity to accumulate savings and without a shred of
residential security. Full proletarianization also entailed the loss of inheritance-
based family continuity. Young people could no longer count on parents to
secure their livelihoods and futures; and parents, for their part, could no longer
rely on their children to support them in old age. These were deeply unset-
tling circumstances for both generations, but perhaps especially for the elderly.
We will consider these changes in greater detail subsequently.

The prospects of losing inheritance-based family continuity furnished a
powerful motive for resisting full proletarianization. The labouring poor
fought bitterly against all measures, from enclosures to the introduction of
factory machinery, which politically suppressed or economically displaced alternative livelihoods. Every independent means of livelihood, from hunting
and fishing rights to a knitting frame, a cow and a garden, were vigilantly
defended and intensely worked. The poor often stuck with alternative livelihoods at levels of real income which were beneath those available at going
wage rates for regular employment, making their own independence paramount even as they sunk into poverty.[136] Far from becoming habituated to
wage work, they tried to use their wages to re-establish independent livelihoods, scrimping and saving in order to purchase a bit of land, buy a loom,
start up a small shop and so on. In short, they resisted full proletarianization
every step of the way – not because 'they had no choice', but rather because
they considered wage work under the employer's nose, on a permanent basis,
to be a step down from their prior livelihoods, a loss of independence and
self-esteem, a debasement of their persons. The effect of mass refusal was to
absorb underemployment locally, limiting the supply of proletarian labour-
power, retarding the development of capitalism. The English breakthrough
was based, in large part, on dismantling this reservation.

To summarize: in the early modern context, semi-proletarian arrangements
of all sorts proliferated because they were immediately advantageous to employers and employees, each for their own reasons. Since both classes resisted
full proletarianization, the transition to industrial capitalism was neither inexorable nor foreordained.

The Land-Poor and the Landless, the Settled and the Vagrant

With vigorous population growth and the concentration of choice arable and
enclosed pasture in fewer hands, the 'long' sixteenth century saw a massive
proliferation of land-poor and landless households. Thus far in this account,
these two strata have been mentioned in the same breath, as if the propertyless

were a subclass of peasant cottagers who had slipped further down the slope of
rural poverty without altering their class relations. While this assumption was
adequate in a discussion of the Middle Ages, it becomes untenable in the early
modern era. There is a basic difference in the labour supply conditions of the
two strata.[137] Those who retained a foothold on the land could resist the lure
of employment elsewhere; the households of smallholders were able to absorb
their own underemployment to some extent. The landless lacked the resources
to do this and were thus open to full proletarianization. The state played a role
in deepening this cleavage. While the 'settled poor' had a recognized place in
society and were generally eligible for local poor relief, the 'rogues and vagabonds' were uprooted and marginalized, hounded by state authorities wherever they went.[138] To appreciate this divergence, we shall consider the fate of
each stratum in turn.

What portion of the swelling populace subsisting on wage income was
utterly propertyless, divorced from the land and lacking any domestic means
of production? How rapidly did this portion increase before the spread of the
factory system? It is extremely difficult to answer these questions with much
precision. With the polarization of peasant holdings in the sixteenth century,
it becomes meaningless to dwell on their average size. A better measure for
our purposes is the proportion of all holdings beneath a minimum threshold
of self-sufficiency for a typical family group. While such a cutoff point is
quite arbitrary (and will vary with the composition of the household, the level
of rent, the soil type and crops being farmed), a benchmark of this sort nevertheless provides a rough estimate of the proportion of producer families on
the land needing supplementary income to get by. The share rises in the
sixteenth and early seventeenth centuries. In seven parishes in the Paris basin,
94 per cent of all holdings were less than 5 hectares, and in an area south of
Poitou, 88 per cent were less than 2.5 hectares. At Serignan in Languedoc,
the number of 'ridiculously tiny holdings' more than doubled in three decades from 1520 to 1550. Everitt reckons that 'peasant labourers' living on
five acres or less made up a quarter to a third of the entire population of
England in Tudor and early Stuart times. Gregory King's survey for 1688,
which has stood the test of time remarkably well, estimated 'labouring people
and out servants' at 23 per cent of the English population; 'cottagers and
paupers' at 24 per cent, while another 3 per cent were 'freeholders of a lesser
sort'. Together, these strata comprised half of the entire population; probably
a majority of them held some land, while working for wages at least part of
the year. Within the burgeoning ranks of the smallholders, those with the
least land were multiplying most rapidly. On a sample of forty-three English
manors before 1560, cottagers with just a garden comprised 11 per cent of all
tenants holding less than six acres; by 1600–10, their proportion had risen to
35 per cent.[139]

It was the grain-growing side of traditional peasant farming that most often collapsed, as holdings were reduced to little more than extensive gardens with perhaps a toft and close or small orchard attached. At a time when grain prices were rising, peasant cottagers had to enter the local market as purchasers of bread. The same price hikes which enriched neighbouring yeomen impoverished cottagers. Everitt's survey of English probate inventories indicates that all but the poorest kept livestock: one or two cows supplying milk, cheese and butter for home use, and perhaps a few sheep furnishing wool for domestic production. Extending Everitt's probate sample, Carole Shamas has calculated the proportion of English 'peasant labourers' owning a cow from the late sixteenth to the early eighteenth centuries. While holding steady in the North, cow ownership in the rest of England declined dramatically. Roughly two in three labourers owned a cow at the start of the period; only one in five did at the close. In a survey of rural labourers' households in 1787–96, only 1 per cent possessed cows, 15 per cent pigs, and 33 per cent gardens. Most of their food was purchased from tradesmen, pedlars or at market.[140] By the end of the eighteenth century, the majority of English labourers were evidently devoid of any productive property. On the continent, the proportions were reversed. In rural Saxony, Fischer found a pattern much more like the North of England. In two centuries of massive proletarianization, 'the small non-peasant property holders had risen more than fifteen times, by far the highest growth rate within the Saxonian population, the growth of the propertyless class being 49 per cent and that of the peasants 16 per cent, the lowest of all groups.'[141]

As long as they could retain their use rights in commons, cottagers could still eke out an existence, avoiding complete dispossession. Grazing rights on common pastures were thus critical to the smallholder's livelihood. A loss of animals often removed the only protein from the family's diet.[142] But other traditional commons rights were also invaluable: access to stone quarries and gravel pits for house and fence repair; and to the woods for building materials, fuel and small game. Even in England, where the drive to enclosure had gone the furthest, most smallholders retained their essential common rights through the seventeenth century; on the continent, except for the Low Countries, the vast majority did. But local forests furnished less of a subsistence cushion than they had two hundred years earlier; they had been cut way back. Fallen timber and wild game were not as easy to come by. In England, an acute timber shortage developed in the sixteenth and seventeenth centuries, the price of firewood leapt up, and coal became an essential household energy source, despite widespread revulsion against 'that noxious mineral'.[143] Under the Crown's domain, the largest forests were increasingly closed to plebeian use. When the arable side of small-scale agriculture collapsed, it was harder to retreat into forest and fen than it had been in the medieval era, though many squatter communities did spring up in the sixteenth and seventeenth centuries. In France, the Water and Forest Ordinance of 1669 was a major turning point, producing 'a positive revolution in the conception of human settlement'. Thereafter, the forests were turned over to professional managers for the sole purpose of producing trees, and the poor were increasingly barred from the woods.[144]

A few livestock, a garden, even a small field or two, were not enough for a family to live on. Hard-pressed households thus needed to develop a non-agricultural moneymaker to supplement their land-based income. There were two main options: to seek employment outside the house or to establish a cottage industry; often they were pursued in combination. Both livelihoods were headwaters of the great proletarian river whose rural tributaries would eventually converge in nineteenth-century industrial towns. While the former developed a direct and increasing reliance on wage income, the latter proceeded indirectly, detouring through a phase of petty commodity production. Let us look briefly at each stream.

The great bulk of common rural labourers were farm hands; most of the rest were miners and quarrymen. Proto-industrial households relied exclusively on family labour and did not normally hire other workers. Farm hands who held land in a village sought work locally and lived at home. Their lives were very different from those of farm servants, who lived in their master's house and came under his supervision and authority twenty-four hours a day.[145] While live-in servants were generally young and single, day labourers were more likely to be married and living with their own families. For many cottagers, the two types of farm employment defined basic stages in their lives. After being servants from their teens to their twenties, they would quit service to marry. Setting up their own households, cottagers would then require supplementary income and hire out as day labourers. Episodic employment suited cottagers still rooted on the land. Unlike landless labourers who were looking for steady employment, local cottagers were primarily oriented to their own land and domestic industries, and sought short-term wage labour close at hand to supplement their income. This selective and locally confined orientation to the labour market was predicated on possession of a holding which still furnished the majority of a family's food provision. Smallholders were often hampered by scheduling conflicts at times of peak demand for agricultural labour-power. If they were growing the same basic crop mix as their more prosperous neighbours, they had their own planting and harvest schedules to meet in the weeks when the large estates were hiring:

> The landholding peasant had too much to do on his own land to be able to spare much time for work outside the holding. ... [But he] welcomed occasional short contracts; weeding, harvesting, hedging and ditching or part-time tanning or wheel-making.[146]

Over time, however, this orientation shifted, as smallholdings splintered further, grain-growing became unviable, and families required more off-farm income to survive. As their own harvests disappeared, cottagers more eagerly sought out peak-season employment with prosperous yeomen and gentlemen farmers. They found themselves in direct competition with itinerant farm labourers and with hordes of poor townsfolk streaming down country roads in search of harvest work. 'Two factors assumed vital dimensions in their lives: namely, the number of days' work they could get in a year and the amount of real wages that could be earned in a day.'[147]

If the position of land-poor 'peasant labourers' was economically tenuous, their neighbours who were completely dispossessed sank into utter destitution. As a general rule, the more reliant families were on wage income, the poorer they became relative to other members of the community. Land loss had other less noted effects on early modern families. In the first place, they were compelled to rearrange their members' labour-power:

> The more men's economic activities came to be located outside the cottage or croft or directed to specialized trades and crafts, the more activities women assumed in and around the home. ... Furthermore, the periodic absence of men gave women responsibility for a number of decisions concerning the family and household economy.[148]

The daily exit of men from the household to go to work for others, wherever family members did not accompany them, was a far-reaching change in family relations, undermining traditional forms of patriarchal authority. Paradoxically, the same shift often increased the reliance of families on men as primary breadwinners, thus inaugurating a new, distinctly proletarian, form of patriarchal power. David Davies, writing in 1795, commented on the effects of enclosures on the family economy: '[formerly] not only the men occupying those tenements, but also their wives and children too, could ... employ themselves profitably at home, whereas now, few of these are constantly employed ... so that almost the whole burden of providing for their families rests upon the men.'[149] This form of patriarchal authority, based on the prerogatives accruing to the family's major breadwinner, will be discussed at length in *Weathering the Storm*.

The landless could remain residentially settled in durable family groups only if their members were able to obtain a minimal level of employment on an annual basis. If the local demand for wage labour was insufficient, proletarian tenants failed to meet their rents, debts would mount, and evictions or desertions would follow, as individuals took to the road in search of work. Since employment in the early modern era was typically seasonal, short-term and task-oriented, it was impossible for most of those who were devoid of any productive property to remain settled in a community for very long. The cleavage between residentially settled and transient wage-earners is perhaps the most significant division in the ranks of the proletarianizing populace, giving rise to considerable antagonism. The local state authorities persistently tried to regulate this relationship through poor law measures, keeping the two populations separate.

Yet a clear majority of the entire rural wage-earning populace seem to have remained rooted and residentially stable in the sixteenth and seventeenth centuries. Transience increased markedly in the eighteenth century, particularly in the latter half, as genuinely national labour markets emerged. This relative stability was due to land retention, not to the availability of year-round employment. King placed the 'vagrant' population of England at a mere 0.5 per cent (30,000) in 1688. While this figure appears far too low, we could multiply it by ten and still have a stratum less than a quarter the size of either 'cottagers and paupers' or 'labouring people and out servants'. In France, Goubert places vagrants at 200,000 in the seventeenth-century, which again represents only 0.6 per cent of the entire population, and a fraction of the settled, semi-proletarian populace.[150]

The upper classes became obsessed with the growth and behaviour of the utterly destitute at the bottom of the proletarian heap: 'vagabonds, rogues, masterless men, and idle persons'. 'No century has been so conscious of the poor as the sixteenth.'[151] The literature and public rhetoric of the time produced a seething cauldron of alarmist imagery, an intoxicating mix of ecclesiastical wrath, lurid sexual projection and ruling-class paranoia. In a typical ouburst, a Kent magistrate castigated 'vagrant and flying beggars who infect and stain the earth with pilfery, drunkenness, whoredom, bastardy, murder and infinite like mischiefs'.[152] Vagrants were not a new sight in the back alleys and roadsides of early modern Europe; why did they attract such opprobrium and state repression in the sixteenth century? In part it was the obvious multiplication of their ranks and their aggressive approach to public begging. In 1594, twelve times as many beggars swarmed the streets of London as in 1517.[153] The prelates of Brabant declared: 'We find ourselves in such great poverty that it is not possible to describe it. We cannot prevent the country dwellers from leaving as they have already done in many places.' Many itinerants ventured far from home; 22 per cent of a large sample of vagrants in seventeenth-century England were picked up more than a hundred miles from their place of birth. A fifth of the vagrants passing through Amiens in the same period had come from Normandy.[154]

Outside the cities, hordes of vagabonds and journeymen, mostly young single males, roamed the countryside in search of employment, alms, and poaching opportunities in unsupervised fields and woods. Settlements of squatters sprang up in forests and around the edges of commons. In 1573, the established residents of Feckenham Forest in Worcestershire, numbering five hundred, brought suit before the Court of Requests declaring that 'the population of the Forest was above five thousand people'. Squatters asserted the customary right to remain resident in cottages erected on waste overnight, though the claim was rarely upheld by early modern courts. Two paupers from Kent explained that they had 'adventured upon' the construction of their huts 'for they were destitute of houses, and had seen other cottages upon the same wastes built by other poor men.'[155] Forest congregations, however, could rarely be considered settled communities; they were more often temporary camping grounds for wayfarers, frequently raided and dispersed by wardens. Growing landlessness placed tremendous pressure on available housing stock, severing the connection between dwellings and holdings. The consolidation of holdings emptied older and inferior dwellings, which then fell into disrepair and were torn down.

The inevitable corollary of male transience was family desertion. The rolls of village poor relief reflected the residuum of the tramping phenomenon; a majority of claimants were women with children. Poor law records disclose that many poor women were deserted by suitors and husbands.[156] The spectre of family disintegration among the poor – a complete rupture with conjugal monogamy and durable cohabitation – haunted the imaginations of the propertied classes. Repeated references in sixteenth-century tracts, sermons, and court sentences to sexual iniquities (bastardy, whoredom and sodomy) registered moral panic: familial norms were being flouted, with dire consequences for future generations. While the poor were generally blamed for their failure to replicate the prevailing family forms of the propertied classes, it is not difficult to discern in such outbursts a more cogent ruling-class concern with the disruptive effects of proletarianization upon the cohesion of poor families. Certainly landlessness and its attendant ills, penury and vagrancy, were associated with high rates of both wife desertion and extramarital childbirth.[157] Arthur Young, one of the more astute observers of his day, clearly saw the connection between enclosure and increasing desertion.

> Is [desertion] not a common crime at present in every parish in the Kingdom? And why do they do it? Because under the present laws they have not the motive to abstain from it, which they would have if they were in a better situation. The system of [renewed access to] land would probably be found the best prevention of this crime.[158]

In subsequent conjunctures, the detrimental impact of proletarianization on poor families would be broached in different terms, but the underlying problem, and the fear of its consequences, persists down to the present day.

The response of state authorities to surging vagrancy was repression. Between 1522 and 1545 sixty towns across Western Europe introduced ordinances which prohibited begging or strictly licensed beggars and tightened the administration of poor relief.[159] The essential thrust of these measures was to deter the migration of the poor and compel the able-bodied to compete for jobs at the going wage rates. Social policy was based on a sharp distinction between the 'impotent poor' (the disabled, sick, senile and orphaned) who deserved assistance from the community; and the able-bodied poor who were held to be idle by choice – 'without their poverty resulting from the mischance of war or other honest causes, but solely from waywardness and pure sloth, through not wishing to work or toil to earn their bread and living', as a sixteenth-century decree put it.[160] Hospitals were built for the former, and workhouses for the latter. Poor people accepted almost any kind of work to stay out of the workhouse.

Early Proto-industrialization: The Kaufsystem

Rural handicrafts expanded considerably in the 'long' sixteenth century. The growth was centred in textiles, metal and wood products, meeting needs for clothing, shelter and domestic furnishings. Cottage by-employments of this nature had roots in the Middle Ages, when production had taken place on a small scale, utilizing hand tools, working up local raw materials into commodities for village exchange. Every substantial medieval village had its blacksmith, carpenter, tanner, baker, mason and potter, as we have seen. The spread of cottage industry in the sixteenth century may appear to be an outgrowth of its medieval predecessor. It set off from the same constricted domestic foundation; its household site and manual technology would not be superseded until the factory system finally displaced cottage industry in the last half of the nineteenth century.

However 'organic' this connection seems at first sight, proto-industrialization was a qualitatively new development.[161] From the outset, it was sponsored by merchant capitalists who organized long-distance distribution networks for rural producers still rooted on the land; cottage producers became increasingly dependent on them over time. On the eve of the Industrial Revolution, merchants ended up owning the cottagers' means of production, supplying them with raw materials and setting quotas for their work. In the putting-out system, domestic producers became proletarians working for a piece-rate wage.[162] In this section I shall focus on the first stage of proto-industrialization, the 'Kaufsystem' of cottage householders – petty commodity producers still rooted on the land and oriented to the seasonal rhythms of agricultural production.[163] This arrangement prevailed in the countryside of Western Europe until the eighteenth century. In a later section, I shall resume discussion of the second stage, the 'Verlagssystem', as it flourished in the period 1750–1850, when more and more cottagers became domestically based proletarians, effectively landless, responding to the business and trade cycles of industrial capitalism.

Until the sixteenth century, market demand for non-food consumer goods was basically dichotomized: (a) long-distance interregional trade in luxury goods, fabricated in cities and towns; (b) local and intraregional trade in subsistence essentials, produced mainly in the countryside. In the sixteenth century, this bifurcation gradually began to break down. On the one hand, the growth of the prosperous middle classes – gentlemen and yeomen in the country, businessmen and professionals in the city – generated demand for cheaper finery (silk, linen, fancy houses and carved furniture) which could be met by rural craftspeople. On the other hand, the swelling ranks of wage-earners began, for the first time, to generate a substantial monetary demand for cheap non-food essentials (leatherware, woollens, broadcloth, cooking-ware and furniture). This also stimulated cottage industry, though here the market remained primarily intraregional.[164]

Cottage industries became increasingly specialized in the seventeenth century. In a typical medieval village, there had been one ironsmith, a few carpenters, and one or two masons; now a *majority* of households in a village would set up as framework knitters, silk-weavers, linen-makers, or metalworkers.[165] The proto-industrial economy was characterized by the massing of production of a given commodity in a particular region, saturating its markets and forcing producer households to rely for their subsistence on long-distance trade, and hence on merchants. Handicraft cottagers certainly strove to remain self-sufficient. They tolerated crushing poverty and resisted proletarianization, clinging tenaciously to their way of life.[166] But as soon as they needed to sell their wares beyond the local market town, they had no alternative but to rely on merchants as retailers. Taking advantage of the dispersion of atomized producers, merchant companies controlled the distribution of commodities and their terms of trade. Extending in times of hardship a line of credit to families which the poor found increasingly difficult to repay, merchants were able to stick a capitalist toe in the cottage door, paving the way for eventual takeover and the spread of the putting-out system.[167]

The form of cottage industry which began to flourish in the sixteenth century engaged the poorer strata of village communities. They were not specialized craftsmen in life-trades with skills developed through long years of apprenticeship; they were semi-skilled family labour teams which set up in a line of business very quickly, adapting to shifts in market demand. Their small-scale means of production required vast quantities of cheap labour to produce competitively priced goods for national and international markets. Merchants looked to areas of cheap labour close to major commercial and trading cities. The fewer alternatives villagers had to generate extra income, the lower the opportunity costs of their labour time. For their part, peasant manufacturers, still oriented to the land, sought forms of handicraft which meshed with the rhythms of agricultural work, generating income in the off-season. Proto-industrial production thus tended to mushroom in pastoral areas of weak manorial control and poor soil, in upland and moorland zones, where poverty was endemic and underemployment acute.[168]

Per unit costs in the cottage economy were well beneath those of the artisan workshops of the towns, which is why merchant capitalists found them so attractive. What accounts for this cost differential? In the first place, peasant cottagers retained an agrarian subsistence base which urban households lacked. The costs of reproducing their labour-power were thus partially offset. Secondly, they usually worked in their cottages, not in separate workshops; rent and overhead expenses were lower. Thirdly, they substituted family members – wives and children – for the mostly male apprentices of the town guilds, exploiting the unpaid labour-power of the domestic group more fully, lowering the dependency ratio of their households in the process.[169] If their reproduction costs were much lower, rural cottagers were also in a much weaker position: plentiful, dispersed, and unorganized. Unable to restrict their own labour supply as the urban guilds could, cottagers bid down its price in ruinous competition with one another.

The family economy of cottage proto-industrialists was fundamentally different from that of either urban artisans or self-sufficient peasant agriculturalists. This had important consequences for household composition, the domestic division of labour, and the form of the family cycle. The labour team of proto-industrial households was normally comprised exclusively of family members. Parents could not afford to retain live-in servants or hire others, but they had every interest in retaining their own children on-site until they married. Generally, they were successful in doing so. As indoor work intensified and field work at a distance from the cottage declined, the traditional division of labour between spouses broke down.[170] Freed from the patrilineal bias of the male-dominated guilds, women were able to play a far more instrumental role in rural cottages than they ever could in the households of urban artisans. (The redistribution of spousal power in the Verlagssystem will be considered in a later section of the chapter.)

The modalities of generational turnover shifted as the arable base of peasant subsistence declined. Rapid land subdivision, bequeathing tiny plots to all sons, seems to have been widespread in zones of cottage industry. In part, this manifests a bias in original location: cottage industry flourished in pastoral areas of weak manorial jurisdiction where partible inheritance was customary.[171] But it also appears to reflect change over time: even in impartible zones of stronger seigneurial pressure, the loss of viable arable and the development of a second income source relaxed the impartible imperative.[172] This was particularly the case if common rights could be retained for all heirs no matter how minuscule their holdings. As we have seen, the desire to compensate all offspring had exerted a constant pressure on holding integrity throughout the feudal epoch. Once the livelihood of future generations was no longer dependent on arable acreage, the impartible rule was placed in abeyance. With this shift, inheritance itself began to decline as the infrastructural grid of the family cycle:

> The foundation and continuing existence of the family as a unit of production and consumption was no longer necessarily tied to the transmission of property through inheritance. It was replaced by the possibility of founding a family permanently as a unit of labour. This reduced not only the parents' control over the marital relations of the young, but it also loosened the structural connection between the generations, in so far as it had been guaranteed by property inheritance and patriarchal domination.[173]

Foundations of the Western European Marriage Pattern

Despite continuing uncertainty as to its origins, the late and non-universal marriage pattern was definitely prevalent across Northwestern Europe in the seventeenth century. By 1650, when village reconstitution studies become sufficiently numerous to render the generality of the pattern indubitable, the average age of women at first marriage was twenty-four or over, 7 to 20 per cent of women never married, and the incidence of childbirth out of wedlock was below 3 per cent.[174] This marital pattern restricted fertility massively. A very considerable minority of women remained single and bore no children; those who married bore none for the first ten years of their fecund life-phase, on average. If they had their last child at the age of forty, their entire reproductive careers would span roughly fifteen years, a long time by modern standards but remarkably brief in a pre-transition context. Resulting fertility was less than half the rate that would have been achieved if all women between fifteen and fifty were married.[175]

If fertility was regulated *by means of* marriage, does this imply that family limitation *within* marriage was non-existent? Family historians and demographers typically assert that birth control was not practised by pre-transition women in a regime of 'natural fertility'. This assumption is inaccurate and ethnocentric, taking the modern form of birth control as the only 'real' form.[176] To be sure, it was rare for couples to adopt the modern practice of deliberately halting childbearing once they had raised a definite number of surviving children. However, birth spacing was subject to various influences; whether these were deliberately manipulated by women to prolong the intervals between children is unclear.[177] The average span between first and second births in early modern Europe was about two years, considerably longer than the minimum. The main inhibitor of fertility within marriage was almost certainly prolonged and vigorous breastfeeding, which tended to suppress ovulation for as long as a mother nursed, delaying her next conception.[178] Poorer women nursed their own infants on a demand basis for two to three years, having fewer births than rich women who often availed themselves of wet-nurses.[179] In some early modern communities, post-partum intercourse taboos and seasonal labour migration (taking husbands away from home, reducing coital frequency) also appear to have prolonged birth intervals, lowering marital fertility. There is certainly literary evidence of intentional fertility suppression in early modern Europe. As we have seen, priests and ministers denounced preventive measures as interfering with God's will. They were convinced that their parishioners frequently employed all manner of potions and techniques to suppress ovulation, intercept sperm, induce miscarriage and perform abortions.[180] It is extremely difficult to gauge the extent to which such measures were used, much less their demographic impact in aggregate terms; but this is no reason to ignore their existence or to assume, a priori, that such effects were unintended.[181]

This said, there can be no doubt that fertility in the early modern era was primarily curtailed by means of marriage and not within it. The delay of marriage was, in Chaunu's phrase, 'la véritable arme contraceptive de l'Europe classique'. A difference of three years in the mean age of women at first marriage (i.e., between twenty-three and twenty-six), would alter the rate of marital fertility by 25 per cent.[182] If such a divergence were sustained over time, the effect would be compounded, since later marriage lengthened the interval between one generation's births and the next. In the absence of countervailing forces, a change in marriage age of this magnitude could sponsor a massive cumulative shift in a country's overall growth rate.[183] The discovery of the Western European marriage pattern has had a number of salient ramifications for social and economic history. By bringing the regulation of marriage and household formation to centre-stage in historical demography, it has discredited the Malthusian image of pre-industrial populations breeding 'naturally', growing exponentially beyond the resources at their disposal, only to be cut down to size by swingeing mortality crises.[184] What was formerly considered to be a high-pressure demographic system, where the 'positive check' of mortality played the primary role in slowing growth, is now seen to have been a relatively low-pressure regime, where the rate of household formation was slowed in response to a tightening land market and declining wages, checking fertility well short of frequent mortality crises.

Reflecting a Malthusian preoccupation with checks to population growth, most scholars have focused on the restrictive function of the 'nuptial valve'. But equally significant is the obverse capacity: to facilitate a rise in the birth rate by means of earlier or more universal marriage in sensitive response to shifts in the mode of labour-power's employment and consumption. Apparently for the first time anywhere, the peoples of Western Europe forged a marital regime which extended the life-phase from puberty to first birth to ten years, thus creating a sizeable latent fertility reserve amenable to flexible adjustment in response to changing conditions of household formation. The quick-release facility of the nuptial valve seems to have played a catalytic role in the acceleration of proto-industrial growth, with the latter, in turn, furnishing a springboard to the Industrial Revolution.[185] We will return to this development later on.

Given the undoubted importance of this distinct nuptial regime, it is important to illuminate the underlying determinants of the pattern. In my view, late and non-universal marriage ought to be conceived as the inadvertent result of a specific interplay of social forces, not as a normative custom in its own right. Late marriage was not consciously sought as a desideratum by any sector of early modern society. The distribution of ages at first marriage tended to be widely spread, with some women marrying in their teens. Such marriages were not scorned as premature, providing they were adequately provisioned. The nobility and gentry tended to marry several years earlier than peasants did, arriving at the late/non-universal pattern later than their social inferiors. They certainly did not impart a prescriptive norm opposed to early marriage. If they had exerted exemplary influence, it would have been in the opposite direction (which suggests that whatever influence they possessed was slight). Guilds often forbade apprentices to marry before a certain age, but this had more to do with the control of entry to a trade and the enforcement of full-length apprenticeship than it did with a cultural norm of late marriage. Church authorities, Catholic and Protestant, did not inveigh against early marriage. Their concern was that the union and its progeny should be sanctified by a church wedding, that the couple should explicitly consent, and that no one declare any legitimate impediment to marriage at the publishing of the banns. Far from exemplifying the great virtue of prudence, as Parson Malthus proposed, delayed marriage was widely held to be a moral blight. 'Many a poor man refrains from matrimony', decried Martin Luther, 'because he cannot see how to provide for a family. This is the chief obstacle to married life, and the cause of all whoredom.'[186] It is misleading, then, to refer to late marriage as a rule or custom, as John Hajnal has done.[187] It is a norm only in the weakest sense of the term (i.e., prevalent or most frequent). Late marriage was tolerated as a necessity. Among the younger generation, impatient to get on with life, waiting to wed was a source of great frustration and conflict, not only with parents but among siblings competing for favourable treatment in the allocation of meagre resources.

The value that *was* inculcated, with strong support in the community, was that a young man and woman contemplating marriage ought not to rush into it prematurely, lest the resulting match be impermanent. This concern was well founded: youthful marriages were more likely to end in break-up and desertion.[188] A couple needed to achieve some measure of viability in a liveli-hood, to have income and productive resources at their command, so that they could begin having children almost immediately and be in a position to sup-port them. The main reason late marriage was prevalent in early modern Western Europe was that it was difficult to do this when productive resources were tied up by the older generation, who retained a veto over marriage. There was a structural blockage in the transmission of productive resources between generations on the land. This obstacle was a manifestation of the nexus of class and patriarchal power.[189] With the spread of wage labour based on independent (market) hiring, capitalism would eventually forge a path round this obstacle in the latter half of the eighteenth century. But in the meantime, local employment opportunities and wage levels were insufficient to facilitate mass circumvention.

In seeking to identify the structural preconditions of the Western European marriage pattern, most scholars have focused attention on neo-locality – the tendency of newly married couples to set up their own households apart from their parents. The pattern is treated as a rule or custom. It is perhaps more accurate to conceive of neo-locality as two norms, or preferred courses of action, operating at cross-purposes; delayed marriage is the result, arising as an eventual resolution in the conflict between fathers and sons (patriarchs in residence and future patriarchs). Sons elected to wait rather than marry and reside under their fathers' roofs. 'When thou art married', grooms were ad-vised, 'live of thyself with thy wife, in a family of thine own.' Two masters under one roof leads to 'unquietness of all parties'.[190] For their part, fathers were unwilling to retire and relinquish control of the holding. The deadlock arose because fathers in Northwestern Europe did not have sufficient authority to force their sons to 'marry in', while sons were in no position to make their fathers retire early. Both generations possessed the (negative) veto power to withstand the other; neither enjoyed the (positive) instrumental power to pro-ceed unilaterally with marriage. The preferred course of each generation was thus blocked by the other, and each opted for second best. Marital deferral became a routine stalling tactic employed by the senior generation in the deadly serious game of patrimonial allocation.

This was the micro-context of delayed and non-universal marriage, but the familial waiting game was not played out in a void. The nuptial impasse was shaped by the compensatory impartible inheritance bind and driven by the scarcity of non-family land and the inferiority of alternative livelihoods. So inheritance remained the best (and often the only) way for young adults to acquire agricultural means of production, marry, establish viable households and raise families. Hypothetically, land could be purchased or leased, but young, single villagers, relying on their own resources, could not afford to enter the land market. The vast majority of places which became available on the land were opened by the deaths of incumbent tenants. The pace of new household formation was dependent on the rate of adult mortality, mediated by the price of land. Age of marriage was therefore correlated with life expectancy at the mean age of parenthood.[191] As the land market tightened and it became harder to compensate children who married out, nuptials were postponed and an increasing minority of children never married. This set of constraints has come to be known as the 'land niche system'. The model's analytical value has been to clarify an equilibrating feedback mechanism *from* adult mortality *through* the land market *to* fertility *by means of* the patriarchal control of marriage. The demographic system could therefore be comprehended in homeostatic terms.[192] As land-clearing initiatives ran their course and labour productivity stagnated, the system provided a fertility check, obviating a full-scale mortality crisis. If the rural producers were still caught in a demographic bind, they could at least draw back from the Malthusian brink.

Is the land niche model valid as one component of an explanation for nuptial delay in the early modern era? There are a number of potential objections. The first is that if I am right in placing the formation of the pattern in the late medieval depression, then 'tight land' cannot be seen as an inaugural prerequisite. On the contrary, the system emerged in a conjuncture of abundant arable, where good land could be acquired so readily that young men did not feel constrained to wait for their family portions. However, the conditions which forge a social structure in the first instance are typically distinct from those that foster its regular reproduction in a subsequent period. The two processes must not be conflated. Once nuptial deferral had become entrenched as a vehicle of devolutionary control, the duration of the delay became responsive to the regional availability of non-family land. This is especially evident at the close of the 'long' sixteenth-century boom, when the nuptial valve tightened in response to rising land prices and the scarcity of decent arable.

A second objection to the land niche model is that retirement contracts were commonplace in many regions of Western Europe, as a component of *inter vivos* inheritance. The turnover of family holdings need not therefore await the death of landholders. Most retirement contracts, however, were components of men's wills, meant to secure the subsistence of widows. Such arrangements were not antithetical to the general practice of delaying the final disposition of the holding until the death of the patriarch; they were an integral facet of it. There were, however, other retirement arrangements involving elderly couples ceding their places in production to heirs marrying in. Would these not invalidate the land niche model as it has been outlined above? They would if such practices were common, but it does not appear that they were. Couple retirements were rare in the early modern era – even in Austria, where the *Ausgedinge* contract was customary.[193]

A third objection is that the land market of the sixteenth and seventeenth centuries was sufficiently generalized to overrun an inheritance-based system of household formation among the rural producers of Western Europe. The basic cause of the late marriage pattern could not lie here. But the land market in these centuries did not subvert the barriers to marriage for small and middling peasants. The market was dominated by rich gentlemen and prosperous yeomen; its dynamic was towards concentration of ever greater acreage in fewer hands. Those of modest means simply could not compete. For them, the compensatory impartible bind was tighter than ever. If young adults were to acquire a viable land parcel and form a household of agricultural producers, they would need to obtain most of their initial fixed capital through inheritance.

A fourth objection is more telling. With the mass proletarianization of the sixteenth and seventeenth centuries, household formation was no longer dependent on acquiring a self-sufficient holding for the majority of rural producers in England and a substantial minority on the continent. While agricultural viability remained a pervasive *objective*, it was no longer a *precondition* to marrying and establishing a household; regular employment and off-farm income were. This is a cogent argument: it means that the land niche model cannot stand on its own. If, as is widely thought, proletarianization tended to ease barriers to marriage, why does the nuptial valve tighten in the late sixteenth and seventeenth centuries, during a phase of very substantial proletarianization? There seem to be three possible responses to this problem, bearing in mind that any thesis on seventeenth-century blockage and stagnation should lay the groundwork for a follow-up thesis on the demographic flood-tide of the eighteenth century.

The first response is simply to revise the terminology of the model from 'places on the land' to 'viable livelihoods', stressing that the rule of neo-locality applied to *all* adults contemplating marriage. Analysts working in the modernization paradigm make no clear distinction between peasant and proletarian marriage patterns, subsuming both within a looser terminology. Since family forms among all classes are more or less the same, the Western European marriage pattern does not require class-specific obstacles to marriage and household formation.[194] The term neo-locality is ambiguous (as discussed in the last chapter); it is being used here in reference to quite diverse modes of household formation.

A second response takes the difference between peasant and proletarian social relations seriously, and elaborates a 'double block' model. The specific difficulties of proletarian youth in forming households and getting married have little or nothing to do with land inheritance. The obstacles are more likely to involve irregular employment, low wage rates, uprooting mobility, skewed sex ratios among itinerants, and the repressive organization of local poor relief. In a double block conception, one postulates a 'tight land, low labour demand' situation prevailing in the seventeenth century, with proletarian obstacles being thrust aside in the mid eighteenth century, as capitalist labour demand accelerated rapidly and the patriarchal and community control of courtship and marriage disintegrated. This is the alternative I prefer.

A third response would be to propose that household formation among the proletarian populace was *not* blocked in the late sixteenth and seventeenth centuries. Proletarians married earlier and bred faster than peasants did from the outset of mass proletarianization in the sixteenth century. This is the position taken by Charles Tilly in his important article on the 'components of growth'; he envisages no basic alteration in proletarian fertility rates between 1500 and 1800, and a rapid indigenous increment of 0.5 per cent per annum averaged across the entire period.[195] I shall weigh the merits of this thesis below, after examining the dynamics of the seventeenth-century depression.

Seventeenth-Century Stagnation and the Last Feudal–Agrarian Cycle

The demographic boom of the 'long' sixteenth century ebbed after 1550 and ground to a near standstill in the next century. By 1700, Western Europe as a whole was only about 9 per cent more populous than it had been a century earlier. Southern Europe contracted, while the North edged forward, but even there the pace of advance was glacial. Some regions suffered grievous losses: the population of Germany was smashed in the Thirty Years War (1618–1648), dropping almost 40 per cent; Spain lost 30 per cent of its people between 1590 and 1650, as the overextended Habsburg Empire unravelled. Other countries experienced minor dips which were not quickly made up in the midst of longer term stagnation.[196]

Did worsening mortality, declining fertility, or some combination of the two terminate the boom and inaugurate a century of stagnation? In zones of war and army occupation, horrendous death rates accounted for most of the contraction, due more to pillage, famine and epidemics in the midst of ecological devastation than to military combat *per se*. The entire region of the Holy Roman Empire lost more than a quarter of its population in the Thirty Years War, while the populations of Brandenburg, Saxony and Bavaria were cut in half.[197] These were the deepest losses on a supraregional scale since the Black Death. Beyond war zones as well, mortality seems to have increased. In England, where the evidence is best, crude death rates rose from a low plateau of around twenty-four (per thousand per annum) in the 1566–1606 period to thirty in the years 1666–1731. On the basis of more fragmentary data, it appears that mortality also rose in France between 1600 and 1695, and in Spain between 1570 and 1650. The 'little ice age' of the seventeenth century, with frequent winters of unusual severity and length, probably contributed to the shortening of life expectancy.[198]

While deteriorating mortality certainly played a substantial role in the demographic depression of the seventeenth century, declining fertility also contributed. In England, the crude birth rate diminished from 38.5 in the decade 1541–51 (when Wrigley and Schofield's back projection begins), to a nadir of 27.5 in 1651–61.[199] It is surprising to find that changes in marital timing played no role at all in diminishing fertility; women's mean age at first marriage was already late in the 1560s (at twenty-seven) and was no higher a century later. In the same period, the proportion never marrying leapt from 4 to 23 per cent.[200] This is an astounding rise in itself, but it is all the more remarkable when one considers that the strictures barring single women from bearing children were tightened considerably at the same time. In a sample of twenty-four English parishes, bastardy rates (as a proportion of all births) fell from around 4.5 per cent in 1605 to less than 1 per cent sixty years later (rising thereafter).[201] As Puritan insurgence grew, 'leakage' around the nuptial valve completely dried up, indicating a formidable suppression of the libidinal energies of young adults in their sexual prime.

On the continent, fertility also appears to have declined.[202] As in England, the reduction was achieved by nuptial constraint, although the specific configuration was very different. In France, women's mean age at first marriage was evidently around twenty-two in the sixteenth century, three or four years younger than in England, and rose thereafter to around twenty-four and a half by 1690. Celibacy probably increased in France, though this trend is more difficult to assess.[203] In the South German town of Nordlingen, the age of women at first marriage rose from 25.1 in 1611–50 to a very late 30.2 by 1691–1730.[204]

Illegitimacy rates on the continent also came down. In rural France, births out of wedlock hovered around 1 per cent in the seventeenth century.[205] By any standard, this is an extraordinarily low rate, revealing how effective the nuptial valve could be. Bridal pregnancy rates declined in this period as well, indicating a general curtailment of premarital sex. In England, roughly one first birth in eight was the result of conception out of wedlock; on the continent one in ten was. By early modern standards, these are low rates.[206] Yet roughly 80 per cent of premarital pregnancies were sanctified by matrimony before the birth took place. Upon the discovery of pregnancy, the full brunt of patriarchal power was brought to bear on recalcitrant suitors who had obtained maidens' consent to coitus by pledging to marry them.[207] Evidently the 'conversion ratio' of betrothal promises to nuptials was already high and climbing in the seventeenth century. In the eighteenth century, with mass proletarianization of a highly mobile sort, these patriarchal safeguards weakened and illegitimacy rates rose abruptly. We will examine this conjuncture below.

In sum, then, rising death rates and declining birth rates both made very substantial contributions to the termination of the long boom in Western Europe and to a stagnant, episodically contracting, seventeenth century. Only with the English data can we weigh their respective contributions to the slump. While both were influential, fertility decline was clearly the dominant factor, especially from 1631 to 1661, as the intrinsic growth rate turned negative.[208]

As a century and a half of sustained population growth ground to a halt in the closing decades of the sixteenth century, the concomitant price boom ebbed. The first major breach in the price edifice opened in the 1590s when grain prices, leaders of the inflationary binge, plummeted.[209] Despite the simultaneity of the initial break, the ensuing slump was staggered; some regions recovered for a time while others failed to. In France, grain prices plunged for twelve consecutive years, bottoming out at less than half their 1590 peak, not to be surpassed until the nineteenth century.[210] German grain prices spiralled upward in the first decade of the Thirty Years War and then crashed in the wake of heavy population loss. English prices remained buoyant the longest, flattening out in the 1630s and finally turning down at mid century as population began to contract. In the last half of the century, the depression was generalized across Western Europe; prices in every major social formation zigzagged down.[211] What happened to real wages in the seventeenth-century depression? The data are thinner here than for the price series, but the overall trend is tolerably clear, and not as uneven regionally as in earlier periods. In most places proletarians made moderate gains, due more to the recession of consumer prices than to the rise of money wages. But these advances did not recoup the losses of the previous century; proletarian living standards in 1700 were probably inferior to those their class ancestors had enjoyed in 1500. In England, wages rose about 12 per cent against a basket of consumer goods from 1640–79 to 1710–49.[212] In France, Germany and Italy, real income advances by wage labourers in the course of the seventeenth century were temporarily wiped out in its closing decades as food prices jumped upward, but were then regained, as price moderated until the 1740s.[213]

Throughout the Middle Ages and the post-plague depression, population growth rates had substructured food prices. During growth phases, cereal prices rose; in periods of demographic stagnation or contraction, prices tumbled. Did the mass proletarianization of the sixteenth and seventeenth centuries subvert this relationship, transforming the basic dynamics of the agrarian–seigneurial cycle? The answer is evidently no; the pattern remained firmly entrenched in Western Europe until the end of the eighteenth century. Wrigley and Schofield have depicted this correlation for England, where the price trend for a basket of consumables (dominated by grain) tracked the population curve remarkably closely over the course of two and a half centuries – from 1541 (when their investigation begins) to 1791: 'If population over a quarter century was rising by one per cent per annum, food prices rose by about one and a half per cent per annum. Equally, during the period of falling population, food prices tended to fall slightly faster.'[214] Thenceforth, the relationship was abruptly breached, as food prices fell while population growth accelerated, marking the final supersession of the agrarian cycle. The same basic correlation pertained on the continent, until the generalized agrarian depression in the first quarter of the nineteenth century.[215]

What accounts for the persistence of this cycle through to the terminal disintegration of the *ancien régime*? The massive growth of the waged labour force in the sixteenth and seventeenth centuries involved very little movement of labour-power from agriculture to industry. The net intersectoral flow from the former to the latter constituted a minor component of proletarian growth before the late eighteenth century. Consequently, the basic relationship of labour productivity to price movements was still anchored firmly in agriculture. Given the ecological and class constraints on land-clearing, and the lack of sustained improvement in farming technique, population trends were bound to exert a powerful influence on food prices in the long term.

One of the distinctive traits of the long agrarian–feudal cycle is the tendency for consumer prices and wages to move in opposite directions over most of it. Both are driven by underlying demographic dynamics: as population grows, land becomes relatively scarce; in the midst of a demographic slump, these tendencies are reversed. Industrial capitalist cycles exhibit the obverse correlation: real wages tend to rise through the boom as full employment is approached, and then take a beating during slumps in the midst of mass unemployment. In a developed capitalist formation, demographic dynamics are mediated by national labour markets and exert a more diffuse influence. Consumer prices and wages generally move in tandem except near the turning points where, in the early stages of a rise, wages lag behind and then remain buoyant longer than most commodity groups at the crest (are 'sticky downward', as economists say).

By these criteria, the early modern cycle was still feudal–agrarian in nature. In the context of population growth and a food price boom, wages eroded badly during the 'long' sixteenth century. In the subsequent phase of demographic stagnation and downward drifting prices in the seventeenth and early eighteenth centuries, real wages advanced. In this regard, the seventeenth-century depression had more in common with its late medieval predecessor than with subsequent industrial capitalist recessions. But there were also very significant differences. Of course the amplitude of the long wave was much less in the latter downturn than in the catastrophic depression following the Black Death. And while the supply of proletarian labour-power dried up in the late medieval depression, the ranks of wage-earners continued to swell throughout the seventeenth century.

193

Proletarian Self-Expansion before 1750?

Was proletarian fertility comparable to that of other classes in the seventeenth century? I have the impression that it was no greater and may well have been less. At the same time, proletarian mortality, particularly infant death, was probably higher than it was among the propertied classes. I am therefore inclined to reject Charles Tilly's model of impetuous proletarian self-expansion from 1500 on.[216] He proposes no change in proletarian vital rates coincident with the overall acceleration of the mid eighteenth century, but a later quickening in the nineteenth century. It seems more likely that the ranks of wageearners were swelled primarily by the extrusion of rural youth from other classes. While proletarian households would lead the vital revolution in the second half of the eighteenth century, their indigenous growth rates were similar to, or smaller than, those of other classes before 1750. The evidence I am able to adduce in support of this assertion is fragmentary and indirect.[217]

In medieval Europe, as noted in the last chapter, prosperous peasants generally had larger households than their land-poor and landless brethren. This pattern persisted through the seventeenth century. In Goodnestone-next-Kent in 1676, the mean size of yeomen households was 5.8, while for tradesmen it was 3.9, labourers, 3.2, and for poor men, 2.1. The average number of co-resident children per household was 2.5 for yeomen, 1.7 for tradesmen, 1.3 for labourers and 0.9 for the poor.[218] Mitterauer and Sieder report a parallel finding in Central Europe, and Flandrin also finds household size to be positively correlated with wealth in France.[219] Gregory King's demographic survey of England in 1688 was in general accord with these reports. He estimated the family size of 'persons in land' at 7, 'freeholders of the better sort' at 7 as well, 'shopkeepers and tradesmen' at 4.5, 'labouring people and out servants' at 3.5, and 'cottagers and paupers' at 3.25.[220] While marked disparities in mean household size do not directly reflect equivalent fertility differentials, it is fair to say that King's estimates furnish no sign of a demographic insurgence among proletarian families in the late seventeenth century. Instead, they incline us to draw the opposite conclusion.

Consider another kind of evidence. Zones of cottage industry organized by merchants on a putting out basis have generally been associated with prolific population expansion. When does the acceleration begin? In the rural canton of Zurich in the seventeenth century, the highland regions in which proto-industry developed grew only slightly faster than the lowland farming regions, remaining more sparsely settled. Between 1700 and 1762, by contrast, the population of the upland districts spurted ahead, expanding 84 per cent in just over six decades, while the farming areas grew only 15 per cent.[221] Clearly, the rapid reproduction of proto-industrial households got under way in the eighteenth century, but not before. In Shepshed, England, where framework knitting burgeoned, the village did not grow in the seventeenth century. From 1640 to 1660 fertility fell, and then recovered slowly, surpassing its 1640 level around 1700. From then on, the birth rate accelerated until 1750, when it exploded upward in a 'radical demographic discontinuity'.[222] Marriage frequency roughly parallels fertility, remaining low until after 1700, then rising slowly until 1750. Women's mean age at first marriage, which was a very high 28.1 in the seventeenth century, fell only one year in the first half of the eighteenth, but then declined rapidly, dropping another four years in the second half.[223] There is no sign of proletarian expansion in seventeenth-century Shepshed; the nuptial valve remained constricted to 1750, bursting open thereafter.

In sum, it appears that rural proletarians did not produce children any faster than other classes before the eighteenth century.[224] And even if, in some regions, proletarian fertility exceeded that of other classes, the surplus would almost certainly have been nullified by higher than average infant and child mortality.[225] So the net result of proletarian fertility minus infant and child mortality was no higher – and in fact was probably lower – than the 'surviving children' rates of other classes.

If proletarian fertility was under substantial constraint in the seventeenth century, one wants to know why. (The question is of particular relevance, since I shall argue that the breach of these strictures was crucial in the population explosion of the following century.) The exigencies of inheritance in a land-tight era cannot explain delayed and non-universal marriage among those whose reliance on land possession for subsistence was in terminal decline, where it had not already ceased. The answer lies in the character of proletarianization in this period, which was predominantly negative. Expropriation, and hence need for wage income, ran far in advance of employer demand for wage labour capable of satisfying that need. It was an era of proletarian immiseration and chronic underemployment.

Early proletarians found it difficult to marry and start households, tending to marry later than peasant women did. And when they did marry, the rural poor often lacked incentives to bear children. Many researchers attribute their relatively low fertility to prolonged breastfeeding. This makes economic sense. Children's contribution to the families of agricultural labourers was bound to be minimal when the demand for day labour was weak, highly seasonal, and often filled by itinerants. The voracious absorption of children into wage labour, a hallmark of industrial capitalism, lay in the future. Most rural youth from land-poor families were sent into service at sixteen to eighteen. As their numbers swelled in seventeenth-century England, service furnished a major impediment to early marriage and independent household formation. The propertied classes and the village authorities made it extremely difficult for 'unattached' poor people to obtain accommodation: 'In order to establish a household landless people were dependent upon landowners. Permission was needed to build a cottage on the waste-land, to rent land in the outfields or turn loose a couple of sheep to graze in the heather.'[226] Steady employment was a prerequisite to settling down and raising a family in one locale. Yet labour demand was so irregular that it was necessary for many landless labourers to lead a peripatetic existence, moving frequently in search of work.

Not only were employment opportunities sporadic and wages very low, but essential supplementary income and maintenance provisions available through poor relief were generally organized so as to exclude migrants not residing permanently in the parish. The effect was to drive a wedge between the settled and the unsettled poor, pinning the rooted down in their home villages in order to retain welfare entitlements, while forcing the uprooted to move on as soon as they were laid off and could obtain no further employment locally. In many cases, the poor were forbidden to marry by poor-law wardens who sought to forestall the children of such unions becoming a future burden on the parish, swelling its tax rolls.[227] Women risked forfeiting their claims to poor relief by marrying outsiders: 'Magistrates could and did insist that whenever an outsider wanted to marry into the community, he or she should meet stringent property qualifications.'[228] In these ways, state authorities curtailed household formation among the poor, exacerbating the demographic imbalance between the settled and transient populations, with many more men than women on the road. This was the case in seventeenth-century Terling, for example, where,

> abetted by the Settlement Laws and the parochial machinery of poor relief, local officials controlled the village size in such a way that surviving children in excess of the replacement level had to find their niches elsewhere, and immigration became more difficult.[229]

In many places, the sex ratio of young adults was sharply skewed. Most early modern cities and towns had more females than males overall, and further asymmetries were built into the age structure of the sexes.[230] These imbalances delayed women's marriages, shortening their childbearing careers. The immigrants to towns and cities were overwhelmingly poor and propertyless. Could this population have been a source of proletarian self-expansion? It is very unlikely. Most early modern cities grew entirely by influx; within city limits, deaths chronically exceeded births. It was not long-standing urban residents but newcomers who failed to reproduce their numbers. Their mortality rates were extraordinarily high, while their marriage and birth rates fell beneath those of the rest of the urban populace. The flow to the cities constituted a very considerable subtraction from population growth as a whole, and from the self-expansion of the proletariat more particularly. London, for example, soaked up half of the excess of births over deaths for the whole of

England between 1625 and 1775. Until the nineteenth century, urbanization slowed the pace of proletarian formation.[231]

We must conclude that before 1750 the growth of the proletariat was a product more of peasant polarization and increasing landlessness than of demographic self-expansion. Yet a century later, the first national censuses indicate that the situation had been reversed. The working class was growing rapidly by means of an excess of births over deaths, and wage-dependent households had become larger than those of the propertied classes. During the century from 1750 to 1850, a crucial, if unobtrusive, inversion occurred which has major implications for our understanding of the demographic transition. For the first time in European history, stretching back as far as we can dimly perceive at present, the households of the land-poor and propertyless become larger on average than those of their class superiors. Until 1850, the inversion was due more to the enlargement of proletarian households (including proto-industrial variants) than to any contraction of co-resident size among the propertied classes. My guess is that the inversion reflects underlying changes in both vital rates: a reduction of class differentials in mortality, together with the opening up of fertility differentials (the disparity becoming particularly noticeable when family limitation began to spread among the propertied classes in the second half of the nineteenth century). We shall examine the vital revolution's takeoff in a later section of this chapter.

Domestic Service in Husbandry

As a life-stage occupation for youth, rural service probably had early modern origins. Swelling numbers of young men and women were sent into service, as the age of marriage rose and the life-phase from puberty to marriage was stretched out. The majority of servants worked for and lived with a farm family, but a very substantial minority made their way into the nearest town to take up employment there. We shall concentrate here on the former segment of the servant population. How prevalent was domestic service in Western Europe? In a superb study of the institution in England, Ann Kussmaul estimates that 60 per cent of youth aged fifteen to twenty-four were servants at any point in time in the first half of the eighteenth century. Hufton informs us that poor country youth in France typically left home at the age of fourteen to go into service. In a group of Danish rural parishes in the late eighteenth century, over half the population aged fifteen to twenty-four were servants; in nine Flemish villages, 38 per cent were, and in three Norwegian areas, 33 per cent. In England, the Low Countries and Scandinavia in the eighteenth century, servants resided in roughly 28 to 35 per cent of rural households.[232] The proportion of adults who had been servants at some point in their youth must have approached half. Clearly, domestic service was a standard (though by no means universal) experience for young adults in Northwestern Europe, particularly if they were from land-poor families. The attraction of employing servants for those who could afford them was that they provided extra hands without establishing inheritance claims upon the holding. The institution flourished in a peasant economy where labour-power was adjusted to available land over the course of the family cycle rather than vice versa, as in Eastern Europe, where farm servants were rare.

For the vast majority of those who entered service, it was not an adult career but a transitional occupation, to be begun soon after puberty and terminated shortly before marriage.[233] Living in their masters' households, servants worked under the direct supervision of the household or his wife. Until the nineteenth century, the term 'family' was taken to include non-kin members of the household.[234] In a cohabiting sense, servants were part of the family. Not only did they work shoulder to shoulder with family members, but they ate at the same table and slept in the same room, often in the same bed. Furthermore, a substantial minority of servants were related to the families they lived with, since parents normally attempted to make their children's first placements with kin, and were often successful in doing so.[235]

Servants worked on a contract basis, normally for one-year stints with the reciprocal option of renewal.[236] While first placements were usually arranged by parents negotiating over their children's heads, subsequent hirings occurred on a face-to-face basis, with terms agreed upon by the employee, who received, in turn, the monetary part of his or her wage, much of it held in reserve and paid out in a lump sum at the end of the contract. In addition to room and board, the non-monetary component of the contract often included the servant's right to plant a small garden on the farmer's land or to run a sheep or two with his herd.[237] Servants were legally obliged to remain in their master's employ until the contract had run its course; deferral of payment provided a powerful economic incentive to do so. They came under the master's paternal jurisdiction twenty-four hours a day, seven days a week, and were not free to leave his employ with impunity. The latter enjoyed custodial prerogatives *in loco parentis,* and often disciplined servants as if they were his own children. Service was not an *alternative* to the prolonged subordination of young adults to patriarchal authority, but an *extension* of familial discipline with a change of masters.

Both masters and servants had many reasons for declining to renew contracts; the result was high turnover. In England, the majority appear to have moved on after a year; in Andrichfurt, Germany, the average stay was only one and a half years.[238] Most, however, did not move very far; the average distance between postings was a few kilometres, rarely exceeding fifteen. Interludes between hirings were the best time to return home, and many servants did so when they were unable to find work or their parents needed their assistance. Yet – perhaps as an indication of familial alienation – 'many did not even see parents then'.[239]

Since many couples failed to have the number of children they wished for, the institution of domestic service compensated, in pragmatic terms, by organizing a massive and continuous exchange of youth between households. The hiring and release of servants fluctuated over the domestic cycle, though servants might be found in some households in every phase. Families took on servants most frequently when their own labour teams were short-handed, particularly when offspring were too young to do a full day's work.[240] Servants came from households at every level of the village community, but they were drawn disproportionately from the ranks of cottagers and labourers.[241] Land-poor families could not put their children to work very productively on tiny plots, nor could they afford to furnish substantial dowries and portions when they married and left. Regardless of the stratum of village society their families inhabited, youths took up service in the households of their parents' social superiors. This status differential satisfied both sets of parents, meeting the objectives of paternalist socialization. It also had the effect of raising labour productivity in agriculture, since it redistributed labour massively from poor to thriving land.[242]

Sending teenagers into service relieved parents of mouths to feed, while enabling youths to accumulate their own marital portions. 'Ten years of a type of bondage ... with only a few hours of leisure each month would, it was hoped, provide [a servant girl] with a dowry' of 500 livres if she were fortunate to work steadily for a decade and lay aside a little from her paltry wages.[243] The average sum saved by servant couples intending to marry in eighteenth-century England was £50 to £60. Most sent money home in the first years of service, saving more for their own marriages in later years.[244] A compelling reason for sending one's children out was that it eased the cumulative tension of marital postponement and testamentary indecision. Not only did parents need some distance from impatient offspring (especially those who were slated to be losers in the eventual inheritance lottery), but one suspects that siblings welcomed the chance to live apart, alleviating the strains of being forced to compete with one another for the choice pieces of a meagre pie.[245] In any case, live-in service absorbed youths' time and energies away from home, while in no way jeopardizing their right to return to claim at the time of devolution.

As a stepping-stone to marriage and adulthood, live-in service was not an alternative to family inheritance. Rather, it was an indispensable component of the land niche/late marriage system, developed in response to the bind of the compensatory impartible custom, as non-family land became scarce and prohibitively expensive. The institution exhibited a good deal of flexibility in adjusting to changes in the availability of new places on the land. Since the paramount goal of male servants was to save enough money to acquire a modest holding, and for females to build up their dowries, the going price of land and domestic provision in relation to servants' wages would affect how long young people remained in service. If this ratio deteriorated, a servant might be persuaded to endure another year or two before leaving to marry. This delay, in turn, would reduce the number of children that women eventually bore.[246]

Day labourers and servants represented competing types of extrafamilial labour-power. Labourers were more often employed in grain-growing where farmers needed additional hands on a peak-season basis; servants were generally preferred in animal husbandry, with more even year-round labour requirements. Whereas servants, working on long contracts, were single and lived in, day labourers, hired on a short-term basis, were usually married and lived out. Any economic condition which induced farmers to alter the proportions of servants and labourers therefore had demographic consequences. In the low-fertility period in England from 1650 to 1749, servants comprised 14 per cent of the population; in the subsequent period of rising and high fertility, from 1750 to 1821, this proportion fell to 11 per cent.[247] While the increase in the servants' share of agricultural labour in the period 1650–1700 was but one factor affecting the population trend, its depressive effect on household formation and fertility is clear.[248] The institution was very effective in tying up young people, facilitating the postponement of marriage and childbearing.

PART III: THE POPULATION BOOM: SPRINGBOARD TO INDUSTRIAL CAPITALISM

In the middle decades of the eighteenth century, the peoples of Northwestern Europe, unbeknown to themselves, embarked on a process of demo-economic expansion that would culminate in the Industrial Revolution. In the last part of this chapter we shall examine the demographic takeoff, focusing in particular on the way positive proletarianization, in galvanizing the process of conjugal formation, broke up the slow-growth equilibrium of the *ancien régime*.

In the first half of the eighteenth century, there was no dramatic rebound from the demographic stagnation of the seventeenth; nothing presaged the vital revolution to come. Growth resumed across Western Europe in the last quarter of the seventeenth century, but at a sluggish pace of 0.1 to 0.2 per cent per year in most regions. At this rate, the peoples of England, France, Italy, Belgium, Austria-Bohemia and Germany enlarged their numbers less than 15 per cent from 1700 to 1750; the Dutch grew not at all.[249] In economic terms as well, the period appears more as a lingering extension of the seventeenth-century slump than as a staging ground for an era of unprecedented development.

Across Western Europe, population growth began to accelerate around 1750.[250] By 1800, numbers in most regions were swelling at rates in the range of 0.75–1.5 per cent per year; this pace continued unabated, or even accelerated, during the nineteenth century. There were historical precedents for growth in the 1–1.5 per cent range. But in the early modern era, such spurts had not been as durable nor as widespread; they tended to last a decade or two, were interrupted by devastating epidemic losses and followed by phases of protracted stagnation, as socioeconomic ceilings of growth were reached. After 1750, all such contractions became progressively more subdued; a century later they had been eliminated. Population expansion persisted decade after decade, without offsetting cyclical regression. Sustained growth at this pace was novel in European history.[251]

The continental sweep of the acceleration can best be appreciated by viewing it in the longer term. Europe (without Russia) grew 7 per cent in the seventeenth century, 54 per cent in the eighteenth, and 102 per cent in the nineteenth. From 1750 to 1900, the peoples of Western Europe almost trebled their numbers.[252] Moreover, they did so despite emigration to overseas colonies of some 45 million people from 1800 to 1914, 'probably ... the greatest transfer of population in the history of mankind'.[253] Explaining the population explosion has become 'the single most important problem in the whole field of modern demographic history'.[254]

Since net migration throughout the period was consistently outward, the entire acceleration must be accounted for by an increasing excess of births over deaths. How is this surplus to be explained? Historical demographers have approached the problem as if it were a mathematical exercise in quantifying components of growth, debating whether falling mortality or rising fertility was 'the prime mover' in the population boom. In my view, this perspective has diverted attention from the underlying – and far more fundamental – question: why did the vital rates diverge radically for over a century before the birthrate began to decline?

The initial phase of the demo-economic liftoff appeared to be inauspicious, resembling the upswing of previous cycles: (a) an abatement of epidemics, resulting in a quickening of population growth; (b) an uneven expansion of agricultural output, barely keeping pace with swelling numbers, lagging behind in some areas, resulting in a general rise in cereal prices; (c) a somewhat faster expansion of industrial production, also demand-led, met primarily through the rural extension of the putting-out system. But towards the end of the century, these growth trends surmounted their traditional land-based limits and broke out on their own. The historical novelty of the situation is striking. As the impoverished ranks of the rural landless proliferated, fertility did not decline nor did mortality crises become more frequent and severe, as they had in the past. What had breached the homeostatic limits of the *ancien régime*? While many factors must be taken into account, one key was the rapid escalation of a specifically capitalist demand for labour-power in the countryside, particularly via the putting-out system. In an earlier era, those who were squeezed off the land had to flee to the cities, only to have been decimated therein. In the second half of the eighteenth century, by contrast, the growth of rural industry enabled proletarians to remain in the countryside, prolonging life and boosting childbirth. The tremendous expansion of capitalist labour demand in rural industry prevented the reconvergence of birth and death rates as the landless population exploded, dissolving the homeostatic regime.

The demographic dimension of the takeoff will be examined at length in a moment. First, let us briefly consider two crucial facets of the economic upturn: the agricultural revolution and the spread of rural industry.

The Agricultural Revolution and the Decline of Service

Industrialization entails a massive shift of labour-power from agriculture to industry. The numbers of people involved in food production in Northwestern Europe did not contract absolutely, but the proportion began to decline quite dramatically in the latter decades of the eighteenth century (earlier in England). The positive contribution of this intersectoral shift to the development of industrial capitalism is obvious: it generated a massive labour reserve, responsive to employment opportunities, prepared to move into rapidly expanding industrial towns. Yet this reallocation could not have proceeded very far (barring massive food imports) unless the growth of agricultural output was sufficient to meet the minimal needs of an expanding population uninvolved in food production. Failure in this regard would lead to chronic grain shortages and escalating cereal prices, absorbing an increasing proportion of the family budgets of wage-earners. This in turn would result in a constriction on consumer demand for non-food commodities, throttling industrial growth. This growth-aborting chain reaction had engendered seventeenth-century stagnation: would history repeat itself?

In fact, Western Europe barely avoided population-driven strangulation in the latter decades of the eighteenth century. The sure sign of demand strain on agriculture, caused by accelerating population growth and intersectoral shifts in the labour force, was a sustained rise in grain prices over the long term. Between 1730–40 and 1800–10, a composite price of the principal bread grains rose 163 per cent in France, 210 per cent in Germany, 250 per cent in England, and 253 per cent in Sweden.[255] The price ratio of agricultural to industrial goods rose steeply as well. Towards the end of the eighteenth century, many industrial regions were becoming economically depressed. Nominal wage hikes did not keep pace with food price increases over the last six decades of the eighteenth century.[256] Both urban and rural proletarians suffered. In seventeen of twenty-one European towns surveyed by Johan Söderberg, the 'bread wage' of general labourers declined from 1730 to 1789. The real wages of agricultural labourers also deteriorated in the last half of the eighteenth century.[257]

If the grain price spiral had not been broken, as it was in the first two decades of the nineteenth century, the Industrial Revolution would have been stillborn. Just as Torrens, Malthus and Ricardo were expounding upon 'the law of diminishing returns from the land', the population–cereal price correlation was decisively breached. This breakthrough, coming very late in the day, was the result of an intensive 'agricultural revolution'. Rising revenues to landowners throughout the eighteenth century eventually resulted in technologically dynamic forms of capital reinvestment in agriculture – a capitalist pattern – in contrast to the traditional mode of extensive growth, limited productivity gains, and diminishing returns to increasingly marginal land.

The primary axis of eighteenth-century improvement (impressive enough by early modern standards) was still of an extensive nature. In England, there had been a substantial rise in agricultural output and yield per hectare between 1660 and 1740. This advance permitted a redistribution of the labour force towards industry, with less than half the active population remaining in agriculture by 1759, far lower than on the continent. Between 1740 and 1790, however, English agriculture stagnated, and around 1770 the country went from being a net grain exporter to an importer.[258] Grain production in France increased roughly 40 per cent in the eighteenth century, only keeping pace with the rise in numbers over the same period, permitting very little leeway for the redistribution of the labour force, whose agricultural component stood at roughly 75 per cent in 1750 and had dipped to 65 per cent by 1800.[259] In other parts of the continent, the expansion of grain output was of a similar order.

The increase was the result of a several changes. 'All over Europe, ... great expanses of heathland were ploughed up, marshes drained, forests cleared and pasture converted to arable.'[260] Contemporaries spoke in alarmed terms of a 'greed for soil' and a 'ploughing mania'. Major land-clearing initiatives were undertaken in Belgium, Germany, the northern Netherlands and Spain.[261] Together with this expansion, landowners promoted a far-reaching privatization of property rights in land: field enclosures; the suppression of commons use rights; and the termination of collectively enforced crop selection, planting and harvest schedules. All this enabled farmers to be more profit-oriented, responsive to shifting market prices for various agricultural commodities – ploughing up grassland, for example, as grain prices outstripped those for animal products, varying their crop mix accordingly. Towards the end of the century (earlier in England) these methods of extending the acreage under crops began to be supplemented by a series of intensive measures: a reduction of fallow through superior crop rotations and the gradual elimination of grazing on the stubble; the increasing use of nitrogen-fixing legumes, the seed drill, and a major intensification of agricultural labour. These innovations raised the productivity of land and labour-power sharply, bursting the age-old link between population growth rates and grain prices.

With the transformation of agricultural relations of production, domestic servants were increasingly replaced by hired hands. Service in husbandry went into gradual decline in England in the middle decades of the eighteenth century. Farmers began to replace servants working on annual contracts with labourers hired on a short-term basis; concomitantly, hired hands moved out of the households of their masters into their own quarters. In southern England, these two trends accelerated in the 1780s, were temporarily halted by labour scarcities during the Napoleonic Wars, then resumed their advance from 1815 on.[262] By the mid nineteenth century, the venerable institution of rural service was all but extinct, fading into oblivion somewhat later on the continent. What accounts for its demise?

Under the impetus of rising cereal prices, grassland was ploughed up and agrarian farming expanded at the expense of pasturage. As mentioned, servants had been concentrated in animal husbandry, where the employment of youth on yearly contracts ensured a stable labour force in all seasons. Labour requirements in grain growing were more uneven: peak demands for a few weeks were interspersed with long fallow seasons during which a farmer's own family could easily handle the workload. From the landowner's standpoint, it made good sense to employ hired hands on a daily basis at planting and harvest times, laying them off as soon as these jobs were finished. With grain prices rising faster than wages, employers were inclined to replace the food provisions to which servants were entitled with money payments to labourers. In England, furthermore, people qualified for the poor rates by claiming residence in a parish for a year; the community's propertied classes thus sought to reduce the welfare rolls by discouraging employers from issuing annual contracts.[263]

The sheer prosperity of commercial farmers in this era of rising revenues unleashed the desire for increased distance between the families of landowners and their hired hands.[264] With the separation of living space, class snobbery escalated. 'Since farmers lived in parlours, labourers were no more found in kitchens.'[265] The farmer's family was 'unwilling to associate with the labourers, and a second table was out of the question'.[266] Farmers complained that sources of respectable servants had dried up: 'The best domestics used to be found among the sons and daughters of little farmers; ... but since that valuable order of men has been so greatly reduced ... servants are of necessity taken from a lower description of persons.'[267] For their part, farm hands became increasingly hostile towards high-handed employers: 'They feel – to use their own words – that they are "treated like slaves". It is seldom that the farmer will condescend to speak to them except in terms of reproach or abuse.'[268]

If farmers had many reasons for wanting to replace live-in servants with hired hands residing elsewhere, there was nevertheless one precondition for the move that was beyond their control. They were utterly dependent upon being able to obtain labourers readily when extra hands were required, precisely in the same weeks of the year that their neighbours were also hiring. By the latter decades of the eighteenth century, rural labour supplies were plentiful all across Western Europe. Except at the height of the Napoleonic Wars, peak demands for labour-power did not engender serious scarcities. This general condition of labour surplus (at least in quantitative terms) was sustained right through the nineteenth century. Sooner or later, the extinction of domestic service in husbandry was assured: in England by 1850, on the continent roughly a half century later. 'Farmers, singly and collectively, had destroyed the niche where youths could be placed, relieving their parents of the expense of maintaining them.'[269]

The release of masses of young people from an institution that had prevented them from considering marriage much before their mid twenties must have facilitated earlier nuptials and independent household formation. Michael Anderson has estimated that a shift of one-fifth of the farm labour force from live-in service to day labour would have increased marital fertility by 6 per cent in agricultural areas.[270] Accelerating population growth was both a cause and an effect of the shift in the agricultural labour force from servants to day labourers.

The Verlagssystem's Expansion and Shifts in the Conjugal Division of Labour

Most industrial growth in the latter half of the eighteenth century was confined to specific regions of the European countryside. Entire villages were swept up in the production of particular lines of standard consumer goods, as merchants extended putting-out (the Verlagssystem), by-passing the urban guilds. Cottage industry flourished in diverse areas: in Westphalia, Saxony, the Zurich uplands, Alsace, Flanders, Brittany, Lancashire, Yorkshire and Ulster. The major product lines were in textiles, but putting-out also became the leading mode of mass-producing inexpensive goods for popular markets in light metalwork, pottery, leatherware and wood-furnishings.

The social relations of production in the domestic industries were mixed and transitional. In the early stages, most cottagers owned their own knitting frames, looms, smithies and kilns. But the tendency over time was for merchant capitalists, exploiting the periodic debt crises of the most impoverished families, to assume ownership of the means of production, gaining greater control of the production process. In the full Verlagssystem, merchants and their agents supplied cottagers with tools and raw materials, stipulated a product quota to be completed in a week, and returned at week's end to collect the finished goods, paying producers a piece rate for articles that passed their inspection. Most vestiges of independent production had thus been lost. This was an industrial capitalist form of production, albeit one still conducted in the producers' homes. Dispersed, unorganized, dependent on merchants for access to distant markets, cottagers were powerless to resist the encroachments of capital seeking control of production.[271]

The population of these proto-industrial zones grew quickly in the eighteenth century through a combination of in-migration and a rising excess of births over deaths. Between 1700 and 1789, the interior of Flanders grew more than twice as fast as the coastal area of commercial farming.[272] In the canton of Zurich, the people of the proto-industrial highlands almost trebled their numbers between 1700 and 1833, while lowland farming areas grew by half.[273] In the Wupper valley, in the heart of the Rhineland's textile industry, small villages of a few hundred mushroomed in a decade into towns of several thousand.[274] The English transformation was phenomenal: while the country as a whole grew by one-third from 1751 to 1801, the industrial Northwest spurted 110 per cent.[275]

The modalities of this extraordinary expansion will be explored more fully in a discussion of regional demographic trends. Here it is sufficient to note that precocious marriage and high childbearing rates were frequently (but not invariably) found in proto-industrial villages. On the one hand, the increasing landlessness of the cottagers and their willingness to subdivide small plots removed all remaining barriers to marriage associated with land transmission. It was thus much easier for the offspring of poor cottagers to get married and set up new households. There was also a positive incentive to marry early. Proto-industrialization raised the potential value of children to their parents' households. It was therefore a rational strategy (if not necessarily a conscious one) to get on with childbearing, entering the most draining phase of the family cycle while the couple were still in their prime. The eldest children would then be in a position to begin making a substantial contribution to the family economy as the productivity of their elders went into decline.[276] Except in times of economic depression, adults endeavoured to keep their offspring at home, working from an early age as members of the family labour team. This retention marked a sharp departure from the early modern pattern of land-poor families, who had typically sent their children into service to prevent them 'from eating their parents out'.[277]

Under the putting-out system, cottage industry was based on the labour of women and children, as it had been traditionally. But in the latter half of the eighteenth century, there was a marked intensification of the working day and younger children were pressed into service as assistants.[278] Merchants and their agents tightened the screws of labour discipline by implementing stricter product quotas, quality-control screening, tighter delivery schedules and elaborate subcontracting networks.[279] The driving force behind the pervasive speed-up of this era was the lowering of piece rates under the competitive whip of technological innovation and the initial spread of the factory system. To make the same income, cottagers had to double or treble their output.

In the face of this acceleration, cottagers broke with the traditional land-based division of spheres, where men worked in the fields and women in and around the house. As families lost their land and commons use rights, men came inside to work alongside their wives, transforming the 'sexual geography' of daily life.[280] Domestic industry forced family members to work together at close quarters, placing a premium on face-to-face teamwork. The need to combine industrial work with childcare and housework at one site fostered a much greater flexibility in the allocation of tasks between spouses. When a wife went out to do business with the contractor, her husband would take care of the home, mind the children, tend the garden and milk the cows.[281] In these circumstances, the sex-typing of skills and areas of responsibility, so pronounced in peasant households, was frequently blurred and sometimes inverted. It was not unusual to find women working as cutlers and nailmakers, and men as spinners and lacemakers. Middle-class observers were troubled that men in weaving villages 'cook, sweep, and milk the cows in order never to disturb the good diligent wife in her work'.[282] The shake-up of male and female work routines in the course of proto-industrialization undoubtedly had far-reaching subjective effects, but it could hardly have meant that cottagers became impervious to gender distinctions in daily work. Yet this is what Hans Medick implies in stating that family teamwork proceeded 'without regard for sex or age'.[283] Jean Quataert concurs, writing that conjugal 'roles were exchangeable and not defined by gender'.[284] Studies of rapid gender flux in the labour process of the early textile mills and in heavy industry in the Second World War do not reveal the dissolution of sex distinctions in these situations; rather, they indicate that a rapid redrawing of the gender map occurs, after a brief period of uncertainty and confusion.[285]

Quataert has argued that the traditional prerogatives available to artisan and peasant patriarchs were largely absent in proto-industrial households; women were able to assert their rights more or less on a par with their husbands. In the homeweaving villages of Saxony, she found a number of practices that may be taken as indices of women's power. The absence of patrilineal guild regulations permitted women to gain greater access to the means of production.

Women brought valuable tools and substantial savings into marriage, helping to establish new households. Husbands recognized looms and knitting frames as the property of their wives, keeping them separate from other household goods. The distinction was preserved in wills, as men made provision for their wives to continue the family business after their deaths. In their frequent role as hawkers of their families' wares, women brought home considerable income, becoming major breadwinners.[286]

All these practices were predicated on the producers maintaining independent family businesses, in full possession of their tools and selling their own goods on an open market. In these circumstances, it appears that cottage industry did indeed foster a very substantial redistribution of spousal power to women's advantage. But it is unlikely that their base of strength would have been sustained as merchants took over ownership and control of the means of production. As Sonya Rose notes in her study of the English hosiery industry, with families operating under the putting-out system,

> men ordinarily directed the household production process and were held responsible by hosiers for the work done by members of the family labour team. This does not suggest that women's work was unimportant or that their work was not valued, [but it does imply] that men had authority over women in the making of hosiery.[287]

Nancy Osterud concurs: '[In the putting-out system] women held primary responsibility for childcare and household chores, so they did not participate in paid labour on equal terms with their husbands.'[288] Merchants promoted male householdship, doing business with husbands as the natural representatives of their families and paying them lump sums for the finished products of the group's labour. State agencies also typically insisted that family businesses be registered in the husband's name and account books made out in his family name.[289] It is surely an exaggeration to place women on an equal footing with men in the cottage economy, particularly as it gets caught up in the putting-out system.

The Mortality Decline after 1750

The last of Western Europe's classical subsistence crises occurred in the 1740s.[290] Mortality abated thereafter. French mortality declined consistently from mid century; in the Scandinavian countries, the turning point came in the 1770s and in England a decade later.[291] The greatest gains were registered in countries with the most room for improvement. As a result, mortality differentials between nations in Northwestern Europe converged, while urban/rural differences persisted until the last decades of the nineteenth century.

Improvement in life expectancy was almost entirely due to the waning of epidemics, which flared less often, were more confined and were not as lethal. In England, for example, there were six years of crisis mortality in the first half of the eighteenth century, averaging 30 per cent above 'trend' (a 25-year moving average centred on the crisis year); in the second half, five crisis years averaged 15 per cent above trend.[292] In the meantime, normal 'background' mortality, the experience of non-crisis years, declined very little before 1800, and hardly at all in the cities until the second half of the nineteenth century. Since epidemic diseases killed poor people in much greater proportions than the rich, their subsidence reduced class differentials in mortality.[293] This was a key factor in enabling poor couples, for the first time in history, to raise larger families than their wealthier counterparts.

Before inquiring into the causes of diminished epidemic mortality, the other early modern killers – war and famine – should be briefly addressed. There is no doubt that the eighteenth century was a more tranquil century for Europe as a whole than the tumultuous seventeenth. Not as many men were killed in combat, army hygiene improved, and with a shift to naval warfare, fewer communities were ravaged by military occupations and pillage.[294] All these changes saved lives. But in so far as military aggression had always been overshadowed by infectious diseases as a means of mass death, its moderate lessening in the eighteenth century cannot be considered a major factor in the overall decline.

Death from starvation became a rarity after the subsistence crisis of the 1740s, with the tragic exception of the Irish Famine. Overall, food production in Western Europe kept pace with population growth, while Eastern European grain imports made up the difference in regions with a deficit. Perhaps the most significant amelioration in this regard was in transport and the spatial distribution of food supplies,

> producing a shift from intensely acute local difficulties to a more generalized, less acute, chronic difficulty. ... [This explains] an apparent contradiction: that it was fully possible for relative emancipation from famine and plague to produce a greater number of poor than ever before. A starving population ... cannot reproduce itself; an undernourished one has no difficulty in so doing.[295]

McKeown has claimed that nutritional improvement occurred at this time, making a prime contribution to mortality decline. In terms of caloric intake, this seems dubious. Households were growing less of their own food, becoming ever more reliant on wages to purchase basic foodstuffs from the baker, butcher and grocer. Without a widespread rise in real wages, it is therefore implausible to postulate substantial gains in this period.[296] But in the second half of the eighteenth century, real wages declined across Western Europe. There is some evidence of improvements in grain *quality*, however, with the curtailment of mould poisoning.[297] This would have reduced food contamination and improved people's health, but not enough to effect a dramatic reduction in the death rate.

The primary factor in the mortality decline was evidently the diminution of epidemic crises. The causes of this abatement have been the subject of intense controversy.[298] The range of plausible theories has recently been narrowed somewhat; scholars agree that several reciprocally reinforcing factors were at work. But firm answers are beyond reach before the twentieth century, owing to the paucity of the types of evidence required to assess changes in the virulence of infectious diseases. Plague had subsided in the second half of the seventeenth century, but the mortality decline cannot be attributed to this. Other killers had taken its place: typhus, cholera, tuberculosis and smallpox, a relative newcomer.[299] Medical intervention made an appreciable difference only in the latter case. By the early eighteenth century, smallpox had become a major killer, accounting for perhaps 10 to 15 per cent of all deaths. The first mass-inoculation measures were undertaken around 1740. Though dangerous (infecting the patient with mild strains of the disease), they were also partially effective, reducing the lethality and spread of smallpox outbreaks considerably. Around the turn of the century, a safer (cowpox) vaccination was introduced, cutting epidemic deaths to a fraction of their former magnitude in the first half of the nineteenth century.[300] In the absence of smallpox vaccination campaigns, it is doubtful that English urbanization would have proceeded at the unprecedented pace that it did (in an era before effective waste disposal) without provoking mortality crises of growth-halting proportions. Other epidemic diseases became less lethal in the century from 1750 to 1850; they were also more confined. Several factors probably contributed to this amelioration: the development of less virulent pathogen strains; the strengthening of human antibody resistance; the cyclical decline of rodent and insect carriers and increased rat resistance and immunity; changes in the handling of livestock with new forms of husbandry; and a moderation in climate.[301] As mentioned, it is well beyond present historical knowledge to weigh the respective contributions of such variables to the subsidence of epidemic mortality.

One factor, more readily observed and pre-eminently social, has been persuasively shown to have made a difference: the population controls increasingly exercised by state authorities in response to local outbreaks of recognizably contagious diseases.[302] As epidemic patterns were more carefully observed and systematically recorded (if not yet understood in a scientific sense), the emergency measures of quarantine and migratory control taken by state officers to prevent diffusion became more concerted, uniform and efficient.[303] The *cordon sanitaire* thrown up by the Habsburgs along the border with the Ottoman Empire, and the French government's pre-emptive isolation of a plague flare-up in Marseille, were particularly effective initiatives by increasingly centralized states.[304] Such interventions were most likely to succeed in combating the dispersion of airborne diseases (tuberculosis, whooping cough, diphtheria, measles and scarlet fever).

The absence of two factors of potentially major influence in reducing death from infectious diseases deserves mention here, since both have played key roles in the twentieth century: improvements in water supply and waste disposal; and use of medicinal drugs and the extension of hospital care. There was probably some deterioration in the provision of safe drinking water and sewerage between 1750 and 1850, due to rapid urbanization, slum overcrowding and an abominable lack of underground drains. The most telling index here is the urban/rural mortality differential, which persisted and may even have increased in this period. In the second half of the nineteenth century, on the other hand, improvements in urban water supplies and waste disposal were considerable. Undoubtedly, they played a major role in prolonging life in this period.[305]

As for drugs and hospitals, it is unlikely that they had a major impact on survival rates much before 1850, with the notable exception of smallpox vaccine, medicine's only real success story in the preceding century.[306] McKeown has demonstrated in convincing detail that eighteenth-century doctors, regardless of their earnestness and compassion, had no effective antidotes for the diseases killing their patients. His pessimistic view that hospitals raised mortality by becoming hotbeds of infection has been convincingly refuted.[307] General hospitals seem to have had a modestly positive impact on mortality between 1750 and 1850, yet no one has presented a well-documented case that they could have played a decisive role in the first century of the mortality decline in Western Europe. To conclude: the primary ingredient in the mortality decline was evidently the reduction of epidemic deaths. This was due to a rather fortuitous combination of biological, social and ecological changes (the three dimensions listed here in their probable order of importance).

While the objective measures of the mortality decline are straightforward and can be readily charted, the subjective response of people to this amelioration is elusive and almost impossible to measure. Yet it is clear that the lasting improvement in survival rates changed the quality of family life and consciousness in subtle but profound ways. In a low-mortality context where the great majority of us survive to old age, it stretches the limits of our imagination to consider people's family experience in a high-mortality world of random impermanence, where loved ones were struck down, suddenly and before their time, with such awful frequency. Improvements in the life-chances of children and adults made family life less chaotic: marriages lasted longer and fewer children were orphaned; if infants endured the first year of life, they stood a much better chance of surviving to old age. Unexpected death could still devastate a family, as it does today, but when pestilence struck less often, it became possible to count on family members surviving and on family bonds

211

enduring, enabling people to plan for the future with greater confidence. The life-chances of a community's members would need to improve for several decades at least before a new sense of familial stability could take root. The transition from a relatively high- to a low-mortality world took place over two centuries in Western Europe, and the life-prospects of urban slum-dwellers did not improve much, if at all, until the last half of the nineteenth century. So we are contemplating a gradual and diffuse transformation; we cannot infer that a shift in familial consciousness would follow immediately upon a major improvement in life expectancy until such time as it became evident that prior death rates would not recur. There is no sound reason, on the other hand, to ignore or discount the subjective effects of a change of this magnitude merely because it is elusive and unquantifiable.

Against all odds, the common folk of pre-industrial Europe struggled to shape their familial destinies. Even during the most horrendous periods of war and epidemic, we find no substantial evidence that people gave up and abandoned their kin to the grim reaper. Accounts of numbed stoicism in the face of mass death should not be mistaken for abject passivity. Popular resignation was the result, above all, of having very little control over births and deaths in the family. People typically thought about these events in mystical ways: 'God had sent them' and then, for reasons beyond human comprehension, He would 'carry them away'. This did not prevent people from acting deliberately to reduce risk, but it limited the form of action that could be contemplated. With the decline in mortality, the scope for effective intervention was broadened. The life-choices that structure family continuity through time had more predictable consequences; critical objectives could be achieved more regularly. Increasingly, the problem of uncontrolled randomness in life's fortunes was addressed through the calculus of probabilities, rather than through ritual, prayer, pleas for divine intercession, and stoicism in the face of the invisible perils of disease or unwanted pregnancy. Families were beginning to be 'what you made them'; a long, slow transition was under way to the modern sense of family determination. The spread of birth control within marriage, and the eventual adoption of family planning to fulfil an ideal target size, marked a turning point in the development of this new sensibility. We will return to these themes in examining the fertility decline in the sequel to this volume, *Weathering the Storm: Working-Class Families from the Industrial Revolution to the Fertility Decline*.

Explaining the Population Boom

Historical demographers have long argued whether falling mortality or rising fertility furnished the driving force of the demographic revolution after 1750.

Swept up in the dynamic of polarized debate, most have plumped for the unilateral role of one factor, while minimizing or denying outright the force of the other. I have seen no compelling evidence or argument thus far presented to enter the lists for either camp. A balanced weighing of the evidence indicates that both stimuli were operative, though their respective contributions varied greatly between countries, regions and classes. How have demographers estimated the respective contributions of rising fertility and declining mortality at a national level?

Wrigley and Schofield feel they have resolved the conundrum for England: 'the fertility rise contributed about two and a half times as much to the rise in growth rates as the mortality fall.'[308] Fertility rose 38 per cent between 1741 to 1816, the jump being due almost entirely to a remarkable decline of 3.3 years in the mean age of women at first marriage from a peak of 27 in 1710 to a nadir of 23.7 a century later.[309] De Vries notes that in the Netherlands as well, a fertility rise furnished the primary impetus to rapid growth, particularly between 1809 and 1837.[310] These results are remarkable in the light of the prevailing view that declining mortality was the main stimulus in the population explosion. So confident have most scholars been in this summary verdict that the centre of controversy shifted in the 1960s and 1970s to an adequate explanation of prolonged life expectancy.[311] Wrigley and Schofield's immense reconstruction in *The Population History of England* has broken up the consensus for England at least.[312]

In most of the other states of Western Europe, aggregate evidence points thus far in the opposite direction: to declining mortality as the primary (and in some cases the sole) vital rate change in the population takeoff. France is evidently the antipodal case to England, and the one most thoroughly documented. The French birth rate drifted down from 1755 on; in the wake of the Revolution the decline grew steeper, persisting through most of the nineteenth century.[313] So in a mathematical sense, France's growth was *wholly* due to declining mortality. French life expectancy lengthened from a wretched twenty-five years in 1750 to forty-one years a century later.

The French began deliberately limiting fertility a full century before other Europeans. The reasons for their precociousness are not clear, and intense controversy surrounds the subject.[314] The French Revolution seems to mark off two distinct phases of descent. Under the *ancien régime*, the nuptial valve was still functioning. The average age of women at first marriage rose 1.4 years from 1700 to 1789; the proportion never marrying increased from 6 to 10 per cent in the same period.[315] In the nineteenth century, the decline was effected within marriage, no longer by means of it. French women married two years earlier in 1900 than they had in 1800, yet cut their fertility by a third during the century.[316]

Scandinavia is the other area of Western Europe for which there are satisfactory archival materials from 1750 on: 'In Sweden, the bulk of the acceleration in intrinsic growth rates between 1750 and 1850 is attributable to declining mortality rates, without which there would have been no consistent and significant change in growth rates.'[317] In Norway from 1735 to 1865, the population multiplied 2.8 times in 130 years. During that time, the birth rate rose 7 per cent while the death rate fell 32 per cent, so declining mortality clearly made the biggest difference.[318] The population of Denmark grew at a more moderate pace than Norway over the same period, but its vital rates developed along very similar lines.[319] Here too, prolonged life expectancy made by far the biggest contribution, in mathematical terms, to the population rise.

Having waded patiently through the foregoing summary of the components of growth, you will probably be wondering, as I have, whether unifying strands of an integral explanation can possibly be found here. Employing the standard demographic measures, and taking the state as the primary unit of aggregation and analysis, the picture is indeed a bewildering one – a cacophony of disparate trends, with each nation exhibiting a unique demographic transition. Yet out of this dissimilarity, a surprisingly congruent result emerged: a broadly simultaneous population expansion of unprecedented scope and duration. On the face of it, we confront an intractable conundrum. This immense historical watershed appears to have been generated by 'opposite' causes in different states: by a fertility rise in England and the Netherlands, and a mortality decline elsewhere. Is there anything here which would enable us to make sense of the vital revolution and its role in the Industrial Revolution? One response to the apparent scarcity of common denominators has been to abandon the quest for general causes as a chimera.[320] The simultaneity and spread of the demographic acceleration is thus treated as a coincidental result of dissimilar causes working in particular contexts – an entirely contingent outcome.

Some historians may rest content with this resolution of the problem; eschewing grand theorizing, they prefer to generate careful descriptions of the specific context and unique trajectory of the demographic transition in particular regions. While benefiting enormously from sharply etched local studies of the transition, analysts with social-scientific ambitions will balk at a research strategy which forsakes hypothesis formation at the international level in order to respect regional differences. Large-scale forces necessarily become manifest as agencies of change by working through specific local and regional formations, whose diversity induces marked variation in the ways in which sweeping change occurs. The full recognition of such unevenness, of distinct routes in transition, need not defeat attempts to explain far-reaching changes by means of macro-dynamic models. In marxist terms, this is the problem of uneven and combined development. We need to identify those forces, acting unevenly, that combined to disintegrate the early modern demographic regime in the disparate regions of Western Europe, galvanizing the vital revolution and generating a remarkably general, though by no means uniform, result.

Owing to the highly polarized debate over 'the prime mover', the question of the *interaction* of fertility and mortality has too often been submerged. Until this dynamic interplay is conceived in a theoretically informed way, it would be a mistake to jump to the conclusion that these patterns are really as antinomous as they appear in a mathematical account based on a diachronic calculation of components of growth. Reasoning of this sort treats the two vital rates in isolation from one another and ignores the question of their interaction. Let us assume, for example, that demographers have firmly established that the population boom in a given country was 'entirely due' to a decline in mortality, with the birth rate persisting at its former level. From a comparative static perspective, the question has been answered; in a dynamic framework, we must still inquire *why the birth rate did not fall* as landlessness increased. For in the homeostatic regime entrenched in Western Europe before 1750, fertility rates had persistently followed mortality trends down when the latter declined for a whole period, as places on the land filled up and the nuptial valve tightened. After 1750, this no longer occurred. If the birth rate had traced its former course (as it did in Finland, and in France to a degree), the expansion would have been moderate and halting, much like previous growth phases. By the same reasoning, wherever fertility rates rose, and this was the primary component of growth (as in England), we must ask why the poor did not die with increasing frequency as a consequence of overcrowding, as they had repeatedly in high-pressure zones of early modern Europe. When considering an initiatory role for either factor, we need to inquire immediately about the other.

There is nothing intrinsically wrong with the *calculation* of components of growth, based on reasonable estimates of birth and death rates over time. The problem with the discussion lies in a form of *reasoning* in which the explanation of a phenomenon is treated as if it were self-evidently inherent in the mathematical finding which furnishes a summary measure of the pattern under investigation.[321] This short-circuits the problem of interpretation; mathematical findings do not speak for themselves. The fact that they are routinely presented as if they did is indicative of a statistical positivism rife in the discipline of demography. As David Coleman and Roger Schofield have remarked, 'any subject which finds it necessary, or indeed possible, to consider its material divorced from an appropriate body of theory must be in trouble. This seems to be the case with demography at present, and it raises many questions.'[322] Components-of-growth reasoning epitomizes the divorce of 'facts' from an appropriate body of theory.

Let us now examine the dynamics of the demographic revolution from the standpoint of region and class, endeavouring to ascertain, from both angles, what caused vital rates to diverge on an enduring basis.

Migration and Regional Demographic Trends

It is invaluable to have a solid set of demographic estimates for nation-states, dating back to the mid eighteenth century at least, as has now been achieved for England, France and the Scandinavian countries. But we would do well to avoid the fixation of most demographers with comparisons between national averages ('the French versus the English pattern'). Nation-states are far too heterogeneous socially to be illuminating units of aggregation. The compositional effect is to mask variance between regions and social classes over the long run, since their vital rates are often out of phase conjuncturally, tending to offset one another. The resulting totals appear before our eyes as direct measures of 'real structures', much more stolid and slow to change than the diverse forces comprising them. More revealing breakdowns of vital rates optimally require theoretically informed categories, where 'region' is more than a territorial subunit of a state, and 'social class' is not uncritically construed simply by reiterating the occupational nomenclature used by census-takers long ago. Unfortunately, most historical demographers continue to labour within the modernization paradigm, where such distinctions are of marginal concern. They have furnished marxists and feminists, latecomers to the field, with an empirically rich but badly misconceived body of evidence and measurement.

The methodology of regional classification is extremely underdeveloped; every analyst invents his or her own system. In summarizing the work of others, one inevitably inherits their eclecticism. Under the circumstances, it would be spurious to present an elaborate typology. Instead, I shall estimate demographic trends in three basic zones of Northwestern Europe: established cities; industrial regions, mostly rural but including new towns arising in the course of population build-up; and rural agricultural regions. Let us consider each in turn.

Cities: Before the Industrial Revolution, the great cities of Western Europe were primarily centres of finance, commerce, trade and state administration. To be sure, much commodity production took place within their gates, but in most cities this was a secondary component of the economy. While wage labour was the norm in urban milieus, the influence of guilds, with their apprenticeship arrangements, was still very strong. Even in manufacturing cities, wage labour was seldom fully proletarian. Early industrial capitalists sought to avoid hiring urban labour, bypassing the guilds in favour of cheaper rural labour. With few exceptions, the Industrial Revolution in its early stages was not centred in pre-existing cities, nor was the demographic boom of the period. Cities were certainly growing, but not much faster than the countryside. In 1750, 13.6 per cent of the population of Northwestern Europe lived in cities (population above 10,000); by 1800, this portion had increased modestly to 14.9 per cent.[323] More people were buried in cities than were baptized in them; they grew entirely by influx. Towards the end of the eighteenth century the deficit had diminished, but reproduction rates did not turn positive in most cities until sometime in the nineteenth century.[324] While birth rates in urban areas were usually comparable to those in their regional hinterlands, death rates were far worse, roughly one and a half times rural rates.[325] As noted, this disparity was not closed until the latter part of the nineteenth century.

Rural Industry: The fastest growing regions in the first phase of the boom were rural areas of industrial production, in textiles, mining and metalworking. The rapidity of population build-up in these regions was remarkable, as we have seen. In-migration and indigenous increase both contributed to this unprecedented expansion. Since the great majority of newcomers were young adults who wed just before or soon after they arrived, migration had the effect of raising the birth rate of industrial regions. Growth was thus partly due to the age effect of in-migration, making it difficult to weigh the respective contributions of the two sources. Mass entry probably played a dominant role in the initial stages, with a tendency for the indigenous ingredient to strengthen over time.

In comparison with major cities and agricultural districts, birth rates in industrial regions were usually high. Between 1730 and 1800, fertility in the industrial districts of Nottinghamshire was on average 29 per cent above levels in nearby agricultural villages.[326] Between 1751 and 1830, birth rates in northwest England were the highest in the country, averaging 7 per cent in excess of the other regions combined.[327] These patterns are clear enough in England, where the documentation is adequate. The continent presents a murkier picture, though the same trends – fast growth based on a combination of in-migration and local increase – are evident in cottage textile districts in Brittany, Flanders, Lombardy, Saxony, Basel, Piedmont and the canton of Zurich. In these zones, high birth rates were almost certainly due to earlier and more universal marriage. By the nineteenth century, the situation on the continent was clearer. Wrigley has contrasted regions of heavy industry and coal mining in northern France, southern Belgium and the Rhineland with adjacent agricultural areas and great cities. In 1860, the general fertility of coal-mining districts was roughly 20 per cent above that of neighbouring agricultural areas.[328] In Sweden, the birth rate in rural industrial regions was 18 per cent higher than that of the other regions combined, while the rate of natural increase was 59 per cent greater than the rest.[329]

217

Mass migration into rapidly growing proto-industrial areas rerouted the landless poor, permitting them to remain in the countryside. Earlier generations of the itinerant landless had no choice but to trek into cities, only to be decimated there. Since the mortality rates of country folk were substantially less than those of urban residents, particularly newcomers, poor migrants stood a much better chance of living through their reproductive years, marrying and bearing children, if they could avoid residing for any length of time in lethal cities. The rapid increase of employment in rural industrial districts gave them the opportunity to do just that.[330] The detouring of migratory flows thus worked on both sides of the demographic equation: it increased the population of reproductive age living in milieus of relatively high nuptiality and marital fertility, and it lengthened their life expectancy. For the first time, the landless began to register a persistent excess of births over deaths. To be sure, the traditional rural–urban flow continued; however, the portion of the rural surplus attracted to the cities fell off dramatically, reaching a low point in the second half of the eighteenth century.[331] Consequently, the rate of urbanization in this century was moderate; most of it was due to the growth of smaller centres, those beneath 10,000 population. New towns were forged as nodal intersections in rapidly crowding zones of rural industry. This pattern was in marked contrast to early modern urbanization, where a relatively few great cities attracted almost the entire influx.

Rural absorption was the by-product of positive proletarianization; in my view, this is the key to the first stage of the population boom. Its full importance cannot be appreciated if one focuses exclusively on fertility differentials between peasants and proletarians, as the debate over the demographic impact of proto-industrialization has tended to do.

Agricultural Regions: Overall, the population of agricultural districts grew in the first phase of the vital revolution, but not as rapidly as in other regions; farm districts thus held a diminishing portion of the entire population. The proportional reduction was due entirely to mass exodus, quickening from 1750 on. The pace of absolute growth was highly uneven; in most agricultural regions numbers rose at least modestly, while in a few areas the population shrank through massive emigration in the wake of enclosures, engrossment or economic stagnation. Labour supply in agriculture – increasingly proletarian – remained plentiful, a remarkable phenomenon in view of the rising tide of out-migration. The surplus kept farm wages down, preserving the traditional differential between industrial and agrarian wages (roughly on the order of 3:2), furnishing a persistent incentive for the unemployed to migrate to zones of new industry. Low farm wages also proved a boon to the capital accumulation of landowners, since returns to labour did not keep pace with rising agricultural productivity or food price inflation.

The primary impetus to demographic acceleration in the farm regions appears to have been the abatement of mortality crises. The nuptial valve opened in England (with the decline of farm service), but on the continent it tightened. In France, Belgium, Germany and the Scandinavian countries, the mean age of women at first marriage rose in most agricultural areas in this period.[332] While a rise in marital fertility may have offset this, the net result cannot have been a rise in fertility. Population growth accelerated because more children were survived to become productive and fertile adults. The biggest improvement was in the life-chances of the itinerant poor, who often left agricultural regions in search of work.

Summarizing the regional picture: the demographic takeoff was generated by a particular interaction between a declining death rate in the countryside; a mass intersectoral flow from agriculture to industry absorbed within the countryside, inhibiting rural–urban migration; and unusually high fertility in the rural industrial districts, in mining, metallurgy and textile communities particularly.

Proletarianization and the Vital Revolution

Did proletarianization quicken population growth rates from 1750 on? An impressive group of scholars have answered in the affirmative, presenting a wide range of evidence from various regions of Northwestern Europe.[333] Most have identified nuptiality as the mediating variable, arguing that proletarians usually found it easier to marry than peasants, tending to do so earlier and more universally. Higher birth rates followed, even where there was no difference between peasant and proletarian fertility rates within marriage. This position has not gone uncontested. Other scholars, examining different communities, have found no consistent difference between peasants and proletarians in the mean age of women at first marriage or proportions ever marrying; a few have even found the reverse disparity, with peasants marrying earlier.[334] They have concluded that the posited connection between proletarianization and high and rising fertility is non-existent or, at the very least, unproven.

The main reason for the dispute, in my view, is the regionally uneven nature of the pattern itself. The proponents of the thesis have studied proto-industrial zones where the correlation is manifest; the sceptics have found that in other areas there is no class difference in marriage or fertility rates. Both sides have tended to overgeneralize from specific patterns. What I want to do here is to offer a tentative explanation for this unevenness. I shall refrain from a detailed dissection of the vast proto-industrialization literature on a case-by-case basis; this would be necessary to clinch the argument. But I think I can show why a mixed result is both logical and to be expected.

I am of the view that there are connections – indeed, pivotal connections

219

– between proletarianization and accelerated population growth, but that the cause-and-effect relationship is multifaceted and highly mediated. In this regard, there are two major problems with the discussion. In the first place, the reproductive connection has been posited to work through fertility, when, from a dynamic standpoint, the essential issue is the widening differential between fertility and mortality. As mentioned, the provision of sustained employment for a chronically underemployed and land-poor populace can certainly prolong people's lives, particularly if it enables them to avoid living in cities for any length of time. And if people live longer, they have more opportunity to couple, procreate and raise children. This point has been discussed in the last section and will not detain us here.

The second deficiency has been the failure to distinguish between different patterns of proletarianization. Amid the welter of claims and refutations, it is possible to discern some fairly broad patterns. Proletarianization *in general* does not promote earlier and more universal marriage; *certain kinds* of proletarianization do. The location and strength of the capitalist demand for labour are decisive. In the stagnant seventeenth and early eighteenth centuries, growing landlessness offered no inducement to marry in the absence of vigorous employer demand. It was *positive* proletarianization, with an opening up of rural and small-town employment opportunities for men and children, that was most frequently associated with earlier and more universal marriage. Relatively high wages for male industrial labourers and an early peak in their earning curve were strongly correlated with early marriage and rapid population growth.[335] Domestic service, on the other hand, retarded marriage, checking fertility.[336] Proletarian migration promoted earlier and more universal marriage (and hence higher fertility) wherever it freed young men and women from parental and community regulation of courtship and brought them into casual concourse in roughly equal numbers. Where mass migration skewed the sex ratio and segregated the sexes in workplace and residence, it suppressed fertility.[337] Women working outside the home generally married later, while cottage industry and the putting-out system have tended to foster earlier marriage and higher fertility. Within marriage, the extra-domestic employment of married women on an inflexible shiftwork basis limited fertility, promoted mercenary wet-nursing, and exacerbated the problem of infant loss, thus slowing growth.[338] Women toiling in textile mills exhibited these patterns. Women cottagers retained some flexibility in their work schedules, preserving a minimal compatibility between productive and reproductive labour that the factory system subsequently destroyed. Their fertility rates were often relatively high, both in and out of wedlock.

Specifically on the question of marriage rates, how do we explain very mixed findings? The conceptual key is to see that two conditions were required to foster earlier and more universal marriage. In the first place, the barriers that had inhibited marriage in the early modern era had to be displaced or circumvented. Secondly, a positive balance of incentives and opportunities was necessary to induce those proletarians in a position to marry to do so, earlier and more universally. Most advocates of the proletarianization–fertility connection have focused unduly on the first condition. There has been a tendency to envision the Western European marriage system as a dam, holding back the immense forces of a prolific river.[339] As soon as proletarianization bursts the nuptial floodgates, people marry earlier and have more children, just as surely as water rushes downhill. With this naturalist assumption, one overlooks the fact that it is not enough to be *free* to marry; young men and women must also *have an interest* in doing so. It was correct to highlight the importance of the proletarian subversion of the traditional land-based blocks to early marriage; it was wrong to assume that such release was a sufficient condition of earlier and more universal marriage. If the correlation between proletarianization and earlier and more universal marriage arises under certain circumstances and not others, as the evidence indicates, we must conclude that either or both of the above conditions have been unevenly met. Perhaps the nuptial valve was not loosened everywhere in the second half of the eighteenth century; perhaps proletarianization failed to provide youth in some communities with a strong incentive to marry early. Both these qualifications are persuasive.

Consider first the dismantling and circumvention of barriers. For single youth of either sex, the growth of employment opportunities furnished a mass alternative to rural domestic service and parentally arranged apprenticeship as preludes to marriage. Instead of being sent into service or a trade, youth increasingly obtained their own employment. The development of *national* labour markets, stimulating the long-distance migration of independent youth (mostly males), delivered a severe blow to parental influence in mate selection and courtship. Domestic service in husbandry waned and farm labourers tended to live apart from their employers, reducing paternalist supervision of their lives off the job. The growth of commercial housing markets, with private accommodation becoming more readily available at the payment of a week's rent from one's own wage, also undermined the community control of youth. All these developments made it easier for young adults to court in their own way, choose mates independently, establish households and set their own wedding dates. However, the spread of wage labour did not loosen the nuptial valve everywhere in the short term. For a while at least, patriarchal leverage over children's marital choices could often be shored up by the community. Earlier marriages tended to occur in thriving open villages and industrial towns, where free market employment was plentiful for youth and there were no serious impediments to setting up independent households. In closed villages, cheap rental accommodation was not readily available to unattached young adults, and the authorities opposed early marriage. Where the local control of poor relief remained vigorous, it was difficult to marry an outsider. Where employment was limited and effectively circumscribed by the local elite, and wages were paid largely in kind, paternalist supervision of labourers' lives off the job remained extensive. In these circumstances, weddings tended to be delayed and many never married at all.

Now consider the second factor, the balance of incentives to marry. The assumption that almost all young adults would wish to wed early if they could is based on implicit premises of a rather timeless sort concerning the twin drives of sex and procreation. These presumptions ought to be openly confronted: first, that young adults, especially men, would naturally be keen to wed in order to enjoy legitimate sex; and second, that sexually mature women would want to begin childbearing without delay, fulfilling maternal instincts. Sexual desire and the wish to have children furnish powerful motives to wed in most societies, but the incentive to marry in order to satisfy these desires depends upon the social organization of marriage and the divergent consequences of pursuing these objectives in and out of wedlock. Increased freedom from parental constraint in mate selection may just as easily lead to the postponement of nuptials as to their hastening. The relaxation of patriarchal and community control over dating and courtship may dissipate one of the most compelling motives for rushing into marriage: the desire to consummate a love interest, and to do so openly without serious stigma.[340] If this is assumed to be the main motive for marriage, then we would not predict that the dismantling of controls would lead to earlier marriage. Proletarianization generally made it easier to engage in premarital sex and for men to evade the obligation to marry in the event of conception. For women, on the other hand, proletarian 'freedoms' often entailed an increased vulnerability – both economic and sexual – inducing them to seek out marriage partners at an early age.[341] It seems generally true to say that proletarian women were keener than men to marry.

Did the residential circumstances of single youth in their late teens and early twenties affect marital timing? Consider young adults living in three situations: (a) remaining at home with parents; (b) 'living in' as servants and apprentices; and (c) residing on their own in relatively unsupervised accommodation. In these conditions, the obstacles and incentives to marry varied directly with one another, thus tending to wash out independent effects and making residential circumstances an unreliable predictor of age at marriage. While living with one's parents furnished a powerful motive for marriage, regular wage remission made it difficult to set aside earnings for the future. A decent rate of current earnings was evidently more important as a requisite to working-class marriage than a saving fund; yet the absence of any savings gave proletarians reason to pause. At the opposite extreme, in independent circumstances, men who were earning their own wage and living on their own found it comparatively easy to wed but lacked an immediate incentive to do so. As

Malthus realized, 'the labourer who earns eighteenpence or two shillings a day and lives his ease as a single man, will hesitate a little before he divides that pittance among four or five which seems to be not more than sufficient for one.'[342] In peasant communities, it was widely recognized that a landholder needed to take a wife to help him manage his property; it was almost impossible to cope alone. He was also anxious to procreate within marriage to ensure himself a legitimate heir. For the proletarian male, by contrast, the drive to assure his own continuity beyond the grave was no longer harnessed to the transmission of property in the means of production. In the short term, his living standard would be higher residing independently than if he chose to marry and cohabit. On the other hand, if he valued security in old age, it made sense to get started on forming a family. Thus, for many men, short- and long-term interests worked in opposite directions, engendering a mixed and indeterminate result.

Where children lived at home with their parents, the generations tugged in different directions. As the opportunities for child labour increased, the rising value of children to the family economy led parents to keep children at home until well into their twenties, handing over wages faithfully, in order to safeguard their own security in old age. The same trend furnished youth with the opposite incentive: early childbearing made financial sense in the long term for those whose labour-power was being prematurely exhausted. If couples got an early start, they would pass through the perilous phase of a high dependency ratio while the main breadwinner's earnings were still at or near their peak. They would then be in a position to 'age gracefully', approaching their twilight years with the considerable assistance and remitted earnings of several offspring in their teens and early twenties.[343] If, as seems clear, parents strove to keep their working children at home as long as possible, while young adults wished to leave and get married as soon as they could, then the timing of their departure was largely dependent upon the balance of power between the generations. Once again we find an indeterminate equation, liable to generate diverse results in terms of the mean age at first marriage.

In conclusion: mass proletarianization did make it somewhat easier for wage-earning youth in *most* regions to determine the timing of their own marriages; but this relaxation was by no means universal. Some of the difference in nuptial patterns noted by scholars may be due to the regionally uneven dismantling of the traditional patriarchal controls on mate selection, courtship and marriage. The effect of proletarianization on the balance of incentives to marry was also highly varied, depending on the residential and employment circumstances of youth. Hypothetically, there were as many possibilities for a negative balance as a positive one. Yet the overall impact in the phase of early industrialization appears to have been positive, both in boosting fertility and lengthening life expectancy. In the transition to industrial

223

capitalism, proletarians exhibited high birth rates in and out of marriage; not invariably higher than those of surrounding classes, but very often so. The rapid expansion of employment for poor men and children in particular was almost certainly a major impetus to the population explosion.

I have arrived at this positive conclusion partly because I do not think that evidence cited by the sceptics (finding that in some areas there was no appreciable difference in the marriage patterns of peasants and proletarians) constitutes a decisive refutation of the connection between proletarianization and population growth. As well as operating in a class-specific way, the effect of proletarianization might have been manifest more broadly at an interregional level. If the rapid expansion of labour demand outside agriculture succeeded in engaging a surplus population of young adults, many of whom would otherwise have stayed put and fought for scarce places on the land, then the resulting proletarianization would probably enhance the inheritance, dowry and marriage prospects of youth remaining behind in agriculture. Their mean age at marriage might then decrease, or at least be inhibited from rising, as it would have in an earlier era prior to the widespread availability of industrial employment. Such an indirectly stimulative effect on the reproduction rates of the young people remaining in agriculture would contribute to overall population growth, while tending – all else being equal – to diminish or efface the marriage and birth rate differentials between peasants and proletarians. Due to the counterfactual nature of this argument, the 'diffuse regional effect' thesis is impossible to prove or disprove. None the less, it seems to be eminently plausible, and might partly account for the mixed and contradictory nature of the direct evidence on class-specific fertility differentials.

The full significance of positive proletarianization to the vital revolution is best appreciated by contrasting population growth differentials by social class before and after 1750. In the medieval and early modern eras, landless labourers had much lower rates of growth than land-based agriculturalists. As we have seen, this deficit was the combined result of higher mortality, later marriage, and lower marital fertility. The ranks of the underclass thus grew primarily, and often entirely, by means of the steady stream of downwardly mobile youth who had lost out in the competition for scarce village land. After 1750, the ranks of the proletariat (especially its rural components) began to swell by an excess of births over deaths. When this endogenous expansion was combined with a continuing influx from the displaced peasantry, the result was a much quicker overall growth rate than that of the propertied classes. Whether this reversal was due to declining mortality or rising fertility is not nearly so important as the fact that it occurred. As the pattern of class demography was transformed, it eventually inverted the prevailing direction of generational mobility between classes and between strata within classes. The mainstream of intergenerational mobility had formerly been downward, from the ranks of the propertied to the propertyless. By the late nineteenth century it had been reversed, with upward mobility becoming predominant: from the ranks of the proletariat into the lower echelons of the middle class, and within the working class, from blue-collar to white. Despite the fact that growth rate differentials would engender great alarm as middle-class birth rates declined, the truth was that the gap turned out to be one of capitalism's greatest strengths – its capacity to keep the dream and illusion of upward mobility alive for the sons and daughters of the working class.

Proletarianization and the Rise of Extramarital Childbirth

The rate of childbirth outside marriage rose all across Western Europe after 1750. In England, less than 2 per cent of births were 'illegitimate' in 1700; a century later over 5 per cent were. The French rate almost quadrupled: from 1.2 per cent in 1740–49 to 4.7 per cent by 1800–1809. Swedish rates nearly trebled from 1750 to 1820, while in Norway and Finland they more than doubled between 1750–70 and 1790–1820. The rise in Germany was even steeper, from 2.5 per cent before 1750 to a very high 11.9 per cent in 1780–1820.[344] It is striking that illegitimacy rates surged everywhere, regardless of trends in the birth rate. Fertility and illegitimacy trends closely paralleled one another in England, rising together from 1655 on as the pace of marriage quickened.[345] In France, by contrast, illegitimacy rose from 1740 on, while the nuptial valve closed and fertility slowed. Extending one's comparative horizon beyond England to the rest of Western Europe reveals no consistent correlation between fertility rates in and out of marriage.[346]

There was, on the other hand, a very strong pattern of persistence within regions. When the illegitimacy rates of the districts of a state (counties, departments, cantons, deaneries or provinces) are rank-ordered at a given point in time, they tend to retain their order in future periods over many decades. Regional persistence was strongly manifest in nineteenth-century Sweden (24 units), England (41), Germany (66), and twentieth-century Portugal (18).[347] Evidence from England indicates that such local perdurance was operative throughout the early modern era.[348] This commends the importance of recognizing locally reproduced cultural norms in matters of courtship, betrothal sex, free unions, customary marriage, abortion and the treatment of unwed mothers. In his pioneering survey of the Norwegian countryside a century ago, Sundt examined neighbouring districts with contrasting levels of illegitimacy. He found that in the low-rate district the mating rituals of youth were closely supervised, with more arranged marriages and less night-courting. Servants' sleeping quarters were usually located in the peasants' main house. In the high-rate district, parents recognized their children's right to select their own mates, night-courting was approved, and illegitimate pregnancies were likely to be regarded more as bad luck than as evidence of moral turpitude.[349] Working beneath the more uniform and centralized reactions of Church and state authorities, diverse community responses to nonconformist behaviour were evidently deeply ingrained, influencing levels of extramarital intercourse and childbirth.

The other side of the coin should not be forgotten: irrespective of their diversity at the outset, the rate of illegitimate births rose in almost all regions in the second half of the eighteenth century.[350] What accounts for the generality of this rising share of births outside marriage? First, we ought to establish whether proletarian single women were in fact much more likely to conceive and bear children than their counterparts in other social classes. Allowing for the typical imprecisions surrounding the conversion of occupational classifications into class categories, the answer appears to be yes: 'the rising number of pregnancies before marriage was basically a working-class phenomenon.'[351] In seven villages in eighteenth-century Norway, over half the cottar women were pregnant at marriage, while only a third of peasant women were.[352] In nineteenth-century Sweden, areas with a large rural proletariat tended to have higher rates of extramarital childbirth. Furthermore, within regions, over twice as many landless women as peasant women were pregnant or had already borne a child at marriage: 'Both illegitimacy and premarital conception were so common among the landless population that it must be assumed that it was an integral part of their marriage system.'[353] In the English parishes of Aldenham, Alcester and Colyton in 1790–1830, 'a much greater number of bastard-bearers seem to have been the children of labourers, or of married people known to have been labourers or servants, than those groups constituted of the whole population.' Flandrin reported the same pattern in France.[354] In short, there are sound empirical grounds for placing proletarianization, and the concomitant dissipation of parental authority and community controls over courtship, at the centre of an explanation of the rise of childbirth outside marriage in the late eighteenth and nineteenth centuries.

Several conditions had been crucial in maintaining tight community control over courtship in early modern Europe. Substantial dowries and landholdings, resources under parental control, were prerequisites to marriage and independent household formation. Young men and women who were unrelated did not normally work together or have much occasion to socialize informally, independent of adult supervision, in the course of daily life. Relations between unmarried men and women were mainly conducted in public on special occasions, at festivals, hiring fairs, holiday dances and wakes. These were well-supervised affairs, staged in ritualized fashion, replete with customs designed to guarantee the circulation of eligible males, preventing premature pairing and undue intimacy.[355] Active suitors tended to be local lads with

roots in the community and family reputations at stake. If conception occurred in the wake of a betrothal pledge, they could almost always be persuaded to marry.

Proletarianization disrupted these structures, integrating the sexes in daily
work and increasing mobility. Wages obviated the need to wait for land to be
made available and dowries to accumulate. Parental approval of betrothal was
still highly desirable, but it was no longer essential in order to proceed with
viable marriage plans.[356] Mate selection was opened to a broader field of eligibles, and courting was freed from highly orchestrated special events, becoming
more frequent, spontaneous and explicitly erotic. As chaperones and go-
betweens were jettisoned, the adult community could no longer supervise
courtship, delay pairing off, and ensure that the 'right' partners were chosen.
The loss of patriarchal power was greeted with a 'crescendo of complaints
about the immoral sexual activity of the young'.[357] The community's 'better
sort' were scandalized: 'girls open their chambers to these night boys and abandon themselves in the uncertain hope that, in the case of pregnancy, they will
not be left to their shame.'[358] Specific accusations of sexual impropriety were
part of a much broader condemnation of a plebeian culture of hedonism and
conspicuous consumption. Proletarian youth, 'this voluptuous class of people',
were accused of 'carelessness and frivolity, lack of concern for the future, ...
[spending] their ample earnings on luxuries'. This was the typical refrain of
merchants, clerics, doctors and government officials.[359]

Did the transformation of courtship practices and youth culture lead to an
increase in premarital sex, or did it merely result in a much lower proportion
of betrothal conceptions being legitimated by timely marriages before pregnancies had come to term? Edward Shorter has proposed that proletarianization gave rise to a veritable sexual revolution among young working-class
women between 1750 and 1850. After dispensing with a series of alternative
possibilities, he concluded that the rise in extramarital births was the result of
a sharp increase in sexual activity among young adults aged eighteen to
twenty-five, the large majority of whom were single. Since 'we can probably
assume that men have always been avid for sexual intercourse ... how do we
explain this new ... willingness on the part of women to climb into the sack
with them?' Shorter's answer was that

> The new proletarians of the eighteenth century were the vanguard of the sexual
> revolution because they were the first to be caught up in the market economy.
> ... From one end of Europe to the other, young unmarried women ... were
> rejecting traditional occupations in favour of paid employments within a
> capitalist setting. ... Not only did paid work give young women the inclination
> to escape the sexual constraints of their parents and town fathers, it also gave
> them the *possibility* of doing so. The dawning of the wish to be free had aroused
> within them a desire for personal independence and sexual adventure.[360]

This thesis generated considerable heat, to put it mildly, among family historians. In perhaps the most substantive response, Tilly, Scott and Cohen rebutted Shorter's thesis in detail, arguing that the key change for newly proletarian youth was the shift of courtship and mate selection from a community-regulated, parentally supervised liaison to an interpersonal affair.[361] A goodly number of early modern peasant women, as we have seen, were willing to engage in premarital sex on the basis of a verbal promise of marriage which their parents were in a position to enforce in the event of pregnancy, buttressed by pressure from the Church and the village's 'better sort'. But proletarian women and servants were more vulnerable. Courtship was likely to be an anonymous 'free market' affair, lacking the dotal negotiation between family heads which had formerly ensured its marital conclusion. Tilly, Scott and Cohen argued that a rising proportion of single women, pursuing traditional sexual practices on the basis of traditional values, were abandoned by transient men upon the discovery of pregnancy. In addition, most domestic servants were now hired on an open market, in contrast to earlier arrangements between family heads. This left young women, migrating further away from home in search of work, increasingly exposed to the sexual advances and impositions of their employers. With seasonal unemployment and desperate poverty, prostitution and infant abandonment also spread in this period.

Taken together, these trends furnish an alternative explanation for abruptly rising rates of unmarried childbirth between 1750 and 1820. Tilly, Scott and Cohen concluded that it was not premarital sexual *practices* that had changed so much as the *social context* within which they were conducted. The measure of single women's increasing vulnerability was this: a much lower proportion of their pregnancies were converted into 'legitimate' births by timely marriages.[362] The thesis has much in common with Shorter's, though this was obscured in the heat of polarized polemic. Both explanations are predicated on the profound social effects of proletarianization; both postulate a transformation of courtship and mate selection, involving the demise of traditional inheritance-based patriarchal and community controls over the behaviour of increasingly mobile youth. The disagreement was essentially over what had changed as these controls disintegrated: sexual practices or marital norms.

Can any quantitative evidence be brought to bear on this controversy? We know that the rate of bridal pregnancy rose steeply in the demographic transition. As with illegitimacy, the trend was extremely widespread across Western Europe. In a broad sample of English parishes in 1690, 15 per cent of first births occurred within eight months of nuptials; by 1800, it was 34 per cent.[363] In France the proportion doubled, rising from a much lower level of 6 per cent in the period 1690–1739 to 12 per cent in 1790–1819.[364] In Germany, the initial rate of 13 per cent before 1750 resembles the English level, while the subsequent climb was more moderate: to 24 per cent by 1780–1820.[365] By combining the illegitimacy and bridal pregnancy rates, it is possible (after making some adjustments) to estimate the proportion of first births conceived outside marriage; Wrigley has done this for England.[366] When both rates were at their lowest in the mid seventeenth century, about one first birth in eight originated in the pregnancy of an unmarried woman. By the end of the eighteenth century, when both rates were peaking, roughly one first birth in two was conceived by an unmarried woman. Knodel found a similar rise in six German villages: from 28 per cent of first births conceived out of wedlock in 1700–49 to 53 per cent by 1800–49.[367]

These trends corroborate Shorter's principal thesis. The twin rise of illegitimacy and bridal pregnancy rates on such a widespread basis indicates that there must have a very substantial rise in premarital sexual relations in this period.[368] In the absence of such a change, it is difficult to believe that the rate of first births conceived outside marriage could quadruple in a century and a half while bridal pregnancy rates doubled in less than a century, at a time when contraceptive devices were rarely used by the vast majority of couples. But this argument in no way invalidates Tilly, Scott and Cohen's thesis that pregnant single women were increasingly vulnerable to male desertion at this time. In the six German villages, for example, Knodel found that a declining proportion of first births conceived out of wedlock ended in marriage. He provides a three-way breakdown. In 1700–49, 60 per cent of first pregnancies ended in marriage before birth; 8 per cent in marriage after birth, and 33 per cent of the time, the couple did not marry. By 1800–49, only 35 per cent of the couples married before birth; 19 per cent married subsequently, and 46 per cent never did.[369] My own rough calculations on the English data point to the same deteriorating trend. The chances that a single woman's first pregnancy would result in birth within marriage declined from a relatively secure 79 per cent in 1670 to 63 per cent by 1800.[370] The thesis of increasing vulnerability is confirmed, but should not be counterposed to a very substantial increase in premarital intercourse. Instead, the two appear to have risen together.

The Demographic and Industrial Revolutions

What were the effects of rapid population growth on capitalist industrialization? Economic historians have proposed two lines of argument that appear, at first glance, to be flatly contradictory. The first thesis focuses on *the acceleration of capital accumulation*. The population boom kept the lid on wages despite an escalating demand for labour-power, permitting employers to increase their share of the value generated by rising productivity. In this way, capital formation could proceed apace. In the absence of quickening population growth, labour shortages would have arisen, wages would have climbed, and the ta-keoff would soon have been aborted. Secondary effects of the population boom were also beneficial. Overcrowding placed a premium on space, boost-ing returns to property owners both on the land and in the housing market in industrial towns. Inequality of income and wealth increased. In the early stages of industrialization, this is what 'primitive accumulation' (as Marx termed it) was all about. The advocates of this view point to rapid population increase and stagnant or declining real wages in the second half of the eighteenth cen-tury. By negative example, the failure of the Low Countries to industrialize in the eighteenth century, despite the comparative advantage of the most ad-vanced commercial agriculture in the world, has been attributed to stagnant population, labour scarcity and a high wage barrier to capital accumulation.

The apparently opposite argument concentrates on *technological change* as the key to the Industrial Revolution. Its proponents maintain that abundant labour supplies and low wages create a disincentive to capital investment and labour-saving mechanization and are thus antithetical to technological breakthrough. They point out that English wages were relatively high in the eighteenth century, in comparison with those on the continent. This competitive disparity generated a powerful incentive to capital-deepening, labour-displacing forms of investment in England – a major reason why that nation pioneered the Industrial Revolution. The argument postulates beneficial secondary effects as well: higher wages strengthen the home market demand for consumer goods, raising the share of household budgets spent on non-food, industrially pro-duced, commodities.

Both theses are cogent, leading one historian to comment that 'there was no pre-determined path from labour-intensive to capital-intensive forms of industrial organization in the eighteenth and nineteenth centuries.'[371] The two may be reconciled if the first is treated as an argument that *wages must not rise* as profits increase at an early, vulnerable, phase of industrialization; accelerating population growth is essential to that end. The second postulates *high wages in the vanguard region*, in comparison with adjacent areas, to spur technological innovation. In fact, both conditions prevailed in the late eighteenth century. Wages generally did not rise in the initial phases of the transformation *throughout the European arena* of industrialization, including England; and rela-tively high wages acted as a stimulus to technological change *in England*. The Industrial Revolution was simultaneously labour-saving in the technological vanguard, and vastly labour-intensive and job-creating everywhere else. For every unit of labour time saved through mechanization, two were required to handle manual labour spin-offs from new industrial processes. Strong incen-tives to technological change and a durable acceleration of capital accumula-tion were integral facets of rapid industrialization. Both preconditions had to be met; in England, they were.

Recognizing that accelerating population growth is a necessary precondition of rapid industrialization does not, however, imply that the former automatically stimulates the latter. In the sixteenth-century boom, the growth of industry and population had increasingly come into conflict, eventually precipitating generalized stagnation in the seventeenth century. After 1750, the accelerating tempo of industrial and population growth rates positively reinforced one another. What had changed, in the meantime, in their relationship with one another? Consider two fundamental differences between the eras. The first lay in the productivity of farm labour, the size of the commercial sector in agriculture, and the responsiveness of farmers to changing conditions of market demand. In the sixteenth century, the population build-up generated a burgeoning demand for basic foodstuffs that European agriculture, still deeply entrenched in seigneurial relations of production, failed to meet in the long run. Given the waste endemic to its mode of surplus extraction and reinvestment, the system could not translate rising grain revenues into sustained improvement in yields per hectare. Output was expanded mainly by means of arable extension on to new and increasingly marginal lands, subject ultimately to diminishing returns. Grain prices continued to spiral upward. The demand for basic food staples absorbed an increasing portion of family budgets, eventually strangling consumer demand for the products of industry.

In the run-up to the Industrial Revolution, by contrast, agricultural output lagged at first, but then recovered, to grow in step with swelling numbers and the shift of the labour force into industry. The initial rise in grain prices in the eighteenth century provided such a stimulus to capital investment in commercial agriculture that production leapt forward, overtaking demand, and the price spiral was abruptly broken in the early nineteenth century. The swelling ranks of the proletariat, dissociated from the land, were able to purchase sufficient food to stay alive and work productively in expanding industries, while themselves constituting an increasing portion of the market for non-food consumer goods.

The second crucial difference between the two eras was in the nature of labour demand and its impact upon the demographic system. As the impoverished ranks of the rural landless swelled in the last decades of the eighteenth century, fertility did not decline, nor did mortality crises become more frequent and severe, as they had in the past. I have argued that the new ingredient was the specifically capitalist demand for labour-power in the countryside, particularly via the putting-out system. The rapid expansion of rural industry in this period prevented the reconvergence of birth and death rates as the landless population exploded, permanently breaching the homeostatic regime.

4

Conclusion

In the first chapter, theoretical guidelines were set out for the conduct of this inquiry. My working hypothesis was that modes of production facilitate the reproduction of certain family forms while inhibiting or precluding the development of others. Familial alignment is primarily affected by the ways in which prevailing modes of production harness and consume the creative powers of producers, and families obtain the means of subsistence. The immediate corollary was to propose that this relationship is reciprocal: that family forms shape the development of modes of production, in the first place because they are central in the production of people and their capacities for work. Since producer families mediate the relationship between labour supply and demand, population growth-trends in a given society will be conditioned by the ways family forms and production regimes interact. The broad survey of the second and third chapters explored the relevance of this theoretical initiative for historical materialism, refining it in the process. Let us conclude by taking stock of this endeavour.

Family Change from Feudalism to Capitalism

If modes of production structure family forms in history, then it ought to be clear that the familial relations of producer classes changed in far-reaching ways in the transition from feudalism to capitalism. This is what I have endeavoured to show, taking issue with the Cambridge Group's continuity thesis. The following alterations were fundamental:

1. As families became increasingly divorced from the means of production, they lost the capacity to transmit productive property from one generation to the next through inheritance. The property infrastructure of familial

continuity was surpassed. Now the livelihoods of youth were secured by turning outward to the labour market to seek their fortunes in a world where wage labour was the primary means of obtaining subsistence. Children's support for elderly parents was no longer secured by the latter's control of essential property; retirement contracts and inheritance preroga- tives became moot, formally intact but substantially superseded. I have defined this as a shift from a stem to a nuclear family form; others describe the same reorientation as a move from a centripetal to a centrifugal family cycle. The terminology employed is a secondary consideration; what is essential is to recognize the full ramifications of the alteration in property relations. All the changes outlined below are bound up with this one.

2. With the separation of labourers from the means of production, their households gradually ceased to be centres of commodity production. The typical work team was no longer comprised primarily of kin and household members. Increasingly, the only thing households produced for sale was their members' labour-power. This engendered the daily exit of wage- earners to work elsewhere. In these circumstances, male householders ceased to preside as the direct on-site managers of their own households. Entering the employer's premises, coming directly under his authority, wage-earners were compelled to labour at times and under circumstances that were not essentially of their choosing.

3. As households gradually ceased to make any of the goods their members consumed, neighbourly exchange declined. The means of subsistence were now acquired, almost entirely, by monetary means, and wages became the near-exclusive source of the proletarian family's income. This shift fostered a new form of householdship based on men's status as primary wage- earners, and a new form of dependency for married women based on the loss of opportunities to generate independent income while working at home. The monetization of domestic provisioning created a new and onerous responsibility – managing the family purse in the never-ending struggle to 'make ends meet' – a job that fell to women within the normal conjugal division of labour.

4. With the separation of households from workplaces and the full monetiza- tion of the wage, employers were unable to intervene in their employees' domestic affairs; moreover, they no longer had a direct interest in doing so. The residential sphere of the labouring class was established as an autonomous domain of private property under the control of its owner- occupants and rent-paying tenants. However, the autonomy of the family group in the private household was limited by the requisites of external

employment: residential location was circumscribed by the necessity of daily transit to and from the workplace; family time 'off work' became a residual of shift (and school) times; meals and sleep had to be scheduled accordingly. The rhythms of domestic work and leisure were thus geared to the exigencies of capitalist work-time discipline. The nature of housework was correspondingly transformed.

5. Domestic service and formal apprenticeship declined as parentally arranged stepping-stones in the preparation of youth for adult occupations; compulsory schooling eventually took their place. The intimate connection between work and training in the domestic setting was lost. This change was part of a larger transformation in the mode of transmitting knowledge between generations. In the protracted shift from a predominantly oral to a literary culture, the community's elders (the traditional repositories of wisdom in an oral universe) were gradually replaced by teachers, and eventually by a host of state officials and professionals who supervised childrearing. The scope of parental authority was thus constrained.

6. Marriage lost its character as a property transaction and an alliance between two families. For proletarians, the union focused more squarely on the partnership of the younger generation. Parental and community influence over courtship and mate selection declined, as did the capacity to veto a match or to force a wedding where the daughter was pregnant. The bride's dowry – where it continued to exist – ceased to be a gift from her parents and became the product of her own arduous scrimping and saving as an independent wage-earner. Betrothal lost its character as a publicly regulated prelude to marriage, mutating into the rite of engagement. Courtship became more informal and less supervised. The social space available for romance was broadened, and its venues became more anonymous and commercial. Mate selection assumed the character of quasi-market activity, with men bidding against one another and women competitively advertising their wares. The ideology of marriage as a love-match between two individuals now flourished, freed from the fetters of familial property exchange. Attraction was now conceived to be inherent in individuals, rather than in the accumulated property and family status they brought to the match. Living together became a frequent precursor to marriage; the legal wedding itself was treated more casually. True-love ideology did not terminate, or even seriously erode, social class endogamy, but it did obscure the operation of class and status considerations in mate selection.

7. In the transition to capitalism, the positive correlation between wealth and family size was inverted. As labour demand burgeoned and mortality crises

abated, the poor and propertyless began to have larger families than the prosperous and propertied classes. By the end of the nineteenth century, with middle-class birth rates plummeting, the urban poor were generating the bulk of Western Europe's demographic expansion. The vital revolution transformed prevailing patterns of intergenerational mobility, as the family cycle mutated. Population growth under feudalism had fostered a process of familial extrusion; those young adults who failed to secure family land moved *out* to the periphery of established settlements and *downward* through disinheritance. Under industrial capitalism, the main trends of population growth and mobility in advanced zones were reversed; young people moved *into* the cities in search of work and subsequently *upward*, as urban working-class living standards gradually improved.

This perspective stands in stark contrast to the Cambridge Group's nuclear family continuity thesis, propounded initially in *Household and Family in Past Time*. The first pillar of the continuity thesis is mean household size, aggregated across all phases of the family cycle. The Group and their research associates found that the mean size of co-resident groups remained remarkably constant at about 4.75 persons per household across Northwestern Europe from the seventeenth to the early twentieth century. Peter Laslett speculated that this 'might cover the Middle Ages as well'.[1] The second pillar is household composition; the predominant co-resident group was found to be simple and nuclear (a married couple and offspring), undergoing no basic alteration in the course of industrialization and urbanization. Richard Wall found 'no dramatic changes ... in the form of the English household between the seventeenth and nineteenth centuries.'[2]

More recently, the Cambridge scholars have grown uneasy with their reputation for depicting domestic arrangements over the centuries in an unduly static fashion. Wall now concludes that 'there has been a considerable amount of change over the past three centuries in the structure of English households.'[3] He makes no attempt either to reconcile this with his earlier evaluation or to acknowledge that he has changed his mind. I suppose one could argue that there had been 'no dramatic change' and 'a considerable amount of change' at the same time; yet there can be no doubt as to whether the Cambridge Group have left the glass of family history half empty or half full. Since Laslett's polemic against the stem family interpretation in his Introduction to *Household and Family in Past Time*, the Group's members and international research associates have been the primary exponents of the nuclear continuity thesis.

The Cambridge Group's well-documented findings concerning the stability of mean household size and the predominance of one- or two-generation co-resident groups were certainly useful in debunking a bucolic image of large, vertically extended peasant households in pre-industrial Europe. However, the

Group's preoccupation with counting co-resident heads and classifying house-holds by composition had the inadvertent effect of replacing one stereotype with another.[4] When scholars applied the Hammel–Laslett classification system to household census data, profound domestic stasis and near-universal nu-clearity appeared almost everywhere they cared to look. In the United States, for example, Rudy Seward, employing the Cambridge methodology, found that 'the appropriate historical image of the American family structure is one of stability ... the presumed dramatic effects that [industrialization and urban-ization] were to have had upon the family never occurred.'[5]

Historians who prefer to view domestic relations through a family-cycle prism tend to be much more impressed with dimensions of change in the transition to industrial capitalism than with the elements of continuity empha-sized by the Cambridge Group. The fundamental difference is conceptual. Empirical questions are not central to the controversy; the ways evidence is used and interpreted are. The debate focuses on the facets of family form that analysts choose to highlight; it hinges on the connection of these dimensions with the structures of the surrounding social formation.[6]

Despite the fact that the Cambridge Group's co-residence paradigm has been widely criticized, Laslett's attack on the stem family interpretation was remarkably successful.[7] The nuclear continuity thesis has become the new or-thodoxy, widely reiterated by historians and sociologists of diverse persuasions, even by those who reject the Cambridge paradigm.[8] The irony is that the argument about nuclear family continuity is based on the co-residence frame-work. If this conception is found wanting (as it now seems to be by most family historians), then the substantive thesis is vitiated. It is a testament to the theoretical vacuity of the discipline that this implication has been so seldom drawn.

Flowing from the Cambridge Group's focus on household composition, nuclear persistence is held to be a function of a neo-local residence 'rule', the strongly held disposition (presumably on the part of both parents and their children) for newlyweds to establish separate households. Why such an incli-nation should persist over centuries, and what conditions engendered it in the first place, are questions the Cambridge historians have never seriously ad-dressed.

The residential tendency to which these scholars refer is indeed an import-ant and distinctive characteristic of Western European family cycles. There is no disagreement here. The pattern can be traced back to the early medieval era, as we have seen. I have taken issue with the ambiguity inherent in the neo-local designation and the notion that this behaviour is best explained in consensual terms. It is not hard to understand why young marrieds would wish to set up their own households and take over the family enterprise. Nor is it difficult to appreciate why elder patriarchs would strive to cling to the reins of domestic power in their waning years and resist being pushed aside. We have, then, the makings of a conflict of interest between the generations. Under what circumstances are young marrieds able to get out from under their parents' tutelage without cutting themselves off from the family estate? What margin of independence is an heir able to exercise in relation to his parents, and what resources can a couple muster at the time of marriage? The longer young people are compelled to wait, the greater will be their capacity to obtain their own domestic space immediately. Paradoxically, by effectively repressing the sexuality of young adults and delaying nuptials, the *ancien régime* enabled them to accumulate resources, set up households, and take over the management of family property at, or very soon after, marriage. Children marrying in their late teens would never have been in a position to do this. The problem of explicating the late marriage system and the distinctly 'Western' family form are thus inextricably related.

What were the preconditions of this family system? Long before late marriage emerged (at the close of the medieval era, by my reckoning) the seeds of this nuptial regime had been sown. My inclination is to locate the origin of the eventual tendency to residential separation in the ascendance of the conjugal bond within the larger matrix of kin affiliation. Employing admittedly sparse evidence, I have endeavoured to trace the rise of conjugal primacy during the transition from Antiquity to feudalism, under the burgeoning influence of the Christian Church. With the dissolution of the Roman West, *sine manu* marriage collapsed, delivering a massive blow to the capacity of elderly patriarchs to rule over their married children. On the other side of the feudal amalgam, with the enervation of the Germanic Sippe, the prerogatives of natal families (particularly the househead's siblings) were rendered subordinate to the inheritance claims of the children of a legitimate union. The conjugal family of the younger generation thus achieved a measure of autonomy in the deployment of domestic power and a primacy in the disposition of family property which it had not formerly enjoyed. The Church's insistence on the explicit consent of the principals buttressed this elevation.

It seems especially important in a study which foregrounds elements of change to recognize this decisive strand of continuity in Western family history. It is not necessary to take on all the ideological baggage of the nuclear family thesis to appreciate the point. The structure of conjugal primacy persisted through the centuries, coming into its own with the formation of the distinctive regime of late and non-universal marriage in Western Europe. Behind its emergence we find a rise in dotal settlements, the spread of Christian influence in regulating marriage, and a stiffening enforcement of nuptial prerequisites in the village community. The erection of obstacles to ill-prepared coupling furnished newlyweds with the capacity to wield resources and assert their interests from the outset of the union. This resulted in a marked tendency to residential independence at marriage, operating within the framework of inheritance.

As noted in the Introduction, the debate over the nature of Western family forms in the past resonates with current concerns about 'the decline of the family'. In the concluding chapter of *Weathering the Storm*, I shall return to the latter controversy, presenting my own views on the contribution that family history potentially brings to the discussion of familial change today.

Western European Marriage and the Rise of Industrial Capitalism

Now let us reverse the causal equation and pose the question: did the dominant form of the family in Western Europe influence the development of the prevailing mode of production in the region, and if so, in what ways? Was there a familial impetus to the historical breakthrough of industrial capitalism in Western Europe?

There is as yet no satisfactory explanation of the genesis of industrial capitalism in Western Europe. Several societies had achieved comparable or superior levels of technological capacity in earlier periods, only to stagnate and regress. Is the late/non-universal marriage system a missing piece of the puzzle? One's suspicions are aroused in light of a double-barrelled coincidence. This nuptial regime has been found in no other pre-industrial social formation save the region that inaugurated industrial capitalism. Secondly, within Western Europe, the English pioneered the Industrial Revolution, and it appears that the late marriage pattern developed among them earlier and more strongly than it did on the continent. Are such concurrences accidental? It seems unlikely.

What contribution could the Western European marriage system have made to the breakthrough of industrial capitalism? Seven factors seem to have been advantageous (several of them closely interrelated):

1. The delay and deterrence of marriage improved life security by checking population growth before the pressure on marginal land became perilous. After the Black Death, Western Europe did not suffer mortality crises of such depth or sweep as have periodically decimated peoples elsewhere, in Africa and Asia, for example.[9] It is likely that this relatively benign experience was at least partly due to the forging of the distinctive Western European marital regime (which, if I am right, crystallized in the century after the Black Death). On a regional basis within Europe, life expectancy appears to be positively correlated with the presence and strength of nuptial regulation. Since in a pre-industrial society the vast bulk of dependants are young, increased longevity lessens the dependency ratio of the population

as a whole. When people die young, parental investment in their childhood is wasted; when the elderly die, they have already made a productive contribution and their passing relieves the community of an economic burden. The higher the proportion of a population surviving to old age, the more efficient it is economically.

2. A society that sets extraordinarily high economic hurdles to marriage stimulates savings – hence capital formation – further down the socioeconomic pyramid than in other societies with comparable levels of wealth and *per capita* income.[10] Couples who enter childbearing with a greater fund of capital (land, domestic goods and cash) are better able to provide for children and keep the household together during the next phase of peak drain in the family cycle.

3. Restrictive marriage raised the productivity of female labour-power in comparison with societies where young women married at puberty or soon after. By preventing a great number of women from marrying at all, the regime preserved their entire adult lives for productive labour. Delaying the onset of childbearing for the rest, late marriage established a period of ten or more years from puberty to the mid twenties, when women in their prime could devote themselves entirely to productive work without the energy-draining, time-consuming diversions of repeated childbirth and the frequent injuries associated with it. Furthermore, a reduction in the sheer number of births in communities living close to the margin of subsistence improved the life-chances of infants, thus raising the efficiency of women's reproductive labour.

4. Men were normally only one or two years older than their spouses in Western Europe. In societies where females marry shortly after the onset of menses, the age gap tends to be much greater: from five to seven years. The Western European marriage system was thus more likely to pair a man and a woman in their primes, increasing the average duration of marriage as a productive partnership. When women reached their latter childbearing years and household resources were stretched, their husbands were younger and more productive; fewer men died at this stage, leaving their wives and young children bereft. The economic benefits to producer households of 'age-egalitarian' marriages were considerable.

5. Life-phase domestic service was an integral facet of the late marriage system. The institution was economically advantageous in three ways. Service (a) furnished an opportunity for pre-nuptial accumulation; (b) redistributed youthful labour from poor farms to more productive holdings; and (c)

introduced youth to a range of farm settings, valuable training for adult vocations.

6. The frustrations of marital delay furnished a powerful motive for youth unlikely to be favoured in the devolution of the patrimony to leave home in search of work, a future spouse, and independent accommodation.[11] Under such a repressive nuptial regime, the youth population was more open to *proletarian* employment opportunities (based on independent market hiring and an individuated money wage) than in social formations where it was easier for young adults to marry and gain access to household space on their parents' land or in the immediate vicinity. Once the demand for labour-power picked up, a virtually inexhaustible stream of cheap, mobile labour-power poured through the breach as nuptial barriers were lowered. Industrializing capital could draw upon this reserve without fully funding, via the wage, the costs of its generational replacement.

7. It is the *restrictive* function of the nuptial valve that has attracted the most attention, reflecting a Malthusian preoccupation with checks to population growth. But equally significant is the obverse capacity: to unleash a sustained *rise* in the birth rate by means of earlier and more universal marriage, in sensitive response to shifts in the mode of labour-power's employment and consumption. This occurred in zones of rural industry in the late eighteenth century.

All these are plausible candidates for consideration as factors furnishing Western Europe in the early modern era with economic advantages relative to other societies. Taken together, they qualify nuptial restriction, at first through its build-up and later through its rupture, as a probable catalytic agent in the advent of capitalism and subsequently in the Industrial Revolution.

What happened to the late marriage pattern in the population boom after 1750? Did the nuptial valve open wide, spring a leak, or was it swept away? If we fixate on changes in the age of marriage, then we must say that marriage remained 'late'. Almost nowhere did women's mean age at first marriage dip beneath twenty-three (the minimum set by Hajnal, and conventionally employed by historical demographers in identifying the pattern). Shifts did occur above the line, as we have seen. In England, women's age at first marriage fell very substantially (an estimated two and a half years during the eighteenth century, to twenty-four), as it did in most industrial zones on the continent. But elsewhere there is little evidence of a decline, and in many regions there was a slight rise. This 'mixed' picture has been taken by many scholars as a clear refutation of arguments put forward by Levine and others which centre on the relationship between proletarianization, nuptiality and fertility. As I argued in the last chapter, the critics have largely missed the point. Readers will recall the distinction drawn earlier between late marriage and nuptial equilibration. As the demographic system lost its slow-growth equilibrium after 1750, fertility ceased to be constrained by marriage as it had been formerly. If the age of marriage did not fall almost everywhere, this is of little import. The decisive fact is that the nuptial valve *failed to tighten* in response to falling mortality and a massive increase in rural landlessness, as it had in the past (most notably in the seventeenth century). The homeostatic mechanism was completely overrun.

The nuptial valve sprang a leak, as a sharply rising portion of births occurred out of wedlock. In a profound cultural shift, proletarians began to treat marriage more casually. Increasingly, young couples lived together and bore children without submitting to a Church wedding or securing a marriage licence, practices that had been almost unheard of a century earlier. By the time of the Napoleonic Wars, it has been estimated that a fifth of the English population lived at one time or another in common-law unions. The rise of casual cohabitation among the swelling ranks of the proletariat has also been noted in France and Germany.[12] Mass proletarianization swamped the nuptial valve as a demographic regulator by undermining the control that parents, village communities and churches had traditionally exercised over the processes of conjugal union: courtship, betrothal, the wedding, first coitus and the inauguration of childbearing. Young people seized the initiative, their actions increasingly governed by the balance of market forces as they sought jobs, unsupervised accommodation and eligible marriage partners. The demographic result was a protracted divergence between the two vital rates, with fertility remaining buoyant for more than a century as life expectancy lengthened.

Women and Patriarchy in the Transition to Capitalism

Did patriarchy wither away in the transition to capitalism, to be replaced by companionate unions, with egalitarian relations between spouses and permissive childrearing practices? Many scholars have written as if this were the case. Le Play was the first social scientist of note to make this claim, deploring the disintegration of traditional patriarchal peasant families in nineteenth-century France. From a very different perspective a century later, Christopher Lasch has recently lamented the enervation of paternal authority. While for most analysts nowadays it is more congenial to welcome the advent of the liberal family, the substantive content of Le Play's assessment has not been altered in the mainstream of modern historiography. Lawrence Stone, in *The Family, Sex and Marriage in England, 1500–1800,* traces the decline of the patriarchal family and the rise of affective individualism among the aristocracy in the late seventeenth and eighteenth centuries. Peter Laslett, in *The World*

We Have Lost, covering the same period for the popular classes in England, describes a similar evolution. As mentioned, Edward Shorter, in *The Making of the Modern Family,* perceives a veritable sexual revolution at the end of the eighteenth century, led by young proletarian women, with the eclipse of the patriarchal control of courtship and mate selection. Steven Ozment portrays a benevolent masculine dominance among Protestants in Reformation Europe in *When Fathers Ruled,* the past tense of the title implying that they do so no longer. In *The European Family* (subtitled *Patriarchy to Partnership from the Middle Ages to the Present*), Michael Mitterauer and Richard Sieder extend this general picture to the whole of Northwestern and Central Europe. Finally, sociologists Michael Young and Peter Wilmott, in *The Symmetrical Family,* concur with the historians' consensus portraying the demise of patriarchy, although they see the decisive shift to companionate marriage occurring much later, in the current century.

Feminists have taken strong exception to this benign and complacent view of more or less continuous progress from 'the Bad Old Days' (in Shorter's words) towards equality in modern families.[13] Undoubtedly there have been major changes in the scope and form of patriarchal authority in the passage from inheritance-based peasant families to the modern nuclear families of urban wage-earners. To argue otherwise would be to contradict the discontinuity thesis just propounded. But these alterations have not entailed the terminal demise of patriarchal authority so much as its intergenerational truncation and the reconstruction of spousal hierarchy on new material foundations.

The power of fathers over their adult children (particularly when the latter have moved out on their own) was gradually dissipated in the course of mass proletarianization, as we have seen; it has never been restored under capitalism. Other powers, however, over wives and young children, were not lost, though they were certainly shaken by men's daily exit from the household to work elsewhere for an employer. Under the demands of capitalist shiftwork, husbands could no longer supervise the work of other family members directly. Patriarchal dominance was reconsolidated in the second half of the nineteenth century, with the deepening fetishism of the individuated wage, the concomitant devaluation of unpaid domestic labour, and the entrenchment of a male breadwinner–dependent housewife conjugal ideal, which became an ideological fixture in Western societies until very recently. These themes will be explored more fully in *Weathering the Storm,* so I shall be extremely brief here. We can assess the change in women's position at three distinct life-stages: as young single adults, as wives in the midst of childbearing, and as widows in old age.

The wage was a potentially powerful instrument of economic independence for youth of both sexes, but in this period very few young women received their own wage as a money payment with no strings attached. The great majority of employed single women lived with their parents until they married, or resided as servants in private households. Normally, those remaining at home would hand their entire pay over to their mothers, perhaps receiving a small amount of pocket money in return. Proletarianization certainly increased people's mobility outside the district of their upbringing. Yet here, too, the gains for young women were limited. Most migrated in the company of other family members. In the event that they had to move away from home on their own to obtain work elsewhere, employment was typically prearranged, with 'suitable accommodation' an integral facet of the contract worked out by parents and employers over their heads. Such women normally resided in private households or supervised boarding houses, where they were not free to keep their own hours or entertain friends at their leisure.

The dissipation of parental control over courtship, mate selection and the timing of marriage was undoubtedly a real gain for young adults. But newfound freedoms in the marriage market were not as easy for women to enjoy as for men. The sexual double standard still prevailed, and single women were increasingly vulnerable to being deserted by suitors upon the discovery of pregnancy. Nor was it any easier than it had been in peasant communities for women to refuse marriage and live independently:

> The girl who failed to marry and so obtain an independent roof over her head faced a predictably bleak future. She could anticipate nothing but destitution. She might be described as the woman most likely in old age to be found on the list of a *bureau de charité*, lacking adequate clothing, food and fuel. Such a ghost of Christmas future must have served to heighten a girl's realization that marriage was the only possible salvation.[14]

If there were modest gains for young single women in achieving a stronger voice in choosing a partner, their position deteriorated once they wed. In peasant households, wives had been full members of a joint production team. In fully proletarian households, the interdependence of husbands and wives was now transmuted into an economic dependency of female homemakers on male breadwinners. As wages became the dominant mode of recognizing and rewarding labour, women's unpaid domestic contribution began to disappear as real work. The new material basis of patriarchal authority became the male control of the primary wage. The deeper a family's reliance on the husband's income, the greater were his breadwinner prerogatives, regardless of whether he exercised them in a brutal or a more enlightened fashion. The way to break this dependency was for women to remain employed throughout their childbearing years. But very few did, as capitalism made it more difficult for women to combine productive work outside the home with infant nurture and childcare responsibilities. Adult mortality was a sure sign of the problem, as women's death rates exceeded men's in many working-class communities in the nineteenth century.

The situation of older working-class women was grim by comparison with their peasant predecessors. Peasant widows rose in community stature upon their husbands' decease, controlling children's fortunes as executors of family estates. Proletarian women sunk into abject poverty, were often bereft and had to appeal to their children for support. Significantly, the probability of remarriage declined across Western Europe from the sixteenth to the nineteenth century, as the ranks of the proletariat swelled.[15] Women were far less likely to remarry than men.

Overall, the advent of industrial capitalism brought limited gains to younger single women, and setbacks to married women of the working class, especially the elderly. This is not to say that they were worse off absolutely but that their standing *in relation to men* had deteriorated, especially in marriage. The emancipatory promise of the bourgeois revolution would not begin to be fulfilled for another century. Women's major advances – in property rights, the vote, easier divorce, and in gaining greater control over fertility – were not won until the late nineteenth and early twentieth centuries. The last of these achievements will be taken up in some detail in the *Weathering the Storm: Working-Class Families from the Industrial Revolution to the Fertility Decline*.

Appendix:
A Note on the Brenner Debate

In an article published in *Past & Present* in 1976, Robert Brenner launched a far-reaching attack on the reigning neo-Malthusian model of the European economy in the early modern era. Brenner's critique of the demographic interpretation (most closely associated with Michael Postan, Emmanuel Ladurie and Wilhelm Abel) provoked considerable controversy, as did his alternative – a class struggle approach. In subsequent issues of the journal, the editors published two direct rebuttals by Ladurie and by Postan and Hatcher (the latter two tracing the heritage of their own views rather more to Ricardo's theory of land rent than to Malthus's population theories), plus a number of related contributions. Finally, Brenner replied at length to his critics. Readers unfamiliar with the debate are urged to read it in the original; all the articles have been usefully assembled within the covers of a book, entitled *The Brenner Debate*.[1] I cannot possibly do justice to the authors' positions here, nor is it my purpose to recapitulate the main lines of argument. But since many matters discussed in the text touch on issues that came under scrutiny in the debate, I decided to attempt a unified response in the form of an appendix, rather than scatter brief comments in notes and digressions.[2]

Entering the highly polarized terrain of the debate is problematic for two reasons. Postan, Hatcher and Ladurie from one side, then Brenner in reply, accused each other of misrepresenting their positions; the attempt to characterize arguments fairly is thus fraught with problems. Secondly, I find myself caught in the middle – though it is not, from my standpoint, a question of sitting on the fence. I would be glad to side with Brenner, my marxist colleague, but I must dissent from the way that he has set the parameters of discussion and drawn the lines of demarcation. As readers will have noted, I owe a great deal to the scholarship of Postan, Ladurie and Abel; to their elucidation of a long feudal–agrarian cycle in particular, and their empirical documentation of correlations in secular rates of change in population, grain

247

prices, land rent and real wages. For the past four decades, these scholars have painstakingly reconstructed the approximate contours of the agrarian cycle from an immense range of archival materials. They have demonstrated beyond all reasonable doubt the existence of these dynamic regularities, persisting across Western Europe throughout the medieval and early modern eras; they deserve full credit for their discovery. I have used the turning points of this two-phase cycle to periodize the early modern era and to organize the third chapter's exposition.

Whether they have adequately interpreted the causal genesis of the patterns they have unearthed is another matter entirely. I agree with Brenner that they have not, and concur with many of the specific faults he finds with their explanatory framework: the narrowness of its ecological focus and its abstraction from class relations of exploitation in particular. Since very similar objections have been raised at several points in the text, I will refrain from rehearsing these matters here. This said, my appreciation of the long feudal–agrarian cycle is profoundly at variance with Brenner's. The discovery of periodic cycles of growth and stagnation operating in the very long run; the attention paid to systemic limits and equilibrating mechanisms; the identification of cumulative contradictions that foster, sooner or later, stagnation and relapse; the recognition that crises, however devastating in human terms, clear the ground for renewed cycles of growth within the system's modified structure: does all this sound familiar, especially to marxist ears? Indeed, it is strikingly reminiscent of Marx's elucidation of the 'laws of motion' of capitalism.

The difference, of course, is that Marx located capitalism's drives and barriers within the processes of capital accumulation; the neo-Malthusians have situated the cyclical dynamics of the feudal economy in the equilibration of land and labour-power – ultimately in the relationship between human reproduction and agrarian ecology. From a historical materialist standpoint, part of this difference can be justified. These are disparate modes of production whose relationship with nature is profoundly dissimilar; the historical specificity of each ought to be respected. The direct connection established within peasant households between procreation and the social relations of exploitation does not exist under capitalism, where the relationship between proletarian reproduction and the labour-power consumed in capitalist production is mediated by the labour market. (This disconnection will be analysed in the first chapter of *Weathering the Storm*.)

On the other hand, the difference between the marxist analysis of industrial capitalist cycles and the neo-Malthusian analysis of agrarian–feudal cycles is also due to the theoretical gulf between the two schools of thought: the mode-of-production paradigm of the former and the naturalist, ecological framework of the latter. For Brenner, this leads to a radical downplaying of the explanatory significance of the feudal cycle. I would prefer (as would the French marxist Guy Bois – see his contribution to the debate) to recast and incorporate the generative structure of the agrarian cycle into a rounded analysis of the feudal mode of production. The crucial specification, in this regard, is to establish connections between the seigneurial mode of extracting a surplus from the dependent peasant cultivators, the characteristic form of land use in the manorial economy, and the predominantly extensive pattern of expansion on to increasingly marginal land. This linkage has been explicated in the third chapter and needs no reiteration here.

Curiously, Brenner and the neo-Malthusians, approaching the problem from opposite directions, arrive at the same stumbling block. Postan and Ladurie recognize social classes and class contention over the distribution of the agrarian product. But they do not see that this struggle, and the property structures within which it is played out, deeply condition the cyclical dynamics they have elucidated. Brenner recognizes the long agrarian cycle, but he does not see that this cycle, by modifying the land–labour-power ratio, profoundly conditions the terms of struggle on the land and the strategic objectives for which both lords and peasants are impelled to strive in different phases of the cycle. An adequate appreciation of the genuine reciprocity of influence here is evidently lacking on both sides. This is why the counterposed terms of the debate are miscast; we are being required to designate the independent and the dependent variables in a one-way model. The choice ought to be refused.

Brenner disparages more than a particular perspective on the long agrarian cycle; he belittles the explanatory significance of the phenomenon itself. This fault is magnified, for me, by an unfortunate legacy of classical marxism: the tendency to dismiss almost any analyses of demographic structures and population growth dynamics as 'Malthusianism'. This promiscuous derogation has deterred marxists from devoting sustained attention to the analysis of demographic forces within our own paradigm. Brenner is hardly to blame for this legacy, but his radical depreciation of the importance of population dynamics in the feudal mode of production certainly perpetuates it.

Brenner's fundamental argument against the neo-Malthusian interpretation is compelling. The outcome of class struggles in a given conjuncture is not determined, in a necessary or sufficient sense, by the partiucular demo-economic circumstances in which dependent peasants and lords find themselves. Different results may well arise in adjacent regions undergoing roughly similar demo-economic processes. When this happens, class relations may be altered in ways that exert cumulative effects on the regions' social structures over time, propelling them along increasingly divergent paths of socioeconomic development in the medium and long term. He argues his case with principal reference to two regional contrasts: (a) East Elbian and Western Germany in the aftermath of the deep fourteenth-century depression; and (b) England and France, from the fifteenth through the seventeenth century. I will return to the latter contrast in a moment.

Brenner's general thesis here is cogent and persuasively argued (particularly in his reply to critics, a more nuanced exposition than his initial foray). Furthermore, he provides a far superior framework for understanding uneven developments in the transition from feudalism to capitalism than Ladurie's vague 'unilineal drift' thesis. But his argument needs tempering. While different outcomes of class struggle *may* generate enduring divergences in regional social structures and economic development, they *will not necessarily* do so. Opposite results in conjunctural struggles are rarely sufficient to account for persistent socioeconomic differences between regions in the long run. (I doubt if Brenner would argue that they were, but he often presents specific cases in these terms.) The effects of divergent outcomes of conjunctural struggles may turn out to be temporary and ephemeral. I would argue that this eventuality is more likely than structural differentiation.

Social revolutions are the obvious (and momentous) exception, where the victorious consolidation of state power by an insurgent class *does* lead, more or less directly, to deep transformations in the prevailing mode of production, and often (but not invariably) to the subsequent displacement of one mode by another. But Brenner is referring to cases of defensive struggles with partial gains, where subordinate classes are not able to end their subordination forthwith. Because the property relations that buttress ruling–class power are not breached in any fundamental sense, particular prerogatives that have been wrested from the powerful in struggle can usually be taken back, as revolts ebb and a modicum of social peace is restored. While ruling classes can often make considerable encroachments on the rights of their subordinates in times of relative quiescence, it is much more difficult for the latter to extend their rights in a molecular and juridically settled fashion without engaging in collective forms of defiance. This does not diminish the importance of Brenner's argument concerning divergent outcomes, nor the cases he draws to our attention. It is precisely because conjunctural differences in struggle outcomes do not normally eventuate in profound and enduring divergences between regions (ultimately to changes in the prevailing mode of production in a given region, far in advance of its neighbour) that the instances when this does occur are historic. I am persuaded that he has correctly identified two of them; this alone is an outstanding contribution.

Comparing England and France

The choice of an analytical framework for a text imposes its own implacable logic on the results achieved. The arguments of the present book are set forth in a highly condensed sketch of developments in Northwestern Europe as a whole. In the process, I have had to generalize in ways that ignore or down-play unevenness between regions. The frequent mention of such disparities (while keeping the author humble and readers alert to the hazards of sweeping generalization) is none the less gestural, in so far as regional differences are not addressed in a sustained and comparative fashion. I therefore welcome the opportunity to step briefly outside the self-imposed limits of the text, offering some thoughts on the contrast Brenner develops between France and England in the transition to capitalism.

Why was England the pioneering site of the Industrial Revolution, and not France? I agree with Brenner's stress on the superior productivity of English agriculture as it developed within an essentially capitalist structure, in contrast with France, where the seigneurial framework and peasant land rights re-mained firmly entrenched. I have reservations about his tendency to read the English breakthrough to capitalist agriculture too far back in time – to the late fifteenth and sixteenth centuries – depicting subsequent developments as on-ward and upward from then on. He writes that England was 'largely exempt' from the seventeenth-century crisis, but makes no sustained argument for this view.

There is not one turning point in the transition to industrial capitalism but several; some obstacles were finally swept aside very late in the day. After substantial gains had been achieved between 1660 and 1730 (with English wheat yields reaching almost twice France's by the latter date), English agricul-ture appears to have stagnated in the next six decades, falling behind quicken-ing population growth from 1750 on. This resulted in grain price rises on a par with those on the continent and the conversion of Britain from being a net food exporter to a very considerable importer after 1770. The 'upward spiral that extended into the Industrial Revolution' would likely have been halted in its tracks, if the failure of home agriculture to meet the compound demand of accelerating population growth and the proportional shift of the labour force out of food production had not been rectified.[3] This correction (a decisive advance for intensive agriculture) was achieved in the early decades of the nineteenth century.

If the contrast in rural class structures and agricultural productivity was certainly one crucial difference, let me suggest two others, arising from the subjects under discussion in this book: (a) the efficiency of English population growth, relative to that of France; (b) the profusion of rural proletarianization in England, compared with its restraint in France. These differences, gener-ated in part by variant family forms in the two social formations, are best grasped by conceiving of demographic infrastructures and family forms as in-tegral features of prevailing modes of production. Let us consider each in turn.

Vital Rate Differences between England and France: Between 1600 and 1750, the peoples of England and France increased their numbers very slowly, with several decades of absolute contraction in the seventeenth century. Contrary to Brenner's assertion, there does not appear to have been much difference between the growth rates of the two countries during this century and a half.[4] The best current estimates are that England grew about 40 per cent and France roughly 30 per cent.[5] (Divergence occurred after 1750, as the English proliferated much more quickly.) Despite a roughly similar outcome in the early modern period, population expansion was achieved more efficiently in England, with lower vital rates and far less squandering of maternal labour-power. This difference is one key to the faster acceleration in England after 1750.

By 1740 (the earliest date for which comparable national records are available) there is solid evidence for lower English vital rates. At that time, the birth rate in England was roughly four-fifths of the French rate, and mortality about three-quarters.[6] For earlier times, we must compare weighted means for dozens of parishes; due to regional variation, this is a dubitable procedure. Yet the disparities between French and English parishes are so consistent that it seems reasonable to project the country-level difference back at least to 1600.[7] In the early modern era, the English demographic system was evidently a 'low-pressure' regime relative to that of France.[8]

What accounts for the difference? While superior grain yields and various ecological factors might conceivably have generated a lower English death rate, it seems more likely that most of the difference originated with nuptiality, and a marked difference in the resulting vigour of the preventive check. As noted, the Western European marriage pattern probably emerged in England in the late medieval era, with women postponing first marriage until the age of twenty-three or older, and at least 10 per cent never marrying. By 1600, the mean age of English brides was roughly twenty-six, and the proportion never marrying had risen above 20 per cent.

There is less evidence concerning marriage patterns in France before 1740, but available studies indicate a relatively unrestrained system. The average age of brides in Normandy, for example, was about twenty-one in the sixteenth century; in four towns in Lorraine, they married on average at eighteen.[9] Thereafter, the nuptial regime appears to have tightened, with brides marrying at twenty-four, on average, by the second half of the seventeenth century.[10] The proportion marrying also fell; yet the English rates of lifelong celibacy were easily double French rates in the seventeenth century.

If the mortality rates of the two countries had been similar, a persistent difference in marriage rates of this magnitude would have resulted in a very substantial divergence in population growth to France's advantage. But they were dissimilar, as we know. Virtually the entire difference in death rates was due to higher infant and child mortality in France (indicating that variant procreative regimes account for the difference, rather than wholly exogenous factors). French women bore two more infants than English women on average, but lost them, mostly in the first months of life. Their privation constituted a vast squandering of female labour-power, energy that would otherwise have been available for productive purposes in the family economy.

Contrasting Patterns of Proletarianization: Patterns of proletarianization in France and England were different from the outset; they became more so over time. In the sixteenth and seventeenth centuries, as we have seen, increasing numbers of land-poor cottagers in both France and England had to resort to wage labour to supplement farm income. But in England, much more frequently than in France, the land-*poor* became land*less,* and were forced to rely ever more exclusively on selling their labour-power to subsist. In France, the resistance of multi-occupational smallholders to full proletarianization was more successful; a far greater proportion of the rural poor clung tenaciously to a small plot, an extended garden and commons use rights. In England, where small plots were more often engrossed, farms consolidated and community use rights abrogated, the movement from a semi-proletarian to a fully proletarian existence proceeded apace. The result was a more mobile and employment-responsive labour force in England, uprooted from the land – a comparatively easy labour force for merchants and industrial capitalists to harness.

Brenner has discussed a major source of this difference in the divergent class relations of agricultural production, but has largely ignored the familial dimension. While marked regional variations in family forms within both countries make national comparisons problematic, there do appear to be discernible differences between the two countries in at least three facets. In *land inheritance,* the tradition of unigeniture was stronger in England, with partible customs contributing to the morcellization of peasant holdings in many regions of France. Secondly, in *residence norms,* neo-locality was nearly universal in England; except in the Paris Basin, young married couples in France were more likely to live with parents or right next door to them. Thirdly, in *mate selection,* French youth and their parents were more inclined to choose a marriage partner from their home village or proximate settlement; north of the Channel, the marital pool tended to be drawn more widely. As a result, kin networks in English villages were not nearly so dense as in their French counterparts.

The upshot of all three differences was that English family forms fostered the emigration of young men from the village of their birth. In France, there was more support and pressure from parents and kin to remain in the local community, if not in co-residence with parents and married siblings then at least close by. Peasant families tended to make room for secondary children as they grew up, married, and sought to establish adult livelihoods, distributing work and domestic provisions more evenly through the extended kin network, locally based. This type of family regime checked mobility, absorbed the underemployed, and restrained full proletarianization under conditions of land poverty. In England, more typically, non-heirs were encouraged to leave and 'make their own way in the world'. The tradition of generational independence was more ingrained. With this family norm, the wage-reliant population lost their places on the land and became more mobile, seeking full-time employment wherever they could find it. In short, English family forms tended to foster rural proletarianization; French family forms to impede the process. Anyone who wishes to argue that a plentiful, cheap and employment-responsive labour supply was a necessary condition of the first Industrial Revolution ought to take cognizance of this difference. If modes of production shape the family forms that develop within them, the converse is also true. Specific family structures may make – or brake – the development of a mode of production. The foregoing is an instance of this effect.

Notes

Introduction

1. See, for example, Ronald Fletcher, *The Shaking of the Foundations: Family and Society* (London, 1988); and Brigitte Berger and Peter Berger *The War over the Family: Capturing the Middle Ground* (New York, 1984).

2. 'The Road to Polygamy', *New York Review of Books*, vol. 36, no. 3, 1989, pp. 12–15.

3. David Kertzer and Caroline Brettell, 'Advances in Italian and Iberian Family History' in Tamara Hareven and Andrejs Plakans, eds, *Family History at the Crossroads* (Princeton, 1987), p. 88.

4. In my view, 'post-Marxian thought' (which came into vogue among certain sectors of the Left intelligentsia in the late 1970s as the entire ideological spectrum shifted to the right) has caricatured marxism, obfuscating its historical diversity and evacuating its considerable strengths without offering the offsetting benefit of redressing its profound weaknesses. From Eugen von Bohm-Bawerk's *Karl Marx and the Close of His System* (first published in 1896) to David Conway's *A Farewell to Marx: An Outline and Appraisal of His Theories*, appearing ninety years later, pundits have repeatedly sounded the death knell of historical materialism, only to see it rise from the ashes every time the world economy went into crisis or capitalism was challenged in some corner of the globe. While the collapse of the Stalinist regimes throughout Eastern Europe certainly compels a fundamental (and welcome) rethinking of its basic tenets, the current spate of 'good riddance' obituaries for marxism strikes me as yet another case of wishful thinking.

Breaking with convention, I have chosen not to capitalize *marxism* in the text. This is intended to register the fact that historical materialism is a generic body of thought and not a secular religion based upon the inerrant texts of its founder.

5. In a recent article on the family farm, for example, Michael Winter begins by acknowledging the importance of kin relations and then proceeds to counsel that 'we must look beyond kinship and family characteristics in order to find the key explanatory features of a particular mode of production': 'Agrarian Class Structure and Family Farming' in T. Bradley and P. Lowe, eds, *Locality and Rurality: Economy and Society in Rural Regions* (Norwich, 1984), p. 117. Why should we ignore kinship and family in order to focus our attention on the 'underlying' mode of production? Does this mean that modes of production are non-familial by their very nature? Instead of perpetuating the conceptual disjunction we ought to bridge it, embedding family forms *in* modes of production, as in reality they are.

6. Here I am in complete agreement with Laslett, who has registered a strong objection to *l'histoire conjuncturel* as applied to familial change: 'The Character of Familial History', in Tamara Hareven and Andrejs Plakans, eds, *Family History at the Crossroads* (Princeton, 1987), pp. 273–4.

Chapter 1

1. Heidi Hartmann, 'The Unhappy Marriage of Marxism and Feminism: Towards a More Progressive Union', in Lydia Sargent, ed., *Women and Revolution: A Discussion of the Unhappy Marriage of Marxism and Feminism* (London, 1981), p. 2. Marxist–feminists have sought to rectify this deficiency in a variety of ways. In addition to the articles in the Sargent

collection, see also Maxine Molyneux, 'Androcentrism in Marxist Anthropology', in *Critique of Anthropology*, vol. 3, nos 9/10 (1977), pp. 55–82; and Karen Sachs, *Sisters and Wives: The Past and Future of Sexual Equality* (Westport, 1979).

2. Despite his salutary criticism of the naturalism inherent in Malthus's theory of population growth, Marx's approach to the reproduction of the working class slips in a similar direction: 'The maintenance and reproduction of the working class remains a necessary condition for the reproduction of capital. But the capitalist may safely leave this to the worker's drives for self-preservation and propagation', *Capital: A Critique of Political Economy*, vol. 1 (New York, 1977) p. 718.

3. Social relations of production refer to the organized ensemble of relations between persons and/or groups of persons engaged in a given production process, directly or indirectly. Anyone with a right or responsibility towards any facet of the design, direction, implementation and output of a production process should be included in the conceptualization of this matrix. In any set of production relations there will be a hierarchy of rights and responsibilities, with minor and flexible prerogatives subject to much greater local variation than critical and limiting conditions. One could not have capitalism, for example, if capitalists did not enjoy the right to appropriate labour's product at the end of the shift. This is a limit-condition of capitalism as a mode of production, congealed in its property form and upheld by bourgeois states everywhere. On the other hand, labour's *de facto* right to control work detail, or to refuse to work in exceptionally hazardous conditions, varies widely from country to country, industry to industry, firm to firm and time to time. These are variations *of* capitalist relations, variations within the range of possible relations in the capitalist mode of production. We should therefore distinguish between limit-conditions of a set of production relations, and normative standards established and adjudicated within limits. This also applies to the social relations of labour-power's production.

4. Engels placed the production of people on the same footing as the production of goods in this justly renowned passage: 'According to the materialistic conception, the determining factor in history is, in the final instance, the production and reproduction of immediate life. This, again, is of a twofold character: on the one side, the production of the means of existence, of food, clothing, and shelter and the tools necessary for that production; on the other side, the production of human beings themselves, the propagation of the species. The social organization under which people of a particular historical epoch live is determined by both kinds of production': *The Origin of the Family, Private Property and the State* (New York, 1972), pp. 71–2. Unfortunately, his very promising initiative was not incorporated in mainstream marxism, where 'the production of human beings themselves' has been persistently ignored in conceptualizing modes of production.

5. There are some notable exceptions. See Claude Meillassoux, *Maidens, Meal and Money: Capitalism and the Domestic Community* (London, 1981); Martha Giminez, 'Population and Capitalism', *Latin American Perspectives*, vol. 15, no. 4 (1977), pp. 5–36. In *Population Theories and Economic Interpretation* (London, 1957), Sidney Coontz laid impressive groundwork for a marxist integration of demography within political economy three decades ago, emphasizing the role of labour demand. His work, largely unheralded in the West at the time, is now receiving belated attention from radical demographers in search of some roots in the discipline. It is amusing to read non-marxists inveighing against 'the marxist theory of population', for the real problem is that we do not have any in a coherent and developed sense: Richard M. Smith, 'Fertility, Economy and Household Formation in England over Three Centuries', *Population and Development Review*, vol. 7 (1981), p. 611. One hardly looks East for inspiration. Soviet demographers typically introduce their work with an obligatory quote from Marx or Lenin, reminding us that populations are comprised of social classes. This is followed by the bombastic assertion that 'Marxist-Leninist theory alone makes it possible to substantiate scientifically the social essence of population': D. I. Valentey, *An Outline Theory of Population* (Moscow, 1980), p. 9. Having dispensed with the preliminary incantations, they then proceed to indulge in arid number-crunching exercises which bear an uncanny resemblance to the classless abstractions of their bourgeois counterparts in the West. One hopes that in the open debates of the glasnost era this sterility would be surpassed, but the Soviet intelligentsia is in such a hurry to embrace the most conservative

nostrums of Western social science, while jettisoning all vestiges of marxism, that the possibilities of the latter's creative reform seem to be precluded in the Soviet Union at this time.

6. Marx, *Capital,* vol. 1 (New York, 1977), p. 784.

7. Karl Marx, *Grundrisse: Introduction to the Critique of Political Economy* (New York, 1983), p. 100.

8. I will discuss the population explosion preceding the Industrial Revolution at some length in ch. 3. On the Neolithic Revolution, see M. N. Cohen, *The Food Crisis in Prehistory: Overpopulation and the Origins of Agriculture* (New Haven, 1977).

9. The tendency to abstract away from nature in marxist inquiry is part of an unfortunate legacy: the equation of social development with the technological conquest of nature by humankind. When technological progress is wrought through the unnecessary and enduring deterioration of a society's natural environment, its dominant conception of human progress should be questioned. Most marxists have been slow to do so, exhibiting an uncritical attachment to this same nineteenth-century notion of progress.

10. See Molyneux, 'Androcentrism in Marxist Anthropology'; Deborah Bryceson and Ulla Vuorela, 'Outside the Domestic Labor Debate: Towards a Theory of Modes of Human Reproduction', *Review of Radical Political Economy,* vol. 16, nos 2/3 (1984), pp. 137–66.

11. Joan Kelly, 'The Doubled Vision of Feminist Theory', *Feminist Studies,* vol. 5 (1979) pp. 216–27. See also Rosalind Petchesky, 'Dissolving the Hyphen: A Report on Marxist-Feminist Groups 1–5', in Zillah Eisenstein, ed., *Capitalist Patriarchy and the Case for Socialist Feminism* (New York, 1979).

12. Nancy M. Tanner, *On Becoming Human,* (London, 1981) chs 3–6.

13. Richard B. Lee, *The !Kung San: Men, Women and Work in a Foraging Society* (New York, 1979), p. 490.

14. Karl Marx, *A Contribution to the Critique of Political Economy* (Moscow, 1970), p. 42.

15. The remarkable cross-cultural consistency of this domestic task allocation, anchoring the division of labour by gender in an immense range of societies, remains a great conundrum in the social sciences. Most scholars take the sexual division of labour for granted, failing to recognize that there is anything here, beyond biology, that needs to be explained. However, there have been a number of bold and thought-provoking attempts by feminist anthropologists to frame an answer: Adrienne Zihlman, 'Women in Evolution. Subsistence and Social Organization among Early Hominids', *Signs,* vol. 4 (1978), pp. 4–20; Rita Mae Blumberg, *Stratification: Socio-economic and Sexual Inequality* (Dubuque, 1978); Peggy R. Sanday, *Female Power and Male Dominance: On the Origins of Sexual Inequality* (Cambridge, 1981); and Nancy Tanner, *On Becoming Human* (London, 1981).

16. Kathleen Gough, 'The Origin of the Family', in Rayna Reiter, ed., *Toward an Anthropology of Women* (New York, 1975), p. 64.

17. Blumberg, *Stratification,* p. 17.

18. Tanner, *On Becoming Human,* pp. 269–71.

19. Peter J. Wilson, *Man, the Promising Primate: The Conditions of Human Evolution* (New Haven, 1980), p. 43.

20. See Linda Gordon, *Woman's Body, Woman's Right: A Social History of Birth Control in America* (Harmondsworth, 1976), p. 39; Norman Himes, *Medical History of Contraception* (New York, 1963); Angus McLaren, *A History of Contraception from Antiquity to the Present* (Oxford, 1990).

21. Lee, *The !Kung San,* pp. 310–25.

22. Patricia Draper, '!Kung Women: Contrasts in Sexual Egalitarianism in Foraging Societies', Reiter, ed., *Toward an Anthropology of Women,*.

23. Demographers treat all forms of fertility regulation except modern contraceptive practice as instances of 'natural fertility'. This misleading concept is discussed on pp. 184–5.

24. Blumberg, *Stratification,* p. 14; Ansley J. Coale, 'The Decline of Fertility in Europe Since the Eighteenth Century as a Chapter in Human Demographic History', in Ansley J. Coale and Susan C. Watkins, eds, *The Decline of Fertility in Europe* (Princeton, 1986), p. 6.

25. The full implications of such an onerous and frequently debilitating travail ought

to be squarely faced. As Roberta Hamilton has remarked: 'it is hard not to conclude that the effect of biological difference on the position of women is an embarrassment to marxists' and, one might add, to feminists: *The Liberation of Women, A Study of Patriarchy and Women* (London, 1978), p. 81.,

26. Alison Jolly estimates that the following primate species achieve a comparable level of independence from constant adult care at these ages: lemur, 0.5 year; macaque, 1.5 years; gibbon, 2 years; chimpanzee, 3 years; orang-utan, 3.5 years; human, 6 years: *The Evolution of Primate Behaviour* (New York, 1972), p. 215.

27. Adrienne Rich, *Of Woman Born* (New York, 1976); Nancy Chodorow, *The Reproduction of Mothering, Psychoanalysis and the Sociology of Gender* (Berkeley, 1978); Dorothy Dinnerstein, *The Mermaid and the Minotaur: Sexual Arrangements and Human Malaise* (New York, 1976).

28. Mary O'Brien, *The Politics of Reproduction* (London, 1981).

29. 'Woman the Gatherer: Male Bias in Anthropology', in Reiter, ed., *Toward an Anthropology of Women*, pp. 46–7.

30. *The Forest People* (New York, 1961).

31. *Family Life and Illicit Love in Earlier Generations* (Cambridge, 1977), p. 104.

32. *The Anti-social Family* (London, 1982), p. 36.

33. George Murdock, 'Comparative Data on the Division of Labour by Sex', *Social Forces*, vol. 15 (1937), pp. 551–3.

34. Ester Boserup, *Women's Role in Economic Development* (New York, 1970).

35. In *Maidens, Meal and Money: Capitalism and the Domestic Community* (London, 1981), Claude Meillassoux highlights the relations between past, present and future producers in the reproduction cycle of labour-power in his analysis of what he terms the domestic mode of production of lineage-based horticulturalists in Africa. His work has furnished a powerful stimulus to my own conception in this chapter.

36. Nancy Folbre has correctly insisted on this point: 'Exploitation Comes Home: A Critique of the Marxian Theory of Labour Power', *Cambridge Journal of Economics*, vol. 6, no. 4 (1982).

37. Gary R. Lee, *Family Structure and Interaction: A Comparative Analysis* (Minneapolis, 1982), ch. 3. It is misleading to speak of 'the family' (or 'the British family') as if families, in their diversity, were replicas of a master institution. Yet this reified reference is still commonplace in family sociology: see, for example, Ronald Fletcher, *The Shaking of the Foundations* (London, 1988).

38. Lutz Berkner and Franklin Mendels, 'Inheritance Systems, Family Structure and Demographic Patterns in Western Europe, 1700–1900', in Charles Tilly, ed., *Historical Studies of Changing Fertility* (Princeton, 1978).

39. Scholars speak, in this regard, of 'family-formation strategies'. The term's strength lies in recognizing people's capacity to shape family cycles in pursuing their own ends. Too often, however, a strategy is simply imputed to the family as a whole on the basis of the end-result, as if it were jointly achieved by all family members acting in harmony. The essential question of whose strategy prevailed is obscured.

40. Laslett, 'Introduction: The History of the Family', *Household and Family in Past Time*, pp. 1–89.

41. Ibid., pp. 24, 27.

42. 'Family and Kinship in Western Europe: The Problem of the Joint Family Household', *Journal of Interdisciplinary History*, vol. 5 (1975), pp. 601–8.

43. 'The difficulty of placing any particular usage of the term family is not merely a technical or academic one. It underlines the many contradictions in analyses of household, sexuality and kinship, and is the root of the apparently inexplicable failure to develop a systematic understanding of the history of these arrrangements': Barrett and McIntosh, *The Anti-social Family*, p. 85.

44. See Sylvia Yanagisako, 'Family and Household: The Analysis of Kin Groups', *Annual Review of Anthropology*, vol. 8, 1979, pp. 161–205; Rayna Rapp, Ellen Ross and Renate Bridenthal, 'Examining Family History', *Feminist Studies*, vol. 5 (1979), pp. 174–200. J. E. Goldthorpe, *Family Life in Western Societies* (Cambridge, 1987), p. 3.

45. Laslett, *Household and Family in Past Time*, p. 27.

46. Laslett, 'Introduction', *Household and Family in Past Time;* Wall, 'The Household: Demographic and Economic Change in England, 1650–1970', in Richard Wall, ed., *Family Forms in Historic Europe* (Cambridge, 1972).

47. Laslett, *Household and Family in Past Time*, p. 61.

48. Many scholars have criticized the way household composition tables have been permitted to structure the conceptual field of family history, despite the fact that co-residence per se is not the key to family structure. See, for example, Michael Anderson, *Approaches to the History of the Western Family, 1500–1914* (London, 1980), esp. ch. 2.

49. See, for example, the predominant orientation of articles published in the *Journal of Family History* and the *Journal of Interdisciplinary History*. As an adjunct to family-cycle analysis, many scholars have recently developed a 'life-course' approach, based on the propensity of individuals at various ages to take specific steps (to leave home, get married, bear their first child, and so on). For a useful introduction to this analysis, see Glen Elder's article 'Families and Lives: Some Developments in Life-Course Studies' in Tamara Harevan and Andrejs Plakans, eds, *Family History at the Crossroads* (Princeton, 1987). Life-course analysis makes very high demands upon data sources, thus eliminating most historical records compiled before the mid nineteenth century. As a statistical method, the technique usefully illuminates shifts in the timing of life-course steps by cohort. As with the Cambridge tables, however, it runs the risk of being inflated into a paradigm. This seems especially dangerous because the life-course approach tends to efface families as collectivities, treating them simply as the nodal intersections of atomized individuals pursuing their own interests. On this point, see Martine Segalen, 'Life-Course Patterns and Peasant Culture in France: A Critical Assessment', in *Family History at the Crossroads*.

50. See in particular the work (listed in the bibliography) of Lutz Berkner, Rudolph Braun, John Gillis, David Levine, Hans Medick, Franklin Mendels, Joan Scott, Louise Tilly and Charles Tilly.

51. See Veronica Beechey, 'On Patriarchy', *Feminist Review*, no. 9 (1979), pp. 66–82; Sheila Rowbotham, Sally Alexander and Barbara Taylor, 'Debate on Patriarchy', in Raphael Samuel, ed., *People's History and Socialist Theory* (London, 1983).

52. Rosalind Coward, *Patriarchal Precedents: Sexuality and Social Relations* (London, 1983).

53. It may be useful to distinguish between two basic axes of male dominance. The first operates through women's systematic exclusion from – or drastic underrepresentation in – arenas of power. The second works through face-to-face relations, wherein men dominate women; the domestic sphere is normally the primary site of the latter oppression. Owing to its subject matter, this text focuses almost exclusively on the second mode of male dominance. This emphasis ought not to be construed as implying that I regard the first process (of institutional exclusion or marginalization) as a minor, secondary or derivative avenue of women's subordination.

54. Varda Burstyn, 'Masculine Dominance and the State', in *Socialist Register,* Ralph Miliband and John Saville, eds (London, 1983); Carol Brown, 'Mothers, Fathers, and Children: From Private to Public Patriarchy', in Lydia Sargent, ed., *The Unhappy Marriage of Marxism and Feminism* (London, 1981).

55. *Women's Oppression Today: Problems in Marxist Feminist Analysis* (London, 1980), p. 16.

56. Note that two possible answers are rejected here in the way the question is posed: (a) that marriage, as historically constituted, is not an oppressive institution for women, and (b) that most women do not wish to marry, but are forced to by others. These propositions deserve to be considered on their empirical merits; I have not rejected them a priori. However, I find them both to be overwhelmingly refuted by the historical evidence for the societies under consideration here. A third possibility – that patriarchal relations *do* objectively oppress women, but that women do not find them oppresive – is considered below.,

57. The standard meaning of the terms 'choice' and 'decision-making' connotes processes which are far too concentrated in time and deliberative to convey what goes on in households as people evolve subsistence-optimizing strategies in a groping, culturally im-

mersed, trial-and-error fashion. The choice-theoretic paradigm, as it is conceived in mainstream economics, is more appropriate to decision-making in executive offices and boardrooms, where explicit agendas are set and profit-maximizing choices are considered in the light of market research, comparative cost estimates, etc. This is one of the main problems in simply transferring the framework of neo-classical decision-making in the firm to the proletarian household, as human-capital theorists do: Gary Becker, *A Treatise on the Family* (Cambridge, Mass., 1981). There are, however, interesting moves afoot to develop a fully marxist micro-economics, where power disparity and divergent interests between agents are embraced theoretically from the outset. See the work of Sam Bowles on capitalist firms: 'The Production Process in a Competitive Economy: Walrasian, Neo-Hobbesian and Marxian Models', *American Economic Review,* vol. 75 (1985), pp. 16–35; and Nancy Folbre on proletarian households: 'Exploitation Comes Home', *Cambridge Journal of Economics,* vol. 6 (1982). My own thoughts on the latter are elaborated in 'Reflections on the Domestic Labour Debate and Prospects for Marxist–Feminist Synthesis', in Roberta Hamilton and Michèle Barrett, eds, *The Politics of Diversity* (London, 1986).

58. On this point, see Marshall Sahlins's provocative polemic with vulgar materialism, *Culture and Practical Reason* (Chicago, 1976). He asks us to consider the most elementary necessity: the subsistence quest for food. We must eat to survive, therefore we are forced to choose particular foods from the range of edibles available. In doing so, we make certain classes of edibles 'food' and reject others. Pragmatic necessity cannot be invoked to explain our choices; even in the most rudimentary societies, food is culturally construed literally from the ground up.

59. Diane Elson criticized a draft of this section for treating the dispositions of rational actors as a priori, failing to take adequate account of the fact that people are changed by the life-options they pursue. The point was well taken, and I have endeavoured to rid the argument of residual traces of an abstract economism based on 'cost accounting' models of rationality. Radical versions of choice-theoretic modelling claim that macro-structures (such as states and modes of production) are explicable in terms of the accretion of individual actions over time. My own theoretical dispositions are far removed from this type of epistemological individualism.

60. See Barbara Ehrenreich's *The Hearts of Men* (New York, 1983) for a cultural exposition of this paradox as it has operated in the postwar context of male breadwinner/dependent homemaker arrangements in the United States.

61. Exploring master–slave relations in the antebellum US South, Eugene Genovese, in *Roll, Jordan, Roll: The World the Slaves Made* (New York, 1976), provides an exemplary marxist analysis of the intimate dialectic of oppression and attachment, moving far beyond models of false consciousness and psychological abnegation. In theoretical terms, his analysis has a great deal to offer students of domestic patriarchy.

62. See Louise Lamphere, 'Strategies, Cooperation, and Conflict Among Women in Domestic Groups', in Michelle Rosaldo and Louise Lamphere, eds, *Woman, Culture and Society* (Stanford, 1974); Rayna Reiter [Rapp], 'Men and Women in the South of France: Public and Private Domains', in Reiter, ed., *Toward an Anthropology of Women;* Meg Luxton, *More Than a Labour of Love: Three Generations of Women's Work in the Home* (Toronto, 1980); Ellen Ross, 'Survival Networks: Women's Neighbourhood Sharing in London before World War I', *History Workshop Journal,* no. 15 (1983), pp. 4–27.

63. Lynne Segal makes an effective socialist–feminist response to radical feminists on this point in *Is the Future Female?* (London, 1987), ch. 3.

64. Cf. Michelle Rosaldo, 'Woman, Culture and Society: A Theoretical Overview', and Sherry Ortner, 'Is Male to Female as Nature Is to Culture?', in Rosaldo and Lamphere, eds, *Woman, Culture and Society.*

65. Frances Dahlberg, ed., *Woman the Gatherer* (New Haven, 1981), pp. 1–33; Karen Sachs, *Sisters and Wives: The Past and Future of Sexual Equality* (Westport, 1979), pp. 65–95.

66. Dahlberg, *Woman the Gatherer,* p. 19. Eleanor Leacock has argued that virtually all manifestations of male dominance in hunter-gatherer societies stem from the malevolent effects of colonialism: 'Women's Status in Egalitarian Society: Implications for Social Evolution', *Current Anthropology,* vol. 19 (1978), pp. 247–75. Certainly a growing depend-

ency on Western imperialism can be shown to have had pernicious consequences for foraging peoples, not least in altering their gender relations; yet it is doubtful that every expression of male dominance can be attributed to the impact of world capitalism.

67. Real strides have recently been taken towards an adequate explanation, however; see in particular Stephanie Coontz and Peta Henderson, eds, *Women's Work, Men's Property: The Origins of Gender and Class* (London, 1986); and Gerda Lerner, *The Creation of Patriarchy* (New York, 1986).

68. Eleanor Leacock, Introduction to F. Engels, *The Origin of the Family, Private Property and the State* (New York, 1972).

Chapter 2

1. Perry Anderson, *Passages from Antiquity to Feudalism* (London, 1974), pp. 462–549.

2. I am following Marc Bloch here in locating the essence of the feudal mode of production in the characteristic conjunction of the fief and the manor: 'A very simple and striking test proves that there was some relationship between feudal institutions and the essentials of the seignorial system. Most [medieval European] societies which had no *seigneuries* – such as Friesland, Dithmarschen, Norway – also had no vassalage and no fiefs. ... Regions imperfectly "seignorialized" were also imperfectly feudalized. ... These coincidences cannot be the result of chance; and in fact the relation between the two sides of the social structure is tolerably clear': 'The Rise of Dependent Cultivation and Seignorial Institutions', in M. M. Postan, ed., *The Cambridge Economic History of Europe*, vol. 1 (Cambridge, 1966), p. 266. See also Georges Duby, *The Early Growth of the European Economy* (New York, 1974), pp. 168–9, and Perry Anderson's cogent discussion in *Passages from Antiquity to Feudalism*, pp. 401–31.

3. M. M. Postan, *The Medieval Economy and Society: An Economic History of Britain in the Middle Ages* (Harmondsworth, 1975), p. 88.

4. Eleanor Searle, 'Seigneurial Control of Women's Marriage: The Antecedents and Function of Merchet in England', *Past & Present*, no. 82 (1979), p. 8.

5. Marc Bloch, *Feudal Society*, vol. 1 (Chicago, 1961), p. 266.

6. Perry Anderson, *Lineages of the Absolutist State* (London, 1974), pp. 397–461.

7. George C. Homans, *English Villagers of the Thirteenth Century* (Cambridge, Mass., 1941), pp. 149–51.

8. Chris Middleton, 'Peasants, Patriarchy and the Feudal Mode of Production in England: A Marxist Appraisal' (part 1), *Sociological Review*, vol. 29 (1981), p. 116.

9. Madeleine Jeay, 'Sexuality and Family in Fifteenth Century France', *Journal of Family History*, vol. 4 (1979), p. 336.

10. An argument to this effect is presented at the outset of the next chapter.

11. Duby writes: 'In the upper levels of society, family ties were being arranged within a rigid framework calculated to safeguard the unity of the inheritance – in a word, lineage. For each family there would be one line of male descent. On succeeding his father, the eldest son would exercise control over the common property handed down from his forebears, as a guarantee that the family might maintain its ascendancy. Against this relatively clear-cut background, the wish to counter the effects of partible inheritance imposed limits on collateral descent. The family would permit only one son – the eldest, or two at the most – to be party to a legitimate marriage; as far as possible, the others would be secured high-ranking positions in the upper clergy or in monasteries; in other words, they would rely on the Church's resources to avoid relegation. This same desire led to the practice of giving a dowry in movable goods to daughters who were about to marry, depriving them of any claim on the landed inheritance. It slowly brought acceptance of the idea that the eldest son should enjoy preferential treatment by receiving the lion's share, if not the whole, of his father's estate': *The Early Growth of the European Economy*, p. 171.

12. In the twelfth century, the jurist Glanvill explained the principle in English common law: 'Since legally, a woman is completely in the power of her husband, it is not

surprising that her dower and all other property are clearly deemed to be at his disposal.'

13. Unilineal descent had previously been assumed, but is now considered dubious.

14. As Jack Goody has noted, the term *lineage* is used in different ways by anthropologists and historians: *The Development of the Family and Marriage in Europe* (London, 1983), pp. 227–32. I find it important to emphasize here both the ascendancy of the conjugal relation against the claims of extended kin groups, and the clear preference to pass land (and other productive property) to sons, designating daughters only in lieu of sons. To capture both facets I have termed this conjugal patriline, as distinct from patrilineage (referring to a more extended kin group) and also in contrast to Goody's 'bilateral diverging devolution', which conveys the misleading impression that the inheritance prerogatives of daughters were on a par with those of sons in medieval Europe. Goody's conception is discussed further on pp. 105-6 and note 297.

15. While patriarchy and patriline were normally complementary principles, they could occasionally work at cross-purposes. In these cases, it is revealing to observe which prevails. If a landholding widow remarried and then died, whose children were entitled to claim portions from the property she had brought to the second union? Her new husband could exercise his patriarchal prerogative to manage her estate, treating it as an integral part of his own, but he could not normally dispose of it without her consent, and upon her decease it reverted in most cases to her sons, not to his. In the end, natal patriline prevailed. The considerable social power of widows – on which many have remarked – was based paradoxically on their testamentary prerogative as transitional guardians of the patriline. Ravensdale cites cases in fourteenth-century Coltenham where the second husband's sons acquired their stepmother's patrimony, but this appears to be exceptional: 'Population Changes and the Transfer of Customary Land on a Cambridgeshire Manor in the Fourteenth Century', in Richard M. Smith, ed., *Land, Kinship and Life-Cycle* (Cambridge, 1984), p. 202.

16. E. A. Wrigley, 'Fertility Strategy for the Individual and the Group' in Charles Tilly, ed., *Historical Studies of Changing Fertility* (Princeton, 1978), p. 139.

17. Marc Bloch, *Slavery and Serfdom in the Middle Ages* (Berkeley, 1975), pp. 38–43.

18. Chris Middleton, 'Peasants, Patriarchy and the Feudal Mode of Production in England: A Marxist Appraisal', *Sociological Review,* vol. 29 (1981), p. 139.

19. Frédéric Le Play, *L'Organisation de la famille* (Tours, 1871). 'Strong', because the authority of the senior patriarch must be vigorous to induce the heir to marry in while retaining the reins of domestic power and resisting retirement. The father does not possess this power in the weak-stem situation. On the prevalence of the strong-stem family cycle throughout central and southern France in the early modern era, see Pierre Goubert, 'Family and Province: A Contribution to the Knowledge of Family Structures in Early Modern France', *Journal of Family History,* vol. 2 (1977), pp. 179–95; and Alain Collomp, 'Tensions, Dissensions, and Ruptures inside the Family in Seventeenth and Eighteenth-Century Haute Provence', in Hans Medick and David Sabean, eds, *Interest and Emotion* (Cambridge, 1984). Virilocality appears to have been customary throughout Mediterranean Europe, but this also gave rise to joint families where two or more sons married in, as was commonplace in medieval Italy: David Herlihy and Christiane Klapisch-Zuber, *Tuscans and Their Families: A Study of the Florentine Catasto of 1427* (New Haven, 1985), pp. 290–336; Richard M. Smith, 'The People of Tuscany and Their Families in the Fifteenth Century: Medieval or Mediterranean?', *Journal of Family History,* vol. 6 (1981), pp. 119-21.

20. The existence of the weak-stem family cycle in the Middle Ages is not in doubt; its predominance is. However, the number of scholars who have detected inheritance and residential arrangements in conformity with the weak-stem cycle in various regions of Northwestern Europe is impressive. See, for example, G. G. Coulton, *Medieval Village, Manor, and Monastery* (Cambridge, 1925), p. 99; George C. Homans, *English Villagers in the Thirteenth Century* (Cambridge, Mass. 1941), pp. 145–6; E. A. Kosminsky, *Studies in the Agrarian History of England in the Thirteenth Century* (Oxford, 1956), pp. 207; Marc Bloch, *French Rural History* (London 1966), p. 163; Georges Duby, *Rural Economy and Country Life in the Medieval West* (Columbia, S.C., 1968), pp. 32–3; Pierre Goubert, 'Family and Province', *Journal of Family History,* vol. 2 (1977), pp. 179–95; Emily Coleman, 'Medieval

Marriage Characteristics: A Neglected Factor in the History of Medieval Serfdom', in R. I. Rotberg and T. K. Rabb, eds, *Marriage and Fertility* (Princeton, 1980), p. 5; Alan Mayhew, *Rural Settlement and Farming in Germany* (London, 1973), p. 35; and Erik Gronseth, 'Notes on the Historical Development of the Relation between Nuclear Family Kinship System and Wider Social Structure in Norway', in R. Hill and R. Konig, eds, *Families in East and West* (Paris, 1970), p. 232. The work of these scholars (with additional corroboration furnished below) is cited to provide an evidentiary basis for the generalization being proposed. The designation 'weak-stem' cycle is, however, mine alone.

21. Michael Mitterauer and Reinhard Sieder, *The European Family, Patriarchy to Partnership from the Middle Ages to the Present* (Oxford, 1982), p. 33; Rodney H. Hilton, *The English Peasantry in the Later Middle Ages* (Oxford, 1975), pp. 29–31; Ian Blanchard, 'Industrial Employment and the Rural Land Market 1380–1520', in Richard M. Smith, ed., *Land, Kinship and Life-Cycle* (Cambridge, 1984), pp. 270–75; Chris Dyer, 'Changes in the Size of Peasant Holdings in Some West Midland Villages', in ibid., p. 289. While retirement contracts of various sorts are plentiful in early modern wills, their origins in the Middle Ages have often been questioned. However, David Gaunt has established their medieval roots in Northwestern Europe through a wide-ranging examination of law codes: 'The Property and Kin Relationships of Retired Farmers in Northern and Central Europe', in Richard Wall, ed., *Family Forms in Historic Europe* (Cambridge, 1983). He finds evidence for retirement practices and *inter vivos* land transfer in Danish and Swedish laws dating from the thirteenth century (pp. 251–2), in German laws from the early fourteenth century (p. 254); and recalls Homan's evidence for 'champion country' England: *English Villagers*, pp. 144–59. On medieval England, see also J. A. Raftis, *Warboys: Two Hundred Years in the Life of an English Medieval Village* (Toronto, 1974), pp. 42–6.

22. Homans, *English Villagers*, pp. 145–7; John Hajnal, 'Two Kinds of Pre-industrial Household Systems', *Population and Development Review*, vol. 8 (1982), p. 482.

23. Jack Goody, *Production and Reproduction: A Comparative Study of the Domestic Domain* (Cambridge, 1976), p. 30; Barbara Hanawalt, *The Ties That Bound: Peasant Families in Medieval England* (New York, 1986), p. 81. In sixteenth-century Cambridgeshire, Margaret Spufford found frequent stipulations in men's wills that their widows were 'to be given house-room and a small acreage on which to support herself', with the heir tilling her plot and granting her 'free egresse and regresse' to the house: *Contrasting Communities: English Villagers in the Sixteenth and Seventeenth Centuries* (Cambridge, 1974), pp. 112–13. She is of the view that this right 'in no way implies a separate entrance for the widow, and a separate dwelling', but it is unclear why this inference could not reasonably be drawn. She endeavours to reconcile this very common retirement arrangement with Laslett's finding that such vertical extension was rare in early modern England, admitting that 'there seems to be a flat contradiction here' (p. 114). A more plausible reconciliation of the evidence than the one Spufford offers is simply to admit the possibility of separate dwellings or adjoined space with separate entrances, and hence discrete households in the narrow sense of the term.

24. Cicely Howell, *Land, Family and Inheritance in Transition: Kibworth Harcourt, 1280–1700* (Cambridge, 1983); Alan Mayhew, *Rural Settlement and Farming in Germany* (London, 1973); Goody, *Production and Reproduction*, p. 29; C. G. Coulton, *Medieval Village, Manor, and Monastery* (Cambridge, 1975), p. 99.

25. *Economy and Society*, vol. 1 (Berkeley, 1978), pp. 359–60.

26. Perry Anderson, *Passages from Antiquity to Feudalism* (London, 1974), pp. 107–42.

27. Malcolm Todd, *The Northern Barbarians, 100 BC – AD 300* (London, 1975); Jean Chapelot and Robert Fossier, *The Village and House in the Middle Ages* (London, 1985).

28. P. A. Brunt, *Italian Manpower, 225 BC – 14 AD* (Oxford, 1971); G. E. M. de Ste Croix, *The Class Struggle in the Ancient Greek World* (London, 1981), pp. 140–7, 226–8.

29. P. R. C. Weaver, *Familia Caesaris: A Social Study of the Emperor's Freedmen and Slaves* (Cambridge, 1972), p. 172; Susan Treggiari, 'Family Life among the Staff of the Volusii', *Transactions of the American Philological Association*, vol. 105 (1975), p. 395.

30. Brunt, *Italian Manpower*, p. 708; de Ste Croix, *Class Struggle in the Ancient Greek World*, pp. 234–9.

31. Susan Treggiari, 'Women as Property in the Early Roman Empire', in D. Kelly

Weisberg, ed., *Women and the Law* (Cambridge, Mass., 1982), p. 19.

32. William Westermann, *The Slave Systems of Greek and Roman Antiquity* (Philadelphia, 1955), p. 146.

33. *The Class Struggle in the Ancient Greek World*, p. 239.

34. A. H. M. Jones, 'Slavery in the Ancient World', *Economic History Review*, 9 (1956), pp. 185–99; de Ste Croix, *Class Struggle in the Ancient Greek World*, p. 237; M. I. Finley, *Ancient Slavery and Modern Ideology* (Harmondsworth, 1980), pp. 129–49; Peter Garnsey, 'Non-Slave Labour in the Roman World', in Garnsey, ed., *Non-Slave Labour in the Greco-Roman World* (Cambridge, 1980), p. 40.

35. Perry Anderson, *Passages from Antiquity to Feudalism*, p. 141.

36. Marc Bloch, 'The Rise of Dependent Cultivation and Seignorial Institutions', in M. M. Postan, ed., *The Cambridge Economic History of Europe*, vol. 1 (Cambridge, 1966), p. 246.

37. Georges Duby, 'Private Power, Public Power' in Georges Duby, ed., *A History of Private Life*, vol. 2 (Cambridge, Mass., 1988), p. 22.

38. In fact, villein rights were never to be explicitly codified in the Middle Ages. In England, according to the Royal Court, villeins were the chattel property of their lords. They could be sold as slaves, and their property was unequivocally considered to be the property of the lord. Nowhere in common law was the familial right of villeins to designate or be designated heirs, acknowledged: Paul R. Hyams, *Kings, Lords and Peasants in Medieval England: The Common Law of Villeinage in the Twelfth and Thirteenth Centuries* (Oxford, 1980), pp. 3–16, 66–79. The central courts consistently assigned lords an absolute power over their peasant subjects which they did not enjoy in practice. Local manor courts were necessarily more pragmatic and conditional concerning the lords' real powers, and were forced to acknowledge certain villein rights which were held to have existed 'as is the custom of the manor, since time out of mind'. As this phrase suggests, these customary rights predated the formation of the feudal order; the medieval aristocracy was in no position to abrogate them.

39. Bloch, 'The Rise of Dependent Cultivation', pp. 251–4. The decisive difference between serfs and slaves was the former's effective possession of the means of producing their own subsistence. This prerogative, as we have seen, was vested as a family's right through the householder; domicile rights to subsistence independence and inheritance rights were corollaries to the familial prerogative that slave families lacked. The social relations of generational reproduction were thus starkly divergent for the two classes' domestic groups, since the imperatives of the land-inheritance system did not exist for slaves, nor were peasant families broken up through sale, or freely alienated from the land as individual chattels; slaves were.

40. Westermann, *The Slave Systems of Greek and Roman Antiquity*, pp. 139–49.

41. N. J. G. Pounds, *An Economic History of Medieval Europe* (New York, 1974), p. 17.

42. Pierre Dockès, *Medieval Slavery and Liberation* (Chicago, 1982), p. 96.

43. David Herlihy, *Medieval Households* (Cambridge, Mass., 1985), p. 62. See also Duby, 'Private Power, Public Power', p. 7.

44. Brent D. Shaw and Richard P. Saller, 'Close-kin Marriage in Roman Society?', *Man*, vol. 19 (1984), pp. 432–44.

45. Beryl Rawson, 'The Roman Family', in Rawson, ed., *The Family in Ancient Rome* (New York, 1986), pp. 20, 32.

46. G. Clark, 'Roman Women', *Greece and Rome*, 2nd ser., vol. 28 (1981), p. 204.

47. Alan Watson, *The Law of Persons in the Later Roman Republic* (Oxford, 1967), pp. 17–18; Keith Hopkins, 'The Age of Roman Girls at Marriage', *Population Studies*, vol. 18 (1965), p. 319; Susan Treggiari, 'Digna Condicio: Betrothals in the Roman Upper Class', *Echos du monde classique, Classical Views*, vol. 28 (1984), p. 421.

48. Richard Saller, 'Roman Dowry and the Devolution of Property in the Principate', *Classical Quarterly*, vol. 34 (1984), pp. 195–205.

49. Sarah B. Pomeroy, *Goddesses, Whores, Wives and Slaves* (New York, 1975), p. 155; Saller, 'Roman Dowry', p. 196.

50. J. A. Crook comments: 'it looks as if sweeping away all male heirs ... but one

was not very nice; you could do it but you must come clean about it. Sweeping away daughters is, perhaps, not minded so much: you can leave them legacy of their dowry. ...' 'Women in Roman Succession', in Rawson, ed., *The Family in Ancient Rome*, pp. 65, 77.

51.   Emiel Eyben, 'Family Planning in Greco-Roman Antiquity', *Ancient Society*, vol. 11, no. 2 (1980).

52.   Marleen Flory, 'Family in Familia, Kinship and Community in Slavery', *American Journal of Ancient History*, vol. 3 (1978), p. 82; Susan Treggiari, 'Women as Property in the Early Roman Empire', in Weisberg, ed., *Women and the Law*, p. 19.

53.   K. R. Bradley, *Slaves and Masters in the Roman Empire* (New York, 1987), p. 49.

54.   Ibid., p. 53.

55.   'Close-kin Marriage in Roman Society?' pp. 432–44; see also Brent Shaw, 'Latin Funerary Epigraphy and Family Life in the Later Roman Empire', *Historia*, vol. 33 (1984), pp. 457–97.

56.   Patrick J. Geary, *Before France and Germany: The Creation and Transformation of the Merovingian World* (Oxford, 1988), pp. 39–41.

57.   R. C. Hoffman, 'Medieval Origins of the Common Fields', in W. N. Parker and E. L. Jones, eds, *European Peasants and Their Markets* (Princeton, 1975), pp. 38–9.

58.   Malcolm Todd, *The Northern Barbarians, 100 BC – AD 300* (London, 1975), pp. 123–8.

59.   Jean Chapelot and Robert Fossier, *The Village and House in the Middle Ages* (London, 1985), p. 23.

60.   Todd, *The Northern Barbarians*, p. 157.

61.   We have a clearer picture of the Celtic Sept in Ireland, due to the absence of manorialization there and the preservation of an extremely rich hagiographic literature: cf. David Herlihy, *Medieval Households* (Cambridge, Mass., 1985), pp. 30–43. The best overview of Germanic kinship is Alexander Murray's meticulous survey of key passages in the legal texts of the successor states, above all the Lex Salica: *Germanic Kinship Structure* (Toronto, 1983). Devoting most of his attention to a convincing critique of earlier schemas of unilineal descent groups, the author refrains from advancing an alternative construction, which he would maintain is premature. Given the tenacious misconceptions fostered by previous paradigms, his reluctance to create another grand theory is understandable. Yet in the last analysis, Murray's reticence is evasive. For he *has* a conceptual framework (which generates a continuity thesis concerning the transition from Antiquity to feudalism). He simply fails to make it explicit, and therefore to submit it to the same intensive scrutiny he accords his opponents.

62.   These scholars were theoretically imprisoned in the formalist jural models of the anthropological orthodoxy of their day, culminating in Radcliffe-Brown's grand descent typology. Unilineal and cognatic kin systems were typically conceived as mutually exclusive opposites. The latter were treated as residual, receiving very little examination despite the fact that an estimated one-third of all tribal societies are organized along the lines of bilateral descent: Roger M. Keesing, *Kin Groups and Social Structure* (New York, 1975), pp. 91–2. Even in patrilineal systems, descent groups do not define the sum total of kin relations. In subsuming kinship within the overarching categories of agnatic descent, various forms of identity and affiliation through women have been ignored.

63.   E. A. Thompson, *The Early Germans* (Oxford, 1965). Julian Thomas has recently hypothesized a transformation from a lineage mode of production, based on unilineal descent groups, to a Germanic system, where the kindred is a looser federation of independent households: 'Relations of Production and Social Change in the Neolithic of Northwest Europe', *Man*, vol. 22 (1987), pp. 405–30. Eschewing technological determinism while focusing on the social relations of production, he associates this protracted and uneven transition with the acceptance of plough agriculture, primitive metallurgy and animal traction, technologies that had been known in the previous millennium but shunned by ruling elders in lineage communities as being subversive of their reproductive priorities. This is a speculative model-building endeavour, as Thomas freely admits, but it is informed by a broadly based survey of recent archaeological findings that have advanced our knowledge of Neolithic Europe very considerably. Ironically, if he is right, the debate about the nature

of the Germanic clans may now be revived, but located, this time round, two to three millennia earlier.

64. Alexander Murray, *Germanic Kinship Structure* (Toronto, 1983), p. 25.

65. *The Development of the Family and Marriage in Europe* (London, 1983), p. 234. The point is that it is meaningless to discuss kin groups without specifying what they actually do. The result of an excessive preoccupation with questions of taxonomic classification has too often been the failure to distinguish between different levels of constitutive adhesion: (a) the recognition of affiliation; (b) the formation of action groups; and (c) the reproduction of corporate entities: Keesing, *Kin Groups and Social Structure* (New York, 1975), p. 11.

66. The particular combination of bilateral descent groups with agnatic primacy is commonplace in cognatic descent systems. See Keesing's discussion in *Kin Groups and Social Structure*, pp. 91–100; Robin Fox, *Kinship and Marriage* (Harmondsworth, 1967), pp. 152–5; and Goody, *The Development of the Family and Marriage in Europe*, pp. 222–39.

67. *Everyday Life of the Barbarians: Goths, Franks and Vandals* (London, 1972), p. 38.

68. Murray, *Germanic Kinship Structure*, pp. 67, 80, 101; T. M. Charles-Edwards, 'Kinship, Status and the Origins of the Hide', *Past & Present*, no. 56 (1972), pp. 3–33; K. J. Leyser, 'The German Aristocracy from the Ninth to the Twelfth Century', *Past & Present*, no. 41 (1968); Herlihy, *Medieval Households*, pp. 51–2.

69. 'Kinship, Status and the Origins of the Hide', pp. 29, 32.

70. Geary, *Before France and Germany*, pp. 52–3.

71. Murray, *Germanic Kinship Structure*, p. 101.,

72. In *Pre-capitalist Economic Formations*, Marx contrasts the oriental and Germanic modes of agricultural production according to the ways they link household and communal property. In the latter, he emphasizes the primacy of independent households, characterizing the kindred as 'an association, not a union. ... In the Germanic form, ... independent family settlement, guaranteed by means of its association with other such settlements by men of the same tribe, and the occasional assembly for purposes of legal disputes, etc. which establishes their mutual surety. ... Communal property as such appears as a communal accessory to the individual kin settlements and land appropriations': *Pre-capitalist Economic Formations* (New York, 1965), p. 80.

73. H. R. Loyn, 'Kinship in Anglo-Saxon England', in Peter Clemoes, ed., *Anglo-Saxon England*, vol. 3 (Cambridge, 1974), p. 199; Murray, *Germanic Kinship Structure*, p. 101.

74. Herlihy, *Medieval Households*, p. 47.

75. Loyn, 'Kinship in Anglo-Saxon England', p. 205.

76. J. M. Wallace-Hadrill, *The Barbarian West: The Early Middle Ages, AD 400–1000* (London, 1962), pp. 121–3.

77. Ibid., p. 125.

78. John Bossy, *Christianity in the West, 1400–1700* (Oxford, 1985), p. 48.

79. Wallace-Hadrill, *The Barbarian West*, p. 122.

80. Bloch, *Feudal Society*, p. 125.

81. Wendy Davies and Paul Fouracre, *The Settlement of Disputes in Early Medieval Europe* (Cambridge, 1986).

82. Herlihy, *Medieval Households*, pp. 50–51.

83. Suzanne Wemple, *Women in Frankish Society, Marriage and the Cloister, 500–900* (Philadelphia, 1981), pp. 70-71.

84. Tacitus, *The Agricola and The Germania* (Harmondsworth, 1948), p. 118.

85. Geary, *Before France and Germany*, pp. 46–8.

86. Herlihy, *Medieval Households*, pp. 52–3.

87. Tacitus, *The Agricola and The Germania*, p. 118.

88. Ester Boserup, *Women's Role in Economic Development* (New York, 1970).

89. Wemple, *Women in Frankish Society*, p. 28.

90. Geary, *Before France and Germany*, pp. 37–8.

91. Colin McEvedy, *The Penguin Atlas of Medieval History* (Harmondsworth, 1961), p. 14.

92. Chapelot and Fossier, *The Village and House in the Middle Ages*, p. 28.

93. J. C. Russell, 'The Control of Late Ancient and Medieval Population', *Memoirs*

of the American Philosophical Society, vol. 160 (1985). Devastation on this scale is roughly on a par with the Black Death.

94. Ibid., p. 36.

95. Georges Duby, *The Early Growth of the European Economy,* p. 184.

96. Ibid., p. 183.

97. David Levine, *Reproducing Families: The Political Economy of English Population History* (Cambridge, 1987), p. 10; Renée Doehaerd, *The Early Middle Ages in the West: Economy and Society* (Amsterdam, 1978), p. 44.

98. P. Anderson, *Passages from Antiquity to Feudalism,* pp. 107–11; Vianna Muller, 'The Formation of the State and the Oppression of Women: Some Theoretical Considerations and a Case Study in England and Wales', *Review of Radical Political Economics,* vol. 9 (1977), p. 14.

99. Duby, *The Early Growth of the European Economy,* pp. 38, 47.

100. Pounds, *An Economic History of Medieval Europe,* pp. 51–2.

101. Duby, *The Early Growth of the European Economy,* pp. 39–40; Pounds, *An Economic History of Medieval Europe,* pp. 51–2.

102 Doehaerd, *The Early Middle Ages in the West,* p. 33; Goody, *The Development of the Family and Marriage in Europe,* pp. 103–6.

103. Bloch, *Feudal Society,* p. 245; Pounds, *An Economic History of Medieval Europe,* pp. 52–3; Duby, *The Early Growth of the European Economy,* p. 45.

104. Goody, *The Development of the Family and Marriage in Europe,* p. 17; Loyn, 'Kinship in Anglo-Saxon England', p. 199; Wallace-Hadrill, *The Barbarian West,* p. 125.

105. In a survey of forty-six peasant communities around the world, Walter Goldschmidt and Evalyn Kunkel discovered that in none did extended kin groups control land; yet this is 'a pattern which is found widely among horticultural producers': 'The Structure of the Peasant Family', *American Anthropologist,* vol. 73 (1971), p. 1060. Goody found the same correlation in samples of horticulturalists and peasants drawn from the Ethnographic Atlas: 'Inheritance, Property and Women: Some Comparative Considerations', in Jack Goody, Joan Thirsk and E. P. Thompson, eds, *Family and Inheritance: Rural Society in Western Europe, 1200–1800* (Cambridge, 1976).

106. Bloch, *Feudal Society,* p. 247.

107. P. Anderson, *Passages from Antiquity to Feudalism,* pp. 117–18.

108. Loyn, 'Kinship in Anglo-Saxon England', p. 199.

109. Alan Macfarlane, *The Origins of English Individualism* (Oxford, 1978).

110. Bloch, *Feudal Society,* p. 191.

111. Vassalage, of course, did not diminish the power of kinship alliance in war and patronage at the apex of the feudal pyramid, where the king presided as the vassal of no man. It was here, in the persona of the royal family, that the ancient (pre-feudal) ideology of the chieftains' dynastic rule by divine right was appropriated and amplified with decisive ramifications. Arranged marriages between royal families sealed political alliances from one end of Europe to the other, and succession feuds sent armies to war and shook dynasties.

112. Georges Duby, 'Private Power, Public Power', in Duby, ed., *A History of Private Life,* vol. 2, p. 20.

113. Bloch cites many reasons for the failure of fief reversion to take hold as feudalism developed in medieval Europe: the incapacity of noble magnates to attract and hold loyal vassals should they have refused to concede the right of patrimony; the unwillingness of knights to risk death in battle for their overlords without assurance that their sons would inherit their fiefs; the difficulty of royal suzerains asserting the divine right of their own progeny to inherit their crowns without granting the same right to lesser nobles; the ideological power of this principle of reciprocity at every level of the aristocratic hierarchy: *Feudal Society,* pp. 191–5. Bloch focuses here strictly on relations within the ruling class. But surely one powerful reason for the still-birth of the 'pure' feudal principle of tenure reversion among the aristocracy lies in its absence down below, defeated by the entrenched inheritance prerogatives of the peasant producers in the early medieval era. It would have been difficult for feudal magnates to vassalize local landowners by denying them a right that the latter's inferiors – the tillers of the soil – had enjoyed, and tenaciously defended, for centuries.

114. Guy Fourquin, *Lordship and Feudalism in the Middle Ages* (London, 1976), p. 188.

115. Bloch, *French Rural History* (London, 1966), pp. 179–80.

116. Bloch, *Feudal Society*, p. 190.

117. Zvi Razi, 'Family, Land and the Village Community in Later Medieval England', *Past & Present*, no. 93 (1981), p. 27.

118. E. Gronseth, 'Notes on the Historical Development of the Relation between Nuclear Family Kinship System and Wider Social Structure in Norway', in R. Hill and R. Konig, eds, *Families in East and West* (Paris, 1970), p. 227.

119. R. C. Hoffman, 'Medieval Origins of the Common Fields', in W. N. Parker and E. L. Jones, eds, *European Peasants and Their Markets* (Princeton, 1975), pp. 61, 44.

120. Bloch, *Feudal Society*, pp. 243–6; Duby, *The Early Growth of the European Economy*, p. 35; Herlihy, *Medieval Households*, p. 57; Pounds, *An Economic History of Medieval Europe*, p. 53.

121. Georges Duby, *Rural Economy and Country Life in the Medieval West* (Columbia, S.C., 1968), p. 29.

122. Bloch, *Feudal Society*, p. 203.

123. Howell, *Land, Family and Inheritance*, pp. 15–16.

124. In a field of scholarship not noted for consensus, there is a general agreement among historians on the close association between seigneurial jurisdiction and the impartibility of arable land. See Jean Louis Flandrin, *Families in Former Times: Kinship, Household and Sexuality* (New York, 1979), p. 80; Goody, *The Development of the Family and Marriage in Europe*, p. 119; Cicely Howell, 'Peasant Inheritance Customs in the Midlands, 1280–1700', in J. Goody, J. Thirsk and E. P. Thompson, eds, *Family and Inheritance*, p. 116; Emmanuel Le Roy Ladurie, 'A System of Customary Law: Family Structures and Inheritance Customs in Sixteenth Century France' in R. Forster and O. Ranum, eds, *Family and Society: Selections from the Annales* (Baltimore, 1976), pp. 45–6; Georges Duby, *Medieval Marriage: Two Models from Twelfth-Century France* (Baltimore, 1978), pp. 8–9; R. Hajdu, 'Family and Feudal Ties in Poitou, 1100–1300', *Journal of Interdisciplinary History*, vol. 8 (1977), p. 133; Homans, *English Villagers*, pp. 32–43; Herlihy, *Medieval Households*, p. 87; Lutz Berkner and Franklin Mendels, 'Inheritance Systems, Family Structure and Demographic Patterns in Western Europe, 1700–1900', in Charles Tilly, ed., *Historical Studies of Changing Fertility* (Princeton, 1978).

125. Diane Hughes, 'From Brideprice to Dowry in Mediterranean Europe', *Journal of Family History*, vol. 3 (1978), pp. 262–96.

126. Ibid., pp. 265–7.

127. Ibid., p. 271.

128. Rosamond Faith, 'Peasant Families and Inheritance Customs in Medieval England', *Agricultural History Review*, vol. 14 (1966), p. 91.

129. Luke 2:43–50. Luke informs us that his parents were baffled by their son's response. All biblical citations are from the new King James version.

130. Matthew 12:46–50. See also Mark 3:31–5 and Luke 8:19–21.

131. Luke 18:28.

132. John 7:5; Matthew 13:57; Mark 6:4.

133. Matthew 8:21–22; Luke 9:59–60.

134. Matthew 10:34–38. Jesus is here quoting with approval the Old Testament.

135. Matthew 23:9.

136. Luke 14:26.

137. Matthew 19:29; Luke 18:29–30.

138. Matthew 19:9. The author of the Gospel of Matthew appears to have found Jesus's unconditional repudiation of divorce too dire, and softened his injunction by inserting the phrase 'except for sexual immorality'. This qualification reconciled the Christian position with the conservative variant of Jewish marriage custom: Elaine Pagels, *Adam, Eve and the Serpent* (New York, 1988), p. 22.

139. Matthew 19:12; Luke 20:34–35.

140. Luke 23:29.

141. Ironically, it is orthodox Christians, ardent 'pro-family' advocates, who are most

inclined to insist on the New Testament's inerrancy. Quoting selectively, they have evaded an unflinching confrontation with Jesus's radical antagonism to domesticity and familial devotion. Biblical scholars provide no consolation; they find that alterations and fraudulent supplements to the original Gospels of Jesus and Paul consistently serve to moderate their uncompromising anti-familial counsel.

142. Roger Lane Fox, *Pagans and Christians* (London, 1986), pp. 359, 373.

143. I Corinthians 7:32–33. See Peter Brown's superb account in *The Body and Society: Men, Women and Sexual Renunciation in Early Christianity* (New York, 1988), pp. 53–57, 160.

144. I Corinthians 6:16; 7:29.

145. Pagels, *Adam, Eve and the Serpent*, p. 80.

146. Ibid., p. 23.

147. Ephesians 5:22–33. Contrast this passage with Paul's use of the same phrase from Genesis ('the two shall become one flesh') in I Corinthians (6:16), where he refers to the dissipation of men who visit prostitutes!

148. Alan Macfarlane, *Marriage and Love in England, 1300–1840* (Oxford, 1986), p. 151. The phrase, from the Prayer Book, is recited in marriage services.

149. Pagels, *Adam, Eve and the Serpent*, p. 112.

150. In Augustine's conception, Adam and Eve's initial impulse of wilful disobedience was not sexually driven, since they were innocents in Eden, free from libidinal urges. However, their transgression empowered Satan, who unleashed his temptations; thenceforth, humans were destined to suffer the torment of lust.

151. Peter Brown, *The Body and Society*, pp. 402–3.

152. Pagels, *Adam, Eve and the Serpent*, pp. 91–7.

153. Brown, *The Body and Society*, p. 205.

154. This account follows Michael Sheehan, 'Choice of Marriage Partner in the Middle Ages', *Studies in Medieval and Renaissance History*, vol. 1 (1978), pp. 3–33. See also James Brundage's panoptic survey of canonical developments in *Law, Sex and Christian Society in Medieval Europe* (Chicago, 1987).

155. In Gratian's *Decretum*, the canon law of the Western Church symmetrically recuperated the minimal requisites of marriage as found in its Roman and Germanic precursors: from the former, the doctrine of consent; from the latter, coital consummation. See Brundage, *Law, Sex and Christian Society in Medieval Europe*, p. 236.

156. Michael Sheehan, 'Choice of Marriage Partner in the Middle Ages', *Studies in Medieval and Renaissance History*, vol. 1 (1978), pp. 4–5.

157. See Brown, *The Body and Society*, p. 345: 'In the Italy of Ambrose, treatises on virginity no longer circulated as exhortations to a sheltered piety. They were written so as to change upper-class opinion – to persuade emperors, prefects, and provincial governors to allow wealthy widows and virgins to remain dedicated to the Church, and to tolerate the redirection of parts of the wealth of great families, through such women, to pious causes.' See also Goody, *The Development of the Family and Marriage in Europe*, p. 123.

158. Roger Lane Fox, *Pagans and Christians*, pp. 340–55. Despite the modern stereotype of late Roman decadence, pagan culture had not been sexually permissive. Within marriage, great emphasis had been placed on correct decorum; a man's virility was preserved through sexual restraint.

159. Brown, *The Body and Society*, p. 31. See also Brundage, *Law, Sex and Christian Society in Medieval Europe* (Chicago, 1987).

160. Madeleine Jeay, 'Sexuality and Family in Fifteenth Century France', *Journal of Family History*, vol. 4 (1979), pp. 338–40.

161. Bossy, *Christianity in the West*, p. 123.

162. Aron Gurevich, *Medieval Popular Culture: Problems of Belief and Perception* (Cambridge, 1988), p. 93.

163. Brundage, *Law, Sex and Christian Society in Medieval Europe*, p. 241.

164. Shulamith Shahar, *The Fourth Estate: A History of Women in the Middle Ages* (London, 1983), pp. 71, 278.

165. Overt discrimination does not often appear in papal pronouncements and canon

law texts concerning sexual conduct. On the whole, they are remarkably even-handed. Only when the selective enforcement of such stipulations is considered, together with their dissimilar results, is the systematic nature of the Church's patriarchal bias manifest.

166. R. I. Moore, 'Duby's Eleventh Century', *History*, vol. 69 (1984), p. 40.

167. Christopher Hill, *Puritanism and Revolution, Studies in Interpretation of the English Revolution of the Seventeenth Century* (London, 1958), p. 384.

168. Carol Delaney, 'The Meaning of Paternity and the Virgin Birth Debate', *Man*, vol. 21 (1986), pp. 494–513.

169. Brown, *The Body and Society*, pp. 148–9.

170. Fox, *Pagans and Christians*, p. 367.

171. Ibid., pp. 366–7.

172. Ibid., p. 367.

173. R. W. Southern, *Western Society and the Church in the Middle Ages* (Harmondsworth, 1970), p. 311.

174. Galatians 3:27–28.

175. Southern, *Western Society and the Church*, pp. 17–18.

176. Bossy, *Christianity in the West*, p. 14.

177. The baptismal ritual thus replicated the creation story of Genesis, where the maternal reality of human birth had been effaced (with Adam issuing from God, and Eve from Adam's side). Male dominance in marriage was justified on these grounds in the New Testament: 'I do not permit a woman to teach or to have authority over a man, but to be in silence. For Adam was formed first, then Eve. And Adam was not deceived, but the woman being deceived fell into transgression' (I Timothy, 2:12–14).

178. Joseph H. Lynch, *Godparents and Kinship in Early Medieval Europe* (Princeton, 1986), p. 337.

179. Robin Lane Fox has argued vigorously (and on the whole persuasively) against any form of a continuity thesis which would see Christians and pagans as members of a 'common Mediterranean religious culture'. He does concede, however, that 'the degree to which people were ever Christianized is a problem which still runs through medieval history, the "age of faith"': *Pagans and Christians*, p. 21.

180. See in particular Keith Thomas, *Religion and the Decline of Magic* (Harmondsworth, 1978), pp. 27–57, and Gurevich, *Medieval Popular Culture: Problems of Belief and Perception*, pp. 1–77.

181. As noted in the first chapter, techno-structures are never pure expressions of their modes of production, but bear the direct impress of the diverse natural environments within which they are embedded. In contrast to European mixed agriculture, the feudal mode of production in Japan was based on riziculture. This difference had a direct impact on cultivation technology, the organization of the fields, the seasonal tempo of labour exertion, the minimum size threshold of viable peasant holdings, the density of the rural population, the configuration of village settlement, clothing and housing forms, and so on. See Perry Anderson, *Lineages of the Absolutist State*, p. 436.

182. Kosminsky, *Studies in the Agrarian History of England in the Thirteenth Century* (Oxford, 1956).

183. The inhibition against village specialization within the economy of a region was not due to the modest size of village settlements nor to the distance between them, but rather to a particular mode of exploitation that fostered a strong peasant preference for production for local use, selling off the surplus to pay the rent and not primarily to make a profit. As such, the constraint on the development of agricultural technology entailed in aversion to cash-crop specialization must be considered endemic to the mode of production. To the extent that the manorial straitjacket was loosened in the early modern era and village autarchy breached, the formerly tight interlacing of agrarian and pastoral farming unravelled and commodity production for extra-local exchange surged ahead in crops and handicrafts. These developments marked the beginning of the end for the feudal–seigneurial mode of production on the land.

184. Macfarlane, *The Origins of English Individualism*.

185. C. G. A. Clay, *Economic Expansion and Social Change: England 1500–1700*

(Cambridge, 1984), pp. 64–5; George Huppert, *After the Black Death: A Social History of Early Modern Europe* (Bloomington, 1986), p. 7; Henry Kamen, *European Society, 1500–1700* (London, 1984), p. 18.

186. Flandrin, *Families in Former Times*, p. 36.

187. Gurevich, *Medieval Popular Culture*, pp. 24, 93.

188. Martine Segalen, *Love and Power in the Peasant Family* (Oxford, 1983), pp. 44–5; Martin Ingram, *Church Courts, Sex and Marriage in England, 1570–1640* (Cambridge, 1987), p. 245.

189. Segalen, *Love and Power*, p. 46; Gurevich, *Medieval Popular Culture*, p. 93. But see Georges Duby, 'Private Power, Public Power,' in Duby, ed., *A History of Private Life*, vol. 2 (Cambridge, Mass., 1988) for an apposite insistence on the validity of distinguishing between public and private domains throughout the feudal epoch.

190. Flandrin, *Families in Former Times*, p. 107.

191. 'Everywhere, woman neighbours lent their assistance. ... In the Pyrenees, custom even prescribed in detail the obligations of each man and woman neighbour in these circumstances. In the case of a death, for example, it was the duty of the closest neighbours to hurry and inform the kinsfolk and friends of the deceased person, and to prepare the house, while the second neighbour cooked the meal and attended to the livestock. The closest woman neighbour stood, in church, at the side of the bereaved; and it was often the four closest neighbours who carried the coffin. They were taken into account even in the regulations which attempted to limit the ostentation of funerals': (Ibid., pp. 36–7).

192. Homans, *English Villagers*, p. 217; Macfarlane, *The Origins of English Individualism*.

193. Keith Wrightson and David Levine, *Poverty and Piety in an English Village: Terling, 1525–1700* (New York, 1979), pp. 82–91.

194. Judith M. Bennett, 'Medieval Peasant Marriage: An Examination of Marriage License Fines in Liber Gersumarum', in J. A. Raftis, ed., *Pathways to Medieval Peasants* (Toronto, 1981), p. 121.

195. R. A. Dodgshon, 'The Early Middle Ages, 1066–1350', in R. A. Dodgshon and R. A. Butlin, eds, *An Historical Geography of England and Wales* (London, 1978), pp. 89, 94.

196. Richard M. Smith, 'Kin and Neighbours in a Thirteenth-Century Suffolk Community', *Journal of Family History*, vol. 4 (1979), p. 248.

197. Richard M. Smith, 'Some Reflections on the Evidence for the Origins of the European Marriage Pattern in England', in C. C. Harris, ed., *Sociology of the Family: New Directions for Britain* (Keele, 1979), p. 97; Chris Dyer, *Lords and Peasants in a Changing Society* (Cambridge, 1980), p. 366.

198. Flandrin, *Families in Former Times*, pp. 34–5.

199. Goody, *The Development of the Family and Marriage in Europe*, p. 186.

200. Scanning the feudal horizon beyond Western Europe, we confront a far greater variation than within it. In Japan, for example, village communities were collectively responsible for raising dues and paying them to the lord's agent: Perry Anderson, *Lineages of the Absolutist State*, p. 447. In the Baltic countryside, by contrast, separate farmsteads dealt directly with the lord, with no mediation from the village community at all: Andrejs Plakans, 'Seigneurial Authority and Peasant Family Life: The Baltic Area in the Eighteenth Century', *Journal of Interdisciplinary History*, vol. 4 (1975), p. 638.

201. Emmanuel Le Roy Ladurie, *Montaillou: The Promised Land of Error* (New York, 1979), p. 24.

202. Hanawalt, *The Ties That Bound*, p. 118.

203. On the strong link between the marital division of labour and 'spheres of inheritance' among European peasants, see Elliot Leyton, 'Spheres of Inheritance in Aughnabay', *American Anthropologist*, vol. 72 (1970), pp. 1378–88; Ovar Löfgren, 'Family and Household among Scandinavian Peasants', in Michael Anderson, ed., *Sociology of the Family*, 2nd edn (Harmondsworth, 1980); Rayna Reiter [Rapp], 'Men and Women in the South of France: Public and Private Domains', in Reiter, ed., *Toward an Anthropology of Women* (New York, 1975). Löfgren identifies the division of labour as the prime cause in this relation. In a Danish island community, where patterns of household organization were transformed, 'the women took over all agricultural activities while men concentrated on

marine activities. As a result, in many cases farms came to be transmitted from mother to daughter' (p. 107). Rapp's study suggests, however, that lines of property transmission may foster a strong sense of distinct male and female domains, even when the practical division of labour transgresses these spheres to some degree; see note 208 below.

204. Lucienne Roubin, 'Male Space and Female Space within the Provençal Community', in Robert Forster and Orest Ranum, eds, *Rural Society in France* (Baltimore, 1977).

205. Flandrin, *Families in Former Times*, p. 109.

206. Hanawalt, *The Ties That Bound*, pp. 101–25. This medieval verse has a surprisingly modern ring: 'Some respit to husbands the weather may send/but huswives affaires have never an end': Chris Middleton, 'The Sexual Division of Labour in Feudal England', *New Left Review*, no. 113/114 (1979), p. 163.

207. Barbara Hanawalt, 'Peasant Women's Work in the Context of Marriage', in Hanawalt, ed., *Women and Work in Preindustrial Europe* (Bloomington, 1986), p. 119. It was village communities, not households, that strove for self-sufficiency in the production of food, clothing and shelter. Terms such as 'natural' and 'subsistence' economy, and the concept 'production for use' effectively lump together a great variety of economic forms and modes of production. As Hanawalt has correctly stressed, the medieval peasant economy was markedly different from the frontier settlements of the New World.

208. This flexibility (and hence the ensuing sketch) was much more true for Northwestern Europe than for the Mediterranean, where women were often excluded from field work on the grounds that it dishonoured their husbands: Goody, *The Development of the Family and Marriage in Europe*, p. 30. Such exclusion, however, may well be normatively maintained as a collective fiction, while being pragmatically relaxed as the occasion requires. In the traditional village of Colpeid in the southern French Alps, Rapp found that 'women claim to hate agricultural work and know nothing about it ... but most cut lavender every summer and in the fall they harvest grapes, as needed. Neither of these tasks is considered "work" by either sex': Reiter [Rapp], ed., *Toward an Anthropology of Women*, pp. 270–71.

209. David Gaunt and Ovar Löfgren, 'Remarriage in the Nordic Countries: The Cultural and Socio-economic Background', in Jacques Dupâquier et al., eds, *Marriage and Remarriage in the Past* (New York, 1981), p. 51.

210. Middleton, 'The Sexual Division of Labour in Feudal England', p. 156.

211. Gaunt and Löfgren, 'Remarriage in the Nordic Countries', p. 51.

212. Hilton, *The English Peasantry in the Later Middle Ages*, p. 105.

213. Pierre Goubert, *The French Peasantry in the Seventeenth Century* (Cambridge, 1986), p. 37.

214. Hanawalt, *The Ties That Bound*, p. 146; Miranda Chaytor, 'Household and Kinship: Ryton in the Late Sixteenth and Early Seventeenth Centuries', *History Workshop Journal*, no. 10 (1980), pp. 25–60.

215. Hanawalt, *The Ties That Bound*, p. 146; Middleton, 'The Sexual Division of Labour in Feudal England', p. 163.

216. Hanawalt, *The Ties That Bound*, p. 146.

217. The thesis of maternal indifference in medieval and early modern Europe was first propounded by Ariès, reiterated by Shorter, and then rendered in its most sensational and tendentious form by the French feminist Elisabeth Badinter, who sought to counter the notion of a timeless maternal instinct by citing court records of severe cases of infant abuse and neglect: Philippe Ariès, *Centuries of Childhood* (London, 1962); Edward Shorter, *The Making of the Modern Family* (New York, 1975), pp. 168–204; Elisabeth Badinter, *Mother Love: Myth and Reality* (New York, 1981). The argument has been rebutted by Ladurie, Shahar, Wilson and with great patience by Pollock, whose meticulously catalogued evidence from a wide range of early modern letters and diaries should suffice to put the thesis to rest: Ladurie, *Montaillou*, pp. 208–12; Shulamith Shahar, *The Fourth Estate: A History of Women in the Middle Ages* (London, 1983), pp. 232–4; Stephen Wilson, 'The Myth of Motherhood Myth: The Historical View of European Child-rearing', *Social History*, vol. 9 (1984), pp. 181–98; Linda Pollock, *Forgotten Children: Parent–Child Relations from 1500 to 1900* (Cambridge, 1983).

218. Hanawalt, *The Ties That Bound*, p. 147.
219. Introduction to A. Clark, *Working Life of Women in the Seventeenth Century*, (London, 1982 [1919]), p. xxiv.
220. Hanawalt, *The Ties That Bound*, pp. 124.
221. Ibid., pp. 184–5.
222. 'Sanctity and Power: The Dual Pursuit of Medieval Women' in Renate Bridenthal and Claudia Koonz, eds, *Becoming Visible: Women in European History* (Boston, 1977), p. 107.
223. 'The Cheshire Cat: Reconstructing the Experience of Medieval Women', in Bernice A. Carroll, ed., *Liberating Women's History: Theoretical and Critical Essays* (Chicago, 1976), p. 226.
224. Roubin, 'Male Space and Female Space within the Provençal Community', pp. 156–7.
225. Flandrin, *Families in Former Times*, pp. 122–9.
226. Middleton, 'The Sexual Division of Labour in Feudal England', p. 121.
227. Martin Ingram, *Church Courts, Sex and Marriage in England, 1570–1640* (Cambridge, 1987), p. 143–4; see also S. D. Amussen, 'Gender, Family and Social Order, 1560–1725' in Anthony Fletcher and John Stevenson, eds, *Order and Disorder in Early Modern England* (Cambridge, 1985), pp. 196–217.
228. E. A. Kosminsky, *Studies in the Agrarian History of England*, p. 216.
229. As Guy Bois notes, 'The family-type holding was the most efficient unit in the framework of intensive polyculture, closely combining crops and stock-raising, at least when it was of optimum size, which means when it permitted the maintenance and full employment of a plough team and the mobilization of the full work potential of the domestic group. Above and below this optimum, the productivity of labour declined': *The Crisis of Feudalism: Economy and Society in Eastern Normandy, 1300–1550* (London, 1984), p. 249.
230. Bloch warns against the tendency to equate the medieval freeholder with a farmer in the bourgeois epoch: 'Above all, let us not conceive of the free peasants as mere farmers, maintaining with the supreme master of the soil, only the cold relationships of debtor and creditor. ... [T]hese people were not only obliged to render to the lord the multifarious rents or services with which the house and field were burdened; they owed him in addition aid and obedience': *Feudal Society*, p. 265. It would thus be wrong to treat villeins and freeholders as two different classes of agriculturalists, thereby restricting feudalism to serfdom and situating freehold cultivators outside the feudal mode of production proper. Wherever allodialists worked land that was within or adjacent to a lord's domain, they were inevitably subject to his political sway and economic exploitation. Only where cleared land and molecular hamlets were remote from manorial settlement and beyond the practical grasp of seigneurial jurisdiction did they fall outside the feudal mode of production proper. In self-sufficient settlements of this nature (which extended over great stretches of Western Europe in the Middle Ages) we can perceive a sedentary–pastoral mode of production, regionally distinct from – but dependent upon, and largely resident within – an overarching feudal state formation: Michael Hechter and William Brustein, 'Regional Modes of Production and Patterns of State Formation in Western Europe', *American Journal of Sociology*, vol. 5 (1980), pp. 1061–94.
231. Kosminsky, *Studies in the Agrarian History of England*, pp. 92, 227–8.
232. Postan, *Medieval Economy and Society*, pp. 82, 161.
233. Kosminsky, *Studies in the Agrarian History of England*, p. 254; Postan, *Medieval Economy and Society*, p. 162. As well as harnessing villein labour to work in their own households and fields, lords also employed full-time servants who lived on the demesne. In the early Middle Ages, the *famuli* were often slaves. In the Domesday Census (1086), 9 per cent of the recorded population were slaves; almost all would have been servants attached directly to the households of landowners. The dividing line between slaves and serfs was not a sharp one in the medieval epoch; slaves often lived as families and held small tenures which they worked when not toiling directly for the lord: Georges Duby, 'Medieval Agriculture, 900–1500', in Carlo M. Cipolla, ed., *The Fontana Economic History of Europe*, vol. 1 (New York, 1972), p. 185. The lord's servile retinue were further subdivided (in ways reminiscent of slave plantations) between domestic servants of the household who resided

in the lord's manse and ploughmen, carters, oxherds, shepherds and dairy maids, who worked in the fields and lived in separate dwellings on the demesne: Rodney H. Hilton, *Bond Men Made Free: Medieval Peasant Movements and the English Rising of 1381* (London, 1977), p. 37.

234. Bois, *The Crisis of Feudalism,* p. 183.

235. David Herlihy, *Medieval Households* (Cambridge, Mass., 1985), p. 71.

236. *Reproducing Families: The Political Economy of English Population History* (Cambridge, 1987), pp. 19–21.

237. Pierre Goubert, *The Ancien Régime: French Society 1600–1750* (New York, 1973), p. 103.

238. Hilton, *Bond Men Made Free,* pp. 37–8.

239. Ibid., pp. 35–6; Ivy Pinchbeck, *Women Workers and the Industrial Revolution, 1750–1850* (London, 1981 [1930]), p. 53.

240. Howell, *Land, Family and Inheritance,* pp. 242, 244–7.

241. Anne R. de Windt, 'Redefining the Peasant Community in Medieval England: The Regional Perspective', *Journal of British Studies,* vol. 26 (1987), pp. 163–207.

242. Jerome Blum, *The End of the Old Order in Rural Europe* (Princeton, 1978), chs 3 and 4.

243. Postan, *Medieval Economy and Society,* p. 140.

244. Emmanuel Le Roy Ladurie, *The Peasants of Languedoc* (Chicago, 1974), p. 40.

245. Postan, *Medieval Economy and Society,* p. 141.

246. E. A. Wrigley, 'Fertility Strategy for the Individual and the Group', in Charles Tilly, ed., *Historical Studies of Changing Fertility* (Princeton, 1978), p. 146.

247. De Windt, 'Redefining the Peasant Community in Medieval England', p. 190.

248. For this reason, feudal crises become manifest as ecological crises of 'overpopulation' on the land. The accounts which Postan and Ladurie have constructed of this dimension of the fourteenth-century crisis are entirely compelling, but they have failed to link peasant demography and agrarian ecology to the mode of seigneurial exploitation. In this regard, the marxist critique of the neo-Malthusian framework by Robert Brenner was very much to the point: 'Agrarian Class Structure and Economic Development in Pre-industrial Europe', *Past & Present,* no. 70 (1976), pp. 30–75. But as Bois remarked in a response to the debate triggered by Brenner's polemic, the latter had 'over-corrected' his opponents, tending to counterpose class struggle dynamics to demographic forces: 'Against the Neo-Malthusian Orthodoxy', *Past & Present,* no. 79 (1978), pp. 60–69. Some brief reflections on Brenner's contribution are offered in an appendix at the end of the text (see pp. 247–54).

249. Pauperized rural youth went in two other directions as well: into armies venturing forth to war, and into cities in search of work. In both cases, these were lethal (and thus effective) 'absorption' mechanisms. While the point is obvious for armies, it is not so for large urban centres; many more youth entered cities in the Middle Ages than ever came out alive, or reproduced their numbers within them. For a careful assessment of the evidence on early modern European cities, see Jan de Vries, *European Urbanization, 1500–1800* (Cambridge, Mass., 1984). See pp. 216–17.

250. 'Recombinant Family Formation Strategies', *Journal of Historical Sociology,* vol. 2, no. 2 (1989) p. 94.

251. Herlihy, *Medieval Households,* p. 77.

252. Richard M. Smith, 'Hypothèses sur la nuptialité en Angleterre aux XIIIᵉ – XIVᵉ siècles', *Annales: Economies, sociétés, civilisations,* vol. 38 (1983), pp. 107–36; H. E. Hallam, 'Age at First Marriage and Age of Death in the Lincolnshire Fenland, 1252–1478', *Population Studies,* vol. 39 (1985), pp. 55–69. John Hajnal, who first identified the unusual late and non-universal marriage pattern, doubted that it was of medieval origin: 'European Marriage Patterns in Perspective', in D. V. Glass and D. E. C. Eversley, eds, *Population in History: Essays in Historical Demography* (London, 1965), p. 120. He postulated its consolidation across Western Europe in the fifteenth and sixteenth centuries. For England, Hajnal construed evidence from the poll tax of 1377 as indicating early and non-universal marriage, but Smith has carefully reworked his calculations and shows this inference to be dubious: 'Hypothèses

sur la nuptialité en Angleterre'.

253. Smith, 'The People of Tuscany and Their Families in the Fifteenth Century: Medieval or Mediterranean?', *Journal of Family History*, vol. 6 (1981), p. 111; Herlihy, *Medieval Households*, pp. 103–7.

254. Ibid., p. 144.

255. Pierre Bourdieu, 'Marriage Strategies as Strategies of Social Reproduction', in Forster and Orest , eds, *Family and Society: Selections from the Annales*, p. 132; Eugen Weber, *Peasants into Frenchmen* (Stanford, 1976), pp. 175–7.

256. Lutz Berkner and Franklin Mendels, 'Inheritance Systems, Family Structure and Demographic Patterns in Western Europe, 1700–1900', in Charles Tilly, ed., *Historical Studies of Changing Fertility* (Princeton, 1978).

257. Lloyd Bonfield, 'Normative Rules and Property Transmission: Reflections on the Link between Marriage and Inheritance in Early Modern England', in Lloyd Bonfield, Richard M. Smith and Keith Wrightson, eds, *The World We Have Gained* (Oxford, 1986), pp. 157–8.

258. This is what Berkner and Mendels have termed systems of preferential partibility, which 'aim at a compromise between the goal of keeping the family farm totally intact by naming only one successor and the opposite goal of providing each child with an equal portion of land. These systems operate by compensating certain children (especially the girls) with monetary payments instead of land, or using wills and other contracts to transfer the bulk of the holding to one heir, while other children receive only small plots. ... The inheritance law does not require that the land be divided in order to assure equality, and ... peasant customs appear to be extremely flexible in the variety of compensations that are deemed acceptable. ... At times such a system may operate exactly like impartibility': 'Inheritance Systems, Family Structure and Demographic Patterns', pp. 213–14.

259. Richard M. Smith, 'Some Issues Concerning Families and Their Property in Rural England, 1250–1800', in Richard M. Smith, ed., *Land, Kinship and Life-Cycle* (Cambridge, 1984), pp. 53–4.

260. E. Gronseth, 'The Relation Between Nuclear Family Kinship System and Wider Social Structure', p. 231; Margaret Spufford, 'Peasant Inheritance Customs and Land Distribution in Cambridgeshire from the Sixteenth to the Eighteenth Centuries', in J. Goody, J. Thirsk and E. P. Thompson, eds, *Family and Inheritance* (Cambridge, 1976), p. 164; Cicely Howell, 'Peasant Inheritance Customs in the Midlands, 1280–1700' in *Family and Inheritance*, p. 118; Jack Goody, 'Inheritance, Property and Women', in *Family and Inheritance*, p. 27; Barbara Hanawalt, *The Ties That Bound*, p. 57.

261. By impartible I mean that the arable part of the family's main landholding was preserved as a single unit with its customary tenure and use rights intact. I am not suggesting that the entire wealth of the family remained undivided. Nor should we assume that impartibility necessarily entailed unigeniture, the designation of a single heir to take over the holding. While this was the norm in most regions of Northwestern Europe, in Mediterranean France and east of the Elbe the transmission of the family holding to two married sons was common.

262. Howell, 'Peasant Inheritance Customs in the Midlands', p. 113.

263. Zvi Razi, 'Family, Land and the Village Community in Later Medieval England', *Past & Present*, no. 93 (1981), pp. 6–7.

264. Löfgren, 'Family and Household among Scandinavian Peasants', p. 103.

265. Lutz Berkner, 'Inheritance, Land Tenure and Peasant Family Structure: A German Regional Comparison', in J. Goody, J. Thirsk and E. P. Thompson, eds, *Family and Inheritance*, p. 74; Smith, 'Some Issues Concerning Families and Their Property in Rural England', pp. 41–54; Hanawalt, *The Ties That Bound*, p. 50; David Sabean, 'Aspects of Kinship Behaviour and Property in Rural Western Europe Before 1800' in J. Goody, J. Thirsk and E. P. Thompson, eds, *Family and Inheritance*, pp. 106–7; Bonfield, 'Normative Rules and Property Transmission', pp. 157–8; Martine Segalen, '"Avoir sa part": Sibling Relations in Partible Inheritance Brittany', in Hans Medick and David Sabean, eds, *Interest and Emotion* (Cambridge, 1984), p. 129; Natalie Davis, 'Ghosts, Kin and Progeny: Some Features of Family Life in Early Modern France', in Alice Rossi and Tamara Hareven, eds,

The Family (New York, 1978), p. 91; Barbara Harvey, *Westminster Abbey and Its Estates in the Middle Ages* (Oxford, 1977), p. 296; Gronseth, 'Notes on the Historical Development of the Relation between Nuclear Family Kinship System and Wider Social Structure in Norway', p. 231.

266. *Feudal Society,* pp. 130–31.

267. P. D. A. Harvey, *The Peasant Land Market in Medieval England* (Oxford, 1984), p. 355.

268. Goody, 'Inheritance, Property and Women', p. 17.

269. Razi, 'Family, Land and the Village Community in Later Medieval England', p. 7.

270. Homans, *English Villagers;* Rosamond Faith, 'Peasant Families and Inheritance Customs in Medieval England', *Agricultural History Review,* vol. 14 (1966), pp. 77–95; Edmund King, *Peterborough Abbey, 1086–1310: A Study in the Land Market* (Cambridge, 1973); Howell, *Land, Family and Inheritance,* pp. 250–53.

271. Smith, 'Some Issues Concerning Families and Their Property in Rural England 1250–1800', p. 14.

272. Howell, *Land, Family and Inheritance,* p. 251.

273. Ian Blanchard, 'Industrial Employment and the Rural Land Market 1380–1520', in Richard Smith, ed., *Land, Kinship and Life-Cycle* (Cambridge, 1984), p. 242.

274. Bonfield, 'Normative Rules and Property Transmission'.

275. Hanawalt, *The Ties That Bound,* p. 53.

276. J. A. Barnes, 'Land Rights and Kinship Rights in Two Brennes Hamlets', *Journal of the Royal Anthropological Institute,* vol. 87 (1957), pp. 31–56.

277. Flandrin, *Families in Former Times,* p. 80.

278. Gronseth, 'The Relation between Nuclear Family Kinship System and Wider Social Structure', p. 231; Howell, *Land, Family and Inheritance,* p. 222. With the benefit of family reconstitution studies, the rate of male and female householdship can often be calculated. Richard Wall has done this for nine communities in early modern England, finding that 90 per cent of men sixty years of age and older were still householdeads: 'Does Owning Real Property Influence the Form of the Household? An Example from Rural West Flanders', in Wall, ed., *Family Forms in Historic Europe* (Cambridge, 1983), p. 39. The practice of retirement was clearly a minority arrangement in these parishes.

279. Flandrin, *Families in Former Times,* p. 152.

280. Goody, *Production and Reproduction,* p. 29; Hanawalt, *The Ties That Bound,* p. 75; Bonfield, 'Normative Rules and Property Transmission: Reflections on the Link Between Marriage and Inheritance in Early Modern England', pp. 160–61.

281. Wrightson and Levine, *Poverty and Piety in an English Village,* p. 131.

282. *Life, Marriage and Death in a Medieval Parish* (Cambridge, 1980), p. 60.

283. M. Mitterauer and R. Sieder, *The European Family* (Oxford, 1982), p. 164.

284. David Sabean, *Power in the Blood: Popular Culture and Village Discourse in Early Modern Germany* (Cambridge, 1984), p. 173.

285. Alan Macfarlane, *Marriage and Love in England, 1300–1840* (Oxford, 1986), p. 270.

286. Hanawalt, *The Ties That Bound,* pp. 158–9.

287. Blanchard, 'Industrial Employment and the Rural Land Market', p. 242.

288. J. W. Cole, 'Social Process in the Italian Alps', *American Anthropologist,* vol. 75 (1973), pp. 773–5.

289. This is a central flaw in Alan Macfarlane's *Marriage and Love in England, 1300–1840.* While commending Goode for warning us of this pitfall (p. 119), he then proceeds to adopt it (p. 292). After acknowledging that parents could bring 'enormous pressure' to bear in determining their children's marriage partners and discussing numerous cases of autocratic imposition, he reverts to this vulgar dichotomy, terming the English regime an 'open, non-pressurized marriage system': p. 293.

290. Jack Goody, 'Inheritance, Property and Women: Some Comparative Considerations', in J. Goody, J. Thirsk and E. P. Thompson, eds, *Family and Inheritance,* p. 23.

291. Bossy, *Christianity in the West,* p. 20.

292. A similar marital-inheritance configuration occurred in town guilds, where the general principle of excluding women from a trade through all-male apprenticeship rules was attenuated somewhat by their entry through marriage and by the family nature of the enterprise. Workshops and stores normally adjoined residential space, and family members toiled there alongside apprentices. In these circumstances, the master's wife became his *de facto* business partner (often managing the financial and marketing side of the operation). When he died, she inherited the enterprise and ran it as a going concern. 'Custom appears always to have secured to the widow, rather than to the son, the possession of her husband's business': Alice Clark, *Working Life of Women in the Seventeenth Century* (London, [1919] 1982), p. 160. The presence of widows with inheritance rights thus made it almost impossible for guilds to exclude women entirely; but as long as daughters were not apprenticed on an equal footing with sons, the patriarchal nature of the enterprise was reproduced from generation to generation. Clark shows that by the constant complaints of unlawful entry and trading 'it was difficult to enforce rules of apprenticeship in a trade which was so habitually used by women for domestic purposes': Ibid., p. 214.

293. Goody, *The Development of the Family and Marriage in Europe,* p. 19.

294. Macfarlane, *Marriage and Love in England,* p. 272.

295. Ibid., p. 268.

296. Ibid., p. 272. This was not invariably true for wealthy women whose portions included substantial land parcels. While husbands were normally permitted to manage such properties as integral parts of their own estates, they were not entitled, in most cases, to absorb them upon her death. They reverted to her family, not to his: Ibid., p. 274; Barbara Diefendorf, 'Widowhood and Remarriage in Sixteenth-Century Paris', *Journal of Family History,* vol. 7 (1982), p. 383. For peasants, however, the requisites of the conjugal household clearly predominated over any residual prerogative of natal lineage for daughters in property.

297. Goody has always endeavoured to specify the relation of conjugal forms to economic structures within a broad comparative framework. In this respect, his work has been a direct stimulus and inspiration to my own, and our differences should not obscure my considerable intellectual debt to him. *The Development of the Family and Marriage in Europe* breaks new ground in the analysis of changing kinship and marital forms in the early and high Middle Ages, particularly in explicating the role of the Church in these changes. I find, however, that Goody's conceptual framework renders an unduly positive impression of women's position in medieval families, minimizing their oppression. He does not fail to mention most of the marital and inheritance practices which disadvantaged women, but he consistently makes too little of them. They cut against his primary concern in comparing African bridewealth to European dowry. He emphasizes bilateral devolution in Europe, minimizing the significance of the fact that land was generally passed through male hands (p. 257). He stresses women's dowry rights, making very little of their subsequent exclusion. He quibbles with Hughes's use of the term disinheritance to describe this exclusion, while failing to grapple with her substantive point (p. 238). The designation of daughters as residual heirs is treated as a breach in patriline, while the routine resumption of son inheritance is underplayed. Despite issuing repeated warnings about the pitfalls of sterile counterpositions, in the end Goody effectively opposes bilaterality to patriline (pp. 232–9).

298. Goody, *Production and Reproduction,* p. 17.

299. The norm of dotal exclusion, and the circumstances of its relaxation, changed in the early modern era: Ladurie, 'A System of Customary Law: Family Structures and Inheritance Customs in Sixteenth Century France', in R. Forster and O. Ranum, eds, *Family and Society,* p. 49. Bourgeois jurists, indifferent or hostile to community use rights, sought to terminate exclusion and re-establish a departed daughter's claim, in clear preference to the continued reliance of elderly women on the archaic dower and their interference in the estate business of their sons. But in the Middle Ages, both the dower's subsistence provision and dotal exclusion in normal circumstances appear to have been well entrenched on the manorial lands of Western Europe.

300. *The Development of the Family and Marriage in Europe,* p. 257.

301. Eleanor Searle, 'Seigneurial Control of Women's Marriage', *Past & Present,* no.

82 (1979), pp. 9, 31.

302. Coulton, *Medieval Village, Manor, and Monastery*, p. 102.

303. 'The Tie That Binds: Peasant Marriages and Peasant Families in Late Medieval England', *Journal of Interdisciplinary History*, vol. 15 (1984), pp. 111–29.

304. Bourdieu, 'Marriage Strategies as Strategies of Social Reproduction', in Forster and Ranum, eds, *Family and Society*, p. 132.

305. The widespread reality of skewed sex ratios, with a deficit of females, is no longer in dispute. Whether selective infanticide and neglect were primary causes of this imbalance is still an open question, however, though the preponderance of evidence indicates that they were at least contributing factors. The sceptics are Carl J. Hammer, 'Family and Familia in Early Medieval Bavaria' in Wall, ed., *Family Forms in Historic Europe*, p. 231; and Hanawalt, *The Ties That Bound*, p. 79. Those who detect evidence of sex-selective infanticide or at least infant neglect: Barbara Kellum, 'Infanticide in England in the Later Middle Ages', *History of Childhood Quarterly*, vol. 1 (1973), pp. 36788; G. G. Coulton, *Medieval Village, Manor, and Monastery*; Emily Coleman, 'Infanticide in the Early Middle Ages', in S. M. Stuard, ed., *Women in Medieval Society* (Philadelphia, 1976); Richard C. Trexler, 'Infanticide in Florence: New Sources and First Results', *History of Childhood Quarterly*, vol. 1 (1973), pp. 98–116; Richard R. Ring, 'Early Medieval Peasant Households in Central Italy', *Journal of Family History*, vol. 4, no. 1 (1979); Herlihy and Klapisch-Zuber, *Tuscans and Their Families* (New Haven, 1985).

306. Herlihy and Klapisch-Zuber, *Tuscans and Their Families*, p. 114.

307. Ibid., p. 147.

308. Weber, *Peasants into Frenchmen*, p. 172.

309. Herlihy and Klapisch-Zuber, *Tuscans and Their Families*, pp. 136–7.

310. Shahar, *The Fourth Estate*, p. 223.

311. Judith Bennett, 'Medieval Peasant Marriage: An Examination of Marriage License Fines in Liber Gersumarum', in J. A. Raftis, ed., *Pathways to Medieval Peasants* (Toronto, 1981), pp. 208–11.

312. Razi, *Life, Marriage and Death*, p. 46.

313. Rebecca Colman, 'The Abduction of Women in Barbaric Law', *Florilegium*, vol. 5 (1983), p. 70; Macfarlane, *Marriage and Love in England*, p. 131.

314. The ecclesiastical doctrine of consent was bound up with another objective: to prevent parents from blocking their children's entry into religious orders as an alternative to marriage: Huppert, *After the Black Death*, p. 120.

315. Martin Ingram, *Church Courts, Sex and Marriage in England, 1570–1640* (Cambridge, 1987), pp. 189–90. Michael Sheehan has very usefully documented the evolution of medieval ecclesiastical doctrine on marriage and its eventual impact on the parish priests' conduct of the wedding ceremony. He correctly stresses the Church's firm commitment to the freely given consent of the bride and groom as the supreme canonical criterion of a valid marriage. Yet his account generally exaggerates the degree to which the Church's increasing role in nuptial regulation curtailed the practical power of parents and lords in matchmaking. Within an interpretative framework that distances the symbolic impact of the wedding ceremony, conducted on a single occasion, from the ongoing exigencies of marriage as an economic union, Sheehan none the less notes that 'there was no attempt to give ritual statement to the notion that the couple was capable of marriage without or against the wishes of their kin': 'Choice of Marriage Partner in the Middle Ages', *Studies in Medieval and Renaissance History*, vol. 1 (1978), p. 32.

316. André Burguière, 'From Malthus to Max Weber: Belated Marriage and the Spirit of Enterprise', in Robert Forster and Orest Ranum, eds, *Family and Society* (Baltimore, 1976), p. 247.

317. Hanawalt, *The Ties That Bound*, p. 165.

318. Sheehan, 'Choice of Marriage Partner in the Middle Ages', p. 12.

319. Macfarlane, *Marriage and Love in England*, p. 125; Huppert, *After the Black Death*, p. 120.

320. Hanawalt, *The Ties That Bound*, pp. 166–8; Pierre Goubert, *The French Peasantry in the Seventeenth Century* (Cambridge, 1986), p. 63; Flandrin, *Families in Former Times*, p.

132; Linda Pollock, 'Courtship and Marriage from the Middle Ages to the Twentieth Century', *The Historical Journal*, vol. 39 (1987), p. 492. Even Macfarlane, who characterizes English marriage as one of individual choice, admits that parents 'could put enormous physical, moral and economic pressure on the individuals': *Marriage and Love in England*, p. 128. In fact, while the English norm was multilateral consent, Macfarlane presents evidence of more cases in which parents forced the union than those in which children married in defiance of their parents' orders.

321. *Marriage and Love in England*, p. 132.

322. Homans, *English Villagers*, p. 163; Hanawalt, *The Ties That Bound*, pp. 166–7; Flandrin, *Families in Former Times*, pp. 130–33; Goubert, *The French Peasantry*, pp. 63, 68; Keith Wrightson, *English Society, 1550–1680* (London, 1982), pp. 72–5; John Gillis, 'Peasant, Plebeian and Proletarian Marriage in Britain, 1600–1900', in David Levine, ed., *Proletarianization and Family History* (New York, 1984), p. 132; Macfarlane, *Marriage and Love in England*, p. 122.

323. John Gillis, *For Better, For Worse: British Marriages, 1600 to the Present* (New York, 1985), p. 17.

324. Martine Segalen, *Love and Power in the Peasant Family* (Oxford, 1983), pp. 18–19.

325. Gillis, *For Better, For Worse*, pp. 21–34; Flandrin, *Families in Former Times*, p. 35. These rituals drew upon a rich repertoire of anti-matrimonial satire wherein women were blamed for all manner of marital misfortune. Men were portrayed as unwitting fools who fell for women's schemes and were forced to marry them, like so many insects snared in spiders' webs: Jeay, 'Sexuality and Family in Fifteenth Century France'.

326. Goody, 'Inheritance, Property and Women', p. 23; Edward Shorter, *The Making of the Modern Family* (New York, 1975), pp. 150–51.

327. Martine Segalen, *Historical Anthropology of the Family* (Cambridge, 1986), pp. 119–20.

328. Ovar Löfgren, 'Family and Household among Scandinavian Peasants', in Michael Anderson, ed., *Sociology of the Family* (Harmondsworth, 1980), p. 96; Segalen, *Love and Power in the Peasant Family*, p. 21.

329. *Historical Anthropology of the Family*, p. 119; Hans Medick, 'The Structures and Function of Population Development under the Proto-industrial System', in Peter Kriedte, Hans Medick and Jürgen Schlumbohm, *Industrialization before Industrialization* (Cambridge, 1981), p. 265, fn. 78.

330. Gillis, *For Better, For Worse*, p. 52; Macfarlane, *Marriage and Love in England*, p. 295.

331. David Gaunt and Ovar Löfgren, 'Remarriage in the Nordic Countries: The Cultural and Socio-economic Background', in Jacques Dupâquier et al., eds, *Marriage and Remarriage in the Past* (New York, 1981), p. 51; Shorter, *The Making of the Modern Family*, pp. 138–48.

332. Segalen, *Love and Power in the Peasant Family*, p. 16; Macfarlane, *Marriage and Love in England*, p. 206.

333. This is the false dichotomy that Hans Medick, David Sabean and their colleagues have so usefully addressed in *Interest and Emotion* (Cambridge, 1984).

334. Gillis, *For Better, For Worse*, pp. 43–83. Yet for the wife, adulthood was not fully attained until she bore her first child: Jeay, 'Sexuality and Family in Fifteenth Century France', p. 336.

335. Eleanor Searle, 'Seigneurial Control of Women's Marriage: The Antecedents and Function of Merchet in England', *Past & Present*, no. 82 (1979), p. 26; Razi, *Life, Marriage and Death*, p. 65; Mitterauer and Sieder, *The European Family*, p. 124; Homans, *English Villagers*, pp. 164–6. Women were sometimes obliged to wed if their original trothplight had been publicly witnessed; for them, 'informed consent' was a once-only proposition: Huppert, *After the Black Death*, pp. 122–3.

336. Gillis, *For Better, For Worse*, pp. 50–51.

337. Gillis, 'Peasant, Plebeian and Proletarian Marriage in Britain, 1600–1900', p. 133.

338. Segalen, *Love and Power in the Peasant Family*, p. 20.

339. Ingram, *Church Courts, Sex and Marriage in England*, p. 226.

340. Ibid., pp. 219–37.

341. Chris Wilson, 'The Proximate Determinants of Marital Fertility in England, 1600–1799', in L. Bonfield, R. M. Smith and K. Wrightson, eds, *The World We Have Gained* (Oxford, 1986), p. 214. The measure is derived from baptisms recorded within eight months of nuptials and varied radically over space and time.

342. Homans, *English Villagers*, p. 172.

343. Gillis, 'Peasant, Plebeian and Proletarian Marriage', p. 134.

344. John Bossy, 'Blood and Baptism: Kinship, Community and Christianity in Western Europe from the Fourteenth to the Seventeenth Centuries', in D. Baker, ed., *Sanctity and Secularity: The Church and the World* (Cambridge, 1973), pp. 131–2.

345. Segalen, *Love and Power in the Peasant Family*, p. 26.

346. Hanawalt, *The Ties That Bound*, p. 170.

347. Gillis, 'Peasant, Plebeian and Proletarian Marriage', p. 134.

348. Ibid., p. 135; see also Segalen, *Love and Power in the Peasant Family*, p. 31.

349. M. M. Postan and J. Z. Titow, 'Heriots and Prices on Winchester Manors', in M. M. Postan, ed., *Essays on Medieval Agriculture and General Problems of the Medieval Economy* (Cambridge, 1983), pp. 159–60; Razi, *Life, Marriage and Death*, p. 57.

350. Hilton, *The English Peasantry in the Later Middle Ages* (Oxford, 1975), p. 101.

351. Christiane Klapisch, 'Household and Family in Tuscany in 1427', in Peter Laslett, ed., *Household and Family in Past Time* (Cambridge, 1972), p. 273.

352. Hanawalt, *The Ties That Bound*, pp. 124, 185.

353. Ladurie, *Montaillou*, p. 197.

354. Herlihy and Klapisch-Zuber, *Tuscans and Their Families*, p. 143.

355. The term 'free bench' originally expressed just such a meagre provision (the widow's right to a seat before the fireplace in her son's home), but in England it subsequently became a general synonym for dower, reflecting the strengthening of widows' dotal prerogatives in the medieval era.

356. Goody, *Production and Reproduction*, pp. 30–31; James A. Raftis, *Tenure and Mobility: Studies in the Social History of the Medieval English Village* (Toronto, 1964), p. 36.

357. Howell, *Land, Family and Inheritance*, p. 257; Mitterauer and Sieder, *The European Family*, pp. 162–6; David Gaunt, 'The Property and Kin Relationships of Retired Farmers in Northern and Central Europe', in Wall, ed., *Family Forms in Historic Europe*; Hanawalt, *The Ties That Bound*, pp. 194–5. A variant of the retirement contract was the corrody, an old-age pension which a well-to-do heir purchased for his mother from a monastery, consisting of a daily ration of bread and ale, firewood, a room, and candles: F. Gies and J. Gies, *Women in the Middle Ages* (New York, 1978), p. 157.

358. Wrightson and Levine, *Poverty and Piety*, pp. 97–8.

359. Shahar, *The Fourth Estate*, p. 238.

360. Routine transfer among servile tenants is sharply at odds with the situation among the nobility, where an overriding concern with preserving family lineages held this particular patriarchal prerogative at bay.

361. Raftis, *Tenure and Mobility*, p. 40.

362. Bloch, *Feudal Society*, p. 136; Mitterauer and Sieder, *The European Family*, p. 122.

363. H. S. Bennett, *Life on the English Manor: A Study of Peasant Conditions, 1150–1400* (Cambridge, 1937), p. 242; Raftis, *Tenure and Mobility*, p. 40.

364. Shahar, *The Fourth Estate*, p. 239; Middleton, 'Peasants, Patriarchy and the Feudal Mode of Production', p. 142.

365. Barbara Harvey, *Westminster Abbey and Its Estates in the Middle Ages* (Oxford, 1977), p. 298.

366. Searle, 'Seigneurial Control of Women's Marriage', p. 10.

367. R. M. Smith, 'Some Reflections on the Evidence for the Origins of the European Marriage Pattern in England', in C. C. Harris, ed., *Sociology of the Family* (Keele, 1979), p. 94.

368. Jack Ravensdale, 'Population Changes and the Transfer of Customary Land on a Cambridgeshire Manor in the Fourteenth Century', in R. M. Smith, ed., *Land, Kinship and Life-Cycle* (Cambridge, 1984), p. 203.

369. Goody, *Production and Reproduction*, p. 12.

370. Howell, *Land, Family and Inheritance*, p. 257.

371. Miranda Chaytor, 'Household and Kinship: Ryton in the Late Sixteenth and Early Seventeenth Centuries', *History Workshop Journal*, no. 10 (1980), p. 48.

372. Natalie Davis, 'The Reasons of Misrule: Youth Groups and Charivaris in Sixteenth-Century France', *Past & Present*, no. 50 (1971), p. 52.

373. Alain Bideau, 'A Demographic and Social Analysis of Widowhood and Remarriage: The Example of the Castellany of Thoissey-en-Dombes, 1670–1840', *Journal of Family History*, vol. 5 (1980), pp. 40–43.

374. On this point (and many others), see Vivien Brodsky's fascinating discussion, 'Widows in Late Elizabethan London: Remarriage, Economic Opportunity and Family Orientations' in L. Bonfield, R. Smith and K. Wrightson, eds, *The World We Have Gained*.

375. Smith, 'Origins of the European Marriage Pattern', p. 94.

376. Gaunt and Löfgren, 'Remarriage in the Nordic Countries', p. 53.

377. H. E. Hallam, *Rural England, 1066–1348* (New York, 1981), p. 259.

378. Hanawalt, *The Ties That Bound*, p. 189; Margaret Spufford, *Contrasting Communities: English Villagers in the Sixteenth and Seventeenth Centuries* (Cambridge, 1974), p. 117.

379. Shahar, *The Fourth Estate*, p. 238.

380. Middleton, 'Peasants, Patriarchy and the Feudal Mode of Production in England'.

381. *Household and Family in Past Time*, p. 136. The problem of taking the proportion of households as one's measure of prevalence applies to most of the Cambridge Group's principal findings. More people lived in extended households than in simple ones, for example, but Laslett tabulates the percentage of extended households (finding that it is 'low') instead of the percentage of the population living in extended households, which would be much higher.

382. Hanawalt, *The Ties That Bound*, pp. 68–81.

383. Using the demographic parameters of England in the first half of the eighteenth century (from Wrigley and Schofield's *Population History of England*), Steven Ruggles has estimated that only 22 to 29 per cent of the population could have lived in three-generation vertically extended households: *Prolonged Connections: The Rise of the Extended Family in Nineteenth-Century England and America* (Madison, 1987), p. 121.

384. *Statistical Studies of Historical Social Structure* (New York, 1978).

385. *Prolonged Connections*, pp. 80–82. Ruggles's alternative model measures the propensity of individuals to reside with kin in various types of households (instead of taking the household as the unit of analysis as the Cambridge researchers had done), thus avoiding the confoundment of a co-varying numerator and denominator that had been inherent in earlier measures. While I am not competent to assess his micro-simulation model, I find his argument as to the superiority of the individual propensity measure upon which it is based to be entirely compelling. It will have a salutary impact on the quantitative side of family history, which must rely on records that permit us to assess the distribution of household composition in a community, and often little else.

386. Ibid., p. 121. From the outset, critiques of the Cambridge research – in the first instance by Lutz Berkner – centred on the conceptual framework and taxonomic preoccupations of the Group: the synchronic tabulation of household co-residence and subsequent classification by means of a standard typology. No one disputed the accuracy of their finding of a predominance of small and simple households. Rather, critics doubted that this was a useful way to think about family forms, suggesting that it generated its own misleading stereotypes, above all of an atomized household unit. Ruggles's objections are of a different order, focusing on more technical issues of the appropriate unit of measures of propensity and the assumptions of simulation modelling. While his critique appears devastating on this ground, and will undoubtedly rehabilitate the earlier notion of a pervasive stem family type (at least at the level of familial ideal), paradoxically, his conceptual framework is almost a replica of the Cambridge Group's, based on co-resident kin composition and impervious to the underlying structure of the family cycle. On this point, see the next note.

387. Ibid., p. 122. I have two reservations in taking Ruggles's work as corroborating a stem family thesis. In the first place, he defines stem families strictly in terms of household

composition, failing to distinguish between a stem formation and a nuclear family living in a vertically extended household. (In his framework, the latter is a contradiction in terms.) I find this to be a critical distinction, as will become clear in this book's sequel, *Weathering the Storm*, where we shall examine nineteenth-century households of increasing complexity. Secondly, he does not allow for the possibility that delayed marriage may arise from the strong aversion of both generations to living together, with the younger generation 'waiting their parents out'. Part of the population he claims are demographically precluded from stem co-residence (in my terms, from choosing a strong-stem option) are probably deliberately waiting to marry until the death of the elder generation eliminates this obligation.

388. *Household and Family in Past Time*, p. 73.

389. John Hajnal, 'Two Kinds of Pre-industrial Household Systems', *Population and Development Review*, vol. 8 (1982), p. 482. Twelve years after he wrote the Introduction to *Household and Family in Past Time*, Laslett defined neo-locality in a different way: 'Neo-localism requires each newly married couple to set up on their own, to live by themselves, and not with the families of either set of parents, to take charge of their own domestic enterprise': 'Family and Household as Work Group and Kin Group: Areas of Traditional Europe Compared', in Wall, ed., *Family Forms in Historic Europe*, p. 531. Here he would appear to include meaning (d), and possibly (b), as well as (a) (see text below). In what sense can the acquisition of family land be termed neo-local under this definition?

390. The anthropologist Goody, for example, terms the prevailing post-marital residence norm virilocal in the early medieval era: 'women went to live with their husbands who in turn often resided with or near their fathers': *The Development of the Family and Marriage in Europe*, p. 19.

391. Goody, *Production and Reproduction*, pp. 20–22. In this sense, one can recognize a vital grain of truth in the neo-local designation without adopting the Cambridge paradigm. A strong aversion to living with parents after marriage and a clear preference for setting up one's own household are important cultural dispositions, becoming manifest in family formation strategies. The pattern is widely recognized, but it has yet to be adequately explained – a major conundrum for family history. I see it as a stalemated outcome of intergenerational struggle. Some preliminary thoughts on the matter are offered in the next chapter; see pp. 150–57 and pp. 186–87.

392. Within different paradigms, others have recognized this difference between what Thomas Held calls 'the classical and the retirement type stem families'; or, in Michaelson and Goldschmidt's terms, patricentric and filiocentric households: Held, 'Rural Retirement Arrangements in Seventeenth to Nineteenth Century Austria: A Cross-Community Analysis', *Journal of Family History*, vol. 7 (1982), p. 229.

393. Ovar Löfgren, 'Family and Household among Scandinavian Peasants', in Michael Anderson, ed., *Sociology of the Family*, p. 111.

394. Macfarlane, *Marriage and Love in England*, p. 96.

395. Hanawalt, *The Ties That Bound*, p. 168; Bennett, 'Medieval Peasant Marriage'.

396. John W. Cole, 'Social Process in the Italian Alps', *American Anthropologist*, vol. 75 (1973), p. 744.

397. Razi, *Life, Marriage and Death*, pp. 57–60; Shahar, *The Fourth Estate*, p. 229.

398. Hallam, *Rural England, 1066–1348*, p. 264.

399. Smith, 'Origins of the European Marriage Pattern', p. 246.

400. Razi, *Life, Marriage and Death*, pp. 83–5. See also Hanawalt, *The Ties That Bound*, p. 81.

401. Herlihy and Klapisch-Zuber, *Tuscans and Their Families*, p. 113.

402. David B. Grigg, *Population Growth and Agrarian Change* (Cambridge, 1980), p. 53.

403. Duby, *Rural Economy and Country Life*, p. 103.

404. Slicher van Bath, *The Agrarian History of Western Europe* (London, 1963), pp. 32–64; P. Anderson, *Lineages of the Absolutist State*, p. 183; D. B. Grigg, *Population Growth and Agrarian Change*, pp. 74–5.

405. In writing of this as an extension on to 'new' land, I do not wish to imply that it was virgin soil. In fact, the likelihood is that most of it had been under some form of

cultivation and settlement in Antiquity, but had subsequently been abandoned in the massive contractions of the late fifth and sixth centuries. In England, for example, 'few, if any, medieval settlements were built on virgin land which had not previously been cultivated. ... Many of the later forests had regenerated over previously occupied land': Ian Longworth and John Cherry, *Archaeology in Britain since 1945* (London, 1986), p. 204.

406. N. J. G. Pounds, *An Economic History of Medieval Europe*, pp. 165–80; van Bath, *Agrarian History of Western Europe*, pp. 151–5.

407. Grigg, *Population Growth and Agrarian Change*, pp. 71–3.

408. R. I. Moore, 'Family, Community and Cult on the Eve of the Gregorian Reform', *Transactions of the Royal Historical Society*, 5th ser., vol. 30 (1980), p. 58.

409. Duby, *Early Growth of the European Economy*, p. 183.

410. van Bath, *Agrarian History of Western Europe*, pp. 134, 314; Hilton, *Bond Men Made Free*, pp. 27–8; Grigg, *Population Growth and Agrarian Change*, p. 68; Postan, *Medieval Economy and Society*, pp. 63–5, 69.

411. Herlihy, *Medieval Households*, p. 145.

412. Razi, *Life, Marriage and Death*, pp. 94, 97.

413. P. Anderson, *Lineages of the Absolutist State*, p. 200.

414. Ibid., p. 201.

415. Carlo M. Cipolla, *Before the Industrial Revolution: European Society and Economy* (New York, 1980), p. 214; van Bath, *The Agrarian History of Western Europe*, pp. 132–44; Duby, *Rural Economy and Country Life*, p. 307; Postan, *The Medieval Economy and Society*, pp. 39–44. Interestingly, Wilhelm Abel, generally regarded as a neo-Malthusian, dissents. He agrees that 'a certain population limit may have been reached', but insists that Malthus's theory of an endogenous population cycle 'does not stand up to the facts': *Agricultural Fluctuations in Europe* (New York, 1980), pp. 40–42. See David Grigg's review of the question of overpopulation in European history: *Population Growth and Agrarian Change*.

416. *Population and Technological Change: A Study of Long-Term Trends* (Chicago, 1981).

417. Grigg, *Population Growth and Agrarian Change*.

Chapter 3

1. Linda Pollock has recently noted the 'current fashionable historiographical stress on continuity over change': 'Courtship and Marriage from the Middle Ages to the Twentieth Century', *The Historical Journal*, vol. 39 (1987), p. 490. She quite correctly insists that the two must be kept in continuous dialectical tension. Conservatives naturally feel most comfortable foregrounding continuity, while radicals prefer to highlight change. Beyond the question of emphasis, however, lies the analytical imperative to offer a convincing explanation of both in their complex relation with one another.

2. If capitalism is our destination, how can I discuss the transition to it without addressing the general structure of this mode? In reality, the historical genesis of a mode of production and its ongoing reproduction are distinct processes, and hence separable in conception and exposition. In this chapter, I shall introduce only those elements of the capitalist mode which bear directly on the process of proletarianization, leaving to the sequel study a fuller discussion of the ongoing reproduction of proletarian family forms within capitalism.

3. Wilhelm Abel, *Agricultural Fluctuations in Europe* (New York, 1980). The long agrarian wave has been thoroughly documented by the historians Wilhelm Abel, Emmanuel Ladurie and Michael Postan. In view of its neo-Malthusian pedigree, some readers may find it odd that it plays such a prominent role in a marxist account. Yet I find it a remarkably significant phenomenon, providing it is set adequately in a mode-of-production framework. From Marx on, historical materialists have been concerned to clarify the 'laws of motion' of prevailing modes of production. What the Kondratieff cycle is to capitalism, the long agrarian wave is to feudalism – the secular growth dynamic endemic to the mode of production in question. This perspective is elaborated in a note on the Brenner debate (pp. 247–54).

4. David E. Davis, 'The Scarcity of Rats and the Black Death: An Ecological

History', *Journal of Interdisciplinary History*, vol. 16 (1986), pp. 460–61. The Black Death is usually considered to be an exogenous factor, as is most epidemic mortality in medieval and early modern Europe. In my view, it is more accurately termed semi-exogenous. The lethal agent was introduced into Europe from the outside, and certainly had independent effects; in fact, it changed the course of history. But the ensuing crisis which the plague set off was of a generalized character, the product of the backlogged contradictions of the feudal system, and by no means confined to population loss. It is significant that between 1315 and 1347 the population of Europe suffered a series of severe subsistence crises, had ceased growing, and in some areas was contracting. It seems hardly coincidental that the one previous European pandemic on a comparable scale, in AD 541–44, in the reign of Emperor Justinian, also struck at a time of widespread systemic crisis, with the Roman Empire in the process of terminal collapse. Population loss in that disaster has been estimated at one-third: J. C. Russell, 'Population in Europe 500–1500', in Carlo M. Cipolla, ed., *Fontana Economic History of Europe: The Middle Ages* (New York, 1972), p. 38.

5. Georges Duby, *Rural Economy and Country Life in the Medieval West* (Columbia, 1968), p. 308; K. F. Heilleiner, 'The Population of Europe from the Black Death to the Eve of the Vital Revolution', in E. E. Rich and C. H. Wilson, eds, *The Cambridge Economic History of Europe*, vol. 4 (Cambridge, 1967), p. 9.

6. Graham Twigg has cast considerable doubt on the conventional wisdom that bubonic plague was the primary disease of the Black Death: *The Black Death: A Biological Reappraisal* (London, 1984). A zoologist with an expertise in the problem of animal diseases transmitted to humans, Twigg demonstrates that certain features of Black Death accounts, as reconstructed by historians, are inconsistent with modern medical knowledge of plague, its mode of transmission, symptoms and mortality pattern. He postulates anthrax as an alternative. David Davis struck a second blow against the old consensus by concluding, after reviewing every form of evidence, that the black rat (the presumed carrier of the plague bacillus) was rare and erratically dispersed across Europe at the time of the Black Death: 'The Scarcity of Rats and the Black Death: An Ecological History', *Journal of Interdisciplinary History*, vol. 16 (1986), pp. 455–70. Whatever the ultimate verdict on the primary lethal agent, 'it is likely that in addition to one main, new disease there was a spectrum of con-current illnesses which were attributed to the more spectacular arrival': Twigg, *The Black Death*, p. 221. Twigg's argument against the bubonic bacillus is persuasive, but it leaves me with the practical problem of what to call this undetermined agent of death which persisted in stalking Europe throughout the early modern period. I shall simply refer to it as 'the plague', using the term in a generic sense, more traditional and colloquial than modern and medical.

7. John Hatcher, *Plague, Population and the English Economy, 1348–1530* (London, 1977), pp. 57–62; Heilleiner, 'The Population of Europe', pp. 10–11; J. C. Russell, *British Medieval Population* (Albuquerque, 1948), pp. 260–70; N. J. G. Pounds, *An Economic History of Medieval Europe* (New York, 1974), p. 139; David Herlihy and Christiane Klapisch-Zuber, *Tuscans and Their Families: A Study of the Florentine Catasto of 1427* (New Haven, 1985), p. 80.

8. The towns and villages of medieval Europe had suffered countless epidemics, but none with anything approaching the level of mortality witnessed in the Black Death. What was different about it? The severity of population loss due to an epidemic disease is basically a function of four factors: its lethality (the proportion of those infected who die); duration; frequency of recurrence; and contagion, hence geographic spread. The Black Death's extraordinary devastation appears to have been due primarily to the last factor, its continental dissemination. Its lethality, duration and frequency of recurrence were not unusual by medieval standards, nor would they be in early modern times.

9. Hatcher, *Plague, Population and the English Economy*, pp. 69–71; D. B. Grigg, *Population Growth and Agrarian Change* (Cambridge, 1980), p. 102.

10. Guy Bois, *The Crisis of Feudalism: Economy and Society in Eastern Normandy, 1300–1550* (London, 1984), pp. 59–66.

11. Herlihy and Klapisch-Zuber, *Tuscans and Their Families*, pp. 62–71.

12. Abel, *Agricultural Fluctuations in Europe*, pp. 80–86; Maurice W. Beresford, *The*

Lost Villages of England (London, 1954); Slicher van Bath, *The Agrarian History of Western Europe* (London, 1963), pp. 162–9.

13. Maurice Aymard, *Dutch Capitalism and World Capitalism* (New York, 1982), p. 135.

14. Herlihy and Klapisch-Zuber, *Tuscans and Their Families*, p. 71.

15. Jan de Vries, *European Urbanization, 1500–1800* (Cambridge, Mass., 1984), p. 39.

16. Rodney Hilton, *Bond Men Made Free: Medieval Peasant Movements and the English Rising of 1381* (London, 1977), pp. 96–134.

17. Peasant support for these open revolts extended well beyond the regions where they took place, and reciprocally, the rebellions had catalytic effects in areas peripheral to the insurgence. Christopher Dyer, for example, describes the exemplary influence of the English Rising in emboldening simmering peasant resistance in the West Midlands: *Lords and Peasants in a Changing Society* (Cambridge, 1980,) p. 275.

18. Abel, *Agricultural Fluctuations in Europe*, p. 90.

19. Dyer, *Lords and Peasants*, pp. 267–9.

20. Some of the most notorious examples were the Statute of Labourers, 1351, in England; the Cortes of Aragon's wage controls in 1350; an ordinance in Castille in 1351; a series of laws passed by the Portuguese Crown between 1349 and 1400; French decrees by John the Good in 1351 and 1354; and a Bavarian ordinance in 1352. See Catharina Lis and Hugo Soly, *Poverty and Capitalism in Pre-industrial Europe* (Atlantic Heights, 1979), pp. 48–52.

21. Christopher Dyer, 'Changes in the Size of Peasant Holdings in Some West Midland Villages', in Richard M. Smith, ed., *Land, Kinship and Life-Cycle* (Cambridge, 1984), p. 281.

22. P. D. A. Harvey, *The Peasant Land Market in Medieval England* (Oxford, 1984), p. 325.

23. The breach in landlord solidarity, while widespread, was by no means universal. In northern Italy and eastern Germany, the demesne remained profitable and there was no move to lease it out, largely because 'the princely and urban authorities had taken measures energetic enough to keep conditions of employment favourable to the lord, notably by hindering the flight from the land and by binding the peasants to the soil': Duby, *Rural Economy and Country Life*, pp. 321–2. Elsewhere, such repression was attempted initially but proved ineffective, and peasants moved about at will. This regional variance in class struggle outcomes in the face of a broadly similar demographic development provides a further corroboration of Robert Brenner's central point against neo-Malthusian historians in what became known as 'The Brenner Debate' (see pp. 000–00).

24. Bois, *The Crisis of Feudalism*, p. 156.

25. Jerome Blum's encyclopaedic survey of rural class relations in the last century of the *ancien régime* is an excellent antidote for the all too prevalent view of the 'free peasant farmers' of Western Europe: *The End of the Old Order in Rural Europe* (Princeton, 1978). The conventional underestimation of seigneurial prerogative west of the Elbe is at least partly a function of comparison with the East, against which, of course, Western peasants in the early modern era appear very free. Such interpretation is never far removed from the ideological vapours of the Cold War, where it is comforting to establish a continuity with the past, contrasting the 'free West' with the 'totalitarian East'.

26. L. R. Poos, 'Population Turnover in Medieval Essex', in Lloyd Bonfield, Richard Smith and Keith Wrightson, eds, *The World We Have Gained* (Oxford, 1986).

27. Due to the scope of this study, I have left aside questions of the feudal relations of benefice and fealty, and of their persistence and mutation with the rise of Absolutist States. On this, see Perry Anderson, *Lineages of the Absolutist State* (London, 1974), pp. 15–42.

28. Herlihy and Klapisch-Zuber, *Tuscans and Their Families*, p. 14.

29. Dyer, *Lords and Peasants in a Changing Society*, p. 352.

30. Emmanuel Le Roy Ladurie, *The Peasants of Languedoc* (Chicago, 1974), p. 13.

31. Bois, *The Crisis of Feudalism*, p. 151; Bruce Campbell, 'Population Pressure, Inheritance and the Land Market in a Fourteenth-Century Peasant Community', in Richard M. Smith, ed., *Land, Kinship and Life-Cycle* (Cambridge, 1984), p. 103; Dyer, *Lords and*

Peasants, p. 300; Ladurie, *The Peasants of Languedoc,* p. 28; Lis and Soly, *Poverty and Capitalism in Pre-industrial Europe,* p. 42; Zvi Razi, *Life, Marriage and Death in a Medieval Parish: Economy, Society and Demography in Halesowen, 1270–1400* (Cambridge, 1980), p. 147. The redistribution of land and village wealth in England in the late medieval period has been sharply debated. Postan has advanced a thesis of 'economic promotion' in the wake of population decline, stressing the benefits to labourers and smallholders: *The Medieval Economy and Society: An Economic History of Britain in the Middle Ages* (Harmondsworth, 1975), pp. 156–8. Hilton and others saw 'social polarization', emphasizing land acquisition by the wealthiest peasant stratum that exceeded all medieval precedents by the mid fifteenth century: *The Economic Development of Some Leicestershire Estates in the Fourteenth and Fifteenth Centuries* (Oxford, 1947), pp. 94–105. While the terminology of these accounts may be irreconcilable, the two dynamics they highlight are not, at least in this period. Precisely because of the unusual availability of land, the accumulation of the nascent yeomanry advanced simultaneously with much more modest improvements by smallholders. As land became scarce again in the sixteenth and seventeenth centuries, this would no longer be possible. Polarization was then the rule, promotion the exception, as the yeoman stratum accumulated at the direct expense of the increasingly landless village poor.

32. Razi, *Life, Marriage and Death in a Medieval Parish,* p. 151.
33. P. Anderson, *Lineages of the Absolutist State,* p. 17.
34. Ibid., pp. 24–8.
35. Joyce Youings, *Sixteenth Century England* (Harmondsworth, 1984), p. 47.
36. Dyer, *Lords and Peasants,* p. 310.
37. Ladurie, *The Peasants of Languedoc,* p. 30.
38. R. A. Faith, 'Peasant Families and Inheritance Customs in Medieval England', *Agricultural History Review,* vol. 14 (1966), pp. 77–95; Harvey, *Westminster Abbey and Its Estates in the Middle Ages,* p. 4; Ladurie, *The Peasants of Languedoc,* p. 30; J. A. Raftis, *Tenure and Mobility: Studies in the Social History of the Medieval English Village* (Toronto, 1964), pp. 33–4; Richard M. Smith, 'Some Issues Concerning Families and Their Property in Rural England, 1250–1800', in Smith, ed., *Land, Kinship and Life-Cycle* (Cambridge, 1984), pp. 58–9.
39. Cicely Howell, *Land, Family and Inheritance in Transition: Kibworth Harcourt, 1280–1700* (Cambridge, 1983), pp. 241–2.
40. Campbell, 'Population Pressure, Inheritance and the Land Market', p. 100.
41. Dyer, 'Changes in the Size of Peasant Holdings', p. 286.
42. Howell, *Land, Family and Inheritance,* p. 228.
43. Dyer, *Lords and Peasants;* Harvey, *Westminster Abbey and Its Estates,* p. 278.
44. Dyer, 'Changes in the Size of Peasant Holdings'; Razi, *Life, Marriage and Death in a Medieval Parish,* pp. 120–21; Richard Sieder and Michael Mitterauer, 'The Reconstruction of the Family Life Course: Theoretical Problems and Empirical Results', in Richard Wall, ed., *Family Forms in Historic Europe* (Cambridge, 1983), pp. 318–19; Howell, *Land, Family and Inheritance,* p. 210.
45. Dyer, 'Changes in the Size of Peasant Holdings', p. 289.
46. Elaine Clarke, 'Some Aspects of Social Security in Medieval England', *Journal of Family History,* vol. 7 (1982), p. 307.
47. 'Industrial Employment and the Rural Land Market, 1380–1520', in Richard M. Smith, ed., *Land, Kinship and Life-Cycle,* p. 243.
48. Howell, *Land, Family and Inheritance,* pp. 115–21.
49. Razi, 'Family, Land and the Village Community in Later Medieval England', *Past & Present,* no. 93 (1981).
50. In the thirteen-month epidemic of 1645–46 in Colyton, one-third of the population was lost. Yet 73 per cent of the parish's married couples survived intact, and in only 6 per cent of all cases did both partners perish. Roger Schofield, 'Anatomy of an Epidemic: Colyton, November 1645 to November 1646', in *The Plague Reconsidered* (Matlock, 1977), p. 120.
51. Herlihy and Klapisch-Zuber, *Tuscans and Their Families,* p. 90.
52. Dyer, 'Changes in the Size of Peasant Holdings', p. 292.

53. Ibid., p. 31.

54. *The Peasants of Languedoc*, pp. 32–3.

55. Razi, *Life, Marriage and Death*, p. 143; Howell, *Land, Family and Inheritance*, p. 235; Dyer, 'Changes in the Size of Peasant Holdings'; Blanchard, 'Industrial Employment and the Rural Land Market 1380–1520', pp. 256–7.

56. Blanchard, 'Industrial Employment and the Rural Land Market, 1380–1520', pp. 258–9.

57. Ester Boserup, *Population and Technological Change: A Study of Long-Term Trends* (Chicago, 1981).

58. Robert Brenner, 'Agrarian Class Structure and Economic Development in Pre-industrial Europe', *Past & Present*, no. 70 (1976), pp. 30–75.

59. Blanchard, 'Industrial Employment and the Rural Land Market 1380–1520', p. 256.

60. Ladurie, *The Peasants of Languedoc*, p. 30.

61. Dyer, *Lords and Peasants*, pp. 293–305, and 'Changes in the Size of Peasant Holdings', p. 284.

62. Dyer, *Lords and Peasants*, p. 304.

63. Blanchard, 'Industrial Employment', p. 265.

64. Collating and evaluating a wide range of evidence, John Hatcher has been instrumental in updating the case (originally made by Russell in *British Medieval Population*) for the deep and protracted nature of the population decline in England. He concludes his review by placing his own estimate of the net decline at 60 per cent, and the resumption of sustained growth somewhere in the third quarter of the fifteenth century. In seeking to explain this massive loss he puts the entire burden on extraordinary plague-induced mortality. His rejection of any role for curtailed fertility is cursory, however. Because of easy land access and buoyant wages, Hatcher finds it 'more logical to believe that the population fell despite an increase in the marriage rate and fertility than to believe that it fell, or failed to recover, because of a decrease in the marriage rate and fertility. But it must be admitted that there are scarcely any reliable data on these basic aspects of medieval life and that there is a pressing need for more research': *Plague, Population and the English Economy*, pp. 56–7, 69–71. With recent work by Razi, Howell, Hallam and Smith, we are no longer completely in the dark on nuptiality and fertility rates in late medieval England: Razi, *Life, Marriage and Death,*; Howell *Land, Family and Inheritance;* H. E. Hallam, 'Age at First Marriage and Age at Death in the Lincolnshire Fenland, 1252–1478', *Population Studies*, vol. 39 (1985), pp. 55–69; and R. M. Smith, 'Hypothèses sur la nuptialité en Angleterre aux XIIIe – XIVe siècles', in *Annales: Economies, sociétés, civilisations*, vol. 38 (1983), pp. 107–36.

65. Campbell, 'Population Pressure, Inheritance and the Land Market', pp. 128–9; Duby, *Rural Economy and Country Life*, p. 310; Dyer, *Lords and Peasants*, p. 234; Heilleiner, 'The Population of Europe', pp. 69–70; George Huppert, *After the Black Death: A Social History of Early Modern Europe* (Bloomington, 1986), p. 13.

66. Heilleiner, 'The Population of Europe', p. 71.

67. Herlihy and Klapisch-Zuber, *Tuscans and Their Families*, pp. 251–2.

68. G. G. Coulton, *Medieval Village, Manor, and Monastery* (Cambridge, 1925), p. 244.

69. Herlihy and Klapisch-Zuber, *Tuscans and Their Families*, p. 251.

70. *A Patriarchal Mode of Production* (unpublished MS, 1984), p. 15.

71. This assumption is itself a disputed issue among demographers, but I am willing to make it. See Ron Lesthaeghe et al., 'Child-Spacing and Fertility in Sub-Saharan Africa: An Overview of the Issues', in Hilary J. Page and Ron Lesthaeghe, eds, *Child-Spacing in Tropical Africa: Tradition and Change* (New York, 1981).

72. 'European Marriage Patterns in Perspective', in D. V. Glass and D. E. C. Eversley, eds, *Population in History: Essays in Historical Demography* (London, 1965).

73. Thus, while merchet fines tended to decline after the Black Death, heriot fines rose drastically in Coltenham: 'It is difficult not to interpret its height after the Black Death as punitive': Jack Ravensdale, 'Population Changes and the Transfer of Customary Land on a Cambridgeshire Manor in the Fourteenth Century', in R. M. Smith, ed., *Land, Kinship and Life-Cycle* (Cambridge, 1984), p. 211.

74. C. O'Grada, 'The Population of Ireland, 1700–1900: A Survey', in *Annales de démographie historique* (1979), pp. 293–4; Grigg, *Population Growth and Agrarian Change*, pp. 135–8.

75. The village of Colyton in Devon, England, also experienced a protracted demographic depression for a century after the plague outbreak of 1645–46 had taken perhaps one-fifth of its population. In a pioneering family-reconstitution study, Wrigley demonstrated that subsequent mortality levels could account for only a small part of this depression; women's age at marriage had risen substantially from 1647 to 1719; and those who married younger than the average had checked fertility *within* marriage: 'Mortality in Pre-Industrial England: The Example of Colyton, Devon over Three Centuries', *Daedalus*, 97 (1968), pp. 546–80. This latter form of fertility regulation was rare in early modern Europe, as studies of other villages have shown. In a follow-up study of Colyton, David Levine argued that the villagers' response to deindustrialization accounted for the no-growth regime established there, not their instinctive prudence, as Wrigley had postulated: *Family Formation in an Age of Nascent Capitalism* (New York, 1977), p. 104.

76. Herlihy and Klapisch-Zuber, *Tuscans and Their Families*, pp. 89, 230.

77. Bengt Ankarloo, 'Agriculture and Women's Work: Directions of Change in the West, 1700–1900', *Journal of Family History*, vol. 4 (1979), pp. 111–20.

78. Michael Mitterauer and Richard Sieder, *The European Family: Patriarchy to Partnership from the Middle Ages to the Present* (Oxford, 1982), p. 38.

79. It is women's age at first marriage which is singled out here, for two reasons: (a) because the timing of female nuptials has far greater effects on fertility than male timing does (especially when women continue to bear children until menopause, as they did in early modern Europe); and (b) because female marriage age varies much more than men's does in the early modern period, furnishing a more sensitive index of underlying changes in the economic and cultural parameters of the prevailing fertility regime.

80. Richard M. Smith, 'The People of Tuscany and Their Families in the Fifteenth Century: Medieval or Mediterranean?' *Journal of Family History*, vol. 6 (1981), pp. 109–11.

81. *Tuscans and Their Families*, pp. 87–8.

82. Ibid., p. 224.

83. Cited in Diane Hughes, 'From Brideprice to Dowry in Mediterranean Europe', in Marion Kaplan, ed., *The Marriage Bargain: Women and Dowries in European History* (New York, 1985), p. 43.

84. Smith, 'Hypothèses sur la nuptialité', pp. 114–15.

85. Ibid., pp. 111–12.

86. Hallam, 'Age at First Marriage and Age at Death', p. 60–61. Since it was necessary for Hallam to estimate mean marriage age by indirect means, the assumptions he makes in doing so could be subject to future query and revision by historical demographers. His premises appear reasonable to me, but I am not really competent to judge them. However, since the same methods were used to calculate mean age before and after the Black Death, the fact of the rise itself is likely to remain solid, even if the absolute ages generated by his calculations are called into question.

87. *Life, Marriage and Death in a Medieval Parish*, pp. 136–7.

88. Howell, *Land, Family and Inheritance*, p. 225.

89. 'Population Pressure, Inheritance and the Land Market', pp. 128–9.

90. R. S. Gottfried, *Epidemic Disease in Fifteenth Century England: The Medical Response and the Demographic Consequences* (New Brunswick, N.J., 1978), pp. 177, 191, 221.

91. C. McEvedy and R. Jones, *Atlas of World Population History* (Harmondsworth, 1978), p. 68.

92. T. H. Hollingsworth, *Historical Demography* (London, 1969), p. 384; Hatcher, *Plague, Population and the English Economy*, p. 63.

93. Grigg, *Population Growth and Agrarian Change*, p. 102; Ladurie, *The Peasants of Languedoc*, p. 52; Bois, *The Crisis of Feudalism*, p. 69.

94. Carlo M. Cipolla, 'Four Centuries of Italian Demographic Development', in D. V. Glass and D. E. C. Eversley, eds, *Population in History: Essays in Demographic History* (London, 1965), p. 160.

95. Grigg, *Population Growth and Agrarian Change*, p. 55. Grigg has brought together a useful summary of the best guesses from AD 1000 on (pp. 52–5). The margin of error in such estimates is rather large.

96. One might hypothesize that this difference was due to the earlier consolidation of the late, non-universal marriage regime in England than on the continent. It is doubtful that English mortality was worse in the period 1450–1600; life expectancy may well have been longer. One is drawn therefore to an explanation for the more gradual English build-up that focuses squarely on a substantially lower fertility rate, and hence to a difference in household formation and the nuptial matrix.

97. Heilleiner, 'The Population of Europe', pp. 71, 75–6.

98. *Epidemic Disease in Fifteenth Century England*. In Tuscany, fertility proved remarkably resilient in the aftermath of epidemic losses in the early fifteenth century. 'This feat of producing babies is more remarkable when we consider that the epidemics were not lenient on young adults of childbearing age': David Herlihy, 'Deaths, Marriages, Births and the Tuscan Economy ca. 1300–1550', in R. D. Lee, ed., *Population Patterns in the Past* (New York, 1977), p. 154.

99. Heilleiner, 'The Population of Europe', p. 79.

100. Bois, *The Crisis of Feudalism*, p. 370–71.

101. *The Dutch Rural Economy in the Golden Age, 1500–1700* (New Haven, 1974), p. 111.

102. Dyer, *Lords and Peasants*, pp. 224–35.

103. E. A. Wrigley and R. S. Schofield, *The Population History of England, 1541–1871: A Reconstruction* (London, 1981), pp. 242–4.

104. Grigg, *Population Growth and Agrarian Change*, p. 55.

105. De Vries, *European Urbanization*, p. 39. It is conventional to regard the opening century of the early modern era as a time of marked urbanization, but this perception is based more on the growth of particular cities than on the proportion of the overall population living in cities. To be sure, the expansion of certain centres was spectacular (the population of Lyon, for example, quadrupled from 1450 to 1550). But the number of urban centres with a population exceeding 10,000 (thus arbitrarily qualifying as cities) rose only modestly in Northwestern Europe: from thirty in 1500 to forty in 1600. De Vries's pathbreaking study furnishes, for the first time, reasonable estimates of these proportions for the various regions of Europe from 1500 on.

106. Abel, *Agricultural Fluctuations in Europe*, pp. 101–6.

107. Herman Kellenbenz, *The Rise of the European Economy* (London, 1976), pp. 99–102.

108. Abel, *Agricultural Fluctuations in Europe*, pp. 116–17.

109. P. Bowden, 'Agricultural Prices, Wages, Farm Profits and Rents', in J. Thirsk, ed., *The Agrarian History of England and Wales*, vol. 5, pt 2 (Cambridge, 1985), p. 15.

110. Eric Kerridge, 'The Movement of Rent, 1540–1640', *Economic History Review*, vol. 6 (1954), pp. 16–34; Abel, *Agricultural Fluctuations in Europe*, p. 26; Ladurie, *The Peasants of Languedoc*, p. 116; Bois, *The Crisis of Feudalism*, p. 383.

111. Abel, *Agricultural Fluctuations in Europe*, pp. 120, 135; Ladurie, *The Peasants of Languedoc*, p. 107; Giuseppe Felloni, 'Italy', Frederic Mauro and Geoffrey Parker 'Spain', and Michel Morineau, 'France', in Charles Wilson and Geoffrey Parker, eds, *An Introduction to the Sources of European Economic History, 1500–1800* (Ithaca, 1977), p. 28, 56, 183; Peter Kriedte, *Peasants, Landlords and Merchant Capitalists: Europe and the World Economy, 1500–1800* (Cambridge, 1983), p. 52.

112. Ladurie, *The Peasants of Languedoc*, pp. 110–14; Shulamith Shahar, *The Fourth Estate* (London, 1983), p. 243.

113. Ladurie, *The Peasants of Languedoc*, p. 94.

114. Pierre Goubert, 'The French Peasantry of the Seventeenth Century', in Trevor Aston, ed., *Crisis in Europe, 1560–1660* (London, 1965), p. 163.

115. Margaret Spufford, 'Peasant Inheritance Customs and Land Distribution in Cambridgeshire from the Sixteenth to the Eighteenth Centuries', in J. Goody, J. Thirsk and E. P. Thompson, eds, *Family and Inheritance: Rural Society in Western Europe*, pp. 160–61.

116.   Howell, *Land, Family and Inheritance*, p. 208.

117.   Kriedte, *Peasants, Landlords and Merchant Capitalists*, p. 55.

118.   C. G. A. Clay, *Economic Expansion and Social Change: England, 1500–1700* (Cambridge, 1984), p. 93.

119.   Bois, *Crisis of Feudalism*, p. 249.

120.   Solvi Songer, '"A Prudent Wife Is from the Lord": The Married Peasant Woman of the Eighteenth Century in a Demographic Perspective', *Scandinavian Journal of History*, vol. 9 (1984), pp. 113–33.

121.   Ovar Löfgren, 'Family and Household: Images and Realities, Cultural Change in Swedish Society', in Robert McC. Netting, Richard R. Wilk and Eric J. Arnould, eds, *Households: Comparative and Historical Studies of the Domestic Group* (Berkeley, 1984), p. 96.

122.   Robert Brenner, 'Agrarian Class Structure and Economic Development in Pre-industrial Europe', in *Past & Present*, no. 70 (1976), pp. 30–75; 'The Agrarian Roots of European Capitalism', *Past & Present*, no. 97 (1982), pp. 16–113.

123.   Charles Tilly, 'Demographic Origins of the European Proletariat', in David Levine, ed., *Proletarianization and Family History* (New York, 1984), p. 49.

124.   Charles Tilly, *As Sociology Meets History* (New York, 1981), p. 179; Louise Tilly, 'Food Entitlement, Famine and Conflict', in Robert I. Rotberg and Theodore K. Rabb, eds, *Hunger and History* (Cambridge, 1983), p. 145.

125.   Note, however, that this is a statement concerning the aggregate balance of supply and demand. While there was a surfeit of general labourers, experienced hands with specific skills were often scarce, as the frequent complaints of employers make clear.

126.   Karl Marx, *Capital*, vol. 1 (New York, 1976), p. 273. Marx made the initial formulation of this conception in his study of 'primitive accumulation', focusing primarily on England. Highlighting the political elimination of alternative livelihoods on the land by means of enclosure and abrogation of communal use rights, he stressed that proletarianization had occurred against the will and considerable resistance of the labouring poor: Ibid., Part 8, pp. 873–942. More than a century later, with the benefit of vast advances in historical research, we may fault him for overemphasizing the enclosure movement (though the prevailing wisdom, following Chambers, now bends the stick too far in the opposite direction). The real problem is not the precise relevance of his model of proletarianization for English history, but the tendency in many marxist studies to treat the peasant expropriation scenario as universal and thus to inhibit genuine inquiry into the rich historical diversity of proletarianization.

127.   C. Tilly, 'Demographic Origins of the European Proletariat', p. 49.

128.   It is this sense of trade-off between subsistence provision and a culturally valued way of life which Edward Thompson evokes so brilliantly in *The Making of the English Working Class* (Harmondsworth, 1968), summarizing his perspective in the standard of living debate: 'It is perfectly possible to maintain two propositions which, on a casual view, appear to be contradictory. Over the period 1790–1840 there was a slight improvement in average material standards. Over the same period there was intensified exploitation, greater insecurity, and increasing human misery. By 1840 most people were "better off" than their forerunners had been fifty years before, but they had suffered and continued to suffer this slight improvement as a catastrophic experience' (p. 231).

129.   Catharina Lis and Hugo Soly, 'Poverty and Capitalism in Pre-industrial Europe: Policing the Early Modern Proletariat, 1450–1850', in Levine, ed., *Proletarianization and Family History*. Modern capitalist states still manipulate these 'welfare' alternatives to ensure that they remain inferior to the lowest levels of the labour market, rendering them more noxious whenever they threaten to undermine the competitive supply of labour-power to the worst jobs available. This is a central purpose of cutbacks in state social expenditure, as important to capitalism as the more easily legitimated objective of balancing government budgets.

130.   One envisages calamitous chain-reactions of downward mobility here, but brighter scenarios are conceivable, as Marx realized: escape from a slave plantation and clandestine migration to a district of free wage labour, for instance: *Capital*, vol. 1, p. 1033.

131.   Olwen Hufton, *The Poor of Eighteenth-Century France, 1750–1789* (Oxford, 1974), p. 69.

132. *The Capitalist World Economy* (Cambridge, 1979), p. 148.

133. Frederick Engels, 'The Housing Question', in Karl Marx and Frederick Engels, *Selected Works* (Moscow, 1958), p. 553.

134. For this reason, I do not concur with the gradualist reinterpretation of capitalist industrialization currently in vogue among economic and social historians. While the Industrial Revolution as a big bang theory certainly merited demotion, the overall effect has been to de-emphasize watersheds: conjunctures of impasse, rupture, release and sharp reorientation. Breaking capitalist dependency on cheap wages and rural recruitment was one such revolutionary turning point, coming very late in the day.

135. Christopher Hill, 'Pottage for Freeborn Englishmen: Attitudes to Wage Labour in the Sixteenth and Seventeenth Centuries', in C. H. Fernstein, ed., *Socialism, Capitalism and Economic Growth* (Cambridge, 1967).

136. Hans Medick, 'The Structures and Function of Population Development under the Proto-industrial System', in Peter Kriedte, Hans Medick and Jürgen Schlumbohm, *Industrialization before Industrialization* (Cambridge, 1981), p. 49.

137. David Levine, *Reproducing Families: The Political Economy of English Population History* (Cambridge, 1987), p. 21.

138. Keith Wrightson, *English Society, 1550–1680* (London, 1982), p. 141.

139. Grigg, *Population Growth and Agrarian Change*, pp. 104–5; Ladurie, *The Peasants of Languedoc*, p. 92; Alan Everitt, 'Farm Labourers', in J. Thirsk, ed., *The Agrarian History of England and Wales*, vol. 4 (Cambridge, 1967), pp. 398, 402; J. F. C. Harrison, *The Common People: A History from the Norman Conquest to the Present* (London, 1984), p. 114.

140. Carole Shamas, 'The Eighteenth-Century Diet and Economic Change', *Explorations in Economic History*, vol. 21 (1984), pp. 256, 264.

141. Wolfram Fischer, 'Rural Industrialization and Population Change', *Comparative Studies in Society and History*, vol. 15 (1973), p. 165.

142. Everitt, 'Farm Labourers', pp. 413–15, 418; Hufton, *The Poor of Eighteenth-Century France*, p. 53.

143. J. Langton, 'Industry and Towns, 1500–1730', in R. A. Dodgshon and R. A. Butlin, eds, *An Historical Geography of England and Wales* (London, 1978), p. 179.

144. Andrée Corvol, 'L'Offouage au XVIIIᵉ siècle: Intégration et exclusion dans des communautés d'Ancien Régime', *Annales: Economies, sociétés, civilisations*, vol. 36 (1981), pp. 390–407.

145. Everitt, 'Farm Labourers', p. 396.

146. Howell, *Land, Family and Inheritance*, p. 182.

147. Ibid., p. 175.

148. Ovar Löfgren, 'The Potato People: Household Economy and Family Patterns among the Rural Proletariat in Nineteenth Century Sweden', in Sune Åkerman, Hans Christian Johansen and David Gaunt, eds, *Chance and Change: Social and Economic Studies in Historical Demography in the Baltic Area* (Odense, 1978), p. 103.

149. K. D. M. Snell, *Annals of the Labouring Poor: Social Change and Agrarian England, 1600–1900* (Cambridge, 1985), p. 169.

150. Pierre Goubert, *The Ancien Régime: French Society, 1600–1750* (New York, 1973), p. 106.

151. Henry Kamen, *European Society, 1500–1700* (London, 1984) p. 167.

152. Ibid., p. 169.

153. Lis and Soly, *Poverty and Capitalism*, p. 78.

154. Clay, *Economic Expansion and Social Change*, p. 221; Kamen, *European Society*, p. 170.

155. Everitt, 'Farm Labourers', pp. 410–11.

156. Kamen, *European Society*, p. 168; David Levine, 'Production, Reproduction and the Proletarian Family in England, 1500–1851', in Levine, ed., *Proletarianization and Family History* (New York, 1984), p. 94.

157. Snell, *Annals of the Labouring Poor*, p. 360–63.

158. Ibid., p. 360.

159. Lis and Soly, *Poverty and Capitalism*, pp. 87–9.

160. Kamen, *European Society*, p. 170.

161. The term 'proto-industrialization' was coined by Franklin Mendels in a salient article which altered the way in which the Industrial Revolution was conceived and discussed: 'Proto-industrialization: The First Phase of the Industrialization Process', *Journal of Economic History*, vol. 32 (1972), pp. 241–61. It served to highlight the crucial importance of burgeoning cottage industry in areas of the countryside that were staging grounds for the Industrial Revolution. Proto-industrial regions were hothouses for capital accumulation and population growth in the 1750–1850 period; both were indispensable to the industrial takeoff.

162. Jürgen Schlumbohm, 'Relations of Production – Productive Forces – Crises in Proto-industrialization', in P. Kriedte, H. Medick and J. Schlumbohm, *Industrialization before Industrialization* (Cambridge, 1981), p. 98–107.

163. Several weaknesses in the concept of proto-industrialization have been pointed out: Maxine Berg, Pat Hudson and Michael Sonenscher, *Manufacture in Town and Country before the Factory* (Cambridge, 1983), pp. 16–20; Rab Houston and K. D. M. Snell, 'Proto-Industrialization? Cottage Industry, Social Change, and Industrial Revolution', *The Historical Journal*, vol. 27 (1984), pp. 473–92; D. C. Coleman 'Proto-industrialization: A Concept Too Many', *Economic History Review*, vol. 36 (1983), pp. 435–48; L. A. Clarkson, *Proto-industrialization: The First Phase of Industrialization?* (London, 1985). In the prevailing discourse, the term suggests (a) a very stylized model of the kind of areas which fostered proto-industrialization, subject to numerous exceptions; (b) a presumably successful transition to factory production, though many proto-industrial areas stagnated in the nineteenth century and were bypassed in the course of industrialization; (c) a fixation on textile industries, to the exclusion of others, particularly mining and metal-making; and (d) a glossing over of the wide variety of social relations of production and exchange which were entailed in this transitional form. While these criticisms are well taken, I see no reason to eschew the term, preferring instead to render it more precise. From a marxist standpoint, it is particularly important to rectify the last deficiency, specifying social relations as they are manifest in a spectrum from petty commodity to capitalist production under the putting-out system.

164. This source of market demand was limited, however, by rising grain and bread prices which absorbed probably half the wage's value. In times of subsistence crises, when grain prices soared, the demand for clothing and household amenities was severely curtailed, as food staples consumed a rising portion of the proletarian family's budget. This bottleneck choked off promising proto-industrial growth spurts time and again, until subsistence crises abated in the latter part of the eighteenth century.

165. While one usually thinks of textile industries in this regard, the regional density of metalworkers in England had become considerable by the late seventeenth century. In the Birmingham to Wolverhampton area, metalworker households were in a majority in four townships between 1660 and 1710. Metalworkers comprised 43 per cent of those whose occupations were listed in a sample of probate inventories in Sheffield between 1695 and 1729: Langton, 'Industry and Towns, 1500–1730', p. 180.

166. Hans Medick, 'The Proto-industrial Family Economy', in P. Kriedte, H. Medick and J. Schlumbohm, *Industrialization before Industrialization* (Cambridge, 1981), p. 49.

167. Schlumbohm, 'Relations of Production', pp. 98–9.

168. Clarkson, *Proto-industrialization*, pp. 20–21.

169. Schlumbohm, 'Relations of Production', p. 95.

170. Medick, 'The Proto-industrial Family Economy', pp. 61–2.

171. Everitt, 'Farm Labourers', p. 456.

172. Medick, 'The Proto-industrial Family Economy', p. 55.

173. Ibid., p. 56.

174. Daniel Scott-Smith, 'A Homeo-Static Demographic Regime: Patterns in Western European Family Reconstitution Studies', in R. Lee, ed., *Population Patterns in the Past* (New York, 1977); Michael W. Flinn, *The European Demographic System, 1500–1800* (Brighton, 1981).

175. Ansley Coale, 'The Decline of Fertility in Europe since the Eighteenth Century as a Chapter in Human Demographic History', in A. J. Coale and S. C. Watkins, eds, *The*

Decline of Fertility in Europe (Princeton, 1986), p. 8.

176. The term 'natural fertility' originated with the Italian economist Corrado Gini and was subsequently elaborated by the French demographer Louis Henry: 'Some Data on Natural Fertility', *Eugenics Quarterly*, vol. 8 (1961), pp. 81–91. Henry defined it as the absence of deliberate birth control and family size limitation in marriage. The term is now in widespread use among demographers; perhaps the best overview of the concept is John Knodel's 'Natural Fertility: Age Patterns, Levels, Trends', in Rudolfo Bulatao and Ronald Lee, eds, *Determinants of Fertility in Developing Countries* (New York, 1982). A population is held to be in a condition of natural fertility when birth patterns show no evidence of being 'parity-related'. In other words, women do not cease to bear children on the basis of the number of currently living children they have already borne; no 'target' of ideal family size is operative. If the fertility curve of a given cohort of married women corresponds broadly to their natural fecundity curve, even through their late thirties and early forties, a regime of natural fertility is held to prevail. Customs and practices which affect birth-spacing, but are not parity-dependent (such as breastfeeding norms and post-partum intercourse taboos), do not contravene a regime of natural fertility.

177. The distinction between two modes of fertility regulation within marriage – the first by means of birth-spacing and the second by means of pre-menopausal stopping – is of capital importance. But the terminology of natural fertility has had pernicious ideological effects, sponsoring a simplistic dichotomy between 'natural' fertility in 'traditional' societies giving rise to 'high' birth rates, and 'controlled' fertility in 'modern' societies engendering 'low' birth rates. This conception obfuscates the regulatory techniques common among pre-industrial peoples and the wide diversity of fertility patterns produced from their differential use in particular settings. In fact, the birth rates of most pre-industrial populations could be more precisely described as moderate, not high, being in the range of 40 to 60 per cent of capacity. While admitting that natural fertility is a problematic concept, most demographers persist in using it. This seems to be due to its congeniality with modernization theory, which is predicated upon the same crude and misleading traditional/modern dichotomy.

178. Flinn, *The European Demographic System*, pp. 112–15; Ulla-Britt Lithell, *Breast-feeding and Reproduction* (Uppsala, 1981); Dorothy McLaren, 'Marital Fertility and Lactation, 1570–1720', in Mary Prior, ed., *Women in English Society, 1500–1800* (London, 1985).

179. D. McLaren, 'Marital Fertility and Lactation', p. 33.

180. Angus McLaren, *Reproductive Rituals: The Perception of Fertility in England from the Sixteenth to the Nineteenth Century* (London, 1984), pp. 57–112.

181. Most demographers assume that practices such as prolonged nursing are not manipulated by individual women, but are culturally determined, imposing an 'unconscious rationality' on natural fertility: E. A. Wrigley, 'Fertility Strategy for the Individual and the Group', in Charles Tilly, ed., *Historical Studies of Changing Fertility* (Princeton, 1978). In Third World surveys, they often find that their informants profess no knowledge of such effects, and so conclude that the benefits of restriction are unrecognized, working against people's express desire for more children. But given strong religious taboos against birth control, we should be wary about accepting the statements of informants on this issue. In some contemporary Third World contexts, there is evidence that women deliberately manipulate nursing and abstinence customs to postpone further conception, optimizing the life-chances of existing infants: John Knodel, 'Family Limitation and the Fertility Transition: Evidence from the Age Patterns of Fertility in Europe and Asia', *Population Studies*, vol. 31 (1977), p. 220. On this issue, see also Ron Lesthaeghe et al., 'Child-Spacing and Fertility in Sub-Saharan Africa: An Overview of the Issues', in H. J. Page and R. Lesthaeghe, eds, *Child-Spacing in Tropical Africa: Tradition and Change* (New York, 1981).

182. Wrigley and Schofield, *The Population History of England*, p. 256.

183. Ron Lesthaeghe, 'Nuptiality and Population Growth', *Population Studies*, vol. 25 (1971), pp. 415–32; H. J. Habakkuk, *Population Growth and Economic Development* (Leicester, 1971), pp. 38–9; Levine, 'Production, Reproduction and the Proletarian Family', pp. 108–11.

184. While I do not share the recent enthusiasm for reclaiming Malthus's analytical

insights without sober regard for the reactionary impact of his moral and political ideas in history, a serious reconsideration of his intellectual legacy from the standpoint of historical materialism is long overdue. A great deal of value in the later editions of *An Essay on the Principle of Population* has been effectively buried beneath the avalanche of invective from the Left that was heaped on the book's first edition, with its notoriously crude (and demagogically effective) pamphleteering projections ('arithmetic' increments of food resources being outstripped by 'geometric' population growth). Malthus is remembered for advocating celibacy and delayed marriage as a panacea, while excoriating all forms of contraception as immoral. Yet he was also perfectly aware that late and non-universal marriage had already become the main factor in restraining European population growth: *An Essay on the Principle of Population* (London, 1973 [1872]), p. 315. The full significance of this discovery had not been adequately recognized until recently.

185. Hajnal, 'European Marriage Patterns in Perspective', p. 132; J. D. Chambers, *Population, Economy and Society in Pre-Industrial England* (Oxford, 1972), p. 58.

186. Heilleiner, 'The Population of Europe from the Black Death to the Eve of the Vital Revolution', p. 70.

187. Hajnal has identified three rules common to pre-industrial Northwestern 'simple household systems': (a) late marriage for both sexes, women over twenty-three and men over twenty-six; (b) a couple in charge of their own household after marriage (the husband is the head of the household); and (c) young people often circulate between households as servants before marriage. He compares these rules with a comparable set for Eastern European 'joint household systems': 'Two Kinds of Pre-industrial Household Systems', *Population and Development Review*, vol. 8 (1982), p. 452. Only the second pattern, in my view, was normatively upheld.

188. Snell, *Annals of the Labouring Poor*, p. 363.

189. As Lesthaeghe has remarked: 'In traditional societies, the regulation of the right to reproduce constitutes an appropriation of female labour resources and of sexual gratification by those who, by virtue of their age and descent, form the ruling group. ... If their objective is to maintain such privileges, others must practice restraint': 'On the Social Control of Reproduction', *Population and Development Review*, vol. 6 (1980), p. 530.

190. Wrightson, *English Society*, p. 69.

191. P. G. Ohlin, 'Mortality, Marriage and Growth in Pre-industrial Populations', *Population Studies*, vol. 14 (1961), pp. 190–97.

192. Roger Schofield, 'The Relationship between Demographic Studies and Environment in Preindustrial Western Europe', in W. Conze, ed., *Sozialgeschichte der Familie in der Neuzit Europas* (Stuttgart, 1977).

193. Thomas Held, 'Rural Retirement Arrangements in Seventeenth to Nineteenth Century Austria: A Cross-Community Analysis', *Journal of Family History*, vol. 7 (1982), pp. 227–54.

194. Modernization theorists do not state this explicitly, but since they have nothing much to say about proletarianization, we must infer that they think class does not matter in family history, or else that early modern Europe was a 'one class society', as Laslett proposed for England: *The World We Have Lost* (London, 1971). Laslett sees his own approach as being very much at odds with modernization theory, but the divergence escapes me. He works in the traditional/modern idiom, eschews periodization, frequently neglects to characterize the societies he studies, and treats 'the past' as an infinitely receding horizon. Note the absence of societal specificity or periodization in the titles of the books he has (co)authored: *The World We Have Lost; Household and Family in Past Time; Family Life and Illicit Love in Earlier Generations; Statistical Studies of Historical Social Structure; Family Forms in Historic Europe*.

195. Tilly, 'Demographic Origins of the European Proletariat', p. 51.

196. Kriedte, *Peasants, Landlords and Merchant Capitalists*, pp. 3, 61; Frederic Mauro and Geoffrey Parker, 'Spain', in Wilson and Parker, eds, *An Introduction to the Sources of European Economic History, 1500–1800* (Ithaca, 1977), p. 37; Giuseppe Felloni, 'Italy', in Ibid., p. 4; Hermann Kellenbenz, 'Germany', in Ibid., p. 192; Wrigley and Schofield, *The Population History of England*, pp. 290, 528; Grigg, *Population Growth and Agrarian Change*, pp. 55–7,

111; Henry Kamen, *Spain in the Later Seventeenth Century, 1665–1700* (New York, 1980), p. 39.

197. De Vries, *The Economy of Europe in an Age of Crisis, 1600–1750* (Cambridge, 1976), p. 4; Kriedte, *Peasants, Landlords and Merchant Capitalists,* p. 61.

198. Wrigley and Schofield, *The Population History of England,* p. 528; Jacques Dupâquier, *La Population française aux XVIIe et XVIIIe siècles,* (Paris, 1979), pp. 12, 44; Mauro and Parker, 'Spain', p. 39; de Vries, *The Economy of Europe in an Age of Crisis,* pp. 12–13.

199. Wrigley and Schofield, *The Population History of England,* p. 528.

200. Roger Schofield, 'English Marriage Patterns Revisited', *Journal of Family History,* vol. 10 (1985), p. 9. The measure is calculated as the percentage of both sexes surviving to the age of forty who do not marry. The nuptial complex was realigned after 1700, as shifts in marital timing assumed a more prominent role in shaping fertility rates.

201. Peter Laslett, *Family Life and Illicit Love in Earlier Generations* (Cambridge, 1977), p. 153. Keith Wrightson has argued persuasively that the latter estimate is too low, but the downward trend in the first six decades of the seventeenth century is not in doubt: 'The Nadir of English Illegitimacy in the Seventeenth Century', in Peter Laslett, Karla Oosterveen and Richard Smith, eds, *Bastardy and Its Comparative History* (Cambridge, Mass., 1980).

202. See Morineau, 'France', p. 158; Dupâquier, *La Population française,* p. 12; Mauro and Parker, 'Spain', p. 39; Felloni, 'Italy', p. 9.

203. Dupâquier, *La Population française,* pp. 26, 60; Grigg, *Population Growth and Agrarian Change,* p. 113. Though tightening in the seventeenth century, the nuptial valve in France was not nearly so constrictive as it was in England, with the age of women at first marriage about four years younger and the portion never marrying less than half the English rate. In the course of the eighteenth century, the national trends crossed paths as the nuptial regime relaxed in England while continuing to close in France: E. A. Wrigley, 'Marriage, Fertility and Population Growth in Eighteenth-Century England', in R. B. Outhwaite, ed., *Marriage and Society* (New York, 1981), p. 177.

204. C. R. Friedrichs, 'Marriage, Family and Social Structure in an Early Modern German Town', *Historical Papers of the Canadian Historical Association,* (1975), p. 29.

205. Dupâquier, *La Population française,* p. 59. See also Mauro and Parker, 'Spain', p. 41.

206. Peter Laslett, 'Introduction: Comparing Illegitimacy over Time and between Cultures', in Laslett, Oosterveen and Smith, eds, *Bastardy and Its Comparative History,* p. 24; E. A. Wrigley, 'Marriage, Fertility and Population Growth in Eighteenth-Century England', p. 162; Flinn, *The European Demographic System,* pp. 121–2.

207. In addition to an unconditional promise, many versions of a conditional pledge were revealed in early modern court testimony: 'I will marry you *if:* (a) your father puts up a dowry, (b) I can get a job, or (c) save up enough money, (d) you get pregnant and (e) cannot get an abortion, (f) you cannot persuade Jack that it is his child and he should marry you, or (g) all else fails …' On these and other variants of marital trothplight, see Geoffrey R. Quaife, *Wanton Wenches and Wayward Wives* (London, 1979).

208. Wrigley and Schofield, *The Population History of England,* p. 243. Wrigley and Schofield write: 'Fertility and mortality contributed equally to the steady fall in *r* [the intrinsic growth rate] from 1601 to 1671' (p. 244). Yet the graph upon which this assessment is based does not indicate equal influence (p. 243). The slope between 1601 and 1671 would be a 45 degree diagonal if fertility and mortality were equally influential, but it is much steeper, indicating that the vertical axis (fertility) predominated over the horizontal (mortality).

209. Abel, *Agricultural Fluctuations in Europe,* p. 117.

210. Kriedte, *Peasants, Landlords and Merchant Capitalists,* p. 4.

211. Mauro and Parker, 'Spain', p. 53; Abel, *Agricultural Fluctuations in Europe,* pp. 150, 153–5, 158; Wrigley and Schofield, *The Population History of England,* p. 403.

212. P. Bowden, 'Agricultural Prices, Wages, Farm Profits and Rents', in Joan Thirsk, ed., *The Agrarian History of England and Wales,* vol. 5, pt 2 (Cambridge, 1985), p. 4.

213. Morineau, 'France', pp. 179–81; Kellenbenz, 'Germany', p. 220; Abel, *Agricultural Fluctuations in Europe,* p. 182; Felloni, 'Italy', p. 28.

214. Wrigley and Schofield, *The Population History of England,* p. 404.

215. Abel, *Agricultural Fluctuations in Europe*, pp. 220–38.

216. C. Tilly, 'Demographic Origins of the European Proletariat', p. 51.

217. The parish records which have furnished such a treasure-trove for family reconstitution studies note people's occupations intermittently and seldom reveal anything of household wealth or property holdings. These records can often be combined with other documentary sources, particularly tax rolls; regrettably, very little of this work has been done: Nigel Goose, 'Household Size and Structure in Early-Stuart Cambridge', *Social History*, vol. 5 (1980), p. 347.

218. Laslett, *The World We Have Lost*, p. 66. The households of various strata in Cambridge in the 1620s were similarly composed: Goose, 'Household Size and Structure in Early-Stuart Cambridge', pp. 368, 372.

219. Mitterauer and Sieder, *The European Family*, p. 42; Jean-Louis Flandrin, *Families in Former Times: Kinship, Household and Sexuality* (New York, 1979), pp. 58, 215. These authors note a correlation between domestic wealth and fertility, while I am making a class-specific argument. But since early modern proletarians were overwhelmingly poor, their more general findings reflect the same class differentials.

220. Laslett, *The World We Have Lost*, p. 36.

221. Rudolph Braun, 'Protoindustrialization and Demographic Changes in the Canton of Zurich', in Charles Tilly, ed., *Historical Studies of Changing Fertility* (Princeton, 1978), pp. 295–7.

222. Levine, *Family Formation*, p. 59.

223. Ibid., pp. 61–3.

224. The evidence cited here is for the seventeenth century. Is it possible that the reproduction rate of proletarians in the 'long' sixteenth century was unusually high relative to that of other classes? We have no direct evidence to bring to bear on this, but it is interesting to look at the villages of Colyton and Terling, where parish records run continuously through the latter half of the sixteenth century; both experienced early proletarianization. Colyton expanded rapidly between 1538 and 1599, as the textile industry boomed, with an average annual growth rate of 1.18 per cent, before contracting in the seventeenth century. In the sixteenth century, childbearing women had 3.45 surviving children on average: Levine, *Family Formation*, p. 111. In Terling, where engrossment proceeded apace in the sixteenth century and agricultural labour was heavily proletarianized, the village population also grew briskly at 0.86 per cent per annum in the period 1550–1624, tapering only slightly in the remainder of the seventeenth century. Terling women averaged 2.88 surviving children in the initial period, this rate declining slightly to 2.65 in the seventeenth century: Levine, *Family Formation*, p. 122. Colyton and Terling were in step with the widespread slowdown of population growth in the late sixteenth century, but there is no evidence that their proletarianizing inhabitants had exceptionally high birth rates before the deceleration.

225. B. Derouet, 'Une démographie sociale différentielle', *Annales: Economies, sociétés, civilisations*, vol. 35 (1980), p. 21; J. C. Giacchetti and M. Tyvaert, 'Argenteuil, 1740–1790', *Annales de démographie historique* (1969), p. 56; M. Terrisse, 'Un faubourg du Havre: Ingouville', *Population*, vol. 16 (1961), p. 291.

226. Löfgren, 'The Potato People', p. 98.

227. Levine, 'Production, Reproduction and the Proletarian Family', p. 95.

228. Friedrichs, 'Marriage, Family and Social Structure in an Early Modern German Town', p. 22.

229. Levine, *Family Formation*, p. 122.

230. De Vries, *European Urbanization*, p. 178; Richard Wall, 'The Composition of Households in a Population of Six Men and Ten Women: South-East Bruges in 1814', in Richard Wall, ed., *Family Forms in Historic Europe* (Cambridge, 1983), p. 428–35. The female surplus of urban Europe in the early modern era contrasts with the sex ratios of cities and towns on other continents as capitalist industrialization begins. Russian, Chinese and Indian cities, for example, have had male surpluses at a comparable stage of development: de Vries, *European Urbanization*, p. 178.

231. Wrigley and Schofield, *The Population History of England*, pp. 168–9; de Vries,

European Urbanization, pp. 194–5, 235–7.

232. Kussmaul, *Servants in Husbandry in Early Modern England* (Cambridge, 1981), p. 1; Hufton, *The Poor of Eighteenth-Century France*, pp. 24, 31; Hajnal, 'Two Kinds of Pre-industrial Household Systems', p. 471; Laslett, *Family Life and Illicit Love*, pp. 32–3.

233. Laslett, *The World We Have Lost*, pp. 16, 263–4; Hufton, *The Poor of Eighteenth-Century France*, p. 29.

234. Kussmaul, *Servants in Husbandry*, p. 2; Flandrin, *Families in Former Times*, p. 140.

235. Kussmaul, *Servants in Husbandry*, pp. 40–41; Erik Gronseth, 'Notes on the Historical Development of the Relation between Nuclear Family Kinship System and Wider Social Structure in Norway', in R. Hill and R. Konig, eds, *Families in East and West* (Paris, 1970), p. 239; Mitterauer and Sieder, *The European Family*, p. 329.

236. Kussmaul, *Servants in Husbandry*, p. 3.

237. Löfgren, 'The Potato People', p. 99.

238. Kussmaul, *Servants in Husbandry*, p. 223; P. Schmidtbauer, 'The Changing Household: Austrian Household Structure from the Seventeenth to the Early Twentieth Century', in R. Wall, ed., *Family Forms in Historic Europe*, p. 363.

239. Snell, *Annals of the Labouring Poor*, p. 285; Kussmaul, *Servants in Husbandry*, pp. 228–9; Richard Wall, 'Work, Welfare and the Family: An Illustration of the Adaptive Family Economy', in L. Bonfield, R. M. Smith and K. Wrightson, eds, *The World We Have Gained* (Oxford, 1986), p. 273.

240. Lutz Berkner, 'The Stem Family and the Developmental Cycle of the Peasant Household: An Eighteenth Century Austrian Example', *American Historical Review*, vol. 77 (1972), p. 414; Ovar Löfgren, 'Family and Household among Scandinavian Peasants', in Michael Anderson, ed., *Sociology of the Family* (Harmondsworth, 1980), p. 88; Richard Wall, 'Does Owning Real Property Influence the Form of the Household? An Example from Rural West Flanders', in R. Wall, ed., *Family Forms in Historic Europe*, p. 394; Luc Danhieux, 'The Evolving Household: The Case of Lampernisse, West Flanders', in Ibid., p. 418.

241. Laslett, *Family Life and Illicit Love*, pp. 43–5; Martine Segalen, 'The Family Cycle and Household Structure: Five Generations in a French Village', *Journal of Family History*, vol. 2 (1977), p. 231; Blanchard, 'Industrial Employment and the Rural Land Market', p. 262; Kussmaul, *Servants in Husbandry*, p. 77.

242. Richard M. Smith, 'Some Issues Concerning Families and Their Property in Rural England, 1250–1800', in Smith, ed., *Land, Kinship and Life-Cycle*, p. 38.

243. Olwen Hufton, 'Women, Work and Marriage in Eighteenth Century France', in R. B. Outhwaite, ed., *Marriage and Society* (New York, 1981); Hufton, *The Poor of Eighteenth–Century France*, pp. 28–9.

244. Snell, *Annals of the Labouring Poor*, p. 347–8; Löfgren, 'The Potato People', p. 99.

245. Macfarlane has postulated incest avoidance as a primary reason for sending children into service, noting that most departed at puberty or shortly thereafter: *The Family Life of Ralph Josselin* (Cambridge, 1970), p. 205. This seems implausible, since incestuous desires and the drive to suppress them are ubiquitous in human societies, while the departure of adolescents from their families at puberty is not. Service in husbandry on this scale appears unique to Western Europe. Are we to infer that incestuous desires were stronger here than anywhere else?

246. R. M. Smith, 'Fertility, Economy and Household Formation in England over Three Centuries', *Population and Development Review*, vol. 7 (1981), pp. 595–622.

247. R. Wall, 'The Household: Demographic and Economic Change in England, 1650–1970', in Wall, ed., *Family Forms in Historic Europe*, p. 498; Smith, 'Some Issues Concerning Families and Their Property', p. 81.

248. Smith, 'Fertility, Economy and Household Formation in England', pp. 602–5.

249. Abel, *Agricultural Fluctuations in Europe*, pp. 158–93. The exception to this sluggish exit from the seventeenth-century slump was Scandinavia, which expanded at a very substantial pace after the catastrophic crisis of the 1650s. The kingdom of Denmark, for example, grew at an average of about 0.8 per cent per year from 1660 to 1769: Aksel Lassen, 'The Population of Denmark, 1660–1960', *Scandinavian Economic History Review*, vol. 14 (1966), p. 134. In the century from 1650 to 1750, Scandinavia as a whole is estimated to

have grown about 40 per cent – not spectacular, but much more than the rest of Northwestern Europe; England, by comparison, grew only 10 per cent: de Vries, *European Urbanization*, p. 36; Wrigley and Schofield, *The Population History of England*, p. 528.

250. Jacques Dupâquier, *La Population française aux XVIIe et XVIIIe siècles*, (Paris, 1979), p. 81; Wrigley and Schofield, *The Population History of England*, p. 528; Kriedte, *Peasants, Landlords and Merchant Capitalists*, p. 102. The French pattern, however, is atypical, for while the growth rate accelerated sharply at mid century, momentum was not sustained. Growth in the first half of the eighteenth century has been estimated at 11 per cent; the population of France was only 19 per cent greater in 1800 than it was in 1750: Dupâquier, *La Population française*, pp. 81–2.

251. It was not a novelty in world history, however, as is often supposed. The population of China grew from an estimated 150 million in 1700 to 330 million in 1800, advancing to 435 million by 1850, almost trebling in 150 years: Jean-Noël Biraben, 'Essai sur l'évolution du nombre des hommes', *Population*, vol. 34 (1979), p. 16. This is about the same rate of growth as Europe experienced from 1750 to 1900, starting a half-century later. The Chinese case defies the conventional wisdom, based on the European experience, that a demographic expansion on this scale requires an industrial revolution to sustain it. It is indicative of the Eurocentric character of demographic theorizing that verities such as this can be repeated endlessly without paying serious attention to pre-industrial China.

252. Biraben, 'Essai sur l'évolution du nombre des hommes', p. 16.; de Vries, *European Urbanization*, p. 36.

253. André Armengaud, 'Population in Europe, 1700–1914', in Carlo M. Cipolla, ed., *Fontana Economic History of Europe*, vol. 3 (New York, 1973), p. 70.

254. Flinn, *The European Demographic System*, p. 81.

255. Abel, *Agricultural Fluctuations in Europe* (New York, 1980), pp. 197–8.

256. Ibid., p. 200.

257. Johan Söderberg, 'Real Wage Trends in Urban Europe, 1730–1850: Stockholm in a Comparative Perspective', *Social History*, vol. 12 (1987), pp. 161–2, 166.

258. R. V. Jackson, 'Growth and Deceleration in English Agriculture, 1660–1790', *Economic History Review*, vol. 38 (1985).

259. D. B. Grigg, *Population Growth and Agrarian Change* (Cambridge, 1980), p. 197; Grigg, *The Dynamics of Agricultural Change* (London, 1982), p. 103.

260. Abel, *Agricultural Fluctuations in Europe*, p. 206.

261. Ibid., pp. 206–7; Kriedte, *Peasants, Landlords and Merchant Capitalists*, p. 106.

262. Kussmaul, *Servants in Husbandry*, pp. 120–25; Snell, *Annals of the Labouring Poor*, p. 81.

263. Kussmaul, *Servants in Husbandry*, pp. 122–5; Snell, *Annals of the Labouring Poor*, pp. 70–77.

264. P. O. Christiansen, 'The Household in the Local Setting: A Study of Peasant Stratification', in S. Åkerman, H. C. Johansen and D. Gaunt, eds, *Chance and Change: Social and Economic Studies in Historical Demography in the Baltic Area* (Odense, 1978), p. 57; Löfgren, 'Family and Household among Scandinavian Peasants', p. 90.

265. Kussmaul, *Servants in Husbandry*, p. 128.

266. Ibid.

267. Ibid., p. 121.

268. Snell, *Annals of the Labouring Poor*, p. 101.

269. Kussmaul, *Servants in Husbandry*, p. 129.

270. 'Marriage Patterns in Victorian Britain', *Journal of Family History*, vol. 1 (1976), p. 76. See also Kussmaul, *Servants in Husbandry*, pp. 112–13.

271. Schlumbohm, 'Relations of Production – Productive Forces', pp. 101–7.

272. Franklin F. Mendels, 'Agriculture and Peasant Industry in Eighteenth-Century Flanders', in P. Kriedte, H. Medick and J. Schlumbohm, *Industrialization before Industrialization*, p. 172.

273. Rudolph Braun, 'Protoindustrialization and Demographic Change in the Canton of Zurich', in Charles Tilly, ed., *Historical Studies of Changing Fertility* (Princeton, 1978), p. 301.

274. Herbert Kisch, 'The Textile Industries in Silesia and the Rhineland: A Comparative Study in Industrialization', in P. Kriedte, H. Medick and J. Schlumbohm, *Industrialization before Industrialization*, pp. 189–90.

275. R. Lawton, 'Population and Society, 1730–1900', in R. A. Dodgshon and R. A. Butlin, eds, *An Historical Geography of England and Wales* (New York, 1978), p. 36.

276. The work of Hans Medick and David Levine has been particularly insightful in illuminating the intergenerational dynamics of proto-industrial households; see in particular Medick's 'The Proto-industrial Family Economy' and Levine's *Family Formation in an Age of Nascent Capitalism*.

277. Löfgren, 'The Potato People', p. 103.

278. Maxine Berg, *The Age of Manufactures, 1700–1820* (London, 1985), pp. 129–58.

279. Berg, 'Women's Work, Mechanization and the Early Phases of Industrialization in England', in P. Joyce, ed., *The Historical Meanings of Work* (Cambridge, 1987), p. 76.

280. Rayna Reiter [Rapp], 'Men and Women in the South of France: Public and Private Domains', in Rayna Reiter, ed., *Toward an Anthropology of Women* (New York, 1975), p. 261.

281. Jean H. Quataert, 'Teamwork in Saxon Homeweaving Families in the Nineteenth Century', in Ruth-Ellen B. Joeres and Mary J. Maynes, eds, *German Women in the Eighteenth and Nineteenth Centuries* (Bloomington, 1986), p. 15.

282. Medick, 'The Proto-industrial Family Economy', p. 62.

283. Ibid., p. 62.

284. 'Teamwork in Saxon Homeweaving Families', p. 15.

285. Cf. William Lazonick, 'The Subjugation of Labour to Capital: The Rise of the Capitalist System', *Review of Radical Political Economics*, vol. 10 (1978), pp. 1–31; Sonya Rose, 'Gender Segregation in the Transition to the Factory: The English Hosiery Industry, 1850–1910', *Feminist Studies*, vol. 13 (1987), pp. 163–84; Ruth Milkman, 'Redefining Women's Work: The Sexual Division of Labor in the Auto Industry in World War Two', *Feminist Studies*, vol. 8 (1982), pp. 337–72.

286. 'Teamwork in Saxon Homeweaving Families', pp. 12–15.

287. 'Gender Segregation in the Transition to the Factory', p. 182.

288. 'Gender Divisions and the Organization of Work in the Leicester Hosiery Industry', in Angela V. John, ed., *Unequal Opportunities: Women's Employment in England, 1800–1918* (Oxford, 1986), p. 57.

289. Quataert, 'Teamwork in Saxon Homeweaving Families', p. 7.

290. John D. Post, *The Last Great Subsistence Crisis in the Western World* (Baltimore, 1977).

291. Dupâquier, *La Population française*, p. 98; Erland Hofsten and Hans Lundström, *Swedish Population History, Main Trends from 1750 to 1950* (Stockholm, 1976); Otto Anderson, *The Population of Denmark* (New York, 1977), p. 14; Michael Drake, *Population and Society in Norway, 1735–1865* (Cambridge, 1969), p. 49; Wrigley and Schofield, *The Population History of England*, p. 528.

292. Wrigley and Schofield, *The Population History of England*, p. 331. Mortality crises are conventionally identified as occurring in those years in which the death rate is at least twice the rate of surrounding non-crisis years. The 'background' level is established as the average of five or ten non-crisis years before and after the crisis: Flinn, *The European Demographic System*, pp. 47–8. The technical problem with this index is the difficulty of arriving at a formula for defining normal years. Wrigley and Schofield sidestep the issue by developing a different measure, designating a crisis as occurring in any year in which the crude death rate is more than 10 per cent above 'trend', the baseline denominator being calculated as a 25-year unweighted moving average, centred on the given year. This trades in one problem for another. Since the measure includes the crisis year, and all other crisis years in the twenty-five year span, it fosters a deceptively diminished impression of the actual year-to-year variance of mortality in the early modern era.

293. Kamen, *European Society*, p. 35.

294. Stephen J. Kunitz, 'Speculations on the European Mortality Decline', *Economic History Review*, vol. 36 (1983), p. 253.

295. Hufton, *The Poor of Eighteenth-Century France,* p. 15.

296. McKeown's thesis [see T. McKeown, *The Modern Rise of Population* (London, 1976)], is also dubious because, short of outright starvation, the relation between malnutrition and mortality is a highly mediated one. See Nevin S. Scrimshaw, 'The Value of Contemporary Food and Nutrition Studies for Historians', in R. Rotberg and T. K. Rabb, eds, *Hunger and History* (Cambridge, 1983), p. 211.

297. Mary K. Matossian, 'Mold Poisoning and Population Growth in England and France, 1750–1850', *Journal of Economic History,* vol. 44 (1984), pp. 669–86.

298. McKeown, *The Modern Rise of Population;* William H. McNeill, *Plagues and Peoples* (New York, 1976); John D. Post, 'Famine, Mortality and Epidemic Disease in the Process of Modernization', *Economic History Review,* vol. 29 (1976), pp. 14–37; M. W. Flinn, 'Plague in Europe and the Mediterranean Countries', *Journal of European Economic History,* vol. 8, no. 1 (1979); Andrew Appleby, 'The Disappearance of Plague: A Continuing Puzzle', *Economic History Review,* vol. 33 (1980), pp. 161–73; Paul Slack, 'The Disappearance of Plague: An Alternative View', *Economic History Review,* vol. 34 (1981), pp. 469–76; Kunitz, 'Speculations on the European Mortality Decline', *Economic History Review,* vol. 36 (1983), pp. 349–64.

299. Flinn, *The European Demographic System,* pp. 62–3.

300. A. J. Mercer, 'Smallpox and Epidemiological-Demographic Change in Europe: The Role of Vaccination', *Population Studies,* 39 (1985), pp. 287–307.

301. McNeill, *Plagues and Peoples,* pp. 218–20.

302. Slack, 'The Disappearance of Plague: An Alternative View'; Flinn, *The European Demographic System,* pp. 58–61.

303. This is not to suggest that the increasingly vigorous intervention of the constabulary and the army in controlling population movement and the use of public space was entirely salutary. Contagious disease control often provided the authorities with a pretext for politically repressive crowd control, prohibiting demonstrations and disbanding public meetings. Since times of peak mortality often coincided with periods of acute grain shortage, emergency public health measures, and the extraordinary powers which they conferred upon the police, were useful in quelling bread riots and nipping various forms of insurgency in the bud: Louise Tilly, 'The Food Riot as a Form of Political Conflict in France', *Journal of Interdisciplinary History,* vol. 1 (1971), pp. 23–57.

304. Kunitz, 'Speculations on the European Mortality Decline', p. 354.

305. Samuel H. Preston and Etienne van de Walle, 'Urban French Mortality in the Nineteenth Century', *Population Studies,* vol. 32 (1978), pp. 275–97; Robert Woods and P. R. Andrew Hinde, 'Mortality in Victorian England: Models and Patterns', *Journal of Interdisciplinary History,* vol. 18 (1987), p. 53.

306. McNeill, *Plagues and Peoples,* p. 212.

307. E. M. Sigworth, 'Gateways to Death? Medicine, Hospitals and Mortality, 1700–1850', in P. Mathias, ed., *Science and Society, 1600–1900* (Cambridge, 1972); John Woodward, *'To Do the Sick No Harm': A Study of the British Voluntary Hospital System to 1875* (London, 1974); S. Cherry, 'The Hospitals and Population Growth: The Voluntary General Hospitals, Mortality and Local Populations in the English Provinces in the Eighteenth and Nineteenth Centuries' [in two parts], *Population Studies,* vol. 34 (1980), pp. 59–75, 251–65; Anders Brändström and Goran Brostrom, 'Life-Histories for Nineteenth-Century Swedish Hospital Patients: Chances of Survival' (unpublished MS, 1988).

308. E. A. Wrigley, 'The Growth of Population in Eighteenth Century England: A Conundrum Resolved', *Past & Present,* no. 98 (1983), p. 131.

309. Wrigley and Schofield, *The Population History of England,* p. 529. Surprisingly, the proportion never marrying grew in the same period, and a concomitant rise in birth outside marriage was not sufficient to offset this. In the meantime, marital fertility remained remarkably stable in England throughout the demographically revolutionary eighteenth century: Wrigley, 'Marriage, Fertility and Population Growth in Eighteenth-Century England', in R. B. Outhwaite, ed., *Marriage and Society* (New York, 1981), p. 145.

310. 'The Population and Economy of the Preindustrial Netherlands', *Journal of Interdisciplinary History,* vol. 15 (1985), p. 664.

311.   W. R. Lee, *European Demography and Economic Growth* (London, 1979), pp. 14–15.

312.   The thesis that English population expansion in the Industrial Revolution was fertility-led and marriage-driven had earlier proponents, most notably Habakkuk and Krause: cf. H. J. Habakkuk, 'English Population in the Eighteenth Century', *Economic History Review*, vol. 6 (1953), pp. 117–33; J. T. Krause, 'Some Neglected Factors in the English Industrial Revolution', *Journal of Economic History*, vol. 19 (1959), pp. 528–40. But their contributions were effectively submerged in the 1960s and 1970s by the preponderant consensus forged by the proponents of declining mortality as the prime mover: Michael W. Flinn, *British Population Growth, 1700–1850* (London, 1970); Thomas McKeown, *The Modern Rise of Population* (London, 1976).

313.   Dupâquier, *La Population française*, p. 98; David Weir, 'Fertility Transition in Rural France, 1740–1829', *Journal of Economy History*, vol. 44 (1984), p. 32.

314.   The early descent of *marital* fertility in France is indeed unique, but the decline of the French *birth rate* was not unprecedented, nor even the steepest. The crude birth rate in Finland fell from a very high 46 (live births per 1000 population per year) in 1755 to a trough of 32 in 1825: O. Turpeinen, 'Fertility and Mortality in Finland since 1750', *Population Studies*, vol. 33 (1979), p. 102. It would be useful to compare the socioeconomic and cultural circumstances of the French and Finnish descents. If this has been done, I am not aware of it. A Gallic conceit concerning 'the uniqueness of the French experience' seems to have retarded intellectual advance. Such ethnocentric vanity is sustained on both sides of the English Channel, furnishing a convenient foil for 'the uniqueness of the English experience'. The history of every society is unique, of course, as is the history of every region, village, family and person. How could it be otherwise? Fuelled by parochial nationalism, steeped in the cognitive universe of bourgeois individualism, this endless insistence on the peculiarity of a phenomenon, its difference from every other, is the bane of theoretically informed history. A militant internationalism, rigorously comparative, is required here, as elsewhere.

315.   Wrigley, 'Marriage, Fertility and Population Growth in Eighteenth-Century England', in R. B. Outhwaite, ed., *Marriage and Society*, p. 177.

316.   Louis Henry and Jacques Houdaille, 'Célibat et âge au mariage aux XVIIIᵉ et XIXᵉ siècles en France', *Population*, vol. 34 (1979), p. 412; Wrigley, 'The Fall of Marital Fertility in Nineteenth Century France: Exemplar or Exception?', *European Journal of Population*, vol. 1 (1985), p. 42.

317.   Wrigley and Schofield, *The Population History of England*, p. 247.

318.   Michael Drake, *Population and Society in Norway, 1735–1865* (Cambridge, 1969), pp. 44.

319.   Otto Anderson, *The Population of Denmark* (New York, 1977), p. 14.

320.   Allan Sharlin, 'Urban–Rural Differences in Fertility in Europe during the Demographic Transition', in Ansley Coale and Susan Watkins, eds, *The Decline of Fertility in Europe* (Princeton, 1986), p. 257.,

321.   The epistemological naturalism of many studies in historical demography is related to the discourse on 'natural fertility'. If the birth rate remains stable over time, its persistence requires no explanation beyond that which was given for its past amplitude. Complacent assumptions of this sort, drawing on a fallacious analogy with physical laws of inertia and momentum, are misleading here, as they invariably are in the social sciences.

322.   *The State of Population Theory* (Oxford, 1986), p. 1.

323.   De Vries, *European Urbanization*, p. 39.

324.   Ibid., pp. 231–7; Adna F. Weber, *The Growth of Cities* (Ithaca, 1899), pp. 236–40.

325.   De Vries, *European Urbanization*, p. 194.

326.   J. D. Chambers, *Population, Economy and Society in Pre-Industrial England* (Oxford, 1972), p. 64.

327.   Lawton, 'Population and Society, 1730–1900', p. 42.

328.   E. A. Wrigley, *Industrial Growth and Population Change* (Cambridge, 1961), p. 141.

329.   Staff of the Institute of Social Sciences, Stockholm University, *Population Movements and Industrialization: Swedish Counties, 1895–1930* (Stockholm, n.d.) p. 330.

330.   Medick, 'The Structures and Function of Population Development under the

Proto-industrial System', p. 84.

331. De Vries, *European Urbanization*, pp. 206–7.

332. Flinn, *The European Demographic System*, pp. 124–7; Wrigley, 'The Fall of Marital Fertility in Nineteenth Century France', p. 46; Erlund Hofsten and Hans Lundström, *Swedish Population History: Main Trends from 1750 to 1950* (Stockholm, 1976).

333. The following scholars have advanced some version of the proletarianization – relatively high birth rate thesis (for most, through the mediation of proto-industrialization): J. C. Benavente, 'Structural Transformation and Early Fertility Decline: The Case of Catalonia', paper presented at the Population Association of America, 1984; Rudolph Braun, 'Protoindustrialization and Demographic Change in the Canton of Zurich'; Jonathan Chambers, *Population, Economy and Society in Pre-Industrial England*; Pierre Deyon, 'La Diffusion rurale des industries textiles en Flandre française à la fin de l'Ancien Régime et au début du XIXᵉ siècle', *Revue du nord*, vol. 61 (1979), pp. 83–96; Wolfram Fischer, 'Rural Industrialization and Population Change'; Peter Kriedte, *Peasants, Landlords and Merchant Capitalists*; David Levine, *Family Formation in an Age of Nascent Capitalism*; Ovar Löfgren, 'The Potato People'; Hans Medick, 'The Structures and Function of Population Development under the Proto-industrial System'; Franklin Mendels, 'Proto-industrialization: The First Phase of the Industrialization Process'; Charles Tilly, 'Demographic Origins of the European Proletariat'; Louise Tilly and Joan Scott, *Women, Work and Family*. Most of the discussion has fixated on the proto-industrial stream within the great proletarian conflux – on cottage industry, especially textiles. Yet this was one of several proletarian wellsprings; there needs to be more study of others. Making extensive use of comparative materials, Michael Haines has documented very similar patterns (of early and universal marriage, high fertility and rapid population growth) in mining districts in the nineteenth and early twentieth centuries: *Fertility and Occupation: Population Patterns in the Past* (New York, 1979).

334. The list of naysayers is equally impressive: Michael Drake, *Population and Society in Norway;* John Knodel, *Demographic Behaviour in the Past: A Study of Fourteen German Village Populations in the Eighteenth and Nineteenth Centuries* (Cambridge, 1988); N. W. Mogensen, 'Structures et changements démographiques dans vingt paroisses normandes sous l'Ancien Régime', in *Annales de démographie historique* (1975); Thomas Nilsson, Hans Norman and John Rogers, 'Family Building and Family Planning in Pre-industrial Sweden', in John Rogers, ed., *Family Building and Family Planning in Pre-industrial Societies* (Uppsala, 1980); Roger Schofield, 'English Marriage Patterns Revisited', *Journal of Family History*, vol. 10 (1985), pp. 2–20; C. Winberg, 'Population Growth and Proletarianization: The Transformation of Social Structures in Rural Sweden during the Agrarian Revolution', in S. Åkerman, H. Johansen, and D. Gaunt, eds, *Chance and Change*; and E. A. Wrigley, 'The Growth of Population in Eighteenth Century England: A Conundrum Resolved', *Past & Present*, no. 98 (1983) pp. 121–50.

335. Haines, *Fertility and Occupation*; John Knodel and Mary Jo Maynes, 'Urban and Rural Marriage Patterns in Imperial Germany', *Journal of Family History*, vol. 1 (1976), p. 156.

336. M. Anderson, 'Marriage Patterns in Victorian Britain', *Journal of Family History*, vol. 1 (1976), p. 76.

337. R. I. Woods and P. R. A. Hinde, 'Nuptiality and Age at Marriage in Nineteenth-Century England', *Journal of Family History*, vol. 10 (1985), pp. 119–44; Knodel and Maynes, 'Urban and Rural Marriage Patterns in Imperial Germany', pp. 156–7.

338. Johanna Brenner and Maria Ramas, 'Rethinking Women's Oppression', *New Left Review*, no. 144 (1984), pp. 33–71.

339. I made this mistake in 'Marxism and Demography', *New Left Review*, no. 137 (1983), pp. 22–47.

340. An increased incidence of premarital sex has an indeterminate effect on the marriage rate; it certainly does not consistently promote earlier marriage. The rise of premarital sex and its association with proletarianization will be examined below.

341. Louise Tilly, Joan Scott and Miriam Cohen, 'Women's Work and European Fertility Patterns', *Journal of Interdisciplinary History*, vol. 6 (1976), p. 464.

342. *An Essay on the Principle of Population*, p. 237.

343. Michael Haines has documented this tendency for miners and metalworkers in the nineteenth century: *Fertility and Occupation*. Marx tied the tendency of industrial workers to marry early directly to capital's voracious consumption of labour-power in the initial stage of industrialization: 'The consumption of labour-power by capital is so rapid that the worker has already more or less completely lived himself out when he is only half-way through his life. ... The absolute increase of this section of the proletariat must take a form which swells their numbers, despite the rapid wastage of their individual elements. Hence, rapid replacement of one generation of workers by another. ... This social requirement is met by early marriages, which are a necessary consequence of the condition in which workers in large-scale industry live, and by the premium that the exploitation of the workers' children sets on their production': *Capital*, vol. 1, p. 795.

344. Wrigley, 'Marriage, Fertility and Population Growth in Eighteenth-Century England', p. 157; Yves Blayo, 'Illegitimate Births in France from 1740 to 1829 and in the 1960s', in Laslett, Oosterveen and Smith, eds, *Bastardy and Its Comparative History*, p. 282; Hofsten and Lundström, *Swedish Population History*, table 2.4; Flinn, *The European Demographic System*, pp. 119–20; Edward Shorter, *The Making of the Modern Family*, pp. 332–6.

345. In England, Hardwick's Marriage Act of 1753 made an official church wedding necessary for marriage. Thereafter, parish clerks were less inclined to grant legitimacy to the children of consensual unions: Roy Porter, *English Society in the Eighteenth Century* (Harmondsworth, 1982), p. 164. This factor alone undoubtedly raised the English bastardy rate in the second half of the eighteenth century, though we should not infer that the entire increase was an artifact of altered recording practices. On the conceptual plane, Richard Smith has quite correctly warned of the pitfalls of treating the legitimate–illegitimate distinction in an overly dichotomous way. He writes of 'a gradient of situations ranging from celibacy ... through free union and consensual union, to customary, religious and civil marriage': 'Marriage Processes in the English Past: Some Continuities', in Bonfield, Smith and Wrightson, eds, *The World We Have Gained* (Oxford, 1986), p. 44.

346. Peter Laslett, 'Introduction: Comparing Illegitimacy over Time and between Cultures', in Laslett, Oosterveen and Smith, eds, *Bastardy and Its Comparative History*, p. 40. There is no uniform legal standard concerning the status of marriage in Christian Europe, nor are parish recording practices necessarily commensurate. The classification of illegitimate and legitimate births must therefore be blurred about the line of demarcation. Comparisons between states of the sort being made here should be treated circumspectly. On the assumption that changes over time in a locality's legal codes and recording practices are likely to have less effect on such compilations than differences between places, I regard comparisons between trends over a given period to be more reliable than comparisons of absolute values at any point in time. Consequently, I have emphasized diachronic contrasts in this discussion.

347. Ibid., p. 38.

348. Laslett, *The World We Have Lost* (London, 1971), p. 137.

349. Michael Drake, *Population and Society in Norway,*; see also 'Norway', in W. R. Lee, ed., *European Demography and Economic Growth* (London, 1979), pp. 305–6.

350. Laslett, 'Introduction: Comparing Illegitimacy', pp. 31–40.

351. Martine Segalen, *Historical Anthropology of the Family* (Cambridge, 1986), p. 131.

352. Solvi Songer, '"A Prudent Wife Is from the Lord": The Married Peasant Woman of the Eighteenth Century in a Demographic Perspective', *Scandinavian Journal of History*, vol. 9 (1984), p.121.

353. Jonas Frykman, 'Sexual Intercourse and Social Norms: A Study of Illegitimate Births in Sweden, 1831–1933', in *Ethnologia Scandinavica*, (1975), pp. 111–50; Ingrid Eriksson and John Rogers, *Rural Labour and Population Change* (Stockholm, 1978), p. 121.

354. Karla Oosterveen and Richard Smith, 'Bastardy and the Family Constitution Studies of Colyton, Aldenham, Alcester and Hawkshead', in Laslett, Oosterveen and Smith, eds, *Bastardy and Its Comparative History* (Cambridge, Mass., 1980); Flandrin, *Families in Former Times*, p. 215. See also S. Stewart, 'Bastardy and the Family Constitution Studies of Banbury and Hartland', in Laslett, Oosterveen and Smith, eds, *Bastardy and Its Comparative History*.

355. John Gillis, 'Peasant, Plebeian and Proletarian Marriage in Britain, 1600–1900', in D. Levine, ed., *Proletarianization and Family History* (New York, 1984).

356. Ibid., p. 141.

357. Shorter, *The Making of the Modern Family*, p. 95.

358. John Gillis, *Youth and History: Tradition and Change in European Age Relations, 1770–Present* (New York, 1981), p. 46.

359. Medick, 'The Proto-industrial Family Economy', p. 64.

360. Shorter, *The Making of the Modern Family*, pp. 260–61, original emphasis.

361. 'Women's Work and European Fertility Patterns', *Journal of Interdisciplinary History*, vol. 6 (1976), pp. 447–76.

362. Songer reached a similar conclusion on the basis of a national sample of rural Norway conducted in 1801: 'The illegitimate children were born of parents acting in harmony with the norms of rural society. They were the outcome of a general youth culture, which had prenuptial sexuality as an important element. The abnormality of the situation was that a prenuptial conception did not result in a wedding but in an illegitimate birth': '"A Prudent Wife Is from the Lord"', p. 121.

363. Wrigley, 'Marriage, Fertility and Population Growth', p. 157.

364. Ibid., p. 181.

365. Flinn, *The European Demographic System*, pp. 122–3.

366. Wrigley, 'Marriage, Fertility and Population Growth', p. 162.

367. *Demographic Behaviour in the Past: A Study of Fourteen German Village Populations*, p. 221.

368. Unfortunately, Shorter insisted on burdening his core argument for an increase in premarital intercourse with heavy breathing about 'a surge of sentiment' which blew across Europe towards the end of the eighteenth century in a gale of randy romance. This idealist dross has been justly dismissed, but his basic thesis was empirically supported with extensive documentation and deserves serious consideration on its merits.

369. *Demographic Behaviour in the Past*, p. 221.

370. Derived from Wrigley, 'Marriage, Fertility and Population Growth', p. 157.

371. L. A. Clarkson, *Proto-industrialization: The First Phase of Industrialization?* (London, 1985), p. 31.

Chapter 4

1. Peter Laslett, *Household and Family in Past Time* (Cambridge, 1972), p. 48.

2. 'Regional and Temporal Variations in English Household Structure from 1650', in John Hobcraft and Philip Rees, eds, *Regional Demographic Development* (London, 1977), p. 109.

3. 'The Household: Demographic and Economic Change in England, 1650–1970', in Wall, ed., *Family Forms in Historic Europe* (Cambridge, 1983), p. 501.

4. Laslett has recently acknowledged that the widespread reiteration of this taxonomic procedure by historians, as if it furnished by itself an adequate and rounded picture of family structures, 'may have stood in the way of more searching comparisons, better modelling, more penetrating analysis': 'The Character of Familial History, Its Limitations and Proper Pursuit', in Tamara Hareven and Andrejs Plakans, eds, *Family History at the Crossroads* (Princeton, 1987), p. 280. With this admission, one can readily concur.

5. *The American Family: A Demographic History* (Beverly Hills, 1978), pp. 178–9.

6. Laslett complains that through a misreading of his Introduction to *Household and Family in Past Time*, the Cambridge paradigm 'became associated with a static approach to the analysis of the family', while admitting that 'there has been an unwillingness to face problems of systematic familial change.' Recognizing that historians adopting a family-cycle perspective have been more inclined to foreground elements of change, he contends that 'the actual definition of a family cycle ... presents excessively difficult problems' and the mustering of comparable evidence in this framework may 'turn out to be a virtually un-

realizable historical project': 'The Character of Familial History', pp. 275–6. With unwarranted pessimism, Laslett, in effect, dismisses the tremendous gains that have been achieved in the past decade by social historians utilizing family-cycle and life-course approaches.

7. He has recently complained that this Introduction was horribly misunderstood, blaming his audience for being statistical illiterates who failed to grasp his analogous use of the null hypothesis (that all households ought to be presumed to be nuclear unless proved otherwise): 'The Character of Familial History', pp. 277–81. The author's mistake, we are assured, was to overestimate his readers. 'Family historians were not up to it in the 1970s, and this still unfortunately seems to be the case': Ibid., p. 279.

8. Tamara Hareven, a prominent critic of Laslett's conception of family structure, none the less accepts the nuclear family continuity thesis and in doing so reverts to the co-residence paradigm: 'The myth about the existence of a three-generation extended *family* in the pre-industrial past ... was exploded by demonstrating that the nuclear *household* had been the dominant pre-industrial form of *family* organization and that *it* had experienced a continuity in Western society at least for the past two centuries': *Family Time and Industrial Time* (Cambridge, 1982), p. 2 (emphasis added). Note the conceptual slippage back and forth between family and household; the Cambridge studies are replete with this conflation. To what, then, does 'it' refer in the above passage – the entity that is ostensibly continuous through the ages? The referent is the household; family is thus reduced to co-resident kin.

9. Peter Laslett, 'The European Family and Early Industrialization', in J. Baechler, J. A. Hall and M. Mann, eds, *Europe and the Rise of Capitalism* (London, 1988), p. 235.

10. John Hajnal, 'European Marriage Patterns in Perspective', in D. V. Glass and D. E. C. Eversley, eds, *Population in History: Essays in Demographic History* (London, 1965); P. Ogden, 'Marriage Patterns and Population Mobility: A Study of Rural France', Research Paper no. 7, School of Geography, Oxford University, 1973; H. J. Habakkuk, *Population Growth and Economic Development* (Leicester, 1971).

11. Laslett, 'The Family and Industrialization: A "Strong Theory"', unpublished paper for the Bad Homburg Symposium, 1975.

12. John Gillis, *For Better, For Worse: British Marriages, 1600 to the Present* (New York, 1985), p. 219; Louis Chevalier, *Laboring Classes and Dangerous Classes in Paris during the First Half of the Nineteenth Century* (Princeton, 1973), pp. 311–13. See also Lenard Berlanstein, 'Illegitimacy, Concubinage and Proletarianization in a French Town, 1760–1914', *Journal of Family History,* vol. 5, no. 3 (1980), p. 370; Knodel *Demographic Behaviour in the Past: A Study of Fourteen German Village Populations in the Eighteenth and Nineteenth Centuries* (Cambridge, 1988), pp. 220–21.

13. Michèle Barrett and Mary McIntosh, *The Anti-social Family* (London, 1982).

14. Olwen Hufton, 'Women, Work and Marriage in Eighteenth Century France', in R. B. Outhwaite, ed., *Marriage and Society* (New York, 1981), p. 189.

15. John Knodel and Katherine Lynch, 'The Decline of Remarriage: Evidence from German Village Populations in the Eighteenth and Nineteenth Centuries', *Journal of Family History,* vol. 10 (1985), pp. 34–59; E. A. Wrigley and R. Schofield, *The Population History of England, 1541–1871: A Reconsideration,* p. 212.

Appendix

1. T. H. Aston and C. H. E. Philpin, eds, *The Brenner Debate: Agrarian Class Structure and Economic Development in Pre-Industrial Europe* (Cambridge, 1985).

2. Ellen Wood, in vehement response to one such note in a draft of this text, persuaded me that I must address these issues more adequately. I thank her for taking issue, though it is doubtful that my perspective will be to her liking.

3. *The Brenner Debate,* p. 327.

4. Ibid., p. 24.

5. J. Dupâquier, *La Population française aux XVIIᵉ et XVIIIᵉ siècles* (Paris: Presses Universitaires de France, 1979), pp. 9–11; E. A. Wrigley and R. Schofield, *The Population History*

of England, 1541–1871 (London, 1981), pp. 528–9.

6. D. Weir, 'Fertility Transition in Rural France, 1740–1829', *Journal of Economic History*, vol. 44, no. 2 (1984), p. 32.

7. M. W. Flinn, *The European Demographic System, 1500–1800* (Brighton, 1981), pp. 103–5, 130.

8. Wrigley and Schofield, *The Population History of England*, p. 451; Flinn, *The European Demographic System*, pp. 103–5.

9. G. Bois, *The Crisis of Feudalism: Economy and Society in Eastern Normandy, 1300–1550* (Cambridge, 1984), pp. 370–71; D. B. Grigg, *Population Growth and Agrarian Change* (Cambridge, 1980), p. 113.

10. Louis Henry and Didier Blanchet, 'La Population de l'Angleterre de 1541 à 1871', *Population*, vol. 38 (1983), p. 795.

Bibliography

Abel, W. *Agricultural Fluctuations in Europe*. New York: Methuen, 1980.

Åkerman, S., Johansen, H. C. and Gaunt, D., eds, *Chance and Change: Social and Economic Studies in Historical Demography in the Baltic Area*. Odense: Odense University Press, 1978.

Alfoldy, G. *The Social History of Rome*. London: Croom Helm, 1985.

Almquist, E. L. 'Pre-famine Ireland and the Theory of European Proto-industrialization: Evidence from the 1841 Census'. *Journal of Economic History*, vol. 39, no. 3, 1979, pp. 699–718.

Amussen, S. D. 'Gender, Family and Social Order, 1560–1725'. In A. Fletcher and J. Stevenson, eds, *Order and Disorder in Early Modern England*. Cambridge: Cambridge University Press, 1985.

Anderson, M. 'Marriage Patterns in Victorian Britain'. *Journal of Family History*, vol. 1, 1976, pp. 55–78.

———. *Approaches to the History of the Western Family, 1500–1914*. London: Macmillan, 1980.

———. *Population Change in North-Western Europe, 1750–1850*. London: Macmillan, 1988.

Anderson, O. *The Population of Denmark*. New York: Cicred, UN, 1977.

Anderson, P. *Lineages of the Absolutist State*. London: Verso, 1974.

———. *Passages from Antiquity to Feudalism*. London: Verso, 1974.

Ankarloo, B. 'Agriculture and Women's Work: Directions of Change in the West, 1700–1900'. *Journal of Family History*, vol. 4, no. 2, 1979, pp. 111–20.

Appleby, A. 'The Disappearance of Plague: A Continuing Puzzle'. *Economic History Review*, 2nd ser., vol. 33, no. 2, 1980, pp. 161–73.

Ariès, P. *Centuries of Childhood, A Social History of the Family*. London: Cape, 1962.

Armengaud, A. *La Population française au XIXe siècle*. Paris: Presses Universitaires de France, 1971.

———. 'Population in Europe, 1700–1914'. In Carlo M. Cipolla, ed., *Fontana Economic History of Europe*, vol. 3. New York: Fontana, 1973.

Aston, T. H. and Philpin, C. H. E., eds, *The Brenner Debate: Agrarian Class Structure and Economic Development in Pre-industrial Europe*. Cambridge: Cambridge University Press, 1985.

Aymard, M. *Dutch Capitalism and World Capitalism*. New York: Cambridge University Press, 1982.

Badinter, E. *Mother Love: Myth and Reality*. New York: Macmillan, 1981.

Barnes, J. A. 'Land Rights and Kinship Rights in Two Brennes Hamlets'. *Journal of the Royal Anthropological Institute*, vol. 87, 1957, pp. 31–56.

Barrett, M. *Women's Oppression Today: Problems in Marxist Feminist Analysis*. London: Verso, 1980.

Barrett, M. and McIntosh, M. *The Anti-social Family*. London: Verso, 1982.

Becker, G. *A Treatise on the Family*. Cambridge, Mass.: Harvard University Press, 1981.

Beechey, V. 'On Patriarchy'. *Feminist Review*, vol. 9, 1979, pp. 66–82.

Benavente, J. C. 'Structural Transformation and Early Fertility Decline: The Case of Catalonia'. Paper presented at the Population Association of America, 1984.

Bennett, H. S. *Life on the English Manor: A Study of Peasant Conditions, 1150–1400*. Cambridge: Cambridge University Press, 1937.

Bennett, J. M. 'Medieval Peasant Marriage: An Examination of Marriage License Fines in Liber Gersumarum'. In J. A. Raftis, ed., *Pathways to Medieval Peasants*. Toronto: Pontifical Institute of Medieval Studies, 1981.

———. 'The Tie That Binds: Peasant Marriages and Peasant Families in Late Medieval England'. *Journal of Interdisciplinary History*, vol. 15, no. 1, 1984, pp. 111–29.

———. '"History That Stands Still": Women's Work in the European Past'. *Feminist Studies*, vol. 14, no. 2, 1988, pp. 269–83.

Beresford, M. W. *The Lost Villages of England*. London: Lutterworth Press, 1954.

Berg, M. *The Age of Manufactures, 1700–1820*. London: Fontana, 1985.

———. 'Women's Work, Mechanization and the Early Phases of Industrialization in England'. In P. Joyce, ed., *The Historical Meanings of Work*. Cambridge: Cambridge University Press, 1987.

Berg, M., Hudson, P. and Sonenscher, M. *Manufacture in Town and Country before the Factory*. Cambridge: Cambridge University Press, 1983.

Berger, B. and Berger, P. *The War over the Family: Capturing the Middle Ground*. New York: Anchor Doubleday, 1984.

Berkner, L. K. 'The Stem Family and the Developmental Cycle of the Peasant Household: An Eighteenth Century Austrian Example'. *American Historical Review*, vol. 77, 1972, pp. 398–418.

———. 'The Use and Misuse of Census Data for the Historical Analysis of Family Structure'. *Journal of Interdisciplinary History*, vol. 5, no. 4, 1975, pp. 721–38.

———. 'Inheritance, Land Tenure and Peasant Family Structure: A German Regional Comparison'. In J. Goody, J. Thirsk and E. P. Thompson, eds, *Family and Inheritance, Rural Society in Western Europe, 1200–1800*. Cambridge: Cambridge University Press, 1976.

Berkner, L. K. and Mendels, F. F. 'Inheritance Systems, Family Structure and Demographic Patterns in Western Europe, 1700–1900'. In C. Tilly, ed., *Historical Studies of Changing Fertility*. Princeton, N.J.: Princeton University Press, 1978.

Berlanstein, L. 'Illegitimacy, Concubinage and Proletarianization in a French Town, 1760–1914'. *Journal of Family History*, vol. 5, no. 3, 1980, pp. 360–74.

Bideau, A. 'A Demographic and Social Analysis of Widowhood and Remarriage: The Examples of the Castellany of Thoissey-en-Dombes, 1670–1840.' *Journal of Family History*, vol. 5, 1980, pp. 28–43.

Biller, P. P. A. 'Birth Control in the West in the Thirteenth and Early Fourteenth Centuries'. *Past & Present*, no. 94, 1982, 3–26.

Biraben, J. N. 'Essai sur l'evolution du nombre des hommes'. *Population*, vol. 34, no. 1, 1979, pp. 13–25.

Blanchard, I. 'Population Change, Enclosure and the Early Tudor Economy'. *Economic History Review*, 2nd ser., vol. 23, 1970, pp. 427–45.

———. 'Industrial Employment and the Rural Land Market, 1380–1520'. In R. M. Smith, ed., *Land, Kinship and Life-Cycle*. Cambridge: Cambridge University Press, 1984.

Blayo, Y. 'Illegitimate Births in France from 1740 to 1829 and in the 1960's'. In P. Laslett, K. Oosterveen and R. Smith, eds, *Bastardy and Its Comparative History*. Cambridge, Mass.: Harvard University Press, 1980.

Bloch, M. *Feudal Society*, vols. 1 & 2, L. A. Manyon, trans. Chicago: University of Chicago Press, 1961.

———. *French Rural History*. London: Routledge & Kegan Paul, 1966.

———. 'The Rise of Dependent Cultivation and Seignorial Institutions'. In M. M. Postan, ed., *The Cambridge Economic History of Europe*, vol. 1. Cambridge: Cambridge University Press, 1966.

———. *Slavery and Serfdom in the Middle Ages*. Berkeley: University of California Press, 1975.

Blum, J. *Lord and Peasant in Russia from the Ninth to the Nineteenth Century*. Princeton, N.J.: Princeton University Press, 1961.

———. *The End of the Old Order in Rural Europe*. Princeton, N.J.: Princeton University Press,

1978.

Blumberg, R. M. *Stratification: Socio-economic and Sexual Inequality*. Dubuque, Iowa: Wm. C. Brown, 1978.

Bois, G. 'Against the Neo-Malthusian Orthodoxy'. *Past & Present*, no. 79, 1978, pp. 60–69. Repr. in T. H. Aston and C. H. E. Philpin, eds, *The Brenner Debate: Agrarian Class Structure and Economic Development in Pre-industrial Europe*. Cambridge: Cambridge University Press, 1985.

———. *The Crisis of Feudalism: Economy and Society in Eastern Normandy, 1300–1550*. Cambridge: Cambridge University Press, 1984.

von Bohm-Bawerk, E. *Karl Marx and the Close of His System*. New York: A. M. Kelley, 1949 [1896].

Bonfield, L. 'Normative Rules and Property Transmission: Reflections on the Link between Marriage and Inheritance in Early Modern England'. In L. Bonfield, R. M. Smith and K. Wrightson, eds, *The World We Have Gained*. Oxford: Basil Blackwell, 1986.

Bonfield, L., Smith, R. M. and Wrightson, K. *The World We Have Gained*. Oxford: Basil Blackwell, 1986.

Boserup, E. *Women's Role in Economic Development*. New York: St. Martin's Press, 1970.

———. *Population and Technological Change: A Study of Long-Term Trends*. Chicago: University of Chicago Press, 1981.

Bossy, J. 'Blood and Baptism: Kinship, Community and Christianity in Western Europe from the Fourteenth to the Seventeenth Centuries'. In D. Baker, ed., *Sanctity and Secularity: The Church and the World*. Cambridge: Cambridge University Press, 1973.

———. *Christianity in the West, 1400–1700*. Oxford: Oxford University Press, 1985.

Bouchard, G. 'L'Etude des structures familiales pré-industrielles: Pour un renversement des perspectives'. *Revue d'histoire moderne et contemporaine*, vol. 28, 1981, pp. 545–71.

Bourdieu, P. 'Marriage Strategies as Strategies of Social Reproduction'. In R. Forster and O. Ranum, eds, *Family and Society: Selections from the Annales*. Baltimore: Johns Hopkins University Press, 1976.

Bowden, P. 'Agricultural Prices, Wages, Farm Profits and Rents'. In J. Thirsk, ed., *The Agrarian History of England and Wales*, vol. 5, pt 2. Cambridge: Cambridge University Press, 1985.

Bowles, S. 'The Production Process in a Competitive Economy: Walrasian, Neo-Hobbesian and Marxian Models'. *American Economic Review*, vol. 75, no. 1, 1985, pp. 16–35.

Bradley, K. R. *Slaves and Masters in the Roman Empire*. New York: Oxford University Press, 1987.

Brändström, A. and Broström, G. 'Life-Histories for Nineteenth-Century Swedish Hospital Patients: Chances of Survival' (unpublished MS, 1988).

Braudel, F. *Capitalism and Material Life, 1400–1800*. New York: Harper Colophon, 1973.

———. *Civilization and Capitalism, 15th–18th Century*. Vol. 1 of *The Structures of Everyday Life*. London: Fontana, 1985.

Braun, R. 'Protoindustrialization and Demographic Changes in the Canton of Zurich'. In C. Tilly, ed., *Historical Studies of Changing Fertility*. Princeton, N.J.: Princeton University Press, 1978.

Brennan, E. R., James, A. V. and Morrill, W. T. 'Inheritance, Demographic Structure and Marriage: A Cross-cultural Perspective'. *Journal of Family History*, vol. 7, no. 3, 1982, pp. 289–98.

Brenner, J. and Ramas, M. 'Rethinking Women's Oppression'. *New Left Review*, no. 144, 1984, pp. 33–71.

Brenner, R. 'Agrarian Class Structure and Economic Development in Pre-industrial Europe'. *Past & Present*, no. 70, 1976, pp. 30–75. Repr. in T. H. Aston and C. H. E. Philpin, eds, *The Brenner Debate: Agrarian Class Structure and Economic Development in Pre-industrial Europe*. Cambridge: Cambridge University Press, 1985.

———. 'The Agrarian Roots of European Capitalism'. *Past & Present*, no. 97, 1982, pp.

16–113. Repr. in T. H. Aston and C. H. E. Philpin, eds, *The Brenner Debate: Agrarian Class Structure and Economic Development in Pre-industrial Europe*. Cambridge: Cambridge University Press, 1985.

Britton, E. *Community of the Vill: A Study of the History of the Family and Village Life in Fourteenth Century England*. Toronto: Macmillan, 1977.

Brodsky, V. 'Widows in Late Elizabethan London: Remarriage, Economic Opportunity and Family Orientations'. In L. Bonfield, R. M. Smith and K. Wrightson, eds, *The World We Have Gained*. Oxford: Basil Blackwell, 1986.

Brooke, C. N. L. *Marriage in Christian History*. Cambridge: Cambridge University Press, 1978.

Brown, C. 'Mothers, Fathers and Children: From Private to Public Patriarchy'. In L. Sargent, ed., *Women and Revolution: A Discussion of the Unhappy Marriage of Marxism and Feminism*. London: Pluto Press, 1981.

Brown, P. *The Body and Society: Men, Women and Sexual Renunciation in Early Christianity*. New York: Columbia University Press, 1988.

Brundage, J. *Law, Sex and Christian Society in Medieval Europe*. Chicago: University of Chicago Press, 1987.

Brunt, P. A. *Italian Manpower, 225 BC – AD 14*. Oxford: Oxford University Press, 1971.

Bryceson, D. and Vuorela, U. 'Outside the Domestic Labor Debate: Towards a Theory of Modes of Human Reproduction'. *Review of Radical Political Economy*, vol. 16, nos 2/3, 1984, pp. 137–66.

Bullough, D. A. 'Early Medieval Social Groupings: The Terminology of Kinship'. *Past & Present*, no. 45, 1969, pp. 3–18.

Burguière, A. 'From Malthus to Max Weber: Belated Marriage and the Spirit of Enterprise'. In R. Forster and O. Ranum, eds, *Family and Society: Selections from the Annales*. Baltimore: Johns Hopkins University Press, 1976.

Burstyn, V. 'Masculine Dominance and the State'. *In R. Miliband and J. Saville, eds, Socialist Register*, London: Merlin Press, 1983.

Butlin, R. A. *The Transformation of Rural England, C. 1580–1800*. New York: Oxford University Press, 1982.

Campbell, B. 'Population Pressure, Inheritance and the Land Market in a Fourteenth Century Peasant Community'. In R. M. Smith, ed., *Land, Kinship and Life-Cycle*. Cambridge: Cambridge University Press, 1984.

Casey, K. 'The Cheshire Cat: Reconstructing the Experience of Medieval Women'. In B. A. Carroll, ed., *Liberating Women's History: Theoretical and Critical Essays*. Chicago: University of Chicago Press, 1976.

Caspard, P. 'Conceptions prénuptiales et développement du capitalisme dans la Principauté de Neuchâtel (1678–1820)'. *Annales: Economies, sociétés, civilisations*, vol. 29, no. 4, 1974, pp. 989–1009.

Chambers, J. D. *Population, Economy and Society in Pre-Industrial England*. Oxford: Oxford University Press, 1972.

Chapelot, J. and Fossier, R. *The Village and House in the Middle Ages*. London: Batsford, 1985.

Charles, L. and Duffin, L. *Women and Work in Pre-Industrial England*. London: Croom Helm, 1985.

Charles-Edwards, T. M. 'Kinship, Status and the Origins of the Hide'. *Past & Present*, no. 56, 1972, pp. 3–33.

Chaytor, M. 'Household and Kinship: Ryton in the Late Sixteenth and Early Seventeenth Centuries'. *History Workshop Journal*, no. 10, 1980, pp. 25–60.

Cherry, S. 'The Hospitals and Population Growth: The Voluntary General Hospitals, Mortality and Local Populations in the English Provinces in the Eighteenth and Nineteenth Centuries'. *Population Studies* (in two parts), vol. 34, no. 1, 1980, pp. 59–75; vol. 34, no. 2, 1980, pp. 251–65.

Chevalier, L. *Laboring Classes and Dangerous Classes in Paris during the First Half of the Nineteenth Century*. Princeton, N.J.: Princeton University Press, 1973.

Chodorow, N. *The Reproduction of Mothering: Psychoanalysis and the Sociology of Gender.* Berkeley: University of California Press, 1978.

Christiansen, P. O. 'The Household in the Local Setting: A Study of Peasant Stratification'. In S. Åkerman, H. C. Johansen and D. Gaunt, eds, *Chance and Change: Social and Economic Studies in Historical Demography in the Baltic Area.* Odense: Odense University Press, 1978.

Cipolla, C. M. 'Four Centuries of Italian Demographic Development'. In D. V. Glass and D. E. C. Eversley, eds, *Population in History.* London: Edward Arnold, 1965.

———. *Before the Industrial Revolution: European Society and Economy,* 2nd edn. New York: Norton, 1980.

Clark, A. *Working Life of Women in the Seventeenth Century.* London: Frank Cass & Co., 1919; Routledge & Kegan Paul, 1982.

Clark, E. 'Some Aspects of Social Security in Medieval England'. *Journal of Family History,* vol. 7, no. 4, 1982, pp. 307–20.

Clark, G. 'Roman Women'. *Greece and Rome,* 2nd ser., vol. 28, no. 2, 1981, pp. 193–212.

Clarkson, L. A. *Proto-Industrialization: The First Phase of Industrialization?* London: Macmillan, 1985.

Clay, C. G. A. *Economic Expansion and Social Change: England, 1500–1700.* Cambridge: Cambridge University Press, 1984.

Coale, A. J. 'The Decline of Fertility in Europe since the Eighteenth Century as a Chapter in Human Demographic History'. In A. J. Coale and S. C. Watkins, eds, *The Decline of Fertility in Europe.* Princeton, N.J.: Princeton University Press, 1986.

Cohen, M. N. *The Food Crisis in Prehistory: Overpopulation and the Origins of Agriculture.* New Haven, Conn.: Yale University Press, 1977.

Cole, J. W. 'Social Process in the Italian Alps'. *American Anthropologist,* vol. 75, no. 3, 1973, pp. 765–86.

Coleman, D. C. 'Proto-industrialization: A Concept Too Many.' *Economic History Review,* 2nd ser., vol. 36, no. 3, 1983, pp. 435–48.

Coleman, D. C. and Schofield, R. *The State of Population Theory.* Oxford: Basil Blackwell, 1986.

Coleman, E. 'Infanticide in the Early Middle Ages'. In S. M. Stuard, ed., *Women in Medieval Society.* Philadelphia: University of Pennsylvania Press, 1976.

———. 'Medieval Marriage Characteristics: A Neglected Factor in the History of Medieval Serfdom'. In R. I. Rotberg and T. K. Rabb, eds, *Marriage and Fertility.* Princeton, N.J.: Princeton University Press, 1980.

Collomp, A. 'Tensions, Dissensions, and Ruptures inside the Family in Seventeenth- and Eighteenth-Century Haute Provence'. In H. Medick and D. Sabean, eds, *Interest and Emotion.* Cambridge: Cambridge University Press, 1984.

Colman, R. V. 'The Abduction of Women in Barbaric Law'. *Florilegium,* vol. 5, 1983, pp. 62–75.

Comminel, G. C. *Rethinking the French Revolution: Marxism and the Revisionist Challenge.* London: Verso, 1987.

Conway, D. *A Farewell to Marx: An Outline and Appraisal of His Theories.* Harmondsworth: Penguin, 1987.

Coontz, S. *Population Theories and Economic Interpretation.* London: Routledge & Kegan Paul, 1957.

Coontz, S. and Henderson, P., eds, *Women's Work, Men's Property: The Origins of Gender and Class.* London: Verso, 1986.

Corbett, P. E. *The Roman Law of Marriage.* Oxford: Oxford University Press, 1930.

Corvol, A. 'L'Affouage au XVIIIᵉ siècle: Intégration et exclusion dans les communautés d'Ancien Régime'. *Annales: Economies, sociétés, civilisations,* vol. 36, no. 3, 1981, pp. 390–407.

Coulton, G. G. *Medieval Village, Manor, and Monastery.* Cambridge: Cambridge University Press, 1925.

Coward, R. *Patriarchal Precedents: Sexuality and Social Relations.* London: Routledge & Kegan

Paul, 1983.

Crook, J. A. 'Women in Roman Succession'. In B. Rawson, ed., *The Family in Ancient Rome*. New York: Cornell University Press, 1986.

Dahlberg, F., ed. *Woman the Gatherer*. New Haven, Conn.: Yale University Press, 1981.

Danhieux, L. 'The Evolving Household: The Case of Lampernisse, West Flanders'. In R. Wall, ed., *Family Forms in Historic Europe*. Cambridge: Cambridge University Press, 1983.

Davies, W. and Fouracre, P. *The Settlement of Disputes in Early Medieval Europe*. Cambridge: Cambridge University Press, 1986.

Davis, D. E. 'The Scarcity of Rats and the Black Death: An Ecological History'. *Journal of Interdisciplinary History*, vol. 16, no. 3, 1986, pp. 455–70.

Davis, N. Z. 'The Reasons of Misrule: Youth Groups and Charivaris in SixteenthCentury France'. *Past & Present*, no. 50, 1971, pp. 41–75. Repr. in N. Z. Davis, *Society and Culture in Early Modern France*. Stanford, Calif.: Stanford University Press, 1975.

———. 'Ghosts, Kin and Progeny: Some Features of Family Life in Early Modern France'. In A. Rossi and T. Hareven, eds, *The Family*. New York: W. W. Norton, 1978.

Delaney, C. 'The Meaning of Paternity and the Virgin Birth Debate'. *Man*, vol. 21, 1986, pp. 494–513.

Derouet, B. 'Une démographie sociale différentielle: Clés pour un système auto-regulateur des populations rurales d'Ancien Régime'. *Annales: Economies, sociétés, civilisations*, vol. 35, no. 1, 1980, pp. 3–41.

Deyon, P. 'La Diffusion rurale des industries textiles en Flandre française à la fin de l'Ancien Régime et au début du XIXᵉ siècle'. *Revue du nord*, vol. 61, 1979, pp. 83–96.

Diefendorf, B., 'Widowhood and Remarriage in Sixteenth-Century Paris'. *Journal of Family History*, vol. 7, no. 4, 1982, pp. 379–95.

Dinnerstein, D. *The Mermaid and the Minotaur: Sexual Arrangements and Human Malaise*. New York: Harper Colophon, 1976.

Dobb, M. *Studies in the Development of Capitalism*, rev. ed. New York: International Publishers, 1963.

Dockès, P. *Medieval Slavery and Liberation*. Chicago: University of Chicago Press, 1982.

Dodgshon, R. A. 'The Early Middle Ages, 1066–1350'. In R. A. Dodgshon and R. A. Butlin, eds, *An Historical Geography of England and Wales*. London: Academic Press, 1978.

Doehaerd, R. *The Early Middle Ages in the West: Economy and Society*. Amsterdam: North Holland, 1978.

Dovring, F. 'The Transformation of European Agriculture'. In H. J. Habakkuk and M. Postan, eds, *The Cambridge Economic History of Europe*, vol. 6, pt 1. Cambridge: Cambridge University Press, 1966.

Drake, M. *Population and Society in Norway, 1735–1865*. Cambridge: Cambridge University Press, 1969.

———. 'Norway'. In W. R. Lee, ed., *European Demography and Economic Growth*. London: Croom Helm, 1979.

Draper, P. '!Kung Women: Contrasts in Sexual Egalitarianism in Foraging Societies'. In R. Reiter, ed., *Toward an Anthropolgy of Women*. New York: Monthly Review Press, 1975.

Duby, G. *Rural Economy and Country Life in the Medieval West*. Columbia, S.C.: University of South Carolina Press, 1968.

———. 'Medieval Agriculture, 900–1500'. In C. M. Cipolla, ed., *The Fontana Economic History of Europe*, vol. 1. New York: Fontana, 1972.

———. *The Early Growth of the European Economy*. New York: Cornell University Press, 1974.

———. *Medieval Marriage: Two Models from Twelfth-Century France*. Baltimore: Johns Hopkins University Press, 1978.

———. 'Private Power, Public Power'. In G. Duby, ed., *A History of Private Life*, vol. 2. Cambridge: Cambridge University Press, 1988.

———. *The Knight, the Lady and the Priest: The Making of Modern Marriage in Medieval France*. New York: Pantheon, 1983.

Duncan-Jones, R. *The Economy of the Roman Empire*, 2nd edn. Cambridge: Cambridge University Press, 1982.

Dupâquier, J. *La Population française aux XVIIe et XVIIIe siècles*. Paris: Presses Universitaires de France, 1979.

Dyer, C. *Lords and Peasants in a Changing Society*. Cambridge: Cambridge University Press, 1980.

———. 'Changes in the Size of Peasant Holdings in Some West Midland Villages'. In R. M. Smith, ed., *Land, Kinship and Life-Cycle*. Cambridge: Cambridge University Press, 1984.

Edholm, F., Harris, O. and Young, K. 'Conceptualizing Women'. *Critique of Anthropology*, nos 9/10, 1977, pp. 101–30.

Ehrenreich, B. *The Hearts of Men: American Dreams and the Flight from Commitment*. Garden City, N.Y.: Anchor Press, 1983.

Eisenstein, Z. R., ed. *Capitalist Patriarchy and the Case for Socialist Feminism*. New York: Monthly Review Press, 1979.

Elder, G. 'Families and Lives: Some Developments in Life-Course Studies'. In T. Hareven and A. Plakans, eds, *Family History at the Crossroads*. Princeton, N.J.: Princeton University Press, 1987.

Engels, D. 'The Use of Historical Demography in Ancient History'. *Classical Quarterly*, vol. 34, no. 2, 1984, pp. 386–93.

Engels, F. 'The Housing Question'. In K. Marx and F. Engels, *Selected Works*. Moscow: Progress Publishers, 1958.

———. *The Origin of the Family, Private Property and the State*, E. B. Leacock, intro. New York: International Publishers, 1972.

Eriksson, I. and Rogers, J. *Rural Labour and Population Change*. Stockholm: Almquist, 1978.

Etienne, M. and Leacock, E. B. *Women and Colonization*. New York: Praeger, 1980.

Everitt, A. 'Farm Labourers'. In J. Thirsk, ed., *The Agrarian History of England and Wales*, vol. 4. Cambridge: Cambridge University Press, 1967.

Eyben, E. 'Family Planning in Greco-Roman Antiquity'. *Ancient Society*, vol. 11, no. 2, 1980, pp. 5–82.

Faith, R. 'Peasant Families and Inheritance Customs in Medieval England'. *Agricultural History Review*, vol. 14, 1966, pp. 77–95.

Farb, P. *Humankind*. New York: Bantam, 1980.

Feil, D.K. 'Beyond Patriliny in the New Guinea Highlands'. *Man*, vol. 19, 1984, pp. 50–76.

Felloni, G. 'Italy'. In C. Wilson and G. Parker, eds, *An Introduction to the Sources of European Economic History*. Ithaca, N.Y.: Cornell University Press, 1977.

Finley, M. I. *Ancient Slavery and Modern Ideology*. Harmondsworth: Penguin, 1980.

Fischer, W. 'Rural Industrialization and Population Change'. *Comparative Studies in Society and History*, vol. 15, no. 1, 1973, pp. 158–70.

Fisher, E. *Woman's Creation: Sexual Evolution and the Shaping of Society*. New York: McGraw-Hill, 1979.

Flandrin, J. L. *Families in Former Times: Kinship, Household and Sexuality*. New York: Cambridge University Press, 1979.

Fletcher, R. *The Shaking of the Foundations: Family and Society*. London: Routledge, 1988.

Flinn, M. W. *British Population Growth, 1700–1850*. London: Macmillan, 1970.

———. 'Plague in Europe and the Mediterranean Countries'. *Journal of European Economic History*, vol. 8, no. 1, 1979.

———. *The European Demographic System, 1500–1800*. Brighton: Harvester, 1981.

Flory, M. 'Family in Familia: Kinship and Community in Slavery'. *American Journal of Ancient History*, vol. 3, no. 1, 1978, pp. 78–95.

Folbre, N. 'Exploitation Comes Home: A Critique of the Marxian Theory of Labour Power'. *Cambridge Journal of Economics*, vol. 6, no. 4, 1982, pp. 317–29.

———. *A Patriarchal Mode of Production*. Unpublished paper, 1984.

Fortes, M. 'Introduction'. In J. Moody, ed., *The Developmental Cycle of the Domestic Group*.

Cambridge: Cambridge University Press, 1958.

Foster-Carter, A. 'The Modes of Production Controversy'. *New Left Review,* no. 107, 1978, pp. 47–77.

Fourquin, G. *Lordship and Feudalism in the Middle Ages.* London: Allen & Unwin, 1976.

Fox, R. *Kinship and Marriage.* Harmondsworth: Penguin, 1967.

———. *Pagans and Christians.* London: Penguin, 1986.

Franzoi, B. *At the Very Least She Pays the Rent: Women and German Industrialization, 1871– 1914.* Westport, Conn.: Greenwood Press, 1985.

Friedrichs, C. R. 'Marriage, Family and Social Structure in an Early Modern German Town'. *Historical Papers of the Canadian Historical Association,* 1975, pp. 17–40.

Frykman, J. 'Sexual Intercourse and Social Norms: A Study of Illegitimate births in Sweden, 1831–1933'. *Ethnologia Scandinavica,* 1975, pp. 111–50.

Garnsey, P. 'Non-Slave Labour in the Roman World'. In P. Garnsey, ed., *Non-Slave Labour in the Greco-Roman World.* Cambridge: Cambridge Philological Society, 1980.

Gaunt, D. 'Illegitimacy in Seventeenth- and Eighteenth-Century East Sweden'. In P. Laslett, K. Oosterveen and R. M. Smith, eds, *Bastardy and Its Comparative History.* Cambridge, Mass.: Harvard University Press, 1980.

———. 'The Property and Kin Relationships of Retired Farmers in Northern and Central Europe'. In R. Wall, ed., *Family Forms in Historic Europe.* Cambridge: Cambridge University Press, 1983.

———. 'Rural Household Organization and Inheritance in Northern Europe'. *Journal of Family History,* vol. 12, no. 1, 1987, pp. 121–41.

Gaunt, D. and Löfgren, O. 'Remarriage in the Nordic Countries: The Cultural and Socio- Economic Background'. In J. Dupâquier et al., eds, *Marriage and Remarriage in the Past.* New York: Academic Press, 1981.

Geary, P. J. *Before France and Germany: The Creation and Transformation of the Merovingian World.* Oxford: Oxford University Press, 1988.

Genovese, E. *Roll, Jordan, Roll: The World the Slaves Made.* New York: Vintage Books, 1976.

Giacchetti, J. C. and Tyvaert, M. 'Argenteuil, 1740–1790'. *Annales de démographie historique,* 1969, pp. 40–61.

Gies, F. and Gies, J. *Women in the Middle Ages.* New York: Crowell, 1978.

Gillis, J. R. *Youth and History: Tradition and Change in European Age Relations, 1770 to Present.* New York: Academic Press, 1981.

———. 'Peasant, Plebeian, and Proletarian Marriage in Britain, 1600–1900'. In D. Levine, ed., *Proletarianization and Family History.* New York: Academic Press, 1984.

———. *For Better, For Worse: British Marriages, 1600 to the Present.* New York: Oxford University Press, 1985.

Giminez, M. 'Population and Capitalism'. *Latin American Perspectives,* vol. 15, no. 4, 1977, pp. 5–36.

Glass, D. V. and Eversley, D. E. C., eds, *Population in History: Essays in Demographic History.* London: Edward Arnold, 1965.

Goffart, W. *Barbarians and Romans, AD 418–584: The Techniques of Accomodation.* Princeton, N.J.: Princeton University Press, 1980.

Goldschmidt, W. and Kunkel, E. J. 'The Structure of the Peasant Family'. *American Anthropologist,* vol. 73, no. 4, 1971, pp. 1058–76.

Goldthorpe, J. E. *Family Life in Western Societies.* Cambridge: Cambridge University Press, 1987.

Goody, J. 'The Evolution of the Family'. In P. Laslett, ed., *Household and Family in Past Time.* Cambridge: Cambridge University Press, 1972.

———. 'Inheritance, Property and Women: Some Comparative Considerations'. In J. Goody, J. Thirsk and E. P. Thompson, eds, *Family and Inheritance: Rural Society in Western Europe, 1200–1800.* Cambridge: Cambridge University Press, 1976.

———. *Production and Reproduction: A Comparative Study of the Domestic Domain.* Cambridge:

Cambridge University Press, 1976.

———. *The Development of the Family and Marriage in Europe*. Cambridge: Cambridge University Press, 1983.

Goody, J., Thirsk, J. and Thompson, E. P., eds, *Family and Inheritance: Rural Society in Western Europe, 1200–1800*. Cambridge: Cambridge University Press, 1976.

Goose, N. 'Household Size and Structure in Early-Stuart Cambridge.' *Social History*, vol. 5, no. 3, 1980, pp. 347–85.

Gordon, L. *Woman's Body, Woman's Right: A Social History of Birth Control in America*. Harmondsworth: Penguin, 1976.

Gottfried, R. S. *Epidemic Disease in Fifteenth Century England: The Medical Response and the Demographic Consequences*. New Brunswick, N.J.: Rutgers University Press, 1978.

———. *The Black Death: Natural and Human Disaster in Medieval Europe*. New York: The Free Press, 1983.

Goubert, P. 'The French Peasantry of the Seventeenth Century'. *Past & Present*, no. 10, 1956, pp. 55–77. Repr. in T. H. Aston, ed., *Crisis in Europe, 1560–1660*. London: Routledge & Kegan Paul, 1965.

———. *The Ancien Régime: French Society, 1600–1750*. New York: Harper & Row, 1973.

———. 'Family and Province: A Contribution to the Knowledge of Family Structures in Early Modern France'. *Journal of Family History*, vol. 2, no. 3, 1977, pp. 179–95.

———. *The French Peasantry in the Seventeenth Century*, Cambridge: Cambridge University Press, 1986.

Gough, K. 'The Origin of the Family'. In R. Reiter, ed., *Toward an Anthropology of Women*. New York: Monthly Review Press, 1975.

Grigg, D. B. *Population Growth and Agrarian Change*. Cambridge: Cambridge University Press, 1980.

———. *The Dynamics of Agricultural Change*. London: Hutchinson, 1982.

Gronseth, E. 'Notes on the Historical Development of the Relation between Nuclear Family Kinship System and Wider Social Structure in Norway'. In R. Hill and R. Konig, eds, *Families in East and West*. Paris: Mouton, 1970.

Gullickson, G. L. 'Proto-Industrialization, Demographic Behavior and the Sexual Division of Labor in Auffay, France, 1750–1850'. *Peasant Studies*, vol. 9, no. 2, 1982, pp. 106–18.

Gurevich, A. *Medieval Popular Culture: Problems of Belief and Perception*. Cambridge: Cambridge University Press, 1988.

Gutmann, M. and Leboutte, R. 'Rethinking Protoindustrialization and the Family'. *Journal of Interdisciplinary History*, vol. 14, no. 3, 1984, pp. 587–607.

Habakkuk, H. J. 'English Population in the Eighteenth Century'. *Economic History Review*, 2nd ser., vol. 6, no. 2, 1953, pp. 117–33.

———. *Population Growth and Economic Development*. Leicester: Leicester University Press, 1971.

Haines, M. R. *Fertility and Occupation: Population Patterns in the Past*. New York: Academic Press, 1979.

Hajdu, R. 'Family and Feudal Ties in Poitou, 1100–1300'. *Journal of Interdisciplinary History*, vol. 8, no. 1, 1977, pp. 117–39.

Hajnal, J. 'European Marriage Patterns in Perspective'. In D. V. Glass and D. E. C. Eversley, eds, *Population in History: Essays in Historical Demography*. London: Edward Arnold, 1965.

———. 'Two Kinds of Pre-Industrial Household Systems'. *Population and Development Review*, vol. 8, no. 3, 1982, pp. 449–94.

Hallam, H. E. 'Some Thirteenth-Century Censuses'. *Economic History Review*, 2nd ser., vol. 10, 1958, pp. 340–61.

———. 'Further Observations on the Spalding Serf Lists'. *Economic History Review*, 2nd ser., vol. 16, 1963, pp. 338–50.

———. *Rural England, 1066–1348*. New York: Fontana, 1981.

———. 'Age at First Marriage and Age at Death in the Lincolnshire Fenland, 1252–1478'.

Population Studies, vol. 39, 1985, pp. 55–69.

Hamilton, R. *The Liberation of Women: A Study of Patriarchy and Women.* London: Allen & Unwin, 1978.

Hammel, E. A. 'The Zadruga as Process'. In P. Laslett, ed., *Household and Family in Past Time.* Cambridge: Cambridge University Press, 1972.

Hanawalt, B. A. 'Childrearing among the Lower Class of Late Medieval England'. *Journal of Interdisciplinary History,* vol. 8, no. 1, 1977, pp. 1–22.

———. 'Peasant Women's Work in the Context of Marriage'. In B. A. Hanawalt, ed., *Women and Work in Preindustrial Europe.* Bloomington, Ind.: Indiana University Press, 1986.

———. *The Ties That Bound: Peasant Families in Medieval England.* New York: Oxford University Press, 1986.

Hareven, T. *Family Time and Industrial Time.* Cambridge: Cambridge University Press, 1982.

Hareven, T. and Plakans, A., eds, *Family History at the Crossroads.* Princeton, N.J.: Princeton University Press, 1987.

Harrison, J. F. C. *The Common People: A History from the Norman Conquest to the Present.* London: Fontana, 1984.

Hartmann, H. 'The Unhappy Marriage of Marxism and Feminism: Towards a More Progressive Union'. In L. Sargent, ed., *Women and Revolution: A Discussion of the Unhappy Marriage of Marxism and Feminism.* London: Pluto Press, 1981.

Harvey, B. *Westminster Abbey and Its Estates in the Middle Ages.* Oxford: Oxford University Press, 1977.

Harvey, P. D. A. *The Peasant Land Market in Medieval England.* Oxford: Oxford University Press, 1984.

Hasbach, W. *The History of the English Agricultural Labourer.* London: Frank Cass, 1966 [1908].

Hatcher, J. *Plague, Population and the English Economy, 1348–1530.* London: Macmillan, 1977.

Hechter, M. and Brustein, W. 'Regional Modes of Production and Patterns of State Formation in Western Europe'. *American Journal of Sociology,* vol. 5, 1980, pp. 1061–94.

Heilleiner, K. F. 'The Vital Revolution Reconsidered'. In D. V. Glass and D. E. C. Eversely, eds, *Population in History.* London: Edward Arnold, 1965.

———. 'The Population of Europe from the Black Death to the Eve of the Vital Revolution'. In E. E. Rich and C. H. Wilson, eds, *The Cambridge Economic History of Europe,* vol. 4. Cambridge: Cambridge University Press, 1967.

Held, T. 'Rural Retirement Arrangements in Seventeenth to Nineteenth Century Austria: A Cross-Community Analysis'. *Journal of Family History,* vol. 7, no. 3, 1982, pp. 227–54.

Henry, L. 'Some Data on Natural Fertility'. *Eugenics Quarterly,* vol. 8, 1961, pp. 81–91.

Henry, L. and Blanchet, D. 'La Population de l'Angleterre de 1541 à 1871'. *Population,* vol. 38, nos 4/5, 1983, pp. 781–825.

Henry, L. and Houdaille, J. 'Célibat et âge au mariage aux XVIIIᵉ et XIXᵉ siècles en France'. *Population,* vol. 34, 1979, pp. 403–41.

Herlihy, D. 'Deaths, Marriages, Births and the Tuscan Economy (ca. 1300–1550)'. In R. D. Lee, ed., *Population Patterns in the Past.* New York: Academic Press, 1977.

———. 'The Making of the Medieval Family: Symmetry, Structure and Sentiment'. *Journal of Family History,* vol. 8, no. 2, 1983, pp. 116–30.

———. *Medieval Households.* Cambridge, Mass. Harvard University Press, 1985.

Herlihy, D. and Klapisch-Zuber, C. *Tuscans and Their Families: A Study of the Florentine Catasto of 1427.* New Haven, Conn.: Yale University Press, 1985.

Hill, C. *Puritanism and Revolution: Studies in Interpretation of the English Revolution of the Seventeenth Century.* London: Secker & Warburg, 1958.

———. *Society and Puritanism in Pre-Revolutionary England.* Harmondsworth, Penguin, 1986 [1964].

———. 'Pottage for Freeborn Englishmen: Attitudes to Wage Labour in the Sixteenth and Seventeenth Centuries'. In C. H. Fernstein, ed., *Socialism, Capitalism and Economic Growth.* Cambridge: Cambridge University Press, 1967.

BIBLIOGRAPHY

Hillgarth, J. N. *Christianity and Paganism, 350–750*. Philadelphia: University of Pennsylvania Press, 1986.

Hilton, R. H. *The Economic Development of Some Leicestershire Estates in the Fourteenth and Fifteenth Centuries*. Oxford: Oxford University Press, 1947.

———. *The English Peasantry in the Later Middle Ages: The Ford Lectures for 1973 and Related Studies*. Oxford: Clarendon Press, 1975.

———. *Peasants, Knights and Heretics: Studies in Medieval English Social History*. Cambridge: Cambridge University Press, 1976.

———, ed. *The Transition from Feudalism to Capitalism*. London: Verso, 1976.

———. *Bond Men Made Free: Medieval Peasant Movements and the English Rising of 1381*. London: Methuen, 1977.

———. 'A Crisis of Feudalism'. *Past & Present*, no. 80, 1978, pp. 3–19.

Himes, N. *Medical History of Contraception*. New York: Gamut Press, 1963.

Hindess, B. and Hirst, P. Q. *Pre-Capitalist Modes of Production*. London: Routledge & Kegan Paul, 1975.

Hoffman, R. C. 'Medieval Origins of the Common Fields'. In W. N. Parker and E. L. Jones, eds, *European Peasants and Their Markets*. Princeton, N.J.: Princeton University Press, 1975.

Hofsten, E. and Lundström, H. *Swedish Population History: Main Trends from 1750 to 1950*. Stockholm: Urval, 1976.

Hollingsworth, T. H. *Historical Demography*. London: Sources of History, 1969.

Holmes, D. R. and Quataert, J. H. 'An Approach to Modern Labor: Worker Peasantries in Historic Saxony and the Friuli Region over Three Centuries'. *Comparative Studies in Society and History*, vol. 28, no. 2, 1986, pp. 191–216.

Homans, G. C. *English Villagers of the Thirteenth Century*. Cambridge, Mass.: Harvard University Press, 1941.

Hopkins, K. 'The Age of Roman Girls at Marriage'. *Population Studies*, vol. 18, 1965, pp. 309–27.

———. *Conquerors and Slaves*. Cambridge: Cambridge University Press, 1978.

Houston, R. and Snell, K. D. M. 'Proto-Industrialization? Cottage Industry, Social Change, and Industrial Revolution'. *The Historical Journal*, vol. 27, no. 2, 1984, pp. 473–92.

Howell, C. 'Stability and Change, 1300–1700: The Socio-Economic Context of the Self-Perpetuating Family Farm in England'. *Journal of Peasant Studies*, vol. 2, no. 4, 1975, pp. 468–82.

———. 'Peasant Inheritance Customs in the Midlands, 1280–1700'. In J. Goody, J. Thirsk and E. P. Thompson, eds, *Family and Inheritance: Rural Society in Western Europe, 1200–1800*. Cambridge: Cambridge University Press, 1976.

———. *Land, Family and Inheritance in Transition: Kibworth Harcourt, 1280–1700*. Cambridge: Cambridge University Press, 1983.

Hufton, O. *The Poor of Eighteenth-Century France, 1750–1789*. Oxford: Oxford University Press, 1974.

———. 'Women and the Family Economy in Eighteenth Century France'. *French Historical Studies*, vol. 9, 1975, pp. 1–22.

———. 'Women, Work and Marriage in Eighteenth Century France'. In R. B. Outhwaite, ed., *Marriage and Society*. New York: St. Martin's Press, 1981.

Hughes, D. 'From Brideprice to Dowry in Mediterranean Europe'. *Journal of Family History*, vol. 3, no. 3, 1978, pp. 262–96. Repr. in M. A. Kaplan , ed., *The Marriage Bargain: Women and Dowries in European History*. New York: Harrington Park Press, 1985.

Huppert, G. *After the Black Death: A Social History of Early Modern Europe*. Bloomington, Ind.: Indiana University Press, 1986.

Hurst, J. G. 'The Changing Medieval Village in England'. In J. A. Raftis, ed., *Pathways to Medieval Peasants*. Toronto: Pontifical Institute of Medieval Studies, 1981.

Hyams, P. R. *Kings, Lords and Peasants in Medieval England: The Common Law of Villeinage in the Twelfth and Thirteenth Centuries*. Oxford: Oxford University Press, 1980.

Ingram, M. *Church Courts, Sex and Marriage in England, 1570–1640*. Cambridge: Cambridge University Press, 1987.

Jackson, R. V. 'Growth and Deceleration in English Agriculture, 1660–1790'. *Economic History Review*, 2nd ser., vol. 38, no. 3, 1985, pp. 333–51.

Jacquart, J. 'French Agriculture in the Seventeenth Century'. In P. Earle, ed., *Essays in European Economic History, 1500–1800*. Oxford: Oxford University Press, 1974.

James, E. *The Origins of France, from Clovis to the Capetians, 500–1000*. London: Macmillan, 1982.

Jeay, M. 'Sexuality and Family in Fifteenth Century France'. *Journal of Family History*, vol. 4, no. 4, 1979, pp. 328–45.

Jochens, J. M. 'En islande médiévale: A la recherche de la famille nucléaire'. *Annales: Economies, sociétés, civilisations*, vol. 40, no. 1, 1985, pp. 95–112.

Jolly, A. *The Evolution of Primate Behaviour*. New York: Macmillan, 1972.

Jones, A. H. M. 'Slavery in the Ancient World'. *Economic History Review*, 2nd ser., vol. 9, 1956, pp. 185–99.

Kamen, H. *Spain in the Later Seventeenth Century, 1665–1700*. New York: Longman, 1980.

———. *European Society, 1500–1700*. London: Hutchinson, 1984.

Kaplan, M. A. *The Marriage Bargain: Women and Dowries in European History*. New York: Harrington Park Press, 1985.

Keesing, R. M. *Kin Groups and Social Structure*. New York: Holt Rinehart, 1975.

Kellenbenz, H. 'Rural Industries in the West from the End of the Middle Ages to the Eighteenth Century'. In P. Earle, ed., *Essays in European Economic History, 1500–1800*. Oxford: Oxford University Press, 1974.

———. *The Rise of the European Economy: An Economic History of Continental Europe from the Fifteenth to the Eighteenth Century*. London: Weidenfeld & Nicolson, 1976.

———. 'Germany'. In C. Wilson and G. Parker, eds, *An Introduction to the Sources of European Economic History, 1500–1800*. Ithaca, N.Y.: Cornell University Press, 1977.

Kellum, B. 'Infanticide in England in the Later Middle Ages'. *History of Childhood Quarterly*, vol. 1, 1973, pp. 367–88.

Kelly, J. 'The Doubled Vision of Feminist Theory'. *Feminist Studies*, vol. 5, 1979, pp. 216–27.

Kent, F. W. *Household and Lineage in Renaissance Florence*. Princeton, N.J.: Princeton University Press, 1977.

Kerridge, E. 'The Movement of Rent, 1540–1640'. *Economic History Review*, 2nd ser., vol. 6, no. 1, 1953, pp. 16–34.

Kertzer, D. and Brettell, C. 'Advances in Italian and Iberian Family History'. In T. Hareven and A. Plakans, eds, *Family History at the Crossroads*. Princeton, N.J.: Princeton University Press, 1987.

King, E. *Peterborough Abbey 1086–1310: A Study in the Land Market*. Cambridge: Cambridge University Press, 1973.

Kisch, H. 'The Textile Industries in Silesia and the Rhineland: A Comparative Study in Industrialization'. In P. Kriedte, H. Medick and J. Schlumbohm, *Industrialization before Industrialization*. Cambridge: Cambridge University Press, 1981.

Klapisch, C. 'Household and Family in Tuscany in 1427'. In P. Laslett, ed., *Household and Family in Past Time*. Cambridge: Cambridge University Press, 1972.

Klapisch-Zuber, C. *Women, Family and Ritual in Renaissance Italy*. Chicago: University of Chicago Press, 1985.

Klassen, J. 'The Development of the Conjugal Bond in Late Medieval Bohemia'. *Journal of Medieval History*, vol. 13, 1987, pp. 161–78.

Knodel, J. 'Family Limitation and the Fertility Transition: Evidence from the Age Patterns of Fertility in Europe and Asia'. *Population Studies*, vol. 31, no. 2, 1977, pp. 219–49.

———. 'Natural Fertility in Pre-industrial Germany'. *Population Studies*, vol. 32, no. 3, 1978, pp. 481–510.

———. 'Natural Fertility: Age Patterns, Levels, Trends'. In R. A. Bulatao and R. D. Lee, eds, *Determinants of Fertility in Developing Countries*. New York: Academic Press, 1982.

———. *Demographic Behaviour in the Past: A Study of Fourteen German Village Populations in the Eighteenth and Nineteenth Centuries*. Cambridge: Cambridge University Press, 1988.

Knodel, J. and Hochstadt, S. 'Urban and Rural Illegitimacy in Imperial Germany'. In P. Laslett, K. Oosterveen and R. M. Smith, eds, *Bastardy and Its Comparative History*. Cambridge, Mass.: Harvard University Press, 1980.

Knodel, J. and Lynch, K. 'The Decline of Remarriage: Evidence from German Village Populations in the Eighteenth and Nineteenth Centuries'. *Journal of Family History*, vol. 10, no. 1, 1985, pp. 34–59.

Knodel, J. and Maynes, M. J. 'Urban and Rural Marriage Patterns in Imperial Germany'. *Journal of Family History*, vol. 1, no. 2, 1976, pp. 129–61.

Knodel, J. and van de Walle, E., 'Lessons from the Past: Policy Implications of Historical Fertility Studies'. In A. J. Coale and S. C. Watkins, *The Decline of Fertility in Europe*. Princeton, N.J.: Princeton University Press, 1986.

Koebner, R. 'The Settlement and Colonization of Europe'. In M. Postan, ed., *Cambridge Economic History of Europe*, 2nd edn, vol. 1. Cambridge: Cambridge University Press, 1966.

Kosminsky, E. A. *Studies in the Agrarian History of England in the Thirteenth Century*, R. H. Hilton, ed. Oxford: Basil Blackwell, 1956.

Krause, J. T. 'Some Neglected Factors in the English Industrial Revolution'. *Journal of Economic History*, vol. 19, 1959, pp. 528–40.

Kriedte, P. *Peasants, Landlords and Merchant Capitalists: Europe and the World Economy, 1500–1800*. Cambridge: Cambridge University Press, 1983.

Kuhn, A. and Wolpe, A. M. *Feminism and Materialism: Women and Modes of Production*. London: Routledge & Kegan Paul, 1978.

Kula, W. 'The Seigneury and the Peasant Family in Eighteenth Century Poland.' In R. Forster and O. Ranum, eds, *Family and Society: Selections from the Annales*. Baltimore: Johns Hopkins University Press, 1976.

Kunitz, S. J. 'Speculations on the European Mortality Decline'. *Economic History Review*, 2nd ser., vol. 36, no. 2, 1983, pp. 349–64.

———. 'Mortality since Malthus'. In D. Coleman and R. Schofield, eds, *The State of Population Theory: Forward from Malthus*. Oxford: Basil Blackwell, 1986.

Kussmaul, A. S. 'The Ambiguous Mobility of Farm Servants'. *Economic History Review*, 2nd ser., vol. 34, no. 2, 1981, pp. 222–35.

———. *Servants in Husbandry in Early Modern England*. Cambridge: Cambridge University Press, 1981.

Ladurie, E. *The Peasants of Languedoc*. J. Day, trans. Chicago: University of Illinois Press, 1974.

———. 'A System of Customary Law: Family Structures and Inheritance Customs in Sixteenth Century France'. In R. Forster and O. Ranum, eds, *Family and Society: Selections from the Annales*. Baltimore: Johns Hopkins University Press, 1976.

———. *Montaillou: The Promised Land of Error*, B. Bray, trans. New York: Vintage Books (Random House), 1979.

Lamphere, L. 'Strategies, Cooperation and Conflict among Women in Domestic Groups'. In M. Z. Rosaldo and L. Lamphere, eds, *Woman, Culture and Society*. Stanford, Calif.: Stanford University Press, 1974.

Lancaster, L. 'Kinship in Anglo-Saxon Society'. *British Journal of Sociology*, vol. 9, 1958, pp. 230–50; 359–77.

Langton, J. 'Industry and Towns, 1500–1730'. In R. A. Dodgshon and R. A. Butlin, eds, *An Historical Geography of England and Wales*. London: Academic Press, 1978.

Lasch, C. 'Reagan's Victims'. *New York Review of Books*, vol. 35, no. 12, 1988, pp. 7–8.

Laslett, P. *The World We Have Lost*, 2nd edn. London: Methuen, 1971.

———. 'Introduction: The History of the Family'. In P. Laslett, ed., *Household and Family in Past Time*. Cambridge: Cambridge University Press, 1972.

———. 'Mean Household Size in England since the Sixteenth Century'. In P. Laslett, ed.,

Household and Family in Past Time. Cambridge: Cambridge University Press, 1972.

————. 'The Family and Industrialization: A "Strong Theory"'. Unpublished paper for the Bad Homburg Symposium, 1975.

————. *Family Life and Illicit Love in Earlier Generations*. Cambridge: Cambridge University Press, 1977.

————. 'Introduction: Comparing Illegitimacy over Time and between Cultures'. In P. Laslett, K. Oosterveen and R. M. Smith, eds, *Bastardy and Its Comparative History*. Cambridge, Mass.: Harvard University Press, 1980.

————, eds. *Bastardy and Its Comparative History*. Cambridge, Mass.: Harvard University Press, 1980.

————. 'Family and Household as Work Group and Kin Group: Areas of Traditional Europe Compared'. In R. Wall, ed., *Family Forms in Historic Europe*. Cambridge: Cambridge University Press, 1983.

————. 'The Character of Familial History, Its Limitations and Proper Pursuit'. In T. Hareven and A. Plakans, eds, *Family History at the Crossroads*. Princeton, N.J.: Princeton University Press, 1987.

————. 'The European Family and Early Industrialization'. In J. Baechler, J. A. Hall and M. Mann, eds, *Europe and the Rise of Capitalism*. Oxford: Basil Blackwell, 1988.

Lassen, A. 'The Population of Denmark, 1660–1960'. *The Scandinavian Economic History Review*, vol. 14, no. 1, 1966, pp. 134–57.

Latouche, R. *The Birth of the Western Economy*. London: Methuen, 1967.

Lawton, R. 'Population and Society, 1730–1900'. In R. A. Dodgshon and R. A. Butlin, eds, *An Historical Geography of England and Wales*. New York: Academic Press, 1978.

Lazonick, W. 'The Subjugation of Labour to Capital: The Rise of the Capitalist System'. *Review of Radical Political Economics*, vol. 10, no. 1, 1978, pp. 1–31.

Leacock, E. B. 'Introduction'. In F. Engels, *The Origin of the Family, Private Property and the State*. New York: New World Books, 1972.

————. 'Women's Status in Egalitarian Society: Implications for Social Evolution'. *Current Anthropology*, vol. 19, 1978, pp. 247–75.

Lee, G. R. *Family Structure and Interaction: A Comparative Analysis*, rev. edn. Minneapolis, Minn.: University of Minnesota Press, 1982.

Lee, R. B. *The !Kung San: Men, Women and Work in a Foraging Society*. New York: Cambridge University Press, 1979.

Lee, W. R. *Population Growth, Economic Development and Social Change in Bavaria, 1750–1850*. New York: Arno Press, 1977.

————, ed. *European Demography and Economic Growth*. London: Croom Helm, 1979.

————. 'The Impact of Agrarian Change on Women's Work and Child Care in Early Nineteenth Century Prussia'. In J. C. Fout, ed., *German Women in the Nineteenth Century*. New York: Holmes & Meier, 1984.

Le Play, F. *L'Organisation de la famille suivant le vrai modèle signalé par l'histoire de toutes les races et tous les temps*. Tours: Maine, 1871.

Lerner, G. *The Creation of Patriarchy*. New York: Oxford University Press, 1986.

Lesthaeghe, R. 'Nuptiality and Population Growth'. *Population Studies*, vol. 25, 1971, pp. 415–32.

————. 'On the Social Control of Reproduction'. *Population and Development Review*, vol. 6, no. 4, 1980, pp. 527–48.

Lesthaeghe, R., Ohadike, P. O., Kocher, J. and Page, H. J. 'Child-Spacing and Fertility in Sub-Saharan Africa: An Overview of the Issues'. In H. J. Page and R. Lesthaeghe, eds, *Child-spacing in Tropical Africa: Tradition and Change*. New York: Academic Press, 1981.

Leveau, P. 'La Ville antique et l'organisation de l'espace rural: villa, ville, village'. *Annales: Economies, sociétés, civilisations*, vol. 38, no. 4, 1983, pp. 920–42.

Levine, D. *Family Formation in an Age of Nascent Capitalism*. New York: Academic Press, 1977.

————. 'Production, Reproduction and the Proletarian Family in England, 1500–1851'. In

D. Levine, ed., *Proletarianization and Family History*. New York: Academic Press, 1984.

———. '"Sooty Faces and Elysian Glades": The Labour Process and the Industrial Revolution of Tyneside'. Unpublished MS, 1984.

———. 'Industrialization and the Proletarian Family in England'. *Past & Present*, no. 107, 1985, pp. 168–203.

———. *Reproducing Families: The Political Economy of English Population History*. Cambridge: Cambridge University Press, 1987.

———. 'Recombinant Family Formation Strategies'. *Journal of Historical Sociology*, vol. 2, no. 2, 1989, pp. 89–115.

Levy, M. J. 'Aspects of the Analysis of Family Structure'. In A. J. Coale et al., eds, *Aspects of the Analysis of Family Structure*. Princeton, N.J.: Princeton University Press, 1965.

Leyser, K. J. 'The German Aristocracy from the Ninth to the Twelfth Century'. *Past & Present*, no. 41, 1968, pp. 25–53.

Leyton, E. H. 'Spheres of Inheritance in Aughnaboy'. *American Anthropologist*, vol. 72, no. 6, 1970, pp. 1378–88.

Lis, C. and Soly, H. *Poverty and Capitalism in Pre-industrial Europe*. Atlantic Heights, N.J.: Humanities Press, 1979.

———. 'Policing the Early Modern Proletariat, 1450–1850'. In D. Levine, ed., *Proletarianization and Family History*. New York: Academic Press, 1984.

Lithell, U. B. *Breast-Feeding and Reproduction*. Uppsala: University of Uppsala, 1981.

Loengard, J. S. '"Of the Gift of Her Husband": English Dower in the Year 1200'. In J. Kirshner and S. F. Wemple, eds, *Women of the Medieval World*. Oxford: Basil Blackwell, 1985.

Löfgren, O. 'The Potato People: Household Economy and Family Patterns among the Rural Proletariat in Nineteenth Century Sweden'. In S. Åkerman, H. C. Johansen and D. Gaunt, eds, *Chance and Change: Social and Economic Studies in Historical Demography in the Baltic Area*. Odense: Odense University Press, 1978.

———. 'Family and Household among Scandinavian Peasants'. In M. Anderson, ed., *Sociology of the Family*, 2nd edn. Harmondsworth: Penguin, 1980.

———. 'Family and Household: Images and Realities, Cultural Change in Swedish Society'. In R. McC. Netting, R. R. Wilk and E. J. Arnould, eds, *Households: Comparative and Historical Studies of the Domestic Group*. Berkeley: University of California Press, 1984.

Longworth, I. and Cherry, J. *Archaeology in Britain since 1945*. London: British Museum Publications, 1986.

Loyn, H. R. 'Kinship in Anglo-Saxon England'. In P. Clemoes, ed., *Anglo-Saxon England*, vol. 3. Cambridge: Cambridge University Press, 1974.

Luxton, M. *More Than a Labour of Love: Three Generations of Women's Work in the Home*. Toronto: The Women's Press, 1980.

Lynch, J. H. *Godparents and Kinship in Early Medieval Europe*. Princeton, N.J.: Princeton University Press, 1986.

Macfarlane, A. *The Family Life of Ralph Josselin*. Cambridge: Cambridge University Press, 1970.

———. *The Origins of English Individualism*. Oxford: Basil Blackwell, 1978.

———. *Marriage and Love in England, 1300–1840*. Oxford: Basil Blackwell, 1986.

MacMullen, R. *Christianizing the Roman Empire, AD 100–400*. New Haven, Conn.: Yale University Press, 1984.

McEvedy, C. *The Penguin Atlas of Medieval History*. Harmondsworth: Penguin, 1961.

McEvedy, C. and Jones, R. *Atlas of World Population History*. Harmondsworth: Penguin, 1978.

McIntosh, M. 'Servants and the Household Unit in an Elizabethan Community'. *Journal of Family History*, vol. 9, no. 1, 1984, pp. 3–23.

McKeown, T. *The Modern Rise of Population*. London: Edward Arnold, 1976.

McLaren, A. *Birth Control in Nineteenth Century England*. London: Croom Helm, 1978.

———. *Sexuality and Social Order: The Debate over the Fertility of Women and Workers in France,*

1770–1920. New York: Holmes & Meier, 1983.

———. *Reproductive Rituals: The Perception of Fertility in England from the Sixteenth to the Nineteenth Century*. London: Methuen, 1984.

———. *A History of Contraception from Antiquity to the Present*. Oxford: Basil Blackwell, 1990.

McLaren, D. 'Marital Fertility and Lactation, 1570–1720'. In M. Prior, ed., *Women in English Society, 1500–1800*. London: Methuen, 1985.

McNamara, J. and Wemple, S. F. 'Sanctity and Power: The Dual Pursuit of Medieval Women'. In R. Bridenthal and C. Koonz, eds, *Becoming Visible: Women in European History*. Boston: Houghton Mifflin, 1977.

McNeill, W. H. *Plagues and Peoples*. New York: Anchor Press, 1976.

Maitland, F. W. *The Domesday Book and Beyond*. Cambridge: Cambridge University Press, 1897.

Malthus, T. R. *An Essay on the Principle of Population*. London: Dent & Sons, 1973 [1872].

Marx, K. *Pre-Capitalist Economic Formations*. New York, International Publishers, 1965.

———. *A Contribution to the Critique of Political Economy*. Moscow: Progress Publishers, 1970.

———. *Grundrisse: Introduction to the Critique of Political Economy*. New York: Vintage, 1973.

———. *Capital: A Critique of Political Economy*, vol. 1. Intro. by E. Mandel. New York: Vintage, 1977.

Marx, K. and Engels, F. *The German Ideology*, ed. and intro. by C. J. Arthur. New York: International Publishers, 1970.

Matossian, M. K. 'Mold Poisoning and Population Growth in England and France, 1750–1850'. *Journal of Economic History*, vol. 44, no. 3, 1984, pp. 669–86.

Mauro, F. and Parker, G. 'Spain'. In C. Wilson and G. Parker, eds, *An Introduction to the Sources of European Economic History, 1500–1800*. Ithaca, N.Y.: Cornell University Press, 1977.

Mayhew, A. *Rural Settlement and Farming in Germany*. London: Batsford, 1973.

Medick, H. 'The Proto-Industrial Family Economy: The Structural Function of Household and Family during the Transition from Peasant Society to Industrial Capitalism'. *Social History*, vol. 3, 1976, pp. 291–315.

———. 'The Proto-Industrial Family Economy'. In P. Kriedte, H. Medick and J. Schlumbohm, *Industrialization before Industrialization*. Cambridge: Cambridge University Press, 1981.

———. The Structures and Function of Population Development under the Proto-Industrial System'. In P. Kriedte, H. Medick and J. Schlumbohm, *Industrialization before Industrialization*. Cambridge: Cambridge University Press, 1981.

———. 'Plebian Culture in the Transition to Capitalism'. In R. Samuels and G. Stedman Jones, eds, *Culture, Ideology and Politics*. London: Routledge & Kegan Paul, 1982.

———. 'Village Spinning Bees: Sexual Culture and Free Time among Rural Youth in Early Modern Germany'. In H. Medick and D. Sabean, eds, *Interest and Emotion*. Cambridge: Cambridge University Press, 1984.

Medick, H. and Sabean, D., eds, *Interest and Emotion*. Cambridge: Cambridge University Press, 1984.

Meillassoux, C. 'The Economic Bases of Demographic Reproduction'. *Journal of Peasant Studies*, vol. 11, no. 1, 1983, pp. 50–61.

———. *Maidens, Meal and Money: Capitalism and the Domestic Community*. Cambridge: Cambridge University Press, 1981.

Mendels, F. F. 'Industry and Marriages in Flanders before the Industrial Revolution'. In P. Deprez, ed., *Population and Economics*. Winnipeg: University of Manitoba Press, 1970.

———. 'Proto-industrialization: The First Phase of the Industrialization Process'. *Journal of Economic History*, vol. 32, 1972, pp. 241–61.

———. 'Social Mobility and Phases of Industrialization'. *Journal of Interdisciplinary History*, vol. 7, no. 2, 1976, pp. 193–216.

———. 'Seasons and Regions in Agriculture and Industry'. In S. Pollard, ed., *Region und*

Industrialisierung. Göttingen: Vandenhoek & Ruprecht, 1980.

——. 'Agriculture and Peasant Industry in Eighteenth-Century Flanders'. In P. Kriedte, H. Medick and J. Schlumbohm, *Industrialization before Industrialization.* Cambridge: Cambridge University Press, 1981.

Mercer, A. J. 'Smallpox and Epidemiological-Demographic Change in Europe: The Role of Vaccination'. *Population Studies,* vol. 39, 1985, pp. 287–307.

Meyer, J. 'Illegitimates and Foundlings in Pre-Industrial France'. In P. Laslett, K. Oosterveen and R. M. Smith, eds, *Bastardy and Its Comparative History.* Cambridge, Mass.: Harvard University Press, 1980.

Middleton, C. 'The Sexual Division of Labour in Feudal England'. *New Left Review,* nos 113/114, 1979, pp. 147–68.

——. 'Peasants, Patriarchy and the Feudal Mode of Production in England: A Marxist Appraisal'. *Sociological Review,* vol. 29, no. 1, 1981, pp. 105–54.

Milkman, R. 'Redefining Women's Work: The Sexual Division of Labor in the Auto Industry in World War Two'. *Feminist Studies,* vol. 8, no. 2, 1982, pp. 337–72.

Mitterauer, M. and Sieder, R. 'The Developmental Process of Domestic Groups: Problems of Reconstruction and Possibilities of Interpretation'. *Journal of Family History,* vol. 4, no. 3, 1979, pp. 257–84.

——. *The European Family: Patriarchy to Partnership from the Middle Ages to the Present.* Oxford: Basil Blackwell, 1982.

Mogensen, N. W. 'Structures et changements démographiques dans vingt paroisses Normandes sous l'Ancien Régime'. *Annales de démographie historique,* 1975, pp. 343–67.

Molyneux, M. 'Androcentrism in Marxist Anthropology'. *Critique of Anthropology,* vol. 3, nos 9/10, 1977, pp. 55–82.

Moore, R. I. 'Duby's Eleventh Century'. *History,* vol. 69, 1984, pp. 36–49.

——. 'Family, Community and Cult on the Eve of the Gregorian Reform'. *Transactions of the Royal Historical Society,* 5th ser., vol. 30, 1980, pp. 49–69.

Morineau, M. 'France'. In C. Wilson and G. Parker, eds, *An Introduction to the Sources of European Economic History, 1500–1800.* Ithaca, N.Y.: Cornell University Press, 1977.

Muller, V. 'The Formation of the State and the Oppression of Women: Some Theoretical Considerations and a Case Study in England and Wales'. *Review of Radical Political Economics,* vol. 9, no. 3, 1977, pp. 7–21.

——. 'Origins of Class and Gender Hierarchy in Northwest Europe'. *Dialectical Anthropology,* vol. 10, nos 1/2, 1985, pp. 93–105.

Murdock, G. 'Comparative Data on the Division of Labour by Sex'. *Social Forces,* vol. 15, 1937, pp. 551–3.

Murray, A. *Germanic Kinship Structure.* Toronto: Pontifical Institute of Medieval Studies, 1983.

Musset, L. *The Germanic Invasions: The Making of Europe, AD 400–600.* University Park, Pa.: Pennsylvania State University Press, 1975.

Nilsson, T., Norman, H. and Rogers, J. 'Family Building and Family Planning in Pre-industrial Sweden'. In J. Rogers, ed., *Family Building and Family Planning in Preindustrial Societies.* Uppsala: University of Uppsala, 1980.

O'Brien, M. *The Politics of Reproduction.* London: Routledge & Kegan Paul, 1981.

Ogden, P. 'Marriage Patterns and Population Mobility: A Study of Rural France'. Research Paper 7, School of Geography. Oxford University, 1973.

O'Grada, C. 'The Population of Ireland, 1700–1900: A Survey'. *Annales de démographie historique,* 1979, pp. 281–99.

Ohlin, P. G. 'Mortality, Marriage and Growth in Pre-Industrial Populations'. *Population Studies,* vol. 14, no. 3, 1961, pp. 190–97.

Oosterveen, K. and Smith, R. M. 'Bastardy and the Family Constitution Studies of Colyton, Aldenham, Alcester and Hawkshead'. In P. Laslett, K. Oosterveen and R. M. Smith, eds, *Bastardy and Its Comparative History.* Cambridge, Mass.: Harvard University Press, 1980.

Ortner, S. B. 'Is Male to Female as Nature Is to Culture?' In M. Z. Rosaldo and L. Lamphere, eds, *Woman, Culture and Society*. Stanford, Calif.: Stanford University Press, 1974.

——. 'The Virgin and the State'. *Feminist Studies,* vol. 4, no. 3, 1978, pp. 19–36.

Osterud, N. G. 'Gender Divisions and the Organization of Work in the Leicester Hosiery Industry'. In A. V. John, ed., *Unequal Opportunities: Women's Employment in England, 1800–1918*. Oxford: Basil Blackwell, 1986.

Outhwaite, R. B., ed. *Marriage and Society: Studies in the Social History of Marriage*. New York: St. Martin's Press, 1981.

Ozment, S. *When Fathers Ruled: Family Life in Reformation Europe*. Cambridge, Mass.: Harvard University Press, 1983.

Pagels, E. *Adam, Eve and the Serpent*. New York: Random House, 1988.

Parsons, T. 'The American Family: Its Relation to Personality and the Social Structure'. In T. Parsons and R. F. Bales, eds, *Family, Socialization and Interaction Process*. New York: Free Press, 1955.

Pasternak, B., Ember, C. R. and Ember, M. 'On the Conditions Favoring Extended Family Households'. *Journal of Anthropological Research* (formerly *Southwestern Journal of Anthropology*) vol. 32, no. 2, 1976, pp. 109–23.

Pehrson, R. N. 'Bilateral Kin Groupings'. In J. Goody, ed., *Kinship: Selected Readings*. Harmondsworth: Penguin Books, 1971.

Perrenoud, A. Le Biologique et l'humain dans le déclin séculaire de la mortalité'. *Annales: Economies, sociétés, civilisations,* vol. 40, no. 1, 1985, pp. 113–35.

Petchesky, R. 'Dissolving the Hyphen: A Report on Marxist-Feminist Groups 1–5'. In Z. R. Eisenstein, ed., *Capitalist Patriarchy and the Case for Socialist Feminism*. New York: Monthly Review Press, 1979.

Pinchbeck, I. *Women Workers and the Industrial Revolution, 1750–1850*. London: Virago, 1981 [1930].

Plakans, A. 'Seigneurial Authority and Peasant Family Life: The Baltic Area in the Eighteenth Century'. *Journal of Interdisciplinary History,* vol. 4, 1975, pp. 629–54.

——. *Kinship in the Past: An Anthropology of European Family Life, 1500–1900*. Oxford: Basil Blackwell, 1984.

Pollock, L. *Forgotten Children: Parent–Child Relations from 1500 to 1900*. Cambridge: Cambridge University Press, 1983.

——. 'Courtship and Marriage from the Middle Ages to the Twentieth Century'. *The Historical Journal,* vol. 39, no. 2, 1987, pp. 483–98.

Pomeroy, S. B. *Goddesses, Whores, Wives and Slaves*. New York: Schocken, 1975.

——. 'The Relationship of the Married Woman to Her Blood Relatives in Rome'. *Ancient Society,* vol. 7, 1976, pp. 215–27.

Poos, L. R. 'The Rural Population of Essex in the Later Middle Ages'. *Economic History Review,* 2nd ser., vol. 38, no. 4, 1985, pp. 515–30.

——. 'Population Turnover in Medieval Essex'. In L. Bonfield, R. M. Smith and K. Wrightson, eds, *The World We Have Gained*. Oxford: Basil Blackwell, 1986.

——. 'The Pre-history of Demographic Regions in Traditional Europe'. *Sociologia Ruralis,* vol. 36, nos 3/4, 1986, pp. 228–48.

Porter, R. *English Society in the Eighteenth Century*. Harmondsworth: Penguin, 1982.

Post, J. D. 'Famine, Mortality and Epidemic Disease in the Process of Modernization'. *Economic History Review,* 2nd ser., vol. 29, 1976, pp. 14–37.

——. *The Last Great Subsistence Crisis in the Western World*. Baltimore: Johns Hopkins University Press, 1977.

Postan, M. M. *The Medieval Economy and Society: An Economic History of Britain in the Middle Ages*. Harmondsworth: Penguin, 1975.

Postan, M. M. and Titow, J. Z. 'Heriots and Prices on Winchester Manors'. In M. Postan, ed., *Essays on Medieval Agriculture and General Problems of the Medieval Economy*. Cambridge: Cambridge University Press, 1983.

Pounds, N. J. G. *An Economic History of Medieval Europe*. New York: Longman, 1974.

Powell, C. L. *English Domestic Relations, 1482–1653*. New York: Russell & Russell, 1972 [1917].

Power, E. *Medieval Women*. Cambridge: Cambridge University Press, 1975.

Preston, S. and Van de Walle, E. 'Urban French Mortality in the Nineteenth Century'. *Population Studies*, vol. 32, no. 2, 1978, pp. 275–97.

Prior, M., ed. *Women in English Society, 1500–1800*. London: Methuen, 1985.

Quaife, G. R. *Wanton Wenches and Wayward Wives*. London: Croom Helm, 1979.

Quataert, J. H. 'Combining Agrarian and Industrial Livelihood: Rural Households in the Saxon Oberlausitz in the Nineteenth Century'. *Journal of Family History*, vol. 10, no. 2, 1985, pp. 145–62.

———. 'Teamwork in Saxon Homeweaving Families in the Nineteenth Century'. In R. B. Joeres and M. J. Maynes, eds, *German Women in the Eighteenth and Nineteenth Centuries*. Bloomington, Ind.: Indiana University Press, 1986.

Raftis, J. A. *Tenure and Mobility: Studies in the Social History of the Medieval English Village*. Toronto: Pontifical Institute of Medieval Studies, 1964.

———. *Warboys: Two Hundred Years in the Life of an English Medieval Village*. Toronto: University of Toronto Press, 1974.

———, ed. *Pathways to Medieval Peasants*. Toronto: Pontifical Institute of Medieval Studies, 1981.

Rapp [Reiter], R., ed. *Toward an Anthropology of Women*. New York: Monthly Review Press, 1975.

———. 'Gender and Class: An Archaeology of Knowledge Concerning the Origin of the State'. *Dialectical Anthropology*, vol. 2, no. 4, 1977, pp. 309–16.

Rapp R., Ross, E. and Bridenthal, R. 'Examining Family History'. *Feminist Studies*, vol. 5, no. 1, 1979, pp. 174–200.

Ravensdale, J. 'Population Changes and the Transfer of Customary Land on a Cambridgeshire Manor in the Fourteenth Century'. In R. M. Smith, ed., *Land, Kinship and Life-Cycle*. Cambridge: Cambridge University Press, 1984.

Rawson, B. 'Family Life among the Lower Classes of Rome in the First Two Centuries of the Empire'. *Classical Philology*, vol. 61, no. 2, 1966, pp. 71–83.

———, ed. *The Family in Ancient Rome*. New York: Cornell University Press, 1986.

Razi, Z. *Life, Marriage and Death in a Medieval Parish: Economy, Society and Demography in Halesowen, 1270–1400*. Cambridge: Cambridge University Press, 1980.

———. 'Family, Land and the Village Community in Later Medieval England'. *Past & Present*, no. 93, 1981, pp. 3–36.

Razzell, P. E. *The Conquest of Smallpox*. Fule, Sussex: Caliban Books, 1977.

Rebel, H. *Peasant Classes, the Bureaucratization of Property, and Family Relations under Early Hapsburg Absolutism, 1511–1637*. Princeton, N.J.: Princeton University Press, 1983.

Reiter [Rapp], R., ed. *Toward an Anthropology of Women*. New York: Monthly Review Press, 1975.

———. 'Men and Women in the South of France: Public and Private Domains'. In R. Reiter, *Toward an Anthropology of Women*. New York: Monthly Review Press, 1975.

Rich, A. *Of Woman Born*. New York: W. W. Norton, 1976.

Riche, P. *Daily Life in the World of Charlemagne*. Liverpool: Liverpool University Press, 1978.

Ring, R. R. 'Early Medieval Peasant Households in Central Italy'. *Journal of Family History*, vol. 4, no. 1, 1979, pp. 2–25.

Roberts, M. 'Sickles and Scythes: Women's Work and Men's Work at Harvest Time'. *History Workshop Journal*, 7, 1979, pp. 3–28.

Rosaldo, M. Z. 'Woman, Culture and Society: A Theoretical Overview'. In M. Rosaldo and L. Lamphere, eds, *Woman, Culture and Society*. Stanford, Calif.: Stanford University Press, 1974.

Rose, S. 'Gender Segregation in the Transition to the Factory: The English Hosiery Industry, 1850–1910'. *Feminist Studies*, vol. 13, no. 1, 1987, pp. 163–84.

Ross, E. 'Survival Networks: Women's Neighbourhood Sharing in London before World War I'. *History Workshop Journal,* no. 15, 1983, pp. 4–27.

Roubin, L. 'Male Space and Female Space within the Provençal Community'. In R. Forster and O. Ranum, eds, *Rural Society in France.* Baltimore: Johns Hopkins University Press, 1977.

Rowbotham, S., Alexander, S. and Taylor, B. 'Debate on Patriarchy'. In R. Samuel, ed., *People's History and Socialist Theory.* London: Routledge & Kegan Paul, 1983.

Russell, J. C. *British Medieval Population.* Albuquerque, N.M., 1948.

———. 'Population in Europe 500–1500'. In C. M. Cipolla, ed., *Fontana Economic History of Europe,* vol. 1. New York: Fontana, 1972.

Russell, J. C. 'The Control of Late Ancient and Medieval Population'. *Memoirs of the American Philosophical Society,* vol. 160, 1985.

Sabean, D. 'Aspects of Kinship Behaviour and Property in Rural Western Europe before 1800'. In J. Goody, J. Thirsk and E. P. Thompson, eds, *Family and Inheritance: Rural Society in Western Europe, 1200–1800.* Cambridge: Cambridge University Press, 1976.

———. *Power in the Blood: Popular Culture and Village Discourse in Early Modern Germany.* Cambridge: Cambridge University Press, 1984.

Sachs, K. *Sisters and Wives: The Past and Future of Sexual Equality.* Westport, Conn.: Greenwood Press, 1979.

Sahlins, M. *Culture and Practical Reason.* Chicago: University of Chicago Press, 1976.

de Ste Croix, G. E. M. *The Class Struggle in the Ancient Greek World.* London: Duckworth, 1981.

Saller, R. 'Familia, Domus, and the Roman Conception of the Family'. *Phoenix,* vol. 38, no. 4, 1984, pp. 336–55.

———. 'Roman Dowry and the Devolution of Property in the Principate'. *Classical Quarterly,* vol. 34, no. 1, 1984, pp. 195–205.

Saller, R. and Shaw, B. 'Tombstones and Roman Family Relations in the Principate: Civilians, Soldiers and Slaves'. *Journal of Roman Studies,* vol. 74, 1984, pp. 124–56.

Sanday, P. R. *Female Power and Male Dominance: On the Origins of Sexual Inequality.* Cambridge: Cambridge University Press, 1981.

Schlumbohm, J. 'Relations of Production – Productive Forces – Crises in Proto-Industrialization'. In P. Kriedte, H. Medick and J. Schlumbohm, *Industrialization before Industrialization.* Cambridge: Cambridge University Press, 1981.

Schmidtbauer, P. 'The Changing Household: Austrian Household Structure from the Seventeenth to the Early Twentieth Century'. In R. Wall, ed., *Family Forms in Historic Europe.* Cambridge: Cambridge University Press, 1983.

Schofield, R. 'Anatomy of an Epidemic: Colyton, November 1645 to November 1646'. In *The Plague Reconsidered.* Matlock, Derbyshire: Local Population Studies, 1977.

———. 'The Relationship between Demographic Studies and Environment in Preindustrial Western Europe'. In W. Conze, ed., *Sozialigeschichte der Familie in der Neuzit Europas.* Stuttgart: Klett Verlag, 1977.

———. 'English Marriage Patterns Revisited'. *Journal of Family History,* vol. 10, no. 1, 1985, pp. 2–20.

Scott, J. W. 'Men and Women in the Parisian Garment Trades: Discussions of Family and Work in the 1830s and 1840s'. In P. Thane, G. Crossick and R. Floud, *The Power of the Past: Essays for Eric Hobsbawm.* Cambridge: Cambridge University Press, 1984.

———. '"L'Ouvrière! Mot impie, sordide ... " Women Workers in the Discourse of French Political Economy, 1840–1860'. In P. Jouce, ed., *The Historical Meaning of Work.* Cambridge: Cambridge University Press, 1987.

Scott-Smith, D. 'A Homeo-Static Demographic Regime: Patterns in Western European Family Reconstitution Studies'. In R. Lee, ed., *Population Patterns in the Past.* New York: Academic Press, 1977.

Scrimshaw, N. 'The Value of Contemporary Food and Nutrition Studies for Historians'. In

BIBLIOGRAPHY

R. I. Rotberg and T. K. Rabb, eds, *Hunger and History*. Cambridge: Cambridge University Press, 1983.

Searle, E. 'Seigneurial Control of Women's Marriage: The Antecedents and Function of Merchet in England'. *Past & Present,* no. 82, 1979, 3–43.

Seccombe W. 'Marxism and Demography'. *New Left Review,* no. 137, 1983, pp. 22–47. Repr. in J. Dickinson and B. Russell, eds, *Family, Economy & State.* Toronto: Garamond Press, 1986.

———. 'Reflections on the Domestic Labour Debate and Prospects for Marxist-Feminist Synthesis'. In R. Hamilton and M. Barrett, eds, *The Politics of Diversity.* London: Verso, 1986.

———. 'The Western European Marriage Pattern in Historical Perspective: A Response to David Levine'. *The Journal of Historical Sociology,* vol. 3, no. 1, 1990, pp. 50–74.

Segal, L. *Is the Future Female? Troubled Thoughts on Contemporary Feminism.* London: Virago, 1987.

Segalen, M. 'The Family Cycle and Household Structure: Five Generations in a French Village'. *Journal of Family History,* vol. 2, no. 3, 1977, pp. 223–36.

Segalen, M. *Love and Power in the Peasant Family.* Oxford: Basil Blackwell, 1983.

———. '"Avoir sa part": Sibling Relations in Partible Inheritance Brittany'. In H. Medick and D. Sabean, eds, *Interest and Emotion.* Cambridge: Cambridge University Press, 1984.

———. *Historical Anthropology of the Family.* Cambridge: Cambridge University Press, 1986.

———. 'Life-Course Patterns and Peasant Culture in France: A Critical Assessment'. In T. Hareven and A. Plakans, eds, *Family History at the Crossroads.* Princeton, N.J.: Princeton University Press, 1987.

Sella, D. 'European Industries 1500–1700'. In C. M. Cipolla, ed., *The Fontana Economic History of Europe,* vol. 2. London: Fontana Books, 1974.

Seward, R. R. *The American Family: A Demographic History.* Beverly Hills: Sage Publications, 1978.

Shahar, S. *The Fourth Estate: A History of Women in the Middle Ages.* London: Methuen, 1983.

Shamas, C. 'The Eighteenth-Century Diet and Economic Change'. *Explorations in Economic History,* vol. 21, 1984, pp. 254–69.

Sharlin, A. 'Urban-Rural Differences in Fertility in Europe during the Demographic Transition'. In A. J. Coale and S. C. Watkins, eds, *The Decline of Fertility in Europe.* Princeton, N.J.: Princeton University Press, 1986.

Shaw, B. D. 'Latin Funerary Epigraphy and Family Life in the Later Roman Empire'. *Historia,* vol. 33, no. 3, 1984, pp. 457–97.

Shaw, B. D. and Saller, R. P. 'Close-kin Marriage in Roman Society?' *Man,* vol. 19, 1984, pp. 432–44.

Sheehan, M. 'Choice of Marriage Partner in the Middle Ages'. *Studies in Medieval and Renaissance History,* vol. 1, 1978, pp. 3–33.

Shorter, E. *The Making of the Modern Family.* New York: Basic Books, 1975.

Sieder, R. and Mitterauer, M. 'The Reconstruction of the Family Life Course: Theoretical Problems and Empirical Results'. In R. Wall, ed., *Family Forms in Historic Europe.* Cambridge: Cambridge University Press, 1983.

Sigworth, E. M. 'Gateways to Death? Medicine, Hospitals and Mortality, 1700–1850'. In P. Mathias, ed., *Science and Society, 1600–1900.* Cambridge: Cambridge University Press, 1972.

Slack, P. 'The Disappearance of Plague: An Alternative View'. *Economic History Review,* 2nd ser., vol. 34, no. 3, 1981, pp. 469–76.

Slocum, S. 'Woman the Gatherer: Male Bias in Anthropology'. In R. Reiter, ed., *Toward an Anthropology of Women.* New York: Monthly Review Press, 1975.

Smith, R. M. 'Population and Its Geography in England, 1500–1730'. In R. A. Dodgshon and R. A. Butlin, eds, *An Historical Geography of England and Wales.* London: Academic Press, 1978.

————. 'Kin and Neighbours in a Thirteenth-Century Suffolk Community'. *Journal of Family History,* vol. 4, 1979, pp. 219–56.

————. 'Some Reflections on the Evidence for the Origins of the European Marriage Pattern in England'. In C. C. Harris, ed., *Sociology of the Family: New Directions for Britain.* Keele: University of Keele, 1979.

————. 'The People of Tuscany and Their Families in the Fifteenth Century: Medieval or Mediterranean?' *Journal of Family History,* vol. 6, no. 1, 1981, pp. 107–28.

————. 'Fertility, Economy and Household Formation in England over Three Centuries'. *Population and Development Review,* vol. 7, no. 4, 1981, pp. 595–622.

————. 'Hypothèses sur la nuptialité en Angleterre aux XIIIᵉ – XIVᵉ siècles'. *Annales: Economies, sociétés civilisations,* vol. 38, no. 1, 1983, pp. 107–36.

————. 'Some Issues Concerning Families and Their Property in Rural England, 1250–1800'. In R. M. Smith, ed., *Land, Kinship and Life-Cycle.* Cambridge: Cambridge University Press, 1984.

————, ed. *Land, Kinship and Life-Cycle.* Cambridge: Cambridge University Press, 1984.

————. 'Marriage Processes in the English Past: Some Continuities'. In L. Bonfield, R. M. Smith and K. Wrightson, eds, *The World We Have Gained.* Oxford: Basil Blackwell, 1986.

Snell, K. D. M. *Annals of the Labouring Poor: Social Change and Agrarian England, 1600–1900.* Cambridge: Cambridge University Press, 1985.

Söderberg, J. 'Real Wage Trends in Urban Europe, 1730–1850: Stockholm in a Comparative Perspective'. *Social History,* vol. 12, no. 2, 1987, pp. 155–75.

Songer, S. '"A Prudent Wife Is from the Lord": The Married Peasant Woman of the Eighteenth Century in a Demographic Perspective'. *Scandinavian Journal of History,* vol. 9, no. 2, 1984, pp. 113–33.

Southern, R. W. *Western Society and the Church in the Middle Ages.* Harmondsworth: Penguin, 1970.

Spufford, M. *Contrasting Communities: English Villagers in the Sixteenth and Seventeenth Centuries.* Cambridge: Cambridge University Press, 1974.

————. 'Peasant Inheritance Customs and Land Distribution in Cambridgeshire from the Sixteenth to the Eighteenth Centuries'. In J. Goody, J. Thirsk and E. P. Thompson, eds, *Family and Inheritance: Rural Society in Western Europe, 1200–1800.* Cambridge: Cambridge University Press, 1976.

Staff. *Population Movements and Industrialization: Swedish Counties, 1895–1930.* Stockholm: Institute for Social Sciences, Stockholm University, n.d.

Stewart, S. 'Bastardy and the Family Constitution Studies of Banbury and Hartland'. In P. Laslett, K. Oosterveen and R. M. Smith, eds, *Bastardy and Its Comparative History.* Cambridge, Mass.: Harvard University Press, 1980.

Stone, L. *The Family, Sex and Marriage in England 1500–1800,* abridged edn. New York: Harper Colophon, 1977.

————. 'The Road to Polygamy'. *New York Review of Books,* vol. 36, no. 3, 1989, pp. 12–15.

Stuard, S. M., ed. *Women in Medieval Society.* Philadelphia: University of Pennsylvania Press, 1976.

Tacitus. *The Agricola and The Germania.* Harmondsworth: Penguin, 1948.

Tanner, N. M. *On Becoming Human.* Cambridge: Cambridge University Press, 1981.

Terrisse, M. 'Un faubourg du Havre: Ingouville'. *Population,* vol. 16, 1961, pp. 285–96.

Thirsk, J. *The Agrarian History of England and Wales,* vols 1–5. Cambridge: Cambridge University Press, 1967–85.

Thomas, J. 'Relations of Production and Social Change in the Neolithic of Northwest Europe'. *Man,* vol. 22, 1987, pp. 405–30.

Thomas, K. *Religion and the Decline of Magic.* Harmondsworth: Penguin, 1978.

Thompson, E. A. *The Early Germans.* Oxford: Oxford University Press, 1965.

Thompson, E. P. *The Making of the English Working Class.* Harmondsworth: Penguin, 1968 [1963].

Thrupp, S. L. 'The Problem of Replacement Rates in Late Medieval English Population'. *Economic History Review,* 2nd ser., vol. 18, 1965, pp. 101–19.

Tilly, C. 'The Historical Study of Vital Processes'. In C. Tilly, ed., *Historical Studies of Changing Fertility.* Princeton, N.J.: Princeton University Press, 1978.

———. 'Did the Cake of Custom Break?' In J. Merriman, ed., *Consciousness and Class Experience in Nineteenth Century Europe.* New York: Holmes & Meier, 1979.

———. *As Sociology Meets History.* New York: Academic Press, 1981.

———. 'Proletarianization and Rural Collective Action in East Anglia and Elsewhere, 1500–1900'. *Peasant Studies,* vol. 10, no. 1, 1982, pp. 5–34.

———. 'Demographic Origins of the European Proletariat'. In D. Levine, ed., *Proletarianization and Family History.* New York: Academic Press, 1984.

Tilly, L. 'The Food Riot as a Form of Political Conflict in France'. *Journal of Interdisciplinary History,* vol. 1, 1971, pp. 23–57.

———. 'Food Entitlement, Famine and Conflict'. In R. I. Rotberg and T. K. Rabb, eds, *Hunger and History.* Cambridge: Cambridge University Press, 1983.

Tilly, L., Scott, J. W. and Cohen, M. 'Women's Work and European Fertility Patterns'. *Journal of Interdisciplinary History,* vol. 6, 1976, pp. 447–76. Repr. in M. Gordon, ed., *The American Family in Social-Historical Perspective,* 2nd edn. New York: St Martin's Press, 1978.

Todd, M. *Everyday Life of the Barbarians: Goths, Franks and Vandals.* London: Batsford, 1972.

———. *The Northern Barbarians, 100 BC – AD 300.* London: Hutchinson, 1975.

Treggiari, S. 'Family Life among the Staff of the Volusii'. *Transactions of the American Philological Association,* vol. 105, 1975, pp. 393–401.

———. 'Lower Class Women in the Roman Economy'. *Florilegium,* vol. 1, 1979, pp. 65–86.

———. 'Questions on Women Domestics in the Roman West'. In M. Capozza, ed., *Schiavitu, manomissione e classi dipendenti nel mondo antico.* Rome: L'erma di Bretschneider, 1979.

———. 'Women as Property in the Early Roman Empire'. In D. K. Weisberg, ed., *Women and the Law: A Social Historical Perspective,* vol. 2. Cambridge, Mass.: Schenkman, 1982.

———. 'Digna Condicio: Betrothals in the Roman Upper Class'. *Echos du monde classique, Classical Views,* vol. 28, no. 3, 1984, pp. 419–51.

Trexler, R. C. 'Infanticide in Florence: New Sources and First Results'. *History of Childhood Quarterly,* vol. 1, 1973, pp. 98–116.

Turnbull, C. *The Forest People.* New York: Simon & Schuster, 1961.

Turpeinen, O. 'Fertility and Mortality in Finland since 1750'. *Population Studies,* vol. 33, no. 1, 1979, pp. 101–14.

Twigg, G. *The Black Death: A Biological Reappraisal.* London: Batsford, 1984.

Valentey, D. I. *An Outline Theory of Population.* Moscow: Progress Publishers, 1980.

Van Bath, S. *The Agrarian History of Western Europe.* London: Edward Arnold, 1963.

van de Walle, E. *The Female Population of France in the Nineteenth Century.* Princeton, N.J.: Princeton University Press, 1974.

Vinogradoff, P. *Villeinage in England.* Oxford: Oxford University Press, 1968 [1892].

———. *The Growth of the Manor,* 2nd edn. London: George Allen & Unwin, 1911.

de Vries, J. *The Dutch Rural Economy in the Golden Age, 1500–1700.* New Haven, Conn.: Yale University Press, 1974.

———. *The Economy of Europe in an Age of Crisis, 1600–1750.* Cambridge: Cambridge University Press, 1976.

———. *European Urbanization, 1500–1800.* Cambridge, Mass.: Harvard University Press, 1984.

———. 'The Population and Economy of the Preindustrial Netherlands.' *Journal of Interdisciplinary History,* vol. 15, no. 4, 1985, pp. 661–82.

Wachter, K. W. with E. A. Hammel and P. Laslett. *Statistical Studies of Historical Social Structure.* New York: Academic Press, 1978.

Wall, R. 'Regional and Temporal Variations in English Household Structure from 1650'. In Hobcraft and Rees, eds, *Regional Demographic Development.* London: Croom Helm, 1977.

————. 'Does Owning Real Property Influence the Form of the Household? An Example from Rural West Flanders'. In R. Wall, ed., *Family Forms in Historic Europe*. Cambridge: Cambridge University Press, 1983.

————. 'The Composition of Households in a Population of Six Men and Ten Women: South-East Bruges in 1814'. In R. Wall, ed., *Family Forms in Historic Europe*. Cambridge: Cambridge University Press, 1983.

————. 'The Household: Demographic and Economic Change in England, 1650–1970'. In R. Wall, ed., *Family Forms in Historic Europe*. Cambridge: Cambridge University Press, 1983.

————. 'Work, Welfare and the Family: An Illustration of the Adaptive Family Economy.' In L. Bonfield, R. M. Smith and K. Wrightson, eds, *The World We Have Gained*. Oxford: Basil Blackwell, 1986.

Wallace-Hadrill, J. M. *The Barbarian West: The Early Middle Ages, AD 400–1000*. London: Hutchinson, 1962.

Wallerstein, I. *The Modern World-System: Capitalist Agriculture and the Origins of the European World-Economy in the Sixteenth Century*. New York: Academic Press, 1974.

————. *The Capitalist World Economy*. Cambridge: Cambridge University Press, 1979.

————. 'Household Structures and Production Processes'. *Review*, vol. 5, 1982, pp. 437–58.

Watson, A. *The Law of Persons in the Later Roman Republic*. Oxford: Oxford University Press, 1967.

Weaver, P. R. C. *Familia Caesaris: A Social Study of the Emperor's Freedmen and Slaves*. Cambridge: Cambridge University Press, 1972.

Weber, A. F. *The Growth of Cities*. Ithaca, N.Y.: Cornell University Press, 1899.

Weber, E. *Peasants into Frenchmen*. Stanford, Calif.: Stanford University Press, 1976.

Weber, M. *Economy and Society*, 2 vols. Berkeley: University of California Press, 1978.

————. *The Agrarian Sociology of Ancient Civilizations*. London: Verso, 1976.

Weir, D. 'Fertility Transition in Rural France, 1740–1829' (dissertation summary). *Journal of Economy History*, vol. 44, no. 2, 1984, pp. 612–14.

————. 'Life under Pressure: France and England, 1670–1870'. *Journal of Economic History*, vol. 44, no. 1, 1984, pp. 27–45.

————. 'Rather Never Than Late: Celibacy and Age at Marriage in English Cohort Fertility'. *Journal of Family History*, vol. 9, 1984, pp. 340–54.

Wemple, S. *Women in Frankish Society, Marriage and the Cloister, 500–900*. Philadelphia: University of Pennsylvania Press, 1981.

Westermann, W.L. *The Slave Systems of Greek and Roman Antiquity*. Philadelphia: The American Philosophical Society, 1955.

Wheaton, R. 'Family and Kinship in Western Europe: The Problem of the Joint Family Household'. *Journal of Interdisciplinary History*, vol. 5, no. 4, 1975, pp. 601–28.

Whetham, E. *The Agrarian History of England and Wales*, vol. 7. Cambridge: Cambridge University Press, 1978.

Williamson, J. 'Norfolk: Thirteenth Century'. In P. D. A. Harvey, ed., *The Peasant Land Market in Medieval England*. Oxford: Clarendon Press, 1984.

Wilson, C. 'Natural Fertility in Pre-industrial England'. *Population Studies*, vol. 38, no. 2, 1984, pp. 225–40.

————. 'The Proximate Determinants of Marital Fertility in England, 1600–1799'. In L. Bonfield, R. M. Smith and K. Wrightson, eds, *The World We Have Gained*. Oxford: Basil Blackwell, 1986.

Wilson, P. J. *Man the Promising Primate: The Conditions of Human Evolution*. New Haven, Conn.: Yale University Press, 1980.

Wilson, S. 'The Myth of Motherhood a Myth: The Historical View of European Child-rearing'. *Social History*, vol. 9, no. 2, 1984, pp. 181–98.

Winberg, C. 'Population Growth and Proletarianization: The Transformation of Social Structures in Rural Sweden during the Agrarian Revolution'. In S. Åkerman, H. C. Johansen and D. Gaunt, eds, *Chance and Change: Social and Economic Studies in Historical Demography in the Baltic Area*. Odense: Odense University Press, 1978.

de Windt, A. R. 'Redefining the Peasant Community in Medieval England: The Regional Perspective'. *Journal of British Studies,* vol. 26, 1987, pp. 163–207.

Winter, M. 'Agrarian Class Structure and Family Farming'. In T. Bradley and P. Lowe, eds, *Locality and Rurality: Economy and Society in Rural Regions.* Norwich: Geo Books, 1984.

Woods, R. I. and Hinde, P. R. A. 'Nuptiality and Age at Marriage in NineteenthCentury England'. *Journal of Family History,* vol. 10, no. 2, 1985, pp. 119–44.

———. 'Mortality in Victorian England: Models and Patterns'. *Journal of Interdisciplinary History,* vol. 18, no. 1, 1987, pp. 27–54.

Woodward, J. H. *"To Do the Sick No Harm": A Study of the British Voluntary Hospital System to 1875.* London: Routledge & Kegan Paul, 1974.

Wrightson, K. 'The Nadir of English Illegitimacy in the Seventeenth Century'. In P. Laslett, K. Oosterveen and R. M. Smith, eds, *Bastardy and Its Comparative History.* Cambridge, Mass.: Harvard University Press, 1980.

———. *English Society, 1550–1680.* London: Hutchinson, 1982.

———. 'Kinship in an English Village: Terling, Essex, 1500–1700'. In R. M. Smith, ed., *Land, Kinship and Life-Cycle.* Cambridge: Cambridge University Press, 1984.

Wrightson, K. and Levine, D. *Poverty and Piety in an English Village: Terling, 1525–1700.* New York: Academic Press, 1979.

Wrigley, E. A. *Industrial Growth and Population Change.* Cambridge: Cambridge University Press, 1961.

———. 'Mortality in Pre-Industrial England: The Example of Colyton, Devon over Three Centuries'. *Daedalus,* no. 97, 1968, pp. 546–80.

———. *Population and History.* New York: McGraw-Hill, 1969.

———. 'Fertility Strategy for the Individual and the Group'. In C. Tilly, ed., *Historical Studies of Changing Fertility.* Princeton, N.J.: Princeton University Press, 1978.

———. 'Marriage, Fertility and Population Growth in Eighteenth-Century England'. In R. B. Outhwaite, ed., *Marriage and Society: Studies in the Social History of Marriage.* New York: St Martin's Press, 1981.

———. 'The Growth of Population in Eighteenth Century England: A Conundrum Resolved'. *Past & Present,* no. 98, 1983, pp. 121–50.

———. 'Urban Growth and Agricultural Change: England and the Continent in the Early Modern Period'. *Journal of Interdisciplinary History,* vol. 15, no. 4, 1985, pp. 683–728.

———. 'The Fall of Marital Fertility in Nineteenth Century France: Exemplar or Exception?' (parts 1 & 2). *European Journal of Population,* vol. 1, 1985, pp. 31–60; 141–77.

Wrigley, E. A. and Schofield, R. *The Population History of England, 1541–1871: A Reconstruction.* London: Edward Arnold, 1981.

Yanagisako, S. J. 'Family and Household: The Analysis of Kin Groups'. *Annual Review of Anthropology,* vol. 8, 1979, pp. 161–205.

Youings, J. *Sixteenth Century England.* Harmondsworth: Penguin, 1984.

Young, M. and Willmott, P. *The Symmetrical Family.* New York: Pantheon, 1973.

Zihlman, A. L. 'Women in Evolution: Subsistence and Social Orgnaization among Early Hominids'. *Signs,* vol. 4, no. 1, 1978, pp. 4–20.

———. 'Women as Shapers of the Human Adaption'. In F. Dahlberg, ed., *Woman the Gatherer.* New Haven, Conn.: Yale University Press, 1981.

Index

adoption 61: *see also* godfamilies
agriculture: agrarian cycle *see* feudalism; agriculturalists, cultivators 91; animal husbandry (stockraising) 78, 79, 142, 160; capitalist *see* capitalism, agriculture; cash-crop specialization (monoculture) 143, 163, 165; climate 129, 148, 190; commons 62, 97, 139, 165, 176; conversion of arable to pasture 139–40, 142; conversion of pasture to arable 128, 160, 177, 203; cropping practices (rotation) 52–3, 57, 63, 92, 127, 130, 139, 141, 204; ecological limits 78, 94, 129, 148, 160, 168, 193, 203; extensive growth pattern *see* feudalism; field systems 79, 96, 97, 139, 153; grain-growing 78, 97, 176 *see also* food; prices, grain; harvest 84, 91, 127, 129, 158, 163; horticulture: 16, 59, 89, 267 n105; intensive development 62, 130–31; interlacing of arable and pasture 78, 142; labour *see* farm labourers; labour, supply and demand; pasturage (pastoral zones) 78, 98, 128, 183; productivity 126, 130, 140, 154, 159, 160; sharecropping 91, 141; slash-and-burn 51; soil erosion and nutrient depletion 128, 131, 160; soil restoration 51, 52–3, 78, 148 *see also* land, soil types; subsistence-oriented cultivation 92, 140, 165; technology 127, 130, 140, 148, 203, 204; transition from hoe to plough; 51, 53, 56, 59, 63, 130; yield, variations in 91–2, 126, 130–31, 160, 252: *see also* feudalism; Germanic peoples; land; Malthusianism; peasants
ancien régime 40: *see also* feudalism
anthropology 14, 19, 20, 36, 50, 123, 265 n62
Antiquity: transition to feudalism 2, 44–60: *see also* Roman Empire
apprenticeship 183, 186, 221, 222, 235: *see also* guilds
Aquinas, St Thomas 76

artisans: *see* crafts/craftsmen
Augustine, St 71: *see also* Church, Augustinian

baptism 75–7, 270 n177; adult 67, 75; infant; 76–77: *see also* godfamilies
Barrett, Michèle 31
bastardy: *see* fertility, extramarital
Belgium 200, 203
betrothal 109, 113–4, 225, 235; Church position on 109; conjugal probation, cancelling nuptials; 104, 114; marital bargaining 112–3; neither single nor married 114; and prerequisites to marriage 109; sexual intimacy during 115, 191, 228–9; testing the match 114–15: *see also* courtship; dowry
birth: *see* childbirth
birth control 17–18; abortion 75, 150, 151, 185, 225; abstinence 72, 151; child spacing 151, 184–5, 195; Church opposition to 72, 75, 151–2, 185; contraceptives 48, 72, 150, 185, 212; delay of first birth 184, 188, 289; post-partum intercourse taboos 185: *see also* breastfeeding; fertility, regulation; mortality, infanticide
Black Death: impact 90, 129–30, 283 n4; losses estimated 129, 137–8, 287 n64; lethal agent 136, 283–4 nn4, 6, 8; subsequent pandemics 136–7, 152, 158: *see also* mortality, crises
Bloch, Marc 267 n113, 273 n230
Bois, Guy 249
boys: *see* children
breastfeeding 17, 21–2, 85, 95, 184–5, 195, 293 n181; wetnurses 107, 220
Brenner debate 247–54

Cambridge Group 166; findings 237, 305 n7; family paradigm 27–9, 121–3, 237, 281 nn381, 386, 304 nn4, 6; nuclear family continuity thesis 27, 50, 135, 233, 236; research methods 28–9: *see also* family, household composition

333

approach; Laslett, Peter
capitalism: in agriculture 79, 143, 164–6,
203, 231, 251–3; capital/wage-labour
relation 134; capital accumulation
172–3, 229–30; extensive versus
intensive patterns of accumulation
172–3; and family forms; 26, 134–5;
industrial cycles 140, 182; labour
demand; 163, 173, 190, 202, 220, 230,
231; 'laws of motion' 248; mode of
production 14, 26, 173, 283 n2; origins
134, 239; 'primitive accumulation' 167,
172, 230, 290 n126; reproduction of
labour-power 21, 172, 234; work
discipline and 207, 220, 235: see also
feudalism, transition to capitalism;
historical materialism; proletarianization
Carolingian era 60
celibacy: see Church, celibacy; Western
European marriage pattern
charivari 80, 112
childbirth 9, 240; assistance 18; hazards 18,
257 n25; legitimate 23, 38: see also
baptism; fertility
child-care 9, 85–86; compatibility with
other labour 21, 244; and human
immaturity 18–19, 20; women's work
16
children: boys 83, 95; child labour 83,
195, 207; girls 83, 95, 107; infants and
young children 85; parental investment
in childcare 19; cost and value to
parents 46, 83, 151, 195, 199, 206, 223;
valuing boys, devaluing girls 95, 107–8:
see also fathers; inheritance; mothers;
parent-child relations; sibling group;
youth socialization
Christian religion: Adam and Eve 69;
conflict between faith and family 66–8;
conversion 75, 77; eternal damnation
76; heresy 76; Jesus, teachings of 65–7;
miracles 77; original sin 69, 75, 76;
'popular Christianity' 77; the Second
Coming 67; virgin birth 65, 73
Church: Augustinian 68–9, 72; birth
control, opposition to 72, 75, 151–2,
185; celibacy, veneration of 67, 69, 70,
74, 75; communities of the faithful 67;
confession 54; courts 109, 114; early
sects 67, 75; exorcism 76, 77;
Inquisition 151; land acquisition see
landholding, Church; lay/clerical
relations 70, 77; magic rites 77;
'marrying the Church' 74–5; mass 71;
monastic orders 75, 78, 95, 127, 151;
parish, local; penance 54, 72, 80;

priests/priesthood 72, 74, 76, 77, 80;
sacraments 68, 76; saints 74; of the
whole society 68, 75, 76: see also
baptism; Christian religion; sexuality
Church, doctrines on marriage 109;
Augustinian doctrine of 69, 115; banns
(lets and impediments) 71, 109–10, 238;
consent of the principals 70, 77, 104,
109, 111, 238; derogation 67, 68;
divorce 67, 104; exogamic proscriptions
71, 77, 108, 110; extension of control
over 70–71, 109, 238, 278 n315;
homogenizing norms 71; kin alliance
104; 'marital debt' 72–3; positive
doctrine 68, 69–70; sexual sins 69, 71,
110, 115, 151, 179, 180, 226;
solemnization (Church ceremony,
liturgy) 71, 109–10, 186; strict (radical)
interpretation 109; upholding parental
influence 110
cities 137, 158, 159, 196, 197, 211, 216–17
community 79–81, 139: see also village
commutation of dues: see feudalism;
demesne
concubinage 71, 72, 73
cottagers 175; cottage economy 125–6,
177, 181, 182: see also landlessness;
poor/poverty; proletarianization;
settlement, squatters; vagrancy
contraception: see birth control
courtship: attraction and interests 113–4,
235; and betrothal 115; matchmakers
and chaperones 112, 227; night-visiting
115, 225; parental approval 110, 112;
regulation by community and parents
111, 112, 220, 225, 226–7; dissipation
of control 190, 221–2, 226–9, 235;
rituals 112; romantic love 113–4, 235;
suitor initiative 112; women's role 47;
venues 112–3, 226, 235: see also
betrothal; marriage, mate selection;
sexuality, pre-marital
crafts/craftsmen 89–90, 141, 181, 182

demesne 53, 88, 139, 148, 154; familiae 49,
59, 78, 141: see also labour-service;
manor
demography: see population
Denmark 120, 197, 214
disease 210–11; antibody resistance 57,
136; bubonic plague 136, 283 n4, 284
n 6; carriers 283 n4; contagion, spread
136, 210, 284 n8; hospitals 211;
innoculation 210; lethality 210, 284 n8;
quarantine 210–11, 300 n303: see also
mortality

disinheritance: *see* inheritance
division of labour between sexes 16,
    20–21, 56, 83–5, 90, 257 n15,
    272 n208: *see also* spousal relations
divorce 1, 2, 67, 72, 74, 104, 245: *see also*
    marriage, annulment; remarriage
domestic labour 56, 84–5, 170, 207;
    continuous 16; skilled labour 16, 19–20
domestic manufacture 79
domestic service: *see* service
dowry 102, 155, 277 n297; bargaining 90,
    112, 113; and bride-price 105; dot 104;
    dower 43, 65, 104, 105, 111; exchange
    configuration 64–5, 104; and female
    status 64–5, 105, 277 n297; final claim,
    subsequent exclusion of 65, 98–9, 104,
    105, 277 n299; and inheritance 96, 98,
    112, 226; *morgengabe* 64; preparatory
    provisioning 22; return of 105–6; size
    47, 155, 238; timing 106; woman's
    own contribution 105, 199: *see also*
    betrothal; inheritance; marriage
dwellings 46, 80, 83, 85, 125, 158:
    see also household; residence; village

Early Modern period: terminology 133–4;
    versus Middle Ages 140, 156, 163, 181
Eastern Europe 44, 103, 152, 153, 154,
    209
East/West contrast: *see* feudalism; family
employment: individual hiring 167, 169;
    and paternalist supervision 170; seasonal
    171, 177; subcontracting 27, 169;
    underemployment 172, 195, 220;
    unemployment 172; year–round 173,
    177–8, 195: *see also* proletarian
    condition; labour; capitalism, labour
    demand
Engels, Friedrich 36, 256 n4
England 5, 58, 111, 137, 159, 175, 190,
    192, 197, 200, 204, 205, 225, 228, 230,
    242, 250–54; Alcester 226; Aldenham
    226; Baslow 146; Cambridgeshire 82;
    Chippenham 162; Colyton 226, 288
    n75; Coltishall 144, 156; Derbyshire
    100; East Anglia 81–2;
    Goodnestone-Next-Kent 194;
    Halesowen 97, 99, 101, 125, 146;
    Lincolnshire 82, 155; London 196;
    Kent 81–2; Kibworth Harcourt 90,
    146, 156, 162; Kirby Lonsdale 81;
    Nottinghamshire 217; Redgrave, 82;
    Rutland 155; Shepshed 194; Somerset
    100; Terling 81, 100, 196; West
    Midlands 145, 149; Westminister 118;
    Worcester 82, 139

evidence: archeological fieldwork 43, 44,
    50, 51; census 29, 48; contemporary
    observers, surveys 50, 175; court rolls 4,
    43, 145; legal codes 43, 52; literary 50,
    52, 185; papyrus 49; parish registers 4,
    158; poor law records 180; tomb
    inscriptions 49–50; wills and probate
    inventories 43, 156, 176
exchange: between neighbours 56, 79–80,
    84, 181, 234; within a region 140, 182;
    supraregional trade 92, 140, 182, 203:
    see also market
exogamy: *see* marriage
extramarital fertility: *see* fertility,
    extramarital

family: affinal family 40; alternatives to 31;
    and biology 22; budgets; change and
    continuity 2, 5, 134–5; Church's
    influence 65–77; conflation of terms
    family and *household* 28, 121, 305 n8;
    conjugal primacy 41, 53, 64–5, 238,
    262 n14; cross–cultural definitions of;
    dependency ratio *see* household;
    desertion 145, 180; East/West
    difference 42, 153; economy 92–3, 230;
    enforcement of norms 24, 109–10;
    English versus French family patterns
    111, 147, 252–4; formation strategies
    22, 25–6, 98, 253–4, 258 n39;
    Germanic family forms *see* Germanic
    peoples; history *see* history, family;
    household composition approach
    121–4, 135, 237, 281 nn381, 386, 304
    nn4, 6; labour team 39, 83, 199, 234;
    modern families 1, 212, 243; and mode
    of production 2, 3, 9, 233, 277 n297;
    natal 40, 41, 124, 238; nuclear *see*
    nuclear family; obligation 23, 24, 66,
    98, 100, 117, 151; peasant family *see*
    peasant, family; peopling societies 11,
    233, 256 n4; privacy 80–81; production
    of labour-power 9, 83, 91–5; reputation
    24, 80–81, 111, 227; Roman forms *see*
    Roman Empire; security 23; size and
    wealth correlated *see* households; 'the
    family' 1, 24, 135, 239; 'Western' form
    1, 135, 238: *see also* dwellings; family
    cycle; householdship; household;
    inheritance; kinship; marriage; nuclear
    family; parent-child relations; parenting;
    patriarchy; residence; sibling group;
    slaves, families; stem family
family cycle: 24, 135, 183, 184, 234;
    approach 25–6, 28–9, 259 n49, 304 n6;
    centripetal versus centrifugal 93,

120–21, 125–6, 184, 234; changing dependency ratio by phase 16, 93, 149, 206; turnover phase 25, 183; versus household composition approach 28, 121–4, 135

famine 209; Irish 152, 209

farm labourers 124, 125, 127, 139–40, 141, 142, 145, 164; 177, 195, 200, 204, 218, 221, 231

fathers/fatherhood: custodial rights 30, 40; fathering 19, 83; arranging children's inheritance and marriages 47, 99–102, 111–13, 145, 147, 149; paternal commitment 20, 22, 30; patriarchs see peasants, patriarchs; and sons 148–9: see also generations; inheritance; marriage, parents' role; parent-child relations; parenting; paternity; patriarchy; retirement

females/women: see dowry; gender relations; girls; heiresses; mothers/mothering; patriarchy; spousal relations; widows

feminism/feminists 4, 9, 11, 19, 30, 35, 86, 216: see also history, women's

fertility: birth intervals (child-spacing) 17, 151, 184–5; birth rates 191, 252; class differentials 39, 125, 194–7, 224; fecundity 115, 184; incentives 151, 195, 222–3; legitimated by marriage 32–3, 38, 115; and population growth 158–9; marriage as regulator 38, 152, 184, 185; and menopause 184; and migration 185, 196, 217; and mortality 159–9, 188, 190, 213; 'natural fertility' 184, 293 nn176, 177; premenopausal stopping 184, 212; rates 213–4, 217; regulation of 10, 13, 15, 22, 92, 150, 152, 212; rituals 39, 77: see also birth control; breastfeeding; childbirth; fertility, extramarital; population; procreation; sexuality; Western European marriage pattern

fertility, extramarital (illegitimacy, bastardy) 152, 191, 222, 225–9; bridal pregnancy 115, 191, 228–9; Church repression 72, 74, 115; class differentials: 226; explaining increase 227–29; illegitimacy rate 115, 191, 225: see also betrothal; courtship; proletarianization

feud: see kinship; Germanic peoples

feudalism (feudal–seigneurial mode of production) 2, 26, 37–44, 78, 118, 136, 163; agrarian cycle 135–6, 140, 192–3, 247–9, 283 n3; and ancien régime 40, 133, 140, 193, 201, 238; benefice see

vassalage and benefice; class conflict and the balance of power 138–40, 143; commutation of dues 139–40, 143, 156; crisis of 2, 129, 130–31, 142; definition 37, 140, 261 n2; demographic dynamics ('overpopulation') 93, 126–31, 140, 163–6, 248–9, 274 n248; East/West contrast 26, 153, 285 n25; exploitation (surplus extraction) 37, 91–5, 129, 133; 148, 153, 160, 164; extensive growth pattern 39, 42, 51, 92–3, 94, 124–9; 159–60, 203, 235; family see peasants, family; fief system 37, 60–62, 267 n113; lords' prerogative 38, 39, 41, 61–2, 137–8; origins 43–60; property form 37–8, 98, 133–4, 143, 150; reproduction cycle of labour-power 83, 248; seigneurial domain extended 59, 63, 268 n124; seigneurial exactions, dues, rent 38, 62, 91–2, 108, 138, 140, 164; see also feudalism, exploitation; serfdom, peasant servility 38, 59, 88, 138–9, 140, 264 n38, 273 n230; technostructure 78, 270 n181; tendencies to stagnation 128–31, 160, 231; transition from Antiquity see Antiquity, transition to feudalism; transition to capitalism 3, 27, 133–4, 137, 233–6; vassalage and benefice 37–8, 60: see also landholding; lords; manor; population; peasants

feudalism, state forms 38, 54, 58, 60, 61; legal code 109; local 80, 143; military retinue and 60; royal courts and 55, 58, 61

Finland 301 n314

food 15, 16, 158, 160, 176, 209, 231 see also agriculture; prices, grain

foragers 15, 89; compared with non-human primates 15; Stone Age bands 17, 20; gender relations 35-6; and subsistence 16; Man the Hunter argument 19–20: see also vagrancy; landlessness

forests: deforestation 127–8, 159–60, 176–7; restricted access 160, 177, 180: see also settlement; squatters

France 98, 160, 190, 191, 192, 194, 200, 202, 213, 217, 225, 228, 242, 250–54; Normandy 137, 158, 161, 179, 252; 'Gaul' 56, 58; Haute Provence 137; Île de France, 58; Languedoc 144, 147, 149, 161, 162, 175; Lyon 161; Marseille 94, 210; Mediterranean 98; Montaillou 83; Paris basin 137, 138, 157, 175, 253; Picardy 162; Poitou 175 gender relations 11; conceptualizing 4, 14; dimension of patriarchy 30–31; identitites 19; in pre-class societies 35–6: *see also* division of labour between sexes; patriarchy; spousal relations

generations, relations between 21, 104, 170, 183, 184, 187, 224–5, 235, 238: *see also* father; mother; parent-child relations; retirement; socialization of youth; widows,

Germanic peoples 44, 50–56; agricultural practices 50–51, 56; barbarian states 44, 53, 54, 55; before Roman contact 50; conjugal family 53, 238; dowry 64–5; feud 52; inheritance 53; kindred and lordship 59–60; kinship (the Sippe) 51–5, 59, 238, 265 n61, 266 n72; marriage 55; migration 56–7; *morgengabe* among 64; nomadic and pastoral roots 50; population growth 56; settlements 52–3; technology 51; women's status 55–6

Germany 58, 110, 127, 137, 157, 160, 161, 162, 190, 194, 198, 200, 202, 203, 205, 217, 225, 228, 242, 249

godfamilies, godfathers, godparents 76–7

Goody, Jack 97, 105, 106, 262 n14, 277 n297

grain: *see* agriculture; food; prices, grain

guilds 183, 186, 277 n292: *see also* protoindustrialization, bypassing guilds

Hajnal, John 152, 155, 186, 241, 294 n187

heir/heiress: *see* inheritance

heriot 41, 62, 139

historical materialism (marxism) 134, 140, 167, 233, 247, 255 n4; blindness to family forms 3, 9; and demography 12, 216, 249, 256 nn4, 5; feminist challenge to, criticism of 4, 9, 14, 16; mode-of-production concept *see* mode of production; political economy 3, 10, 12, 134, 140, 148, 248; problem of economism 10–11; theories of false consciousness 33: *see also* Marx; uneven and combined development

history/historians 140; determinism 25; empiricism 7; economic history 185; family history 4, 36, 51–2, 107, 121, 135; historical demography 150, 185, 201, 212; historical sociology 6–7, 10, 39; local studies 4, 6, 214; long view of history 2, 5; revisionist current 29; social history 5, 6, 7, 25, 29, 39, 121, 185; theory 7; women's history 4, 36, 86

householdship: 36, 40, 106, 234; female head 117–19, 276 n278; and kindred 53; male bias 40, 118; transfer of authority 30, 42–3, 102–3, 107, 116, 118, 123–4: *see also* households; patriarchy; residence

households: complex or extended 43 ; composition, co–residence patterns 42, 90, 120, 122–4, 146, 183, 236; dependency ratio 16, 21–2, 92–3, 142, 153, 223, 239; 'domus' 83; formation, conditions of 25, 89, 90, 96, 123–4, 153, 158, 186, 188, 189; 195, 205, 206; simple 43, 121, 236, 294 n187; size 28, 90, 121, 146, 158, 194, 236; size and wealth correlated 38–9, 90, 125, 128, 194, 195, 205, 206: *see also* dwelling, family, household composition approach; neo-locality; peasants; protoindustrialization; residence rules

husbands: *see* patriarchy; spousal relations

ideologies: and interest 33–4, 113–14; theories of false consciousness 33

illegitimacy: *see* fertility, extramarital

industrialization: factory system 181, 207; industrial revolution 181, 186, 203, 214, 216, 230, 291 n134; and the population boom 186, 229–31; shift in labour force 193, 202; technological change 230: *see also* protoindustrialization

infanticide: *see* mortality

inheritance 96–103; agnatic 40, 53, 64, 71, 73, 106, 146, 183, 277 n292; birth order and 95, 101; and collateral kin 106, 145; compensatory impartible 39, 63, 97–9, 104–5, 126, 187, 189, 199, 275 n258; congugal patriline 41, 62; conjugal primacy 38, 41, 65, 71; conversion from partible to impartible 39, 62–4; coparcenary (joint) 53, 98; delaying devolution 100–101; discrimination against females 107; disinheritance 48–9, 110, 236; 'diverging devolution' 98; and dotal exchange 96, 98, 155; egalitarian principles and unequal shares 97, 102, 105; family heritability 42, 61–2, 106, 144–6, 148–50, 261 n11; and fertility 95; formal models of (ideal–types) 96; formal rules of 100; fragmentation of holdings (avoiding) 42, 48, 96, 97–8; and gendered spheres 83; Germanic and

Roman elements blended 64; heirs 39, 64, 71, 101, 104, 117, 124; heiresses: 106–7; impartible 44, 62–5, 96, 128, 152, 183, 184, 268 n124, 275 n261; inside/outside feudal zones 63; land niche system *see* landholding; and land tenure 144; leeway, flexibility and pragmatism 9, 100, 101–2; and lineage; 'loose' and 'tight' systems 96; lords' prerogatives and influence 61–2, 64, 101, 106–7, 118; and marriage 38, 87, 103–8; non-heirs *see* non-heirs; partible 63, 128, 183; patrilineal *see* agnatic; *pre-mortem* or *inter-vivos* 101, 103, 188; primogeniture 53, 100; right of reversion (*retrait lignager*) 61, 145, 149, 165, 199 sibling conflict *see* sibling group; sons preferably, daughters in lieu of sons 40, 64, 106; strategies of heirship 98–103; security in old age *see* old age; retirement; unigeniture 63, 98, 253; and widows 117–18; wills 149, 188; women's prerogatives 40, 87, 104, 277 n297: *see also* dowry; landholding; land, availability; patriarchy; population; retirement
Italy 44, 46, 98, 141, 192, 200; Florence 107, 126, 137, 155; Prato 137, 155; Pistoia 137; Sicily 44, 157; Tuscany 138
joint family 103

King, Gregory 175, 194
kinship 22; afinal kin 107; bilateral (or cognatic) descent 40, 52, 107; Christian form *see* godfamilies; codifying domestic cycle 25, 107; collateral ties 41, 64, 71, 145, 146; density in settlements 81–2, 90, 108, 127, 253; feud 52, 54–5; and feudal relations 40–41, 60–62; formalist paradigm 10, 24, 265 n62, 266 n65; function and structure 52; Germanic kindred *see* Germanic peoples, kinship; involuntary onus 23; kindred 41, 43, 51–3; matrilineal/patrilineal descent 52, 55; reckoning 40, 52; security 54, 55; as support networks 23, 54, 90, 107; 43; unilineal descent groups 51, 52, 59, 60, 265 nn61, 63

labourers: *see* farm labourers
labour-power 14–22; consumption of 92, 154, 158, 183, 73, 185, 223, 303 n343; daily cycle 16, 78, 93; generational cycle 16, 93, 170, 172, 183: *see also* family, peopling societies; mode-of-production concept

labour market: *see* markets
labour service 41, 59, 84–5, 88, 92, 163; relinquishment 139–40, 148, 154: *see also* demesne; feudalism, seigneurial exactions
labour, supply and demand: 11, 16, 91, 92, 138, 141, 152,; 160–61, 163, 167, 173, 175, 182, 193, 203, 282 n405: *see also* capitalism, labour demand
Ladurie, Emmanuel Le Roy 147, 148, 163
land: abundance (vacancy) 138, 142, 148–9, 154; arable 78; availability 90, 91, 148–50, 156, 188, 199–200; clearing initiatives 126, 159, 188, 193, 203, 282 n405; colonization *see* settlement; market *see* markets; scarcity 94, 95, 96, 163; soil types 51, 137: *see also* agriculture; forest; landholding; manor; manse; neo-Malthusianism; population; settlement, colonization
land/population/labour-power 93–4, 96, 97, 129–31, 138, 146, 153, 161, 193, 248: *see also* landholding, niche system
landholding: acquests 53, 63, 97; alienation to outsiders 53; Church acquisition 71, 269 n157; copyhold 149; desertion (absenteeism, vacancy) 90, 99, 139, 140, 142, 145, 163; distribution 88, 128, 142, 148, 149, 162–3; dispossession (enclosure, eviction) 138–9, 162–3, 165, 170–71, 174–6, 178, 180, 197; entry (conditions and fees) 38, 90, 118, 138, 142, 145, 149, 153; family land 42, 52, 62, 97, 144–6, 148, 187, 188 *see also* inheritance, family heritability; fragmentation of holdings 42, 48, 53, 64, 89, 96, 97, 128–9, 163, 175, 183, 253 *see also* inheritance, fragmentation; lease 62, 90, 99, 128; link with marriage 38, 153–4, 187–8; minimum size viable for family 42, 93–4, 127–8, 175; niche system 96, 154, 187–9, 199, 224 *see also* Western European marriage system; squatters *see* settlement, squatters; surveyed 98, 149; tenure forms 88–9, 143–5: *see also* agriculture; inheritance; land; lords; manor; peasants, manse
landlessness 59, 162–3, 174–7: *see also* poverty; proletarian condition; vagrancy
Laslett, Peter 1, 20, 27, 50, 236, 242, 255 n6, 282 n389, 294 n194, 304 n6
Le Play, Frédéric 42
lords: absenteeism 143; class discipline 138–9, 285 n23; thirst for revenues 91, 129, 141: *see also* feudalism; manor

Luther, Martin 186

males/men: *see* fathers/fatherhood; gender
relations; householdship; inheritance,
heirs; patriarchy; spousal relations
Malthus, Thomas 11, 186, 203, 223
Malthusianism 128–31, 152, 185, 188,
241; and marxism 11–12, 293 n184;
neo-Malthusianism 148, 154, 247–9:
see also Brenner debate
manor 41, 78, 140, 153; bipartite structure
59, 78, 143; ecclesiatical 59, 139;
origins 53, 58–9; manor court 61, 62,
125, 143, 150, 238 n38; relation with
village 78, 139–41, 143–4: *see also*
demesne; labour service
manse: *see* peasants, manse
markets: consumer goods (non-food) 182,
230, 231; food 209; housing 221, 230;
labour 179, 187, 193, 221, 234, 248;
land 99, 102, 141, 148–50, 164, 167,
185, 189, 230: *see also* capitalism,
exchange
marriage: by abduction 71, 73; annulment
104, 111 *see also* divorce; bargaining *see*
betrothal; barriers and prerequisites 114,
186, 196, 206, 221, 226, 238;
clandestine 55, 74, 109, 111, 125;
Church regulation *see* Church,
doctrines on marriage; circumscribing
eligibility 25, 41, 74–5, 108, 112–13,
196, 227: *see also* Western European
marriage pattern; companionate 69, 86;
conception, pressure to marry 191, 222,
227, 228–9; consent of the principals
70, 74, 104, 110, 278 n315;
consummation ('marital debt') 64, 72–3,
103; endogamy 41, 58, 82, 108, 153,
165, 235, 253; exogamy 41, 58, 64, 74,
82, 90, 108, 112–13, 153, 165, 227,
235; 253; incentives 112–13, 152, 154,
221–3; and inheritance 25, 103–8, 112,
235; kin alliance 22, 54, 103, 104, 111;
lords' influence 106–7, 108, 118–19,
153–4; mate selection 47, 103, 112,
113–14, 124, 227, 235; monogamy 17,
71, 73; parents' role 71, 77, 103–4,
110, 111, 113, 124–5, 165, 186–7, 221,
226–7, 235, 276 n289, 279 n132; and
patriarchy 30–36, 112; polygyny 55;
prestation *see* dowry; Roman 46–8;
strategies *see* family formation strategies;
timing 98, 104, 113, 134, 228; wedding
115–16, 186–7; women's conjugal duty
to procreate 39, 86: *see also* betrothal;
Church, marriage; courtship; divorce;

dowry; merchet; patriarchy, alternatives
to marriage; remarriage; spousal
relations; Western European marriage
pattern
Marx, Karl 11, 12, 134, 168, 230, 248,
256 n2, 290 n126
marxism: *see* historical materialism
Mediterranean 5, 56, 103, 115, 121, 141,
147, 166
merchants 168, 181, 182
Meillassoux, Claude 258 n35
merchet 41, 62, 107, 108, 125, 153
messuage: *see* peasants, manse
migration 82, 137, 152, 185, 201, 206,
217, 221; to cities 137, 196, 218;
detouring rural–urban flow 216, 218;
'the invasions' 50, 56–7; sex ratio 185,
189, 196, 220: *see also* fertility,
migration; peasants, mobility; vagrancy
mobility: *see* peasants; proletarianization
mode of production: and culture 24, 32;
and demographic regime 12–13, 233,
248; dominant 24, 40, 133, 140, 233;
empirical onus of theory 27; and family
forms 3, 9, 24, 134–5, 233, 254; genesis
of 134–5; infrastructure/superstructure
10–11, 32; labour-power 11, 91, 233;
levels of analysis 26–7, 134; and nature
13, 78, 148, 248, 257 n9; productive
forces 10, 148; revolution of 13, 135;
expanded conception of 4, 255 n3;
social relations of production 10, 133,
256 n3; standard theory of 3, 10–11,
16; and technostructure 13, 270 n181;
transferring wealth between generations
39, 91: *see also* technology
modernization theory 29, 133, 166, 189,
216, 294 n194
mortality: adult 188, 240, 245; background
209, 299 n292; class differentials 194,
195, 197, 209; crises 56, 136, 142, 148,
152, 158, 239, 299 n292; decline
157–8, 208–12, 219; in epidemics 56,
150, 201, 209, 210–11; from famine
209; and hollow age cohorts 136, 150;
infant and child 16, 20, 150, 158, 195,
220, 252; infanticide and fatal neglect
75, 107, 150, 278 n305; life expectancy
117, 154, 239; maternal 18; positive
check 185; response to abatement
211–12; rural/urban ratio 208, 211,
217; sex ratio 107–8, 240, 245; during
war 158, 209: *see also* Black Death,
disease; population, recovery from
mortality crises
mothers, mothering 19, 83; maternal

indifference thesis 272 n217;
mother-child bond 19: *see also*
childbirth; child-care; children; fertility;
parenting; parent-child relations; youth
socialization

nature 91–2; ecological niche 15
neo-locality: *see* residence
neo-Malthusianism: *see* Malthusianism
Netherlands 137, 157, 159, 160, 203, 213
non-heirs (secondary children) 39, 98,
102–3, 124–26, 235, 254; keeping them
in the vicinity 99, 253; emigrating to
the fringes 39, 94, 103, 124, 127, 253;
nuclear family form 124–6
Norway 157, 197, 214, 226
nuclear family 82; continuity thesis 1, 50,
121; isolation of 60; versus stem family
121–6
nuptiality: *see* marriage; Western European
marriage pattern

old age 25, 126, 145, 148, 149, 154, 174,
223: *see also* retirement
overpopulation: *see* feudalism, demographic
dynamics

parent-child relations 25–6, 41, 42, 43, 47,
76, 83, 101–2, 110–12, 123–4, 151,
174, 183, 198, 222–3, 234: *see also*
fathers; inheritance; marriage, parents'
role; mothers; patriarchy; widows
parenting 19–20, 23: *see also* fathers,
mothers, youth socialization
paternity 17, 18, 22, 67, 71, 73
patriarchy 19, 20, 23, 30–36, 40, 55, 76,
86–7, 96; 106, 116, 124, 147, 149, 178,
184, 188, 191, 198, 222, 223, 242–5,
260 n61; alternatives to marriage 31,
75, 119–20, 244; definition 30, 201,
259 n53; and conjugal partnership 30;
male violence and civility 35, 86;
paterfamilias 47; *potestas* 48; proletarian
form 178, 234, 243, 244; public face
30, 86; roots of male dominance 33;
transfer of authority *see* householdship;
upholding familial norms 24, 80–82,
191; and women holding land 40,
118–19: *see also* family; parent-child
relations; householdship; spousal
relations
peasants: *adscripticii* 46; *coloni* 46; cottar
underclass 89, 92, 125–6, 128, 141,
162–3, 174–5, 199; debt 163;
disintegration as a class 165–6; hired
hands (non-family labour) 92, 93, 164,

177, 199 *see also* farm labourers; manse
(holding) 43, 46, 63, 79, 83–4, 97;
merging slaves and freeholders 58–9;
middling 149, 164; mobility 39, 90,
140, 142, 145, 236; patriarchs 40, 42,
100, 102, 113, 118, 145, 147, 187;
polarization 162–6, 197, 285 n31;
resistance (insurgency) 61, 138–9, 160,
165; servility *see* feudalism, serfdom;
smallholders (land-poor) 89, 99, 108,
124–5, 142, 163, 175; stratification 52,
162–6, 285 n31; subjection 38,
subsistence generalists 79; villeins and
freeholders compared 88–9, 273 n230;
villeins 41, 46, 79, 88, 264 n38;
yeomen 89, 141, 163, 164, 189: *see also*
cottagers; demesne; feudalism, serfdom;
land/population/labour-power; lords;
manor; slaves/slavery; village
peasants, family form 38–40, 121–4;
heritability 61–2, 100; labour-team 39,
83, 92–3, 127, 140, 141, 164, 199,
273 n229; 'overflow' branches 93, 103,
124, 127–9, 224, 236
poor/poverty 163, 173, 194, 209;
able-bodied versus 'impotent' 181;
begging (and repression of) 138,
180–81; demography 39, 93, 125, 128;
forest encampments 177; poaching 125,
179; poor relief 163, 175, 179, 180,
196, 204, 222; resistance to full
proletarianization 173–4; ruling-class
response 179–80; squatters, fringe
dwellers 124–5; settled versus transient
174–81, 195; workhouse 181 *see also*
family, desertion; landlessness;
proletarian condition, subproletarian
existence; vagrancy
population: accelerating, rapid growth 57,
200, 205–6, 231; class differentials in
growth rates 219, 224; components of
growth 150, 157–8, 166, 191–2, 201,
212–14; components-of-growth
reasoning 214–15; contraction,
depopulation, losses 56, 57, 136–7,
148–9, 287 n64; debate over prime
mover 150–51, 190–92, 201, 212–16,
224; demographic transition (vital
revolution) 214, 229–31, 236; extensive
growth *see* feudalism, extensive growth;
fertility and mortality, interaction 12,
201, 202, 209, 215, 220, 239 growth,
correlation with cereal prices 160,
192–3, 204, 231, 247–8; growth rates
57, 126, 140, 157, 185, 201;
homeostatic (slow-growth) regime 140,

156, 187–88, 200, 202, 215, 220, 231
240 *see also* land/population/labour
power; low-pressure versus
high-pressure system 185, 252; 'laws of
population' 11–12; 'overpopulation' *see*
feudalism, demographic dynamics;
recovery from mortality crises 136, 150,
157, 201; sex ratio 107–8, 196; and
social classes 12, 206: *see also* Black
Death; demography; fertility; feudalism,
demographic dynamics, agrarian cycle;
land, availability; Malthusianism;
mortality; population trends; settlement
population trends (by period): late
    Antiquity, contraction (AD542–650) 57;
early medieval growth phase 57;
tenth-century acceleration 57, 126;
thirteenth- and fourteenth-century
stagnation 128–31, 135–6; Black Death
and subsequent losses 129, 137–8; 'long'
sixteenth-century growth 136, 157–9;
seventeenth-century stagnation 136,
190–93; mid-eighteenth-century
take-off 136, 200–202, 212–19
prices 140; agricultural–industrial price
    ratio 160, 202; grain (cereal) 74, 92,
141, 142, 160, 163–4, 192, 201–3, 231:
see also wages; land market and rent; *for
secular trends, see* feudalism, ararian cycle;
primates 14, 15, 258 n26
procreation: as a form of production 4;
    biological drive 32–3; women's
conjugal duty 39, 86, 115: *see also*
fertility
proletarian condition 89; absence of
    alternative livelihood 168–9; clarifying
the concept 166–9; contrasting full and
semi-proletarian households 169–70;
fully proletarian households 169–70,
175; need for wage income
(continuum) 166, 168, 169, 195, 209;
negative and positive 167, 195, 218,
220, 224; male breadwinner's
prerogatives 178, 234, 243, 244;
residential instability 174–5, 179–80;
semi-proletarian households 168–9,
172–3, 177; separation of residence and
workplace 178, 204–5, 234;
subproletarian existence 179–80: *see also*
capitalism; employment; landholding,
dispossession; landlessness; industrial
revolution; poor/poverty; wages
proletarianization 2, 124–6, 133–5, 163–5,
166–4; and extramarital fertility 180,
225–9; family cycle 178–9; family
insecurity (disruption) 173–4, 177, 180;

growth of proletarian populace 166,
170–72, 182, 231, 296 n224;
incremental versus sudden progressions
135, 168; inflow/outflow 171; male
desertion 180, 228, 229; marriage rate
187, 219, 220–23, 241; mobility
(upward and downward) 174, 224–5,
290 n130; moving in search of work
174, 179–80, 220, 221, 241, 244, 253;
pre-capitalist origins 168; and
population boom 219–25, 302 nn333,
334; resistance and obstacles 169,
172–4, 182, 253; sources of growth
168, 171–2, 194–7; and state repression
175, 179–81, 196; theory 168, 290
n126; variety of routes, conflux 168: *see
also* capitalism; employment;
landholding, dispossession; landlessness;
industrial revolution; poor/poverty;
wages
property: public/private domains 80–81
protoindustrialization 292 n161; bypassing
    urban guilds 183, 205; conjugal division
of labour; cottage industry 181, 182,
205; definition of concept and critiques
292 nn161, 163; family economy,
labour team 183, 184, 206, 208; and
fertility 206, household composition
177, 183; indebtedness 182, 206;
kaufsystem (petty commodity
production) 181–4, 208; and migration
206, 217–18; and mortality 218; and
population boom 218; origins 181–2;
transition from kaufsystem to
verlagssystem 181, 182, 205–6; textiles
205, 207, 217, 292 n163; verlagssystem
(putting-out system) 181, 201–2,
205–8, 220: *see also* capitalism; merchants

regions 5, 214, 224; contrast between 5,
    39, 42, 55, 82, 216–19, 225–6, 249–54,
301 n314; perspective, as unit of
analysis 216, 250–51
remarriage 1, 43, 71, 74, 86, 104, 117–19
rent 160–61, 164: *see also* feudalism,
exactions; mode of exploitation
residence 42, 48, 90, 222–3; detached
    quarters 43, 124, 187, 263 n23;
impermanence 57, 89, 125, 174, 175,
178–9; neo-locality 42, 122, 123,
237–8, 253, 282 n389, 282 n391;
patrilocality (virilocality) 106, 107, 123;
rules, preferences 42, 237, 253: *see also*
dwelling; Cambridge group, family
paradigm; household; settlement;
Western European marriage pattern;

vagrancy
retirement 154; contracts 43, 117, 188;
    reluctance to retire 42, 43, 101, 187,
    237: *see also* househeadship; inheritance;
    patriarchy; old age
Ricardo, David 203
Roman Empire 44–50; betrothal in (the
    sponsio) 47; disintegration 56–7, 63;
    divorce and remarriage in 47; dowry
    customs 47–8, 64; frontiers 44, 45, 50;
    inheritance rules 48, 63; *latifundia* 45,
    56; law 70; marriage 46–48, 238; and
    Germanic peoples; *latifundia* 45; nuclear
    co-residence 50; principate 45;
    republican era 45, 48; senatorial elite
    49; sexuality in 72: *see also* slaves/slavery

Scandinavian countries *see under names of
    individual countries*
Scott, Joan Wallach 228–9
service/servants 197–202, 228, 297 n245;
    component of late marriage system 94,
    103, 195, 199–200, 220; contracts 198;
    contrast with day-labour 204–5, 315;
    correlation with *inter vivos* inheritance;
    decline 204–5; job turnover 198; as a
    life-stage 177, 198; living with master's
    family 80, 177, 198, 204–5; origins of
    197; prevalence of 197–8; redistribution
    of labour-power 199, 240
settlement: colonization 127, 153, 159;
    freeholding versus manorial zones 82;
    growth of existing settlements 124–5;
    overflow of family branches 93, 124–6;
    population gain, enlargement and new
    settlements 127; population loss,
    disruption and lost villages 57, 136–7;
    squatters 59, 89, 125, 175, 177,
    179–80: *see also* feudalism, extensive
    growth pattern; inheritance, nonheirs;
    land, availability; landholding; peasants,
    family, overflow
sexuality: abstinence, celibacy 67, 74, 151;
    betrothal *see* betrothal, sexual intimacy;
    Church's attitude 72, 73, 74, 116; coital
    frequency 185; conjugal right ('marital
    debt') 22, 30, 72–3, 115–16; and
    courtship 227; dissociability 17–18;
    double standard 73, 151, 244, 269
    n165; female chastity at marriage 55;
    fidelity and paternity 18, 22; fornication
    74, 116; libidinal surplus 17, 22, 69, 72,
    73, 191; 'marital debt' 72–3, 115–16;
    men's freedom, women's vulnerability
    222, 228; monogamy *see* marriage;
    premarital and betrothal sex *see* fertility,

extramarital; procreation 16, 22, 151;
    prostitution 74, 228: *see also* birth
    control; Church, doctrines on marriage;
    fertility; marriage; paternity; Western
    European marriage pattern
Shorter, Edward 227–29, 304 n368
sibling group: competition 75, 102, 103,
    116, 125, 186, 199; compensating
    non-heirs 102–3
slaves/slavery 141; domestic and field 45;
    ergastula 46; exploitation 45; families 45,
    46, 49; *famuli* 46, 141; fertility, slave
    breeding 44, 45, 49, 58; ganged labour
    45, 58; import-replacement versus
    indigenous reproduction 45; owners 45;
    reasons for decline 45; sale and price
    45, 49; sex ratio 44; manumission 45,
    49; marriage among slaves 44; marriage
    with freedpersons; and roman law; *servi
    casati* 46; slaves versus serfs 264 n39,
    273 n233
Spain 46, 127, 138, 157, 161, 190, 203
spousal relations 32–5; autonomy in daily
    life 86; and community vigilance 80;
    desertion 180, 187; devotion 34, 86;
    division of labour 83–4, 106, 178, 183,
    207–8, 234, 243, 272 n208 *see also*
    division of labour between sexes; 'good'
    husbands and wives 35, 86, 243; male
    power 86–7, 243; 'natural' spheres and
    inheritance 83, 271 n203; reciprocity
    34; wife-beating 35, 86: *see also*
    househeadship; marriage; patriarchy;
    remarriage; retirement
state 36, 54, 175, 179, 208, 210, 226,
    300 n303; barbarian states *see* Germanic
    peoples; enforcement of family norms
    24: *see also* feudalism; proletarianization,
    state repression
stem family 42, 82, 122, 234, 281 nn386,
    387; Laslett's critique 236, 237; Le
    Play's conception 42; evidence of
    prevalence 43, 262–3 nn20, 21, 23;
    weak stem variant 43, 122–4; strong
    stem variant 42, 122, 262 n19; stem
    versus nuclear family cycle 121–3, 234,
    282 n392
subsistence 290 n128; crises 208; means of
    9, 15, 233, 234; 'surplus' 21: *see also*
    food; residence
Sweden 98, 202, 214, 217, 225

tenure: *see* landholding; peasants
theory 214–15; family/economy divide 10;
    naturalism 14, 221, 248, 256 n2;
    301 n321; paradigm of constrained

choice 31–2, 259 n57, 168–9, 260 n59; pragmatism 32, 260 n58; relation with evidence 7, 27, 214; structural-functionalism 9: *see also* historical materialism
Tilly, Charles 168, 190, 194
Tilly, Louise 228–9
trade: *see* exchange and markets
trothplight: *see* betrothal

unemployment: *see* employment
uneven and combined development 6, 214–15
urbanization: *see* cities
vagrancy 89, 90–91, 124–6, 138, 169, 174, 177, 179–81, 236, 296 n230; wandering Christian sects 67, 68: *see also* landlessness; landholding, dispossession; poor/poverty; proletarianization
village 163; assemblies 79; autonomy from seigneurial authority 139–40, 271 n200; co-operation, collective endeavour 79, 83, 88; deserted 137; and field systems 139; 'home base' 93; moral regulation 80–81; neighbours 81, 270 n183; offices/officials 85, 196; relations between households 78–82; self-sufficiency 78–9; size 78: *see also* community; settlement
villein: *see* peasant, villein

wages 142, 145, 161, 168, 243; 'bread wage' 161, 203; life earning curve 220; payment in kind 198; piece-rate 181; real wage trends 161, 173, 192, 193, 202–3, 209, 218, 229–30; women's wages versus men's 161: *see also* capitalism; employment; proletarian condition; proletarianization
Wall, Richard 236
war 209; Hundred Years 158; Napoleonic 204, 205; Thirty Years 190, 192: *see also* mortality, causes; war
Weber, Max 43
wedding: *see* marriage
Western European marriage pattern 2, 56, 74–5, 94–5, 116, 152, 154, 184, 187, 188, 239–42; age at first marriage 95, 111, 155–6, 185, 186, 191, 195, 224, 241, 252, 288 nn79, 86; age difference between spouses 94, 155, 240; celibacy

and 74–75, 94, 95, 116, 155–6, 184, 191, 240, 252, 300 n309; and capitalism 156–7, 239–41; Church's influence 71, 74–5; deadlock between fathers and sons 74, 187, 152, 184; determinants 154, 186–9; double-block model 189–90; as fertility restriction 184–6, 188, 219–21, 239, 241; four-sided decision-making 111–12; homeostatic demographic system *see* population; improving life expectancy 185, 239, 289 n96; land niche system 187–9, 199; and land market 185, 187, 188–9; late medieval watershed 112, 156; neo-locality and 153, 187, 189; as a norm or custom 186; nuptial valve 94, 95, 142, 156, 185, 186, 188, 189, 191, 221; origins 74, 94–5, 152–6, 188, 274 n252; prerequisites (threshold) 154, 186, 189; and proletarianization 187, 189, 241–2; service, component of late marriage system 94, 153, 199–200, 240; shift in balance of generational power 112–13: *see also* landholding, niche system; marriage; neo-locality; remarriage; retirement
widowers 86
widows 42–3, 65, 71, 74, 102, 117–20, 163; landholding 101, 117, 120; landless 117; peasant versus proletarian condition 120; pressure (for and against) remarriage 42, 74, 119, 154; prominence in village life 117
women 32; comparing peasant and proletarian 86, 120, 242–5; and self-interest 32; status 55–6, 86–7, 207–8, 242–5; support networks 34–5, 56, 79–80, 84, 151, 271 n191; 'why do women marry?' 31–4, 244, 259 n56: *see also* division of labour between the sexes; dowry; gender relations; heiresses; inheritance, discrimination against females; women's prerogatives; mothers/mothering; patriarchy; spousal relations; widows
wustungen: *see* settlement, population loss and lost villages

youth socialization 9, 18–19, 23, 76, 83, 199, 235, 240: *see also* child-care; parent-child relations; parenting